Shakespeare's Political and Economic Language

ARDEN SHAKESPEARE DICTIONARY SERIES

Series Editor
Sandra Clark (Birkbeck College, University of London)

Class and Society in Shakespeare	Paul Innes
Military Language in Shakespeare	Charles Edelman
Shakespeare's Books	Stuart Gillespie
Shakespeare's Demonology	Marion Gibson
Shakespeare and the Language of Food	Joan Fitzpatrick
Shakespeare's Legal Language	B.J. Sokol & Mary Sokol
Shakespeare's Medical Language	Sujata Iyengar
Shakespeare's Non-Standard English	N. F. Blake
Shakespeare's Plants and Gardens	Vivian Thomas and Nicki Faircloth
Shakespeare's Theatre	Hugh Macrae Richmond
Shakespeare's Religious Language	R. Chris Hassel, Jr
Women in Shakespeare	Alison Findlay

Forthcoming:

Shakespeare's Insults	Nathalie Vienne-Guerrin
Shakespeare and National Identity	Christopher Ivic

Shakespeare's Political and Economic Language

A Dictionary

VIVIAN THOMAS

Bloomsbury Arden Shakespeare
An imprint of Bloomsbury Publishing Plc

B L O O M S B U R Y

LONDON · NEW DELHI · NEW YORK · SYDNEY

Bloomsbury Arden Shakespeare
An imprint of Bloomsbury Publishing Plc

Imprint previously known as Arden Shakespeare

50 Bedford Square	1385 Broadway
London	New York
WC1B 3DP	NY 10018
UK	USA

www.bloomsbury.com

**BLOOMSBURY, THE ARDEN SHAKESPEARE and the Diana logo are trademarks of
Bloomsbury Publishing Plc**

First published 2008, this revised paperback edition published 2015

© Vivian Thomas 2015

British Library Cataloguing in Publication Data
A catalogue record for this book is available from the British Library

ISBN:	PB:	978-1-4725-7338-4
	ePDF:	978-1-4411-5167-4
	ePub:	978-1-4742-1608-1

Library of Congress Cataloging-in-Publication Data
A catalog record for this book is available from the Library of Congress

Typeset by RefineCatch Limited, Bungay, Suffolk
Printed and bound in Great Britain

For
Audrey
Will and Alex
Lorna and Linda

Contents

Acknowledgements

It would be difficult to overstate the value of the David and Ben Crystal *Glossary* (2002) which has been my constant companion since commencing this study. I have benefited from the astute criticism, patience and encouragement of the Series Editor, Professor Sandra Clark. Colleen Coalter and the team at Continuum have been helpful, not least in pressing me to put other tasks in abeyance to complete this volume. Len Rix and Patrick Smith scrutinized the manuscript with rigour and insight, obliging me to rethink and correct several entries. My son, William, contributed to meeting the publisher's technical requirements while my wife, Audrey, prepared the various versions of this text. I am indebted to my students whose inquiring minds have been a source of stimulation over many years. Any errors or inadequacies are my own responsibility. For this paperback edition I owe a debt of gratitude to Margaret Bartley, Emily Hockley and the support staff at Bloomsbury Publishing.

Series Editor's Preface

The Continuum Shakespeare Dictionaries aim to provide the student of Shakespeare with a series of authoritative guides to the principal subject-areas covered by the plays and poems. They are produced by scholars who are experts both on Shakespeare and on the topic of the individual dictionary, based on the most recent scholarship, succinctly written and accessibly presented. They offer readers a self-contained body of information on the topic under discussion, its occurrence and significance in Shakespeare's works, and its contemporary meanings.

The topics are all vital ones for understanding the plays and poems; they have been selected for their importance in illuminating aspects of Shakespeare's writings where an informed understanding of the range of Shakespeare's usage, and of the contemporary literary, historical and cultural issues involved, will add to the reader's appreciation of his work. Because of the diversity of the topics covered in the series, individual dictionaries may vary in emphasis and approach, but the aim and basic format of the entries remain the same from volume to volume.

Sandra Clark
Birkbeck College
University of London

Preface

Academic research while acknowledging Shakespeare's exploration of finance, especially in *The Merchant of Venice* and *Timon of Athens,* has neglected, until relatively recently, to analyse the dramatist's deep engagement with economics, the concepts embodied in the texts and absorption of the values of the market place into the commerce of life. Shakespeare's work exhibits a hyper-sensitivity to the growing application of economic concepts at every level of discourse. As a consequence the plays and poems are replete with words which carry significant economic freight. Shakespeare criticism has been more explorative with respect to the political dimensions of the plays, but there has been no specialized work devoted to the dramatist's political vocabulary. The aim of this dictionary is not only to provide a pathway through the specialist language of political and economic phenomena, but to reveal the ways in which key terms, concepts and modes of thinking animate exchanges which inhabit even the romantic and comic fields of discourse. A striking feature of both plays and poems is the alchemy of verbal transmutation, the ways in which particular words function in disparate semantic fields.

The two decades prior to the first publication of this book in 2008 witnessed the emergence of lively scholarship, most notably the New Economic Criticism, devoted to the analysis of Shakespeare's engagement with the market in all its aspects and manifestations. Subsequently, 'ecocriticism', which embraces Shakespeare's response to the natural world, and 'presentism', are illustrative of theoretical perspectives that extend the terrain of economic and political concerns. Shakespeare's response to 'green desire' and the related financial and intellectual investment in 'botanical capital' is analysed in a recent addition to this series: *Shakespeare's Plants and Gardens.*

'What's aught but as 'tis valued?' (*Troilus and Cressida*, 2.2.52)

'Come buy of me, come; come buy, come buy' (*The Winter's Tale*, 4.4.228)

'Sell when you can, you are not for all markets' (*As You Like It*, 3.5.60)

'Three thousand ducats for three months, and Antonio bound' (*The Merchant of Venice*, 1.3.9–10)

                     'we seize into our hands
His plate, his goods, his money, and his lands' (*Richard II*, 2.1.209–10)

'Master, I marvel how the fishes live in the sea.'
'Why, as men do a-land; the great ones eat up the little ones' (*Pericles*, 2.1.26–9)

'Through tatter'd clothes small vices do appear;
Robes and furr'd gowns hide all' (*King Lear*, 4.6.163–4)

'Be it thy course to busy giddy minds
With foreign quarrels' (*Henry IV, Part 2*, 4.5.213–14)

                     'Who are the violets now
That strew the green lap of the new-come spring?' (*Richard II*, 5.2.46–7)

'I can add colours to the chameleon,
Change shapes with Proteus for advantages,
And set the murderous Machiavel to school' (*Henry VI, Part 3*, 3.2.191–3)

'Men must learn now with pity to dispense,
For policy sits above conscience' (*Timon of Athens*, 3.2.86–7)

Abbreviations

1. *Shakespeare's Works*

ADO	*Much Ado About Nothing*
ANT	*Antony and Cleopatra*
AWW	*All's Well That Ends Well*
AYL	*As You Like It*
COR	*Coriolanus*
CYM	*Cymbeline*
E3	*Edward III*
ERR	*The Comedy of Errors*
HAM	*Hamlet*
1H4	*The First Part of Henry IV*
2H4	*The Second Part of Henry IV*
H5	*Henry V*
1H6	*The First Part of Henry VI*
2H6	*The Second Part of Henry VI*
3H6	*The Third Part of Henry VI*
H8	*Henry the Eighth*
JC	*Julius Caesar*
JN	*King John*
LC	*A Lover's Complaint*
LLL	*Love's Labour's Lost*
LR	*King Lear*
LUC	*The Rape of Lucrece*
MAC	*Macbeth*
MM	*Measure for Measure*
MND	*A Midsummer Night's Dream*
MV	*The Merchant of Venice*
OTH	*Othello*
PER	*Pericles*
PHT	*The Phoenix and the Turtle*
PP	*The Passionate Pilgrim*
R2	*Richard II*
R3	*Richard III*
ROM	*Romeo and Juliet*
SHR	*The Taming of the Shrew*
SON	*Sonnets*
STM	*Sir Thomas More*

TGV	*The Two Gentlemen of Verona*
TIM	*Timon of Athens*
TIT	*Titus Andronicus*
TMP	*The Tempest*
TN	*Twelfth Night*
TNK	*The Two Nobel Kinsmen*
TRO	*Troilus and Cressida*
VEN	*Venus and Adonis*
WIV	*The Merry Wives of Windsor*
WT	*The Winter's Tale*

2. *Others*

ch.	Chapter
Cho	Chorus
ed.	editor(s) or edited by
Epil.	Epilogue
esp.	especially
F1	the 'First Folio' edition of Shakespeare's collected plays, 1623
F.	Folio
I. or II.	line number(s) in poems
Q	quarto
refs	references
trans.	translated by
vol.	volume
fn	footnote
SOD	Shorter Oxford Dictionary

Conventions

Headwords and Entries

In order to facilitate cross-referencing, each headword appearing in any other entry is printed (once) in **bold**. This principle does not apply to quotations. I have adhered to the general practice in these dictionaries. Section (A) provides definitions; (B) explores examples of the ways in which the word is used; (C) offers suggested reading relating to the word, concept or application in one or more of the texts drawn on in this entry. When I recommend an article or chapter and provide details of the book in which it is incorporated, only the volume itself is included in the Bibliography. Subtitles of books are not included in this section but are cited in full in the Bibliography. Punctuation is kept to a minimum. All footnote references are to page numbers.

Quotations

All quotations are intimated by means of an abbreviated title with scene and act divisions (*PER* 2.1.45) unless the title of the play is evident from the discussion. All citations relate to *The Riverside Shakespeare*, second edition, ed. G. Blakemore Evans, which is cued to Marvin Spevack's nine-volume *The Harvard Concordance to Shakespeare*, 1973. Editorial commentaries, generally drawn from the Arden editions, take the following form with page numbers of footnotes after comma, e.g. Arden 2, 241. As a general rule, if a quotation consists of five or more full lines it appears in block quotes. All square brackets within quotations are my interventions. All italics in Shakespeare quotations are my own.

Introduction
The Shakespearean Moment and Shakespeare Studies

There is now abundant evidence to show that an extraordinary economic trans-formation was taking place during Shakespeare's lifetime. Recent studies of the technological developments in the fields of mapmaking, clocks, mirrors, books and military equipment reveal the dramatist's thoroughgoing command of this specialist knowledge. Whether it is warfare, music, religion, law, politics or economics, the extent of Shakespeare's erudition is only fully revealed when experts interrogate the plays and poems with the specific purpose of exploring the linguistic and conceptual embodiment of these features in the text.

The past two to three decades have witnessed a rich outpouring of writing on Shakespeare's engagement with economic developments, concepts and ideas. What has become known as The New Economic Criticism originated as a name devised for a conference that took place in 1991. It was subsequently adopted by Woodmansee and Osteen[1] as the title for a volume devoted to a mapping of this varied and stimulating approach to Shakespeare studies. Mark Shell's seminal *Money, Language and Thought* (1982) was followed by numerous studies devoted to the economic circumstances that shaped early modern England, and the ways in which these forces find expression in the plays.[2] Not only have the princi-ples, structures, assumptions and techniques of economics been explored and incorporated into analyses of the context and texture of the plays, but economics as an area of technical expertise has also been subjected to close scrutiny. There is now a whole body of critical work within schools of economics analysing the ways in which the language of literature shapes economic thinking and practice.

The prolific output in this area of literary study serves, perhaps, to suggest the timely nature of this volume. What makes the study of 'Shakespeare the econo-mist' so rewarding is the conceptual clarity he displays in all things economic along with their understated absorption into the human, social or cultural engagements that occupy his dramatic and non-dramatic works.

Studies devoted to analysing economic change in all its aspects – expansion in the output and range of products coming onto the market, the enlargement of trading networks along with their financial concomitants, both national and international, technological advance, the growth of population and expansion of cities, especially London – bear witness to a marked transformation of Shakespeare's world during his lifetime. As Sandra Clark points out, 'after the fall of Antwerp in 1576 London became the greatest trading city of Europe'.[3] More than half a century ago, C. L. Barber ascribed Shakespeare's peculiar sensitivity to the role of holidays and festivals to the contrast between the rural and urban worlds he traversed. He suggested that 'during Shakespeare's lifetime, England became conscious of holiday custom as it had not been before, in the very period when in many areas the keeping of holidays was on the decline'.[4] More recently, Agnew, Bruster and others have revealed the ways in which theatre itself embodied and reflected the physical, social, economic and psychological changes taking place at this time.[5] This was the moment when the market gained ascendancy and became central to the sensibility of the age. The theatre and its hinterland embodied the spirit of the market: theatre embraced the whole of social life in all its multitudinous workings, from history to contemporary affairs – from monarchs to beggars: Helen of Troy converses with the bawd Pandarus; heroes like Price Hal rub shoulders with Bardolph, Pistol and Nym; the despised plebeians influence political outcomes in *Julius Caesar* and *Coriolanus*; the smell of sweat, so disdained by Octavius Caesar, is frequently found in close proximity to more refined odours.

This was a period of transformation that both facilitated and stimulated the theatrical articulation and interrogation of the concerns, tensions, aspirations, values and imaginative reach of the society. Language, the most significant currency of the age, was being newly minted within the theatre. Here was the imaginative centre of this cosmopolitan city, shaping reality into multifarious patterns. Exoticism, voyeurism and fantasy commingled with the economic realities of destitution and opulence: Romeo's apothecary and *King Lear*'s ragged outcasts occupied the same space as the Lord and wealthy suitors of *The Taming of the Shrew*. This kaleidoscope of generative space juxtaposed extremes of economic circumstances.

Likewise, the political worlds of histories and tragedies exposed ambitions, manoeuvres, collisions and wars. History suddenly acquired a vibrant *presentness*. Flags and banners fluttered in the air, but the bleak realities of *realpolitik* found expression in ways that stimulated critical intelligence. The costs of wars were rendered as vividly as were their glories. Pageantry, power and demystification were intertwined. In the theatre of dreams, economics and politics now held centre stage.

A brief summary of the economic and political pressures animating Shakespeare's society is provided by John J. Joughin:

> Shakespeare's drama emerged at a moment of acute political turbulence; a period of social upheaval, often shorthanded by cultural historians as the 'crisis of the 1590s' – a decade which encompassed a series of catastrophic events including dearth, plague, rapid population expansion, inflation, unemployment, increased immigration and attendant vagrancy, attacks on 'aliens', apprentice riots and a host of other problems.[6]

Here was a crucible of politics and language. Shakespeare's world vibrated with political intrigue and uncertainty; political ideas and institutions were constantly explored and evaluated in the numerous books brought forth by a prolific press catering for an eager public. The recycling of chronicle material found new form and vigour on the stage, transforming the 'then' of the past into the 'now' of the present, so that history walked and talked within touching distance of the audience.

The odours of politics were in the nostrils of every citizen, as persistent and pressing as the economics of everyday life. Never before could the behaviour, motivations and actions of rulers have appeared so available for critical scrutiny – and all for one penny. Without taking ship, the auditor could be transported to Rome, Athens, Alexandria or the New World. Past and present were immediately accessible and, not least, the present *now* reflected in the past. Histories were employed as mirrors of contemporary life. Contrasting constitutional models were subject to impassioned debate and relentless scrutiny. Such discussions were no longer confined to the corridors of power or the debating chambers of the intellectual elite: they were there constantly on the stage before the eyes and ears of the humblest citizens.

Shakespeare's plays are suffused by political life. Assassinations abound; the passion for power seems as inexhaustible as the deviousness employed to attain it. The entire social universe is embraced by political action and reaction. Vigorous, colourful, impassioned plebeians tread the political stage with a presence as vital as the Machiavellians who manipulate and control events, while genuine heroism contends with treachery and fraud. Political contention dominates the histories and tragedies; the problem plays, romances and comedies all have a significant political dimension.

Economic life is equally vibrant. Shakespeare reveals a clear understanding of the difference between resources and money, of the nature and implications of credit and interest, of liquidity and cash flow, of the folly of extravagance and of the pain of destitution. He shows the economic and human costs of war, the significance and irrevocable potency of supply and demand, and the palpability of opportunity cost and tradeoffs. The world of economics dominates both the courts of kings and the operations of the brothel. Indeed, the brothel provides a microcosm of the world's financial structures, dealing with such matters as purchase price, the declining value of the product as it moves from the prime status of virginity to the health hazard of contaminated flesh. Economic realities are inescapable and frequently ugly, as Marina tells the pimp, 'thy food is such/As hath been belched on by infected lungs' (*PER* 4.6.168–9). Even Rosalind and Celia need to carry off all their valuables when absconding from court. The Forest of Arden is an uninviting place until they display the wherewithal to purchase a farm. In both *Timon of Athens* and *The Merchant of Venice*, money, extravagance, debt, borrowing and asset structures constitute the very lifeblood of social reality.

Every play manifests and registers the pulse-beat of economic life – as do the non-dramatic works. Whether the speaker possesses the nimble and assured wit of Rosalind (cautioning Phebe, 'Sell when you can, you are not for all markets' – *AYL* 3.5.60), the brutal precision of Richard Gloucester ('Priests pray for enemies, but princes kill' – *2H6* 5.2.71) or the prophetic force of Joan Pucelle ('Glory is like a circle in the water, / Which never ceaseth to enlarge itself, / Till by broad spreading it disperse to nought' – *1H6* 1.2.133–5), the plays vibrate with the words and concepts of economic and political life.

Alighting on the felicitous expression 'technological confluence', Adam Max Cohen draws attention to the need to acknowledge that what was taking place during Shakespeare's lifetime cannot be calculated by summing up the achievements or changes in each field, even were this possible. Only by attempting to gain an *imaginative* grasp of the consequences arising from the *interactions* of these developments, the physical changes and the ways in which they were apprehended or imposed themselves on the minds of people surrounded by these forces, can this be achieved.[7]

This new world where the market acquired a vigour that inflicted itself both as a physical presence and as an imaginative agency became an inescapable nexus. Such was the influence of the market that many social commentators perceive this period as giving birth to 'commodity fetishism'.[8] Like most social institutions, the newly attained dominance of the market created new opportunities for pecuniary and psychic enrichment while simultaneously undermining traditional modes of social engagement. One thing that seems indisputable is that this material advance facilitated the emergence of a vigorous and profitable theatre. As John Maynard Keynes, the most influential economist of the twentieth century, expressed it: 'We were just in a financial position to afford Shakespeare at the moment when he presented himself!'[9]

The capacity and output of the theatre is indicated by Andrew Gurr's estimate that 'well over fifty million visits were made to playhouses' between the erection of the first purpose-built theatres in the 1560s and their closure in 1642.[10] For Bruster, 'London's playhouses can best be understood in terms of commerce, as centres for the production and consumption of an aesthetic product.'[11] Or, put even more concisely by Brecht, here was an 'acoustic department store'.[12] The theatre that emerged from this milieu formed part of the surge in market relations and activity. 'Thomas Gresham began construction of the Royal Exchange in Lombard Street in London in 1566–67, just as the Red Lion playhouse opened for business.' Dealing in national and international finance, 'the piazzas surrounding it contained around a hundred individual shops . . . A visitor from Germany in 1592 called the Exchange "a palace, where all kinds of beautiful goods are usually to be found" '.[13] The year 1599 saw the opening of Shakespeare's Globe; a year later the second Blackfriars and the Fortune opened for business, coinciding with the receipt of the royal stamp of approval for the East India Company. Within a decade Robert Cecil opened the New Exchange, described by Lawrence Stone as 'a sort of stock exchange and estate agency . . . a kind of bazaar for the upper-class clientele which normally passed along the Strand between the Law Courts and the royal palace at Westminster, and the Inns of Court and the City to the east'.[14]

Bruster sees this concatenation of events as 'the dawn, in London, of institutionalized capitalism'. Emphasizing the coalition of physical presence and imaginative power, he links this 'bank of the world' with the theatre; something captured by Dekker's comment: 'The theatre is your poets' Royal Exchange, upon which their Muses – that are now turned to merchants – meeting, barter away their light commodity of words for a lighter ware than words – plaudits and the breath of the great beast.'[15] If Dekker's 'commodity of words' suggests something insubstantial, 'The placelessness of the Renaissance platform stage worked to exoticize and commodify space.'[16] The theatre provided transportation and transformation, a plethora of psychic riches for those disposed to vicarious travel. Words cast into the air embodied the pleasures and anxieties of the market-place: enriching vocabularies and thought processes for those acquisitive enough to enhance their linguistic store.

The essence of the market is connectedness: innumerable transactions are linked in a complex network, too labyrinthine to be easily comprehended. Agents, factors, go-betweens inhabit a world awash with goods, services, cash and credit. They penetrate every fissure and interstice, filling those spaces with their activity. Monarchs, aristocrats, bourgeoisie and workers are engaged in a scramble to enjoy the fruits of this hectic commercial activity. The market became a process, a phenomenon, a concept, rather than just a place. Malleability and shape-changing inhered in its identity. As the market gained pre-eminence in daily life, it insinuated itself into thought processes. Market and theatre became conceptually and even literally symbiotic. Theatre owed its very existence to the market; its elaborated, mind-enhancing commodity dramatized the genius of the market, its transmutative character, exchange displaying a generative capacity in which everything and everybody changed. At the same time it exposed the inordinate appetite and greed which the market both stimulated and celebrated. The economics of everyday life was shifting from survival and sufficiency to acquisition and accumulation.

Something inevitably missed when focusing exclusively on Shakespeare's vocabulary is his firm grasp of concepts. He reveals a thorough understanding of distinctions between capital, in its physical and monetary forms, and income; stocks and flows; real resources and their monetary expression; the operation of supply and demand in the determination of prices and interest rates; the function of liquidity and reputation. Shakespeare shows the same thorough understanding in the facilitating of financial transactions, in the interdependencies between economic sectors and their vulnerability (for instance, in an excessive tax burden, described in *Henry VIII*); in the economic costs of war – not only in the matter of raising money but also in terms of economic dislocation.

For the most part the economic contribution arising from occupations is unacknowledged by the social elite: the providers of the necessities of life are disparaged. It is Edgar who, having been plunged into the lower depths, expresses compassion for the perilous occupation of samphire collectors, a 'dreadful trade' (*LR* 4.6.15). The skilled artist fares better, winning Iachimo's breathless admiration (*CYM* 2.4.68–84). Shakespeare's only named artist, Julio Romano, also receives general acclaim for his past wonders, even if there is a false ascription of his genius prior to the monument scene (*WT* 5.2.94–100).

Shakespeare infiltrates his plays with the circumstances of the **market-place** and its contentious influence. Old Capulet sends out for an extra batch of cooks to speed up the provision of a wedding feast; Petruchio berates a tailor in mock irritation for his poor workmanship; an old ostler fails to come to terms with a rise in the price of oats; a farm-hand is subject to a fine for leaving a sack at Hinckley fair; a cobbler enjoying a holiday, absorbing the displays and doings of Roman society's shapers, seizes the opportunity to exercise his wit at the expense of his social superiors; the pathetic apothecary, rendered so vividly by Romeo's description, seeking to maintain the appearance of a going concern, employs devices which serve only to expose imminent destitution.

Several critical concepts embedded in the heart of modern economic theory such as opportunity cost and optimization are given expression in diverse ways. The critical significance of the margin or threshold is noteworthy. Not confined to economic **practices** in any restrictive way, this idea relating to all kinds of physical thresholds, such as maps and land distribution, is to be found in *King Lear, Henry IV, Part 1* and *Henry V*, and in the physical and psychological thresholds so vital to *Macbeth*. Bookkeeping, calculation, estate management and education as a form of human capital (*AYL*), conspicuous consumption, saving and investment, debts, bills and bonds are all present. Brokers, entrepreneurs, factors, merchants, moneylenders and tradesmen repeatedly animate the plays, with *The Comedy of Errors* providing striking examples. The language of economics even seeps into the language of love, sometimes being made to serve a higher purpose; on other occasions contaminating courtship with commerce.

Shakespeare illuminates a social universe impregnated, even infected, by the spirit of calculation. Assessment, evaluation, measurement, counterbalance, are shown to be integral to human relationships, and engagements.[17] Frequently the language of the market-place colours discourse in a way that casts an oblique light on a relationship or subverts a romantic connection. For example, Pandarus concludes the mutual love pledges of Troilus and Cressida with the phrase 'Go to, a bargain made' (*TRO* 3.2.197).

On other occasions when the language of the market-place is appropriated by lovers, the conceptual and verbal potency of the commercial sphere vitalizes the articulacy of love. Such is the case in the celebration of mutuality subsequent to Bassanio's choice of the leaden casket. Portia is so passionately assured of the spiritual and emotional wealth that love bestows that the language of economic life does service in a higher sphere, resisting the threat of contamination.[18] Juliet delivers a declaration of love which draws a distinction between the true substance of feeling and the inadequacy of expression. In the process, she reveals the difference between the real wealth that resides in love and the workaday wealth that can be calculated with money:

> Conceit, more rich in matter than in words,
> Brags of his substance, not of ornament;

> They are but beggars that can count their worth,
> But my true love is grown to such excess
> I cannot sum up sum of half my wealth.

ROM 2.5.30–4

The compression and complexity of this speech is startling. 'Conceit', or understanding, celebrates a love which is truly valuable. Juliet puns on the word 'excess' meaning both superabundance and interest on a loan. Such is the growth of her emotional capital that it is beyond calculation. The world of economics and finance is glanced at only to be left behind. Language has been worked creatively, intensely and economically, to point out a key distinction and to intimate the nature of love.

A concept fundamental to modern economics is the complementary relationship between two goods or services. For Shakespeare the most perfect expression of complementarity is the relationship between wind and sails. Here is the embodiment of 'beauty and utility' (*H5* 5.2.53). In the Shakespearean aesthetic nothing quite matches this interdependence. Contemplating the attractive power of the Countess of Salisbury, King Edward III distinguishes two qualities that work in harmony, the rhetorical figure chiasmus reflecting and reinforcing the complementarity: 'Like as the wind doth beautify a sail, / And as a sail becomes the unseen wind, / So do her words her beauty, beauty words' (*E3* 2.1.279–81). Enobarbus (*ANT* 2.2.193–4) and Titania (*MND* 2.1.124–34) employ this concept in ways which bring together the forces of nature, technology, commerce and aesthetics. (See entry on **traders**.)

Of all the elements to be found in Shakespeare's work that go to make up its dramatic mosaic, perhaps the most remarkable is the dramatist's choice of word. Frequently invented or derived from Latin it is transmuted to create a verbal coinage. It is even stretched from its existing range to encompass new fields. It is the colour, weight, texture and seeming odour of the word that makes the auditor or reader respond to the rightness of its choice – frequently an option that was not immediately apparent. Bryan A. Garner provides a useful summary of this augmentation of the English language during this period of linguistic fertility:

> Through the conscious efforts of scholars during the English Renaissance, more words were added to the English language than at any other time in its history. The *Chronological English Dictionary* lists 26,947 words, mostly Latinate, that were added to the English language from 1500 to 1659 . . . the number of loanwords coming into English increased steadily during the sixteenth century, culminating with the period beginning in the 1590s, when Shakespeare and the other great Elizabethan writers were active – after which time the borrowing levelled off.
>
> In the years when Shakespeare was writing, from roughly 1588 to 1612, 7,968 neologisms were brought into English. During this very fecund period of twenty-four years, thirty per cent of all the Renaissance neologisms appeared.[19]

As Steven R. Mentz notes, 'Early modern explorations of economics usually bear traces of multiple discourses'. For example, in England at the start of the seventeenth century 'the modern sense of capital, debt, and interest were still under construction, and terms like "reckoning" and "debt" still carried strong theological senses.'[20] Turner comments, ' "trust", "goods", "save", "value", "means", "redeem", "redemption", "dear", "obligation", "interest", "honour", "company", "worth", "thrift", "use", "will", "partner", "deed", "fair", "owe", "ought", "risk", "royalty", "fortune", "venture", "grace" and so on . . . insist on the incarnation of their noble moral meanings in their base pecuniary ones'.[21]

Differing responses to words under the influence of changing cultural practices have been highlighted by Agnew. For instance, Castiglione's *The Courtyer* 'became for English audiences a symbol of grace *and* guile, propriety *and* policy'. Likewise, such words as ' "cunning", "art", and "craft" no longer evoked the unequivocal meanings of ingenuity, skill, and workmanship. Instead, they implied a capacity for misrepresentation and treachery that, by the late sixteenth century at least, was popularly identified with Machiavellianism.'[22]

Shakespeare seems to have been almost preternaturally alert to the dimensions of a word: its critical impact and opalescent or transmutative potentialities. What meaning is initially perceived or felt weaves or expands under the influence of the word's mobile ambiance. In the case of migratory language, a word that possesses powerful resonance in the religious realm may also inhabit the secular domain. 'Redeem' is noteworthy, in that the original meaning of 'redemen', reaching back to 1415, signifies 'buy back, pay off, free, deliver' but was 'in part possibly a back formation from *redemption*, or at least influenced by *redemption*'.[23] The sense 'spiritually saved' became highly significant in a world dominated by religious ideas. Thus the theological meaning inevitably exerts a pressure on the everyday sense of recouping reputation or providing some form of recompense. Clearly 'redeem' was too fecund a word to resist the colouration attaching it to the religious sphere. Used with frequency in *Henry IV, Part 1*, including the forms 'redeem'd' and 'redeeming', it is strongly associated with Hal when he makes his promise to the audience to create an illusion of wasteful waywardness only to appear all the more magnificent on becoming king:

> My reformation, glitt'ring o'er my fault,
> Shall show more goodly and attract more eyes
> Than that which hath no foil to set it off.
> I'll so offend, to make offense a skill,
> Redeeming time when men think least I will.

> 1.2.213–17

Hal returns to the concepts embedded in the word in his soliloquy at the Battle of Shrewsbury, challenging the fierce Scot, the Douglas, with the words, 'It is the Prince of Wales that threatens thee,/Who never promiseth but he means to pay'

(5.4.42–3). The language of the market-place and tavern-reckonings quickly changes when Hal addresses his father with solicitude, 'how fares your Grace?' only to receive the response, 'Thou hast redeem'd thy lost opinion' (5.4.44–8). 'Redemption' is now *primarily* about *this world*; the judgement that has to be won becomes that of 'opinion'. (See entry on **opinion**.)

Throughout Shakespeare's dramatic career, Machiavellianism is a vital force. Consequently this promotes a political lexicon that is vigorous, muscular and subtle. Deviousness, underhand dealing, and ruthlessness call forth a language that accommodates such ambitions and such passions. Shakespeare employs the word '**Machiavel**' only three times, once as a term of abuse (1H6 5.4.74) and once in a purely comic context (WIV 3.1.101). The one character who employs the word to acknowledge and celebrate his adherence to this principle or code is Richard Gloucester (3H6 3.2.182–95).

The word most frequently associated with Machiavellian activity is '**practice**': it is peculiarly descriptive of the activities of those employed in schemes, plots and manoeuvres designed to bring down political opponents. Someone operating in the service of such '**factions**', is an '**intelligencer**' (though see this entry for the exception – 2H4 4.2.15–21). A fellow schemer is a '**complice**', the scheme itself a '**complot**'. Masters of political intrigue engage in '**policy**'. To be '**politic**' is generally to be at the least circumspect but more usually to be guileful and self-seeking. A '**politician**' is one devoted to self-interest. A term used most powerfully to embody ruthless self-interest and self-regard is '**commodity**', a word used six times by the Bastard Faulconbridge in a single and lengthy speech that dissects the nature of the political world (quoted in full in the entry 'commodity'). The word does, of course, possess other meanings and operates in the field of economics, but nowhere else in Shakespeare's works is it used with such singular force to designate an action, attitude or outlook. It is, as Faulconbridge avers, 'the bias of the world' – the fulcrum on which the world of political opportunism is balanced. A term capable of carrying a sharp political edge is '**consorted**'; '**consort**' is generally neutral, though when Edmund says of Edgar 'Yes, madam, he was of that consort' (LR 2.1.97), the word acquires a stain. Mercutio bridles when Tybalt uses the word, before punning on its musical application (ROM 3.1.45–9). '**Capitulate**' merits an entry because of the divergence between current usage – to surrender or give way – and that employed in the plays, where it is used to signify 'negotiate' or 'to draw up articles of agreement'. A '**customer**' is a prostitute as opposed to someone seeking to purchase goods. '**Convey**' carries the implication of 'to steal' in addition to such meanings as 'escort'. Hence Bolingbroke's command 'convey him to the Tower', elicits Richard's biting riposte, 'Conveyers are you all' (R2 4.1.317–18). Accordingly, some words are included because they carry singular freight in a particular political context.

One consequence of the contestations that animate political discourse, commencing as early as the Henry VI plays, is that antagonists acquire a virtuosity in venting their hostility. Such conflicts as those between Gloucester and Winchester, or between the Yorkists and the Lancastrians, are replete with words that are conceptually refined to excoriate adversaries. '**Contumelious**' is one of the words that carries a particular sting. Integral to this word are insolence, contempt, arrogance, scorn. Regardless of rancour or even hatred, adversaries have access to a rich vocabulary of vituperation that allows them to display contempt while simultaneously being analytical and precise.

'**Pestiferous**' is another such word, carrying the suggestion of moral contagion. When Gloucester uses the term in his confrontation with Winchester it forms part of a comprehensive indictment – which, for all its virulence is forensic (1H6 3.1.8–27). Despite being ungracious, obdurate and strident, these antagonists exercise a masterly control over their political invective. In order to gain a firm appreciation of this rhetorical vivacity it is necessary to appreciate the weight and colour attaching to such words.

Two words infected by sinister implications are '**complice**', a participant in a conspiracy or cynical group – though it is employed once without an adversely pejorative meaning – and '**complot**', a devious scheme designed to bring down or kill enemies. The weight of the word is indicated by Richard's demand for an oath that the exiled Bolingbroke and Mowbray will never meet, 'To plot, contrive, or complot any ill' (R2 1.3.189). The final word draws into itself all the lesser possibilities. This is the ultimate expression of scheming.

Battle-hardened reviewers still find themselves taken aback by the potency of political life in Shakespeare's plays. In a review of the RSC's production of the Henriad (2007–8) a distinguished reviewer commented: 'Shakespeare's Histories, in their interaction between politics and the individual, increasingly seem the core of his creative output.'[24] Even the comedy *As You Like It* has at its centre the matter of usurpation – a theme that dominates histories and tragedies. The same play reveals the interweaving of politics, economics and social life. Orlando, deprived of his rightful inheritance and the benefit of an education, is horrified at the prospect of leaving the security of a productive enterprise to suffer certain destitution.

Just as the precariousness of economic circumstances finds expression in the plays of the period, so too does an obsession with wealth and accumulation. The speech that provides a most compelling picture of the process of commerce, its ships, merchants, trade routes, exotic products, and coinage is Barabas' soliloquy at the opening of Marlowe's *The Jew of Malta*. The global network is described with nonchalance, areas of the world distinguished, their superabundance of sought-after rarities flippantly represented: 'Bags of fiery opals, sapphires, amethysts, / Jacinths, hard topaz, grass-green emeralds, / Beauteous rubies, sparkling diamonds' (1.1.25–7). Yet, like the spider weaving its web, all this traffic is controlled from the centre culminating in 'Infinite riches in a little room' (1.1.37). In 47 lines Marlowe domesticates and commodifies the entire globe, the 'Infinite riches' of Barabus' 'little room' fitting snugly into another little room, Marlowe's theatre: space is constricted; imagination unconfined.

Another potent and symbolic room residing outside Shakespeare's work is Volpone's bedroom. Volpone's opening prayer celebrates the power of gold, but also the usurpation which it has effected: it is now the universal religion: 'Good morning to the day; and, next, my gold! / Open the shrine, that I may see my saint. / Hail the world's soul, and mine!' (1.1.1–3). The opening three lines of this 27-line speech convey the essence of the transformation that has taken place. Accumulation has become an addiction; human imagination and volition are enervated. Those who offer the prospect of gain can be sure of clients ready to be fleeced. The art is, in Volpone's words, a matter of: 'Letting the cherry knock against their lips, / And, draw it, by their mouths, and back again' (*Volpone* 1.1.89–90). Shakespeare and Jonson recognize that 'wants' are socially generated. Appetite and acquisitiveness create a market for any master of manipulation. *The Alchemist*, like *Volpone*, embodies a dream factory. The little rooms of Marlowe and Jonson are, indeed, metaphors for London, the world's market-place.

Frequently, 'economics' is identified as 'financial'. Shakespeare, however, shows a sophisticated awareness of the distinction between productive resources, such as ships and land, which may be almost infinitely malleable, and financial assets such as bonds or cash which constitute a command over such resources. The plays that figure most prominently in this volume are those dominated by finance: *The Merchant of Venice* and *Timon of Athens*. This is largely because Venice, then a great mercantile centre, had at its core an ideological and commercial conflict: the role of the moneylender and the legitimacy of usury or the taking of interest. The earlier play probes the connections between affective bonds and financial bonds. Just as the human heart finds expression in terms of intensity of feeling with love, hate and revenge, so too is it palpable as the physical price Antonio seems about to pay for failure to keep his bond. His ships are, of course, physical resources (capital assets), just as the cargo of spices and silks visualized by Salerio momentarily enrobing the sea after a shipwreck are gorgeously physical (1.1.32–4). Occasionally the physicality of money is emphasized in the theatre, as when Bassanio pours a chest full of coins onto the floor in the trial scene. But central to this play is money as liquidity, the great facilitator, in a world teeming with trade and commerce. At a time when a debate had been raging for two decades (see entry on **usury**), Shakespeare's play engages with the fundamental dispute about the legitimacy of usury. Is it right in principle? Is it inevitable? Should interest *rates* be subject to controls, such as the maximum rate of 10 per cent allowable at the time when the play was performed? Should this be an open market or restricted to one religious group? These are merely a few of the questions to which the play gives rise.

Timon of Athens – that other great financial play, containing around a hundred different words relating to **value, worth** and **exchange** – could hardly be further removed from the milieu of Venice. Remarkably, it embodies an economic 'model'. Timon's house is a centre of affluence and reckless gift-giving: resources in their physical and paper forms pervade the play. Timon, discovering that all his productive assets have been sold or mortgaged, gasps: 'To Lacedaemon did my land extend'. The dramatist lived in a world that appeared to be in a state of permanent expansion as new lands were discovered and new products flowed in, so the riposte of the loyal steward is surprising: 'Oh my good lord, the world is but a word; / Were it all yours, to give it in a breath,/ How quickly were it gone!' (2.2.151–4).

Shakespeare did not have the privilege of beholding our tiny planet spinning in space, yet Timon's steward reveals an intuitive awareness that *all* resources are *finite*. In a world of rapid consumption, resources can be expended in a single 'breath'. The ephemeral nature of the seemingly inexhaustible is rendered vividly. In this most conceptual of Shakespeare's plays the economic universe is sharply delineated. Agriculture, a major source of economic activity, is almost invisible, largely because the focus is on the social elite. They devote themselves to consumption that is *simultaneously* investment. Feasting at Timon's expense they provide him with small offerings and large flattery for which they receive handsome returns in the form of rich gifts. They even lend him money to finance this extravagance, ultimately gaining possession of Timon's lands when they are mortgaged to them.

The human spirit is depicted as frozen or coagulated: 'Their blood is cak'd, 'tis cold, it seldom flows' (2.2.216); compassion is absent: 'Friendship's full of dregs' (1.2.233); 'Pity's sleeping' (4.3.485). Cynicism and duplicity are in the very grain of the society: 'Promising is the very air o' th' time; / It opens the eyes of expectation. / Performance is ever duller for his act' (5.1.22–4). Affluence takes the form of waste: 'our vaults have wept / With drunken spilth of wine, when every room / Hath blaz'd with lights and bray'd with minstrelsy' (2.2.159–61). But its potential for sustaining a more refined sensibility is suggested by Timon's rueful comment, 'But myself, / Who had the world as my confectionary' (4.3.259–60). In a world where 'dishonor traffics with man's nature' (1.1.158), we encounter the incisive oxymoron of 'politic love' (3.3.34).

Self-interest is not merely the primary value, it is the sole animating force. As one of these social parasites observes of Timon, 'Every man has his fault, and honesty is his' (3.1.27–8). When such men turn away Timon's steward, they physically embody this ethos: 'After distasteful looks, and these hard fractions, / With certain half-caps, and cold-moving nods, / They froze me into silence' (2.2.211–13). The physicality links conditions and relationships. A character who denies relief to Timon on the grounds that 'Timon is shrunk indeed' (3.2.61), signalling a financial *and* physical contraction, is the same individual who 'ne'er drinks / But Timon's silver treads upon his lip' (3.2.70–1). 'Shrunk' and 'tread' vivify and intensify. The 'wide sea of wax' (1.1.47) referred to by the Poet is suggestive of mobility but also of cloyment or constriction. 'Wax', so important in this play, also alludes to 'grow greater', but it is subject to a strange contraction when a servant debt-collector describes Timon's changed circumstances: 'the days are wax'd shorter with him' (3.4.11). Wax is associated with the myth of Icarus that shadows the play and represents the seal on documents such as bonds and mortgages which possess a power that displaces, reduces or nullifies human bonds. Just as wax coagulates and hardens into the brittle stamp or seal, even language becomes mortgaged, as Timon's steward acknowledges: 'what he speaks is all in debt; he owes / For ev'ry word' (1.2.198–9). Everything is commodified, acquiring a strange mobility *and* confinement: 'His land's put to their books' (1.2.200). All things can be summed and put into a ledger. Economic circumstances even transform time itself. As Timon's financial position manifests itself, 'The future comes apace' (2.2.148). Contraction and constriction are suddenly everywhere: 'Lord Timon's happy hours are done and past, and his estate shrinks from him' (3.2.6–7). 'Shrinks' contains the physical suggestion of cowering fearfully as well as simply diminishing. The frozen Timonesque landscape is all-embracing. As Timon puts it: 'The place which I have feasted, does it now / (Like all mankind) show me an iron heart?' (3.4.82–3). As the debt-collectors clamour for repayment Timon realizes that fellow-feeling has been dislodged by pecuniary values and categories: 'Cut my heart in *sums*', '*Tell* out my blood', 'Five thousand drops *pays* that' (3.4.93–5). At the very core of this spiritual corruption is the lust for wealth, embodied in the ultimate transformative force: gold. In Timon's words:

> This yellow slave
> Will knit and break religions, bless th' accurs'd,
> Make the hoar leprosy ador'd, place thieves,
> And give them title, knee and approbation
> With senators on the bench. This is it
> That makes the wappen'd widow wed again;
> She, whom the spital-house and ulcerous sores
> Would cast the gorge at, this embalms and spices
> To th' April day again.

> 4.3.34–42

Corruption, economic, political and physical, is as manifest as it is ubiquitous. In furnishing the prostitutes with his new-found gold and the injunction to spread diseases, Timon puns on 'conditions' meaning 'natures' but also 'agreement': 'Spare your oaths; / I'll trust to your conditions' (4.3.139–40). In a world of contracts and waxen seals, the human capacity to act in accordance with the sworn oath has been lost. The distorted relationship between the physical and the financial is captured in his hour of need. Lucullus draws a clear line between affective and financial relationships: 'this is no time to lend money, especially upon bare friendship without security' (3.1.41–3). As the First Stranger observes, 'Men must learn now with pity to dispense, / For policy sits above conscience' (3.2.87–8). When confronted by his honest steward Timon produces an oxymoron that cuts to the core of his society: 'Is not thy kindness subtle, covetous, / If not a usuring kindness, and, as rich men deal gifts, / Expecting in return twenty for one?' (4.3.508–10). 'Kindness' meaning common humanity and compassion or generosity has been transformed into an instrument of deception and acquisition. The usury of this play bears no relationship to the provision of genuine commercial liquidity: it is a mechanism of exploitation.

Timon of Athens is a magnificent play. It concentrates like no other on the corrupting power of the unfettered quest for financial advantage. It reveals that the strands of economic and political life are tightly interwoven. Without the dominance of higher ideals there is no *genuine* society. In the second scene,

Timon maintains: 'what better or properer can we call our own than the riches of our friends?' (1.2.102–3). That key word 'properer' is richly suggestive of propriety, property and proprietorial. Property should flow, not coagulate.

If *Timon of Athens* is the play that probes to the core of the commodified, transactional society, *Henry V* interrogates the pursuit of glory and the role of vested interests. The discussion between Canterbury and Ely during the opening scene provides a perfect example of the interweaving of economic and political matters. Key economic concepts are delineated with precision; the operation of vested interests articulated in a way sufficiently opaque to satisfy the sensibilities of refined politicians. The decision hovering above the heads of the prelates relates to the problem of a parliamentary bill put in abeyance in response to political uncertainties during the previous regime. The two crucial matters raised during the discussion surround the potential costs to the Church and the opportunity available for removing the bill from the political agenda. What is most noteworthy about the dialogue is the clarity of the economic analysis. The Archbishop of Canterbury deals first with 'opportunity cost' in a considered way:

> As much as would maintain, to the King's honor,
> Full fifteen earls and fifteen hundred knights,
> Six thousand and two hundred good esquires;
> And to relief of lazars, and weak age
> Of indigent faint souls past corporal toil,
> A hundred almshouses right well supplied;
> And to the coffers of the King beside,
> A thousand pounds by th' year. Thus runs the bill.

> 1.1.12–19

The audience is made fully aware of the alternative uses of resources and invited to ask what the Church does with its income: for example, how much is spent and could be spent on the poor, weak and infirm? Should the state acquire the land in question, would its allocation of the revenues be more or less socially commendable? At the very least the issue of 'opportunity cost' is being raised. Secondly, there is a clear distinction being made between a capital asset like land and the revenues to which it gives rise. To hand over a large sum of liquid assets is far less damaging than to sacrifice part of the capital base from which the Church derives its income. Providing the finance for a war in France is definitely the better financial option. Failure to seize this opportunity would be to fail the Church. The real art of Machiavellianism is to make the politically advantageous position satisfying both to conscience and opinion. Linking violence and finance, Canterbury's incitement is undeviating:

> With blood and sword and fire, to win your right;
> In aid whereof we of the spirituality

> Will raise your Highness such a mighty sum
> As never did the clergy at one time
> Bring in to any of your ancestors.

1.2.131–5

Henry's apparent hesitancy, on the grounds of possible invasion by the Scots, gives rise to Canterbury's analogy of the operation of the division of labour in the natural world and in economic life. What is so striking about this comparison is that the symbiotic relationship between bees and flowers is both civil and violent:

> Where some, like magistrates, correct at home;
> Others, like merchants, venter trade abroad;
> Others, like soldiers, armed in their stings,
> Make boot upon the summer's velvet buds,
> Which pillage they with merry march bring home
> To the tent-royal of their emperor,
> Who busied in his majesty surveys
> The singing masons buildings roofs of gold,
> The civil citizens kneading up the honey,
> The poor mechanic porters crowding in
> Their heavy burthens at his narrow gate,

1.2.191–201

Thus the hive mirrors the perfectly functioning commonwealth. It is characterized by an efficient division of labour where even violence plays its part. The violence is effected by extravagant poetic licence. What should stand as an exemplum of a peaceful, ordered society is employed as a justification for war without any sense of incongruity on the part of the speaker. The counterpart to this either disingenuous or cynical misrepresentation is provided by Burgundy. Making his plea for peace he identifies the damage inflicted on the economy and the consequent impoverishment of familial, social and cultural structures:

>   let it not disgrace me,
> If I demand, before this royal view,
> What rub or what impediment there is,
> Why that the naked, poor, and mangled Peace,
> Dear nurse of arts, plenties, and joyful births,
> Should not in this best garden of the world,
> Our fertile France, put up her lovely visage?
> Alas, she hath from France too long been chas'd,
> And all her husbandry doth lie on heaps,
> Corrupting in its own fertility.
> Her vine, the merry cheerer of the heart,
> Unpruned dies; her hedges even-pleach'd,

> Like prisoners wildly overgrown with hair,
> Put forth disorder'd twigs; her fallow leas,
> The darnel, hemlock, and rank fumitory
> Doth root upon, while that the coulter rusts
> That should deracinate such savagery;

5.2.31–47

This vision of an economy in disarray with its implications for education and scientific progress is irresistible. It exposes the violence witnessed in the play as shocking and perverse. The pivotal phrase is 'beauty and utility'. Economic activity, revealed as the very foundation of society, also has an aesthetic quality which generates a refinement of sensibility. In Shakespeare's play of war and peace economic reality is vividly represented and its vulnerability to political ambitions made clear.

One of the finest scenes in the exploration of political and economic life occurs in *Henry VIII.* Queen Katherine and the Duke of Norfolk appeal to the King to revoke the recent financial impositions imposed by Cardinal Wolsey. In setting forth her complaint the Queen highlights the political repercussions of special taxes. This speech is unprecedented in Shakespeare's work for its description of the integrated nature of manufacturing industries, and their susceptibility to fracture or collapse consequent upon disruption. The chasm that divides gainful employment from impoverishment and beggary is clearly articulated. This precisely crafted political indictment – in a language conveying fully the indignation these taxes have aroused yet carefully retaining the refinement of diplomacy – is followed up by Norfolk who, completing the argument, delineates the *economic* consequences:

> Not almost appears,
> It doth appear; for, upon theses taxations,
> The clothiers all, not able to maintain
> The many to them 'longing, have put off
> The spinsters, carders, fullers, weavers, who,
> Unfit for other life, compell'd by hunger
> And lack of other means, in desperate manner
> Daring th' event to th' teeth, are all in uproar,
> And danger serves among them.

1.2.29–37

The King's cancellation of Wolsey's tax not only exposes the economic and political costs of such adventures but also displays a keen awareness of the state's dependence on a sound economy:

> Sixth part of each?
> A trembling contribution! Why, we take

> From every tree, lop, bark, and part o'th'timber;
> And, though we leave it with a root, thus hack'd,
> The air will drink the sap.
>
> 1.2.94–8

In an exercise in damage limitation, the thwarted Wolsey seeks to gain credit for this policy reversal: 'let it be nois'd / That through our intercession this revokement / And pardon comes' (1.2.105–7). This incident by no means completes the play's exploration of economic and political manoeuvring, but it provides a telling example of the relationship of a real economy to finance and power.

A persistent representation of the market is the brothel. At first blush this is surprising because it is illicit and occupies the margins of a society dominated by a complex and sophisticated network of production, trade and commerce. A vital feature of the market-place is the facilitator or go-between, the quintessential representative being the bawd. It is hard for any go-between to avoid disrepute by virtue of the infamy attaching to the bawd. The 'factor', agent of the merchant, avoids the opprobrium attaching to bawd, but in most situations the very concept of the go-between is subject to suspicion or odium. The brothel reveals the impersonal nature of market relations in their most stark form. Mistress Quickly and Doll in the Henriad appear more like public benefactors than ruthless exploiters, not least because they are exploited by Falstaff and accordingly benefit from the roseate glow that seems to hover over Eastcheap. No such mitigation is apparent in the admittedly vibrant but sordid underworld of *Measure for Measure*, as depicted with bleak and brutal realism in Simon McBurney's 2004 production for the National Theatre Company and Complicité,[25] or in *Pericles*. But whereas Mistress Overdone, Pompey Bum and their associates are counterbalanced by the corrupt practices of the Deputy, Angelo, no such offsetting influences are to be found in *Pericles*. Paradoxically, it is the first of the Romances, *Pericles*, which provides the most thorough exploration of the economics of the brothel. Here we see life in the lower depths where financial survival leaves no place for sentiment. Indeed, were Marina unable to offer the prospect of profitable diversification, as teacher and entertainer in prosperous households, she would be raped in order to make her compliant.

It is not clear whether a similar compulsion is a factor in *Measure for Measure*. It is evident that disease is a frequent concomitant of provision and receipt of the service rendered by prostitutes. Despite this substantial drawback Lucio insists to the disguised Duke, 'it is impossible to extirp it quite, friar, till eating and drinking be put down' (3.2.102–3). Yet as Marina comments in her short time as captive in the brothel, 'Diseases have been sold dearer than physic' (*PER* 4.6.98). Is the brothel, therefore, a parody of the market or its most potent expression? All demands *that are backed by money*, will be met, no matter how perverse the consumer. (See entry on **bawd**.)

Approach and Methodology

In addition to providing valuable tools for the exploration of Shakespeare's plays, sonnets and narrative poems, these dictionaries constitute a celebration of the dramatist's intellectual curiosity, his omnivorous reading and his prodigious mastery of differing fields of specialized knowledge. Concepts, principles and techniques are employed with such a facility and lightness of touch that they can be used to fertilize other apparently dissociated areas of thought. Moreover, they reveal that Shakespeare is never merely passive or submissive in responding to specialized disciplines such as religion, law, politics or economics. He brings a highly active, interrogative intelligence to bear so that arcane and complex spheres of knowledge are made accessible. These are articulated in diverse ways from the formal and austere through to the sceptical and playful. One of the great pleasures of exploring complex, sophisticated and specialized vocabularies is the light they throw on seemingly playful or superficial exchanges. This explorative layering underlying dialogue enhances awareness of Shakespeare's unique capacity for endowing discourse with multiple strata, never diminishing or obscuring surface meanings, but enriching and enhancing them.

Shakespeare's economic and political language is extensive, vivid and intricate. The ideal situation for the compiler of a dictionary of specialized language would be the discovery of an extensive list of technical or recondite terms that could then be thoroughly explored for the benefit of the non-specialist. In this respect, areas such as Shakespeare's legal or military language are the most favoured. The picture is more complicated with respect to political and economic language. The significance of this particular vocabulary frequently resides in the way in which certain words have changed their meaning through time, or because some words possess a peculiar vitality when operating in the political or economic realms.

Shakespeare's virtuosity is such that a word often contains an entire landscape. Sometimes it is necessary to explore that landscape in order to highlight the peculiar topographical location or configuration of political or economic words and concepts.

Some readers may be disappointed by a failure to discover an entry on a word which has a blush of economic or political significance, or one that occupies the hinterland of an application that resides outside the specialist fields to which this study is devoted. In order to keep this volume within realistic bounds I have disregarded words which could reasonably be expected to fall within the purview of this study where their meanings are obvious. Likewise in selecting quotations I have generally employed examples which are illuminating because of the complexity of application or where they reveal the nuances and mobility of the word in question. I have endeavoured to keep these entries brief in the hope that the reader will want to go immediately to the core of the idea. On occasion I have felt obliged to provide more extensive treatment.

Because they contain several headwords, some passages are cited and discussed more than once. I have preferred to run the risk of overlap or duplication rather than compressing or fragmenting entries by redirecting readers to other headwords. In some instances I have linked two or three closely related words in one entry, e.g. '**faction**', '**factionary**', '**factious**', in order to aid their definition and analysis. On other occasions, for such adjacent terms as '**policy**', '**politic**', '**politician**', '**politicly**', clarity requires separation. There are 233 entries.

When choosing illustrative examples I have occasionally strayed to the limits of my brief in order to convey the mobility of the word in question. This is to reveal either the colouration the word carries into a non-political/economic domain or to indicate ways in which such potential carry-over is expunged.

Choice of words: criteria   To qualify for inclusion a word had to meet one of the following criteria:
(1) A technical term requiring definition and analysis of its range and context, e.g. '**usury**', '**earnest**', '**value**', '**price**', '**practice**'.
(2) A word that has changed in meaning, or possesses additional implications so that confusion in a political or economic context is likely, e.g. '**capitulate**' (which means 'to negotiate' or 'to sign articles of agreement', but does *not* mean 'surrender'); '**competitor**', signifying associate rather than rival; '**rival**', too, usually means associate.

Readers would expect an entry on '**commodity**' because of its role in economics, but it is also critical in the political domain where it signifies unscrupulous pursuit of self-interest, the outstanding example of which occurs in *King John* where Faulconbridge the Bastard employs it six times in one speech (quoted in full under this entry). Likewise, '**innovator**', which would suggest someone engaged in technological change, was not used in this sense in Shakespeare's day. Rather, it intimates radical *political* change or upheaval. '**Subsidy**' denotes a tax or financial imposition rather than supplement, rebate or some form of negative tax as is now suggested in modern discourse. '**Traffic**' has come to be deeply associated with illicit activity whereas in Shakespeare's plays it generally sits comfortably alongside '**trade**' as part of the commerce of everyday life.
(3) Words apparently possessing little economic or political significance in current usage decidedly enter either political or economic realms in the plays; '**beguile**', for instance: although embodying six distinct meanings two-thirds of the applications signify to 'steal' or 'deceive'. '**Opinion**', though still operative today in the field of political discourse, carries nothing like the range and pressure operative in the plays.
(4) There is a concept still fundamental to economics and politics even if Shakespeare's uses of the words differ from current terminology. '**Capital**', in the sense of productive resources, physical or financial, capable of generating income is strongly present in the plays, but is not linked to this particular word. The word is included, nevertheless, so that the reader can discover its precise applications. '**Investments**' has the meaning of 'clothes' rather than 'financial instruments' except possibly on one occasion when Polonius, providing a master-class in double meanings strongly connected to the world of finance, cautions Ophelia: 'Do not believe his vows, for they are

brokers, / Not of that dye which their investments show' (*HAM* 1.3.127–8). It would appear that here is a Shakespearean coinage – all the more likely because 'investments' in the sense of garments is also a coinage. Given this probability the word decidedly merits an entry. The modern sense of an outlay of **money** or resources designed to produce a future stream of income or **profit** occurs first in the period 1613–16 in the letters and journals dealing with the East Indian trade. Chambers adds that the figurative meaning of 'clothe' or 'endow with attributes, qualities', etc., is first recorded in Shakespeare's *Othello* (1604).[26] The sense of 'to clothe in the insignia of an office, install in an office of rank' dates from 1533–34. Shakespeare seems peculiarly drawn to this word with its latent possibilities. Foreman discusses the etymology and implications of investment and investments.[27]

(5)   The world of politics is characterized by fierce exchanges. It would be easy therefore to conceive of some words as being merely vituperative. Several of the words included here have been selected because of the peculiar leverage they exercise by being both *precise* and *potent*. Examples include, '**consorted**', '**contumelious**', '**caterpillar**', '**palter**', '**perfidious**', '**pestiferous**', '**complot**', '**traduce**'. Part of the vocabulary of political invective, they are either analytical or forensic in function. A word like '**temporize**' demands inclusion because it penetrates more deeply than in the broader discourse of everyday life. It occupies a particularly significant role in the most frequently cited *political* play in this volume: *Coriolanus*.

Recommendations for further reading, section (C) in each entry, has been based on the principle that these texts illuminate the word and its concept as it is developed in one or more of the examples cited. Generally, I have been confronted by an embarrassment of riches. This is due to the extensive choice of material now available on virtually every aspect of Shakespeare studies. The criteria I have used are based on the relevance of a word to my discussion, the brevity of that discussion and accessibility. Occasionally I direct the reader to particular pages or chapters; at other times I leave it to the reader to either select the plum or eat the entire pudding. There are many fine volumes in the bibliography that merit close scrutiny though they have not been mentioned under any particular heading. This bibliography will I hope make available to students the numerous islands of scholarship helpful in navigating this particular sea of Shakespeare studies without inhibiting personal exploration.

Notes

1   Woodmansee, Martha and Osteen, Mark, eds, *The New Economic Criticism: Studies at the Intersection of Literature and Economics*, London and New York: Routledge, 1999.
2   For a sense of the range and trajectory of these new approaches to Shakespeare Criticism see: Hawkes, David, *Idols of the Marketplace: Idolatry and Commodity Fetishism in English Literature, 1580–1680*, New York and Basingstoke: Palgrave, 2001; Woodbridge, Linda, ed., *Money and the Age of Shakespeare: Essays in New Economic Criticism*, New York and Basingstoke: Palgrave Macmillan, 2003; Harris, Jonathan Gil, *Sick Economies:*

Drama, Mercantilism, and Disease in Shakespeare's England, Philadelphia: University of Pennsylvania Press, 2004.

3   Clark, Sandra, in *Renaissance Drama*, Cambridge and Malden, MA: Polity, 2007: 151.
4   Barber, C. L., *Shakespeare's Festive Comedy: A Study of Dramatic Form and its Relation to Social Custom*, Princeton, NJ: Princeton University Press, 1959: 16.
5   Agnew, Jean-Christophe, *Worlds Apart: The Market and the Theater in Anglo-American Thought, 1550–1750*, Cambridge and New York: Cambridge University Press, 1986; Bruster, Douglas, *Drama and the Market in the Age of Shakespeare*, Cambridge and New York: Cambridge University Press, 1992; paperback 2004.
6   Joughin, John J., 'Shakespeare and politics: an introduction' in Alexander, ed., *Shakespeare and Politics*, Cambridge: Cambridge University Press, 2004: 6.
7   Cohen, Adam Max, *Shakespeare and Technology: Dramatising Early Modern Technological Revolutions*, New York and Basingstoke: Palgrave, 2006: 171.
8   For an analysis of 'commodity fetishism', including the intersection between Marx and the 'Classical' economists and theological perspectives, see Hawkes, David, *Idols of the Marketplace: Idolatry and Commodity Fetishism in English Literature, 1580–1680*, New York and Basingstoke: Palgrave, 2001: Chapter 2.
9   Keynes, J. M., *A Treatise on Money*, 2 vols, New York: Macmillan, 1930: Volume 2: 154.
10 Gurr, Andrew, *Playgoing in Shakespeare's London*, Cambridge: Cambridge University Press, 1987: 4.
11 Bruster, Douglas, op. cit.: 3.
12 Brecht, Bertolt, 'Radio as a means of communication: a talk on the function of radio' (1930) in Mattelart, Armand and Siegelaub, Seth, eds, *Communication and Class Struggle*, Volume 2: 'Liberation, socialism' (New York: International General, 1983): 169.
13 Bruster, Douglas, op. cit.: 3–4.
14 Stone, Lawrence, 'Inigo Jones and the New Exchange', *Archaeological Journal* 114 (1957): 106–7.
15 Thomas Dekker, *The Gull's Hornbook* (1609), from Pendry, E. D., *Thomas Dekker*, Stratford-upon-Avon Library, Volume 4, Cambridge, MA: Harvard University Press, 1968: 98.
16 Bruster, Douglas, op cit.: 4–8.
17 *Troilus and Cressida* is the play that engages most intensively with the concepts of measurement, calculation, quantification, division and fragmentation. For exploration of their dramatic integration see Thomas, Vivian, *The Moral Universe of Shakespeare's Problem Plays*, Croom Helm, 1987; paperback, Routledge, 1991: 81–102.
18 For exploration of implications arising from words and concepts in this speech and their contemporary resonance see, for example, Netzloff, 'The lead casket: capital, mercantilism, and *The Merchant of Venice*' in Woodbridge, Linda, ed., *Money and the Age of Shakespeare: Essays in New Economic Criticism*, New York and Basingstoke: Palgrave Macmillan, 2003. Netzloff has a penetrating discussion on the melding of pecuniary, heroic and chivalric conceptions in the evolution of Elizabethan commerce. Antonio's 'wealthy *Andrew*' (1.1.27) for instance, 'shares its name with the Spanish galleon captured by Sir Francis Drake in 1596, the same year as the play's initial performance'. Moreover, 'The comparison of Portia to the golden fleece (1.1.169–72; 3.2.241) further evokes an image frequently used to represent the precious metals of the Americas'. However, Netzloff detects a counter-current in commercial discourse where the promiscuity of Spanish gold with its inflationary consequences for sixteenth-century Europe – formulated by Bassanio as 'the guiled shore / To a most dangerous sea' (3.2.97–8) – becomes associated with the suffocating image of Midas, in contrast to creative English industry with its expansive production and export of woollen cloth. As Netzloff expresses the matter: '*The Merchant of Venice* distances its economy from an older chivalric model of "adventure", one still evoked in the literature of English privateering of the 1590s, foregrounding instead an emergent ethos of capitalist "venturing" ' (166–9).

19 Garner, Bryan A., 'Shakespeare's Latinate neologisms' in Salmon, V. and Burness, E., *A Reader in the Language of Shakespearean Drama*, Amsterdam/Philadelphia: John Benjamins Publishing Company, 1987: 209.

20 Mentz, Steven R., 'The fiend gives friendly counsel: Launcelot Gobbo and polyglot economics in *The Merchant of Venice*' in Woodbridge, ed., *Money and the Age of Shakespeare: Essays in New Economic Criticism*, New York and Basingstoke: Palgrave Macmillan, 2003: 179.

21 Turner, Frederick, *Shakespeare's Twenty-First Century Economics: The Morality of Love and Money*, New York and Oxford: Oxford University Press, 1999: 195.

22 Agnew, Jean-Christophe, op. cit.: 76.

23 Barnhart, Robert K., *Chambers Dictionary of Etymology*: 899.

24 Billington, Michael, 'Exciting trilogy with limitations: *Richard II/Henry IV Parts One and Two*', the *Guardian*, 18 August 2007.

25 O'Connor and Goodland, eds, *A Directory of Shakespeare in Performance, 1970–2005*, Volume 1, Basingstoke and New York: Palgrave Macmillan, 2007: 805–6.

26 Barnhart, ed. *Chambers Dictionary of Etymology*: 542.

27 Forman, Valerie, 'Material dispossessions and counterfeit investments: the economies of *Twelfth Night*' in Woodbridge, Linda, ed., *Money and the Age of Shakespeare: Essays in New Economic Criticism*, New York and Basingstoke: Palgrave Macmillan, 2003: 116–18.

abound

(A) Generally straightforward, this word possesses strong economic force in *H8* and *ROM* where the meaning is to prosper or flourish financially.

(B) In the opening scene of *H8*, a group of characters analyse the magnificence and extravagance of the competitive display of **wealth** and theatricality by the English and French kings at the Field of the Cloth of Gold (June 1520). Aburgavenny observes that the enterprise has imposed such a financial burden on friends who participated that their days of prosperity are over: 'I do know / Kinsmen of mine, three at the least, that have / By this so sicken'd their estates, that never / They shall abound as formerly' (*H8* 1.1.80–3). This play, originally entitled *All Is True*, vibrates with political and economic matters.

The Friar, punning on '**use**', meaning to take **interest**, scolds Romeo for his self-indulgent response to banishment: 'Fie, fie, thou shamest thy shape, thy love, thy wit, / Which like a usurer abound'st in all, / And usest none in that true use indeed / Which should bedeck thy shape, thy love, thy wit' (*ROM* 3.3.122–5). The contrast is between the sterility of **usury** and the fruitfulness of rational **expenditure**.

Of the other examples, one requires brief comment because of its political context and singular pressure. Young Malcolm, in probing Macduff's honesty, insists that he lacks all the kingly virtues. Having enumerated them, he concludes: 'I have no relish of them, but abound / In the division of each several crime, / Acting it many ways' (*MAC* 4.3.95–7). This unusual construction means something more than 'abundance'; Malcolm claims that he is extravagantly given to every possible vice and displays virtuosity in the exercise of each.

(C) For a description of the events referred to in *Henry VIII*, see McMullan's Introduction to Arden 3. He also engages with the key concept of temperance 85–93, and spectacle, paying special attention to Greg Doran's use of 'Discreet Spectacle' 53–7 in the acclaimed RSC production of 1996. This excellent essay contains significant comments on the political and economic dimensions of this seriously undervalued work. The essay concludes with a summary of the evidence relating to the question of Fletcher's possible contribution to the play. Also of interest here is Maria Hayward's *Dress at the Court of Henry VIII*. Michael Long's pungent, brief and incisive book explores *Macbeth*'s key concepts including, crucially, the ideas of abounding and reciprocity. Again, if 'brevity is the soul of wit', Cedric Watts' *Romeo and Juliet* delineates the language and structure of *ROM* with panache.

accompt, account
(A) There is no essential distinction between these words: both are used as nouns and verbs. Behind their varied usages lies the idea of the account book or **reckoning**, extending from God's account book to household **bills**. Thus applications range from being called to account morally or financially to a straightforward arithmetical calculation or estimate. Less obviously in *ROM* is the meaning number or assortment, while in *WT* precedent or calculation is signified. The verb is used to intimate '**consider**' and also 'to take account of' or 'to esteem'. The adjective accountant means 'responsible' or 'answerable'.
(B) The notion of account as esteem or estimation is clearly conveyed by Portia:

> You see me, Lord Bassanio, where I stand,
> Such as I am. Though for myself alone
> I would not be ambitious in my wish
> To wish myself much better, yet for you,
> I would be trebled twenty times myself,
> A thousand times more fair, ten thousand times more rich,
> That only to stand high in your account,
> I might in virtues, beauties, livings, friends,
> Exceed account.
>
> *MV* 3.2.149–57

This delicate, generous verbal dance focuses on the subordination of worldly goods to feeling, providing a fine example of the way in which Shakespeare takes a term from its original locale in economic life and applies it to the higher world of the emotions. Significantly, the word is used twice in the last three lines with the passage itself embedded in an exchange where economic terms experience vitalizing transformations, becoming the currency of love as opposed to the currency of the **market-place**.

The sense of rendering an account of actions is found in diverse situations. The *locus classicus* is provided by the Ghost of Old Hamlet who complains of the sudden cutting off of his life so that he had no time to seek forgiveness for his sins:

> Thus was I, sleeping, by a brother's hand
> Of life, of crown, of queen, at once dispatch'd,
> Cut off even in the blossoms of my sin,

> Unhous'led, disappointed, unanel'd,
> No reck'ning made, but sent to my account
> With all my imperfections on my head.
>
> *HAM* 1.5.74–9

Here is a clear sense of life itself, all our actions, being entered into an account book, which is **audited** by God.

The suggestion of being called to a reckoning is expressed with the utmost vigour by Prince Hal when he reassures his father that he will strip Hotspur of his glories, transferring them to himself:

> Percy is but my factor, good my lord,
> To engross up glorious deeds on my behalf;
> And I will call him to so strict account
> That he shall render every glory up,
> Yea, even the slightest worship of his time,
> Or I will tear the reckoning from his heart.
>
> *1H4* 3.2.147–52

Not only is the link established between render, reckoning and account, but the abstract 'glorious' is expressed with the tangible physicality of gold coins. The integration of the financial and honorific spheres is cemented by the term '**factor**' meaning financial agent. The entrepreneurial Hotspur conceives of himself as a self-centred accumulator of renown, but he is busy in the service of Hal.

The simple meaning of account as number is given expression by Richard before the Battle of Bosworth in response to Norfolk's estimate of Richmond's force of 'six or seven thousand': 'Why, our battalia trebles that account' (*R3* 5.3.10–11). The use of the term in the sense of 'consider' is intimated by Richmond in his appeal to God also before the Battle of Bosworth: 'O Thou whose captain I account myself' (*R3* 5.3.108).

Words frequently possess a particular vitality in Shakespeare by virtue of their susceptibility to punning. Such is the case when Catesby uses the word first to mean **value** or esteem when addressing Hastings, and then to indicate 'expect' or 'anticipate' when making a wicked aside to the audience: 'The princes [Richard and Buckingham] both make high account of you – / [Aside] For they account his head upon the bridge' (*R3* 3.2.69–70). This cruel joke takes part of its pressure from the quibble on 'high' meaning 'great' but also physically elevated, i.e. high on the bridge. It is possible that the second 'account' means anticipate or 'in their calculation or account book', the latter being particularly telling as the head is used to intimidate the Mayor and is part of some careful accounting in the political ledger. It could be that anticipate, estimate, calculate all jostle for primacy as account splinters under the concentration of the lines embodying witty mockery – a characteristic feature of this play.

The meaning 'consider', the most frequent application of the term, is clearly articulated by Leontes' loyal servant, Camillo, who accepts his master's injunction to poison his dear friend Polixenes: 'I am his cupbearer: / If from me he have wholesome beverage, / Account me not your servant' (*WT* 1.2.345–7). The word's capacity to be played on is illustrated by Coriolanus in defending himself against the accusation that he has not 'lov'd the common people': 'You should account me the more virtuous that I have not been common in my love. I will, sir, flatter my sworn brother, the people, to earn a dearer estimation of them; 'tis a condition they account gentle' (*COR* 2.3.94–7). The first use means esteem or 'consider me'; the second, estimate. Here is a steely irony in which there is a convergence of meanings. Sandwiched within the sardonic mockery is the economically grounded phrase 'earn a dearer estimation': the **counterfeit** currency, flattery, is passed for the true coin of genuine regard. The contextual paradox is that the haughty hero is incapable of dissembling in order to gain political **advantage**.

A seemingly simple but oblique and strangely moving application occurs in Romeo's haunting description of the impoverished apothecary's shop where the term essentially means 'array' or 'assortment': 'and about his shelves / A beggarly account of empty boxes,/ Green earthen pots, bladders, and musty seeds, / Remnants of packthread, and old cakes of roses / Were thinly scattered, to make up a show' (*ROM* 5.1.44–8). Here the page of the account book is literalized into these shabby scraps of decayed or out-of-date goods. The epithet 'beggarly' employed in conjunction with 'account' is itself a deeply impoverishing phrase, jarring our senses into sympathetic activity. Nowhere else is the term harnessed to create such an evocative response.

The physical account book or material calculation is referred to by Flavius in remonstrating with Timon: 'O my good lord, / At many times I brought in my accompts, / Laid them before you' (*TIM* 2.2.132–4). The Jailer's Daughter, her mind unbalanced, expresses a prosaic application of the principle of making an arithmetical calculation or drawing up a balance sheet. She attributes this clerical skill to a horse: 'A very fair hand, and casts himself th' accounts / Of all his hay and provender' (*TNK* 5.2.58–9). Cade's rebellion also gives rise to this direct specification when the smith denounces the Clerk of Chartam for his mastery of these subversive skills: 'He can write and read and cast accompt' (*2H6* 4.2.85–6).

Portia, disguised as Balthazar, employs the verb when declining financial recompense for her legal services: 'And I, delivering you, am satisfied, / And therein do account myself well paid' (*MV*, 4.1.416–7). She considers Antonio's thanks sufficient reward.

The suggestion of 'responsible' or 'answerable' finds expression in Iago's soliloquy when he reveals the nature of his desire for Desdemona: 'Now I do love her too, / Not out of absolute lust (though peradventure / I stand accomptant for as great a sin)' (*OTH* 2.1.291–3). Only slightly different is Angelo's claim that Claudio is answerable to the law for his crime of fornication: 'And his offence is so, as it appears, / Accountant to the law upon that pain' (*MM* 2.4.85–6). 'Penalty' is the meaning attaching to the word 'pain'.

On the return of Leontes' ambassadors from the Oracle at Delphos much sooner than anticipated, a lord announces: 'So please you, sir, their speed / Hath been beyond accompt' (*WT* 2.3.197–8). The meaning here is calculation.

Shakespeare both adopts and subverts the conceptualizations associated with the economic transformations of the age. God's ledger may have been super-seded by that of the merchant, but the dramatist emphasizes the connections between the moral and material spheres. Moreover, he takes economic concepts and transmutes them into metaphors of love. The compacting potential afforded by this process is illustrated by several of the above examples. Shakespeare has a facility for siphoning off opprobrious or mundane connections while com-mandeering their vitalizing associations. This is shown in his transferring a finan-cial concept to the emotional sphere (as in the Portia example above). On other occasions, they are simultaneously activated to generate agitation. In the Coriolanus example, 'dear' and 'account' retain the hard-edged qualities of economic life while at the same time possessing strong emotional force.

(C) The significance of improved accounting, double-entry bookkeeping and the growth of a whole host of activities designed to capture and sum the complex nexus of economic activities and financial flows are elaborated in diverse ways by Glimp and Warren, eds, *The Art of Calculation*; Crosby, *The Measure of Reality*; Sullivan, *The Rhetoric of Credit*; Turner, *Shakespeare's Twenty-First Century Economics*. For a succinct commentary on the legal dimensions of the word, see Sokol and Sokol, *Shakespeare's Legal Language*. A fascinating account of the religious aspects is to be found in Greenblatt, *Hamlet in Purgatory*. Brockbank, *Coriolanus*, Arden 2, 185, has a footnote on the *COR* example.

achieve, achievement

(A) The essential meaning of the verb achieve is to attain some end, or to gain possession of something, e.g., a crown, territory, a military victory, a woman, or even something more abstract like experience. Hence the noun achievement is something acquired or possessed through endeavour or bought to a successful conclusion. Achievements are attributes or attainments of an individual or a society. Central to these terms is meritoriousness. What is gained is highly valuable. It has been attained through great effort or good fortune.

(B) The word is used in both political and romantic spheres, frequently with interesting nuances. At the straightforward level Aufidius, commenting on Coriolanus' military prowess, concedes that he 'Fights dragon-like, and does achieve as soon / As draw his sword' (*COR* 4.7.23–4). The beauty of this comment is that the victories are secured *effortlessly*, whereas endeavour is usually intrinsic to achievement. Determining to send his son Proteus out into the wider world, Antonio affirms: 'Experience is by industry achiev'd, / And perfected by the swift course of time' (*TGV* 1.3.22–3).

Henry V cautions the French Herald, Mountjoy, who prior to the Battle of Agincourt offers the English king the opportunity of negotiating his ransom: 'Bid them achieve me, and then sell my bones' (*H5* 4.3.91). Earlier in the play the Constable of France has confidently asserted that when Henry is fully acquainted with the nature of his predicament, 'He'll drop his heart into the sink of fear, /

And for achievement offer us his ransom' (3.5.59–60). This is a more complicated construction which probably means that Henry will capitulate and settle for saving his own life by ransom, thereby, 'bringing the matter to an end' – the most likely meaning of achievement here. There is also a play on achievement as 'attainment', in that Henry's survival contrasts sharply with his intended conquest of France.

Movement into the field of romance casts light on the essentials and subtlety of the word. Cassio gives vent to his adoration of Desdemona by reporting that Othello 'hath achiev'd a maid / That paragons description and wild fame' (*OTH* 2.1.61–2). Here he celebrates his commander's great fortune in winning her.

Cressida, however, has a different take on the word. For her the woman who has been 'achieved' has been physically possessed; she has crossed a threshold; her position has been fundamentally transformed. In a remarkable speech she acknowledges that a woman has ascendancy over a man until she surrenders physically to him: 'Women are angels, wooing: / Things won are done, joy's soul lies in the doing / . . . / Therefore this maxim out of love I teach: / Achievement is command; ungain'd, beseech' (*TRO* 1.2.286–93). Here is an interesting crossover point between strategy and love: the essence of Cressida's analysis is power. The lesson is one of sexual politics. Cressida seems to have judged matters rightly, because the morning after their only night of lovemaking she is unable to persuade Troilus to return to bed. There is a twist here which leads to another nuanced application of the term. Before they are properly dressed they discover that Cressida is to be **exchanged** for a Trojan prisoner. Troilus' bewildered response is: 'How my achievements mock me!' (4.2.69). The word 'achievements' is as compacted as the sentence: the physical and emotional surrender by Cressida to him and his release from the torment of seemingly hopeless desire are both lost in the blink of an eye.

The Countess of Auvergne's reference to Talbot's 'achievements' alludes to his conquests and all that attaches to his martial prowess (*1H6* 2.3.8). Hamlet's comment has broader terms of reference when he complains that the Danes' reputation for drunkenness deflects admiration away from their qualities and attainments: 'They clip us drunkards, and with swinish phrase / Soil our addition, and indeed it takes / From our achievements, though perform'd at height, / The pith and marrow of our attribute' (*HAM* 1.4.19–22).

The sense of 'achievements' as 'attributes' that have been earned finds expression in the words of the Countess of Rossillion. Praising Helena she makes a distinction between inherited attributes (potentialities) and those that are cultivated: 'she derives her honesty, and achieves her goodness' (*AWW* 1.1.44–5). In the words of Maria's letter, so eagerly taken up by Malvolio, 'Some are born great, some achieve greatness, and some have greatness thrust upon 'em' (*TN* 2.5.145–6). Occasionally, a by-product of achieving greatness is the ill repute that accompanies it. On his deathbed Henry IV reassures Hal that inheritance of the crown cleanses it from the stain of **usurpation**: 'To thee it shall descend with better quiet, / Better opinion, better confirmation, / For all the soil of the achievement goes / With me into the earth' (*2H4* 4.5.187–90). However, minutes later the dying king incites his son to engage in a military campaign to deflect the attentions of those who may pry into his legitimacy: 'Yet though thou stand'st more sure than I could do, / Thou art not firm enough, since griefs are green, / . . . / . . . Therefore, my Harry, / Be it thy course to busy giddy minds / With foreign quarrels' (202–14).

Hence the king who acknowledges that 'all my reign hath been but as a scene / Acting that argument' (197–8) sets in motion Hal's French campaign, with all its bloody consequences, in order to validate and preserve his 'achievement' – something Hal succeeds in doing in the short run but which eventually culminates in a terrible civil war. Shakespeare's audience, familiar with the *1H6–R3* tetralogy, hearing the above lines from Henry's speech would have recognized their telling dramatic irony.

(C) Hattaway, ed., *The Cambridge Companion to Shakespeare's History Plays*, contains excellent essays relating to this discussion. The Arden 3 editions of *1H6* (Burns), *2H6* (Knowles) and *3H6* (Cox and Rasmussen) are crammed with fascinating details. Saccio's *Shakespeare's English Kings* is exemplary in exploring the relationship between the historical characters and events and Shakespeare's dramatic treatment of them, territory also negotiated in a lively and colourful way by Norwich, *Shakespeare's Kings*. The numerous volumes written from the perspectives of New Historicism and Cultural Materialism include Dollimore and Sinfield, eds, *Political Shakespeare*; Bristol, *Carnival and Theatre*; Tennenhouse, *Power on Display*. Craik, ed., *Henry V*, Arden 3, 230 has a note on 'achievement'. Cressida's plight receives close consideration by Charnes, *Notorious Identity*, and Leggatt, *Shakespeare's Tragedies*.

advance, advanced, advancement

(A) The verb advance has two frequent and unequivocal meanings: the most obvious is literally to raise or lift up; the second is to promote, prefer or elevate to a position of influence or power. A third meaning of advance, found in *TIM*, and used only once, is to enhance. Another possible meaning is to be active or go forward. The adjective advanced intimates held high or raised up; the noun advancement signifies preferment or elevation.

(B) The literal sense of to 'raise up' or 'put forward' arms or flags occurs with considerable frequency; and metaphorically to fine effect in *ROM*. Richmond, in his oration before the Battle of Bosworth, cries: 'Advance your standards, draw your willing swords' (*R3* 5.3.264), a phrase suggesting an eager, orderly action. Berowne uses the phrase metaphorically when leading the courtship assault on the ladies of France: 'Advance your standards, and upon them, lords' (*LLL* 4.3.364). More subtle and moving is Romeo's response to the apparently dead body of Juliet: 'Thou art not conquer'd, beauty's ensign yet / Is crimson in thy lips and in thy cheeks, / And death's pale flag is not advanced there' (*ROM* 5.3.94–6).

In *COR*, a play of intense physicality, arms and swords are raised to telling effect. The eponymous hero expresses his eagerness for action in a way which is both urgent and vivid: 'Filling the air with swords advanc'd and darts, / We prove this very hour' (1.6.61–2). It is no wonder his proud mother says of him, 'Death, that dark spirit, in's nervy arm doth lie, / Which, being advanc'd, declines, and then men die' (2.1.160–1).

To gain advancement in terms of promotion is used with great frequency. Even in the comedy *TN* Valentine assures the recently arrived Viola/Cesario, 'If the Duke continue these favours towards you, Cesario, you are like to be much advanc'd' (1.4.1–2). Less enthusiasm is expressed in the same play for Malvolio's anticipated elevation to the status of Count as Fabian mockingly observes, 'How he jets [struts] under his advanc'd plumes!' (2.5.31).

The histories and tragedies abound in political examples. Typical is Queen Elizabeth's complaint to Richard Gloucester, 'You envy my advancement and my friends" (R3 1.3.74). Less rancorous is Falstaff's ever hopeful assurance to Justice Shallow, 'Fear not your advancements, I will be the man yet that shall make you great' (*2H4* 5.5.78–80). One of the most surprising applications occurs in *TIM* where the recklessly generous Timon offers a rich jewel to one of his flatterers: 'I must entreat you honor me so much / As to advance this jewel; accept it and wear it' (1.2.169–70). Here 'advance' means 'enhance': the **value** of the jewel will be increased by the **worth** of the wearer. This unique expression in Shakespeare is interesting not least because the lines uttered by Timon are so characteristic of his flatterers.

Palamon and Arcite express their reservation about fighting on behalf of their **tyrannical** uncle, Creon, but feel compelled to defend their country against an invading army. This tension is given expression in compacted language: 'But alas, / Our hands advanc'd before our hearts, what will / The fall o'th'stroke do damage?' (*TNK* 1.2.111–13). There is here a suggestion of a disjunction between hands and heart. To 'be active' or 'go forward' is a possible gloss, but equally the meaning could simply be 'raised'.

(C) Smith, *Shakespeare's Drama of Exile*, McDonald, *Shakespeare's Late Style*, and Nuttall, *Timon of Athens*, are relevant here.

advantage, advantageable, advantaging

(A) Remarkable in its range, a few meanings attaching to the word are unique usages – some, surprisingly elusive. The most precise meaning is in the sphere of economics where advantage refers to **interest** on loans. Interpretation of import-ant political moments depends crucially on perceiving distinctions between the following: interest or addition; opportunity; benefit or gain; favourable condi-tion or circumstance; military strategy or superior strategic position; a more convenient time; constriction; circumspection; instrument; hopeful anticipation or maintenance of diminishing strength; superiority or initiative; distortion; pro-tection or benefit; prospect or benefit; **advancement**, elevation or prospective gain; with expedition. Advantaging is employed punningly to mean interest and benefit. The only use of advantageable is straightforward, meaning beneficial.

(B) Shylock considering an accommodation of three thousand ducats cannot resist the temptation to taunt Antonio with inconsistency for soliciting an interest-bearing loan – given that he vociferously denounces such transactions:

'Methoughts you said you neither lend nor borrow / Upon advantage' (*MV* 1.3.69–70). Antonio continues to argue the impropriety of charging interest on 'barren metal' (1.3.134) but is drawn into the 'merry sport' of an interest-free loan. Shylock forgoes one kind of advantage (interest) in order to secure another kind of advantage, namely the prospect of the power of life and death over a hated adversary.

Prince Hal prides himself on repaying **debts**, so it is no surprise that he returns, with interest, the **money** stolen by Falstaff and his associates in the Gadshill affair. As he tells Peto, 'The money shall be paid back again with advantage' (*1H4* 2.4.547–8).

Lines or speeches are frequently enriched by an awareness of advantage as 'interest' and its association with '**use**' as another term for 'interest'. In *TGV* Valentine praises his friend Proteus for having 'Made use and fair advantage of his days' (2.4.68). This courtly exposition to the Duke involves a display of verbal virtuosity by Valentine. Even the possible implication of *excessive* interest, arising from his two puns, is expunged by the epithet 'fair'. Of course, his verbal dexterity cannot be fully appreciated without an understanding of the double meaning attaching to use and advantage. The generative power of a word like 'advantage' and the collocations attaching to such financial terms can be observed in the Countess' comments on her ward, Helena: 'Her father *bequeath'd* her to me, and she herself, without other *advantage* [addition], may lawfully make *title* to as much love as she finds. There is more *owing* her than is *paid*, and more shall be *paid* her than she'll *demand*' (*AWW* 1.3.101–5). The emotional largesse of the Countess is expressed in financial terms, 'advantage' being catalytic. Here is another example of the way in which Shakespeare draws on the prevailing pecuniary terminology to energize expression and to give it an edge: feeling and mental adroitness work to generate emphasis without emotional flaccidity. Richard III, endeavouring to persuade the former Queen Elizabeth to encourage her daughter to marry him, employs 'advantaging' to intimate augmentation:

> Again shall you be mother to a king;
> And all the ruins of distressful times
> Repair'd with double riches of content.
> What? we have many goodly days to see:
> The liquid drops of tears that you have shed
> Shall come again, transform'd to orient pearl,
> Advantaging their love with interest
> Of ten times double gain of happiness.
> *R3* 4.4.317–24

The elegant conceit shocks by virtue of incongruity. Here is a calculation in which Elizabeth is presented with the idea that the murder of her sons will be more than compensated by royal grandchildren. This commingling of the language of financial transactions with delicate imagery forges an audacious proposal deeply cynical even by Richard's standards.

Advantage as 'opportunity' has wide currency in the plays, something easily observed in Sebastian's reassurance to his fellow conspirator Antonio that they will murder Alonso with dispatch when a suitable moment arises: 'The next advantage / Will we take throughly' (*TMP* 3.3.13–14). In a very different situation the jealous Ford soliloquizes on the recklessness of his friend Page affording his wife the opportunity for infidelity: 'He pieces out his wive's inclination; he gives her folly motion and advantage' (*WIV* 3.2.34–5).

Advantage as benefit is given forceful articulation by Isabella in her quest to secure the freedom of her brother condemned to death by Angelo for the crime of fornication: 'I something do excuse the thing I hate, / For his advantage that I dearly love' (*MM* 2.4.119–20). She seeks extenuation for an action she reprehends. The same play provides a good example of advantage used to signify favourable **condition** or circumstance. The Duke, advising Isabella on the setting up of the bed-trick, instructs her: 'agree with his demands to the point; only refer yourself to this advantage: first, that your stay with him may not be long; that the time may have all shadow and silence in it; and the place answer to convenience' (3.1.244–8). A similar meaning is expressed by Puck recounting to Oberon how he alighted upon Bottom separated from his fellow mechanicals:

> The shallowest thick-skin of that barren sort,
> Who Pyramus presented, in their sport,
> Forsook his scene and ent'red in a brake;
> When I did him at this advantage take,
> An ass's nole I fixed on his head.
> *MND* 3.2.13–17

Soliloquizing on his superiority to Posthumus, Cloten's comparisons include: 'not beneath him in fortunes, beyond him in the advantage of the time, above him in birth' (*CYM* 4.1.10–12). Does 'advantage of the time' mean 'in prevailing circumstances'? Or, as the Riverside edition tentatively proposes, more fortunate in 'cultural and social opportunities(?) or worldly experience(?)' (1592). Here the word is locked into the phrase in a way that precludes the acquisition of a meaning from the single word, but heightens our awareness of its remarkable leverage.

Closely related is Palamon's threat to his cousin Arcite: 'Or I will make th'advantage of this hour / Mine own' (*TNK* 3.6.123–4). In essence he intends to decide the quarrel here and now taking all opportunity circumstances afford him. It is possible here to make advantage mean opportunity, but that does less than justice to its integrated nature.

Another very different meaning occurs during the discussion between Helena and Parolles. Helena claims that Parolles was born when Mars was retrograde (in astrological terminology moving in a backward or unfavourable direction) because, as she puts it, 'You go so much backward when you fight.' To which he responds, 'That's for advantage' – meaning that it is a manoeuvre designed to obtain tactical superiority. She, however, retorts with a play on advantage: 'So is running away, when fear proposes the safety' (*AWW* 1.1.200–3). Helena implies that the advantage, gain or benefit of fleeing is the saving of one's life. Parolles promptly leaves the field defeated in a battle of wits that has intertwined an exploration of manoeuvring in sex and war – and, in the process, yielded rich comedy.

Faulconbridge, the Bastard, temperamentally the antithesis of Parolles, uses the word to similar effect when he cries, 'Speed then to take advantage of the field' (*JN* 2.1.297), expressing the necessity of getting to the battleground first in order to occupy the most commanding position. The most straightforward expression of the term to indicate strategic advantage occurs when Belarius encourages his sons in battle with the words, 'Stand, stand! we have th'advantage of the ground' (*CYM* 5.2.11).

The meaning 'at a more convenient time' is evidently present in Hal's decision to postpone the reading of the remaining papers filched from the pockets of the sleeping Falstaff: 'What there is else, keep close, we'll read it at more advantage' (*1H4* 2.4.541–3). From such simplicity of meaning the same play offers a more complicated example. During the final conference held before their assault on Henry IV's crown, the rebel party in anticipation of success divides the king-dom, but then suddenly fall into an odd dispute. Hotspur decides that a key geographical circumstance is depriving him of a fair share of the land and so proposes to redirect the River Trent. Mortimer attempts to mollify his brother-in-law by pointing to the territorial symmetry created by the curve of the river: 'Mark how he bears his course, and runs me up / With like advantage on the other side, / Gelding the opposed continent as much / As on the other side it takes from you' (3.1.107–10). If the word used were 'disadvantage' there would be no problem, but as it stands advantage must mean something like 'constric-tion', 'contraction', 'restraint' or 'confinement'. This is a unique usage and one that has attracted little attention.

Another remarkable and unique usage arises when Mountjoy the French Herald warns Henry V that he is about to pay the price for his reckless invasion, contrasting French restraint or circumspection with English rashness: 'Thus says my King: Say thou to Harry of England, though we seem'd dead, we did but sleep; advantage is a better soldier than rashness. Tell him we could have rebuk'd him at Harfleur, but that we thought not good to bruise an injury till it were full ripe' (*H5* 3.6.118–23). The antithesis makes it plain that advantage means caution, wariness or circumspection.

A surprising, and seemingly unappreciated, meaning is provided by Richard Plantagenet after witnessing the death of his uncle Mortimer. He vows to regain the status attaching to the title Duke of York either by the King's concession or by force: 'And therefore haste I to the parliament, / Either to be restored to my blood, / Or make my will th'advantage of my good' (*1H6* 2.5.127–9). Here advantage must mean 'instrument'. This appears to be its sole use in this sense.

Another problematic usage occurs in the same play when Lucy, upbraiding Somerset, describes the heroic Talbot holding off his French attackers while longing for English reinforcements:

> And whiles the honorable captain there
> Drops bloody sweat from his war-wearied limbs,
> And, in advantage ling'ring, looks for rescue,
> You, his false hopes, the trust of England's honor,
> Keep off aloof with worthless emulation.
>
> 4.4.17–21

Editors are in conflict over this interpretation, Oxford suggesting 'unadvantaged, lingering' while Arden 3 (Burns, fn 240) opposes such emendation on the grounds that Talbot has an advantage (superiority) but one that is slipping away. Riverside proffers, with caution, 'trying to maintain such advantage as the situation affords' (fn 655). The idea of retaining a tenuous superiority is an attractive one. The phrase 'with advantage lingering' is infused with a poetic delicacy that well becomes Talbot's last stand – heightening awareness of the surprising range of this word. In this context advantage could even mean 'hope' or 'expectation' with a conceptual compression being at work so that the single word advantage signifies hopeful anticipation.

A fairly simple example of the word is provided by Titinius when complaining at the Battle of Philippi, 'O Cassius, Brutus gave the word too early, / Who, having some advantage on Octavius, / Took it too eagerly' (*JC* 5.3.5–7). Brutus having gained the initiative or upper hand then squandered it.

The most difficult or perplexing application arises in Faulconbridge's speech on **'commodity'** in which the quest for personal gain or advantage triumphs over all other motives, pushing the world off its moral axis:

> Commodity, the bias of the world –
> The world, who of itself is peised well,
> Made to run even upon even ground,
> Till this advantage, this vile-drawing bias,
> This sway of motion, this commodity,
> Makes it take head from all indifferency,
> From all direction, purpose, course, intent –
>
> *JN* 2.1.574–80

Commodity clearly upsets the natural balance of the world. The series of epithets attaching to and clarifying the meaning of commodity commences with advantage, suggesting perhaps something intrinsically distorting – in which case this is a unique usage. It is possible that what is meant is that advantage is the principle of seeking to gain an edge or superior position by virtue of manoeuvring for prime position. It is significant that this is probably the most assertive political/ economic speech in the canon, conveying as it does the presence of a force so powerful that all relationships and considerations are subordinated to a principle compacted of economic and political elements. (See entry on **commodity**.)

This hugely elastic word does service for 'protection' when the guileful Edmund persuades his brother Edgar to flee, though the meaning 'benefit' also sits comfortably here: 'You have now the good advantage of the night' (*LR* 2.1.22).

When Roderigo finally begins to see that despite an enormous outlay of time and money he is no closer to gaining access to Desdemona, he confronts Iago with the discrepancy between promises and outcomes: 'Every day thou daff'st me with some device, Iago, and rather, as it seems to me now, keep'st from me all conveniency than suppliest me with the least advantage of hope' (*OTH* 4.2.175–8). Here advantage means 'prospect' or 'benefit'. Either term sits snugly in a construction which reveals the comfortable elasticity of the word.

'Advancement' or 'elevation' is probably the meaning when Claudius describes Fortinbras' aspirations in the context of uncertain political circumstances, but equally (as favoured by Jenkins, Arden 2 fn 180) it could mean prospective gain:

> Now follows that you know young Fortinbras,
> Holding a weak supposal of our worth,
> Or thinking by our late dear brother's death
> Our state to be disjoint and out of frame,
> Co-leagued with this dream of his advantage,
> *HAM* 1.2.17–21

Othello, on leaving the Senate, gives the directions: 'Honest Iago, / My Desdemona must I leave to thee. / I prithee let thy wife attend on her, / And bring them after in the best advantage' (*OTH* 1.3.294–7). He is instructing his ensign to expedite the voyage in the most opportune way. The nuances in meaning attaching to this word make it one of the most interesting in Shakespeare's vocabulary.

Henry V instructs his counsellors to pursue negotiations with the French King in such a way that, 'as your wisdoms best / Shall see advantageable for our dignity' (*H5* 5.2.87–8).

(C) Alexander, ed., *Shakespeare and Language,* contains several essays that are relevant here. Gillett, 'Me, U, and non-U' in Salmon and Burness, eds, *A Reader in the Language of Shakespeare's Drama,* 120, has interesting commentary on the Hotspur–Mortimer dispute. For the pressure of words in *H5* see Shapiro, *1599,* esp. 110–11; Walch, '*Henry V* as the working-house of ideology' in Alexander, ed., *Shakespeare and Politics.*

after-debts

(A) Such debts arise from receiving the goods first and paying for them later. The only occurrence is in *AWW.*

(B) Parolles, writing a letter to Diana, warns her to be wary of Bertram's promises: 'He ne'er pays after-debts, take it before' (4.3.226). The caution, though given by a rascal, is both timely and astute as Bertram later displays a remarkable facility for dissimulation.

(C) For commentary on the legally strategic place of **debt** in society see the

Sokols' entry in *Shakespeare's Legal Language* and Jordan and Cunningham, eds, *The Law in Shakespeare*.

agent
(A) In its economic and political application the word means deputy, representative or go-between. The other meanings signify sense organ or faculty; 'doer' or expressive medium of inner faculties.
(B) On arrival in France, King John makes it clear to the French King that he considers himself God's deputy on earth, at least with respect to English possessions – which includes the town of Angiers:

> Peace be to France – if France in peace permit
> Our just and lineal entrance to our own;
> If not, bleed France, and peace ascend to heaven,
> Whiles we, God's wrathful agent, do correct
> Their proud contempt that beats his peace to heaven.
>
> *JN* 2.1.84–8

Suffolk reports that Cardinal Campeius has left the court and 'Is posted, as the agent of our Cardinal, / To second all his plot' (*H8* 3.2.59–60). Campeius is perceived to be Wolsey's deputy – though there is also the suggestion of go-between. Similarly, Pandarus complains: 'O world, world, world! thus is the poor agent despis'd! O traders and bawds, how earnestly are you set a-work, and how ill requited!' (*TRO* 5.10.36–8). As Pandarus is the quintessential bawd, agent carries the sense of go-between, but he is also the deputy who negotiates on behalf of his client. 'Traitors' of Q and F is sometimes amended to traders, but either application accommodates both deputy and go-between. Despite the lively presence of the bawd and the acrid stench of the brothel in *MM*, the direct sense of deputy is present when Lucio denounces Angelo: 'I would the Duke we talk of were return'd again. This ungenitur'd agent will unpeople the province with continency' (3.2.173–5).

Acknowledging her inability to corrupt Pisanio, the Queen in *CYM* sees him as a potent representative of his master Posthumus: 'A sly and constant knave, / Not to be shak'd; the agent for his master, / And the rememberancer of her to hold / The hand-fast to her lord' (1.6.75–8). The fidelity of Pisanio acts as a mirror of his master's loyalty thereby confirming his place in Imogen's heart. Here, agent is no mere instrument. The sense of organ or faculty is best illustrated by Macbeth. Having been persuaded by Lady Macbeth to undertake the assassination he expresses his resolve by calling forth his innermost faculties: 'I am settled, and bend up / Each corporal agent to this terrible feat' (*MAC* 1.7.79–80). *WT* affords an intriguing and unique example. Leontes falling into his fit of jealousy evaluates the behaviour of Hermione with respect to Polixenes: 'This entertainment / May a free face put on, derive a liberty / From heartiness, from bounty, fertile bosom, / And well become the agent; 't may – I grant' (1.2.111–4). The agent is the doer of these things, but there remains the idea of the agent as the expressive force or representation of inner qualities or faculties.

(C) See Sullivan, *The Rhetoric of Credit*; Agnew, *World's Apart*; Long, *Macbeth*; and Muldrew, *The Economy of Obligation*.

assay

(A) Testing the quality of metals is the most obvious meaning of this word. Indeed, it is used, albeit metaphorically, in this sense as characters and situations are tested. Conceptually this word has several applications: to accost or assault either physically or to proposition; to petition; to put to the test; to entice or induce; to estimate or evaluate; to experience; attempt or endeavour; trial of arms or challenge; evidence, proof or intimation.

(B) Expressing indignation at being propositioned in a letter from Falstaff, Mistress Page exclaims: 'What an unweigh'd behaviour hath this Flemish drunk-ard pick'd . . . out of my conversation, that he dares in this manner to assay me?' (*WIV* 2.1.22–5). In addition to the idea of an assault there is also the suggestion of to put to the test her virtue – something of great significance in a play where these citizens feel morally superior to all other social groups, including the nobility.

The straightforward application to mean assault is well illustrated by Henry IV on encountering the fearsome Scot, the Douglas, on the battlefield at Shrews-bury: 'I have two boys / Seek Percy and thyself about the field, / But seeing thou fall'st on me so luckily, / I will assay thee, and defend thyself' (*1H4* 5.4.31–4).

Requesting Lucio persuade Isabella to appeal to the Deputy on his behalf, Claudio uses the word in the sense of petition: 'Implore her, in my voice, that she make friends / To the strict deputy; bid herself assay him'. His misplaced hope resides in her demeanour and articulacy:

> I have great hope in that; for in her youth
> There is a prone and speechless dialect,
> Such as move men; beside, she hath prosperous art
> When she will play with reason and discourse,
> And well she can persuade.
>
> *MM* 1.2.180–6

However, it is not articulacy, compassionate tenderness nor vulnerability that moves Angelo but sexual attraction. Petitioning Angelo, Isabella does indeed assay him, inadvertently exposing the **counterfeit** that has previously passed **current**. Later, the disguised Duke uses the word in the sense of testing when cautioning Claudio against hope of reprieve: 'Angelo had never the purpose to corrupt her; only he hath made an assay of her virtue to practice his judgement with the disposition of natures' (*MM* 3.1.161–4).

In the politically tense atmosphere of the senate scene a sailor sounds a reassuring note claiming that the Turkish fleet is making for Rhodes rather than Cyprus. The First Senator expresses disbelief: 'This cannot be / By no assay of reason; 'tis a pageant / To keep us in false gaze' (*OTH* 1.3.17–19). Clearly assay here means test. The Turkish move is indeed a ruse; their real goal is Cyprus.

A sense of attempt or endeavour is evident in York's denunciation of Queen Margaret when he is taken prisoner: 'But that thy face is vizard-like, unchanging, / Made impudent with use of evil deeds, / I would assay, proud queen, to make thee blush' (*3H6* 1.4.116–18). This meaning occurs in diverse situations ranging from Rosalind's proposal to Celia, 'what if we assay'd to steal / The clownish fool' (*AYL* 1.3.129–30), to Lord Scales' warning that, 'The rebels have assay'd to win the Tower' (*2H6* 4.5.8).

Othello captures the tension between cool judgement and the promptings of passion when, consequent on the brawl guilefully engineered by Iago, he is woken by the alarm bell in Cyprus: 'Now by heaven, / My blood begins my safer guides to rule, / And passion, having my best judgement collied, / Assays to lead the way' (*OTH* 2.3.204–7). Here the meaning is 'attempts': the hero's judgement is darkened and so passion attempts to **achieve** dominance.

Voltemand, the ambassador returned from Norway, assures Claudius that the dangerous Fortinbras has pledged himself 'never more / To give th'assay of arms against your Majesty' (*HAM* 2.2.70–1). 'Trial of arms', or 'challenge' is evidently the meaning here. This play has five applications of the term. The least obvious meaning occurs when Claudius, kneeling in prayer, asks forgiveness for the murder of his brother: 'O wretched state! O bosom black as death! / O limed soul, that struggling to be free / Art more engag'd! Help, angels! Make assay, / Bow, stubborn knees, and heart, with strings of steel' (3.3.67–70). 'Make assay' is glossed as 'make the effort', but the requirement here seems stronger, suggesting that the angels make an assault on his 'limed soul' in the way that Donne calls on God to 'Batter my heart' (*Holy Sonnets* 14) invoking urgency and violence.

Uncomplicated, but interesting, is Gertrude's questioning of Rozencrantz and Guildenstern. Attempting to discover whether they have sought to draw Hamlet into any activity, she asks, 'Did you assay him / To any pastime?' (*HAM* 3.1.14–15), revealing her eagerness for Hamlet's old school-friends to engage with her son so that he will confide in them. 'Entice' or 'induce' are the most appropriate synonyms.

A fascinating usage arises from Polonius' exposition to his servant Reynaldo on the subterfuges employed in life to discover the truth: 'And thus do we of wisdom and of reach, / With windlasses and with assays of bias, / By indirections find directions out' (2.1.61–3). In the metaphor drawn from bowls, the idea is that the bowler attempts to *estimate* or *evaluate* the course of the wood [bowl] by analysing the degree of bias inherent in the object he is propelling along the green. This section of the speech characterizes much of the action of a play in which assessments, manoeuvres and tests are used to draw conclusions and determine actions so that 'with assays of bias' could be a subtitle for *HAM*.

A unique usage occurs in *A Lover's Complaint*: 'experience'. There is an acknowledgement that neither precepts nor the advice of others can determine behaviour. Understanding is achieved through the experience of suffering:

' "But ah, who ever shunn'd by precedent / The destin'd ill she must herself assay, / Or forc'd examples 'gainst her own content / To put the by-past perils in her way?" ' (155–8).

Yet one more meaning has been ascribed to the word, namely, 'evidence', 'proof' or 'indication'. Edmund responds to the challenge of the masked Edgar: 'In wisdom I should ask thy name, / But since thy outside looks so fair and warlike, / And that thy tongue some say of breeding breathes' (*LR* 5.3.142–4). Does 'say' here constitute a contraction of assay? If so the meaning would be evidence, proof or indication. However, the Crystals, who propose this, also cite 'announce' or 'proclaim' as one of the meanings of 'say', which is accommodated by the above example, though trace or indication would probably be a better fit.

(C) Intriguing discussions relating to these and related matters are to be found in the chapters on *MM* and *HAM* in Kermode, *Shakespeare's Language*. White, *The Merry Wives of Windsor*, is insightful on the language and mores of the play.

audit, auditor

(A) The idea of the audit as a cut-off point where the financial **accounts** are assessed, is strong in the plays and sonnets, but not in a literal way: the audit usually refers to the evaluation of the individual's life before God or before posterity. Here is a perfect example of a conception that dominates the age, a careful system of recording and calculating financial transactions, transferred to the moral sphere where a person's life ultimately undergoes the scrutiny of a spiritual audit. There is only one case where the reference to auditors is literal, *TIM*, though there is another example of an exposition of economics, by Lady Macbeth, which is perhaps surprising in a play where the moral audit is a recurring idea. There is also a single reference to 'a kind of auditor' (*1H4* 2.1.57) suggesting an accountant or possibly even an official of the **Exchequer**.

(B) Describing the robbers' prospective victims, Gadshill refers to 'a kind of auditor, one that hath abundance of charge too' (*1H4* 2.1.57–8). This could imply a **treasury** official or more generally an accountant. However, 'his abundance of charge' may intimate not simply lots of baggage to purloin but carriage of substance adding to the probability of it denoting a treasury official.

After Flavius has announced to Timon that he is bankrupt, the prodigal master is incredulous: 'To Lacedaemon did my land extend'. The loyal steward's response is utterly remarkable – almost unthinkable in an epoch when the flood of resources and products poured in from an ever-expanding world: 'O my good lord, the world is but a word; / Were it all yours to give it in a breath, / How quickly were it gone!' To which a crestfallen Timon responds: 'You tell me true.' It is only then that Flavius invites his master to investigate the books and his **husbandry**:

> If you suspect my husbandry or falsehood,
> Call me before th'exactest auditors,
> And set me on the proof. So the gods bless me,

> When all our offices have been oppress'd
> With riotous feeders, when our vaults have wept
> With drunken spilth of wine, when every room
> Hath blaz'd with lights and bray'd with minstrelsy,
> I have retir'd me to a wasteful cock,
> And set mine eyes at flow.
>
> *TIM* 2.2.151–63

This **exchange** merits extensive quotation because it creates a vivid picture of a **wealthy** household pouring forth seemingly endless abundance, married to a clear conception that all resources are finite. Here the steward holds up a mirror to the destructive nature of conspicuous consumption.

The connections between ownership, stewardship, possession and accountability are expressed with precision by Lady Macbeth in response to King Duncan's gracious announcement:

> Duncan: Fair and noble hostess,
>   We are your guest to-night.
> Lady Macbeth: Your servants ever
>   Have theirs, themselves, and what is theirs, in compt,
>   To make their audit at your Highness' pleasure,
>   Still to return your own.
>
> *MAC* 1.6.24–8

In a play where the concept of reciprocity is central, this reply is perfect: the King is the owner of the realm; as stewards, his subjects, even noble ones, manage resources in trust. An unusual interpretation was provided in the Almeida 2005 production. A slyly dominating Duncan (William Gaunt) required an explicit statement of the master–steward relationship and received it. Emma Fielding as Lady Macbeth responded with astute awareness of political realities.

More characteristic is Hamlet's reflection on his father's position in the afterlife when he contemplates **exacting** revenge on the praying Claudius: ' 'A took my father grossly, full of bread, / With all his crimes broad blown, as flush as May, / And how his audit stands who knows save heaven?' (*HAM* 3.3.80–2). The situation is full of ironies because Claudius acknowledges that it is impossible to secure forgiveness while retaining firm possession of those things for which he committed the crimes: his crown and queen. Although Hamlet does not know it, Claudius' audit is in a worse **condition** than Old Hamlet's. Moreover, Hamlet seems to take no account of his own audit. Finally, Hamlet's seeming quest for a wholly satisfactory revenge may be a rationalization that enables him to postpone the act.

(C) See Jordan and Cunningham, eds, *The Law in Shakespeare*, and the Sokols' entry in *Shakespeare's Legal Language*, for the legal aspects, and Greenblatt, *Hamlet in Purgatory*, for the moral and religious dimensions. Appelbaum, *Aguecheek's Beef*, ch. 1, is particularly relevant to *HAM*. Long, *Macbeth*, and Sinfield, ed., *Macbeth*, are both insightful and germane to this discussion.

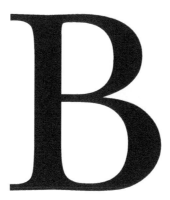

band

(A) A term possessing six distinct meanings, its chief significance here is as a legal instrument specifying a financial obligation. It also means legal commitment or moral obligation; a troop of men; a society or fellowship; shackle; collar or ruff. The arresting officer in *ERR* is referred to humorously as 'the master of the band'.

(B) It is not surprising to find the financial application of this word in the early comedy *ERR*, as the play's action is embedded in a network of commercial transactions. Adriana expresses surprise when required to provide a large sum of money to deliver her husband: 'This I wonder at, / That he unknown to me should be in debt. / Tell me, was he arrested on a band?' The servant cannot resist the opportunity for a pun, pretending to understand band as ruff or collar, replying: 'Not on a band but on a stronger thing: / A chain, a chain!' (4.2.47–51). The debt in question, of course, relates to a gold chain. If the weft of the play consists of commerce, the warp is mistaken identities and comic confusion. Words coming from different spheres transmute through punning, subsuming commercial life into the whirligig of playfulness and romance.

Something that is frequently mentioned in *HAM* is that the territory surrendered by Old Fortinbras to Old Hamlet was not the outcome of some rash encounter but a legally binding commitment instigated by the Norwegian king. Claudius stands firm when Young Fortinbras attempts to regain those lands: 'Lost by his father, with all bands of law, / To our most valiant brother' (1.2.24–5).

Intriguingly, bands in the sense of troops, is used only in reference to the Volscian soldiers in *COR*. The second senator says, 'Take your commission, hie you to your bands' (1.2.26). *1H6, 3H6, ANT* and *CYM* all have a single reference to bands in this sense.

(C) Highly significant here is Perry, 'Commerce, community and nostalgia in *The Comedy of Errors*' in Woodbridge, ed., *Money and the Age of Shakespeare*. The commingling of commerce, sex and romance receives considerable attention in Leggatt, ed., *The Cambridge Companion to Shakespearean Comedy*; Dutton and Howard, eds, *A Companion to Shakespeare's Works – Volume III: The Comedies*. Hopkins, *Shakespeare on the Edge*, has a highly relevant chapter on *HAM*. Barton, 'Livy, Machievelli and Shakespeare's *Coriolanus*' in Alexander, ed., *Shakespeare and Politics*, 185, points out that 'Historically the Volscians were a semi nomadic, cattle-raiding people' and comments insightfully on other aspects of their struggle with the Romans.

bankrout, bankrupt

(A) These words are interchangeable but the former is employed fourteen times; the latter only three. As noun, verb and adjective the word has only the modern sense of financially ruined. The term is, however, employed in a metaphorical as well as a literal sense.

(B) The telling usages are by Shylock, who twice directs the word towards Antonio. In response to the baiting by Salerio and Solanio, Shylock exclaims against Antonio, whose ships appear to have miscarried: 'A bankrout, a prodigal, who dare scarce show his head on the Rialto' (*MV* 3.1.44–6). Likewise in the trial scene when Bassanio cries, 'Why dost thou whet thy knife so earnestly?', Shylock's biting riposte is, 'To cut the forfeiture from that bankrout there' (4.1.120–2). There is a savage logic here: bankrupts are made to relinquish what assets they possess; in financial terms they lose all status and autonomy. Shylock's sentences are incisive and typical of his sharp-edged linguistic fluency. Surprisingly, the other play with a celebrated bankrupt at its centre, *TIM*, employs the word only once. The misanthropic Timon utters a curse calling for a reversal of natural and social processes. In what is possibly the most magnificently vituperative speech in Shakespearean drama his appeals include the following: 'Bankrupts, hold fast; / Rather than render back, out with your knives, / And cut your trusters' throats!' (4.1.8–10).

Bankruptcy is frequently associated with total ruination, even beggary, so that when Juliet uses the word as a metaphor it gathers into itself a singular force and poignancy. The Nurse reports Tybalt's death in a way that leads Juliet to believe that Romeo is dead, so she cries out in anguish: 'O, break, my heart, poor bankrout, break at once! / To prison, eyes, ne'er look on liberty!' (*ROM* 3.2.57–8). Even her eyes lose all right to liberty, and must enter the darkness of the prison – the residence of bankrupts who have lost all.

In a glorious conceit which celebrates the beauty of the young man who has taken unto himself all nature's store of beauty, *SON* 67 concludes:

> Why should he live, now Nature bankrout is,
> Beggar'd of blood to blush through lively veins,
> For she hath no exchequer now but his,
> And proud of many, lives upon his gains?

O, him she stores, to show what wealth she had
In days long since, before these last so bad.

Shakespeare's transference of the language of commerce to the spheres of nature and love provide startling examples of conceptual and linguistic transmigration.

(C) Nuttall's *Timon of Athens* provides a concise and insightful engagement with the financial and human dimensions of the play. Klein's Introduction to the Cambridge edition is also richly explorative. Schiffer, ed., *Shakespeare's Sonnets*, offers diverse approaches to the *SON*s. Mahon and Mahon, eds, *The Merchant of Venice*, affords many significant insights into the play including Szatek's essay '*The Merchant of Venice* and the politics of commerce'.

bargain(s)

(A) This apparently simple word has several discrete meanings, never possessing its unequivocal modern suggestion of a highly **advantageous** transaction in which the purchaser acquires a **commodity** or opportunity significantly below the normal or expected **price**. Most commonly the word means agreement, pledge or commitment. It is also employed as a noun to signify transactions; promised portion; something negotiated, agreed or **achieved**; ridicule. Used as a verb it can span the spectrum of negotiations or engagements in financially competitive activities.

(B) When Shylock complains of Antonio, 'He hates our sacred nation, and he rails / Even there where merchants most do congregate / On me, my bargains, and my well-won thrift, / Which he calls interest' (*MV* 1.3.48–51), and again later, 'He hath disgrac'd me, and hind'red me half a million, laugh'd at my losses, mock'd at my gains, scorn'd my nation, thwarted my bargains' (3.1.54–7), he means transactions. Antonio, of course, sees deriving **interest** from lending money as abhorrent.

The Duke of York, who considers himself the rightful King of England, gives vent to his anguish as his French territories are being diminished by Henry VI: some as gifts in a marriage settlement (Anjou and Maine); others are lost (Paris) or are vulnerable (Normandy). 'So York must sit, and fret, and bite his tongue, / While his own lands are bargain'd for and sold' (*2H6* 1.1.230–1). Auctioned seems the most accurate meaning here, but the suggestion of squabbled over, or competed for, are also present. Accordingly, what is described is something even less dignified than a mere auction.

Promised portion seems the meaning attaching to the term when used by Hal and Poins in exercising their wit at the expense of Falstaff:

Poins: Jack, how agrees the devil and thee about
        thy soul that thou soldest him on Good
        Friday last, for a cup of Madeira and a cold
        capon's leg?
Prince: Sir John stands to his word, the devil shall

> have his bargain, for he was never yet a
> breaker of proverbs. He will give the
> devil his due.
>
> *1H4* 1.2.114–9

The engagement gives Hal the opportunity of exhibiting his quick wit and verbal dexterity. Falstaff is mockingly praised for sticking to the agreement: giving the devil his promised portion (Falstaff's soul) for the cheap price of a glass of wine and a chicken's leg. Even though notorious for breaking his word Falstaff would not break a proverb. At the core of this quibble is the idea of bargain as an agreement, but at the same time the word is given a tilt in the direction of promised portion.

An example of bargain as engagement in a financially competitive activity is provided by Boult the pimp, who says to the brothel-keeper that as he has negotiated the **purchase** of Marina from the pirates, he ought to be allowed to experience her first: 'But, mistress, if I have bargain'd for the joint-'. He does not have to finish his sentence as she does it for him: 'Thou mayst cut a morsel off the spit' (*PER* 4.2.129–31). This is, of course, a particularly sordid **exchange** because the pure Marina has been reduced to **traded** flesh and is described using the imagery of food.

An oral agreement is signified when Henry V says of the glove he has persuaded Fluellen to wear in his cap, 'I by bargain should / Wear it myself' (*H5* 4.7.174–5).

Bargain as an agreement taking the form of a document stamped with a seal finds expression in declarations of love. The voyeuristic Pandarus, having brought his niece Cressida and Troilus to a mutual declaration of love, plays on kiss as 'seal': 'Go to, a bargain made, seal it, seal it, I'll be the witness' (*TRO* 3.2.197–8). Julia too seeks to 'seal the bargain with a holy kiss' (*TGV* 2.2.7). Romeo, in graver circumstances, makes a similar reference (*ROM* 5.3.113–15) as does Venus in a remarkable speech of passionate desire which links legal, commercial and financial terms:

> Pure lips, sweet *seals* in my soft lips *imprinted,*
> What *bargains* may I make, still to be *sealing?*
> To *sell* myself I can be well contented,
> So thou wilt *buy,* and *pay,* and use good *dealing,*
>   Which *purchase* if thou make, for fear of *slips,*
>   Set thy *seal manual* on my wax-red lips.
>
> *VEN* 511–16

Here is a fine example of Shakespeare commandeering the language of the **market-place** to facilitate a witty protestation of love. Less than obvious are the punning references to coinage: 'imprinted' and 'slips', the latter referring to **counterfeit** coins.

During the confusion of mistaken identities Syracusian Antipholus beats his trusty servant Dromio, ostensibly for refusing to take the situation seriously. The indignant servant complains, 'Hold, sir, for God's sake! Now your jest is in earnest, / Upon what bargain do you give it me?' (*ERR* 2.2.24–5). This is likely to puzzle the modern auditor/reader but Dromio, punning on '**earnest**' as a down payment on an agreed purchase, means: 'what agreement or prior arrangement have we come to that affords you the privilege of striking me?'

The sense of agreement being stretched to intimate 'pledge' occurs in *MV* when Gratiano proposes to Bassanio, 'And when your honors mean to solemnize / The bargain of your faith, I do beseech you / Even at that time may I be married too' (3.2.192–4). This is the only case where the construction invites intensification of meaning. This may be seen as a unique usage arising out of the play's deep engagement with bargains. A new meaning is perhaps born out of a natural propensity for thinking of bargains as agreements negotiated in the market-place. The pledge of love, 'bargain', suffers possible contamination consequent on its association with pecuniary matters. As the courtship is encompassed by financial implications (Bassanio confessing his impecunious condition while Portia's **wealth** is as magnetic as her beauty), Gratiano's quite natural use of the word 'bargain' resonates in a way that 'pledge' would not. This may not be a sly insinuation by Gratiano but a culturally induced expression. In the process a new meaning of the word bargain is born.

Suffolk, during his dispute with Gloucester defends the unrewarding aspect of his proposal (that King Henry VI break a previous marriage commitment in order to marry the penniless Margaret of Anjou), by claiming that financial negotiations are relevant to peasants rather than to kings: 'So worthless peasants bargain for their wives, / As market men for oxen, sheep, or horse' (*1H6* 5.5.53–4).

Of no particular economic or political significance, but providing an ambiguous application of the term is the waiting-woman's line in *TNK*: 'That's as we bargain, madam' (2.2.152). The meaning could be determine, negotiate or agree.

There is a complex piece of wordplay in *LLL* which provokes the precocious child Moth into successful mockery of the fantastical Spaniard Armado. The rustic Costard comments, 'The boy hath sold him a bargain, a goose, that's flat. / Sir, your pennyworth is good, and your goose be fat. / To sell a bargain well is as cunning as fast and loose' (3.1.101–3). The nub of the comment is that the boy has made a fool of Armado, but the two references to bargain are interesting because here is the inverse of the modern usage. Rather than emerging from the transaction with a highly favourable outcome, Armado has been short-changed. The phrase 'fast and loose' means to 'cheat'. Goose carries the meaning of a tailor's smoothing iron, hence the play on flat – flat-iron. But goose can also mean 'prostitute' or a 'swelling in the groin arising from venereal disease' – another bad bargain. Conceptually, the entire exchange or negotiation between Moth and Armado has been verbal, but the quest for ascendancy carries us into the mental arena of the market-place, affording Costard the opportunity of summing up in terms of bargaining or competitive activity.

(C) Abundant commentary on the verbal virtuosity of *VEN* and *LLL* are to be found in Cheney, ed., *The Cambridge Companion to Shakespeare's Poetry*, and Londre, ed., *Love's Labour's Lost*. Also pertinent to this entry is Harris, *Sick Economies*.

barren, barren-spirited

(A) The meanings attaching to barren are familiar to a modern audience: infertile in terms of land; incapable of breeding or giving birth; void or empty (of substance, spirit or **intelligence**); unresponsive or indifferent. The single use of barren-spirited signifies lacking originality or ingenuity – a natural follower.

(B) Straightforward is Caliban's recollection that when Prospero first arrived on the island, 'then I love'd thee / And show'd thee all the qualities o'th'isle, / The fresh springs, brine-pits, barren place and fertile' (*TMP* 1.2.336–8). Gonzalo, expressing his fear of the tempest exclaims, 'Now would I give a thousand furlongs of sea for an acre of barren ground, long heath, brown furze, anything' (1.1.65–7).

The most striking usage from the standpoint of economics and politics is Antonio's denunciation of Shylock: 'If thou wilt lend this money, lend it not / As to thy friends, for when did friendship take / A breed for barren metal of his friend?' (*MV* 1.3.132–4). This takes us to the core of **interest**-bearing loans. For Antonio, as money cannot 'breed', it is in no way generative, so taking interest on loans cannot be morally justified. However, Antonio, who provides interest-free loans for his friends (deriving his income from **trade** – a risky activity despised by Shylock) finds himself with a cash-flow crisis. Being asset rich doesn't help when liquidity is so tight. Without individuals who specialize in the **provision** of loanable funds many commercial ventures would simply not be tenable. Moreover, the greater the number of suppliers of loanable funds the lower would interest rates be, as potential borrowers could shop around. Shylock understands this perfectly when complaining that Antonio's penchant for making interest-free loans drives down the going rate of interest. Even were the loans not free they would still exert downward pressure on interest rates because of the increase in the supply of loanable funds. As Shylock expresses it: 'I hate him for he is a Christian; / But more, for that in low simplicity / He lends out money gratis, and brings down / The rate of usance here with us in Venice' (*MV* 1.3.42–5). The moral opprobrium attaching to moneylenders prevents the expansion of the supply of funds and the consequent downward pressure on interest rates, since they are determined by the interaction between the supply and demand for such funds, the degrees of risk associated with the various loans, and the time period for which they are made available. Clearly Bassanio could not acquire a commercial loan himself as he has no collateral (he concedes that he is in **debt**) and his venture is extremely risky (seen from the standpoint of a potential lender).

In *R3*, Queen Elizabeth disdains the unwillingness of her nephew and niece to join her sorrowing for her husband:

> Give me no help in lamentation,
> I am not barren to bring forth complaints.

> All springs reduce their currents to mine eyes,
> That I being govern'd by the watery moon,
> May send forth plenteous tears to drown the world!
>
> 2.2.66–70

Here the idea of barren as lacking fecundity becomes part of a conceit, since the moon controls the tides and fertility. Her own grief is so abundant that she is like the sea which is governed by the moon, an emblem of fertility, as well as, paradoxically, of chastity.

Moving from the economics and sexual aspects of the term, there is the uncomplicated meaning of 'empty' or 'bereft' as exhibited by Perdita when she apologizes for a lack of colourful flowers because of her moral disapproval of carnations:

> the fairest flow'rs o'th'season
> Are our carnations and streak'd gillyvors
> (Which some call Nature's bastards). Of that kind
> Our rustic garden's barren, and I care not
> To get slips of them.
>
> *WT* 4.4.81–5

There is no better example of the word meaning devoid than the line 'When lofty trees I see barren of leaves' (*SON* 12.5).

The sense of being mentally ungenerative or stupid is provided by Malvolio's sneer at Feste's discomfiture: 'I marvel your ladyship takes delight in such a barren rascal. I saw him put down the other day with an ordinary fool that has no more brain than a stone' (*TN* 1.5.83–5). Similarly, Bottom is referred to by Puck as 'The shallowest thick-skin of that barren sort' (*MND* 3.2.13).

Strikingly, Mowbray, banished by Richard II, laments the loss of his native tongue and lacking command of any other: 'Within my mouth you have enjail'd my tongue, / Doubly portcullis'd with my teeth and lips, / And dull unfeeling barren ignorance / Is made my jailer to attend on me' (*R2* 1.3.166–9). This example shows how differently the effect of a word can operate, 'barren' providing the culmination of this copious diction – an acknowledgement of a loss of mental life through lack of the means of expression.

Advising the players Hamlet cautions them, especially the clown, against any improvisation which appeals only to the least insightful spectators: 'for there be some of them that will themselves laugh to set on some quantity of barren spectators to laugh too, though in the mean time some necessary question of the play be then to be consider'd' (*HAM* 3.2.40–3).

Something slightly different from stupid or ungenerative is the reference to Lepidus who is described brutally by Mark Antony as 'A barren-spirited fellow; one that feeds / On objects, arts, and imitations, / Which, out of use and stal'd by other men, / Begin his fashion' (*JC* 4.1.36–9). Evidently what is meant is lacking ingenuity, originality or initiative: the essential spark of life. Thus the condemnation of being mentally barren ranges from Puck's suggestion of thick-headed (*MND* 3.2.13), through Malvolio's insult of lacking mental agility, Mowbray's enforced intellectual deprivation, mentally inactive members of a theatre audience, to Lepidus who is a follower, lacking volition.

(C) Highly relevant to *MV* is Spencer, 'Taking excess, exceeding account' in Woodbridge, ed., *Money and the Age of Shakespeare*; Shell, 'The Wether and the Ewe' in *Money, Language and Thought*; Engle, *Shakespearean Pragmatism*. See also entry on **usury**.

bate, bated, bate-breeding, bateless

(A) Significant in both political and economic spheres, this word also possesses more general applications. In terms of **quantification** it signifies to deduct or diminish; to modify; to omit; to leave out of consideration or disregard; to lose weight. There are distinct references to falconry where bate applies to the beating of wings. Used as a noun, discord or strife is indicated. The adjective bated intimates to be withheld, restrained or greatly diminished. Finally, the word is used as part of a compound to signify the promotion of disputation or strife. Hence bate-breeding means to stir up trouble or discord. The adjective bateless implies incapable of being blunted.

(B) Unequivocal use of the term to mean 'diminish' or 'reduce' occurs in *TMP* where Ariel, faced with a new list of tasks, reminds Prospero of his promise: 'Remember I have done thee worthy service, / Told thee no lies, made thee no mistakings, serv'd / Without or grudge or grumblings. Thou did promise / To bate me a full year' (1.2.247–50). Here is a specification of a contractual agreement that has been amended in Ariel's favour to take account of exemplary service.

Closely related, but lacking the sharp edge of strict quantification, is the meaning 'to modify' or 'lessen'. In the trial scene Antonio declares that it is pointless to plead with Shylock: 'You may as well go stand upon the beach / And bid the main flood bate his usual height' (*MV* 4.1.71–2).

Pistol uses the expression in emotional terms when appealing to Fluellen not to drive him and his associates into the breach where the fighting is fierce: 'Be merciful, great duke, to men of mould. / Abate thy rage, abate thy manly rage, / Abate thy rage, great duke! / Good bawcock, bate thy rage; use lenity, sweet chuck!' (*H5* 3.2.22–5). Pistol has the distinction of employing the word more frequently than any other character, using it as a refrain to mesmerize Fluellen. Also telling, in this example, is the switch from the repeated use of the form 'abate', soothingly descending to the more usual form, 'bate'. This is a miniature master-class in the control of rhythm through diction, assonance and alliteration.

The meaning 'to omit, leave out, or sacrifice' occurs at a critical moment in *COR*. The warrior seeking political office is unwilling to undergo the traditional ceremony of standing before the people in the gown of humility. Sicinius, the tribune, is all too aware of the significance of the ritual and its potential for bringing down their class enemy: 'Sir, the people / Must have their voices; neither will they bate / One jot of ceremony' (2.2.139–41).

In the build-up to the Battle of Shrewsbury, Hotspur, disdainful of a dissolute Prince Hal, is shaken out of his complacency by Vernon's information that the Prince of Wales has arrived with a magnificent force: 'All furnish'd, all in arms; / All plum'd like estridges, that with the wind / Bated like eagles having lately bath'd' (*1H4* 4.1.97–9). There is a pristine quality ascribed to these troops as their plumes ruffle in the wind with the shimmering cleanliness of freshly bathed eagles – also a strength and eagerness, features, augmented by the remainder of this graphic speech.

The adjectival application signifies 'restrained' or 'diminished'. Shylock, in specifying the insults he has had to endure at the hands of the very man who now seeks to borrow from him, asks rhetorically:

> Shall I bend low and in a bondman's key,
> With bated breath and whisp'ring humbleness,
> Say this:
> 'Fair sir, you spet on me on Wednesday last,
> You spurn'd me such a day, another time
> You call'd me dog; and for these courtesies
> I'll lend you thus much moneys'?
>
> *MV* 1.3.123–30

The whole context of Shylock's biting irony is charged with powerful political, economic and social pressures, much of which is captured by the aural/visual hendiadystic phrase 'bated breath and whisp'ring humbleness'.

Falstaff, explaining to Doll why Poins is in favour with Hal, includes the following attributes: 'swears with a good grace . . . and breeds no bate with telling of discreet stories' (*2H4* 2.4.248–50). Here the meaning is discord.

Jealousy, personified in *VEN*, is accused by Venus of provoking strife or discord: ' "This sour informer, this bate-breeding spy, / This canker that eats up Love's tender spring, / This carry-tale, dissentious Jealousy" ' (655–7). This compound 'breed-bating' captures the idea of Jealousy as an *agent provocateur*. This interpretation of the word as 'troublemaker' is confirmed by Mistress Quickly's comment, unique in the plays, that John Rugby can be relied upon for discretion, as he is 'no tell-tale nor no breed-bate' (*WIV* 1.4.12).

The sole reference to bateless occurs in *LUC* where Tarquin's desperate sexual desire cannot be blunted: 'Happ'ly that name of "chaste" unhapp'ly set / This bateless edge on his keen appetite' (8–9).

(C) The conceptual configuration of this word in the sense of 'lower', 'reduce' or 'attenuate' infiltrates the discourse of politics and economics in significant ways. But it is worth drawing attention to the peculiar verbal facility of Pistol whose presence does so much to illuminate key political plays from the margins. Hussey, *The Literary Language of Shakespeare*, 134, comments that 'To penetrate the layers of Pistol's mind would need not a psychologist so much as an archaeologist, for phrases and characters from old plays are overlaid with scraps of colloquial Elizabethan English.' On the topic of flesh and finance in *MV* see

Shell, *Money, Language and Thought*, ch. 3. Also stimulating is Cheney, ed., *Shakespeare's Poetry*.

bawd

(A) The meaning of the word is a go-between, especially in the sense of a procurer. Just occasionally the word is used in the sphere of politics to apply to a fixer, but in such a case the term carries with it the strongly opprobrious sense of the arranger of sexual deals. So pervasive is the bawd in the unofficial or black economy that occasionally a colourful underworld of sexual licentiousness animates the plays. The world of prostitution is most powerfully manifest in the 'problem play' *MM* and is a major component even in the delectable Romance *PER*. The tavern and brothel coalesce in the *H4* plays, displaying a gritty earthiness that has a good deal of sentimental appeal. Inevitably, the term is also used metaphorically with once again the unsavoury aspect of the profession uppermost.

(B) It should come as no surprise that the word in all its forms appears most frequently in *MM* (over twenty times). The play hinges on the decision to clean up Vienna. Pompey Bum is a witty bawd who sees his activity as essential. When challenged by Escalus, the acting magistrate, 'How would you live, Pompey? By being a bawd? What do you think of the trade, Pompey? Is it a lawful trade?', Pompey's riposte is telling: 'If the law would allow it, sir.' The implication is clear: the law is arbitrary. Pompey's rhetorical question: 'Does your worship mean to geld and splay all the youth of the city?' exposes the limitations of the law. Elaborating his **opinion**, Pompey intimates the economic significance of the trade in the city: 'If this law hold in Vienna ten year, I'll rent the fairest house in it after threepence a bay' (2.1.224–42). Characteristically the dramatist is revealing a comfortable understanding of **price** being determined by the interaction of supply and demand and the way in which the unofficial or black economy exerts its influence on the official economy. If prostitution were driven out there would be a collapse in the demand for rented accommodation when brothel-owners decamped to other cities. Earlier, Pompey had revealed the interaction between prostitution and the housing **market** when communicating the thrust of Angelo's new proclamation. Informing Mistress Overdone that 'All the houses in the suburbs of Vienna must be pluck'd down', he reassures her that those in the city 'shall stand for seed. They had gone down too, but that a wise burgher put in for them' (1.2.95–100). This oblique comment suggests that those with resources and contacts have been quick to purchase the houses of ill-repute and will resell them (at a profit) when Angelo's reforming zeal has cooled. With the slightest of touches Shakespeare indicates the interconnections between sectors of the economy and the opportunistic adroitness of those with **money**. As Pompey intimates, there can be no prospect of abolishing prostitution, it is merely a matter of producing new configurations. The disruption will, however, result in a transfer of resources from brothel-owners to respectable profiteers. There is also rich irony in Mistress Overdone's indignant or anguished cry, 'Why, here's a change indeed in the commonwealth!' (1.2.104–5). There is a sense here of the community being accosted by authority. Moreover, by alighting on the term '**commonwealth**', she is adopting a word from the Elizabethan reform tracts, commandeering the terminology of those promoting rigorous policies against vice. It is as if she has inadvertently engaged with a discourse about the very nature of society. Should respect be paid to its organic, evolutionary nature, or should it be beaten into shape on the anvil of political authority by an Angelo or Puritan extremists?

If *MM* is the play most animated by the underworld of prostitution (something exhibited in lurid and repulsive detail in the arresting National Theatre Company and Complicité production (2004)), *PER* is the play where the socio-economic operation of the brothel is most vividly presented. Of the three characters who run the establishment, one is designated Bawd and another Pander, so that these generic terms for bawd become personalized. Bawd is female. Along with her husband/partner she supervises the enterprise, employing Boult as the general factotum. Every element of the business is delineated, commencing with the inability to take **advantage** of favourable market conditions because of lack of working **capital**: the failure to replace or supplement their diseased prostitutes. Consequently returns have fallen to a level where **profits** are almost outweighed by risks: 'the commodity wages not with the danger' (4.2.31).

Boult buys Marina in the **market-place**. Price is negotiated on the strength of her virginity and appearance. He makes a down payment, '**earnest**', before the deal is approved and then closed by Bawd. Careful consideration is given to market strategy in order to maximize **revenue** by advertising and auctioning her initial services. As Boult expresses it, 'I have cried her almost to the number of her hairs, I have drawn her picture with my voice' (4.2.94–5). Bawd's instruction is, 'cry, "He that will give most shall have her first" ' (4.2.59–60). There is a clear conception of her **hire** price declining through time. As a virgin she commands an exceptional rate which will decline gradually until disease and physical degeneration depresses her value below her subsistence **costs**. When this threshold is crossed she will be discarded. The economics of the brothel is universal. (N.B. Natasha's policy with respect to the family servant in Chekhov's *Three Sisters*, Act 3. Responding to Olga's objection, 'She's been with us thirty years', the bourgeois Natasha retorts, 'But she can't work now, can she!')

As honoured customer, the Governor of Myteline could not be further removed from Angelo's puritanical zealotry when he reveals a familiarity in negotiating for Marina:

Boult:	For flesh and blood, sir, white and red, you shall
	see a rose, and she were a rose indeed, if she had but –
Lysimachus:	What, prithee?
Boult:	O, sir, I can be modest.
Lysimachus:	That dignifies the renown of a bawd, no less than
	it gives a good report to a number to be chaste.
Bawd:	Here comes that which grows to the stalk, never
	pluck'd yet, I can assure you.

4.6.34–42

There can hardly be a greater contrast between these scenes and their equivalent in *MM*. Myteline seems to have a dearth of prostitutes. Marina is a sex-slave who has been bought, whereas in *MM* the females seem to have entered the business willingly. Bawd openly boasts of bringing up illegitimate children to be inducted into prostitution – something Boult jokes about (*PER* 4.2.16). Mistress Overdone claims to have raised Lucio's illegitimate child, though whether she will be initiated into the **trade** is not clear. Interestingly, despite being part of this sordid world Boult declines to use the word 'prick'. Lysimachus, stating his business to Marina, is confronted by the depths of his depravity, so he abandons his lecherous desires, asserting that he had no intention of undertaking such a transaction. In Boult's words, 'She sent him away as cold as a snowball, saying his prayers too' (4.6.139–40). In denouncing his **occupation** Marina employs one of the ugliest images in Shakespeare's works: 'thy food is such / As hath been belch'd on by infected lungs'. His riposte is: 'What would you have me do? Go to the wars, would you? where a man may serve seven years for the loss of a leg, and have not money enough in the end to buy him a wooden one?' (4.6.168–73).

The economic and social considerations of the brothel scenes are multiple and frequently cut across each other. Marina's escape, with Boult's help, can be effected only because of her astonishing artistic gifts. The Chorus, describing the range of her talents, makes it clear that Boult's assistance is part of the **mercenary bargain**: 'That pupils lacks she none of noble race, / Who pour their bounty on her; and her gain / She gives the cursed bawd' (5.9–11).

In *H5* the trade of bawd is linked with that of cutpurse, implying that this unsavoury business spills over into other disreputable activities. Gower refers to Pistol as 'a bawd, a cutpurse' (3.6.62), while Pistol acknowledges a future embracing both activities: 'Well, bawd I'll turn, / And something lean to cutpurse of quick hand' (5.1.85–6).

Certainly the trade is despised and becomes synonymous with the absence of morality. Apemantus, the cynical philosopher in *TIM*, berates servants collecting **debts** for their ignoble masters with a phrase that captures precisely the status of bawds: 'Poor rogues, and usurers' men, bawds between gold and want!' (2.2.59–60), culminating with the phrase, 'Go, thou wast born a bastard, and thou't die a bawd' (2.2.84–5).

TIM is the play in which the naked quest for financial gain is seen at its ugliest. Money itself is perceived as a universal bawd acquiring an emblematic status as a go-between of illimitable depravity. In *JN*, a play that plumbs the depths of amorality in politics, the image of the bawd acquires significant status. In Faulconbridge's famous speech on a world governed by '**commodity**' or political cynicism (and quoted in full under the entry on commodity) there is a close linkage between bawd and commodity: 'And this same bias, this commodity, / This bawd, this broker' (2.1.581–2). Constance, having been betrayed by the King of France, for reasons of *realpolitik*, denounces him to her son, Arthur, in a devastating verbal assault at the heart of which is the annihilating emblem of the bawd serving the whore Fortune:

> But Fortune, O,
> She is corrupted, chang'd, and won from thee;
> Sh' adulterates hourly with thine uncle John,
> And with her golden hand hath pluck'd on France
> To tread down fair respect of sovereignty,
> And made his majesty the bawd to theirs.
> France is a bawd to Fortune and King John,
>
> 3.1.54–60

Here is a perfect example of how the commonplace designation of the sexual go-between is so malodorous that it becomes available as a vital resource for invective. The word evidently enters the grain of sensibility in a way that enables it to function as the touchstone of degeneracy and duplicity. A fascinating example of this is to be found in Polonius' chastisement of Ophelia for allowing herself to be taken in by Hamlet's assertion of love:

> Do not believe his vows, for they are brokers,
> Not of that dye which their investments show,
> But mere implorators of unholy suits,
> Breathing like sanctified and pious bonds [bawds],
> The better to beguile.
>
> *HAM* 1.3.128–31

Most editors, rightly I believe, follow Theobald's emendation of 'bawds' for **'bonds'**. The phrase 'sanctified and pious bawds' is oxymoronic: clearly bawds affect a solicitous concern or decorum in their function of drawing the naive, vulnerable or susceptible into their corrupt orbit. No longer is 'bawd' a mere epithet of contempt; its employment conjures up a world of deception and contamination. 'Bawd', then, impregnates the socio-linguistic map in a way that colours and animates the sensibility of the day.

(C) For the issues raised in *MM* on the commonwealth and puritans see Lever, ed., *Measure for Measure*, Arden 2, xlv–xlvi. A wider discussion of this topic is provided by Thomas, *The Moral Universe of Shakespeare's Problem Plays*; Shugar, *Political Theologies in Shakespeare's England*, and Barker, ed., *Shakespeare's Problem Plays*. Skeele, ed., *Pericles*, contains essays that illuminate several aspects of the play, while Hadfield, *Shakespeare and Renaissance Politics*, 203–15, comments on Marx, money and the contemporary resonances in *TIM*. White, *Innocent Victims*, has telling commentary on Ophelia; Ewbank, '*Hamlet* and the power of words' in Alexander, ed., *Shakespeare's Language*, comments insightfully on Polonius' speech. O'Connor and Goodland, eds, *A Dictionary of Shakespeare in Performance: 1970–2005*, affords a brief summary of the production alluded to in the discussion of *MM*.

beguile, beguiling

(A) A word not obviously belonging to the political or economic lexicon, beguile has six meanings, two of which are highly pertinent to the present study.

Significantly, these constitute three-quarters of occurrences. They are: to deceive, trick or manipulate for financial or other material advantage; to rob or deprive of something material or emotional. The remaining four applications are: to captivate or bewitch; to while away the time in a pleasant way; to draw from or entice; to transform, disguise, misrepresent. The noun, beguiling, signifies deception. *OTH* is the play in which the word occurs most frequently, followed by *MND*.

(B) Lady Macbeth is incisive both in analysis and advice when preparing her husband for the assassination of King Duncan:

> Your face, my thane, is as a book, where men
> May read strange matters. To beguile the time,
> Look like the time; bear welcome in your eye,
> Your hand, your tongue; look like th' innocent flower,
> But be the serpent under't.
>
> *MAC* 1.5.62–6

The phrase to 'beguile the time' takes on a metaphysical quality, but the antithesis between appearance and intention is rendered superbly. Deception is the heart of the term. Only once in *ANT* is Octavius Caesar outmanoeuvred. When a guard discovers that Cleopatra has committed suicide, he cries, 'Caesar's beguil'd' (5.2.323).

The meaning 'rob' or 'deprive of' has numerous applications. Mistress Quickly realizes that Falstaff has deliberately provoked her in order to escape his outstanding **debt**: 'I know you, Sir John, you owe me money, Sir John, and now you pick a quarrel to beguile me of it' (*1H4* 3.3.66–7). There is deception here, but the objective is to rob her. Arguably, she compacts both meanings, deception and robbery.

When the Duke attempts to persuade Brabantio to make the best of things and accept the marriage of Othello and Desdemona, on the basis that 'He robs himself that spends a bootless grief', the aggrieved father replies bitterly, 'So let the Turk of Cyprus us beguile, / We lose it not, so long as we can smile' (*OTH* 1.3.209–11).

The third meaning, to be captivated or enchanted by, is also well illustrated by the play in which the word appears more frequently than in any other. Iago, reflecting on the way that the courtesan Bianca appears totally bewitched by Cassio, muses: 'It is a creature / That dotes on Cassio (as 'tis the strumpet's plague / To beguile many and be beguil'd by one)' (4.1.95–7). Here, there is a suggestion of deception as well as enchantment.

The idea of passing away the time pleasantly is captured in an interesting political context, when Northumberland, insinuating himself with Bolingbroke, protests:

> These high wild hills and rough uneven ways
> Draws out our miles and makes them wearisome,
> And yet your fair discourse hath been as sugar,

Making the hard way sweet and delectable.
But I bethink me what a weary way
From Ravenspurgh to Cotshall will be found
In Ross and Willoughby, wanting your company,
Which, I protest, hath very much beguil'd
The tediousness and process of my travel.

R2 2.3.4–12

The sense of 'passing the time' pleasantly is also given expression by the Duke in *MND*. Describing his satisfaction with the mechanicals' performance he observes: 'This palpable-gross play hath well beguil'd / The heavy gait of night' (5.1.367–8).

A more elusive, and seemingly unique, application is the idea of drawing from, or to charm out of. Othello describes to the assembled leaders of Venice how he won Desdemona's affections by narrating his history to her: 'And often did beguile her of her tears, / When I did speak of some distressful stroke / That my youth suffer'd' (*OTH* 1.3.156–8).

There are two telling examples of the sense to 'distract' or to 'divert consciousness from'. Desdemona, seeming to engage in playful banter though aching with fearful anguish as she awaits the arrival of Othello's storm-tossed ship in Cyprus, says in an aside, 'I am not merry; but I do beguile / The thing I am by seeming otherwise' (2.1.122–3). Even more poignantly, Titus contemplating his daughter Lavina, who has been raped and mutilated, can think of only one device for deflecting her consciousness from her suffering: 'Come and take choice of all my library, / And so beguile thy sorrow' (*TIT* 4.1.34–5).

(C) Kolin, ed., *Othello* covers a wide range of material that is highly informative. Heilman's 'Wit and witchcraft: an approach to *Othello*' in Dean, ed., *Shakespeare: Modern Essays in Criticism*, is also engaging. White, *Innocent Victims*, and Foakes, *Shakespeare and Violence*, both engage with Lavinia's plight.

bill
(A) When applied to financial documents the word refers to either a bill of **exchange**, a promissory note, or a financial **reckoning** as is still used in everyday parlance, e.g. 'Here is your bill, Sir.' Other meanings are as a noun: inventory; document; written order (in a military context); proclamation or parliamentary bill; a long-handled weapon; beak; and as a verb: the action of birds rubbing beaks.

(B) Slender takes great pleasure in validating the authority of his uncle Shallow by proclaiming his status as one 'who writes himself *Armigero*, in any bill [of exchange], warrant, quittance [discharge from debt], or obligation [contract]' (*WIV* 1.1.9–11). In this comic endeavour to acquire status by association, Slender is here underlining the pervasive role of pecuniary transactions and financial documents in the economics of everyday life. The significance of 'bill' as 'promissory note' emerges in a starkly contrasting situation in *TIM* where the Steward of the **bankrupt** Timon rebukes the creditors' servants: 'Why then preferr'd you not your sums and bills / When your false masters eat of my lord's meat? / Then they could smile, and fawn upon his debts, / And take down th'int'rest into their glutt'nous maws' (3.4.49–52). Here is a bitter exposure of the dark side of a **credit** economy. Those who have glutted themselves on Timon's hospitality and generosity have willingly financed that activity to make a double gain by charging **interest** on the money used to entertain them. Now that Timon is facing bankruptcy the creditors engage in a competitive race to liquidate their loans.

A fascinating commingling of political and economic elements occurs at the opening of *H5* when Canterbury refers to a delayed parliamentary bill which, had it been passed, would have had serious financial implications for the Church. In order to prevent the revival of this legislation he confides to his fellow cleric, Ely, the **advantages** of offering to finance Henry's proposed war with France. The dialogue that follows begins with 'bill' meaning 'proposed act of parliament' and concludes with the sense of 'bill' as 'financial reckoning':

> Cant.: My Lord, I'll tell you, that self bill is urg'd
> Which in th'eleventh year of the last king's reign
> Was like, and had indeed against us pass'd,
> But that the scambling and unquiet time
> Did push it out of farther question.
> Ely: But how, my lord, shall we resist it now?
> Cant.: It must be thought on. If it pass against us,
> We lose the better half of our possession;
> For all the temporal lands, which men devout
> By testament have given to the Church,
> Would they strip from us; being valu'd thus:
> As much as would maintain, to the King's honor,
> Full fifteen earls and fifteen hundred knights,
> Six thousand and two hundred good esquires;
> And to relief of lazars, and weak age
> Of indigent faint souls past corporal toil,
> A hundred almshouses right well supplied;
> And to the coffers of the King beside,
> A thousand pounds by th'year. Thus runs the bill.
> 1.1.1–19

What is so interesting here is Canterbury's awareness that it is much shrewder to offer a large cash sum in order to preserve those productive assets which will generate an income stream into the indefinite future. This gives the Church a vested interest in promoting the war – something Henry knows full well when he asks Canterbury to provide an impartial adjudication regarding the English monarch's right to rule France. In addition, the speech reveals an acute awareness of **wealth** consisting of productive assets, as opposed to mere cash, and the alternative uses to which the **revenues** from such assets can be put. Here is, then, a sophisticated seminar on economics, enlightening both the educated and uneducated members of the audience.

JC provides examples of the word used in the sense of both proclamation and military order. Messala responds to his associates' comments with his own information on the situation in Rome: 'That by proscription and bills of outlawry / Octavius, Antony and Lepidus / Have put to death an hundred senators' (4.3.173–5). Urgency is palpable at the crucial Battle of Philippi as Brutus conveys his orders: 'Ride, ride, Massala, ride, and give these bills / Unto the legions on the other side' (5.2.1–2).

(C) For a precise and incisive account of the legal dimension of bills and **bonds** see Sullivan, *The Rhetoric of Credit*, 25–6; Agnew, *Worlds Apart*, 70; and the entry in Sokol and Sokol, *Shakespeare's Legal Language*; their entry 'coram' offers further commentary on Slender's discourse. Anthony Brennan's admirable volume, *Henry V*, and Ornstein, *A Kingdom for a Stage*, are both highly relevant here. So too is Muldrew, *The Economy of Obligation*.

bond, bondage

(A) A key term in several plays, bond refers to legal documents designating financial obligations on a set date; a non-financial contract or obligation; bonds, between parents and children, lovers or friends; literal bonds used to restrain physically. *MV* is the play in which financial bonds figure most strongly (referred to 40 times) and are set against emotional bonds; *LR* provides the supreme example of filial and emotional bonds preserved and violated. This word encompasses an enormous span of human relationships from the deepest emotional connection to the dispassionate documents that objectify and depersonalize relationships.

(B) Not only is *MV* the play with the highest number of references to financial bonds, but Shylock twice delivers short speeches in which bond is used three times: 'let him look to his bond. He was wont to call me usurer, let him look to his bond. He was wont to lend money for a Christian cur'sy, let him look to his bond' (3.1.47–50). This powerful repetition with its unassailable rhythm concentrates all relevant matters into that one document, the bond. The exclusion of extraneous considerations, such as mercy, love or charity, is again emphasized by Shylock's triple expression: 'I'll have my bond, speak not against my bond, / I have sworn an oath that I will have my bond' (3.3.4–5). Thus Bassanio's request for a loan of three thousand ducats for three months precipitates a transaction in which the bond of friendship is interwoven with and contained within the financial bond.

Egeon, who enters shackled at the opening of *ERR*, is not released from bondage until the final scene when his wife Emilia, in the role of the Abbess, secures his freedom – 'Whoever bound him, I will loose his bonds, / And gain a husband by his liberty' (5.1.340–1). Thus the physical and emotional bonds are linked in this early comedy which embodies the loss and recovery theme pursued with such persistency in the Late Plays or Romances. The concept of the emotional bond intertwined with a pledge or commitment is pervasive, ranging from Theseus' reference to his forthcoming marriage day, 'For everlasting bond of fellowship' (*MND* 1.1.85) to Cordelia's fateful declaration 'I love your Majesty /

According to my bond, no more nor less' (*LR* 1.1.92–3). Integral to Cordelia's declaration is filial duty or obligation, something that strikes Lear as coldly formal. Use of the word is not, however, restricted to such unambiguous applications. The term gathers around it not only enormous potency but a strident, clamorous force that achieves a peculiar resonance. Timon, besieged by creditors, endows the literal meaning of the term with a metaphorical vigour: 'How goes the world, that I am thus encount'red / With clamorous demands of debt, broken bonds, / And the detention of long since due debts, / Against my honor?' (*TIM* 2.2.36–9). Here, the bonds which have already run beyond their redemption date now appear to be taking on a life of their own, berating Timon for his dilatoriness. The sentence has two meanings that run in parallel: the more literal relating the clamorous quality to those people presenting the bonds; but the frightening vitality and urgency of the assault arises more from the strange suggestion of talking, screaming, date-**broken** bonds. Frequently in the theatre the audience imbibes the stranger meaning, emotionally and without demur, whereas at the slower pace of reading the more literal sense predominates.

Some comment is required about the ultimate bonds that lie between man and God. When witnessing Cressida's betrayal of him, Troilus gives voice to this connection with extreme force: 'Cressid is mine, tied with the bonds of heaven; / Instance, O instance, strong as heaven itself, / The bonds of heaven are slipp'd, dissolv'd, and loos'd' (*TRO* 5.2 .154–6). Troilus avows that what binds them is indissoluble; but that even the bonds of heaven have, in fact, been undone. This instance of the impossible becoming fact is central to his disbelief of a betrayal that he has not just witnessed – but also knows to be true. The invocation of heavenly bonds is then required to resolve an absolute contradiction. Less perplexing but equally urgent and extreme, is Macbeth's appeal to the dark force of night to break his bond with God, the source of compassion:

> Come, seeling night,
> Scarf up the tender eye of pitiful day,
> And with thy bloody and invisible hand
> Cancel and tear to pieces that great bond
> Which keeps me pale!
>
> *MAC* 3.2.46–50

The bond, which is all-powerful, is here seen as taking the physical form of a document which has to be both cancelled *and* torn to pieces. Here is a Faustian longing to break with God: to break the unbreakable bond.

Another example must be cited because of its penetrative insistence on the bond of life. Posthumus, believing himself responsible for the death of his wife, Imogen, is a prisoner waiting to be executed. From the opening phrase of this long speech – 'Most welcome, bondage!' – he dwells on physical bonds: 'locks', 'fetter'd', 'bolt', 'gyves' – before appealing to the gods to release him from life: 'and so, great pow'rs, / If you will take this audit, take this life, / And cancel these cold bonds' (*CYM* 5.4.3–28).

Having confessed his crimes and expressed his remorse it requires only that the gods **audit** or confirm the **account** and release him from life. The extended metaphor is fairly clear (but see Nosworthy) though the '*cold* bonds' remain open to interpretation – is it the document which contains the facts or is it the cold body ready for death? Here is a commingling of bond as document and simultaneously as something else, the divine thread that inhabits the living person. In quite different metaphorical worlds *MAC* and *CYM* exhibit this vision of the ultimate bond just as *TRO* represents a bond beyond all other bonds.

Reassured of his invulnerability by the apparitions, Macbeth determines on a metaphysical contract that he intends to seal with the blood of Macduff: 'But yet I'll make assurance double sure, / And take a bond of fate: thou shalt not live, / That I may tell pale-hearted fear it lies, / And sleep in spite of thunder' (*MAC* 4.1.83–6).

Timon facilitates the marriage of a servant, agreeing to provide him with a sum of **money** equal to the girl's dowry – on the principle of the common bond of fellowship: 'This gentleman of mine hath serv'd me long; / To build his fortune I will strain a little, / For 'tis a bond in men' (*TIM* 1.1.142–4).

A contrary perspective is provided by the cynic philosopher Apemantus in the grace he delivers before his frugal meal: 'Immortal gods, I crave no pelf, / I pray for no man but myself. / Grant I may never prove so fond, / To trust man on his oath or bond' (1.2.62–5). No kind of commitment to fellow beings is to be trusted: neither oaths, expressions of faith, moral imperatives nor written documents. This is the play which above all others probes the connections between hypocrisy, financial exigencies and ideals of fellowship.

However, for Brutus a Roman's word is his bond. Consequently, he rejects the oath-taking proposed by Cassius and the conspirators: 'what other bond / Than secret Romans, that have spoke the word / And will not palter?' (*JC* 2.1.124–6).

Moving from the highly charged political atmosphere of Rome to the coldly calculating world of Vienna, the cynical Angelo, accepting the Duke's congratulations for his **competence** and probity as Deputy, replies: 'You make my bonds still greater' (*MM* 5.1.8). Evidently, he means ties and obligations.

Deep human attachment is signified by Le Beau when describing the relationship between the cousins, Rosalind and Celia: 'whose loves / Are dearer than the natural bond of sisters' (*AYL* 1.2.275–6).

At a critical political moment the bond that constitutes the very essence of human connectedness finds its expression in Coriolanus' anguished cry as his thirst for revenge is undermined by something even stronger: 'My wife comes foremost; then the honor'd mould / Wherein this trunk was fram'd, and in her hand / The grandchild to her blood. But out, affection, / All bond and privilege of nature, break!' (*COR* 5.3.22–5). This intense emotional bond transcends all other commitments and so Rome is reprieved – though its great hero pays with his life.

(C) See Nosworthy, ed., *Cymbeline*, Arden 2, fn 28, 156. The Sokols' entry on bonds, and Jordan and Cunningham, eds, *The Law in Shakespeare*, merit scrutiny. Likewise, Lyon, *The Merchant of Venice*, and the Mahons' volume on the same play are interesting here. On *TRO* see Thomas, *The Moral Universe of Shakespeare's Problem Plays*, and the stimulating essays in Barker, ed., *Shakespeare's Problem Plays*. Fascinating, too, is Nutall, *Timon of Athens*, Turner, *Shakespeare's Twenty-First Century Economics*, esp. 137, 191–2, Ingram, *Idioms of Self-Interest*, esp. 62–71, 114–15 and Danby, *Shakespeare's Doctrine of Nature*, esp. 114–40.

boot(s), to boot, to give the boots, make boot, overboots
(A) The versatility of this word is remarkable. Essentially the term relates to reward or benefit, either financial or personal. To analyse the application of this word is an interesting exercise in tracing the spillage into additional meanings, some of which are detectable only by careful contextual probing. In addition to the nuances discernible in the employment of the word, it gives rise to playful punning via its association with footwear. Possibly one of the meanings arises from a pun on overboots in water (deeply in love). Apart from its literal meaning, footwear, the word has the following meanings: as a noun, applications include compensation, benefit, **profit** or **advantage**; alternative; something thrown in or added; plunder. As a verb it means: to benefit; compensate; pull on one's boots. 'To boot' means 'in addition'. 'To give the boots' is to make a mockery of some-one or subject them to a put-down.
(B) When young Prince Florizel needs a disguise he persuades the rogue Autoly-cus to part with his inferior garments in **exchange**. Camillo, who initiates the scheme, pays Autolycus for his compliance, saying, 'there's some boot', i.e. com-pensation. The rogue confides to the audience, 'What an exchange had this been, without boot! What a boot is here, with this exchange!' (*WT* 4.4.636–76). Even without the financial compensation he would have gained by the exchange: the transaction has produced a double benefit or advantage. Hence compensa-tion and benefit or advantage are two distinct meanings that facilitate a witty piece of verbal juggling.

Allocating prisoners to his associates the Lieutenant says, 'make boot of this' (*2H6* 4.1.13), that is, ransom him.

The idea of paying over the odds or affording someone an advantage is expressed most simply by the hapless Menelaus in his attempt to fend off Cressida's put-down and secure a kiss – or 'three': 'I'll give you boot, I'll give you three for one.' Here the two meanings of compensation and advantage coalesce. But as Cressida wittily implies, rates of exchange are determined by *quality* as well as **quantity**. 'The kiss you take is better than you give; / Therefore no kiss' (*TRO* 4.5.38–40).

The pure meaning of advantage or benefit is expressed by Hermione in the trial scene. When confronted by Leontes' firm conviction of her guilt she says, 'it shall scarce boot me / To say "Not guilty" ' (*WT* 3.2.25–6). An uncertain meaning attaching to the word occurs in *ANT*. Having buffeted the messenger for bring-ing news of Antony's marriage to Octavia, Cleopatra regains momentary control and offers him reward in mollification of his beating: 'the blow thou hadst / Shall make thy peace for moving me to rage, / And I will boot thee with what gift beside / Thy modesty can beg' (2.5.69–72). If she means 'reward' this is a rare usage as a verb. Logic requires this interpretation though compensation is a possibility. Cleopatra has said that the blow has cleared the **debt** incurred by the messenger for putting her into a rage. They are now starting from a position of equality or neutrality, but if he comes up with the right answer he will gain a reward, not compensation. Enrichment is on offer as bait. The only other application of the word in this play arises when Maecenas incites Octavius to take advantage of Antony's predicament by striking quickly: 'Give him no breath, but now / Make boot of his distraction' (4.1.8–9).

The idea of boot as 'prey' or 'plunder' occurs twice in the plays. When employing an analogue for the division of labour, the Archbishop of Canterbury, perversely, compares bees to soldiers, some of whom behave like **merchants** while 'Others, like soldiers, armed in their stings, / Make boot upon the summer's velvet buds' (*H5* 1.2.194–5). The symbiotic act of gathering pollen and fertilizing the flowers is equated with the destructive pillage (boot) of soldiers. Gadshill, in describing an impending robbery, boasts of the quality of his associates, 'nobility and tranquility, burgomasters and great oney'rs', before going on to make a punning joke about how they intend to prey on society: 'for they pray continually to their saint, the commonwealth, or rather, not pray to her, but prey on her, for they ride up and down on her, and make her their boots'. This double pun, which concludes with the **commonwealth** as prey, is picked up by his associate and taken back to its source: 'What, the commonwealth their boots? Will she hold out water in foul way?' (*1H4* 2.1.75–84). In other words, will the commonwealth not only keep your feet dry in muddy byways but will she also protect you in your disreputable activity? Poins has, of course, devised a scheme to relieve the robbers of their 'booty' (1.2.165).

The word is also the equivalent of 'into the **bargain**'. Henry IV, chastising Prince Hal, swears, 'Now by my sceptre, and my soul to boot, / He hath more worthy interest to the state / Than thou the shadow of succession' (3.2.97–9). This usage also seems present when the same character uses the word with reference to his inability to sleep:

> Canst thou, O partial sleep, give then repose
> To the wet sea-boy in an hour so rude,
> And in the calmest and most stillest night,
> With all appliances and means to boot,
> Deny it to a King?
>
> *2H4* 3.1.26–30

The brutal Margaret, weighing the losses of the houses of York and Lancaster, endows the word with a closely related meaning of 'thrown in': 'Thy Edward he is dead, that kill'd my Edward; / Thy other Edward dead, to quit my Edward; / Young York he is but boot, because both they / Match'd not the high perfection of my loss' (*R3* 4.4.63–6). This use of the term is completely appropriate to the former Queen, who weighs deaths in such a callous way that the life of the young prince can be referred to as a trivial extra.

Almost the last word on this term must go to Falstaff. Having been told the news that Hal has acceded to the throne, he urges: 'Master Shallow, my Lord Shallow – be what thou wilt, I am Fortune's steward – get on thy boots. We'll ride all night . . . Boot, boot, Master Shallow! I know the young king is sick for me. Let us take any man's horses, the laws of England are at my commandment' (*2H4* 5.3.129–37). Despite the obvious encouragement to Shallow to hurry up, might there be a suggestion of other meanings such as advantage or easy pickings? Given that Falstaff has already borrowed a thousand pounds from Shallow on the promise of future rewards, titles, and possibly lucrative offices, this is surely a case of a delicious punning conflation. The dramatic irony is enriched because the audience is well aware that Falstaff's self-delusion is at its height – as is Shallow's.

The blind Gloucester, expressing gratitude to his disguised son Edgar, exclaims: 'Hearty thanks; / The bounty and the benison of heaven / To boot, and boot!' (*LR* 4.6.224–6). This clearly means 'in addition': heaven's blessings are to be added to his thanks. Significantly, Albany uses the expression in a similar way when restoring Edgar and Kent to their true positions: 'You, to your rights, / With boot, and such addition as your honors / Have more than merited' (5.3.301–3). 'With boot' suggests 'with advantage'. Intriguingly, the phrase 'and such addition' suggests not only a restoration of the status quo but with additional benefit earned by dedicated loyalty. In these cases the word is powerfully associated with a desire to stretch giving to the limit – something quite natural in a play which stretches everything to the limit, including love and suffering.

Boot as 'alternative' occurs in *R2* when Richard cuts short Mowbray's protestations, claiming he has no alternative but to withdraw from his challenge to Bolingbroke: 'Norfolk, throw down, we bid, there is no boot' (1.1.164) In the event Mowbray refuses this proffered escape route and is exiled as a consequence. Interestingly, when he complains that his services merit reward rather than such grievous punishment, Richard resorts to the word again: 'It boots thee not to be compassionate, / After our sentence plaining comes too late' (1.3.174–5). Protestations are of no benefit or advantage once the decision has been made.

To boot is used by Macduff when Malcolm casts doubt on his sincerity, fearing that he is in the service of Macbeth: 'I would not be the villain that thou think'st / For the whole space that's in the tyrant's grasp, / And the rich East to boot' (*MAC* 4.3.35–7). Space is of singular significance in this play and so the idea of the enormous expanse of the rich and exotic East thrown in or added as part of the bribe is striking.

(C) Correll, 'Scene stealers' in Woodbridge, ed., *Money and the Age of Shakespeare*, and Turner, *Shakespeare's Twenty-First Century Economics*, offer contrasting perspectives on Autolycus and the **market**. Particularly relevant to Falstaff and associates are Ruiter, *Shakespeare's Festive History*, and Bloom, *Shakespeare: The Invention of the Human*.

bootless

(A) Without hope, futile, unavailing is the essence of the word.

(B) Antonio, finding Shylock impervious to his pleas for mercy, acknowledges the futility of his endeavour: 'I'll follow him no more with bootless prayers' (*MV* 3.3.20). Julius Caesar, emphasizing his implacable rejection of the conspirators' appeals on behalf of Publius Cimber, states: 'Doth not Brutus bootless kneel?' (*JC* 3.1.75). Clifford, mortally wounded, utters a bitter critique of the contention between the houses of York and Lancaster, finally acknowledging, 'Bootless are plaints, and cureless are my wounds' (*3H6* 2.6.23). This word is unambiguous but does exercise strategic significance in the **political** lexicon by traversing the whole range of human suffering and despair.

(C) Goy-Blanquet, *Shakespeare's Early History Plays*, and Zander, ed., *Julius Caesar*, are of interest here.

booty, booties

(A) Booty, employed only three times, carries not only its contemporary meaning of stolen goods or loot, but also people taken by force. There is a single use of booties which involves a significant movement from outright theft or conquest to ill-gotten gains or tainted financial acquisition – in a context that is comic.

(B) When introducing the plan to expose and humiliate Falstaff at Gadshill, Poins explains to Hal how they will let the fat knight and his cronies rob the pilgrims, before setting on the successful thieves: 'and when they have the booty, if you and I do not rob them, cut this head off' (*1H4* 1.2.164–6). In contrast to this game or jest, the other references are associated with two of the most violent scenes in Elizabethan drama. Aaron the Moor informs Tamora of the trap that is laid to murder Bassianus and to rape and mutilate his wife. As Aaron sees them approach he says, 'Here comes a parcel of our hopeful booty, / Which dreads not yet their lives' destruction' (*TIT* 2.3.49–50). So the young people constitute the booty, though only part or 'parcel', as Aaron plans the destruction of the entire family of the Andronici.

The other reference has an equally violent context but is slightly ambiguous. Queen Margaret and her bloodthirsty associates, Clifford and Northumberland, bait the captured Duke of York:

> Cliff: Ay, ay, so strives the woodcock with the gin.
> North: So doth the cony struggle in the net.
> York: So triumph thieves upon their conquer'd booty,
> So true men yield, with robbers so o'ermatch'd.
> *3H6* 1.4.61–4

Booty could mean 'gold' or 'goods' but given the qualifying 'conquer'd' it seems more likely to refer to prisoners. Evidently, then, 'booty' refers to something pillaged or taken by overmastering force, and in two of the three cases in Shakespeare the booty in question is human. The only plural example arises when Autolycus refers to the favourable turn of events that rain down financial benefits on him: 'If I had a mind to be honest, I see Fortune would not suffer me: she drops booties in my mouth' (*WT* 4.4.831–2). This is a fascinating example as it does not involve outright theft but **exploitation** of the gullible. The Old Shepherd and his son are enticed into offering the money. 'Booties' here means 'money dubiously acquired but not by outright theft'. More a form of windfall! This represents an interesting process of chronological change.

(C) See Tricomi, 'The aesthetics of mutilation in *Titus Andronicus*' in Alexander, ed., *Shakespeare and Language*. Bloom, *Shakespeare: The Invention of the Human*, engages with the role, status and idiolect of Autolycus. Interesting, too, on Autolycus' language is Carroll, 'Language, politics, and poverty in Shakespearean drama' in Alexander, ed., *Shakespeare and Politics*, esp. 150.

bound, bounded, bounding

(A) In its principal economic application the noun signifies a circumscribed area or territory or more narrowly, productive agricultural land. Significant, too, is boundary or limit. As an adjective, a bound servant is one who is contracted or indentured to a master; to be bound can mean to be under an obligation to behave in a certain way or to be committed to something. The verb involves the idea of to leap or ricochet; also to contain, confine or enclose. Finally, there are the simpler meanings of to set out on a journey to a particular destination; to dress (a wound); to tie up or tie together; to encircle (the head with the laurel, oak or other garlands or symbols of triumph). The adjectives bounded and bounding intimate something confined.

(B) Lear, dividing his kingdom between his daughters, responds to Goneril's flattery with a parade of largesse:

> Of all these bounds, even from this line to this,
> With shadowy forests and with champains rich'd,
> With plenteous rivers and wide-skirted meads,
> We make thee lady.
>
> *LR* 1.1.63–6

The burgeoning, life-enhancing nature of this territory is powerfully articulated in only a few lines. Mortimer, setting out the division of the kingdom between the rebels, allocates the territory of Wales to his father-in-law: 'All westward, Wales beyond the Severn shore, / And all the fertile land within that bound, / To Owen Glendower' (*1H4* 3.1.75–7). Having killed Hotspur at the Battle of Shrewsbury, Prince Hal ruminates:

> Ill-weav'd ambition, how much art thou shrunk!
> When that this body did contain a spirit,
> A kingdom for it was too small a bound,
> But now two paces of the vilest earth
> Is room enough.
>
> 5.4.88–92

The more confined meaning of 'productive agricultural land' gains expression in *AYL* by both Silvius – 'he hath bought the cottage and the bounds' (3.5.107) – and Corin, 'his cote, his flocks, and bounds of feed / Are now on sale' (2.4.83–4).

The idea of 'bound' as 'barrier' or 'limit' is frequently expressed, but most succinctly by Venus: 'The sea hath bounds, but deep desire hath none' (*VEN* 389). Gonzalo, in enumerating the **conditions** that would prevail in his utopia, includes the **provision**, 'Bourn, bound of land, tilth, vineyard, none' (*TMP* 2.1.153). Everything would be held in common. Prospero, when describing the faith he had placed in his treacherous and **usurping** brother, Antonio, uses 'bound' in the sense of 'barrier' or 'boundary': 'As my trust was, which had indeed no limit, / A confidence sans bound' (1.2.96–7).

Talbot acknowledges that his force is completely surrounded: 'How are we park'd and bounded in a pale, / A little herd of England's timorous deer' (*1H6* 4.2.45–6). *TIM* provides a rare example of 'bound' meaning 'indentured' or 'contracted'. The disillusioned misanthrope calls for the breakdown of all order: 'Bound servants, steal' (4.1.10).

The most fascinating example of 'bound' as 'committed to a course of action' or 'tied to an obligation' occurs during Claudius' failed attempt to pray:

> Pray can I not,
> Though inclination be as sharp as will.
> My stronger guilt defeats my strong intent,
> And, like a man to double business bound,
> I stand in pause where I shall first begin,
> And both neglect.
>
> *HAM* 3.3.38–43

This dedication to two opposed actions ('to double business bound') leads to paralysis.

Volumnia, expressing confidence in her son Caius Martius Coriolanus, comments on his past **achievements**: 'To a cruel war I sent him, from whence he return'd, his brows bound with oak' (*COR* 1.3.13–15). Here is the literal meaning, 'encircled'.

Hubert in advancing the proposal of a marriage between King John's niece and the French 'Dolphin' as a means of making peace, praises her breeding: 'Whose veins bound richer blood than Lady Blanche?' (*JN* 2.1.431). Here 'contains' is the meaning.

(C) Consideration of the paradox of reference to the abundantly fertile territory of Britain and the bleakness of the physical landscape in *LR* can be found in Long, *The Unnatural Scene*, ch. 7, while ch. 6 analyses Claudius' predicament. Young's discussion in ch. 6 of *The Action to the Word* encompasses *LR*'s anti-pastoral. McAlindon, *Shakespeare's Tragic Cosmos*, illuminates both plays. Much of the criticism of the 1970s and 80s, e.g. Wilson and Dutton, eds, *New Historicism and Renaissance Drama*, focused on 'bound' in the sense of 'liminal'. Agnew,

Worlds Apart, has an extensive discussion of the liminal in terms of the evolution of the **market-place**. Highly relevant too are the discussions of maps and boundaries: Kinney, *Shakespeare's Webs*; Cohen, *Shakespeare and Technology*; and Hopkins, *Shakespeare on the Edge*.

bountiful, bountifully, bounty

(A) The adjective bountiful is unproblematic, referring to boundless generosity, largesse, giving forth abundantly. While there is generally a strong material or financial dimension, the term does not have this exclusive application. Fortune, for instance, is characterized as bountiful even without suggestion of finance. Likewise the noun bounty is generally employed to refer to exceptional material generosity but is occasionally used to intimate a human capacity for giving emotionally without reserve. The adverb bountifully, employed only once, means abundantly.

(B) At the conclusion of his narration to Miranda, Prospero expresses his gratitude for impending deliverance from the island and the prospect of revenge on those who engineered the **usurpation** of his dukedom. He attributes this situation to Fortune: 'bountiful Fortune, / (Now my dear lady) hath mine enemies / Brought to this shore' (*TMP* 1.2.178–80).

Rosalind, too, refers to the 'bountiful blind woman' Fortune, making particular reference to her gifts of honesty and beauty (*AYL* 1.2.35–6). The idea of having abundance or being abundant is more frequently associated with this word than with mere riches. The Countess plays up to Lavatch's banter with a comment, 'Marry, that's a bountiful answer that fits all questions' (*AWW* 2.2.15–16). Coriolanus provides an abstract use of the term when mocking the **plebeians**' susceptibility to flattery by their superiors: 'And since the wisdom of their choice is rather to have my hat than my heart, I will practice the insinuating nod, and be off to them most counterfeitly; that is, sir, I will counterfeit the bewitchment of some popular man, and give it bountiful to the desirers' (*COR* 2.3.98–102). From now on, Coriolanus protests, he intends to display the false *bonhomie* characteristic of popular **politicians** – though he is incapable of doing so.

Responding to Hotspur's dismissive attitude towards Glendower, Mortimer lists his father-in-law's attributes: 'valiant as a lion, / And wondrous affable, and as bountiful / As mines of India' (*1H4* 3.1.165–7).

References to Timon's bounty pertain primarily to his giving of gifts and feasts. A wealthy and cynical recipient of his largesse turns away Timon's servant, who has made a request for money, with the phrase, 'Thy lord's a bountiful gentleman, but thou art wise' (*TIM* 3.1.39–40). The antithesis places bounty in the category of folly, and personal **advantage** in the category of wisdom. The separation of material giving from well-wishing is brought out with admirable clarity by another of Timon's false friends, who refuses his request for financial aid with the phrase, 'Commend me bountifully to his good lordship' (3.2.52–3). Only commendations are to be abundant. In a situation where the desperate need is for funds rather than words this sole use of the adverb becomes oxymoronic.

The 'capacity to display generosity' is preponderant in the application of this word, though the idea of material **wealth** generally hovers around it. The best example of 'bounty' as 'having magnitude that is infinite' is Juliet's declaration of love to Romeo: 'My bounty is as boundless as the sea, / My love as deep; the more I give to thee, / The more I have, for both are infinite' (*ROM* 2.2.133–5).

The two characters most associated with 'bounty', Timon and Mark Antony, commingle financial generosity with a spirit of emotional abundance. Timon is addressed as 'Magic of bounty!' (*TIM* 1.1.6), and described as 'the very soul of bounty!' (1.2.209). The word and its adjuncts attaches to him more frequently than to any other character – albeit he is the target for parasites seeking to **exploit** his generosity. The play is replete with this word in all its forms. Timon gives away all he has – so that he is ruined. When deserted by his closest associate, Antony sends his treasure after him, 'with / His bounty overplus' (*ANT* 4.6.20–1), provoking the anguished response from Enobarbus: 'O Antony, / Thou mine of bounty, how wouldst thou have paid / My better service, when my turpitude / Thou dost so crown with gold! This blows my heart' (4.6.30–3). It is not the treasure that breaks Enobarbus' heart but the spirit that lies behind the gesture. It is noteworthy to observe that the human quality is here described by a metaphor of a mine. Striking, too, is Enobarbus' acknowledgement of his own 'turpitude' – a word employed only by him and elsewhere by Cressida (*TRO* 5.2.112). In her great encomium on Antony, Cleopatra too emphasizes his bounty: 'For his bounty, / There was no winter in't' (*ANT* 5.2.86–7). The appeal of this attribute is intimated by Malcolm when he lists it among 'The king-becoming graces' (*MAC* 4.3.91). The much less frequent application of the term as 'financial reward' is clearly expressed by Bolingbroke as he reassures those who are supporting him against Richard II: 'Evermore thank's the exchequer of the poor, / Which, till my infant fortune comes to years, / Stands for my bounty' (*R2* 2.3.65–7).

(C) Adelman, *The Common Liar*, Kahn, *Roman Shakespeare*, McAlindon, *Shakespeare's Tragic Cosmos*, Thomas, *Shakespeare's Roman Worlds*, Cantor, *Shakespeare's Rome*, and Miola, *Shakespeare's Rome*, all provide vivid accounts of the characters and the contrasting worlds and **values** embodied in *ANT*. Adamson, *Troilus and Cressida* provides a thorough yet compact exploration of *TRO*, while Thomas, *The Moral Universe of Shakespeare's Problem Plays*, pays close attention to Cressida's betrayal. Jowett's essay, 'Middleton and debt in *Timon of Athens*' in Woodbridge, ed., *Money and the Age of Shakespeare*, is also highly relevant. So too is Ingram, *Idioms of Self-Interest*, esp. 62–71. Hardy, *Shakespeare's Storytellers*, is perceptive in her exploration of characters' narratives.

bourn

(A) Used only nine times in the entire canon, this term means threshold, boundary, demarcation, barrier, confine or frontier. The word has two aspects: firstly the line that demarcates ownership of adjacent plots of ground or territories with a strong implication of property rights, and secondly a physical barrier between these two areas or regions, something which impedes movement between the domains or territories.

(B) When Gonzalo sets out his agenda for the creation of a utopia, he places emphasis on absence of authority or ownership, thereby excluding 'contract, succession, / Bourn, bound of land, tilth, vineyard, none' (*TMP* 2.1.152–3). Bourn suggests 'territorial marker'.

Notable is the application made by the jealous Leontes in cataloguing various forms of faithlessness: 'false / As dice are to be wish'd by one that fixes / No bourn 'twixt his and mine' (*WT* 1.2.132–4). Leontes implies that in this duplicitous world schemers reject the notion of title to property.

The conception of a physical barrier gains strong, though contrasting, expression in *TRO* and *HAM*. Ulysses in his mock praise of Ajax says: 'I will not praise thy wisdom, / Which like a bourn, a pale, a shore, confines / Thy spacious and dilated parts' (2.3.248–50). Here the idea of 'binds-in' is apparent. Bourn as a confining barrier occurs when, in his 'To be, or not to be' soliloquy, Hamlet contemplates that territory beyond life, 'The undiscover'd country, from whose bourn / No traveller returns' (3.1.78–9). This reads like 'confine', and there is an elaborate discussion of this by Jenkins (*Hamlet* Arden 2, 491–2). The possible suggestion of bourn as 'region' seems discounted by usage in *PER* where Gower intimates the nature and contraction of time: 'Thus time we waste, and long leagues make short; / Sail seas in cockles, have and wish but for't, / Making, to take our imagination, / From bourn to bourn, region to region' (4.4.1–4). Here 'boundary' seems to be the suggestion, evidently cancelling 'region' as an alternative possibility.

The idea of 'boundary' is clearly involved in the dialogue between Antony and Cleopatra. When the Egyptian Queen teases Antony, 'I'll set a bourn how far to be belov'd' she precipitates the expansive retort, 'Then must thou needs find out new heaven, new earth' (*ANT* 1.1.16–18). For Antony, love is unconfined; it transcends all boundaries or limits. On neither of the occasions in which the word is used in *LR* is the meaning immediately obvious. When Gloucester expresses astonishment at finding himself alive after his attempted 'leap' to his death, 'But have I fall'n, or no?', Edgar reassures him, 'From the dread summit of this chalky bourn' (4.6.56–7). It would be natural to interpret bourn as 'cliff' here but it would seem that the boundary is the cliff face, which is the barrier between sea and land. More problematic is Mad Tom's line, ' "Come o'er the bourn, Bessy, to me" ' to which the Fool responds, 'Her boat hath a leak' (3.6.25–6). This could mean stream or river, but again separating threshold or boundary seems perfectly logical. 'Burn' also means stream. Here the barrier or boundary in question might well be a 'stream' or 'burn' such that both words can apply simultaneously, so providing a felicitous conflation. There seems little doubt of the general meaning of the word but on occasion there is sufficient uncertainty to provide a plausible alternative suggestion. However, analysis of all nine cases strongly suggests a legal, physical or metaphysical boundary.

(C) Jenkins, ed., *Hamlet*, Arden 2, 491–2; Foakes, ed., *Lear*, Arden 3, fn 288, are both informative. Greenblatt, *Hamlet in Purgatory*, is significant in exploring the life/death boundary while Musgrove, 'Thieves' cant in *King Lear*' in Salmon and Burness, eds, *A Reader in the Language of Shakespearean Drama*, explores both the linguistic and social boundaries. Highly relevant too is Hopkins, *Shakespeare on the Edge*.

break, broken

(A) The sole economic function of this term – as verb, noun or adjective – is to signify **bankruptcy**, including an application to **bonds** that cannot be redeemed. It has numerous other meanings all of which are straightforward.

(B) A very clear and surprising example occurs in *CYM*, where the captive Posthumus lectures the jailer on the ways of the world. He does not seek enfranchisement; rather, protesting, 'I know you are more clement than vild men, / Who of their broken debtors take a third, / A sixt, a tenth, letting them thrive again / On their abatement' (5.4.18–21). Evidently, creditors are occasionally generous to bankrupts, leaving them with a financial base sufficient to rekindle their business. Creditors are 'vile' in Posthumus' mind because he seeks no second chance but only immediate annihilation.

Timon, accosted by creditors demanding immediate payment, calls on Flavius, his steward, to **account** for the situation: 'How goes the world, that I am thus encount'red / With clamorous demands of debt, broken bonds, / And the detention of long since due debts, / Against my honour? (*TIM* 2.2.36–9). Here the bonds are financial instruments carrying a date by which they must be redeemed. As that deadline has already passed, they are 'broken'. There are also other kinds of borrowings or **bill**s awaiting payment that have been outstanding for an excessive period. Within minutes Timon will be informed that he is ruined. It is natural, and characteristic of the concentrated language of the play, that Flavius sees himself and his fellow servants as 'All broken implements of a ruin'd house' (4.2.16). They, too, are now without financial means and are like discarded implements. When, however, rumour spreads of Timon's new-found **wealth** the Poet exclaims, 'Then this breaking of his / Has been but a try for his friends?' (5.1.8–9).

Intriguing is Juliet's response to the Nurse in the mistaken belief that Romeo is dead: 'O, break, my heart, poor bankrout, break at once!' (*ROM* 3.2.57). Bereft, her heart is just like a bankrupt – broken. Awareness of the word attaching to bankrupt intensifies and vivifies her exclamation. A similar play on words occurs in a political and economic context when Willoughby responds to the critique of Richard's financial **exactions** and lavish outlays: 'The King's grown bankrout, like a broken man' (*R2* 2.1.257).

Shylock, seeking to quell Bassanio's misgivings about the **conditions** of the proposed bond, says: 'Pray you tell me this: / If he should break his day, what should I gain / By the exaction of the forfeiture?' (*MV* 1.3.162–4). Here, default is the required meaning. Helena also puts her life in jeopardy by guaranteeing that her medicine will cure the King. As she expresses it: 'If I break time, or flinch in property / Of what I spoke, unpitied let me die' (*AWW* 2.1.187–8).

(C) Klein's introductory essay to his Cambridge edition of *TIM* is relevant here. So too is Jowett, 'Middleton and debt in *Timon of Athens*' in Woodbridge, ed., *Money and the Age of Shakespeare*, and Nuttall, *Timon of Athens*. Also valuable are

Jordan and Cunningham, eds, *Shakespeare and the Law*; Sullivan, *The Rhetoric of Credit*; Turner, *Shakspeare's Twenty-First Century Economics*; and White, ed., *Romeo and Juliet*.

broker

(A) Go-between is the meaning here, whether employed in the financial, political or sexual spheres.

(B) The most versatile use of the term is by Polonius when cautioning Ophelia against accepting Hamlet's love vows. The conceptual hinge of his discourse is that of the go-between as someone practised in deception, his richly punning assault moving between diverse meanings. The word 'tender' is used five times, with one of its applications referring to legal tender, while '**investments**' refers both to financial engagements and clothes. In drawing to a conclusion, he puns on 'broker' in a way that brings together a financial go-between and a **bawd**:

> In few, Ophelia,
> Do not believe his vows, for they are brokers,
> Not of that dye which their investments show,
> But mere implorators of unholy suits,
> Breathing like sanctified and pious bonds,
> The better to beguile.
>
> *HAM* 1.3.126–31

Editors frequently adopt Theobald's emendation of 'bawds' for '**bonds**' in the penultimate line. What is fascinating in the extended dialogue is the way in which Polonius conflates financial and sexual matters through clever punning, putting the relationship in a sordid light, doubly sullied, so that love is squeezed out by sex and money.

The ultimate designation of broker as go-between occurs in the speech of Faulconbridge the Bastard, who sees '**commodity**' or personal advantage as the governing principle of social and political life. This dazzling speech, which is quoted in its entirety under the 'commodity' entry, contains the lines, 'And this same bias, this commodity, / This bawd, this broker, this all-changing word' (*JN* 2.1.581–2). Politics, economics and prostitution are fused to convey a sense of commodity as go-between in human affairs: personal mercenary gain being the ultimate transactional agent. This cynicism regarding the broker is manifest in the soliloquy of the conjuror Hume: 'They say, "A crafty knave does need no broker", / Yet am I Suffolk and the Cardinal's broker' (*2H6* 1.2.100–1). The self-praise arises from his awareness that both Suffolk and the Cardinal are consummate **Machiavels**. There is, however, a dramatic irony as Hume is merely small change in this game of high stakes, used and disposed of with equal facility.

The abject nature of the broker as sexual go-between is summed up by Troilus in his contemptuous dismissal of Pandarus, whose faithless niece Cressida has betrayed him: 'Hence, broker, lackey! Ignominy, shame / Pursue thy life, and live aye with thy name!' (*TRO* 5.10.33–4). Bevington, Arden 3, like many other editors, has the more appealing 'broker-lackey'. Pandarus, because of his role in this famous pairing, gave rise to the common name for bawd: pander.

(C) Ewbank 'Hamlet and the Power of Words', is particularly germane to this discussion, appearing in a rewarding volume of essays, *Aspects of Hamlet*, ed. Muir and Wells, and reprinted in Alexander, ed., *Shakespeare and Language*. Also important in this context is Forman, 'Material dispossessions and counterfeit investments' in Woodbridge, ed., *Money and the Age of Shakespeare*, and Grady, *Shakespeare's Universal Wolf.*

capital

(A) Although Shakespeare has a clear understanding of capital as assets or resources, financial or physical, capable of generating an income stream over time, he never employs the word in this sense. Rather he confines it to the political sphere where it describes an action, usually treason, meriting the death penalty, or when applied more generally to mean pre-eminent or principal. Killing or fatal is a third meaning.

(B) Henry V, responding to the conspirators' advice to inflict serious punishment on a soldier who abused the King's name, proceeds with his scheme of entrapment by declaring: 'If little faults, proceeding on distemper, / Shall not be wink'd at, how shall we stretch our eye / When capital crimes, chew'd, swallow'd, and digested, / Appear before us?' (*H5* 2.2.54–7). The would-be assassins are first castigated by the indignant monarch, then swiftly executed for the capital crime of treason.

Henry uses the word in the sense of 'chief' or 'main' when referring to the role of the French Princess in the peace negotiations: 'Yet leave our cousin Katherine here with us: / She is our capital demand, compris'd / Within the fore-rank of our articles' (5.2.95–7). The reality that lies behind this courtly gallantry becomes apparent a few lines later when Henry wittily proclaims: 'I love France so well that I will not part with a village of it; I will have it all mine. And, Kate, when France is mine and I am yours, then yours is France and you are mine' (5.2.173–6).

Hamlet plays on the word, probably in the sense of 'pre-eminent', when mocking Polonius who has referred to being 'kill'd i'th'Capitol', while playing Julius Caesar at the university: 'It was a brute part of him to kill so capital a calf there' (*HAM* 3.2.103–6). Hamlet puns on Capitol, while calf means fool. To the modern ear 'capital' could suggest 'admirable', but this sense was not recorded before the eighteenth century.

Volumnia provides an interesting application of the meaning 'killing' when pleading with her son to relent. She points out that his family are unable to petition the gods for the victory of Rome because it would mean praying for his destruction:

> Thine enmity's most capital; thou barr'st us
> Our prayers to the gods, which is a comfort
> That all but we enjoy. For how can we,
> Alas! how can we, for our country pray,
> Whereto we are bound, together with thy victory,
> Whereto we are bound?
>
> *COR* 5.3.104–9

(C) See Houston, *Shakespearean Sentences*; McAlindon, *Shakespeare Minus 'Theory'*, on *H5*; Poole, *Coriolanus*; Watts, *Hamlet*; and Coyle, ed., *Hamlet*.

capitulate

(A) Possessing two distinct political applications, this word is problematic for the modern audience because it does not have the modern meaning of give in or surrender. Rather the word means either to negotiate or to sign articles of agreement. The word appears only twice.

(B) As Henry IV chastises Hal, comparing him unfavourably to Hotspur, he lists the formidable forces ranged against him: 'Percy, Northumberland, / The Archbishop's Grace of York, Douglas, Mortimer, / Capitulate against us, and are up' (*1H4* 3.2.118–20). Here the word means that they have drawn up articles of agreement. Equally foreign to modern ears is Coriolanus' expression when attempting to fend off his mother's appeal to spare Rome: 'Do not bid me / Dismiss my soldiers, or capitulate / Again with Rome's mechanics' (*COR* 5.3.81–3). Evidently he means to negotiate or come to terms with. The very idea of engaging in a dialogue with the **plebeians** fills this aristocratic warrior with a feeling of revulsion. Hence the word gathers around it an aura of ignoble activity. As there are no further examples in Shakespeare it is not possible to detect any hint of a bridge between this usage and the modern sense of the word.

(C) See Hopkins, *Shakespeare on the Edge*; Hadfield, *Shakespeare and Renaissance Politics*; Alexander, ed., *Shakespeare and Politics*.

cashier(ed)

(A) Used only five times, twice by Iago, it means discharged or expelled from service. Used only once in the strictly military sense, the association is retained even when a military context is not directly applicable. In a comic episode the drunken Slender, deprived of both his wits and his cash, is described as being cashiered. Here cashiered may apply to both conditions: his wits have been driven out of service but he has also been robbed, so there is scope for an effective pun, 'cash-sheared' meaning fleeced.

(B) Iago provides a perfect example of 'cashiered' employed to indicate loss of military position in approving the consequence of Roderigo's **exploit** – Cassio has been deprived of his position as Othello's lieutenant – when he says: 'Cassio hath beaten thee, / And thou by that small hurt hast cashier'd Cassio' (*OTH* 2.3.374–5). Something close to this direct military usage occurs when Falstaff confides to the Host of the Garter 'I must turn away some of my followers', eliciting the reply, 'Discard, bully Hercules, cashier; let them wag; trot, trot' (*WIV* 1.3.4–7). Timon's loyal steward is also referred to as 'cashier'd' when his master is made **bankrupt** (*TIM* 3.4.60). Very different is the case of the hapless Slender, who complains of having first been made drunk and then robbed by Falstaff's cronies, Bardolph, Nym and Pistol. Bardolph attempts to evade responsibility by explaining: 'Why, sir, for my part, I say the gentleman had drunk himself out of his five sentences . . . And being fap, sir, was (as they say) cashier'd' (*WIV* 1.1.174–9). The malapropism of 'sentences' for 'senses' provokes an entertaining sequence of ideas. No doubt Slender's evening's conversation amounted to little more than five sentences before his wits were cashiered, drummed out of service by drink, so that he was then 'sheared of cash' or 'cashiered'. Indeed, the Folio even spells the word 'casheered'.

(C) Edelman, *Shakespeare's Military Language* supplies an entry on this word. For a really engaging exploration of *WIV* see White's slim volume, *The Merry Wives of Windsor*. Kolin, ed., *Othello*, is wide ranging and highly informative.

caterpillar

(A) This humble insect gave its name to a concept central to the political discourse of the day, namely the parasite. Caterpillar is used to refer to those who derive an income by siphoning off public funds for their personal **advantage**. Intrinsic to this relatively simple usage is the idea that such **exploitative** activity is debilitating to the **commonwealth**. Personal gain is decidedly at the expense of public welfare, with an image of the caterpillar stripping the plant of both its vigour and its sustenance as the perfect representation of an exploitation that is destructive. The word is never used in a way that is calm or detached; it is always **invested** with a mixture of disgust and indignation. Almost exclusively used in the plural the term indicates that such pillage is normally a joint enterprise. Remarkably, a direct application of the connection to the natural world occurs only twice out of its seven usages. Moreover, four of the remaining five cases occur in two plays (twice each in *R2* and *1H6*). Where the word applies directly to the natural world it is employed as an analogy – a means of exposing deep-seated vice: ingratitude and lust. So strongly did the term caterpillar become associated with cynical economic exploitation that it virtually ceased to be a metaphor. The term 'caterpillar' when articulated on the stage *immediately* conjured up the mental image of an exploiting man. It is as if the metaphor had been so effective that the space between origin and application collapsed.

(B) The only use of the term in the singular occurs in *PER* where it is employed in its literal sense. Lysimachus the Governor of Mytilene reassures Helicanus of his willingness to provide his visitors with safe harbour and **provisions**: 'O sir, a courtesy / Which if we should deny, the most just God / For every graff would send a caterpillar, / And so inflict our province' (5.1.58–61). Significantly, the sense of the caterpillar as constituting a destructive infestation is present here, with a caterpillar for *each plant*. This example is also instructive because it is associated with ingratitude, a heinous vice in the Shakespearian moral universe.

The application of the term in the narrative poem, *VEN*, is innocent of political association. Here the caterpillar is perceived as analogous to lust. Adonis complains to Venus:

> Call it not love, for Love to heaven is fled,
> Since sweating Lust on earth usurp'd his name,
> Under whose simple semblance he hath fed
> Upon fresh beauty, blotting it with blame;
>> Which the hot tyrant stains, and soon bereaves,
>> As caterpillars do the tender leaves.
>>> 793–8

The most characteristic use arises in *R2* in relation to the King's infamous train of parasitical associates Bushy, Bagot and Green. Bolingbroke, having returned from exile, informs his uncle York,

> But we must win your Grace to go with us
> To Bristow castle, which they say is held
> By Bushy, Bagot, and their complices,
> The caterpillars of the commonwealth,
> Which I have sworn to weed and pluck away.
>> 2.3.163–7

This process is both justified and camouflaged by representing the extra-judicial action as a necessary public duty rather than as an act of **usurpation**.

Perhaps the *locus classicus* occurs in the play's emblematic garden scene. The garden was seen as a model for the body **politic**, something made explicit by the gardener in delivering instructions to his colleague: 'Go thou, and like an executioner / Cut off the heads of too fast growing sprays, / That look too lofty in our commonwealth: / All must be even in our government.' His elaborate statement, of which the above lines form the core, elicits a churlish response but one which drives home the significance of the analogy:

> Why should we in the compass of a pale
> Keep law and form and due proportion,
> Showing as in a model our firm estate,
> When our sea-walled garden, the whole land,
> Is full of weeds, her fairest flowers chok'd up,
> Her fruit-trees all unprun'd, her hedges ruin'd,

> Her knots disordered, and her wholesome herbs
> Swarming with caterpillars?
>
> 3.4.33–47

This elaborate riposte emphasizes the gardeners' meticulous attention to detail, a scrupulosity which exposes the failure of a monarch to observe the exacting standards of government. It is striking that the image of neglect culminates with the swarming caterpillars. *2H6* also has two references to caterpillars. In the famous scene of Cade's rebellion a messenger provides the King with a vivid picture of the **advancing** rebels – 'His army is a ragged multitude / Of hinds and peasants, rude and merciless' – intimating that they are motivated by a class hatred, insisting that, 'All scholars, lawyers, courtiers, gentlemen, / They call false caterpillars, and intend their death' (4.4.32–7). The brutal murder of the Clerk of Chartam reveals the mindlessness of Cade and his associates, but seen from the bottom up the well fed and well clothed are parasites living off the fruits of the labour of the poor. Exploitation and parasitism lie at the heart of this antagonism. The very structure of the society (clerks, written documents, scholarship), is perceived as a charade designed to fool the poor into subordination and awe. Ultimately, the threat is short lived and though it has its comic aspects the implications are thought-provoking. An ugly view of society finds its definitive expression in the image of the caterpillar – a word of such direct and forceful meaning that it can hardly be thought of as a metaphor: caterpillar *means* parasitical exploiter.

In *2H6* news arrives that after a period of erosion all the English territories in France have been lost. While Henry VI accepts this outcome with stoicism, the Duke of York is angered at the shrinkage of a kingdom which he sees imminently as his rightful inheritance: 'Thus are my blossoms blasted in the bud, / And caterpillars eat my leaves away' (3.1.89–90). Here the images operate like blades of a scissors. The image of buds being blasted by frosts is a favourite of Shakespeare's. The caterpillar image is given an unusual turn since the loss arises not from wilful predation but as a consequence of incompetence.

During his infamous act of highway robbery at Gadshill, Falstaff, possessing a natural facility for inversion, denounces his victims, the pilgrims, as 'whoreson caterpillars! bacon-fed knaves!' (*1H4* 2.2.84). The implication is that over-fed, well-**monied** pilgrims have come by their wealth through parasitical activities. The fulcrum of this expansive, vibrantly witty verbal assault is 'caterpillars'.

(C) Considerations of predation, exploitation, abuse of power and deformation of the body politic find powerful expression in the history plays. Hadfield, *Shakespeare and Renaissance Politics*, 33, points out that, 'three of the best-selling of Shakespeare's printed plays from the1590s were history plays: the quartos of *1 Henry IV* (1598: seven editions in twenty-five years) *Richard III* (1597: five editions in twenty-five years); and *Richard II* (1597: five editions in twenty-five years). Hattaway's recently edited volume, *Shakespeare's History Plays*, provides an admirable guide through the labyrinth of power, and can be profitably augmented by such wide-ranging and contrasting explorations as McAlindon, *Shakespeare's*

Tudor History; Leggatt, *Shakespeare's Political Drama*; Tennenhouse, *Power on Display*; Bristol, *Carnival and Theatre*; Dollimore and Sinfield, eds, *Political Shakespeare*.

chapmen
(A) Used only twice, on both occasions in the plural, this term refers to **traders** or **merchants** but carries the implication of a dealer whose plausible tongue compensates for the inferior quality of the product he is selling, while disparaging the quality of the product he wishes to **purchase**. The chapman's **profit** is a function of his ability to maximize the disparity between the price he pays for products and the price for which he sells them.
(B) What is noteworthy in *LLL* is the way in which the word is embedded in a whole complex of financial markers. The Princess, chastising Boyet, a courtier given to verbal extravagance, suggests paradoxically that his elaborate flattery diminishes her:

> Good Lord Boyet, my beauty, though but *mean*,
> Needs not the painted flourish of your praise:
> Beauty is *bought* by judgement of the eye,
> Not utt'red by base *sale* of *chapmen's* tongues.
> I am less proud to hear you *tell* my *worth*
> Than you much willing to be *counted* wise
> In *spending* your wit in the praise of mine.
> 2.1.13–19

At first this may appear as just a witty riposte surpassing Boyet's verbal virtuosity. But it cuts more deeply. The Princess claims her beauty is 'mean', implying merely commonplace, being perhaps at the mid-point between gorgeous and unremarkable. This begins a process which develops into a subtle critique of verbal **excess**, partly by making words carry genuine freight. 'Painted' refers both to rhetorical excess and to face painting, another form of artifice. (Woudhuysen, *Love's Labour's Lost*, Arden 3, fn 143, draws attention to the proverb, 'a good face needs no paint'.) The transition into the world of commerce, effected by spiralling employment of the language of the **market-place**, exposes verbal and financial inflation while being subject to the Princesses' control. The commercial world is one of glib hyperbole: **commodification** is the name of the game. The array of financial terms – 'sale', 'chapmen's', 'tell', **'worth'**, 'counted', 'spending' – huddle together cheek by jowl, inhabiting a landscape far removed from genuine critical assessment. A space opens up, that is both conceptual and verbal. A key theme in this play is **cheapening** by excess; overrepresentation becoming misrepresentation. The consequence of verbal inflation is the commodification of language. The Princess employs the discourse of the market-place as a means of showing how the predilections and assumptions of commerce can be treated objectively and analytically. The very promiscuity of the market-place, its facility for impregnating thought and expression, has to be acknowledged and restrained.

A complacent Paris receives a rebuff when he asks Diomed whether he or Menelaus is the more worthy of Helen. The Greek warrior exposes Helen as a worthless woman responsible for the deaths of countless Trojans and Greeks. The shaken Trojan prince declares that Diomed is being insincere, devaluing Helen, the very thing he would like to regain for the Greeks: 'Fair Diomed, you do as chapmen do, / Dispraise the thing that they desire to buy' (*TRO* 4.1.76–7). In contrast to *LLL* here the conception of the chapman is of one who uses his **bargaining** acumen to buy cheaply by devaluing the item he seeks to purchase.

(C) Agnew, *Worlds Apart*, 67, comments interestingly on the idiom of chapmen and the circulation of 'canting dictionaries' and quotes Dekker on players as chapmen 119. Londre, ed., *Love's Labour's Lost*, contains interesting essays on many aspects of the play including language, manners and style. Woodmansee and Osteen, eds, *The New Economic Criticism*, and Veblen, *The Theory of the Leisure Class*, explore language, commerce and **values**.

cheap, cheapen

(A) Cheap as simply meaning at a low **price** presents no difficulties. Cheapen, however, is less straightforward. Used only twice it means to **bargain** for, or negotiate a price.

(B) When castigating the tribunes for their antagonism towards Coriolanus, Menenius asserts, 'Yet you must be saying Martius is proud; who, in a cheap estimation, is worth all your predecessors since Deucalion' (*COR* 2.1.89–92). Lowest evaluation is the meaning attaching to Menenius' key phrase, 'cheap estimation'. Cheap is often used in the evaluative non-monetary sense. It is also frequently employed as a means of antithesis. The speaker in the sonnets ruefully confesses to having 'sold cheap what is most dear' (*SON* 110.3), namely reputation.

When Benedick provides an inventory of the qualities he requires in a wife he insists: 'Rich she shall be, that's certain; wise, or I'll none; virtuous, or I'll never cheapen her' (*ADO* 2.3.30–2). 'Cheapen' means to 'bargain for' or 'negotiate'.

Likewise, Bawd in *PER* complains that her new acquisition for the brothel, the youthful and pure Marina, is exerting such a morally wholesome but financially ruinous influence on the clients that, 'she would make a puritan of the devil, if he should cheapen a kiss of her' (4.6.9–10).

(C) Bruster, *Drama and the Market in the Age of Shakespeare*, explores the diverse aspects of the **market** in theory and **practice**.

chronicle, chronicled, chronicler

(A) These words represent an important human and political concept. The primary application relates to the recording of **achievements** in a way that sanctifies the life of an individual or society, giving it a shape that both validates and authenticates action and attainment. The concept is expressed more frequently than the word itself. Time and again in the histories and tragedies characters seek to frame their life; to capture and re-present its significance and to reveal the place they have occupied. The second meaning is merely to give an **account**, or tell a story without this narration necessarily possessing any deep resonance. The first application requires a chronicler to be someone who is an authenticated speaker, or the book itself, the chronicle. The second use of the term relates to someone who knows the sequence of events or tale, but neither the account nor the narrator need take on any historical significance. The chronicler in this routine sense does not possess the status attaching to the chronicler in a more elevated sense. Finally, something that is chronicled has been marked down and can be trivial (*TGV* 1.1.41 and *MND* 3.2.240) or profound (*R2* 5.5.116).

(B) Mark Antony, preparing to do battle with Octavius Caesar, promises Cleopatra: 'I and my sword will earn our chronicle' (*ANT* 3.13.175). These two figures are deeply concerned with **achieving** a place in history and authenticating themselves in the imagination of subsequent generations. Antony's boast is requisite at a moment when they are so palpably sliding to defeat and losing the material world to the acquisitive Caesar. While Antony and Cleopatra look to occupy a space that will be one of eternal glory, Queen Katherine pursues something altogether different. Having heard, to her astonishment, her loyal servant Griffith provide an attractive account of the life of her great and despised enemy, the late Cardinal Wolsey, she comments beautifully:

> After my death I wish no other herald,
> No other speaker of my living actions
> To keep mine honor from corruption,
> But such an honest chronicler as Griffith.
> Whom I most hated living, thou hast made me,
> With thy religious truth and modesty,
> Now in his ashes honor. Peace be with him!
>
> *H8* 4.2.69–75

Unlike the famous lovers, Katherine wishes only to be vindicated, to be honoured after her death as a figure of integrity. Antony's quest is for celebrity – fame; Katherine's for a just appreciation – name.

It is worth noting two other examples which convey a similar awareness of the dimensions of this concept. Hamlet insists that Horatio stay alive so that he can provide a true account of all that has passed:

> O God, Horatio, what a wounded name,
> Things standing thus unknown, shall I leave behind me!
> If thou didst ever hold me in thy heart,
> Absent thee from felicity awhile,
> And in this harsh world draw thy breath in pain
> To tell my story.
>
> *HAM* 5.2.344–9

Whereas Hamlet seeks only vindication of his honourable intentions, not even using the word 'chronicler', Coriolanus defies Aufidius and his associates as he asserts the greatness of his deeds and the reputation he has earned as a warrior: 'If you have writ your annals true, 'tis there / That, like an eagle in a dove-cote, I / Flutter'd your Volscians in Corioles. / Alone I did it. "Boy"!' (*COR* 5.6.113–16). In this Roman play Shakespeare chooses 'annals' rather than 'chronicle' but the concept is the same: the chronicles should contain a true account of men's achievements and their attainment of fame. Intriguingly, before this moment Volumnia has warned her son that if he attacks Rome with his Volscian forces he will relinquish all that he has achieved as a Roman hero:

> if thou conquer Rome, the benefit
> Which thou shalt thereby reap is such a name
> Whose repetition will be dogg'd with curses;
> Whose chronicle thus writ: 'The man was noble,
> But with his last attempt he wip'd it out,
> Destroy'd his country, and his name remains
> To th'ensuing age abhorr'd.'
>
> 5.3.142–8

Name and fame matter, especially to the greatest of all Roman warriors; fame has been achieved on the battlefield; infamy, or loss of name, may result from an act of betrayal – even though it may be an understandable act of revenge.

The lighter meaning is neatly captured by Valentine in mocking Proteus' susceptibility to love: 'Love is your master, for he masters you; / And he that is so yoked by a fool, / Methinks should not be chronicled for wise' (*TGV* 1.1.39–41). Accounted, reputed or **considered** is the meaning here. In a wholly different context Exton castigates himself for murdering Richard II: 'For now the devil that told me I did well / Says that this deed is chronicled in hell' (*R2* 5.5.115–6). Marked down or set down is indicated here: a diabolical deed is recorded not by men but by the devil himself.

Hector in meeting Nestor for the first time embraces him and dignifies him with a title that celebrates or memorializes his antiquity: 'Let me embrace thee, good old chronicle, / That hast so long walk'd hand in hand with time' (*TRO* 4.5.202–3). Here is the physical embodiment, a living recordation of events of historical significance. Iago, in providing an entertainment for the company, delineates the virtues of an exemplary woman, only to conclude, anticlimactically, that she is fit only, 'To suckle fools and chronicle small beer' (*OTH* 2.1.160). In other words to keep or record petty household accounts.

A nice shade is added to the meaning by Cardinal Wolsey in defending himself against accusations of imposing excessive and unjust taxes:

> If I am
> Traduc'd by ignorant tongues, which neither know
> My faculties nor person, yet will be
> The chronicles of my doing, let me say

> 'Tis but the fate of place, and the rough brake
> That virtue must go through.
>
> *H8* 1.2.71–6

That is to say, a great man's actions are inevitably subject to scrutiny and comment. Ignorant people will always set themselves up as authorities on those doings, elevating themselves to chroniclers, whereas their tittle-tattle is risible. The use of chronicles indicates a misconception of their own importance with the word now used to considerable ironic effect.

Hamlet elevates actors when he refers to them as, 'the abstract and brief chronicles of the time' (*HAM* 2.2.524–5). Inherent in this hendiadys is a compaction which celebrates the actors for being able to capture and give expression to the essence of their social universe, making palpable what is nebulous and intangible to the uninitiated. What histories try to achieve in retrospect the actors capture on the wing – history in the process of being made.

The idea of chronicle is aptly rendered by Prospero, who advises his listeners that his life on the island over the past dozen years is not amenable to a brief narration: 'No more yet of this, / For 'tis a chronicle of day by day, / Not a relation for a breakfast, nor / Befitting this first meeting' (*TMP* 5.1.162–5). Amazing though this tale will be, and close to death as Prospero may be, this account does not function like that of Hamlet's or of Coriolanus'. Nor does it function like that of Othello's which is earnest, emphatic, even desperate and aimed at an audience, the Venetians, who will judge him. In this case both name and fame are involved:

> Soft you; a word or two before you go.
> I have done the state some service, and they know't –
> No more of that. I pray you, in your letters,
> When you shall these unlucky deeds relate,
> Speak of me as I am; nothing extenuate,
> Nor set down aught in malice. Then must you speak
> Of one that lov'd not wisely but too well;
>
> *OTH* 5.2.338–44

(C) The relevant chapters in Brower, *Hero and Saint*, McAlindon, *Shakespeare Minus 'Theory'*, Young, *The Action to the Word*, and Matheson, 'Venetian culture and the politics of *Othello*' in Alexander, ed., *Shakespeare and Politics*, all illuminate this topic. So too does Hardy, *Shakespeare's Storytellers*.

clipper

(A) This is a person who clips coins: an illegal **practice**, punished as treason, designed to make a **profit** for the perpetrator.

(B) Used solely in *H5* on the night before the Battle of Agincourt, the disguised King concludes his dispute with Bates and Williams by commenting on military odds. Henry playfully puns on cutting off French heads and clipping coins:

'Indeed the French may lay twenty French crowns to one they will beat us, for they bear them on their shoulders; but it is no English treason to cut French crowns, and to-morrow the King himself will be a clipper' (*H5* 4.1.225–9).

(C) Counterfeiting and tampering with the coinage attracted the unscrupulous opportunist, and even Shakespeare's celebrated fellow dramatist was suspected of the crime. For a vibrant account of Marlowe and the Elizabethan world, Riggs, *The World of Christopher Marlowe*, heads the list of fine volumes, which includes Honan, *Christopher Marlowe, Poet and Spy*, Cheney, ed., *The Cambridge Companion to Christopher Marlowe*, and Nicholl, *The Reckoning*. See also the entry on **counterfeit**.

coffer, coffers up

(A) Possessing two financial meanings, the term can refer to the box or treasury containing either private or public funds or to the funds themselves, whether abundant or negligible. On a few occasions in a more general sense the word appears to apply to boxes or containers (*OTH* 2.1.208; *WIV* 4.2.61). The term 'coffers up', used only once, means to hoard **wealth**.

(B) As Richard II contemplates the death of his uncle, John of Gaunt, he anticipates the prospect of confiscating his wealth in order to finance the Irish campaign: 'The lining of his coffers shall make coats / To deck our soldiers for these Irish wars' (*R2* 1.4.61–2). The witty and incisive imagery celebrates the transformative nature of **money** with coin transmuting into men and equipment.

Henry IV is dismissive of Hotspur's proposal that his captured brother-in-law Mortimer be ransomed from the Welsh: 'Shall our coffers then / Be emptied to redeem a traitor home?' (*1H4* 1.3.85–6).

Mark Antony in his forum speech **fashions** the dead Caesar into a model public benefactor: 'He hath brought many captives home to Rome, / Whose ransoms did the general coffers fill' (*JC* 3.2.88–9).

When the captured sailor, Antonio, asks for money – mistaking Viola (disguised as Cesario) for Sebastian – her answer makes it clear that her coffer means available funds: 'My having is not much; / I'll make division of my present with you. / Hold, there's half my coffer' (*TN* 3.4.345–7).

Lucrece, denouncing human perversity, provides a disquisition on the folly of hoarding wealth: ' "The aged man that coffers up his gold / Is plagu'd with cramps and gouts and painful fits, / And scarce hath eyes his treasure to behold" ' (*LUC* 855–7).

(C) Forman, 'Material Dispossessions and Counterfeit Investments: The economics of *Twelfth Night*' in Woodbridge, ed., *Money and the Age of Shakespeare*, is of interest here. So, too, is Ruiter, *Shakespeare's Festive History*; Cheney, ed., *Shakespeare's Poetry*; Zander ed., *Julius Caesar*.

commerce

(A) Employed only four times the word signifies transactions or intercourse. In only one case is there any possibility that trade is alluded to or incorporated in the meaning.

(B) The only case affording a possible suggestion of the exchange of goods being involved occurs in the famous degree speech in *TRO* which refers to 'Peaceful commerce from dividable shores' (1.3.105). While trading activity frequently creeps into this play its other reference relates purely to non-marketable dealings. Ulysses informs Achilles that the Greek leadership is fully aware of his exchanges with Polyxena: 'All the commerce that you have had with Troy / As perfectly is ours as yours, my lord' (3.3.205–6).

(C) See Adamson, *Troilus and Cressida*, and Engle, *Shakespearean Pragmatism*, esp. ch. 7.

commission, commissioner

(A) Relating to power and authority this is a term with several distinct meanings: warrant or authority; command or power; government commission; a body made up of justices of the peace; a delegation. A commissioner is an official acting on behalf of the King in his absence.

(B) Winchester receives a cold response from York on his arrival in France as he announces that he comes, 'With letters of commission from the King' (*1H6* 5.4.95). York feels that his hard won victories in France are about to be cancelled by a peace treaty. Aufidius embraces his former enemy Coriolanus and divides his authority with him as he prepares to attack Roman territory: 'take / Th'one half of my commission' (*COR* 4.5.137–8). Queen Katherine, providing evidence of the severe taxes imposed by Wolsey, says, 'The subject's grief / Comes through commissions, which compels from each / The sixt part of his substance, to be levied / Without delay' (*H8* 1.2.56–9). This comment gives a clear indication of the power of these instruments of government and of Wolsey who has instituted these proceedings in the King's name but without his knowledge. Much less intimidating is the body consisting of justices of the peace in *2H4*. As Falstaff arrives to recruit soldiers, Shallow informs him, 'it is my cousin Silence, in commission with me' (3.2.87–8). The situation is comic – though not to the recruits. Surrey charges Wolsey with having dispatched a delegation to negotiate without the King's approval: 'you sent a large commission . . . / Without the King's will or the state's allowance' (*H8* 3.2.320–2). Henry V calls forth those who are to undertake specific tasks in his name during his absence: 'Who are the late commissioners?' (*H5* 2.2.61). They are the traitors who are about to become performers in Henry's piece of political theatre.

(C) See Pallister, *The Age of Elizabeth*, ch. 10; Clark, *Renaissance Drama*, ch. 12; Hattaway, ed., *Shakespeare's History Plays*.

commodity

(A) This deceptive word sometimes carries its contemporary meaning of saleable item. Additionally, it can mean any one of the following: quantity, supply or stock; gain, benefit, **advantage; profit**, proceeds; parcel; self-interest or expediency. A quality integral to the word is **merchandise**, something possessing a **market value**. Hence its potential for dividing into pejorative or non-pejorative applications.

(B) When Hermione, indicted for adultery, responds to Leontes' threats with the words, 'To me can life be no commodity' (*WT* 3.2.93) she is using the word in an unusual and direct way to mean benefit. Her husband has rejected and imprisoned her, denounced her newly born daughter as a bastard, and denied her access to her son. Life itself has no value. A movement away from this meaning is provided by Parolles in *AWW*. He cautions Helena that virginity is an asset whose value diminishes through time just like any perishable goods kept too long: ''Tis a commodity will lose the gloss with lying: the longer kept, the less worth' (1.1.153–4). This affected insouciance is characteristic of the man for whom virginity is a marketable item. A straightforward application of the term is occasioned by Antonio's caution to Bassanio that he has a cash-flow problem: 'Neither have I money nor commodity / To raise a present sum' (*MV* 1.1.178–9). Here commodity means merchandise that can be sold for cash.

The rich potential of the word ranges well beyond these straightforward applications. When Pompey refers to the crimes of fellow prisoners he cites Master Rash: 'he's in for a commodity of brown paper and old ginger' (*MM* 4.3.4–5). In other words he is imprisoned for attempting to evade the law, which limits the rate of **interest** to 10 per cent, by supplying part of the loan in the form of commodities at a valuation above their market **price**. Here 'commodity' means simply 'stock' or 'supply', but it is tainted by virtue of its constituent part. Here is a **practice** which gives rise to a term, 'commodity of . . .' and in so doing contaminates a word. Borachio and Conrade quibble on these meanings when arrested by the Watch. Borachio says: 'We are like to prove a goodly commodity, being taken up of these men's bills.' The indignity of being captured by such maladroit yokels provokes laughter or scorn just as the dubious quality of goods provided as part of the deal by a moneylender is apparent. **Bills** here refer to the weapons of the Watch and the securities of the loan. Conrade replies with a further play on the word: 'A commodity in question, I warrant you' (*ADO* 3.3.177–9). Here is a quibble on a commodity much sought after, and 'subject to trial by legal examination' (Stevens, cited by Humphries, ed., *Much Ado About Nothing*, Arden 2, fn 163).

A significant application occurs in *PER* in a discussion relating to profit or financial gain. Pander proposes to his partner Bawd that current market **conditions** afford them such a small profit or return, when set against the risks, legal and spiritual, that they should contemplate retirement: 'O, our credit comes not in like the commodity, nor the commodity wages not with the danger; therefore if in our youths we could pick up some pretty estate, 'twere not amiss to keep our door hatch'd. Besides, the sore terms we stand upon with the gods will be strong with us for giving o'er' (4.2.30–5). The brothel scenes in this play are replete with economic analyses. Here is a careful evaluation of profitability and rates of return. Even a spiritual element is drawn into the economic calculus. High rates of return from immoral activity might be enough to outweigh negative spiritual returns, but here profitability is on the very margin.

Falstaff in mock denigration of his reputation and that of Hal muses, 'I would to God thou and I knew where a commodity of good names were to be bought' (*1H4* 1.2.82–3). Here commodity signifies 'parcel', but a subtle bifurcation reveals Falstaff (by way of a joke) attempting to achieve moral stature by means of a market transaction. Most things can be **purchased** in this culture but name: reputation or moral **worth** is not a transactional phenomenon. Ever pressed financially, Falstaff makes continual resort to sharp practice including taking bribes to exempt strong, healthy men from military service while recruiting the physically unfit. Hence he ends up with 'such a commodity of warm slaves, as had lieve hear the devil as a drum' (*1H4* 4.2.17–18).

Something that emerges from these comic applications of the term is the idea of a parcel of dubious worth. Given the centrality of the market in Elizabethan and Jacobean culture and, to use the Marxist term, the 'commodification' of the world, a seemingly simple, non-pejorative word gradually accretes the suggestion that what the world is really about is acquisition, accumulation and possession. It is this idea that finds early expression in *JN* where the word is used, six times, more frequently than in any other play. Here 'commodity' is **capitalized**, effectively turning unscrupulous personal advantage into a fundamental principle of human activity – it is what makes the world turn and is the chief activator of human behaviour. Faulconbridge, the Bastard, in a rightly admired speech of great energy and drive, exposes a social universe characterized by self-seeking, duplicity and opportunism, balancing his speech on the term 'commodity' just as he represents society balanced on the conceptual fulcrum commodity. It is difficult to appreciate fully the structural significance of the word without quoting the speech in its entirety. All six uses of the word occur in this one speech yet the concept dominates the play. Shakespeare's plays abound in vilification (Timon is the outstanding practitioner in this field) but no character or idea is dissected in the way that commodity is here – nor is any principle granted so much malign power:

> Mad world, mad kings, mad composition!
> John, to stop Arthur's title in the whole,
> Hath willingly departed with a part,
> And France, whose armor conscience buckled on,
> Whom zeal and charity brought to the field
> As God's own soldier, rounded in the ear
> With that same purpose-changer, that sly devil,
> That broker, that still breaks the pate of faith,
> That daily break-vow, he that wins of all,
> Of kings, of beggars, old men, young men, maids,
> Who having no external thing to lose
> But the word 'maid', cheats the poor maid of that,
> That smooth-fac'd gentleman, tickling commodity,
> Commodity, the bias of the world –
> The world, who of itself is peized well,
> Made to run even upon even ground,
> Till this advantage, this vile drawing bias,
> This sway of motion, this commodity,

> Makes it take head from all indifferency,
> From all direction, purpose, course, intent –
> And this same bias, this commodity,
> This bawd, this broker, this all-changing word,
> Clapp'd on the outward eye of fickle France,
> Hath drawn him from his own determin'd aid,
> From a resolv'd and honorable war
> To a most base and vile-concluded peace.
> And why rail I on this commodity?
> But for because he hath not woo'd me yet:
> Not that I have the power to clutch my hand
> When his fair angels would salute my palm,
> But for my hand, as unattempted yet,
> Like a poor beggar, raileth on the rich.
> Well, whiles I am a beggar, I will rail,
> And say there is no sin but to be rich;
> And being rich, my virtue then shall be
> To say there is no vice but beggary.
> Since kings break faith upon commodity,
> Gain, be my lord, for I will worship thee.
>
> 2.1.561–98

(C) See the Sokols' entry on commodity and in this volume the entry on **advantage**. On the purchase of name see Humphries, ed., *Henry IV, Part 1*, Arden 2, fn 128. For Marx and commodification see Egan, *Shakespeare and Marx*; Kamps, ed., *Materialist Shakespeare*; and Howard and Shershow, eds, *Marxist Shakespeares*. Highly significant in this context are Brotton, *The Renaissance Bazaar*; Hawkes, *Idols of the Market Place*; Woodbridge, ed., *Money in the Age of Shakespeare*; Agnew, *Worlds Apart*, esp. 57–87; Bruster, *Drama and the Market in the Age of Shakespeare*, esp. 105; Hadfield, *Shakespeare and Renaissance Politics*. Relevant to *JN* are Vaughan, 'King John' in Dutton and Howard, eds, *Shakespeare's Works – Vol. II: The Histories*; Cavanagh, *Language and Politics in the Sixteenth-Century History Play*; Donawerth, *Shakespeare and the Sixteenth-Century Study of Language*; Smallwood, ed., *Players of Shakespeare 6*.

commonality

(A) When wishing to distinguish that part of the **commonwealth**, the common people, the term 'commonality' is used. There are only two cases, one a prosaic reference to the common people in *H8*; the other, much more significant, is in *COR*.

(B) The denunciation by the common people of the eponymous hero Coriolanus could hardly be more direct: 'he's a very dog to the commonality' (1.1.28–9). Unremitting in his excoriation of the common people this contempt stems from his patrician conception that **plebeians** do not form part of the commonwealth. Shakespeare dramatizes a moment in Roman history, around 396 BC, when the plebeians acquire political representation in the form of tribunes. This institutionalized their position allowing them to become part of the commonwealth. At a moment in the political crisis when tensions are at their highest, Sicinius makes the revolutionary claim, 'What is the city but the people?' (3.1.198). After Coriolanus has been exiled the tribune says, 'The commonwealth doth stand, and so would do, / Were he more angry at it' (4.6.14–15). The 'commonality' are now insiders, part of the commonwealth; the famous warrior Coriolanus has been exiled, thereby becoming an outsider. A new order has been established in which the common people have a voice: they are acknowledged as constituting part of the commonwealth.

In *H8* the surveyor of the Duke of Buckingham has been **suborned** by Wolsey to recount how a monk predicted that the Duke would become King and that in the furthering of this event he should 'strive / To the love o'th' commonality' (1.2.169–70). What is surprising in this case is that an aspirant to the throne whose prospects of attaining the crown are remote, should seek to insinuate himself with the common people. (Buckingham was descended directly from Edward III's second son, Thomas of Woodstock.) The prophecy, it seems, is married to political advice. Though the truth of this narration is brought into question by Queen Katherine, the accusation sticks and Buckingham is executed. This application of the word is in one sense commonplace, but its implication is intriguing: Buckingham is advised to behave in the very way that Bolingbroke is accused of doing by Richard II, who rightly suspects his cousin's aims:

> Ourself and Bushy, Bagot here and Green,
> Observ'd his courtship to the common people,
> How he did seem to dive into their hearts
> With humble and familiar courtesy,
> What reverence he did throw away on slaves,
> Wooing poor craftsmen with the craft of smiles
> And patient underbearing of his fortune,
> As 'twere to banish their affects with him.
> Off goes his bonnet to an oyster-wench,
> A brace of draymen bid God speed him well,
> And had the tribute of his supple knee,
> With 'Thanks, my countrymen, my loving friends',
> As were our England in reversion his,
> And he our subjects' next degree in hope.
>
> *R2* 1.4.23–36

Here is a contemptuously vivid description that reveals just how successfully Bolingbroke plays the common people, affecting humility and humanity. He does, of course, succeed in getting the crown and delivers a seminar to Hal on precisely how he employed the art of political theatre in his quest to gain popular favour, albeit his **account** is somewhat at variance with that provided by Richard. Having characterized his technique he describes the outcome:

> And then I stole all courtesy from heaven,
> And dress'd myself in such humility
> That I did pluck allegiance from men's hearts,
> Loud shouts and salutations from their mouths,
> Even in the presence of the crowned King.
>
> *1H4* 3.2.50–4

This may seem a long way from the brief comment in *H8*, but it illustrates the significance of courting public popularity, of mastering the arts of political theatre, even when the commonality possess negligible power. Coriolanus is singular in courting the antagonism of the plebeians, but even he recognizes that **politicians** invariably seek to ingratiate themselves with the people, no matter how much they disdain or disparage them in private. Sarcastically he declares that he 'will counterfeit the bewitchment of some popular man' (*COR* 2.3.101). An Officer exclaims to his colleague who has protested that Coriolanus 'loves not the common people', 'Faith, there hath been many great men that have flatter'd the people, who ne'er lov'd them' (2.2.6–8). The discourse relating to the relationship between the elite and the common people and the nature of political manipulation is, therefore, highly significant in Shakespeare's plays.

(C) For an analysis of the attitudes to the plebeians and Shakespeare's shaping of Rome, see Thomas, *Shakespeare's Roman Worlds*; Kahn, *Roman Shakespeare*; Cantor, *Shakespeare's Rome, Republic and Empire*; Miola, *Shakespeare's Rome*; Velz, 'The ancient world in Shakespeare: authenticity or anachronism – a retrospect', *Shakespeare Survey* 31: 1–12; Hattaway, 'Tragedy and political authority' in McEachern, ed., *Shakespearean Tragedy*. Shapiro's acclaimed study, *1599*, affords valuable insights into the contemporary scene. Saccio, *Shakespeare's English Kings*, is remarkably clear in tracing the intricacies of the relationships between historical events and the dramatic choices. Excellent essays on political theatre are to be found in Howard and O'Connor, eds, *Shakespeare Reproduced*, Dollimore, *Radical Tragedy*, and Holderness, ed., *Shakespeare's History Plays*.

commonweal, commonwealth

(A) Both these words mean society, state or nation but the application always entails strong awareness of the political dimension of the community so that 'body **politic**' may be an apt rendering, though it risks diminishing the sense of the juices of local and national feeling embodied in the term. The key components are identity, belonging, connectedness, along with institutionalized political structures. Commonwealth is used almost three times as frequently as commonweal (28/10) and of these 38 applications 10 occur in the three parts of *H6*. Intrinsic to the conception of the commonwealth is the idea of an entity embodying the capacities and resources of the community. No abstract term such as social structure or institutional framework can do justice to the expression of something so evidently physical and malleable. The commonwealth in Shakespeare's plays is clearly an organism, membership of which constitutes a privilege and whose very **commonality** calls forth duty and obligation, the antithesis of which is **exploitation**.

(B) The precise flavour of these expressions is clearly revealed by the following examples. Subsequent to the assassination of Julius Caesar, Brutus seeks to reassure the populace by implying that there had been no genuine commonwealth under their great leader: 'Here comes his body, mourn'd by Mark Antony, who, though he had no hand in his death, shall receive the benefit of his dying, a place in the commonwealth, as which of you shall not?' (*JC* 3.2.41–4). Here is a promise of inclusiveness and a reactivation of a living, vitalized social and political reality.

In *TMP*, Gonzalo, having been shipwrecked with the King's party on a seemingly deserted island, is inspired to expound on his vision of an ideal society. Here is a utopia free of work, commerce, conflict or inequality:

> I' th' commonwealth I would, by contraries,
> Execute all things; for no kind of traffic
> Would I admit; no name of magistrate;
>
> . . .
>
> No occupation, all men idle, all;
> And women too, but innocent and pure;
> No sovereignty –

Two cynical auditors, Sebastian and Antonio, point out the flaw in the scheme:

Sebastian: Yet he would be king on't.
Antonio: The latter end of his commonwealth forgets the beginning.
2.1.148–59

The conception expounded by Gonzalo is that the perfect commonwealth is one of equality. Deriding the implausibility of such an idea is easy but the critical issue is that the closer presiding reality is to this model the nearer society approaches a true commonwealth. Tyranny and a commonwealth are incompatible.

Awareness of the vulnerability of the commonwealth and the responsibility for its maintenance is particularly apparent in the *H6* plays. In *Part 1* the young King Henry chastises his quarrelling uncles, Gloucester and Winchester, concluding with a particularly strong metaphor: 'Believe me, lords, my tender years can tell, / Civil dissention is a viperous worm / That gnaws the bowels of the commonwealth' (3.1.71–3).

In *Part 2* Suffolk denounces Gloucester for his performance as Lord Protector: 'Since thou wert king – as who is king but thou? – / The commonwealth hath daily run to wrack' (1.3.123–4). In *Part 3* Montague cautions King Edward against the folly of choosing the widow Lady Grey for his wife in preference to the Lady Bona, the French princess: 'Yet, to have join'd with France in such alliance / Would more have strength'ned this our commonwealth' (4.1.36–7). Here, there

67

is an acute sense of the significance of foreign affairs. Security and prosperity depend on both internal and external relations.

The Duke of Gloucester is described by one of his serving men as 'So kind a father of the commonweal' (*1H6* 3.1.98). By contrast the malicious Cardinal denounces Gloucester for his feigned dedication, 'That smooth'st it so with king and commonweal!' (*2H6* 2.1.22). It is noteworthy that there is a distinction between the king and the larger entity, 'commonweal'. The **Machiavellian** Aaron makes a similar distinction as he anticipates the success of Tamora, in bringing about the destruction of Rome: 'This siren that will charm Rome's Saturnine, / And see his shipwreck and his commonweal's' (*TIT* 2.1.23–4).

While these terms are used most frequently in history plays, it is worth noting their lighter application in the comedies. On the entry of the rustic Costard, the courtier Boyet comments dismissively, 'Here comes a member of the common-wealth' (*LLL* 4.1.41). This could mean, as suggested by the Riverside editor, the 'common people'. More likely is the meaning, 'here's a sample of the citizenry' with irony being extracted from the idea that Costard is a full, though pathetic-ally inadequate, member of society. Later in the play the curate Nathaniel commends the schoolmaster Holofernes for his scholarship and service to the community as a schoolteacher: 'You are a good member of the commonwealth' (4.2.76–7). Here the idea of service to the local community seems to be the ultimate accolade. The sense of community is particularly strong in the comed-ies, possessing an inverted quality, so that the essence of community resides in the locality, its health-giving energy moving upwards. The process of inter-action between people and laws is neatly captured by Mistress Overdone, who on being informed that the **bawdy** houses are to be pulled down as a con-sequence of the new proclamation, exclaims: 'Why, here's a change indeed in the commonwealth!' (*MM* 1.2.104–5).

(C) For an engaging and perceptive exploration of the relationship between common people and commonwealth see Parker's chapter on 'Rude mechanic-als' in *Shakespeare from the Margins*. A highly concentrated exploration of politics, theology and the commonwealth is provided by Shugar in *Political Theologies in Shakespeare's England*. Hankins' insightful essay 'Humanism and the origins of modern political thought' is to be found in Kraye, ed., *Renaissance Humanism*. For further relevant commentary see Stevenson, *Praise and Paradox*; Loomba, *Shakespeare, Race and Colonialism*; Alexander and Wells, eds, *Shakespeare and Race*; Hadfield, *Shakespeare and Republicanism*.

compact

(A) Employed as a noun the word's primary meaning is political, signifying agree-ment or alliance, though it is also used for a marriage covenant. As an adjective it can indicate collusion and also composed or made-up. Used as a verb it signifies to consolidate or reinforce, and to concentrate as in concocting a poison.

(B) When Mark Antony seeks to insinuate himself with the conspirators, Cassius attempts to pin him down: 'I blame you not for praising Caesar so, / But what compact mean you to have with us? / Will you be prick'd in number of our friends, / Or shall we on, and not depend on you?' (*JC* 3.1.214–17). Horatio emphasizes the moral and legal nature of an agreement by which King Hamlet and his Norwegian counterpart, Fortinbras, determined the circumstances of their duel: 'by a seal'd compact / Well ratified by law and heraldry' (*HAM* 1.1.86–7).

A parallel to this legally ratified agreement occurs in *TN*, when the Priest is called upon by Olivia to validate her claim that she is married to Cesario: 'And all the ceremony of this compact / Seal'd in my function, by my testimony' (5.1.160–1). Technically, a compact is meant to be binding. In practice, however, a distinction is made between an agreement ratified by law and ceremony and that which is merely a verbal commitment.

Employed as an adjective to mean 'made' or 'consisting of', there is a fine example at the end of *TIT* when Marcus rehearses Rome's past griefs and suffering: 'My heart is not compact of flint nor steel' (5.3.88).

Oswald employs the adjective when ingratiating himself with Cornwall and Regan claiming to be the innocent party in his quarrel with the disguised Kent: 'It pleas'd the King his master very late / To strike at me upon his misconstruction, / When he, compact, and flattering his displeasure, / Tripp'd me behind' (*LR* 2.2.116–19). Oswald implies that his adversary and Lear were in league or were collusive.

A good example of the use of the word as a verb is also provided in *LR*. Goneril instructs Oswald to take a message to her sister and to ratify or augment her complaints against Lear: 'And thereto add such reasons of your own / As may compact it more' (1.4.338–9). Given Goneril's ruthlessness and Oswald's oily tongue, it would appear that the stronger meaning attaches to the word, so that Oswald is being instructed to contrive his own fabrications to strengthen the tenor of the letter.

(C) The aspects of power and idiom are glanced at from diverse angles in Coyle, ed., *Hamlet*, and in Ryan, ed., *King Lear*. The question of political manoeuvrings receives significant attention in Thomas, *Julius Caesar*; particularly relevant is Kahn's essay on 'Friendship and Emulation' in Zander, ed., *Julius Caesar*. See also Jordan and Cunningham, eds, *The Law in Shakespeare*.

competence
(A) Used only once, sufficient resources to live on rather than the modern suggestion of capability applies here.
(B) The newly crowned King Henry V halts the procession to rebuke Falstaff, 'I know thee not, old man', before intimating that he will be provided with sufficient funds to live on:

> For competence of life I will allow you,
> That lack of means enforce you not to evils,
> And as we hear you do reform yourselves,
> We will, according to your strengths and qualities,
> Give you advancement.
>
> *2H4* 5.5.66–70

(C) Historically much of the commentary on this public annihilation of Falstaff was couched in sentimental terms, but during the past few decades a more hard-edged approach has gained ascendancy. The rejection of the fat knight is now perceived as part of *realpolitik* though this has hardly resulted in a softening towards the new monarch. Grady explores the proposition of Hal/Henry as the prince of **Machiavels** with vigour and vivacity in *Shakespeare, Machiavelli and Montaigne*; Holderness, ed., *Shakespeare's History Plays*, gathers together a strong representation of recent approaches. Ruiter, *Shakespeare's Festive Histories*, and Bloom, *Shakespeare: The Invention of the Human*, highlight important aspects of this social universe.

competency
(A) This word signifies both means of life or adequacy of sustenance; also **provision** that is adequate but not excessive or opulent.
(B) Menenius, delivering his famous fable of the belly, gives voice to the belly's defence against the accusation of being parasitical:

> Because I am the store-house and the shop
> Of the whole body. But, if you do remember,
> I send it through the rivers of your blood,
> Even to the court, the heart, to th'seat o'th'brain,
> And, through the cranks and offices of man,
> The strongest nerves and small inferior veins
> From me receive that natural competency
> Whereby they live.
>
> *COR* 1.1.133–40

'Sustenance' appears to be the meaning here. Surprisingly, his analogy between the human body and the body **politic** succeeds in quelling the starving rioters.

When, however, the wealthy Portia complains, 'my little body is a-weary of this great world', Nerissa is quick to check her:

> You would be, sweet madam, if your
> miseries were in the same abundance
> as your good fortunes are; and yet for
> aught I see, they are as sick that surfeit
> with too much as they that starve with
> nothing. It is no mean happiness therefore
> to be seated in the mean: superfluity
> comes sooner by white hairs, but competency
> lives longer.
>
> *MV* 1.2.1–9

Nerissa states the case for being blessed with sufficiency, or 'competency', rather than with abundant resources.

(C) For analysis of the fable of the belly and its diverse sources and implications see Barton, 'Livy, Machiavelli and Shakespeare's *Coriolanus*' in *Essays Mainly Shakespearean*, and Hadfield, *Shakespeare and Renaissance Politics*, 171–81. Other highly relevant commentary is to be found in McAlindon, *Shakespeare Minus 'Theory'*; Poole, *Coriolanus*; Lieber, *Shakespeare's Festive Tragedies*; Hillman, *Shakespeare's Entrails*.

competent, computent
(A) Financial or material (territorial) equivalence is indicated by the single use of competent. In the case of the variant spelling, computent, the adjectival meaning is real, substantial, or possibly to require a **reckoning**.
(B) Horatio's description of the terms of the duel between King Hamlet and his Norwegian rival, Fortinbras, includes the lines:

> Did forfeit (with his life) all those his lands
> Which he stood seiz'd of, to the conqueror;
> Against the which a moi'ty competent
> Was gaged by our king, which had return'd
> To the inheritance of Fortinbras,
> Had he been vanquisher;
>
> *HAM* 1.1.88–93

Evidently an equivalent portion or territory of equal **worth** is meant by the phrase 'moi'ty competent'.

In contrast, Sir Toby Belch, presenting a challenge to Cesario/Viola on behalf of his associate Sir Andrew Aguecheek, maintains that it is no trivial matter, but a grievance based on a significant and substantial affront to propriety that now necessitates a reckoning: 'Sir, no; his indignation derives itself out of a very computent injury' (*TN* 3.4.246–7). Riverside modernizes 'computent' to 'competent'.
(C) See Hulme, *Explorations in Shakespeare's Language*, 165, for an interesting comment whereby 'in the usual modernisation to "competent", some fine thread of Sir Toby's meaning may be lost'. Jones, *Shakespeare at Work*, Kermode, *Shakespeare's Language*, and Holderness, *Textual Shakespeare*, are valuable in their exploration of *HAM*.

competitor(s)
(A) A dangerous word because it has shifted its meaning. It does *not* mean **rival**, its obvious meaning today, though the context sometimes suggests that it does. The two meanings are: colleague, partner or associate; fellow candidate.
(B) Employed only nine times in all, with three of the occasions in *ANT*, only one character uses the word twice: Octavius Caesar. Complaining to Lepidus about Antony's antics in Egypt and his dilatoriness in responding to a call for assistance, the humourless young man declares in his prologue to a colourful and masterly indictment, 'You may see, Lepidus, and henceforth know, / It is not Caesar's natural vice to hate / Our great competitor' (1.4.1–3). The two leading members

of the triumvirate (Lepidus is a mere makeweight) are indeed covert rivals, but to all intents and purposes they are colleagues – which is what the term overtly means here. Even more potentially misleading is Octavius' encomium on receiving news of Antony's death. The man who has been in fierce conflict with Antony and was intent on disgracing him or hounding him to death, suddenly becomes dewy-eyed:

> I must perforce
> Have shown to thee such a declining day,
> Or look on thine; we could not stall together
> In the whole world. But yet let me lament,
> With tears as sovereign as the blood of hearts,
> That thou, my brother, my competitor
> In top of all design, my mate in empire,
> Friend and companion in the front of war,
> The arm of mine own body, and the heart
> Where mine his thoughts did kindle – that our stars,
> Unreconciliable, should divide
> Our equalness to this.
>
> 5.1.37–48

Arguably, there is no ambiguity as the word is wedged between so many commendatory terms, but if read in the modern sense it can be perplexing. Confusion is also possible in *TGV*. Proteus, having fallen in love with Silvia, the sweetheart of his best friend Valentine, has the task of aiding the lovers in their planned elopement. Thus he soliloquizes:

> I cannot now prove constant to myself,
> Without some treachery us'd to Valentine.
> This night he meaneth with a corded ladder
> To climb celestial Silvia's chamber-window,
> Myself in counsel his competitor.
>
> 2.6.31–5

Although Proteus is now Valentine's friend *and* rival, he is using 'competitor' to mean associate. The second meaning, that of 'co-petitioner', is also open to misunderstanding, especially given the ferocity of the competition between the brothers Saturninus and Bassianus as they manoeuvre to become Emperor of Rome in the opening scene of *TIT*. Bassianus appeals to the citizenry to make way for his entrance through the gates: 'Tribunes, and me, a poor competitor' (1.1.63).

Where 'competitors' is used, the scope for assuming the modern meaning of rivals is particularly strong. For instance, when Aaron chastises the Goth princes for quarrelling over Lavinia, who is already married to the Emperor's brother, he exclaims: 'Why, are ye mad? or know ye not, in Rome / How furious and impatient they be, / And cannot brook competitors in love?' (2.1.75–7). Perhaps the modern inference, 'rivals', would not be seriously misleading here even if, strictly speaking, the term means co-petitioners.

In *R3*, however, the messenger bringing news that the King's enemies are gathering in groups, refers to them first as 'confederates' and then as 'competitors' that 'Flock to the rebels' (4.4.502–5). There is scope for confusion here, though the modern auditor would probably be saved from undue perplexity by the context. Likewise, when Feste announces the entrance of his associates or fellow conspirators Sir Toby Belch and Maria, in the incarceration and mockery of Malvolio, his comment 'The competitors enter' (*TN*4.2.10) is ambiguous. The same is true of *LLL*, where Boyet refers to the King and his associates who have sworn to dedicate themselves to study, abjuring the company of women: 'And he and his competitors in oath' (2.1.82). Less than obvious to the modern ear is the meaning in *ANT* where Menas the pirate proposes to Pompey that he cut the throats of their newly acquired allies. He refers to Octavius Caesar, Mark Antony and Lepidus as, 'These three world-sharers, these competitors' (2.7.70). He means associates, and the actor might well deliver the phrase 'world sharers' and the term 'competitors' with biting contempt. Either way, on page or stage it is possible to misconstrue the meaning. Part of the disdain of Menas for the triumvirate arises from his perception that these nominal allies are in fact bitter rivals.

Intriguingly, either meaning of the word, associate or fellow candidate, is open to misunderstanding, so that the modern meaning of 'rival' could be misapplied by the reader or audience.

(C) Thomas, *Shakespeare's Roman Worlds*, and Adelman, *The Common Liar*, both examine the manoeuvrings in *ANT*; the former also devotes a chapter to *TIT*. Bullough, *Shakespeare's Narrative and Dramatic Sources*, vol. 5, is invaluable for analysing the play in the light of Plutarch's historical material. Metz, *Shakespeare's Earliest Tragedy*, is vital here. Foakes, *Shakespeare and Violence*, and Leggatt, *Shakespeare's Tragedies*, are also insightful. Leggatt, *Shakespeare's Comedy of Love* has a fine chapter on *TN*.

complice(s)

(A) Used only five times – always in the history plays – the term means associates, accomplices or confederates. It can be neutral or pejorative.

(B) On receiving news of the death of his son Hotspur, Northumberland gives way to a histrionic outburst that provokes the Lord Bardolph to remind him of the need for sober judgement: 'Sweet Earl, divorce not wisdom from your honor, / The lives of all your loving complices / Lean on your health, the which, if you give o'er / To stormy passion, must perforce decay' (*2H4* 1.1.162–5).

In the other four cases the word suggests disdain for enemies as, for instance, when Young Clifford spurns Warwick and the Yorkists with the battle cry, 'And so to arms, victorious father, / To quell the rebels and their complices' (*2H6* 5.1.212–13).

(C) Cavanagh, *Language and Politics in the Sixteenth-Century History Play*, is revealing with respect to the implications and associations of words in political discourse and conflict.

complot

(A) The word signifies a devious scheme, the outcome of which is the death of adversaries. Thus although the modern equivalent would be plot or conspiracy, neither word carries the full impact of complot used either as a noun, as in secret plan or agreement, or as a verb, where collude or conspire would be the modern equivalent. Even the sound of the word is suggestive of ruthless machinations. *R2* and *R3* each have two examples, *TIT* three, with a single one in *2H6*. Accordingly the word figures only in the histories and in one tragedy, and only in the first part of Shakespeare's career.

(B) In the scene of mutual denunciation in *R2*, Bolingbroke sums up his catalogue of Mowbray's misdeeds with the lines, 'That all the treasons for these eighteen years, / Complotted and contrived in this land, / Fetch from false Mowbray their first head and spring' (1.1.95–7). The alliterative phrase implies a spider-like weaving of cunning schemes and conspiracies. 'Contrived' carries the suggestion of thought-up, whereas 'complotted', which receives the heavier weight, intimates conspiratorial activities. In sending Bolingbroke and Mowbray into exile, Richard makes them swear that they will not join forces to scheme against him – even though they are deadly enemies. The oath is long and comprehensive, concluding with the lines: 'Nor never by advised purpose meet / To plot, contrive, or complot any ill / 'Gainst us, our state, our subjects, or our land' (1.3.188–90). Richard is seeking to make the oath absolute, but even so the copious diction in the penultimate line seems to give a special status to complot as the ultimate conspiratorial activity.

As Gloucester confronts his enemies who surround him like a pack of dogs, he tells the reluctant Henry VI that the object of their accusations is not only to relieve him of his position as Lord Protector or to remove him from the political scene, but rather, as he protests, 'I know their complot is to have my life' (*2H6* 3.1.147). He uses this strong word and is right to do so as they are plotting his murder.

The word is used twice in a few lines in *R3*, and is given a particularly ugly twist. Buckingham, the puppet who considers himself to be the puppet-master, asks Richard, 'Now, my lord, what shall we do if we perceive / Lord Hastings will not yield to our complots?' The intrigue is the plan to displace the heirs of the deceased Edward. Richard's brutal reply is, 'Chop off his head!' Richard then equivocates before stiffening Buckingham's resolve with the promise of rich rewards when he becomes king, closing the scene with the words, 'Come, let us sup betimes, that afterwards / We may digest our complots in some form' (3.1.191–200). The sound connection between 'digest' and 'complot' is particularly distasteful, the whole expression conveying an indication of how difficult it is to resist producing example after example as each new situation seems to reveal another facet of the word. It flickers ominously in the light of each distinctive configuration.

Finally, the conceptual core of the word, its kinetic intensity, is given expression in *TIT*, when the demonic villain Aaron confesses his crimes to Titus' son, Lucius:

'Twill vex thy soul to hear what I shall speak:
For I must talk of murders, rapes, and massacres,
Acts of black night, abominable deeds,
Complots of mischief, treason, villainies,
Ruthful to hear, yet piteously perform'd.

5.1.62–6

It is as if all really despicable contrivances are 'complots'. The 'complot' gives birth to these dreadful actions, the position of the word in this speech and in its line becoming highly significant.
(C) Metz, *Shakespeare's Earliest Tragedy*, Hadfield, *Shakespeare and Renaissance Politics*, Schoenbaum, 'Richard II and the realities of power' in Alexander, ed., *Shakespeare and Politics*, and Grady, *Shakespeare, Machiavelli and Montaigne*, all engage with the words, concepts and actions that are manipulative and duplicitous.

compose
(A) Possessing two meanings as a verb, the political application of the word is to reach agreement. Its other use is to shape, form or **fashion**.
(B) Antony having returned to Rome for a conference with Octavius regarding the threat of Pompey, turns to Enobarbus and says, 'If we compose well here, to Parthia' (*ANT* 2.2.15). The irony is that even before the confrontation with Octavius has begun, Antony is preparing for his next adventure in the East. But far from effecting an **advantageous** agreement, Antony is drawn into a politically disastrous marriage with Octavia, the sister of Octavius.

Macbeth employs the second meaning when, having been persuaded by Lady Macbeth to undertake the murder of King Duncan, he praises her resolution in terms that produce a startling piece of dramatic irony: 'Bring forth men-children only! / For thy undaunted mettle should compose / Nothing but males' (*MAC* 1.7.72–4). This decision precipitates the death of the pair and the end of the prospect of generation.
(C) Long, *Macbeth*, is particularly valuable with respect to this question of breeding and fertility. Thomas, *Shakespeare's Roman Worlds*, and Adelman, *The Common Liar*, take up contrasting positions on this peace conference. Deats, ed., *Antony and Cleopatra*, includes Fuller's 'Passion and politics' among its many interesting essays.

composition
(A) The primary political application of the term is that of forging an agreement. One use, promised settlement, has financial significance. The word also means compatibility or consistency; **bargain** or arrangement; constitution or make-up.
(B) Faulconbridge the Bastard denounces the folly of King John and the cynicism of the French King and his party in subscribing to a peace treaty: 'Mad world, mad kings, mad composition!' (*JN* 2.1.561). This line is merely the opening salvo in this rightly acclaimed speech on '**commodity**' – the unfettered pursuit of personal **advantage**.

The slippery Angelo, in seeking to conceal his duplicity and corrupt **practices**, claims that he broke off his engagement to Marianna partly because she had failed to fulfil the terms of their financial settlement: 'Partly for that her promised proportions / Came short of composition' (*MM* 5.1.219–20).

Characteristic of the variety of meanings attaching to 'composition' is the ambiguous comment on the evaluation of the size of the Turkish fleet in *OTH*. The Duke, confronted by diverse estimates, emphasizes both the inconsistency and incompatibility of the reports: 'There's no composition in these news / That gives them credit' (*OTH* 1.3.1–2). Consistency is the required meaning here.

(C) See entry on **commodity**. Piesse, '*King John*: changing perspectives' in Hattaway, ed., *Shakespeare's History Plays*, is illuminating on *JN*; Barker, ed., *The Problem Plays*, and Dollimore, *Radical Tragedy* are informative on *MM*.

compt

(A) Impregnated with the idea of being held to **account**, this term in all its applications has behind it the image of the account book. Politically this means being subject to the ultimate control of a higher authority such as the king. In its spiritual dimension it means accountability before God.

(B) In responding to Duncan's thanks for their hospitality, Lady Macbeth protests that everything they possess belongs to the King and is merely held in trust for him: 'Your servants ever / Have theirs, themselves, and what is theirs, in compt, / To make their audit at your Highness' pleasure, / Still to return your own' (*MAC* 1.6.25–8). Both Oxford and Cambridge editions deviate from Folio's 'in compt', preferring instead 'count'. Riverside and Arden 2 follow Folio.

Othello, tormented at having been deceived into murdering Desdemona, surveys her dead body and anticipates their meeting in the afterlife: 'when we shall meet at compt,/ This look of thine will hurl my soul from heaven, / And fiends will snatch at it' (*OTH* 5.2.273–5). *OTH* is permeated with religious ideas. With all the zeal of a convert the Moor turned Christian seems to have imbibed the stark images of a merciless God and horrific hell. According to the pronouncements in the play and prevailing orthodoxy, Othello is doubly condemned to damnation. So too, it appears, is Desdemona: 'She's like a liar gone to burning hell' (5.2.129).

In between these two extremes is the only other use of the word. During the seeming reconciliation in *AWW*, Bertram mollifies the King with a smooth account of his misguided treatment of his apparently dead wife, Helena. The King responds: 'Well excus'd. / That thou didst love her, strikes some scores away / From the great compt' (5.3.55–7). This 'compt' or account is neither narrowly political nor religious: it is a social account involving Bertram's obligations to the King, to his family name, and to the broader human responsibility which every person **owes** to another. Bertram has violated all these codes of conduct so that his account is in a parlous state. Even the magnanimous monarch, seeking to reintegrate a key member of the aristocracy into society, does not go so far as to say that the account has been cleared; merely that Bertram's remorse has mitigated a bad situation.

(C) For a concise, interesting engagement with *AWW*, see Zitner, *All's Well That*

Ends Well. Kolin, ed., *Othello*, Alexander and Wells, eds, *Shakespeare and Race* and *Shakespeare and Sexuality*, all contain several essays that engage with comments made here.

compter, counter

(A) Two of the senses of the word are financial: a piece of metal used for counting up; small change. Used in hunting it signifies in pursuit of the wrong scent.

(B) The young shepherd, designated 'Clown' in *WT*, is defeated in his attempts to calculate **revenues** from the sale of wool. Conceding he requires the help of discs, he muses: 'I cannot do't without compters' (4.3.36). This is probably what Jaques means when challenged by the Duke about his likely conduct if given freedom to excoriate wrongdoers. He asks, 'What, for a counter, would I do but good?' (*AYL* 2.7.63). This ambiguous usage is, apparently, a reference to a playful expression, 'I'll wager a counter you can't tell me.' No 'real' **money** is put at risk in this friendly bet.

The term small change seems applicable when Brutus denounces his colleague Cassius for failing to provide him with funds to pay his soldiers – from enforced **exactions** that he himself could not stoop to acquire directly!

> Should I have answer'd Caius Cassius so?
> When Marcus Brutus grows so covetous
> To lock such rascal counters from his friends,
> Be ready, gods, with all your thunderbolts,
> Dash him to pieces!
>
> *JC* 4.3.78–82

The suggestion is not only that they are insignificant coins (he has, after all, requested 'gold') but also that any coinage is trivial or tarnished when set against honour and friendship.

The hunting image is clear when Gertrude turns on the common people supporting Laertes' bid to supplant Claudius on the Danish throne: 'How cheerfully on the false trail they cry! / O, this is counter, you false Danish dogs!' (*HAM* 4.5.110–11).

(C) Sullivan, *The Rhetoric of Credit*, is rewarding on all aspects of finance. Parker, *Shakespeare from the Margins*, ch. 5, is of particular relevance to *HAM*. So, too, is de Grazia, *'Hamlet' without Hamlet*.

comptless

(A) There is a single occurrence of this word in *VEN*. It means beyond measure or calculation.

(B) Venus, totally enthralled by Adonis, promises that the immeasurable longing and anguish provoked by his rejection will be compensated or **counterpoised** by a single kiss: 'And one sweet kiss shall pay this comptless debt' (*VEN* 84).

(C) Kolin, ed., *Venus and Adonis*, contains several instructive essays on this voluptuous narrative poem.

condition

(A) This innocent-seeming word can be employed in at least ten possible ways. Most of these have political or economic significance: settlement or arrangement; stipulation or proviso; action or the management of affairs; procedure; contract or legal instrument; point of law; character or disposition; attribute or behaviour; nature or circumstances; social rank; way of life. Employed as a verb in *TIM* the word means to make subject to a certain stipulation. The adverb 'conditionally' signifies 'on condition'.

(B) After the Volscian town has been taken by the Romans, a soldier consoles the great warrior Aufidius with the assurance that a satisfactory settlement will be achieved: ' 'Twill be deliver'd back on good condition.' The idea of an agreement being negotiated from a position of weakness is evidently anathema to the Volscian hero: 'Condition? / What good condition can a treaty find / I'th'part that is at mercy?' (*COR* 1.10.2–7).

During the cold-blooded proscription scene in *JC*, the newly formed Triumvirate **bargain** over the fate of friends and foes. Lepidus agrees that his brother shall be placed on the proscription list, but with a proviso: 'Upon condition Publius shall not live, / Who is your sister's son, Mark Antony'. Mark Antony does not pause to cavil: 'He shall not live; look, with a spot I damn him' (4.1.4–6). Another key political moment occurs during the play's famous quarrel scene. Having endured Brutus' 'chastisement', Cassius asserts himself, claiming, 'I am a soldier, I, / Older in practice, abler than yourself / To make conditions' (4.3.30–2). 'Conditions' appears to mean to determine action or the management of affairs.

As the champions prepare for the duel in *TRO*, Aeneas tells Agamemnon that Hector will accept any rules or procedures laid down by the Greeks: 'He cares not, he'll obey conditions' (4.5.72).

Contract or agreement is Shylock's meaning when he specifies the precise details to be incorporated in the **bond**: 'Express'd in the condition' (*MV* 1.3.148).

A problematic usage arises in *R2*. Bolingbroke, having returned from exile without the King's permission, disingenuously asks his uncle York, 'My gracious uncle, let me know my fault, / On what condition stands it and wherein?' Bolingbroke's 'condition' could be a legal term meaning 'what point of law have I infringed?' Equally, it could be a reference to his character. Either way the importance of the word is evident as York pounces on it with his riposte: 'Even in condition of the worst degree, / In gross rebellion and detested treason' (2.3.106–9). Circumstances is the meaning attaching to York's usage. Having become Henry IV, Bolingbroke adopts the same word but to signify 'disposition' or 'temper' when chastising the Northumberland faction:

> My blood hath been too cold and temperate,
> Unapt to stir at these indignities,
> And you have found me, for accordingly
> You tread upon my patience; but be sure
> I will from henceforth rather be myself,
> Mighty and to be fear'd, than my condition,

> Which hath been smooth as oil, soft as young down,
> And therefore lost that title of respect
> Which the proud soul ne'er pays but to the proud.
>
> *1H4* 1.3.1–9

His son, Henry V, employs the word to intimate 'position' or 'station in life', when, on the eve of Agincourt, he soliloquizes on the burdens of kingship: 'We must bear all. O hard condition, / Twin-born with greatness, subject to the breath / Of every fool whose sense no more can feel / But his own wringing!' (*H5* 4.1.233–6). Even so, just before the battle his masterly rhetoric is used to create a feeling of inclusiveness, promising social elevation to those he had dismissed as having no cares beyond concerns for their own stomach ache: 'We few, we happy few, we band of brothers;/ For he to-day that sheds his blood with me / Shall be my brother; be he ne'er so vile, / This day shall gentle his condition' (4.3.60–3). In the same play Gower commends Fluellen's beating of Pistol in the hope that it will change the miscreant's way of life: 'henceforth let a Welsh correction teach you a good English condition' (5.1.78–9).

The sense of 'attribute' is provided by Coriolanus in responding to the charge that he has not 'lov'd the common people'. He promises to adopt the behaviour of a popular politician by flattering them because ' 'tis a condition they account gentle' (*COR* 2.3.93–7).

Henry VI employs the adverb when coming to an agreement with York over the future of the crown:

> I here entail
> The crown to thee and to thine heirs for ever,
> Conditionally that here thou take an oath
> To cease this civil war, and whilst I live
> To honor me as thy king and sovereign,
> And neither by treason nor hostility
> To seek to put me down and reign thyself.
>
> *3H6* 1.1.194–200

The other applications of the term as defined above are prolific and are fascinating but generally unambiguous. Moreover, they do not carry significant economic or political freight.

(C) For a succinct analysis of the episodes in *JC* see Thomas, *Julius Caesar*. Zander, ed., *Julius Caesar*, covers an especially wide range of topics. Wheeler, ed., *Coriolanus*, achieves similar breadth for that play; penetrating and insightful are Brennan, *Henry V*, and McAlindon, *Shakespeare's Tudor History*.

consort, consorted

(A) Employed as a noun, verb or adjective the political connotation of this word is of conspiring. The non-pejorative meaning is accompanying or attendant. It also means a group of musicians.

(B) Consequent upon the revelation of an assassination plot against him, the newly installed King Henry IV in pardoning his cousin Aumerle adopts a more severe attitude towards his co-conspirators: 'But for our trusty brother-in-law and the abbot, / With all the rest of that consorted crew, / Destruction straight shall dog them at the heels' (*R2* 5.3.137–9). It is noteworthy that the conspirators are degraded both here and later in the play when Fitzwater refers to, 'Two of the dangerous consorted traitors / That sought at Oxford thy dire overthrow' (5.6.15–16). They are not simply conspirators but are a rough grouping or 'crew' who commit the ultimate crime of acting against their own country, 'traitors'.

By contrast, Cassius bewails the departure of the eagles that accompanied his force from Sardis to Philippi, as they were omens of good fortune:

> Coming from Sardis, on our former ensign
> Two mighty eagles fell, and there they perch'd,
> Gorging and feeding from our soldiers' hands,
> Who to Philippi here consorted us.
> This morning are they fled away and gone,
> *JC* 5.1.79–83

In the wake of Duncan's murder, Malcolm advises his brother, 'Let's not consort with them' (*MAC* 2.3.135). Here is a seemingly neutral application, but it is edged with distrust. Intriguingly, Edmund seizes on Regan's sly insinuation of a connection between Edgar and Lear's knights: 'Yes, madam, he was of that consort' (*LR* 2.1.97). The choice of word is instructive. A clear example of the potentially negative associations of the term occurs when Tybalt assails his antagonist with the provocative opening, 'Mercutio, thou consortest with Romeo –'. He is quickly cut short by the witty, bitter riposte: 'Consort! what, dost thou make us minstrels? . . . Here's my fiddlestick, here's that shall make you dance. 'Zounds, consort!' (*ROM* 3.1.45–9). The pun on a group of musicians is accompanied by the drawing of Mercutio's sword. The sinister side of the word is also revealed by Richard Gloucester as he turns savagely on Hastings who is in thrall to Mistress Shore. He attributes his sudden (pretended) affliction to 'Edward's wife, that monstrous witch, / Consorted with that harlot, strumpet Shore' (*R3* 3.4.70–1).

The non-pejorative quality of the word finds expression when the Princess of France responds to the King of Navarre's welcome: 'Sweet health and fair desires consort your Grace!' (*LLL* 2.1.177). Even here there is a suspicion of over-elaboration, as the situation is tinged with tension.

(C) Highly relevant in the exploration of this word is Parker, *Shakespeare from the Margins*, ch. 5. The *JC* incident is taken directly from Plutarch's account of events. Bullough, ed., *Shakespeare's Sources, The Roman Plays, Vol. 5*, provides convenient access to this vital source. See also Thomas, *Shakespeare's Roman Worlds*; Danson, ed., *On King Lear*; White, ed., *Romeo and Juliet*; and Freedman, *Power and Passion in Shakespeare's Pronouns*.

contumelious(ly), contumely

(A) This word, employed in all its grammatical forms, is of great significance in the political lexicon of the plays. It draws into itself a whole complex of associated words yet can remain elusive for a modern audience or readership. The following concepts are integral to the word: insolence, disdain, contempt, arrogance, scorn. To be treated contumeliously is to feel stained, subjected to intolerable treatment, violated even. The distribution of this word is intriguing: the adjective is used in the first two parts of *H6*; and afterwards only in the late tragedy, *TIM*. The adverb occurs once only, in *1H6*; the noun only in *HAM*.

(B) Questioned about his treatment as prisoner of the French, the ransomed Talbot rails against the indignities he suffered at the hands of his tormentors: 'With scoffs and scorns and contumelious taunts. / In open market-place produc'd they me / To be a public spectacle to all' (*1H6* 1.4.39–41). The essence of his complaint extending over a dozen lines is embodied in the phrase 'contumelious taunts'.

A fierce clash occurs when Warwick accuses Suffolk of complicity in the murder of Duke Humphrey, thus provoking his antagonist to a bloody challenge. The Queen, however, intervenes on behalf of her favourite, Suffolk. To Warwick's bold assertion, 'What dares not Warwick, if false Suffolk dare him?', she responds, seeking to cut him to the quick: 'He dares not calm his contumelious spirit, / Nor cease to be an arrogant controller' (*2H6* 3.2.203–5). Rebellious, rancorous, overbearing, contemptuous are compacted into the explosive term 'contumelious spirit'. Indeed the word's potency comes close to the accusation of treason. Controller means 'detractor' or 'slanderer', so this brief interjection is venomous.

During the internecine conflict between the Duke of Gloucester and the malign Cardinal of Winchester, the struggle spills over into the streets as their serving men become involved in a violent clash. The indignant Mayor of London rightly berates them for this outrage: 'Fie, lords, that you, being supreme magistrates, / Thus contumeliously should break the peace!' (*1H6* 1.3.57–8). Once again this highly compacted word embodies the suggestion that they are shamelessly haughty, egregiously disdainful of the very law and order that they are charged to maintain. Here is an inveterate hatred impervious to pleas or obligations.

In rejecting the blandishments of the Senators of Athens, Timon expresses his contempt for the Athenians and his enthusiasm for their destruction: 'Giving our holy virgins to the stain / Of contumelious, beastly, mad-brain'd war' (*TIM* 5.1.173–4). This must be the most powerful single-line denunciation of war in the whole of Shakespeare. The sense of violation active in the word contumelious is most apparent here: the 'holy virgins', the embodiment of purity, are to be stained. The epithets that succeed it emphasize the senseless nature of war. 'Contumelious' is not only the headword of the line but is also the link word: with staining there is also the uncompromising, unheeding, reckless, disdainful nature of war. Timon, the master of vituperation, is icily sober in his delineation of the essence of war. Strikingly this is the only use of the adjective outside of the early plays *1H6, 2H6*.

Hamlet provides the sole use of the noun, contumely, and does so in that most famous soliloquy: 'To be, or not to be'. He suggests that the outrages, misfortunes and sufferings that have to be endured are tolerated only because of the uncertainties that lie beyond death:

> For who would bear the whips and scorns of time,
> Th' oppressor's wrong, the proud man's contumely,
> The pangs of despis'd love, the law's delay,
> The insolence of office, and the spurns
> That patient merit of th'unworthy takes,
>
> *HAM* 3.1.69–73

This section of the soliloquy is profoundly concerned with oppressor and oppressed: 'whips and scorns', 'wrong', 'despis'd', 'delay', 'insolence', 'spurns', 'unworthy', are set against 'patient merit'. Locked into the conceptual and rhythmic movement of this passage is 'the proud man's contumely'. High-handedness, arrogance, contempt, disdain all cohere in that telling phrase. In this moment of deep reflectiveness Hamlet bears witness to a sickening egotism that so often contaminates the holder of high office, an egotism which manifests itself in the humiliation and degradation of any subordinate. Here is life seen from the bottom up. In order to encapsulate the social, political and deeply personal dimensions of life, Shakespeare needs to recall this compelling word.

The strong association of this term with the early histories might seem surprising at first blush, but they are plays characterized by deep personal antagonisms, sinister political manoeuvring, factionalism and towering ambition. It is not merely that this particular word captures so well much of the feelings and actions of key participants, but it also accommodates the desire to give expression to them. Well suited to this political arena, it is no accident that the only two characters to employ the word outside these histories are both profoundly alienated, exhibiting feelings of disgust and contamination: Hamlet temporarily; Timon irrevocably.

(C) Schalkwyk, *Speech and Performance in Shakespeare's Sonnets and Plays*, discusses interiority in *Hamlet*; Hillman, *Shakespeare's Entrails*, also has an interesting chapter on the 'inward man' in *HAM*; Bruster, *To Be Or Not To Be*, is devoted to analysing Hamlet's soliloquies. Pendleton, ed., *Henry VI*, and Smallwood, ed., *Players of Shakespeare 6*, are of particular interest here. Knight, *The Wheel of Fire*, contains 'The pilgrimage of hate: an essay on *Timon of Athens*'.

convent, conventicle

(A) The verb convent means to assemble or convene; also to summon. The noun can signify either a clandestine gathering or a mere meeting place.

(B) Sicinius the tribune responds with elaborate formality at the outset of the proceedings designed to elect Coriolanus to the consulship: 'We are convented/ Upon a pleasing treaty, and have hearts / Inclinable to honor and advance / The theme of our assembly' (*COR* 2.2.54–7).

Gardiner, the fanatical Bishop of Winchester, expresses his pleasure that Cranmer has been summoned to face charges of heresy: 'To-morrow morning to the Council-board / He be convented' (*H8* 5.1.51–2).

The Duke of Gloucester concludes a long and powerful speech by indicting the courtiers who have met secretly to plot against him: 'Ay, all of you have laid your heads together – / Myself had notice of your conventicles – / And all to make away my guiltless life (*2H6* 3.1.165–7).

King Edward's usage when addressing his secretary Lodowick possesses the meaning 'meeting place', but there is a political dimension: 'Then in the summer arbor sit by me, / Make it our council house, or cabinet: / Since green our thoughts, green be the conventicle, / Where we will ease us by disburd'ning them' (*E3* 2.1.61–4). Even here there is a conspiratorial connotation, albeit a playful one, because Edward wishes his secretary to pen a love missive to the Countess of Salisbury – who, like the King himself, is already married.

(C) For a vigorous insistence on Shakespeare's sole authorship of this fine play, see Sam's introduction to his edition of *Edward III*. A more cautious approach is to be found in Melchiori's admirable Introduction to the Cambridge edition. For a review of the RSC's production at the Swan Theatre in 2002 by someone who shares Sam's enthusiasm see Thomas, 'Thus from the heart's abundance speaks the tongue' in *Shakespeare at the Centre*, August, 2002. Goy-Blanquet, *Shakespeare's Early History Plays*, is particularly pertinent here.

convey, conveyance, conveyers

(A) What at first sight appears to be a simple word with few meanings, on closer scrutiny proves to cover different kinds of actions and experiences. The following are all distinct applications of the verb though inevitably there are meanings that overlap with at least a few ambiguous usages: transmit as in a letter or by disease; transport, make away with or carry off; accompany or escort – friendship, diplomatic arrangement or rough dispatch; to impart an understanding; steal; hide or conceal; conduct or transact; satisfy or indulge; pass off or pretend. The noun, too, has multiple applications, the most relevant here being conduit; escort; removal; dexterity; guile; underhand dealing; a legal document transferring property. A conveyer is a thief.

(B) Richard III cautions Stanley to ensure his wife transmits no letters to her son Richmond: 'Stanley, look to your wife. If she convey / Letters to Richmond, you shall answer it' (*R3* 4.2.92–3). Convey signifies a more violent transmission when Lear curses Goneril by invoking Nature: 'Into her womb convey sterility, / Dry up in her the organs of increase' (*LR* 1.4.278–9).

The finest example of urgency attaching to the term is provided by the former Queen Margaret in her prayer for Richard to be carried off to hell: 'Earth gapes, hell burns, fiends roar, saints pray, / To have him suddenly convey'd from hence' (*R3* 4.4.75–6).

The implication of convey as secretly removed or stolen away is evident in the Duke's comment on his careful protection or restraint of his daughter, Silvia, locked in her chamber at night: 'And thence she cannot be convey'd away' (*TGV* 3.1.37).

The French ambassadors are dispatched with the minimum of diplomatic ceremony, as Henry brusquely instructs his courtiers, 'Convey them with safe conduct. – Fare you well' (*H5* 1.2.297). The word means escort or accompany or provide them with the requisite guard. The use of the word to mean accompany or escort covers a wide range of circumstances from companionable association (*TGV* 3.1.254), through formal diplomatic protection (*H5*), to the unpleasant extreme of someone being taken off under guard, sometimes without a semblance of dignity (*R2* 4.1.316). There is little ceremony attaching to the execution of Suffolk. The Lieutenant gives the command to lead him off: 'Convey him hence, and on our longboat's side / Strike off his head' (*2H6* 4.1.68–9).

Using the word to mean imparted, Egeon describes the shipwreck that began his troubles: 'For what obscured light the heavens did grant / Did but convey into our fearful minds / A doubtful warrant of immediate death' (*ERR* 1.1.66–8). The phrase, 'convey into our fearful minds' generates a feeling of something more than apprehension or awareness; the expectation of imminent death imposes itself. The Duke, reassuring Isabella, uses the word in the sense imparted or brought to: 'The assault that Angelo hath made to you, fortune hath convey'd to my understanding' (*MM* 3.1.184–5).

Two obscure cases occur in *ANT*. Ventidius, having completed his colloquy with Silius on their success against the Parthians, warns of the danger of offending Antony: 'The weight we must convey with's will permit, / We shall appear before him' (3.1.36–7). The key phrase must mean the substance of which, with his permission, we shall impart to him. Significantly more difficult is Antony's address to Cleopatra in the wake of his undignified flight from the Battle of Actium: 'O, wither hast thou led me, Egypt? See / How I convey my shame out of thine eyes / By looking back what I have left behind / 'Stroy'd in dishonor' (3.11.51–4). It would seem that while Antony's humiliation is mirrored in, and so transmitted by, Cleopatra's eyes, he seeks to remove the shame by consideration of his former **achievements**. Perhaps extract, remove, or 'make away with' is the meaning attaching to convey. Alternatively, it might mean 'apprehend': the apprehension or conviction of his fall from grace is so visible in her eyes that he tries to deflect his sense of shame by averting his eyes from hers to past events which reveal him in a favourable light.

Falstaff, dispatching Bardolf to his new trade of tapster, comments on the blatancy of his thefts, to which Pistol, disparaging such crudity, replies, ' "Convey," the wise call it. "Steal"? foh! a *fico* for the phrase!' (*WIV* 1.3.29–30). This cant word for theft neatly encompasses the idea of something transported from one person to another. Richard II plays on this double meaning when Bolingbroke orders his forced removal to the Tower – 'Go some of you convey him to the tower' – by responding, 'O, good! convey! Conveyers are you all, / That rise thus nimbly by a true king's fall' (*R2* 4.1.317–8). Thus those who have attached themselves to Bolingbroke's regime are dismissed as thieves. There is yet a more telling aspect to this bitter pun, as conveyors are also people who transfer property rights, making this is a vital ingredient in Richard's multi-layered comment.

The meaning 'conceal' occurs in *HAM* when Polonius informs Claudius that he intends to eavesdrop on Gertrude's conference with the Prince: 'Behind the arras I'll convey myself / To hear the process' (3.3.28–9).

Edmund, Gloucester's illegitimate son, persuades his father that Edgar seeks his life. He is, therefore, given licence to 'Frame the business after your own wisdom'. Edmund responds, 'I will seek him, sir, presently; convey the business as I shall find means, and acquaint you withal' (*LR* 1.2.98–102). Evidently he means conduct the business.

In attempting to persuade the apparently reluctant heir to the throne to launch a physical challenge to Macbeth, Macduff reassures Malcolm that his stated vice of 'voluptuousness', or limitless sexual desire, is not an insuperable barrier to kingship: 'You may / Convey your pleasures in a spacious plenty, / And yet seem cold, the time you may so hoodwink' (*MAC* 4.3.70–2). Enjoy or indulge appears to be the required meaning, but manage with stealth or conduct in secret has been proposed.

A unique application is provided by Canterbury in his apologia for Henry's invasion of France. Exposing the fraudulent claimants to the throne of France, he dismisses Charles, Duke of Lorraine, who, 'Convey'd himself as th' heir to th' Lady Lingare' (*H5* 1.2.74). In other words, he passed himself off as heir.

The only application of 'conveying' occurs during the midst of battle when Cominius comforts his troops with the suggestion that Coriolanus and his men are having success on another front: 'Whiles we have strook, / By interims and conveying gusts we have heard / The charges of our friends' (*COR* 1.6.4–6). The battle cries waft on the transporting wind. This vivid phrase provides a compelling example of Shakespeare infusing a battle scene with poetic delicacy.

(C) Of special significance here are Parker, *Shakespeare from the Margins*, ch. 5; Grady, *Shakespeare, Machiavelli and Montaigne*; Schoenbaum, '*Richard II* and the realities of power' in Alexander, ed., *Shakespeare and Politics*; Jordan and Cunningham, eds, *The Law in Shakespeare*, esp. ch. 4 and 5; Gross, *Shakespeare's Noise*, ch. 5.

corrival, co-rival

(A) The noun has two meanings, both occurring in significant political contexts: equal; associate or partner. The verb intimates to vie with or to be a rival.

(B) Hotspur, giving vent to his indignation at the King's unwillingness to ransom his brother-in-law, Mortimer, embraces the prospect of rebellion by delivering a paean to honour:

> By heaven, methinks it were an easy leap,
> To pluck bright honor from the pale-fac'd moon,
> Or dive into the bottom of the deep,
> Where fadom-line could never touch the ground,
> And pluck up drowned honor by the locks,

> So he that doth redeem her thence might wear
> Without corrival all her dignities;
>
> *1H4* 1.3.201–7

Prince Hal shares Hotspur's intolerance of a co-equal – something he makes clear as they prepare for their fatal encounter on the battlefield: 'Two stars keep not their motion in one sphere, / Nor can one England brook a double reign / Of Harry Percy and the Prince of Wales' (5.4.65–7).

The same play gives rise to the other application of the word when the rebellious Archbishop of York provides an impressive catalogue of the King's associates, concluding, 'The noble Westmorland, and warlike Blunt, / And many moe corrivals and dear men / Of estimation and command in arms' (4.4.30–2). Corrivals, carries the suggestion of 'high calibre allies'.

In *TRO*, Nestor employs the verb when drawing an analogy between men and boats. In favourable conditions both the strong and weak look equally impressive as they vie for prominence. It is only when circumstances are demanding that the distinction between them becomes evident: 'Where's then the saucy boat / Whose weak untimber'd sides but even now / Corrivall'd greatness? Either to harbor fled, / Or made a toast for Neptune' (1.3.42–5).

(C) Holderness, ed., *Shakespeare's History Plays: Richard II to Henry V*, contains much of interest on these plays; so too does Leggatt, *Shakespeare's Political Drama*. Adamson's slender volume *Troilus and Cressida* is first class.

cost, costly

(A) The first meaning attaching to the word is simple enough: financial outlay – though even here there is a distinction between coin and the embodiment of such expenditure in rich garments. The second meaning is a unique extension of the first by referring to some project or scheme – a costly development. Thirdly, there is the meaning of richly endowed, either in material goods or residing in human beauty or **worth**. Finally, the verb signifies loss or deprivation: physical or emotional injury, or loss of a crown. The adjective relates to **expense**, lavish outlay, or to what is precious.

(B) The history plays display a sharp awareness of the resources absorbed by military or political engagements. The initial manoeuvrings of the King and his hostile associates, the Northumberland **faction**, pivot on the request that Henry ransom Mortimer. His response is emphatic:

> Shall our coffers then
> Be emptied to redeem a traitor home?
> Shall we buy treason? and indent with fears,
> When they have lost and forfeited themselves?
> No, on the barren mountains let him starve;
> For I shall never hold that man my friend
> Whose tongue shall ask me for one penny cost
> To ransom home revolted Mortimer.
>
> *1H4* 1.3.85–92

The whole speech embraces the concept of costs, worth and **value**. It is an intensely physical and bitingly political analysis in terms of **accountancy** and accountability.

The meaning 'lavish expense' is clearly illustrated by the Duke's protestation to the Friar in *MM*: 'My holy sir, none better knows than you / How I have ever lov'd the life removed, / And held in idle price to haunt assemblies / Where youth, and cost, witless bravery keeps' (1.3.7–10). The contrast is between a life of retirement with one of **fashion**, trivial activity ('idle price') and extravagance.

Perhaps 'outlay' is what Jaques means when railing against the world's vices: 'What woman in the city do I name, / When that I say the city-woman bears / The cost of princes on unworthy shoulders?' (*AYL* 2.7.74–6). Here is an objection to middle-class housewives dressing in clothes more appropriate to the aristocracy. But the outlay here is *embodied* in the garments so that the sumptuousness of the clothes dominates the conceptual field. There is a blending of cost as 'outlay' with cost as 'lavish display'.

Unique in its use in Shakespeare is the sense of an object or scheme that is costly in terms of the resources it has absorbed or embodies. When the Archbishop and his associates weigh up the prospect of successful rebellion against the King, Lord Bardolph responds by way of analogy with a building project. He lays out in detail the procedures followed from initial conception to implementation, emphasizing the need to proceed by means of known resources rather than by promises. Failure to do this will lead them into a false situation:

> Like one that draws the model of an house
> Beyond his power to build it, who, half through,
> Gives o'er, and leaves his part-created cost
> A naked subject to the weeping clouds
> And waste for churlish winter's tyranny.
> *2H4* 1.3.58–62

Successfully completed, the 'cost' or 'project' would render benefits; incomplete because the scheme is beyond the planner's resources, it stands as an indictment of inadequate foresight.

To the modern sensibility, cost is outlay – something that goes into creating a product or providing a benefit, but Shakespeare also uses the word cost to signify the benefit itself: something rich or lavish – or as someone might say today, costly. When in *E3* the Countess makes a long speech designed to fortify her invitation to the King to enter her castle, she conducts her argument by way of an analogy that contrasts a rich inside with an unregarded outside or vice versa:

> For where the golden ore doth buried lie,
> The ground, undeck'd with nature's tapestry,
> Seems barren, sere, unfertile, fructless, dry;
> And where the upper turf of earth doth boast
> His pride, perfumes, and parti-color'd cost,

Delve there, and find this issue and their pride
To spring from ordure and corruption's side:
1.2.149–55

The 'parti-colour'd cost' here is rich beauty. The same idea occurs in *PER* when
the bereft Prince of Tyre encloses a scroll in the coffin along with his seemingly
dead wife: 'I, King Pericles, have lost / This queen, worth all our mundane cost'
(3.2.70–1). Her value or worth transcends all calculation of material objects or
treasures.

Cost as loss or deprivation is vividly expressed by Henry VI in exhibiting fear of
his adversary the Duke of York: 'Whose haughty spirit, winged with desire, / Will
cost my crown' (*3H6* 1.1.267–8). A similar sense of cost as loss is provided by
Hector when responding to Ulysses' prediction of the destruction of Troy: 'The
fall of every Phrygian stone will cost / A drop of Grecian blood' (*TRO* 4.5.223–4).

When Buckingham refers to 'this last costly treaty' (*H8* 1.1.165) which formed
a part of the ceremony of Field of the Cloth of Gold, he is alluding to its lavish
expense.

Antony, soliloquizing over the body of Julius Caesar, means 'precious' when
he cries, 'Woe to the hand that shed this costly blood!' (*JC* 3.1.258).

(C) Hattaway, ed., *Shakespeare's History Plays*, quotes Lord Bardolph's building
analogy and comments: 'The analogy is a time-honoured one, deriving ultimately
from the linked Parables of the Tower Builder and the King going to War in Luke
14.28–32. Bardolph is offering a lesson in "edification": etymologically the word
means "building" and is a recurrent metaphor in the Pauline epistles' (21). The
multiple implications of costs are explored extensively in Sullivan, *The Rhetoric of
Credit* and Hawkes, *Idols of the Marketplace*.

counter-caster

(A) Used only once – disparagingly – this term means arithmetician or one who is
fitted for nothing better than doing sums, perhaps with the help of counters. For
counter see **compter**.

(B) Iago uses the term when scornfully dismissing Cassio's stature as a military
man. Already well into his diatribe with Roderigo he has referred to Cassio
as 'a great arithmetician', implying a mere theorist. He concludes that unlike
himself, a man exceptionally experienced in military matters, Cassio is a mere
'counter-caster' (*OTH* 1.1.19–31).

(C) See Scragg, 'Iago – vice or devil' in Muir and Edwards, eds, *Aspects of Othello*,
and McAlindon, *Shakespeare's Tragic Cosmos*.

counterfeit

(A) The essence of this word in all its grammatical forms and attributions is
imitation; it can apply to a portrait, impersonation, deliberate deception, or an
inauthentic representation of a legitimate coin or emblem such as a royal ring.
Surprisingly, the abundant numismatic applications are nearly all metaphoric.
Only Henry VIII's ring is literal and authentic.

(B) Believing himself the victim of Imogen's infidelity, Posthumus insists that no man can be sure of his legitimacy:

> We are all bastards,
> And that most venerable man which I
> Did call my father, was I know not where
> When I was stamp'd. Some coiner with his tools
> Made me a counterfeit;
>
> *CYM* 2.5.2–6

The coinage image is used wittily rather than bitterly by Mercutio when baiting Romeo about his sudden disappearance: 'You gave us the counterfeit fairly last night'. When Romeo protests his innocence, 'What counterfeit did I give you?' Mercutio responds with a pun on 'slip' or counterfeit coin: 'The slip, sir, the slip, can you not conceive?' (*ROM* 2.4.45–8).

Constance employs the coinage metaphor when denouncing King Philip of France for deserting her cause and forming an alliance with King John: 'You have beguil'd me with a counterfeit / Resembling majesty, which being touch'd and tried, / Proves valueless. You are foresworn, foresworn!' (*JN* 3.1.99–101). There is nothing metaphorical at the crucial moment in *H8* when Gardiner is suddenly thwarted in his attempt to send Cranmer to the tower. Confronted by the King's ring Surrey can only gasp: ' 'Tis no counterfeit' (5.2.137).

Falstaff has the distinction of using the word most often. In a play deeply engaged in the duality of authenticity and misrepresentation, and where the King himself 'hath many marching in his coats' (*1H4* 5.3.25), Falstaff plays dead in order to escape the fearsome Douglas. Relieved at having survived, he exclaims, ' 'twas time to counterfeit', but then, regaining his composure, he evades self-censure with a verbal quibble:

> Counterfeit? I lie, I am no counterfeit. To die is to be a counterfeit, for he is but the counterfeit of a man who hath not the life of a man; but to counterfeit dying, when the man thereby liveth, is to be no counterfeit, but the true and perfect image of life indeed. The better part of valor is discretion, in the which better part I have sav'd my life. 'Zounds, I am afraid of this gunpowder Percy though he be dead. How if he should counterfeit too and rise? By my faith, I am afraid he would prove the better counterfeit.
>
> 5.4.113–24

Falstaff not only exonerates himself but also represents in little the play's serious debate about the role of duplicity in achieving objectives.

Pistol does not escape so lightly as his erstwhile fellow-in-fraud, being denounced by Gower as 'an arrant counterfeit rascal' (*H5* 3.6.61) and 'a counterfeit cowardly knave' (5.1.69).

Counterfeiting is not, however, always opprobrious. Edgar, disguised as Mad Tom, is so discomposed when encountering the mad Lear that he can barely maintain his role: 'My tears begin to take his part so much, / They mar my counterfeiting' (*LR*, 3.6.59–60). In the midst of battle Warwick comments metadramatically on the need to redouble their efforts rather than passively to observe, 'as if the tragedy / Were play'd in jest by counterfeiting actors?' (*3H6* 2.3.27–8). Like those engaged in political manoeuvring, actors are masters in the art of counterfeiting.

Counterfeit as image or representation is intimated when the relieved and delighted Bassanio retrieves Portia's portrait from the casket: 'Fair Portia's counterfeit! What demigod / Hath come so near creation?' (*MV* 3.2.115–16).

Quite different in tone is Timon's response to the duplicitous Painter: 'Thou draw'st a counterfeit / Best in all Athens; th'art indeed the best, / Thou counterfeit'st most lively' (*TIM* 5.1.80–2). The disenchanted Timon, now fully aware of the depths of human artifice, indicts the Painter as himself a counterfeit: a flattering rogue who has simulated affection and affinity. He is perfectly equipped to create representations of men who doubly counterfeit: representations of the real thing; surfaces without humanity.

(C) Of importance here are Turner, *Shakespeare's Twenty-First Century Economics*; Sullivan, *The Rhetoric of Credit*; Hawkes, *Idols of the Marketplace*; Shell, *Money, Language and Thought*; Simmel, *The Philosophy of Money*; and Foreman, 'Marked angels: counterfeits, commodities, and *The Roaring Girl*', *Renaissance Quarterly* 54 (2001): 1–30.

counterpoise

(A) Employed as a noun, this word possesses the meaning counterbalance or equal weight. The verb can signify to match or equal; to counterbalance or offset. In economic, political and social circumstances the word is of strategic significance.

(B) When pirates negotiate a ransom with their prisoners in *2H6*, they balance the lives of colleagues lost and injuries received in the capture against the sums required as compensation and **profit**. The Lieutenant is angered by the initial reluctance of the prisoners to pay handsomely for their freedom:

> What, think you much to pay two thousand crowns,
> And bear the name and port of gentlemen?
> Cut both the villains' throats; for die you shall.
> The lives of those which we have lost in fight
> Be counterpois'd with such a petty sum!
>
> 4.1.18–22

What is instructive about this example is not a matter of verbal complexity, but Shakespeare's exploration of the concepts of honour and **value**. The pirates claim the moral high ground: the victims have injured them (Walter Whitmore has even lost an eye) by resisting, so the normal profit expected from such a ransom has to be supplemented by compensation. Moreover, it has to be offered without prevarication so as not to bruise the dignity and honour of the pirates. Finally, revealing his identity, Suffolk is executed on patriotic grounds: he is condemned for misappropriation of state funds, engineering the contract of a marriage between Henry VI and the daughter of a 'worthless king' (4.1.81), adultery with Queen Margaret, the murder of Duke Humphrey, and bringing about the loss of English territories in France. What is fascinating is the indignation expressed by the pirate, who is a proud patriot. His only peccadillo, which he fails to acknowledge, is deriving a living from piracy. The Lieutenant and his associates employ key political and economic concepts in making judgements and decisions while failing to display any self-awareness of their own wrongdoing. Indeed, such is their righteous indignation that they prefer to execute Suffolk than settle for the huge ransom he can offer. Few scenes in Shakespeare afford such caustic scrutiny of the deployment of political and economic concepts.

Hotspur, having sounded an associate to join the impending rebellion against Henry IV receives a judicious reply: ' "The purpose you undertake is dangerous, the friends you have nam'd uncertain, the time itself unsorted, and your whole plot too light for the counterpoise of so great an opposition" ' (*1H4* 2.3.10–14). 'Counterpoise' is here employed to perfection: the circumstances are weighed and balanced with precision, endowing the dramatic moment with a richly ironic significance. Hotspur dismisses this careful evaluation with blustering contempt only to discover the accuracy of the prediction when Glendower, Mortimer and even his father fail to arrive for the Battle of Shrewsbury.

In a memorable speech to the Senators, the noble Cominius presents Coriolanus' candidature for consulship with the words:

> It is held
> That valor is the chiefest virtue, and
> Most dignifies the haver; if it be,
> The man I speak of cannot in the world
> Be singly counterpois'd.
> *COR* 2.2.83–7

The stature of Coriolanus as the greatest warrior in the world is articulated in a way that sets him apart as the supreme embodiment of his culture: a true Roman without equal. The last phrase possesses a clarity that is self-validating. The very word 'counterpoise'd' is the ideal balancing mechanism in this undecorated speech.

A potentially ambiguous case arises when Coriolanus, having spared Rome, seeks to put a gloss on his **achievements** to the Volscians: 'Our spoils we have brought home / Doth more than counterpoise a full third part / The charges of the action' (5.6.76–8). He probably means that the **revenues** acquired as spoils of war exceed by a third the total cost of the enterprise. Alternatively, it is tempting to assume that the revenues actually cover only a third of the **costs** of the action. This latter interpretation would not be ludicrous because Rome has been humiliated (a big gain in political terms) and military adventures were notorious for failing to produce a profit on the balance sheet.

The word is strategic in financial transactions. The King of France effectively forces Helena on Bertram after the young count has rejected her on grounds of social status. The King concludes the transaction with the words, 'Take her by the hand, / And tell her she is thine; to whom I promise / A counterpoise – if not to thy estate / A balance more replete' (*AWW* 2.3.173–6). The counterpoise or balancing sum is such that Helena is to become richer than Bertram. The financial scale now weighs in her favour.

A similar duty falls on Timon when an Old Athenian complains that his daughter seeks to marry Timon's servant. Rather than warning him off, the wildly generous Timon promises to provide his servant with a dowry equivalent to that of his bride: 'Give him thy daughter; / What you bestow, in him I'll counterpoise, / And make him weigh with her' (*TIM* 1.1.144–6).

(C) See Donawerth, *Shakespeare and the Sixteenth-Century Study of Language*, especially ch. 7; Zitner, *All's Well That Ends Well*; Poole, *Coriolanus*.

cozen, cozener
(A) A word likely to confuse a modern reader, it means to deceive, swindle, cheat, defraud or trick. A cozener is a trickster or fraudster. Curiously, this term appears most frequently in *WIV*, with 12 appearances making up one-third of the total usages.

(B) The most sardonic use occurs in *R3*, where Queen Elizabeth responds to Richard's affected innocence of the murder of the princes in the Tower. When he brazenly protests, 'You speak as if that I had slain my cousins!' her punning riposte is devastating: 'Cousins indeed, and by their uncle cozen'd / Of comfort, kingdom, kindred, freedom, life' (4.4.222–4). This rhetorical figure, asyndeton, in which words are released one after the other without intervening conjunctions, underlines the magnitude of Richard's crime with singular force. Lear, too, uses the word to similar devastating effect when, in his colloquy with the blind Gloucester, he inveighs against the corruption and hypocrisy of authority: 'The usurer hangs the cozener. / Through tatter'd clothes small vices do appear; / Robes and furr'd gowns hide all' (*LR* 4.6.163–5). Here the petty thief is subjected to the full force of the law while a rigorous exploiter who lends **money** at extortionate rates sits administering justice.

A typical act of cozenage is that perpetrated by that seller of knick-knacks, the trickster and petty thief Autolycus. He begins by lifting the purse of the Shepherd's son, designated 'Clown', before fleecing most of the villagers. In response to the importunities of Mopsa, the victim protests, 'Have I not told thee how I was cozen'd by the way, and lost all my money?' The disguised rogue slyly comments, 'And indeed, sir, there are cozeners abroad' (*WT* 4.4.251–3).

Not only do people deceive or cheat; some may be victims of 'cozen'd thoughts' (*AWW* 4.4.23) or hope – a conception articulated by the crestfallen queen expressing her fears for her husband, Richard II:

> I will despair, and be at enmity
> With cozening hope. He is a flatterer,
> A parasite, a keeper-back of death,

> Who gently would dissolve the bands of life,
> Which false hope lingers in extremity.
> *R2* 2.2.68–72

(C) Agnew, *Worlds Apart*, ch. 2, is particularly pertinent to Autolycus, cozenage and the evolution of the **market**. Also focusing directly on this topic is Hartwig, *Shakespeare's Tragicomic Vision*, 117–23. Of interest too is Hopkins, 'The King's melting body: *Richard II*' in Dutton and Howard, eds, *A Companion to Shakespeare's Works, Vol II – The Histories*.

credit, creditor

(A) The concept of credit as deferred payment is implicated in a number of applications, but it is invariably allied to the concept of creditworthiness which is dominant in references to financial arrangements. The other meanings are: reputation – which includes moral or professional standing; credibility or belief; faith or trust; report, news, letters. As a verb it means to give grace to, esteem; trust or have faith in. Creditors are holders of **debt**.

(B) Characteristic of the **use** of credit in a financial context is Hal's grumbling acceptance of Falstaff's admission that the young Prince has paid all the tavern **reckonings**: 'Yea, and elsewhere, so far as my coin would stretch, and where it would not, I have us'd my credit' (*1H4* 1.2.54–6). Hal implies that his credit-worthiness has enabled him to obtain drink by means of deferred payment. The relationship between the two concepts is continued by Falstaff who begins his riposte with a play on this connection: 'Yea, and so us'd it that, were it not here apparent that thou art heir apparent' (1.2.57–8). The unfinished implication is that were it not for his expectations, Hal's ability to borrow would already be exhausted.

Timon's servant expresses disgust when a beneficiary of his master's largesse refuses to come to his aid: 'Timon has been this lord's father, / And kept his credit with his purse; / Supported his estate, nay, Timon's money / Has paid his men their wages' (*TIM* 3.2.67–70). This implies that Timon's outlays have maintained the man's financial standing or 'credit' through Timon being ready to supply him with funds when required. It could also imply that Timon has prevented his **bankruptcy** or calling in of loans by meeting the **interest** payments for him. 'Credit' could, therefore, refer to borrowings as opposed to reputation. Both meanings may be present. One of Timon's creditors, a senator, makes an urgent request for repayment of loans. He complains, 'My uses cry to me; I must serve my turn / Out of mine own. His days and times are past, / And my reliances on his fracted dates / Have smit my credit' (2.1.20–3). Clearly these loans constitute a significant proportion of this man's resources. Timon has failed to repay the loans on the specified dates: they have been 'fracted' or missed. Consequently, the Senator either lacks the funds to meet his necessary outlays, so he is nervous that he will be unable to meet his own debts, or he fears his precarious situation will be perceived, thereby undermining his creditworthiness. Here is a coalescing of meanings because loss of business reputation or creditworthiness undermines his capacity to raise loans. The role of credit in the economy, the potentially damaging impact of the domino effect, and the importance of financial reputation are embodied in a play grounded in financial transactions.

Angelo, the goldsmith, pleads with Antipholus of Ephesus to acknowledge that he has received the chain, and to pay up, so that he can discharge his own debt to a fellow **merchant**. He cautions, 'Consider how it stands upon my credit' (*ERR* 4.1.68). He means his standing as a businessman.

Because an entire network of transactions is effected on the probity of merchants, trust is of paramount importance. Hence, although credit rarely if ever stands for incurring debt, it does occupy a significant place in the financial nexus because of the frequency with which the word attaches to solidity of financial status and the role this plays in commerce.

Mark Antony, confronted by the bloodied hands of the assassins and the corpse of Caesar, accepting their offer of alliance, acknowledges that the conspirators may have doubts about his sincerity: 'Gentlemen all – alas, what shall I say? / My credit now stands on such slippery ground / That one of two bad ways you must conceit me, / Either a coward or a flatterer' (*JC* 3.1.190–3). 'Credit' signifies credibility.

As the rebels produce various accounts of Jack Cade's noble origins, Stafford contemptuously dismisses them with his question: 'And will you credit this base drudge's words, / That speaks he knows not what?' (*2H6* 4.2.151–2). In other words, believe this or put your faith in it becomes the meaning attaching to credit.

Iachimo, having failed in his attempt to persuade Imogen that Posthumus has been unfaithful, pretends that he was merely testing her. His new approach is to celebrate Posthumus' good fortune: 'The credit that thy lady hath of thee / Deserves thy trust, and thy most perfect goodness / Her assur'd credit' (*CYM* 1.6.157–9). Imogen reposes so much trust in Posthumus' fidelity that she merits his integrity and devotion to her. Credit here is a matter of moral estimation and trust.

Sebastian in seeking his guide and mentor, Antonio, uses credit to mean letter – which is not used in this sense elsewhere: 'I could not find him at the Elephant, / Yet there he was, and there I found this credit, / That he did range the town to seek me out' (*TN* 4.3.5–7). As the servants prepare to meet their new mistress, Katherine the shrew, Curtis, parrying Grumio's wordplay, proclaims, 'I call them forth to credit her' (*SHR* 4.1.104). Credit here signifies to do her honour or grace her entrance.

The characters most haunted by creditors are Antonio and Timon. Ironically, before he is left bankrupt and friendless Timon goes immediately to the aid of an acquaintance on hearing 'His means most short, his creditors most strait' (*TIM* 1.1.96). Antonio refers to Shylock as his 'bloody creditor' (*MV* 3.3.34).

As the duke points out in *MM*, Nature is a demanding but beneficent creditor:

> nor Nature never lends
> The smallest scruple of her excellence,

> But like a thrifty goddess, she determines
> Herself the glory of a creditor,
> Both thanks and use.
>
> 1.1.36–40

What attributes or qualities Nature imparts to human beings she expects to be utilized and augmented. 'Use', application and interest on the loan are expected.

(C) Amongst the abundant literature on this topic is Sullivan, *The Rhetoric of Credit*; Agnew, *Worlds Apart*, esp. 43–9; Muldrew, *The Economy of Obligation*; Carruthers, *City of Capital*; Brenner, *Merchants and Revolution*. Particularly pertinent to *ERR* is Parker, *Shakespeare from the Margins*, ch. 2 and Miola, ed., *The Comedy of Errors*. For *TIM* see Chorst, 'Biological finance in Shakespeare's *Timon of Athens*', *English Literary Renaissance*, Autumn 1991, vol. 21 (3): 349–70.

current

(A) In some ways this is an unlikely word to carry significant economic or political freight. When related to coins and the circulation of currency it has the specific sense of genuine or authentic. By a natural extension it operates metaphorically, and is used widely, for evaluating a character, actions, **accounts** or representations: are they authentic, valid, true, or not to be taken at face **value**? It is used neutrally to indicate generally accepted behaviour or current **practice**; and pejoratively as the way of the world. It has both a literal and metaphorical application to the flow of water, events, or life force. Finally, when applied to music in *H8* (1.3.47) it signifies up to date or fashionable.

(B) The conception of authenticity and circulation of currency finds expression in Hotspur's praise of the Douglas before the Battle of Shrewsbury:

> If speaking truth
> In this fine age were not thought flattery,
> Such attribution should the Douglas have
> As not a soldier of this season's stamp
> Should go so general current through the world.
>
> *1H4* 4.1.1–5

Hotspur also resorts to the metaphor when attempting to call into question the claim that he refused to hand over his prisoners – concluding a colourful narrative of the incident with the words: 'And I beseech you, let not his report / Come current for an accusation / Betwixt my love and your high Majesty' (1.3.67–9).

Richard III, having attained the crown, seeks to confirm its possession by murdering his nephews. Turning to his co-conspirator, Buckingham, he prefaces his proposal with the comment, 'Ah, Buckingham, now do I play the touch, / To try if thou be current gold indeed' (*R3* 4.2.8–9). Here the term is used metaphorically: Buckingham is to be tested just as the gold coin is 'touched' to determine its purity. The economic, political and moral elements coalesce in a moment packed with tension and possibility. In the event, Buckingham's hesitation costs him his place as Richard's intimate. Soon after he suffers the loss of his head. Richard, who is himself a false coin, playing the innocent while engaging in murderous duplicity, is strangely drawn to the concept of the authentic. The former Queen Margaret jolts the Marquis of Dorset by reminding him that his newly attained elevation is so recent that his title is barely acknowledged: 'Peace, Master Marquess, you are malapert, / Your fire-new stamp of honor is scarce current' (1.3.254–5).

The Chamberlain confirms the authenticity or truth of the information he imparted to Gadshill on the previous evening – that the tavern contained pilgrims with full purses: 'It holds current that I told you yesternight: there's a franklin in the Wild of Kent hath brought three marks with him in gold' (*1H4* 2.1.53–6). One of those occasions where the precise expression arises naturally out of the subject-matter, this may help explain Shakespeare's facility for creating 'natural' conversation.

When Claudius in soliloquy refers to the 'corrupted currents of this world' (*HAM* 3.3.57) he means natural flows or patterns of behaviour – ways of carrying on. Intentions or design is intimated when Hamlet contemplates the ways in which actions are deflected from their proposed ends: 'And enterprises of great pitch and moment / With this regard their currents turn awry, / And lose the name of action' (3.1.85–7).

Under the pressure of Iago's induced jealousy, Othello uses current to mean flow of life, life blood – of which Desdemona is the source: 'The fountain from which my current runs / Or else dries up' (*OTH* 4.2.59–60).

(C) For further exploration of the authentic/inauthentic duality in the *R2–H5* cycle see entry on **counterfeit**. Relevant here are Newman, 'And wash the Ethiope white' in Howard and O'Connor, *Shakespeare Reproduced*; Parker, *Shakespeare from the Margins*, ch. 7; Turner, *Shakespeare's Twenty-First Century Economics*; Sullivan, *The Rhetoric of Credit*; Ingram, *Idioms of Self-Interest*.

custom, custom-shrunk

(A) At a personal level 'custom' means habitual **practice**, familiar action, usual manner or familiarity. At a social level it means tradition, socially or legally sanctioned principle or action. It is used on one occasion to mean creative capacity, or **trade**. There is also the sense of commercial patronage, which occurs twice only. 'Custom-shrunk' signifies a seriously constricted market or a decline in demand.

(B) On only a single occasion in all his writings does Shakespeare name a real artist, one famed for the realism of his workmanship. Hence the Third Gentleman explains the origin of the statue that everyone has gone to see:

> A piece many years in the doing and now
> newly perform'd by that rare Italian
> master, Julio Romano, who, had he
> himself eternity and could put breath into

his work, would beguile Nature of
her custom, so perfectly he is her ape.
WT 5.2.95–100

Leaving aside two critical caveats, Julio Romano is described as a workman of
such genius that he threatens to **usurp** Nature of her creative function. Ironically,
the seeming statue is really the living Hermione, believed by everyone other than
Emilia to have been dead for 16 years.

Petruchio, as part of his taming technique, calls in the tailor to reveal the
cap and gown he has made for Kate, but affects disgust with the workmanship
before throwing him out: 'Go hop me over every kennel home, / For you shall
hop without my custom, sir' (*SHR* 4.3.98–9).

Bawd, in *PER*, expresses her satisfaction with Boult the pimp when he arrives at
the brothel with the lovely Marina. She gives him **money** and promises that he
will receive further **recompense** for successfully advertising her in the town:
'Boult, spend that in the town. Report what a sojourner we have; you'll lose
nothing by custom' (4.2.137–9). The closing colloquial expression might sound
odd but it is merely an understated way of saying 'you'll be well rewarded'.

In a noteworthy speech, Calchas, the prophet, appeals to the Grecian leadership
to reciprocate the benefits he has bestowed on them by virtue of his desertion of
Troy and his prediction of Grecian victory. In preparing to ask them to trade a
Trojan prisoner of high **worth** for his daughter, Cressida, he points out that his
personal identity has been virtually expunged because of his removal from the
society where every personal and social link has been sundered:

> I have abandon'd Troy, left my possession,
> Incurr'd a traitor's name, expos'd myself
> From certain and possess'd conveniences
> To doubtful fortunes, sequest'ring from me all
> That time, acquaintance, custom, and condition
> Made tame and most familiar to my nature;
> And here, to do you service, am become
> As new into the world, strange, unacquainted.
> *TRO* 3.3.5–12

What is so remarkable is his insistence that our wholeness, or very sense of being,
is anchored in community. Calchas reveals the magnitude of his sense of loss. He
is a truly alienated man. A key word in this confession is 'custom'. What little we
see of Calchas after this point confirms his sense of isolation, of non-being, even
when he regains his daughter, Cressida.

A fine example presents itself when the haughty Antonio, seeking a loan
from Shylock, behaves as if he is willing to bestow a favour on the moneylender:
'Shylock, albeit I neither lend nor borrow / By taking nor by giving of excess, /
Yet to supply the ripe wants of my friend, / I'll break a custom' (*MV* 1.3.61–4).
Clearly Antonio means something much stronger than his usual or habitual way

of doing things. His custom is part of his way of life. It is an integral part of his ideology, a conception of the way the social universe should be constructed. It is, indeed, an action of considerable magnitude that he is willing to seek an **interest**-bearing loan. Viewed in this light he is about to make a serious concession in engaging in this transaction. The weight attaching to the word 'custom' makes a great deal of difference in the degree to which we find him blindly arrogant or genuinely ill at ease in entering upon an arrangement which he conceives as deeply offensive and contrary to his personal and commercial principles.

To appreciate the range of this word it is advantageous to contrast the seriousness of Antonio's meaning with Benedick's response to Claudio's enquiries about Hero: 'Do you question me, as an honest man should do, for my simple true judgement? or would you have me speak after my custom, as being a profess'd tyrant to their sex?' (*ADO* 1.1.166–9). Benedick effectively asks, do you want me to speak honestly or in my usual playful way of disparaging women?

The contrast between custom as a mere affectation or game with something akin to religious observance is revealed by Imogen's insistence that her newly found protectors disregard her illness and proceed with their wonted pattern of hunting: 'So please you, leave me, / Stick to your journal course: the breach of custom / Is a breach of all' (*CYM* 4.2.9–11).

Copeland, arriving in France to render the captured Scottish King David to Edward III, uses the word in the formal sense of customary tribute: 'Receive, dread lord, the custom of my fraught, / The wealthy tribute of my laboring hands' (*E3* 5.1.79–80). The nicely turned phraseology underlines the socio-political nature of the action.

This is the same ingrained institutional principle to which the exasperated Duke of York appeals when denouncing Richard's decision to confiscate Bolingbroke's inheritance:

> Take Herford's rights away, and take from Time
> His charters and his customary rights;
> Let not to-morrow then ensue to-day;
> Be not thyself; for how art thou a king
> But by fair sequence and succession?
>
> *R2* 2.1.195–9

Mistress Overdone, the brothel-keeper, complains about the adverse circumstances that are damaging her business: 'Thus, what with the war, what with the sweat, what with the gallows, and what with poverty, I am custom-shrunk' (*MM* 1.2.82–4). Everything seems to be conspiring to contract her pool of clients. (C) Significant for the statue scene in *WT* is Enterline, *The Rhetoric of the Body from Ovid to Shakespeare*, ch. 6. Also significant here is Appadurai, *The Social Life of Things*. For further discussion of Calchas' speech and its implications in *TRO* see Thomas, *The Moral Universe of Shakespeare's Problem Plays*; Grady, *The Universal Wolf*; and Harris, *Sick Economies*.

customer

(A) Employed twice in the singular the word means prostitute. Used four times in the plural it signifies either client or prostitute. On one occasion the client relates to ordinary commercial activity; on the others to the frequenter of a brothel.

(B) Because of the confusion surrounding Diana's accusation that Bertram has deprived her of her virginity, the King is led to doubt her sincerity and virtue. He suspects that she is a loose woman: 'I think thee now some common customer' (*AWW* 5.3.286). Cassio is even more terse and emphatic in refuting Iago's suggestion that he has promised to marry Bianca. Recoiling in disgust, he gasps, 'I marry her! What? A customer!' (*OTH* 4.1.119). Cassio insists that a prostitute is not fit to be his wife, though he has no qualms about enjoying her sexual favours.

Of the four references to customers in the sense of clients, only one fails to refer to those engaged in the **purchase** of human flesh. A servant in *WT* announces the arrival of Autolycus with his pack of trifles, claiming, 'no milliner can so fit his customers with gloves' (4.4.192).

(C) Pafford, ed., *The Winter's Tale*, Arden 2, esp. 33–4, emphasizes the connections between Autolycus and Green's coney-catching pamphlets in addition to his classical associates deriving from Ovid's *Metamorphoses*. Important, too, is Harris, *Sick Economies*, and Alexander and Wells, eds, *Shakespeare and Sexuality*.

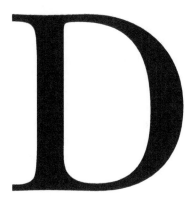

dearth

(A) A word both strong and elemental, it means scarcity or severe shortage – generally of food. In a political context its application is literal; in a romantic or religious context it is metaphorical. Another meaning is costliness or high **value** arising from scarcity or rarity. *HAM* is the source of this unique usage.

(B) Unsurprisingly, the word occurs most frequently (three times) in *COR*, a play which opens tumultuously with starving **plebeians** denouncing the patricians. Menenius employs the word twice in his attempt to quell their rebellious indignation:

> For your wants,
> Your suffering in this dearth, you may as well
> Strike at the heaven with your staves as lift them
> Against the Roman state, whose course will on
> The way it takes, cracking ten thousand curbs
> Of more strong link asunder than can ever
> Appear in your impediment. For the dearth,
> The gods, not the patricians, make it, and
> Your knees to them (not arms) must help.
>
> 1.1.66–74

Of particular interest is Antony's use of the word when responding to Octavius Caesar's interest in Egypt. In a succinct summary, Antony creates a vision of the natural fecundity in which the Nile plays the pivotal role:

> Thus do they, sir: they take the flow o'th' Nile
> By certain scales i'th'pyramid; they know,
> By th'height, the lowness, or the mean, if dearth

> Or foison follow. The higher Nilus swells,
> The more it promises; as it ebbs, the seedsman
> Upon the slime and ooze scatters his grain,
> And shortly comes to harvest.
>
> *ANT* 2.7.17–23

Though this revealing passage generally passes without comment it provides an important glimpse of the Egyptians' scientific approach to agriculture, the association of the Nile with fertility, and, the deep engagement of Octavius with economic realities.

Julia uses the word metaphorically when she confesses to Lucetta her longing for her newly acquired and recently departed Proteus: 'O, know'st thou not his looks are my soul's food? / Pity the dearth that I have pined in, / By longing for the food so long a time' (*TGV* 2.7.14–16). The image is also present, but in a more compressed form, when Venus finally extracts a kiss from the reluctant Adonis: 'Whereon they surfeit, yet complain of drouth; / He with her plenty press'd, she faint with dearth' (*VEN* 544–5).

Whether used literally or metaphorically, an antithetical structure is strongly associated with the employment of this word. It is worth drawing on another verse from *VEN* to illustrate the point:

> Therefore despite of fruitless chastity,
> Love-lacking vestals, and self-loving nuns,
> That on the earth would breed a scarcity
> And barren dearth of daughters and of sons,
> Be prodigal: the lamp that burns by night
> Dries up his oil to lend the world his light.
>
> 751–6

SON 146, which contains the line 'Why dost thou pine within and suffer dearth' (3), is balanced on the antithetical structure of starving the soul while making the body resplendent, once again making central the dearth/abundance antithesis.

In response to Osric's display of verbal elaboration, Hamlet is provoked into a blistering parody of the courtier's extravagant praise of Laertes with the words 'in the verity of his extolment, I take him to be the soul of great article, and his infusion of such dearth and rareness as, to make a true diction of him, his semblable is his mirror' (*HAM* 5.2.115–9). 'Costliness' or 'high value arising from scarcity or rarity' appears to be the meaning here. At the conceptual core of this is economics. The very rarity of someone as extraordinarily gifted as Laertes must inevitably make him costly. Claudius has already suggested to Laertes that they provoke Hamlet into a contest by stirring up his emulation: 'We'll put on those shall praise your excellence, / And set a double varnish on the fame / The Frenchman gave you' (4.7.131–3). Osric's 'double varnish' is of such a quality that Hamlet is driven to biting mockery. No doubt Hamlet also reacts to an ingratiating courtliness which has become or is becoming systemic under

Claudius' regime. The provocation and the resulting animus are not merely aesthetic: they are also political.

(C) Thomas, *Shakespeare's Roman Worlds*, 128–34, engages in a close analysis of the scene on Pompey's galley and the political manoeuvrings that surround it. Poole's volume, *Coriolanus*, is marked by clarity and insight. Orwell's essay on 'Language and politics' is germane to Hamlet's comment. Agnew, *Worlds Apart*, esp. 51, discusses action taken in 1587 to counteract the dearth in England. Harris, *Sick Economies*, 37–8, cites Smith's use of 'dearth' to signify dearness in his economic analysis of 1581. Wilson, *Will Power*, 63–82, considers dearth in England consequent on the enclosures. Pallister, *The Age of Elizabeth*, 154, notes that 'dearth' was used to describe an inflationary situation even when the process arose from an increase in the **money** supply relative to **commodities** coming on the **market**. Thus a term formerly applied to rising **prices** consequent upon poor harvests extended its reach in a rather paradoxical way to inflation engendered purely by monetary forces.

debt, debitor, debtor
(A) An obligation to repay, a debt may be financial, political, moral or social. The word employed in both the singular and plural occurs most frequently in *TIM* (13 times). Residing just as comfortably in the religious and political spheres as in the financial, the concept is striking for the way in which it produces a force field that fuses these seemingly disparate elements. Debitor is the debit column in an **account** book; debtor designates the person responsible for repayment of a debt.

(B) Encountering the Duke disguised as a friar, Escalus congratulates him on having discharged his duty by preparing Claudio for death: 'You have paid the heavens your function, and the prisoner the very debt of your calling' (*MM* 3.2.249–50). The syntactical compression of this sentence brings together the moral and spiritual dimensions of obligation. A servant of God spends his life in spiritual service and acquits himself of obligations to those who suffer by ameliorating their **condition**. He is the conduit between heaven and the sinful or afflicted. What is significant here is the way in which this word, like '**reckoning**', finds a natural habitat in the spiritual sphere, just as it does in the financial, political and social arenas.

The complexity with which Shakespeare uses the term in a financial sense is apparent in *TIM*. The agitated steward Flavius, confronted by further demands to provide lavish presents for Timon's guests, says in an aside, 'His promises fly so beyond his state / That what he speaks is all in debt: he owes / For ev'ry word' (1.2.197–9). Here again is a conceptual compactness that commingles the literal and metaphoric. Without knowing it Timon has been borrowing to finance his gift-giving. As he can't speak without giving, every word he utters incurs a debt.

Refreshingly simple, though rich in paradox, is Worcester's use of the word in setting forth the case for a pre-emptive strike against Henry IV: 'The King will always think him in our debt, / And think we think ourselves unsatisfied, / Till he hath found a time to pay us home' (*1H4* 1.3.286–8). There is logic in the reasoning of this guileful character. He and his brother Northumberland were instrumental in effecting Bolingbroke's **usurpation** of Richard II's throne. Can such a political obligation ever be cleared? If not the remedy may lie in removing the creditor.

Attempting to create calm in the wake of Caesar's assassination, Brutus seeks to reassure the horrified onlookers with the phrase 'ambition's debt is paid' (*JC* 3.1.83). As far as he is concerned Caesar was guilty of a serious crime. With his death he has been exculpated. Moral absolution has been effected. The abstract phrase is chilling in its concision. It is almost mathematical in its expression. Nothing human enters the equation. Ironically, Mark Antony will take the word 'ambition' and turn it into a refrain supercharged with an emotion that will eventually engulf Brutus and his fellow conspirators.

The debt all mortals must pay is death. Even the drunken Stephano acknowledges, 'He that dies pays all debts' (*TMP* 3.2.131). In seeking to provoke his mother into moderating her grief at the loss of her husband, Edward IV, and confronting immediate political exigencies, Dorset frames his message in spiritual terms, employing the word twice:

> Comfort, dear mother, God is much displeas'd
> That you take with unthankfulness his doing.
> In common worldly things 'tis call'd ungrateful
> With dull unwillingness to repay a debt,
> Which with a bounteous hand was kindly lent;
> Much more to be thus opposite with heaven,
> For it requires the royal debt it lent you.
>
> *R3* 2.2.89–95

Although Dorset is not characterized by depth of humanity, there is fineness of sensibility in this speech: what is generously lent should be repaid with reciprocal grace, both in the material and spiritual realms.

A coalition of the spiritual and political is present in Hal's famous soliloquy. He revels in the deceit whereby he proposes to play the wastrel in order to be all the more impressive when he is reborn:

> So when this loose behaviour I throw off
> And pay the debt I never promised,
> By how much better than my word I am,
> By so much shall I falsify men's hopes,
> And like bright metal on a sullen ground,
> My reformation, glitt'ring o'er my fault,
> Shall show more goodly and attract more eyes
> Than that which hath no foil to set it off.
> I'll so offend, to make offence a skill,
> Redeeming time when men think least I will.
>
> *1H4* 1.2.208–17

'Debt', 'reformation', 'redeeming' collaborate powerfully to reconfigure the modern sensibility: are the spiritual and political harnessed together, or has the spiritual been **suborned**?

Debt as obligation is intimated by Hector: 'Nature craves / All dues be ren-d'red to their owners: now, / What nearer debt in all humanity / Than wife is to the husband?' (*TRO* 2.2.173–6). At this point in the famous debate scene the great Trojan warrior is stating the case for surrendering Helen to the Greeks. Within a few lines, however, he decides that their 'joint and several dignities' (193) override all other obligations.

On the eve of the Battle of Agincourt, Williams asserts that 'if the cause be not good, the King himself hath a heavy reckoning to make'. He goes on to describe the nature of dying in war and its consequences: 'some swearing, some crying for a surgeon, some upon their wives left poor behind them, some upon the debts they owe, some upon their children rawly left' (*H5* 4.1.134–41). It is strik-ing that in this description financial debts are embedded in the list of obliga-tions. Moreover, the moral, political and economic calculus includes the King's 'reckoning'.

The way in which the concepts of financial, political and moral obligations permeate Shakespeare's work can be indicated by the following contrasting examples. Announcing the death of Young Siward, Rosse tells his father: 'Your son, my lord, has paid a soldier's debt' (*MAC* 5.9.5). In very different circum-stances Pandarus encourages Troilus to go beyond words in his courtship of Cressida: 'Words pay no debts, give her deeds' (*TRO* 3.2.55). Demetrius, wearied in his pursuit of Hermia, articulates his obligation to sleep by resort to the rich lexicon of finance: 'So sorrow's heaviness doth heavier grow / For *debt* that *bankrout* sleep doth sorrow *owe*; / Which now in some slight measure it will *pay*, / If for his *tender* here I make some stay' (*MND* 3.2.84–7). 'Tender' can mean 'offer' in both pecuniary and non-pecuniary senses.

The Lord Chief Justice seizes on the opportunity for financial wordplay when ordering Falstaff to both pay his debts to Mistress Quickly and to marry her: 'Pay her the debt you owe her, and unpay the villainy you have done with her. The one you may do with sterling money, and the other with current repentance' (*2H4* 2.1.118–21).

Reference to 'debitor' as a column in an account book occurs in the unlikely situation where the jailer is preparing Posthumus for execution: 'A heavy reckon-ing for you, sir. But the comfort is, you shall be call'd to no more payments, fear no more tavern-bills . . . O, the charity of a penny cord! it sums up thousands in a trice. You have no true debitor and creditor but it: of what's past, is, and to come, the discharge. Your neck, sir, is pen, book, and counters; so the acquittance follows' (*CYM* 5.4.157–70). This masterly summary of the clearing of financial and moral obligations, all neatly contained in the columns of the account book, epitomizes this social universe. The world of finance is in the ascendancy.

(C) See entries on 'reckoning', 'redeem' and 'reformation' in Hassel, *Shakespeare's Religious Language*. Shugar, *Political Theologies in Shakespeare's England*, is particu-larly good on the theological and political connections in *MM*. The financial intricacies of debt management are articulated with clarity in Turner, *Shakespeare's Twenty-First Century Economics*, esp. 121–2. Jowett, 'Middleton and debt in *Timon of Athens*' in Woodbridge, ed., *Money and the Age of Shakespeare*, and McAlindon, *Shakespeare's Tudor History*, are highly significant here.

detention
(A) This unique usage refers to withholding of payment.
(B) The unsuspecting Timon is baffled when accosted by **creditors** demanding immediate payment. Totally unaware of his financial situation he turns to his steward for an explanation: 'How goes the world, that I am thus encount'red / With clamorous demands of debt, broken bonds, / And the detention of long since due debts, / Against my honor?' (*TIM* 2.2.36–9).
(C) For some acute observations on this play see Nuttall, *Timon of Athens*; Klein, ed., *Timon of Athens*; Chorst, 'Biological finance in Shakespeare's *Timon of Athens*', *English Literary Renaissance*, Autumn 1991, vol. 21 (3): 349–70; and Ingram, *Idioms of Self-Interest*, esp. 59–71.

earnest, earnest-penny

(A) The financial meaning of earnest is down payment, something submitted in advance as a portion of the total sum due. There is a parallel political application when some honour is bestowed as an indication of something greater to follow. As an adjective the word means serious or genuine. The adverb 'earnestly' has the modern meaning of intently, steadfastly, deliberately, eagerly, urgently. Earnest-penny refers to a sum paid up front in order to guarantee the receipt of the product in due course, but is applied metaphorically in a political or military context to signify guarantee of further damage (*E3* 3.1.151).

(B) When Boult the pimp arrives at the brothel with the captured Marina, he has already made a down payment to the pirates to secure the transaction. He tells his employer, 'If you like her, so; if not, I have lost my earnest' (*PER* 4.2.44–5). Evidently an earnest is a non-returnable deposit paid to ensure the supplier does not change his mind and sell to another **customer**. Likewise, if the purchaser has a change of heart the supplier retains the deposit as compensation for the possibility of missing out on another client.

The politically parallel case occurs twice in *MAC*. Rosse greets Macbeth with showers of praise from King Duncan before announcing the first indication of future honours: 'And for an earnest of greater honor, / He bade me, from him, call thee Thane of Cawdor' (1.3.104–5). Soliloquizing on the accurate prediction made by the weird sisters, Macbeth attempts to evaluate the veracity of their more extravagant promise – the crown: 'This supernatural soliciting / Cannot be ill; cannot be good. If ill, / Why hath it given me earnest of success, / Commencing in a truth?' (1.3.130–3).

H5 provides an interesting example by virtue of combining the financial and political dimensions. Henry, condemning the conspirators who have received a payment for his assassination, exclaims: 'You have conspir'd against our royal person, / Join'd with an enemy proclaim'd, and from his coffers / Receiv'd the golden earnest of our death' (2.2.167–9). Rather than a deposit they have received full payment, but it is an earnest in the sense of an advance payment for carrying out the assassination. Accordingly, an earnest is a means of *binding* a **bargain**.

The meaning serious or genuine is common. The Duke of Buckingham going to his execution recalls the retribution he invited when swearing fidelity to the family of the dying King Edward: 'That high All-Seer, which I dallied with, / Hath turn'd my feigned prayer on my head, / And given in earnest what I begg'd in jest' (*R3* 5.1.20–2). In defending herself against the accusation of instigating the imprisonment of Clarence, Queen Elizabeth protests that she has been 'An earnest advocate to plead for him' (*R3* 1.3.86). Evidently she means 'sincere' or 'genuine'.

'Eagerly' or 'urgently' is the meaning attaching to Bassanio's horrified expression when he says to Shylock: 'Why dost thou whet thy knife so earnestly?' (*MV* 4.1.121).

Pandarus' laconic lament at the close of *TRO* contrasts the eagerness with which **bawds** are employed and the contemptuous way they are dismissed once their services have been rendered: 'O traders and bawds, how earnestly are you set a-work, and how ill requited! Why should our endeavour be so lov'd and the performance so loath'd?' (5.10.37–9).

(C) Dutton and Howard, eds, *A Companion to Shakespeare's Works – Vol. II: The Histories*, contains several essays relating to the political circumstances discussed here. For exploration of the financial aspects arising out of this discussion see Woodmansee and Osteen, eds, *The New Economic Criticism*, and Sullivan, *The Rhetoric of Credit*.

engage

(A) The significant financial meaning of the term is to **mortgage** property: land or other assets. A related and generally non-financial application is to make a pledge or give a guarantee. A third meaning is to accept a challenge, to take up a gage. A further meaning relates to making an assault or a whole-hearted commitment. A significant political and military dimension occurs when someone submits to the power of the enemy to function as a guarantor or hostage. The word also bears the implication of being associated with or forming part of an action. As an adjective, the term is used to mean entangled; and also pledged.

(B) Exposed to the enormity of his outstanding **debts**, Timon responds to his steward with the desperate riposte, 'Let all my land be sold', only to receive even more crushing information, ' 'Tis all engag'd, some forfeited and gone' (*TIM* 2.2.145–6). In order to finance lavish consumption, gifts and banquets for his 'friends', Timon has borrowed against his enormous landholdings: what land remains is mortgaged.

Giving a pledge or guarantee occurs in social, economic and political contexts. Bassanio, on receiving news of Antonio's arrest, explains to Portia, 'I have engag'd myself to a dear friend, / Engag'd my friend to his mere enemy, / To feed my means' (*MV* 3.2.261–3). Here is a noteworthy case of the term 'engaged' providing a lynchpin encompassing word of honour and legal obligation. Bassanio has succeeded in his gamble by winning Portia, but meantime Antonio's collateral, his six ships, have all foundered (or so it appears at this stage), and the date for repayment has expired so that Bassanio's pledge or promise is nullified. Antonio is open to the **exaction** stipulated in the **bond**.

Significantly, Brutus rejects Cassius' proposal of an oath-taking by the conspirators, protesting that the word of a Roman constitutes an absolute pledge:

> what other bond
> Than secret Romans, that have spoke the word
> And will not palter? and what other oath
> Than honesty to honesty engag'd
> That this shall be, or we will fall for it?
>
> *JC* 2.1.124–8

A Roman's word requires no ritual or bond to hold it fast.

Given the strong ritualistic elements in *R2* it is unsurprising that the play affords two examples of engaged being employed in the sense of 'taking up a challenge'. Denouncing Aumerle, a Lord throws down his gage with the words, 'There is my honor's pawn, / Engage it to the trial, if thou darest' (4.1.55–6). Moments later, Surrey challenges Fitzwater: 'there is my honor's pawn, / Engage it to the trial, if thou dar'st' (4.1.70–1). These challenges occur after Bolingbroke has effectively deposed Richard and the scramble to get on side is taking place. What is startling, parodic and amusing in this scene is that the medieval world of ritual has already given way to a new epoch, a **Machiavel**lian world where *realpolitik* has moved from the shadows to come centre stage.

Ulysses describes Troilus' fervent heroism:

> who hath done to-day
> Mad and fantastic execution,
> Engaging and redeeming of himself
> With such a careless force, and forceless care,
> As if that luck, in very spite of cunning,
> Bade him win all.
>
> *TRO* 5.5.37–42

In his determination to avenge Cressida's betrayal, Troilus has evidently chosen the most violent areas of the battlefield and, despite the odds, emerged unscathed.

Hotspur, prior to the Battle of Shrewsbury, lists his grievances against the King, emphasizing the mistreatment of his brother-in-law, Mortimer: 'suff'red his kinsman March / (Who is, if every owner were well plac'd, / Indeed his king) to be engag'd in Wales, / There without ransom to be forfeited' (*1H4* 4.3.93–6). 'Held hostage' is the meaning here.

In responding to Northumberland's grief at the loss of his son, Hotspur, in the rebellion against the King, Lord Bardolph points out: 'We all that are engaged to this loss / Knew that we ventured on such dangerous seas' (*2H4* 1.1.180–1). His subsequent argument that they must try again indicates the significance attaching to 'engaged': an involvement which is complete, whole-hearted.

The sense of 'entanglement' emerges uniquely in *HAM* where the praying Claudius reveals awareness of his predicament as a regicide, now in possession of his brother's crown and wife – all of which he intends to retain: 'O limed soul, that struggling to be free / Art more engag'd!' (3.3.68–9).

Rejecting all the pleas against his participation in the fatal battle, Hector declares that he has pledged himself to fight with specific Greek warriors – most notably Achilles: 'Aeneas is a-field, / And I do stand engag'd to many Greeks, / Even in the faith of valor, to appear / This morning to them' (*TRO* 5.3.67–70).

(C) Coyle, ed., *Hamlet*, offers significant comments on key aspects of the play. Dutton and Howard, eds, *A Companion to Shakespeare's Works – Vol. II: The Histories*, and Sahel, 'Some versions of coup d'etat, rebellion and revolution' in Alexander, ed., *Shakespeare and Politics*, are particularly interesting here. Exceptionally penetrating is McAlindon, *Shakespeare's Tudor History*. Thomas, *The Moral Universe of Shakespeare's Problem Plays*, explores the issues touched on in *TRO*.

engross

(A) The primary meaning of the word is to accumulate, **monopolize**, or absorb either resources, opportunities, or particular kinds of feeling, e.g. grief. Two other, very different meanings, are to fatten or distend; and to set out something in a correct legal form.

(B) The sickly Henry IV provides an excellent example of accumulation when complaining that Hal's disappearance with the crown is characteristic of sons' ingratitude. They make victims, he claims, of industrious fathers:

> For this they have engrossed and pil'd up
> The cank'red heaps of strange-achieved gold;
> For this they have been thoughtful to invest
> Their sons with arts and martial exercises;
> When like the bee tolling from every flower
> The virtuous sweets,
> Our thighs pack'd with wax, our mouths with honey,
> We bring it to the hive, and like the bees,
> Are murd'red for our pains. This bitter taste
> Yields his engrossments to the ending father.
>
> *2H4* 4.5.70–9

Thus the accumulation of **wealth** and power ('strange-achieved gold') by arduous and possibly dubious means, serves only to demonstrate to fathers the fruitlessness of their endeavours. The term being used twice in this speech signifies the nature of accumulation as both the product of superhuman effort and an acknowledgement of the unrewarding nature of the activity. Hal uses the word himself when responding to his father's charge that he lacks Hotspur's heroic manliness: 'Percy is but my factor, good my lord, / To engross up glorious deeds on my behalf; / And I will call him to so strict account / That he shall render every glory up' (*1H4* 3.2.147–50). The exchange is fascinating not least because of the commingling of heroic and commercial language.

The ultimate monopolizer, death, is referred to by Romeo in his memorable suicide speech over the body of Juliet: 'and, lips, O you / The doors of breath, seal with a righteous kiss / A dateless bargain to engrossing death!' (*ROM* 5.3.113–15). There are legal and financial terms embedded in these lines which serve as an acknowledgement of the ubiquitous pressures of these realities imposing themselves on consciousness and verbal formulations even at a moment of such emotional intensity.

The application of the term 'to express writing in an appropriate legal form' occurs at a resonant moment in *R3*. The Scrivener's speech strikes at the heart of political tyranny: for their own safety people pretend not to see through a device which is obvious to everyone:

> Here is the indictment of the good Lord Hastings,
> Which in a set hand fairly is engross'd
> That it may be to-day read o'er in Paul's.
> And mark how well the sequel hangs together:
> Eleven hours I have spent to write it over,
> For yesternight by Catesby was it sent me;
> The precedent was full as long a-doing,
> And yet within these five hours Hastings liv'd,
> Untainted, unexamin'd, free, at liberty.
> Here's a good world the while! Who is so gross
> That cannot see this palpable device?
> Yet who's so bold but says he sees it not?
>
> 3.6.1–12

This moment, like the arrest of Hastings (3.4) had chilling echoes in Stalin's Russia. This play also provides an example of the word being employed to mean to 'fatten' or 'distend the stomach'. In another piece of political theatre, Buckingham, seeking the support of the Mayor and his associates for the crowning of Richard, presents his candidate as a model of restraint and piety: 'Not dallying with a brace of courtesans, / But meditating with two deep devines; / Not sleeping, to engross his idle body, / But praying, to enrich his watchful soul' (3.7.74–7). Those antitheses which form the rhetorical basis of this speech are so outrageous that they promote a daring piece of political pantomime.

(C) There are several fine discussions of the themes and language animating these plays including: Cavanagh, et al., eds, *Shakespeare's Histories and Counter-Histories*; Goy-Blanquet, *Shakespeare's Early History Plays*; Levenson, 'Shakespeare's *Romeo and Juliet*' in Alexander, ed., *Shakespeare and Language*; Davis, 'Death and desire in *Romeo and Juliet*' in Wells and Alexander, eds, *Shakespeare and Sexuality*; Hillman, *Shakespeare's Entrails*.

estate

(A) A richly expansive word that encompasses economics, politics and sociology, the noun can signify any of the following: a kingdom; property; fortune or prosperity; situation or circumstance; high rank; a particular social stratum: high, middle or low; endowment or benefit. The verb means to endow or settle upon. The word occurs most frequently in *TIM*, a play that pivots on Timon's **wealth** and status.

(B) A critical moment occurs when King Duncan, despite heaping plaudits on the hero of the day, Macbeth, makes clear the line of inheritance: 'We will establish our estate upon / Our eldest, Malcolm' (*MAC* 1.4.37–8). From this instant Macbeth knows that the realm of Scotland is unattainable by legitimate means.

Antonio rebuts Salerio's suggestion that anxiety about the safety of his ships provokes his melancholy: 'My ventures are not in one bottom trusted, / Nor to one place; nor is my whole estate / Upon the fortune of this present year' (*MV* 1.1.42–4). Estate may embrace two concepts: 'total financial **worth**'; and 'situation in life'. Uncertainty is not a concern for this careful **merchant** who knows how to spread his risks. By contrast, Bassanio has to confess to his friend that having spent well beyond his income his financial situation is precarious; ' 'Tis not unknown to you, Antonio, / How much I have disabled mine estate, / By something showing a more swelling port / Than my faint means would grant continuance' (1.1.122–5). Again both concepts are involved: his lands and finance; his personal situation in life. However, when Salerio hands Antonio's missive to Bassanio with the words, 'His letter there / Will show you his estate' (3.2.235–6) he means circumstances, **condition**. His miserable situation is, of course, the product of the apparent collapse of his estate in the financial sense – something spelled out in Antonio's own words: ' "Sweet Bassanio, my ships have all miscarried, my creditors grow cruel, my estate is very low" ' (3.2.315–17). In this play estate as condition of life or circumstance is firmly tied to estate as property.

Fortune in the sense of prosperity is intimated when it is said of the ruined Timon, 'his estate shrinks from him' (*TIM* 3.2.6–7). His depleted material fortunes will, in turn, bring about the total collapse of his personal standing.

Olivia, rejecting Orsino's proposal, delivered by Viola, protests that although he has all the necessary personal attributes and is of high status or rank, she cannot love him: 'Yet I suppose him virtuous, know him noble, / Of great estate, of fresh and stainless youth' (*TN* 1.5.258–9). Of course, high social standing implies wealth.

A distinction can be made between high social standing generally and distinct social strata. Buckingham, making his mock plea to Richard Gloucester that he claim the crown, chastizes him for his overly sensitive display of courtesy to his kindred, 'And egally indeed to all estates' (*R3* 3.7.213). It would appear that nobody, however lowly, is beneath Richard's consideration. Here we have a perception of clearly delineated social levels.

The reformed Oliver, in *AYL*, promises to make restitution to his younger brother, Orlando, by endowing him with everything he has inherited from their father: 'for my father's house and all the revenue that was old Sir Rowland's will I estate upon you' (5.2.10–12). By contrast, Menenius, on hearing that he has been sent a personal missive containing news of Coriolanus's triumph over the Volscians, celebrates a different kind of endowment: 'A letter for me! it gives me an estate of seven years' health, in which time I will make a lip at the physician' (*COR* 2.1.114–16).

Estate as a 'piece of property' is intimated in *PER* when Pander sets out the case for early retirement: 'if in our youths we could pick up some pretty estate, 'twere not amiss to keep our door hatch'd' (4.2.32–3). The dialogue encompasses a debate about risks, morals and opportunity-**cost**. Keeping the 'door hatch'd' means to shut up shop. The reference to their 'youths' is either playful or facetious. This play contains some of the most explorative analysis of economic phenomena in the canon.

The most anxious reference to 'estate' in the sense of 'condition' or 'general situation' occurs on the eve of the Battle of Agincourt, when the soldier, Williams, enquires of the disguised King what Erpingham thinks of their position: 'I pray you, what thinks he of our estate?' (*H5* 4.1.96).

(C) For a range of relevant comment see Donawerth, *Shakespeare and the Sixteenth-Century Study of Language*, ch. 6; Lyne, *Shakespeare's Late Work*; McDonald, *Shakespeare's Late Style*; Ward, *As You Like It*; Kamps, ed., *Materialist Shakespeare*; Jordan and Cunningham, eds, *The Law in Shakespeare*.

exact, exacted, exacting, exaction, exactly

(A) Exact and its adjuncts are in the main conceptually unproblematic, but the different meanings and nuances are fascinating, not least because there are occasions when the term embodies a highly compacted concept such that no single word does it justice. As an adjective, exact signifies complete, accomplished, highly skilled or expert; as a verb, to command or enforce, e.g. taxes; the noun exaction implies excessive taxation or an exorbitant demand; also enforcement; the adverb 'exactly' intimates completely or entirely; precisely; expressly.

(B) Narrating their history to Miranda, Prospero describes how his brother's usurpation began by being given too much authority: 'He being thus lorded, / Not only with what my revenue yielded, / But what my power might else exact' (*TMP* 1.2.97–9). 'Command' is probably the best synonym for 'exact' in this case.

Expressing his abhorrence of **usury** whilst attempting to borrow from Shylock, Antonio protests:

> If thou wilt lend this money, lend it not
> As to thy friends, for when did friendship take
> A breed for barren metal of his friend?
> But lend it rather to thine enemy,
> Who if he break, thou mayest with better face
> Exact the penalty.
>
> *MV* 1.3.132–7

'Enforce' is the required meaning here. When Bassanio attempts to dissuade his friend from accepting the terms of the **bond**, Shylock reassures them: 'If he should break his day, what should I gain / By the exaction of the forfeiture?' (1.3.163–4).

Far from obvious is the meaning attaching to Parolles' use when he proposes himself as the right man for the difficult task of retrieving the company's drum from the enemy: 'But that the merit of service is seldom attributed to the true and exact performer, I would have that drum or another, or *hic jacet*' (*AWW* 3.6.60–3). In this lovely example of hendiadys, with the two terms appearing to be parallel but each having its own nuance, the whole is more than the sum of the parts: 'exact' means 'meritorious' or 'accomplished'; 'true' means 'authentic', so the phrase as a whole signifies the nonpareil or authentic hero. Of course, Parolles is an outrageous, albeit appealing, coward: a **counterfeit**.

The most problematic case occurs in *TRO*, when Ulysses describes how Patroclus entertains Achilles with his mockery of the Greek leadership:

> And in this fashion,
> All our abilities, gifts, natures, shapes,
> Severals and generals of grace exact,
>
> . . .
>
> serves
> As stuff for these two to make paradoxes.
> 1.3.178–84

The context here suggests accomplishments, though the meaning of the phrase in question, 'grace exact', implies something more intense, such as the 'very essence of our capabilities, the quintessence'.

When Hotspur receives the news that his father's forces will not after all be arriving for the Battle of Shrewsbury, he overcomes his disappointment by indulging in a characteristic piece of rationalization: 'Were it good / To set the exact wealth of all our states / All at one cast? To set so rich a main / On the nice hazard of one doubtful hour?' (*1H4* 4.1.45–8). 'Exact' means total or complete. If all their resources were gambled on this one battle then defeat would be final, whereas by keeping part of their forces in reserve they have a chance of regrouping and fighting another day. In the event Northumberland's absence is to **cost** them not only the battle, but also their hopes of unseating Bolingbroke.

Horatio describes the Ghost of King Hamlet as 'Armed at point exactly, cap-a-pe' (*HAM* 1.2.200). The meaning here is 'in every particular, with nothing omitted'. This idea is also communicated, in very different circumstances, when Cleopatra informs Octavius Caesar that she has drawn up a detailed and comprehensive list of her valuables: 'This is the brief: of money, plate, and jewels / I am possess'd of; 'tis exactly valued, / Not petty things admitted' (*ANT* 5.2.138–40).

The modern sense of 'precisely' or 'to the letter' is very clear when Prospero commends his trusty sprite: 'Ariel, thy charge / Exactly is perform'd' (*TMP*

1.2.237–8). His orders for further action are couched in the same terms: 'Thou shalt be as free / As mountain winds; but then exactly do / All points of my command' (1.2.499–501).

'Exactitude' and 'precision' are the qualities admired by Iachimo when he describes the workmanship that created the tapestry in Imogen's magnificent bedchamber:

> A piece of work
> So bravely done, so rich, that it did strive
> In workmanship and value, which I wonder'd
> Could be so rarely and exactly wrought,
> Since the true life on't was –
>
> *CYM* 2.4.72–6

Yet here again the word works hard conveying not just the technical skill involved, but an artistry that expresses the very life of the figures, embracing and embodying the life force. 'Exactly' probes deeply, producing a nuance that is unique in the use of this word.

When in *TRO* the great, but unarmed, heroes meet face to face for the first time, Achilles expresses his contempt for his famous adversary: 'Now, Hector, I have fed mine eyes on thee; / I have with exact view perus'd, Hector, / And quoted joint by joint' (4.5.231–3). 'Critical precision' seems to be the meaning conveyed by 'exact view': the survey has been brief but comprehensive, implying that there is not much to Hector – an implication seized upon by the Trojan hero who responds vigorously to the slight. Exact here embodies *both* concepts: precise and expert.

The sense of 'precise' or 'meticulous' is the required meaning when Lear denounces Goneril for referring to his knights as a 'disorder'd rabble': 'My train are men of choice and rarest parts, / That all particulars of duty know, / And in the most exact regard support / The worships of their name' (*LR* 1.4.263–6).

Slightly problematical is Mowbray's use when defending himself against the charges preferred by Bolingbroke. Turning to John of Gaunt, he admits to a serious breach of faith in the past but insists that he has received forgiveness for his transgressions: 'But ere I last receiv'd the sacrament / I did confess it, and exactly begg'd / Your Grace's pardon, and I hope I had it' (*R2* 1.1.139–41). 'Expressly' is the most obvious synonym in this example, though something more is implied given the extreme formalities embedded here: 'with all the rules of propriety duly adhered to'. This is the only example of the word being used in this precise sense.

'Precise, emphatic or unequivocal' are compacted in 'exact' when Hamlet informs Horatio of his discovery by unsealing the orders to execute him: 'Where I found, Horatio – / Ah, royal knavery! – an exact command, / . . . / My head should be strook off' (*HAM* 5.2.18–25). 'Precise' is probably the meaning implied here but it is hard to resist the feeling that 'emphatic' or 'unequivocal' are added ingredients.

The implication 'highly skilled and meticulous' scrutinizers occurs when the steward protests to Timon that his financial plight has not been due to lax or improper administration of his financial affairs: 'If you suspect my husbandry or falsehood, / Call me before th' exactest auditors, / And set me on the proof' (*TIM* 2.2.155–7).

Exacted signifying 'enforced financial obligation' or 'taxes' is well illustrated by Lord Say in defending himself against Cade's rebels: 'Justice with favour have I always done; / Pray'rs and tears have mov'd me, gifts could never. / When have I aught exacted at your hands, / But to maintain the King, the realm, and you?' (*2H6* 4.7.67–70). Say insists that financial impositions have been just taxes required to defray necessary public expenditure.

Quite different are the circumstances in *H8*. The King bridles when confronted by Katherine's exposure of Cardinal Wolsey's financial impositions. She stresses public disquiet, citing Wolsey as 'putter-on / Of these exactions' before proclaiming: 'These exactions / (Whereof my sovereign would have note), they are / Most pestilent to th' hearing, and, to bear 'em, / The back is sacrifice to th' load...' The King retorts, 'Still exaction! / The nature of it? In what kind, let's know, / Is this exaction?' (1.2.24–54). The tension, anxiety and political nervousness apparent in this exchange (no other play employs the term four times) reveals how this word is conceived in terms of 'exploitation' or 'extortion'. The other play which employs the term, in this sense, is *R2*. The wayward King is denounced for his outrageous schemes for raising **money**. Ross complains: 'The commons hath he pill'd with grievous taxes'. Willoughby adds, 'And daily new exactions are devis'd, / As blanks, benevolences, and I wot not what' (2.1.246–50).

The idea of a 'non-pecuniary imposition or enforcement' finds expression in *MM* where the Duke comments on the thwarting of Angelo's intended sexual blackmail of Isabella by the substitution of Marianna: 'So disguise shall by th'disguised / Pay with falsehood false exacting, / And perform and old contracting' (3.2.280–2). What has been imposed by Angelo, sexual intercourse as a fee for freeing Claudio, will be paid by the substitute, Marianna, his former fiancée. Hence, a double falsehood produces a legitimate outcome: the intended exploitation culminating in a legitimate transaction.

(C) Particularly relevant with reference to this topic are: Bradshaw, *Shakespeare's Scepticism*; Schoenbaum, 'Richard II and the realities of power' in Alexander, ed., *Shakespeare and Politics*; Howard and Shershow, *Marxist Shakespeares*; Nuttall, *Timon of Athens*; Kingsley-Smith, *Shakespeare's Drama of Exile*; Shell, *Money, Language and Thought*, esp. ch. 3; Donawerth, *Shakespeare and the Sixteenth-Century Study of Language*, ch. 6; McDonald, *Shakespeare's Late Style*.

excess

(A) A key word in the lexicon of finance, signifying **interest**, or **usury**, it is used more frequently to intimate superabundance, surfeit or extremity. Although excess is used only once in the literal sense of interest, the concept reaches into strata of discourse in a way that generates consciousness of its financial dimension.

(B) Endeavouring to finance Bassanio's pursuit of Portia, Antonio is obliged to resort to securing a loan from Shylock. He immediately claims the moral high ground indicating contempt for Shylock's profession: 'Shylock, albeit I neither lend nor borrow / By taking nor by giving of excess, / Yet to supply the ripe wants of my friend, / I'll break a custom' (*MV* 1.3.61–4). Intriguingly, the word does not recur in their subsequent dialogue, Shylock referring to this kind of transaction as 'upon **advantage**'. When, later in the play, Bassanio chooses the right casket, Portia tries to check her feelings: 'O love, be moderate, allay thy ecstasy, / In measure rain thy joy, scant this excess! / I feel too much thy blessing; make it less, / For fear I surfeit' (3.2.111–14). What she feels is a superabundance of joy – an extremity of emotion which contrasts with the financial augmentation that characterizes moneylending.

Much more focused and concentrated is Juliet's breathless response to Romeo's declaration of love, because she puns on the word, using it as the fulcrum on which her perception is balanced: 'They are but beggars that can count their worth, / But my true love is grown to such excess / I cannot sum up sum of half my wealth' (*ROM* 2.6.32–4). By 'excess' she means both 'super-abundance' and the 'accumulation generated by lending'. She commandeers the language of finance for the expression of love. Through such verbal alchemy purification is achieved.

The blind Gloucester in his humiliated and degraded condition reflects on the material inequalities in society. He advocates a redistribution of income, 'So distribution should undo excess, / And each man have enough' (*LR* 4.1.70–1).

The supreme example of 'excess' as 'unnecessary embellishment' or 'utmost superfluity' occurs in *JN* where Salisbury ridicules the King's second coronation:

> Therefore, to be possess'd with double pomp,
> To guard a title that was rich before,
> To gild refined gold, to paint the lily,
> To throw a perfume on the violet,
> To smooth the ice, or add another hue
> Unto the rainbow, or with taper-light
> To seek the beauteous eye of heaven to garnish,
> Is wasteful and ridiculous excess.
>
> 4.2.9–16

'Guard', of course, means 'to provide elaborate, ornate or expensive lining to a garment', but there is also the secondary meaning of 'protect'.

The most integrated case occurs in *LUC*. Tarquin is so set on ravishing Lucrece that he has no sense of the losses that will outweigh any possible gain arising from his actions:

> Those that much covet are with gain so fond,
> That what they have not, that which they possess,
> They scatter and unloose it from their bond,

And so by hoping more they have but less,
Or gaining more, the profit of excess
   Is but to surfeit, and such griefs sustain
   That they prove bankrout in this poor rich gain.

                                    134–40

The two meanings attaching to excess vitalize the financial analogy.

(C) See Carroll, *Fat King, Lean Beggar*; Watts, *Romeo and Juliet*; Wynne-Davies, 'Intolerance in the *Merchant of Venice*' in Dutton and Howard, eds, *Companion to Shakespeare's Works, Vol. III*, esp. 370–2; also Vaughan, '*King John*' in Vol. II. A parallel to Juliet's compressed expression of the arithmetic of love is Sidney's, 'See Beauties totall summe summ'd in her face', *Astrophel and Stella SON*, 85.10. For *LUC* see Cheney, ed., *Shakespeare's Poetry*, and White, *Innocent Victims*.

exchange

(A) The primary meaning of the word is familiar: giving one thing in order to receive another in return. Surprisingly, rather than financial, exchanges are usually with physical items such as clothes, abstractions like mutual commitments or even people. There is only one reference to financial documents or **bills** of exchange. The word can also mean transformation. A distinct application occurs in *HAM*, where exchange refers to a pass or phase in fencing. Finally, there is the meaning of sexual congress in 'exchange of flesh'.

(B) An exchange of persons takes place when the Trojans give up Cressida in return for their captured warrior Antenor. Cressida's father, Calchas, asks the Greeks to negotiate the transfer of Cressida because at last they have a sufficiently strong **bargaining counter**:

> You have a Troyan prisoner call'd Antenor,
> Yesterday took; Troy holds him very dear.
> Oft have you (often have you thanks therefore)
> Desir'd my Cressid in right great exchange,
> Whom Troy hath still denied, but this Antenor,
> I know, is such a wrest in their affairs
> That their negotiations all must slack,
> Wanting his manage; and they will almost
> Give us a prince of blood, a son of Priam,
> In change of him. Let him be sent, great princes,
> And he shall buy my daughter; and her presence
> Shall quite strike off all service I have done,
> In most accepted pain.
>
>   *TRO* 3.3.18–30

A fascinating aspect of this proposed arrangement is that it is designed to clear all obligations. In practice, the exchange fatally disrupts a crucial compact that has taken place in the previous scene: the exchange of lovers' vows between Troilus and Cressida followed by the physical consummation of their love. The word 'exchange' occurs only once in this play (twice if 'change', which has the same meaning in the same speech, is counted), but it is *the* play most preoccupied with exchanges.

The idea of 'exchange' as unequal – someone getting the better of the transaction – is captured by Claudio in his public exchange of love vows with Hero: 'Lady, as you are mine, I am yours. I give away myself for you, and dote upon the exchange' (*ADO* 2.1.308–9). At first blush this might seem an admirable assertion of love's independence from the world of **mercantile** exchange, but on closer scrutiny it is rather disingenuous. This proposal has been preceded by Claudio's inquiry about whether Hero is an only child (who will inherit her father's property) and is succeeded by a distasteful display of male proprietorial authority. What Claudio has produced is an elegant verbal formulation that ostensibly elevates emotional exchange above the exchange of the market-place. This piece of verbal virtuosity creates the suspicion that suavity substitutes for sincerity as the whiff of commerce attaches to the more delicate aroma of romance.

Camillo, eager to obtain a disguise for the young prince Florizel, offers the wayfarer Autolycus an exchange of garments and financial inducement to expedite the deal. The delighted rogue celebrates an arrangement that has furnished him with better clothes in addition to a cash payment: 'What an exchange had this been, without boot! What a boot is here, with this exchange!' (*WT* 4.4.674–6). (See entry on **boot**.)

Changing sex or identity by means of disguise is fairly common in Shakespeare, something that makes Jessica blush with embarrassment when she adopts the attire of a page to escape from her father, Shylock. As she says to her waiting lover, Lorenzo: 'I am glad 'tis night, you do not look on me, / For I am much asham'd of my exchange' (*MV* 2.6.34–5). Transformation is what she means, but the word 'exchange' reverberates with unconscious suggestion of her religion and social identity. In Darko Tresnjak's superb production for New York's Theatre for a New Audience at the Swan Theatre, Stratford-upon-Avon, in 2007, Nicole Lowrance's Jessica seemed deeply damaged by her experience. This unusually gentle Lorenzo (Vince Nappo) seemed destined for a difficult future.

Othello also uses the word in this sense when he affirms to Iago that he would never suffer the anguish of uncertainty were he to receive any indication of Desdemona's infidelity:

> No! to be once in doubt
> Is once to be resolv'd. Exchange me for a goat,
> When I shall turn the business of my soul
> To such exsufflicate and blown surmises,
> Matching thy inference.
> *OTH* 3.3.179–83

'Transform me into a goat' is Othello's meaning.

The only reference to financial documents known as 'bills of exchange' is to be found in *SHR*, where a character described as Pedant is accosted by Tranio and persuaded that anyone coming from Mantua to Padua does so in peril of his life. The wayfarer replies: 'Alas, sir, it is worse for me than so, / For I have bills for money by exchange / From Florence, and must here deliver them' (4.2.88–90). In one sense this is a completely trivial example, but in a play deeply engaged with emotional, matrimonial and financial exchanges it adds a further touch to this social universe.

Guilefully choreographing the fatal scene of swordplay in *HAM*, Claudius exclaims: 'Set me the stoups of wine upon that table. / If Hamlet give the first or second hit, / Or quit in answer of the third exchange, / Let all the battlements their ord'nance fire' (5.2.267–70). Exchange means 'bout' or 'engagement', which requires an adjudication or concession as to whether a hit has been effected and if so by which party.

(C) For a contextualizing discussion of the Calchas incident and quantification in *TRO* see Thomas, *The Moral Universe of Shakespeare's Problem Plays*. Leggatt, *Shakespeare's Tragedies*, is also highly relevant here. For details on bills of exchange see entries on bills and **bonds**. For thorough exploration of the financial and human dimensions see Sullivan, *The Rhetoric of Credit*; Turner, *Shakespeare's Twenty-First Century Economics*; Magnusson, 'Voice potential: language and symbolic capital in *Othello*' in Alexander, ed., *Shakespeare and Language*; Parker and Hartman, eds, *Shakespeare and the Question of Theory*; Wynne-Davies, ed., *Much Ado About Nothing* and *The Taming of the Shrew*; Bate, *Shakespeare and Ovid*; Lyon, *The Merchant of Venice*.

exchequer

(A) This word simply means the national treasury or large store of finance. Whether employed in a serious or comic context the strategic political significance of finance is strongly in evidence. Interestingly, there are, too, metaphorical applications.

(B) The physical sense of the exchequer as a chest of gold is illustrated three times in *1H4*, with Falstaff evidently anticipating easy access to it when Hal becomes King. During the robbery at Gadshill Falstaff becomes breathless after his associates have concealed his horse. This leads to his gasping avowal: ' 'Sblood, I'll not bear my own flesh so far afoot again for all the coin in thy father's exchequer' (2.2.35–7).

When Hal reveals that he has been reconciled with the King and the trouble over the Gadshill robbery has been resolved, so that now he may 'do anything', Falstaff immediately responds, 'Rob me the exchequer' (3.3.182–3). Falstaff uses the word more frequently than any other character (four times). His fantasy of gaining access to an infinite supply of **money** is illustrated by his vision of transforming the merry wives, Ford and Page, into 'exchequers': 'I will be cheaters to them both, and they shall be exchequers to me' (*WIV* 1.3.69–71). The fat knight works in a neat pun with 'cheaters', as the 'escheate' was an official of the

Exchequer. Hence a verbal quibble can turn deception into authorized activity, a trick Falstaff effects with audacious verbal dexterity in *1H4*, when he endeavours to transform highway robbery into something both legitimate and glamorous: 'Let us be Diana's foresters, gentlemen of the shade, minions of the moon, and let men say we be men of good government, being govern'd, as the sea is, by our noble and chaste mistress the moon, under whose countenance we steal' (1.2.25–9).The closing pun on 'countenance' to mean 'authority' or 'patronage', as well as 'face', clinches the argument. Falstaff's overflowing verbal exchequer is frequently called into service to empty the financial exchequer of other characters.

The dispossessed Bolingbroke provides an intriguing application when expressing his gratitude to those who have come to support him on his return from exile: 'Evermore thank's the exchequer of the poor, / Which, till my infant fortune comes to years, / Stands for my bounty' (*R2* 2.3.65–7). The poor, of course, have only thanks to offer. Bolingbroke's apologetic comment contains within it the prospect of being able to provide more material rewards once he has command of significant financial resources.

It is worth noting the metaphorical use of the term by Valentine when picking up on the financial terms, 'spends', 'borrows', **'bankrupt'**. In his verbal contest with Thurio, he makes a final thrust at his adversary with the comment: 'You have an exchequer of words and, I think, no other treasure to give your followers; for it appears by their bare liveries that they live by your bare words' (*TGV* 2.4.43–6).

SON 67 also employs exchequer metaphorically, incorporating it in a financial conceptual field that includes 'bankrout', 'gains', 'wealth'.

(C) Relevant here is McAlindon's chapter on 'Falstaffian wit' in *Shakespeare Minus 'Theory'*. Parker, *Shakespeare from the Margins*, ch. 4, explores the language of *WIV*. Bloom, *The Invention of the Human*, Ruiter, *Shakespeare's Festive History*, Schiffer, ed., *Shakespeare's Sonnets*, and Edmondson and Wells, *Shakespeare's Sonnets*, are germane to this discussion.

exhibiter

(A) The proposer or mover of a **bill** in parliament is an exhibiter.

(B) Employed only once, in *H5*, Canterbury confides in his colleague Ely that the parliamentary bill designed to deprive the Church of half its assets may yet be thwarted. The key figure is the new King, Henry V: 'He seems indifferent; / Or rather swaying more upon our part / Than cherishing th' exhibiters against us' (1.1.72–4). Canterbury sets out a strategy designed to secure the King's support by offering to finance the war in France.

(C) See Introduction. Also Brennan, *Henry V*; Holderness, ed., *Shakespeare's History Plays*.

exhibition

(A) This word has two meanings: a financial allowance or endowment (a term still current in some British universities) and a gift or present. It is also used once malapropistically by Verges to Dogberry mistaking the word for 'commission' (*ADO* 4.2.5).

(B) Antonio, having determined to send his son Proteus off to court, assures him that he will have financial support equal to that of his friend, Valentine: 'What maintenance he from his friends receives, / Like exhibition thou shalt have from me' (*TGV* 1.3.68–9).

Likewise, accepting his commission to fight against the Ottomites, Othello requests the Duke make appropriate provision for his bride, Desdemona: 'I crave fit disposition for my wife, / Due reference of place and exhibition, / With such accommodation and besort / As levels with her breeding' (*OTH* 1.3.236–9).

CYM provides an additional example which is by no means obvious from the context. Iachimo, attempting to seduce Imogen, claims that her husband Post-humus is spending the money she gave him on prostitutes: 'To be partner'd / With tomboys hir'd with that self exhibition / Which your own coffers yield' (1.6.121–3).

After the chaos of the opening scene of *LR*, the Duke of Gloucester is bewil-dered: 'Kent banish'd thus? And France in choler parted? / And the King gone to-night? Prescrib'd his pow'r, / Confin'd to exhibition? All this done / Upon the gad?' (1.2.23–6). No longer master of the realm's finances, Lear is a dependant.

Emilia uses the word to mean 'gift' or 'present' when confiding to Desdemona that she, like many women, could be seduced:

> Marry, I would not do such a thing for a joint-ring,
> nor for measures of lawn, nor for gowns, petticoats,
> nor caps, nor any petty exhibition; but, for all the
> whole world – 'ud's pity, who would not make
> her husband a cuckold to make him a monarch?
> I should venture purgatory for't.
>
> *OTH* 4.3.72–7

In admitting this she has the wit and sophistry to justify herself!

(C) See Orlin, ed., *Othello*; Schlueter, ed., *Two Gentlemen of Verona*; Crystal, '*Think on my Words': Exploring Shakespeare's Language*.

expense

(A) Financial outlay; lavish expenditure or extravagance; and the using up or exhaustion of resources, are the three meanings attaching to this word.

(B) A messenger responding to Exeter's question about the loss of French terri-tories – 'How were they lost? What treachery was us'd?' – provides a prosaic answer:

> No treachery, but want of men and money.
> . . .
> One would have ling'ring wars with little cost;
> Another would fly swift, but wanteth wings;

> A third thinks, without expense at all,
> By guileful fair words peace may be obtain'd.
>
> *1H6* 1.1.68–77

In this case 'expense' simply means 'financial outlay'.

Quite different is the implication of the aristocratic but impecunious suitor to Mistress Page in *WIV*. Fenton explains to Anne why her father will not countenance him as a son-in-law: 'He doth object I am too great of birth, / And that my state being gall'd with my expense, / I seek to heal it only by his wealth' (3.4.4–6). 'Extravagance' is the implication of 'expense' here. Likewise, when Henry VIII receives an inventory of Cardinal Wolsey's personal possessions he is struck by the magnitude of the financial activity: 'What piles of wealth hath he accumulated / To his own portion! and what expense by th'hour / Seems to flow from him!' (*H8* 3.2.107–9). Unlike the profligate Fenton, Wolsey is more adroit in acquisition than lavish in expenditure.

*SON*s 94 and 129 both employ expense in the sense of 'using up', 'dissipating' or 'exhausting'. Characters, who are virtuous, judicious and circumspect, 'They rightly do inherit heaven's graces, / And husband nature's riches from expense' (94.5–6). Unlike this garnering up of energy and vitality, conserving rather than squandering, lust produces a destructive loss of spiritual and physical resources: 'Th'expense of spirit in a waste of shame / Is lust in action' (129.1–2).

(C) Schiffer, ed., *Shakespeare's Sonnets*, Edmondson and Wells, *Shakespeare's Sonnets*, Fineman, *Shakespeare's Perjured Eye*, all explore the *SON*s with subtlety and insight. McMullan, ed., *Henry VIII*, Arden 3, makes many fine comments on 'Truth and Temperance', 85–93. White, *The Merry Wives of Windsor*, explores the financial and social dimensions of the play with finesse.

exploit, exploits

(A) In the modern application of the word the first syllable is unstressed, the second heavily stressed; here both syllables are stressed with the heavier weight generally falling on the second. The word has two principal meanings: a dangerous enterprise or an honorific, usually military, action. These meanings are usually quite distinct, though there are examples where a character attributes honour to an action about which the audience may have reservations. On two occasions (*MND* and *ERR*) the word is embedded in a comic context. On a single occasion (*TRO*) the word is used to mean sexual intrigue. There is no application of the word in the modern sense of an individual or agency securing a disproportionate or unfair allocation of rewards arising from a transaction involving two or more parties.

(B) Characteristic of the term is its employment in *AWW* where the young French courtiers go off to war in Italy to prove their manhood: 'It well may serve / A nursery to our gentry, who are sick / For breathing and exploit' (1.2.15–17). The Bishop of Ely enthusing Henry V for the assault on France urges: 'and my thrice-puissant liege / Is in the very May-morn of his youth, / Ripe for exploits and mighty enterprises' (*H5* 1.2.119–21).

The achievements of another great military figure, the eponymous hero Titus Andronicus, are hailed by a Goth in similar terms: 'Whose high exploits and honourable deeds / Ingrateful Rome requites with foul contempt' (*TIT* 5.1.11–12). Here the military achievements are accentuated by the adjective 'high' linked with 'honourable deeds'. Exploit as a famous or daring action is made manifest when young John Talbot pleads with his famous father to allow him to stay and fight against the French even though, because of the fearful odds, doing so may **cost** him his life: 'Flight cannot stain the honour you have won, / But mine it will, that no exploit have done' (*1H6* 4.5.26–7).

The term is tarnished, but still employed in the context of fighting, when used by Poins in outlining a strategy for the robbery at Gadshill to expose Falstaff, simultaneously, as a liar and a coward: 'and then will they adventure upon the exploit themselves, which they shall have no sooner achiev'd but we'll set upon them' (*1H4* 1.2.171–3). The Lord Chief Justice perceives the action as a dubious escapade: 'Your day's service at Shrewsbury hath a little gilded over your night's exploit on Gadshill. You may thank th'unquiet time for your quiet o'erposting that action' (*2H4* 1.2.148–51). The check affords the Lord Chief Justice a fine opportunity for exercising his delight in witty antitheses (day's/night's; unquiet/quiet) but shifts the territory covered by the word so that the action involved need not be valorous or in any way admirable. Indeed, the term is occasionally applied to actions that are brutal or have terrible consequences. Macbeth, hearing the news that Macduff has fled to England, thereby thwarting his intended assassination, whispers in an aside, 'Time, thou anticipat'st my dread exploits' (*MAC* 4.1.143–4). Evidently, there is no conception of heroic action here, only unjustified violence. Shockingly, Macbeth, having missed his adversary, orders the slaughter of his wife and children. Richard III asks his page, 'Know'st thou not any whom corrupting gold / Will tempt unto a close exploit of death?' (*R3* 4.2.34–5). The last phrase signifies secret murder. The repugnant nature of this proposition is exacerbated by 'corrupting gold' and 'close': here everything is furtive. Richard is also responsible for devaluing the term when, in a pre-battle oration to his troops, he denounces Richmond's invasion as a 'fond exploit' (5.3.330): a foolish and naive adventure.

In *LUC* the poet makes a comparison between Tarquin's ravishment of Lucrece and marauding soldiers confronting helpless victims: 'Obdurate vassals fell exploits effecting, / In bloody death and ravishment delighting' (429–30). The 'exploits' are clearly vile, murderous actions.

Brutus, hoping his old associate Caius Ligarius will join the conspiracy, is dismayed to find him sick, but is soon reassured: 'I am not sick, if Brutus have in hand / Any exploit worthy the name of honor.' Brutus confidently responds, 'Such an exploit have I in hand, Ligarius, / Had you a healthful ear to hear it' (*JC* 2.1.316–19). It is noteworthy here that exploit is taken to mean bold action or undertaking but for the audience there is no automatic assumption that such an action is honourable. Brutus can conceive of no more honourable action than the preservation of republican democracy, but the action required to achieve this end is bloody assassination.

The Countess of Auvergne, having devised a trap for the English hero, Talbot, reflects: 'The plot is laid. If all things fall out right, / I shall as famous be by this exploit / As Scythian Tomyris by Cyrus' death' (*1H6* 2.3.4–6). Here the word means 'famous action'. What is intriguing is the association of assassination with fame. The infamy of the action is nullified by virtue of being patriotic. Clearly there is an undertow here as Tomyris, even though she killed Cyrus the Great in battle, kept her victim's head in a wineskin filled with blood. The countess appears to be no more squeamish than her historical model so that the 'exploit' hardly carries with it an association of honorific action.

Helena, believing that she is being mocked and ridiculed by Lysander and Demetrius, denounces them for engaging in such an unworthy game: 'A trim exploit, a manly enterprise, / To conjure tears up in a poor maid's eyes / With your derision! None of noble sort / Would so offend a virgin' (*MND* 3.2.157–60). The adjective 'trim', meaning courageous, is employed sarcastically. The implication is that an exploit should be dignified, courageous and honorific.

Uniquely, exploit is used for a romantic intrigue in *TRO*. Paris, noted for his frivolity, asks Pandarus why Troilus will be missing from the royal table: 'What exploit's in hand? Where sups he to-night?' (3.1.81–2).

(C) For a guide to the intricacies of pronunciation in the plays see Coye, *Pronouncing Shakespeare's Words*; Wright provides an extensive exploration of hendiadys and the significance of diverse stress patterns in *Hearing the Measures*. Martindale and Taylor, *Shakespeare and the Classics*, are informative on several points as is Hadfield, *Shakespeare and Republicansim*.

faction, factionary, factious

(A) These words are used in different ways, but the concept that lies at their heart is opposition or dissention. Most frequently the noun is used to designate a knot of people conscious of their opposition to some other group. Usually employed in a neutral way it can have a pejorative application, but in such cases it is qualified by an appropriate adjective, e.g. 'pernicious' faction. Intriguingly, 'factions' is always pejorative, even without a qualifying adjective. Split or division is the second meaning. The process of the formation of a common cause is a third application. The fourth meaning is abuse or insult. Finally, it is used to mean dissention. Factionary, unique to *COR*, means partisan. Factious, broadly implies behaviour which is oppositional. But it is also used in the sense 'to form a faction'. A third application denotes rebellious or seditious action rather than mere opposition.

(B) Faction innocent of political significance is apparent in *TGV*, where the singularly gentle outlaws promptly decide that their latest captive will make an ideal leader of their band: 'This fellow were a king for our wild faction!' (4.1.37).

Thersites comments dismissively on the antagonistic Greek warriors, Ajax, Achilles and Patroclus, 'I will keep where there is wit stirring, and leave the faction of fools' (*TRO* 2.1.118–19). The meaning is 'party of fools', though the irony is that the group is riven by the competitive hostility of Ajax and Achilles.

When Lucius announces that Cassius and unidentifiable associates seek admission to his house, Brutus says in an aside: 'They are the faction' (*JC* 2.1.77) – the conspirators who have united with Cassius to assassinate Julius Caesar.

An oblique but illuminating example occurs in *TIM*. The Second Senator, in dismissing Alcibiades' plea for clemency on behalf of one of his men found guilty of murder, claims that his habitual drunkenness accentuates his violent propensities: 'In that beastly fury / He has been known to commit outrages /

And cherish factions' (3.5.70–2). There is no implication in this play of any political agitation by this shadowy character, but it would appear that there is anxiety that insubordination is in itself subversive. The Senator perceives the behaviour as hovering between political dissension and unruly behaviour. In modern parlance the murderer is something of a 'loose cannon' associating with groups noted for their disrespectful attitude towards authority. That last phrase probably means 'support subversive elements', as the Riverside editors suggest. This leaves open to question the meaning of 'subversive'. Does this interpretation imply 'political agitators' or 'unruly elements'? The latter seems more likely given the little we know of this character, but the expression 'cherish factions' is richly ambiguous – perhaps conveniently so.

1H6 provides three examples of the meaning of an oppositional group, two of which are neutral and one pejorative. Moreover, it also provides another use of the word in the sense of 'split' or 'division'. In the famous Temple Garden scene Richard Plantagenet proclaims the integrity of his group and enduring opposition to the Duke of Somerset and his supporters, symbolically marking the antagonism by the elevation of the white rose over the red rose of his **rivals**: 'And, by my soul, this pale and angry rose, / As cognisance of my blood-drinking hate, / Will I forever and my faction wear, / Until it wither with me to my grave, / Or flourish to the height of my degree' (2.4.107–11). There is no plainer example of faction signifying a clearly defined and determined group.

A coolly neutral application carrying the suggestion of 'party' or 'group', is apparent in *3H6*. Richard Gloucester, weighing up the relative strengths of the forces of the Yorkists and Queen Margaret's Lancastrians, comments: 'If she have time to breathe, be well assur'd / Her faction will be full as strong as ours' (5.3.16–17).

When, in *1H6*, the Duke of Burgundy deserts the English monarch to align himself with the French, his letter proclaims that he has, ' "Forsaken your pernicious faction / And join'd with Charles, the rightful King of France" ' (4.1.59–60). The put-down is emphatic as the English are not only reduced to the level of a mere group, but the qualifying adjective 'pernicious' intimates that they are destructive.

Characteristic of the term 'factions' is its adversely pejorative connotation. The Messenger bringing news of English defeats in France ascribes the setback to rivalries in the English court: 'Amongst the soldiers it is muttered, / That here you maintain several factions; / And whilst a field should be dispatch'd and fought, / You are disputing of your generals' (*1H6* 1.1.70–3). 'Factionalism', then, is inherently destructive of the necessary unity of purpose.

Warwick, again in the Temple Garden scene, emphasizes the historical significance of the conflict that has spilled over into fierce opposition: 'And here I prophesy: this brawl to-day, / Grown to this faction in the Temple Garden, / Shall send between the Red Rose and the White / A thousand souls to death and deadly night' (2.4.124–7). 'Faction' here seems to mean 'split' or 'division' and the formation of two hostile groups. Intrinsic to factionalism is irreconcilable, and possibly bloody, conflict. Indeed, the presence of the beautiful emblems here heightens the incongruity between representations of principles in decorative insignia and the willingness to embrace the wanton destruction of life that must follow from the collision.

The sense of a faction as the *formation* of a united group is given clear expression by means of antithesis when the wily old Nestor refers to the breach between the Greeks' battering rams, Achilles and Ajax: 'their fraction is more our wish than their faction' (*TRO* 2.3.98–9). Their rivalry, Nestor implies, will make it easy for the Greek leadership to manipulate them, whereas any coming together will remove the scope for playing on their mutual distrust and quest for supremacy. The concept of division is of singular significance in this play where even the gods are given to taking sides. As Ulysses puts it, in commenting on the **achievements** of Achilles: 'Whose glorious deeds but in these fields of late / Made emulous missions 'mongst the gods themselves, / And drave great Mars to faction' (3.3.188–90). In Book V of the *Iliad*, Mars does, indeed, intervene on the side of the Trojans.

In expressing his determination to retain the country wench Audrey, Touchstone the Fool unleashes a tirade against her rustic suitor William. Incongruously, but characteristically, his threat to murder or batter the poor yokel includes the warning, 'I will bandy with thee in faction' (*AYL* 5.1.55). In other words, 'trade insults': the only occasion when faction is used in this sense. However, the proximity of this word to the adjective 'factious' is apparent from the phrase 'factious bandying of their favourites' in *1H6* (4.1.190).

Attempting to convince Cleopatra that he must return to Rome, Mark Antony cites the impending confrontation between Octavius Caesar and Pompey: 'Equality of two domestic powers / Breed scrupulous faction' (*ANT* 1.3.47–8). 'Faction' means 'dissention'. People who would normally carry on with their business become quarrelsome even over trivial considerations ('scrupulous') when there is no unitary authority.

In pleading with the Volscian guards to allow him access to Coriolanus, Menenius refers to his past, undeviating, support for his hero: 'Prithee, fellow, remember my name is Menenius, always factionary on the party of your general' (*COR* 5.2.28–30). 'Always taking his side, being a resolute and dependable ally' is what Menenius signifies here. It is not surprising that this sole use occurs in Shakespeare's most political play. In this social universe to be is to be political.

Perversely, Hector seeks to *unite* his quarrelsome enemies so that they can get back to fighting: 'I have a roisting challenge sent amongst / The dull and factious nobles of the Greeks' (*TRO* 2.2.208–9). The hendyadistic 'dull and factious' conveys a lack of vitality so that what energy there is finds expression in querulousness.

Having provided a recitation of his deeds in placing his brother Edward on the throne, Richard Gloucester denounces Queen Elizabeth for her former adherence to the Lancastrian cause: 'In all which time you and your husband Grey / Were factious for the house of Lancaster; / And, Rivers, so were you. Was not your husband / In Margaret's battle at Saint Albans slain?' (*R3* 1.3.126–9). This must mean 'supportive of', displaying 'readiness to ally themselves' with the

Lancastrians or 'forging a group to back them'. The dying King Edward tries to secure amity among the hostile groups surrounding him. Listing them he says, 'You have been factious one against the other' (2.1.20).

Whereas individuals feel no discomfort about identifying themselves with a faction, the term factious is generally applied contemptuously, implying agitator or disturber of the peace, one prone to provoking conflict. Hence as Queen Margaret and her associates prepare to do battle with the Duke of York, Clifford cries, 'He is a traitor, let him to the Tower, / And chop away that factious pate of his' (*2H6* 5.1.134–5). King Henry VI denounces the Duke of York with the words, 'Thou factious Duke of York, descend my throne, / And kneel for grace and mercy at my feet: / I am thy sovereign' (*3H6* 1.1.74–6). He clearly means 'rebellious' or 'seditious'.

The idea that to be factious can be admirable is expressed by Casca, who, having listened to Cassius' diatribe against Caesar, says, 'Hold, my hand. / Be factious for redress of all these griefs, / And I will set this foot of mine as far / As who goes farthest' (*JC* 1.3.117–20). The conception here is that those on the margins of political life have no option but to form oppositional groups if they are to restrain or overcome those wielding power. Casca is, of course, the first of the assassins to strike Caesar.

(C) Several essays in Alexander, ed., *Shakespeare and Politics*, Hattaway, ed., *Shakespeare's History Plays*, and Smallwood, ed., *Players of Shakespeare 6*, are relevant here. Also stimulating is Goy-Blanquet, *Shakespeare's Early History Plays*. Each of Arden 3 editions of the *H6* plays has an excellent Introduction: Burns, ed., *King Henry VI, Part 1*; Knowles, *King Henry VI, Part 2*; Cox and Rasmussen, *King Henry VI, Part 3*.

factor

(A) A factor is an intermediary, agent, **broker** or representative in commercial or political transactions. The direct, literal meaning is purely economic but it acquires significant metaphorical force when employed in the sphere of **politics**. This highly significant concept is employed only six times: twice in designating economic activities, and four times in the political sphere.

(B) In the opening scene of *ERR*, Egeon, in recounting his travails, refers to business **ventures** of his younger days: 'Our wealth increas'd / By prosperous voyages I often made / To Epidamium, till my factor's death, / And the great care of goods at random left, / Drew me from kind embracements of my spouse' (1.1.39–43). Even this brief comment illustrates the role of the factor handling affairs at the local level so that the merchant or principal guides the enterprise from a distance making only periodic visits to each of his transaction sites.

Iachimo is a gentleman of the first rank but uses the term when pretending to Imogen that he has acted as agent for a group of people in acquiring a present for the Emperor: 'Which I (the factor for the rest) have done / In France' (*CYM* 1.6.188–9).

The transfer to the political sphere is well illustrated by Buckingham's appeal for Richard Gloucester to accept the proffered crown and so prevent its contamination by 'illegitimate' princes:

> Which to recure, we heartily solicit
> Your gracious self to take on you the charge
> And kingly government of this your land:
> Not as protector, steward, substitute,
> Or lowly factor for another's gain;
> But as successively, from blood to blood,
> Your right of birth, your empery, your own.
>
> *R3* 3.7.130–6

Significantly, in the mouth of the aristocrat the factor is seen as a mere drudge, the servant to another man's betterment. A vivid example occurs in the same play when the former Queen, Margaret, provides a catalogue of the deaths of the Yorkists who have paid the price for destroying the Lancastrians. Ultimately, she comes to the arch-villain: 'Richard yet lives, hell's black intelligencer, / Only reserv'd their factor to buy souls / And send them thither' (4.4.71–3). Here is a wonderful conception of Richard as hell's spymaster or go-between (**intelligencer**), used by the devil to trade in souls like some assiduous dealer on behalf of the master-**merchant**. This portrayal elevates Richard to the position of the most murderous participant in the Wars of the Roses while simultaneously diminishing him to the status of unknowing servitude. By contrast, Pompey addressing the triumvirs prior to their negotiations refers to them as the most highly elevated factors: 'To you all three, / The senators alone of this great world, / Chief factors for the gods' (*ANT* 2.6.8–10).

Finally, Hal's assurance to his father, Henry IV, that he is about to outclass the charismatic Hotspur, once more reveals the aristocrat's disdain for the mere factor or agent:

> Percy is but my factor, good my lord,
> To engross up glorious deeds on my behalf;
> And I will call him to so strict account
> That he shall render every glory up,
> Yea, even the slightest worship of his time,
> Or I will tear the reckoning from his heart.
>
> *1H4* 3.2.147–52

'Factor', '**account**', '**reckoning**', reveal the way in which the language of commerce is not only commandeered by lovers, as for instance by Portia and Bassanio, but also by politicians and warriors: commerce as the great social fact of the age is employed to illuminate the rates of **exchange** and **profitable** encounters of lovers, who usually expunge any unsavoury contamination by subsuming the language of commerce into the language of love, as well as dealings in the arenas of war and politics where commercial language and concepts are employed but are disparaged in the process.

(C) Agnew, *Worlds Apart*, esp. 175, provides insightful and incisive commentary on the implications of this word. Brenner, *Merchants and Revolution*, Carruthers,

City of Capital, and Stevenson, *Praise and Paradox: Merchants and Craftsmen in Elizabethan Popular Literature*, provide a vivid picture of the network of **trade** and commerce and the human agency involved in this flow of activity. Deats, ed., *Antony and Cleopatra* contains several essays that impinge on the incident cited here, while Thomas, *Shakespeare's Roman Worlds*, 128–33, discusses Pompey and the incident in detail.

far-fet

(A) The single occurrence of this word intimates far-sighted, guileful, or scheming, collocating almost inevitably with '**policy**'.

(B) Somerset, defending his failure in France, sneers at the capacity of his rival York: 'If York, with all his far-fet policy, / Had been the Regent there in stead of me, / He never would have stay'd in France so long' (*2H6* 3.1.293–5). This fascinating compound is saturated with irony, so the term signifies something admirable in the military sense, probably combining far-seeing with strategic cunning.

(C) See Goy-Blanquet, *Shakespeare's Early History Plays*; Knowles, ed., *Henry VI Part 2*, Arden 3, Introduction.

fashion, fashionable, fashion-mongers, fashion-monging

(A) A word with multiple meanings, fashion possesses some interesting economic and political implications. The verb, meaning to form or shape; to transform; or to contrive, is of particular political significance. As a noun the meanings are: workmanship or craftsmanship; the prevailing style of clothes, manners or behaviour; style, mode or observance; disposition or way of viewing matters; conventional or customary behaviour; caprice or whim; type, kind or social group; name, title or character. The plural relates to a disease of the mouth and nose, afflicting horses (*SHR* 3.2.51). The verb 'fashion in' is to 'work in'; the adjective 'fashion-monging' intimates enthusiastic pursuit of the latest fashions – to be a fashion-monger. Fashionable implies shallowness.

(B) *JC* provides some fascinating examples and contains a particularly difficult interpretive problem. Straightforward enough is Brutus' warm response to the suggestion of recruiting Caius Ligarius to the conspiracy: 'Send him hither, and I'll fashion him' (2.1.220). Evidently he means persuade him of the wisdom of the action and prepare him for his role. Put brutally, 'mould him to our purpose'.

Much more testing is his earlier usage in the famous orchard soliloquy when he is persuading *himself* to participate in the conspiracy. Having failed to indict Caesar of **usurp**ing power, he turns to the question of what Caesar might become: 'And since the quarrel / Will bear no color for the thing he is, / Fashion it thus: that what he is, augmented, / Would run to these and these extremities' (2.1.28–31). What does the key phrase 'Fashion it thus' mean? It seems to reside mid-way between the passive, 'consider', 'let's look at it this way', and the more active 'represent', 'let's shape or put the construction in this form'. Brutus' soliloquy is an attempt to examine the case for acting against Caesar, but emotionally the decision has already been made. Brutus is too much attached to the ideas of integrity and nobility to stoop to twist the argument, but that 'fashion' effects a crucial elision. Nowhere else is the application of the word so oblique.

When the detached Cicero responds to Casca's near-hysterical description of strange happenings and the ascription of supernatural causes to them, he provides a sober caution: 'Indeed, it is a strange-disposed time; / But men may construe things after their fashion, / Clean from the purpose of the things themselves' (1.3.33–5). Cicero's 'fashion' means 'manner, disposition or inclination'. The play teems with problems and events that call for interpretation. Despite their shared heritage each individual brings his own peculiar predisposition to analysis and interpretation. Cicero's caution is well aimed and could act as an epigraph for the play. This is a world of flux and uncertainty and each character is susceptible to his predilections and preconceptions.

Similarly, in the previous scene Cassius suggests to Brutus that they ask Casca for an **account** of the off-stage events that he has witnessed: 'And he will (after his sour fashion) tell you / What hath proceeded worthy note to-day' (1.2.180–1). Casca does, indeed, provide a vivid account, but one so coloured by his manner or affected style that it is hardly a disinterested representation.

Even the 'fashion' normally ascribed to clothes and conventional behaviour takes an odd turn in this play. In the pursuit of a dignified death the losers resort to suicide. So prevalent is it that Brutus says, preparing for his own death, 'slaying is the word, / It is a deed in fashion' (5.5.4–5).

This word, so persistent in *JC*, is employed by Mark Antony to comment on the lack of originality in Lepidus. His psychological predisposition is to follow rather than lead; to accept rather than initiate:

> A barren-spirited fellow; one that feeds
> On objects, arts, and imitations,
> Which, out of use and stal'd by other men,
> Begin his fashion. Do not talk of him
> But as a property.
>
> 4.1.36–40

Lepidus' conception of being in the vanguard – adopting the manners and **practices** he ascribes to the man of mode – exposes his stupidity. He lacks the wit to know what is the latest style or technique – or what is 'in fashion'. This oddly brutal dismissal by Antony is instructive because it captures something on the surface of politics. Kudos attaches to the discernment to adapt in such a way as to always appear the new man, possessed of stylish modernity. The irony here is that Antony is addressing Octavius Caesar who possesses that instinct to a remarkable degree – something accentuated much later on Pompey's galley when Antony advises Octavius, 'Be a child o'th'time' (*ANT* 2.7.100). Here is, indeed, the character who is the antithesis of Lepidus: he smells the future on the breeze and responds accordingly. Antony's apparently churlish speech aimed at 'placing' Lepidus, carries within it a great deal of circulatory energy, thanks in large part to this key word 'fashion'. Not only is Octavius always on the cusp of fashion but this attribute also gives him a critical edge in fashioning or shaping events rather than merely responding to them.

Borachio, the character most addicted to the word, employs it in the sense of to 'contrive' or 'manage' when describing his scheme for disrupting the planned marriage between Hero and Claudio: 'I will so fashion the matter . . . that jealousy shall be call'd assurance, and all the preparation overthrown' (*ADO* 2.2.46–50). A little later he describes the process of the deception in a drunken dialogue animated by the word, alighting on a felicitous expression: 'But seest thou not what a deformed thief this fashion is?' (3.3.124). Fashion is a 'deformed thief' because it persuades people to engage in extravagant outlays to maintain appearances – frequently of exaggerated elaboration and **expense**. As Conrade puts it, 'fashion wears out more apparel than the man'. Not only is 'fashion' wasteful, according to Conrade, but by its very nature it is capricious. Criticizing Borachio for losing the thread of his story he adds, 'But art not thou thyself giddy with the fashion too, that thou hast shifted out of thy tale into telling me of the fashion?' (3.3.140–3). Economics, psychology and social behaviour are all subtly interwoven in a dialogue involving two drunks.

This play in which 'fashion' occurs more frequently than elsewhere, also has an interesting case of the verb used in the sense of to form or shape. Don John the Bastard insists that he will not shape his behaviour to gain the approval of the social elite presided over by his brother Don Pedro: 'I had rather be a canker in a hedge than a rose in his grace, and it better fits my blood to be disdain'd of all than to fashion a carriage to rob love from any' (1.3.27–30). Taciturnity is his natural mode; conviviality goes against the grain. Here is a character who refuses to 're-fashion' himself even for political advantage – a strangely attractive characteristic found in this strange villain. He does, nevertheless, exhibit a facility for punning and carefully crafted antitheses.

The capacity to shape and form others need not be something contrived. As Kate points out in extolling the virtues of her charismatic husband Hotspur, he provoked emulation: 'He was the mark and glass, copy and book, / That fashion'd others' (*2H4*, 2.3.31–2).

Irresistible is the paradoxical case provided by the conniving tribune, Sicinius. Stirring the plebeians to revoke their election of Coriolanus to the office of consul, he emphasizes how the eponymous hero revealed his contempt even at the moment of seeking favour:

> forget not
> With what contempt he wore the humble weed,
> How in his suit he scorn'd you; but your loves,
> Thinking upon his services, took from you
> Th'apprehension of his present portance,
> Which most gibingly, ungravely, he did fashion
> After the inveterate hate he bears you.
>
> 2.3.220–6

According to Sinicius, rather than 'fashioning' an appropriate humility, Coriolanus accentuated or 'fashioned' an extreme form of his characteristic arrogance. Coriolanus has, of course, been fashioned into the supreme instrument of war by his mother, who has also inculcated contempt for the **plebeians**. What she can't do is refashion him into a politician. He is incapable of practising the 'insinuating nod' (2.3.99) or stooping, even to the gods.

Having received news of Posthumus' instruction to murder her for presumed infidelity, Imogen employs fashion as clothes: 'Poor I am stale, a garment out of fashion, / And for I am richer than to hang by th'walls, / I must be ripp'd. To pieces with me! O!' (*CYM* 3.4.51–3).

Lear, more straightforwardly, criticizes Mad Tom's sartorial choice: 'You, sir, I entertain for one of my hundred; only I do not like the fashion of your garments. You will say they are Persian, but let them be chang'd' (*LR* 3.6.78–81).

York's objection to Somerset's adoption of the red rose as an insignia is much more severe: here is an observance that is highly provocative: 'Now, by this maiden blossom in my hand, / I scorn thee and thy fashion, peevish boy' (*1H6* 2.4.75–6).

Angelo the goldsmith is thoroughly businesslike when handing over a chain to his client: 'here's the note / How much your chain weighs to the utmost charect, / The fineness of the gold, and chargeful fashion' (*ERR* 4.1.27–9). Workmanship or skilled execution is the meaning here. Characteristic of a play pervaded by economic activity we have a careful break-down of the **bill** for the work with each constituent, quality and **quantity** of material and labour, clearly delineated.

Hermione, protesting at the treatment she has received, maintains that she is not requesting conditions appropriate to her status as Queen, but a standard applicable to *all* women, whatever their personal or social position: 'with immodest hatred / The child-bed privilege denied, which 'longs / To women of all fashion' (*WT* 3.2.102–4). This is, of course, a highly political situation, and part of the immense appeal of Hermione is the dignity, intelligence and vigour with which she demands her rights before the law.

Queen Katherine, on the brink of death, urges her kinsman Lord Capuchius to carry and support her appeal to the King on behalf of her loyal staff. Clearly there is a risk of provoking the King's antagonism because her suit is pressed so fervently. The vigour of the response is a declaration of determination and integrity: 'By heaven, I will, / Or let me lose the fashion of a man!' (*H8* 4.2.158–9). Name, title or stature is the meaning of fashion here. Strikingly in the RSC production at the Swan (1996), Capuchius tore the letter with deliberation as soon as he was out of Katherine's presence, an interpolation that set the demands of political **advantage** over the principles of social duty and personal integrity.

The idea of 'caprice' or 'passing fancy' lies at the heart of Laertes' caution to Ophelia not to be seduced by Hamlet's apparent affection:

> For Hamlet, and the trifling of his favor,
> Hold it as a fashion and a toy in blood,

> A violet in the youth of primy nature,
> Forward, not permanent, sweet, not lasting,
> The perfume and the suppliance of a minute –
> No more.
>
> *HAM* 1.3.5–10

Should the meaning of the word cause any uncertainty, it is resolved in this case by means of elaboration. 'Fashion' here is something lacking fixity or permanence. However, the distinctive flavour is provided by the phrase 'fashion or a toy in blood'. Dalliance is a natural propensity in young men: frivolity, lightness, mobility characterize their inclinations.

Fashion as conventional behaviour is best illustrated by Henry V in his approbation of Fluellen: 'Though it appear a little out of fashion, / There is much care and valor in this Welshman' (*H5* 4.1.83–4). This application includes **custom** or **practice**, something indicated by Rosalind when she appears to deliver the epilogue in *AYL*: 'It is not the fashion to see the lady the epilogue; but it is no more unhandsome than to see the lord the prologue.'

There is a single case of the term 'fashion in', meaning to 'work in'. Troilus in his nervous apprehension seeks to gain some absolute pledge of fidelity from Cressida as she prepares to leave Troy:

> I speak not 'be thou true' as fearing thee,
> For I will throw my glove to Death himself
> That there is no maculation in thy heart;
> But 'be thou true' say I to fashion in
> My sequent protestation: be thou true,
> And I will see thee.
>
> *TRO* 4.4.62–7

This mobile, facilitating, shaping quality of 'fashion' is a vital lubricant affording fluency in the discourse of politics, economics, social life and love.

The unsavoury odour attaching to the sartorial dimension of the word is reflected in 'fashionable' and the compounds 'fashion-mongers' and 'fashion-monging'. Ulysses' famous discourse on the destructive nature of Time includes a telling simile: 'For Time is like a fashionable host / That slightly shakes his parting guest by th'hand, / And with his arms outstretch'd as he would fly, / Grasps in the comer' (3.3.165–8). The '*fashionable* host' is light, inconstant, shallow, facile.

The only other application occurs in another biting play, *TIM*. The Painter, confiding in his equally cynical associate, asserts that the hallmark of fashionable behaviour is to promise without any intention of fulfilling it:

> Promising is the very air o'th'time;
> It opens the eyes of expectation.
> Performance is ever the duller for his act,

And but in the plainer and simpler kind of people
The deed of saying is quite out of use.
To promise is most courtly and fashionable;

5.1.22–7

In this speech the Painter celebrates a fashionable society devoid of honesty or authenticity.

Mercutio railing against modern affectation includes in his diatribe reference to 'these new tuners of accent! ... these strange flies, these fashion-mongers, these pardon-me's, who stand so much on the new form, that they cannot sit at ease on the old bench?' (*ROM* 2.4.29–35).

Equally dismissive, and hardly less eloquent, is the indignant Antonio. Eager to right his niece, he challenges Don Pedro and Claudio, insisting that their swordsmanship and manhood are showy and insubstantial:

I know them, yea,
And what they weigh, even to the utmost scruple –
Scambling, outfacing, fashion-monging boys,
That lie and cog and flout, deprave and slander,
Go anticly, and show outward hideousness,
And speak off half a dozen dang'rous words,

ADO 5.1.92–7

The fashion-monger is the embodiment of the showy, trivial and meretricious style of the fashionable world. To be 'fashionable' is, in general, to be of dubious quality.

It would be difficult to conclude without two further examples of the suspicion attaching to fashion. In providing a catalogue of Richard II's vices and the susceptibilities of youth, Gaunt includes,

Report of fashions in proud Italy,
Whose manners still our tardy, apish nation
Limps after in base imitation.
Where doth the world thrust forth a vanity –
So it be new, there's no respect how vile –
That is not quickly buzz'd into his ears?

R2 2.1.21–6

Intriguingly here is not only the triviality of the new but also its seductiveness. Berowne, in mocking the 'fantastical Spaniard' Armado as 'A man of fire-new words, fashion's own knight' (*LLL* 1.1.178), provides a wonderfully felicitous phrase. Here is a character putting himself forward as the very embodiment of courtly fashion, and in so doing he runs into excess that makes him absurd. 'Fashion', it seems, attracts the naturally weak-minded; the discerning character approaches it with circumspection if not disdain.

135

(C) For a probing of the problematic phrase employed in Brutus' orchard soliloquy, see, for example, Nuttall, *A New Mimisis*, 106–9. Thomas, 'Shakespeare's sources' in Zander, ed., *Julius Caesar*, explores the play's interpretative dilemmas and its multiple presentations and representations; also significant in this context is Drakakis, 'Fashion it thus' in Kamps, ed., *Materialist Shakespeare*. For other essays integral to this discussion, see Alexander, ed., *Shakespeare and Politics*; Wynne-Davies, ed., *Much Ado About Nothing* and *The Taming of the Shrew*; Miola, ed., *The Comedy of Errors*; Londre, ed., *Love's Labour's Lost*; Leggatt, *Shakespeare's Tragedies*; Greenblatt, *Renaissance Self-Fashioning*.

fedary, federary, feodary

(A) Regardless of spelling, this rare word means one who abets: an accomplice or accessory; someone who is a confederate. The three examples combine personal and political implications.

(B) The meaning is unmistakeable in *WT*, where Leontes, crazed with unfounded jealousy, denounces his queen Hermione and his trusty servant Camillo (who has been forced to flee to avoid the King's injunction to poison Polixenes): 'I have said / She's an adult'ress, I have said with whom: / More – she's a traitor, and Camillo is / A federary with her' (2.1.87–90). The emphasis is placed on complicity in underhand dealing of a political nature. The word carries with it a strongly distasteful suggestion of collusion that is profoundly treacherous. The opprobrium attaching to such association is effectively conveyed by Pisano. Having read the letter instructing him to murder Imogen he castigates the material that carries the message: 'O damn'd paper, / Black as the ink that's on thee! Senseless bauble, / Art thou a feodary for this act, and look'st / So virgin-like without?' (*CYM* 3.2.19–22). The implication is clear: the 'feodary' is as morally contaminated as the prime mover; even insensible paper can't evade condemnation! This is a bizarre but unambiguous case, whereas the meaning of Isabella's expression when pleading with Angelo for her brother, who has been condemned to death for the crime of fornication, is anything but self-evident. When Angelo concedes 'We are all frail', her eager riposte is, 'Else let my brother die, / If not a fedary, but only he, / Owe and succeed thy weakness' (*MM* 2.4.121–3). Her argument is that all men are susceptible to sexual temptation. It is, therefore, unjust to execute her brother as the vice or activity cannot be eliminated with his death. The confederates of this vice will continue in the same way.

(C) Lever, ed., *Measure for Measure*, Arden 2, fn 61, has a concise comment on this last example:

> 'Feodary' ('Fedarie' F) combines two meanings: (i) confederate, accomplice . . . from Lat. *foedus*; (ii) feudatory, i.e. hereditary tenant, from *Lat. feodarius*. The sense is thus: 'If my brother has no associates in this weakness you refer to, and no man else will in the way of nature inherit it, then let him die.

For an excellent discussion of this play's language see Kermode, *Shakespeare's*

Language; Ryan, ed., *Shakespeare: The Last Plays*, is also highly relevant to this entry.

fee

(A) This commonplace word has a surprising range of applications, though apart from the sense of payment or reward, which is the most general meaning, the noun is used in other senses uniquely or rarely. They are, **value** or **worth**; possession or property; dependant, vassal or beneficiary. The verb signifies to pay or recompense; to purchase or procure. The adjectival use intimates paid, hired or bribed.

(B) The sense of payment or reward arises frequently. Angelo, the goldsmith – in a play replete with the language of commerce – seeks to secure payment for his chain by recourse to the law: 'Here is thy fee, arrest him, officer' (*ERR* 4.1.76). More colourfully, Buckingham promises that he will be successful in wooing the Mayor and citizens on behalf of Richard: 'Doubt not, my lord, I'll play the orator / As if the golden fee for which I plead / Were for myself' (*R3* 3.5.95–7). Hamlet provides the sole example of fee as 'value' or 'worth' when he protests that he has nothing to fear in following the Ghost: 'I do not set my life at a pin's fee' (*HAM* 1.4.65).

Hippolyta refers to Theseus' neck as her property which she is willing to lend to the kneeling queens who require his aid: 'Prorogue this business we are going about, and hang / Your shield afore your heart, about that neck / Which is my fee, and which I freely lend / To do these poor queens service' (*TNK* 1.1.196–9).

In his feast of mockery the enlightened Timon provides an ironic prayer of welcome to the parasites who have posed as friends. In a unique usage of fees as subjects or vassals, he includes a plea to the gods to deal with the remainder of those yet uncursed by him: 'The rest of your fees, O gods – the senators of Athens, together with the common lag of people – what is amiss in them, you gods, make suitable for destruction' (*TIM* 3.6.79–82). This odd usage calls forth the suggestion from the Riverside editor that their lives are held in fee from the gods: that is, 'in tenure'.

Macbeth informs his wife that Macduff has declined to provide a display of fealty by attending his feast, adding that he has paid spies in every household: 'There's not a one of them but in his house / I keep a servant fee'd' (*MAC* 3.4.130–1). Here the participle intimating Macbeth's procurement of the service of spies gains force by virtue of a homonymic quality which turns the coin of fee into the elemental dependency on Macbeth to feed.

(C) See next entry, **fee-simple**, and the Sokols' entries on 'fee' and 'land' for a clear explication of the legal significance of property holdings and rights. Vital here is Soellner, *Timon of Athens*; Jordan and Cunningham, eds, *The Law in Shakespeare*. Parker, *Shakespeare from the Margins*, ch. 2, provides an interesing discussion of *ERR*.

fee-grief, fee-simple, in fee

(A) Fee-grief suggests private grief rather than loss and suffering pertaining to a group or community. The fee-simple is a private estate held in perpetuity, the heirs being in full possession as opposed to a limited lease. By extension, sold 'in fee' indicates to be in complete possession as opposed to land held on a limited lease and thereby subject to restrictions on rights of inheritance and other legal impediments.

(B) The desperate and destitute rebel Cade is dismayed when, seeking to steal some food from a garden, he is confronted by the owner, Iden. His aside, especially in the light of Iden's complacent soliloquy on his contented state, reveals awareness of the gap between the man in full possession of his property and the possessionless outlaw: 'Here's the lord of the soil come to seize me for a stray, for entering his fee-simple without leave' (*2H6* 4.10.24–6).

The Captain informing Hamlet of the futility of the Norwegian campaign against the Poles intimates the worthlessness of the territory in question: 'To pay five ducats, five, I would not farm it; / Nor will it yield to Norway or the Pole / A ranker rate, should it be sold in fee' (*HAM* 4.4.20–2). Clearly, sold outright rather than leased is the meaning, bringing together an awareness of the expenditure of resources on war, and agriculture as the foundation of human survival. This land could not even be colonized. Moreover, unlike the honour-hungry Fortinbras, the Captain is anchored in economic and social reality.

When Rosse, newly arrived in the English court, is reluctant to impart some of the news he brings from Scotland, Macduff demands, 'What concern they? / The general cause? or is it a fee-grief, / Due to some single breast?' (*MAC* 4.3.195–7). Clearly there is a connection here between fee-grief and fee-simple. Muir, ed., *Macbeth*, Arden 2, fn 133–4, comments:

> An estate in fee-simple is the largest estate in land known to the English law, and Shakespeare here may convey a twofold idea of boundless grief, i.e. the utmost which could be contained in 'some single breast', and of particular ownership as opposed to ownership in common. But Shakespeare may have meant no more than 'a peculiar sorrow, a grief which hath a single owner' (Johnson).

The matter in question, the murder of Macduff's wife and children, is specific to this interlocutor rather than being one of Scotland's general ills. Here is an example of the language of economic life interpenetrating the personal–political discourse. It does so in a way that ignites the broader issue of the authentic owner of the land of Scotland; Malcolm rather than the false possessor, Macbeth.

Sokol and Sokol define and discuss the fee-simple with admirable clarity. Their discussion intimates something of the resonance alluded to here: 'A fee-simple represents the closest English land law comes to absolute ownership of land. It is necessary to qualify absolute ownership in this way because of the operation of tenures, which states that all land is held by the Crown' (120–1). This is something emphasized earlier by Lady Macbeth in her gracious welcome to King Duncan: 'Your servants ever / Have theirs, themselves, and what is theirs, in compt, / To make their audit at your Highness' pleasure, / Still to return your own' (*MAC* 1.6.25–8).

(C) Important here are Sokol and Sokol, *Shakespeare's Legal Language*, and Jordan and Cunningham, eds, *The Law in Shakespeare*. Also relevant here is Hopkins, *Shakespeare on the Edge*, and Long, *Macbeth*.

fifteen, fifteenth

(A) This is a tax of one-fifteenth levied on property or a rate of payment required in return for a service. A **tithe** or **tenth** was commonplace through the longstanding tradition of the entitlement of the Church to a portion of agricultural output.

(B) Indignation is expressed in the opening scene of *2H6*, when it is revealed that Margaret, the newly arrived bride-to-be of the King, brings no dowry, and that territory has been awarded to her father as a reverse dowry. Additionally, even the **cost** of her transport has to be borne by the English. Gloucester is outraged that Suffolk has been allowed to **exact** a tax in order to reimburse himself for these costs: 'A proper jest, and never heard before, / That Suffolk should demand a whole fifteenth / For costs and charges in transporting her!' (1.1.132–4).

Indignation is also evident during Cade's rebellion. Bursting onto the scene, a messenger delivers news of a captive: 'My lord, a prize, a prize! Here's the Lord Say, which sold the towns in France; he that made us pay one and twenty fifteens, and one shilling to the pound, the last subsidy' (*2H6* 4.7.20–3). The first figure, one and twenty fifteenths, represents a tax of 140 per cent, and like so much in this scene is a wild exaggeration, whereas the second, one shilling in the pound, indicates a tax of 5 per cent. This subsidy constituted a parliamentary grant to the monarch and so represented another tax – whereas today 'subsidy' indicates a negative tax, a payment or rebate to the individual or organization. Historically, Cade's proposed reforms included the abolition of taxes.

(C) See entries on **tenth, tithe** and **subsidy**. Hassel's entry on tithe in *Shakespeare's Religious Language* is informative. Knowles, ed., *Henry VI Part II*, Arden 3, provides a thorough introduction to the play: see especially his footnotes on this topic 320; Ornstein, *A Kingdom for a Stage*; Lull, 'Plantagenets, Lancastrians, Yorkists and Tudors . . .' in Hattaway, ed., *Shakespeare's History Plays*, explore these plays in fascinating detail. Bullough, ed., *Narrative and Dramatic Sources of Shakespeare*, Vol. III, provides convenient access to Hall and Holished. Goy-Blanquet, *Shakespeare's Early History Plays* is another source of stimulating commentary.

fraught, fraughtage, fraughting

(A) These words mean freight, cargo or luggage. The noun fraught also means burden or load. As an adjective it means filled, laden or packed. As a verb it means to weigh down or encumber. The noun fraughtage signifies cargo. The adjective fraughting means forming a cargo or constituting the freight.

(B) Salerio imparts the first suggestion of Antonio's troubles when he refers to news of a shipwreck: 'there miscarried / A vessel of our country richly fraught' (*MV* 2.8.29–30). The ship was fully laden with a rich cargo.

By a natural extension, the word is used to signify an emotional burden, something revealed by Othello as he feels the accession of jealousy overtake him: 'Swell, bosom, with thy fraught, / For 'tis of aspics' tongues!' (*OTH* 3.3.449–50).

Less obvious in its metaphorical application of burden is Cymbeline's emphatic dismissal of Posthumus: 'If after this command thou fraught the court / With thy unworthiness, thou diest' (*CYM* 1.1.126–7).

The Prologue in *TRO* gives a dramatic description of the Greeks landing in Troy, the fraughtage in this case being the soldiers: 'To Tenedos they come, / And the deep-drawing barks do there disgorge / Their warlike fraughtage' (11–13).

Miranda's compassion is exquisitely rendered when she employs the word to indicate a cargo of souls – believing she has witnessed a real shipwreck rather than Prospero's magic: 'Had I been any God of power, I would / Have sunk the sea within the earth or ere / It should the good ship so have swallow'd and / The fraughting souls within her' (*TMP* 1.2.10–13).

(C) For an engagement with the last play's language see Ryan, ed., *Shakespeare: The Last Plays*; Hartwig, *Shakespeare's Tragicomic Vision*; Kermode, *Shakespeare's Language*; McDonald, *Shakespeare's Late Style*.

G

garner

(A) The noun signifies a granary or storehouse; the verb to store up or lay up.

(B) Used only twice in the literal sense and once metaphorically, it is a telling word. On hearing news that Rome's enemies are in arms Coriolanus dismisses the starving and rebellious **plebeians** with contempt: 'The Volsces have much corn; take these rats thither / To gnaw their garners' (*COR* 1.1.249–50).

Delivering a blessing on Miranda and Ferdinand, Ceres' song includes the promise of fertility and abundance: 'Earth's increase, foison plenty, / Barns and garners never empty; / Vines with clust'ring bunches growing, / Plants with goodly burthen bowing' (*TMP* 4.1.110–13).

Soul-stricken Othello expresses his sense of annihilation, believing that the loss of Desdemona's love is the only thing that could have **broken** him: 'But there, where I have garner'd up my heart, / Where either I must live or bear no life' (*OTH* 4.2.57–8). The image is of Desdemona as a storehouse where Othello has irrevocably lodged his heart.

(C) For some penetrating appreciation of Shakespeare's most political and visceral play see Poole, *Coriolanus*; Wheeler, ed., *Coriolanus*. Kolin, ed., *Othello*, and Alexander and Wells, eds, *Shakespeare and Race*, have essays particularly pertinent to love in the play. For an exploration of the contemporary resonances arising through crop failures in England see George, 'Plutarch, insurrection, and dearth in *Coriolanus*' in Alexander, ed., *Shakespeare and Politics*.

government

(A) This term relates primarily to the control or management of the state, or any grouping such as an army, or even to a garden. Unlike the modern conception of a political and administrative machine, the sense here is of an individual controller. The second application pertains to self-control.

(B) Even in *MM*, the play which provides the most abstract engagement with

141

government, it is 'governing well' that is referred to by the Duke in his opening address to Escalus:

> Of government the properties to unfold
> Would seem in me t'affect speech and discourse,
> Since I am put to know that your own science
> Exceeds, in that, the lists of all advice
> My strength can give you.
>
> 1.1.3–7

The gardener in *R2*, making an analogy between the garden and the body politic, emphasizes the need for judicious control: 'All must be even in our government' (3.4.36). Hotspur enquires about who is leading his father's army: 'Who leads his power? / Under whose government come they along?' (*1H4* 4.1.18–19). The Earl of Worcester cautions Hotspur about his lack of self-control after he has antagonized their important ally, Glendower. His assertiveness is a two-edged sword, claims the Earl:

> Though sometimes it show greatness, courage, blood –
> And that's the dearest grace it renders you –
> Yet oftentimes it doth present harsh rage,
> Defect of manners, want of government,
> Pride, haughtiness, opinion, and disdain,
>
> *1H4* 3.1.179–83

(C) See Aughterson, *The English Renaissance Part 2*; Bradshaw, *Shakespeare's Sceptism*; Lever, *The Tragedy of State*; Hadfield, *Shakespeare and Renaissance Politics*.

hade land, head land

(A) Used only once, most editors accept the Quarto version 'hade land', thought to refer to land left unploughed as a boundary area, or a strip at the edge of the field left last to facilitate the turning of the plough. The context, however, suggests land previously left fallow but now ready for sowing. Folio's 'head land' refers to a piece of land jutting out from the rest of the arable land.

(B) Davy asks his master Shallow, 'sir, shall we sow the hade land with wheat?' (*2H4* 5.1.14). What seems likely is that the area that has been left fallow is now ready to be cultivated – unless Folio's 'head land' is correct. The particular interpretation is not a matter of great moment in itself, but it forms part of a discourse which draws on the most commonplace details of country living. A feeling is engendered of a deep engagement with the economics of everyday life, establishing a rhythm quite unlike that of the court and its political manoeuvring. This is not a romanticized vision of bucolic existence. Indeed Falstaff provides a contemptuous mockery of it (5.1.60–85), and along with the Gloucestershire scenes in *2H4* reveals the manoeuvres and petty corruption operating well away from court. Nevertheless, the details of rural life that permeate these scenes provide a sense of a distinctive social universe.

(C) Bulman, '*Henry IV Parts 1 & 2*', esp. 172–4, in Hattaway, ed., *Shakespeare's History Plays*, is of interest here. So too is Ruiter, *Shakespeare's Festive History*.

having

(A) Indicating financial means, **wealth** or possessions, the word also means attributes, talent or abilities.

(B) As Anne Page's suitors are weighed in the balance, her father is emphatic in turning down Fenton, not least because he is impecunious: 'The gentleman is of no having ... No, he shall not knit a knot in his fortunes with the finger of my substance' (*WIV* 3.2.71–5).

143

Believing he has encountered his friend Sebastian, the beleaguered Antonio asks for the return of his purse. The puzzled Viola/Cesario shows no recognition but offers half her substance in **recompense** for release from Sir Toby's trap: 'Out of my lean and low ability / I'll lend you something. My having is not much; / I'll make division of my present with you' (*TN* 3.4.344–6).

Turning away from Wolsey, the King enumerates his past favours, claiming that much of his largesse was bestowed at the cost of his own possessions: 'Since I had my office, / I have kept you next my heart, have not alone / Employ'd you where high profits might come home, / But par'd my present havings, to bestow /My bounties upon you' (*H8* 3.2.156–60). A critical political point here is that those in power can enrich others by providing them with lucrative positions without **cost** to themselves. Henry, however, has gone much further, diminishing his own wealth to benefit Wolsey – the rarity of the act accounting for his indignation.

The second sense, of gift or attributes, is to be found in *A Lover's Complaint*, where a nun is esteemed so highly that even the natural world is lost in admiration: 'Whose rarest havings made the blossoms dote' (235).

Anne Bullen protests that she would prefer obscurity to 'a golden sorrow', provoking her **auditor** to affirm, 'Our content / Is our best having' (*H8* 2.3.22–3). Wealth and possessions are all very well, she suggests, but the greatest possession of all is contentment. The dialogue is, of course, richly ironic. Anne is soon to accept financial favours that will culminate in the attainment of a 'golden sorrow', while the philosophical Old Lady is tireless in her pursuit of financial rewards.

(C) White, *The Merry Wives of Windsor*, is highly perceptive in the exploration of 'having', money and class. Rewarding also is Brigden, *New Worlds, Lost Worlds*; McMullan, ed., *King Henry VIII*, Arden 3, Introduction.

hire

(A) Acquisition of some service or payment for services rendered is intimated by hire.

(B) Capulet, in his eagerness to expedite the marriage feast for Juliet, gives orders to secure the services of extra staff for the occasion: 'Sirrah, go hire me twenty cunning cooks' (*ROM* 4.2.2). Those so appointed have to be 'cunning' or skilled.

Volumnia visualizes her magnificent warrior-son Coriolanus exhorting his men and terrorizing his enemies by drawing, surprisingly, on an analogy from agriculture: 'forth he goes, / Like to a harvest-man that's task'd to mow / Or all or lose his hire' (*COR* 1.3.35–7). The contract is such that the whole of the job has to be completed in an agreed time or the worker does not get paid at all. Hence such a worker performs his task with utmost vigour and urgency.

Shylock's narrative designed to justify reward for shrewd dealing, contains an example of payment or wages taking the form of sheep: 'That all the eanlings, which were streak'd and pied / Should fall as Jacob's hire' (*MV* 1.3.79–80).

(C) See Goldman, *Acting and Action in Shakespearean Tragedy*, ch. 7, 'Characterizing

Coriolanus'. With reference to Capulet's kitchen Appelbaum, *Aguecheek's Beef*, is entertaining and illuminating.

husbandry

(A) This word has drifted to the margins of discourse in the modern world but occupies a highly significant place in Shakespeare's lexicon, figuring in a wide range of contexts and possessing seven distinct meanings: maintenance or preservation; sexual fertilization; agricultural activity or land management; household work or chores; household management; thrift or careful use of resources; diligence or industriousness. Most of these meanings relate to the management of resources, making this a key economic term, but there are quite distinct shades of meaning within this broad category each with fascinating applications. The sexual application is more literal than metaphoric.

(B) The trickiest case occurs in *SON* 13, where the speaker encourages the young man to marry, procreate and so maintain or continue his lineage. The term used for lineage is 'house' so that the concept becomes both physiological and material: we 'see' the building while absorbing the idea of family name. The legal terminology of 'lease' and 'determination' accentuate our sense of a physical edifice. Consequently the closing section emphasizes the young man's role in maintenance or preservation of his family line, name and the physical building:

> Who lets so fair a house fall to decay,
> Which husbandry in honor might uphold
> Against the stormy gusts of winter's day
> And barren rage of death's eternal cold?
>   O, none but unthrifts: dear my love, you know
>   You had a father, let your son say so.
>
>   9–14

'Husbandry' seems to possess a unique meaning here of 'maintenance of the physical fabric', but draws into itself the associations of responsibility for nurturing the family's resources and also physical husbandry in the form of impregnating his wife – of being a good husband. Here is someone required to be husband, husbandman, steward and perpetuator of the family name. Not to recognize the peculiarity of the primary meaning of the term here is to miss the matrix which connects these meanings.

Probably the most beautiful expression of the sexual act and ensuing pregnancy anywhere in literature emanates from the tawdry, rather sordid character, Lucio, when he tells the novice Isabella that her brother is in trouble because his fiancée is pregnant:

> Your brother and his lover have embrac'd.
> As those that feed grow full, as blossoming time
> That from the seedness the bare fallow brings

> To teeming foison, even so her plenteous womb
> Expresseth his full tilth and husbandry.
>
> *MM* 1.4.40–4

This may legitimately be conceived as a metaphorical application from agriculture, but that weakens and diminishes the power and beauty of the speech. An analogy is present here but as a build-up to the husbandry of physical procreation: a process central to the whole of nature: the fecundity of man and woman engaged in the mutual expression of love. It does appear, then, that husbandry possesses this distinct sexual significance.

The only other example of this specific use occurs in a non-dramatic context. The speaker, encouraging the young man to marry and have children, pours scorn on one possible obstacle: 'For where is she so fair whose unear'd womb / Disdains the tillage of thy husbandry?' (*SON* 3.5–6).

The essential nature of nurturing the soil and maintaining agricultural productivity is best illustrated by two examples which emphasize the consequences of the failure to undertake these tasks. The Machiavellian Queen Margaret incites King Henry to dispose of Humphrey, Duke of Gloucester, by driving home her argument with a telling metaphor: 'Now 'tis the spring, and weeds are shallow-rooted; / Suffer them now, and they'll o'ergrow the garden, / And choke the herbs for want of husbandry' (*2H6* 3.1.31–3).

Shakespeare, the economist, gives powerful expression to the centrality of agriculture and its maintenance when, towards the close of *H5*, Burgundy makes his impassioned speech on behalf of peace. This is, indeed, the most comprehensive representation of agricultural activity in the canon:

> let it not disgrace me,
> If I demand, before this royal view,
> What rub or what impediment there is,
> Why that the naked, poor, and mangled Peace,
> Dear nurse of arts, plenties, and joyful births,
> Should not in this best garden of the world,
> Our fertile France, put up her lovely visage?
> Alas, she hath from France too long been chas'd,
> And all her husbandry doth lie on heaps,
> Corrupting in its own fertility.
>
> 5.2.31–40

A further 15 lines are devoted to a grim delineation of the collapse of agriculture. This speech suggests that the essence of life is husbandry. It is significant that a play perceived, until relatively recently, as a clarion call to warfare and a celebration of patriotism creates such a space to celebrate peace, agriculture and abundance – the epitome of potential fertility being France, 'this best garden of the world'.

As Falstaff's newly selected recruits attempt to resist the embrace of military service, Mouldy claims that he is irreplaceable at home: 'My old dame will be undone now for one to do her husbandry and her drudgery' (*2H4* 3.2.112–13). These two terms are linked in a way suggesting a proximity that connects to household work or chores. Portia hands over her household management to Lorenzo: 'Lorenzo, I commit into your hands / The husbandry and manage of my house' (*MV* 3.4.24–5). Evidently the word means domestic *management* in this up-market case rather than doing the donkey-work implicit in Mouldy's comment.

Two contrasting examples of the meaning 'good household management' are provided in *TIM* and *COR*. The loyal steward, having revealed Timon's bankruptcy, emphasizes that he is not personally culpable: 'If you suspect my husbandry or falsehood, / Call me before th' exactest auditors, / And set me on the proof' (2.2.155–7). Aufidius concedes that his rival Coriolanus has conducted his affairs in the **interest** of the Volscian state: 'Although it seems, / And so he thinks, and is no less apparent / To th'vulgar eye, that he bears all things fairly, / And shows good husbandry for the Volscian state' (4.7.19–22). The husbandry in this latter case is a long way away from careful household stewardship, but constitutes an overall concern for the society, marshalling its resources by successfully plundering the enemy.

There is a meaning which is close to that of careful household management but is differentiated by suggesting *extreme stringency* in managing resources. The most compelling example is Banquo's beautiful expression embodying the remarkable conceit that the stars are candles lit by angels: 'There's husbandry in heaven, / Their candles are all out' (*MAC* 2.1.4–5). In other words, the unnatural darkness is explained by the desire in heaven to save on candles; no stars are visible because the frugal angels have not yet lit the candles or have extinguished them. This idea is more than fanciful, it is fantastic: the lines constitute sublime poetry that is surely not deconstructed by the audience – something usually invited by conceits.

This meaning of 'thrift' is much more straightforward when incorporated in Polonius' advice to his son as he prepares to leave for France: 'Neither a borrower nor a lender be, / For loan oft loses both itself and friend, / And borrowing dulleth th'edge of husbandry' (*HAM* 1.3.75–7).

'Husbandry' also means 'diligence or assiduousness'. Consequent upon an earth tremor, two gentlemen greet each other having left their homes at an exceptionally early hour. The first says, 'Pure surprise and fear / Made me to quit the house'. To which his neighbour responds: 'That is the cause we trouble you so early, / 'Tis not our husbandry' (*PER* 3.2.17–20). The meaning here is more than simply the need to get on with our daily household or farming activities; it implies 'extreme assiduity in getting things done'.

A fascinating example occurs when Alexander explains that the Trojan hero, Hector, is so eager to compensate for the indignity of being knocked down in battle on the previous day that,

> He chid Andromache and strook his armorer,
> And like as there were husbandry in war,
> Before the sun rose he was harness'd light,

> And to the field goes he; where every flower
> Did as a prophet weep what it foresaw
> In Hector's wrath.
>
> *TRO* 1.2.6–11

This is not easy to explicate, but the antithesis seems to suggest that the people who rise and go to work at dawn are those engaged in husbandry, or farm work, whereas warriors begin their endeavours much later in the day. Such daybreak diligence or assiduity is not the province of the warrior. By conflating meanings, or packing two meanings together, Shakespeare creates an image of the farmer as the embodiment of eager, conscientious endeavour, something now, uncharacteristically, emulated by the warrior. Nature, in the form of each flower, sorrows at the prospect of the victims of Hector's anger, intensifying the incongruity of the warrior striding through the field like a conscientious farmer. The primary meaning here is diligent, though the secondary implication of husbandry as farming activity is so closely compacted that the concepts are married.

When Orlando praises old Adam for his 'pains and husbandry' (*AYL* 2.3.65) he is referring to his conscientious service during a lifetime's devotion to his master's affairs. Here is another compacting of 'diligence' with 'management of household and estate affairs'.

Henry V justifies the exceptionally early start to the day by the proximity of the French army and the impending Battle of Agincourt: 'For our bad neighbor makes us early stirrers, / Which is both healthful and good husbandry' (*H5* 4.1.6–7). Here husbandry must mean 'conscientious behaviour'. What is intriguing is the way in which this meaning connects so closely with the idea of sound household management and of agricultural activity that begins at first light. In both *TRO* and *H5* there is a lurking irony in the juxtaposition of the warrior, the bringer of death, with the farmer and industrious householder engaged in preserving life.

(C) Agnew, *Worlds Apart*, 55–6, discusses the concept in the context of classical Greece. Also relevant here are Hadfield, *Shakespeare and Renaissance Politics*; Barton, *Essays, Mainly Shakespearean*; Warley, *Sonnet Sequences and Social Distinction in Renaissance England*; McEachern, ed., *Shakespearean Tragedy*.

impeach, impeachment

(A) Carrying substantial freight in the language of political contestation, these words straddle a technical vocabulary of chivalry and a more modern spirit of vituperative aggression. To impeach is to charge, accuse, challenge or indict; it also means to call into question, disparage or reproach, occurring twice in a significantly economic context. Impeachment carries both these meanings but has the additional possibility of impediment or obstacle.

(B) In the conflict between Bolingbroke and Mowbray that dominates the formal chivalric world of the opening of *R2*, the King bids his loyal associate to withdraw from the challenge. Mowbray, however, refuses, insisting that to do so would involve a stain on his honour: 'I am disgrac'd, impeach'd, and baffled here, / Pierc'd to the soul with slander's venom'd spear' (1.1.170–1). 'Impeached' carries all the force of a formal accusation, while 'baffled' means dishonoured, carrying with it the implication of being stripped of knighthood. The copious diction of the first line is severely formal, while the imagery of the second line expands into a wider expression of personal malice. Intensity is forged from the precision of formality married to indignation.

A trenchant example of this sense of formal indictment is provided by King Philip of France in his declaration of support for young Arthur. King John of England demands: 'From whom hast thou this great commission, France, / To draw my answer from thy articles?' The riposte takes up the challenge embodied in the word 'articles', meaning items in a formal indictment:

> From that supernal judge that stirs good thoughts
> In any breast of strong authority,
> To look into the blots and stains of right.
> That judge hath made me guardian to this boy,

> Under whose warrant I impeach thy wrong,
> And by whose help I mean to chastise it.
>
> *JN* 2.1.110–17

These formalities, which locate God as the supreme source of kingly authority, soon give way to a quest for cynical personal advantage with the Pope's representative Pandulph displaying all the arts of a confirmed **Machiavel**.

The second application, to 'call into question' or to 'discredit', occurs in *MV*. Salerio tells Bassanio of Antonio's predicament, and of Shylock's threat that the very foundation of the Venetian state will be called into question if his **bond** is not honoured: 'He plies the Duke at morning and at night, / And doth impeach the freedom of the state, / If they deny him justice' (3.2.277–9). As Antonio later points out, the very lifeblood of Venice is commerce. It is impossible, therefore, for the Duke to grant him a special dispensation as this would compromise the integrity and impartiality of Venetian law:

> The Duke cannot deny the course of law;
> For the commodity that strangers have
> With us in Venice, if it be denied,
> Will much impeach the justice of the state,
> Since that the trade and profit of the city
> Consisteth of all nations.
>
> 3.3.26–31

A shocking example occurs when Queen Margaret and her associates capture the Duke of York. Northumberland protests that their honour will not be impugned by carrying out a brutal killing rather than allowing Clifford to fight singly against the exhausted and wounded prisoner: 'It is war's prize to take all vantages, / And ten to one is no impeach of valor' (*3H6* 1.4.59–60). This utterance reveals how far any sense of honour has been left behind. Clifford, of course, has already murdered young Rutland, and a napkin drenched with the child's blood is given to York to wipe away his tears. He is mocked with a paper crown as a prelude to decapitation. His head is then placed on the city walls.

The third meaning, 'impediment' or 'obstruction', is present when Henry tells Mountjoy that he would prefer to withdraw to Calais without engaging the French: 'And tell thy King I do not seek him now, / But could be willing to march on to Callice / Without impeachment' (*H5* 3.6.140–2).

(C) The tremendous power of the *H6* plays has been well attested in recent years by RSC productions. The *H6–R3* cycle was directed by Adrian Noble at the Royal Shakespeare Theatre in 1988–9 under the title of *The Plantagenets*. Michael Boyd directed the *H6–R3* cycle at the RSC's Swan Theatre in 2000–1, and again at the RSC's Courtyard Theatre in 2006–8. In 2001 The Watermill Company (Propeller) produced a visceral and exhilarating adaptation of the *H6* trilogy – a two-part production directed by Edward Hall – designated *Rose Rage*. *JN*, along with the *H6–R3* cycle, has been produced twice by the RSC in recent years (2001 and 2006), on both occasions to great acclaim, revealing just how undervalued this play is. Bloom has many fine things to say on several of the plays but is dismissive of these. Attendance at these productions would surely have changed his views. Good chapters on the play are to be found in Donawerth, *Shakespeare and the Sixteenth-Century Study of Language*; Leggatt, *Shakespeare's Political Drama*; Piesse, 'King John: changing perspectives' in Hattaway, ed., *Shakespeare's History Plays*. Smallwood, ed., *Players of Shakespeare 6*, contains commentaries by actors who performed in both *H6–R3* and *R2–H5* cycles and *JN* in the 2001 season. For further glances at *JN* see the entry on **commodity**. For Venice and **trade** see Brotton, *The Renaissance Bazaar*, and for a thorough exploration of the racial context see Shapiro, *Shakespeare and the Jews*. The significance of honour and chivalry are explored by James, *Society, Politics and Culture*, and Denton, ed., *Orders and Hierarchies in Late Medieval and Renaissance Europe*.

imprese

(A) A term for a heraldic device, it occurs only once, but in a highly charged political situation.

(B) Bolingbroke, newly returned from exile, denounces King Richard's associates, stressing his sufferings and listing their misdeeds, including the seizure of his rightful inheritance: 'From my own windows torn my household coat, / Ras'd out my imprese, leaving me no sign, / Save men's opinions and my living blood, / To show the world I am a gentleman' (*R2* 3.1.24–7). Evidently the heraldic emblem is intrinsic to his sense of identity.

(C) Seimon, *Shakespearean Iconoclasm*, and Bolam, '*Richard II*' in Hattaway, ed., *Shakespeare's History Plays*, are of interest here. See also Shaperio's fascinating *1599*, esp. 33–5, for an account of Elizabeth's shield gallery and Shakespeare's participation in writing the *impressa* 'that the Earl of Rutland displayed at King James' Accession day tournament in March 1613'. Significant too are James, *Society, Politics and Culture*, and Denton, ed., *Orders and Hierarchies in Late Medieval and Renaissance Europe*.

impress

(A) As a noun, conscription or enforced service is the primary meaning of the word. It also signifies imprint or stamp. Used as a verb, the word means to conscript or enlist.

(B) Enobarbus remonstrates with Antony in his futile attempt to persuade him to fight on land with his own battle-hardened soldiers rather than depending on the inadequate Egyptian navy: 'Your ships are not well mann'd, / Your mariners are muleters, reapers, people / Ingross'd by swift impress' (*ANT* 3.7.34–6).

Expressing disbelief at the prospect of Birnan Wood ever approaching Dunsinane hill, a relieved Macbeth rejoices: 'That will never be. / Who can impress the forest, bid the tree / Unfix his earth-bound root?' (*MAC* 4.1.94–6).

Seeking solace in the prospect of a holy war, Henry refers to himself as enlisted or 'impressed' as a dedicated Christian, though most of his accompanying troops will be under a more material impress: 'As far as to the sepulchre of Christ – /

Whose soldier now, under whose blessed cross / We are impressed and engag'd to fight – / Forthwith a power of English shall we levy' (*1H4* 1.1.19–22).

Impress as 'stamp or impression' finds clear expression in the Duke's reassurance to the hapless suitor Thurio that Silvia will soon forget her banished lover Valentine: 'This weak impress of love is as a figure / Trenched in ice, which with an hour's heat / Dissolves to water, and doth lose his form' (*TGV* 3.2.6–8).

(C) Siemon, *Shakespearean Iconoclasm*, Adelman, *The Common Liar*, Kahn, *Roman Shakespeare*, Thomas, *Shakespeare's Roman Worlds*, Goldman, *Acting and Action in Shakespearean Tragedy*, and Long, *Macbeth*, are all relevant here.

increase

(A) This word pertains to generation, both human and agricultural: fertility, growth, crops and offspring. Additionally, it signifies expansion or growth in the more general sense.

(B) Blessing the young couple, Ceres, goddess of agriculture and fertility, promises 'Earth's increase, foison plenty, / Barns and garners never empty' (*TMP* 4.1.110–11).

Queen Margaret sorrowing over the exile of her favourite, Suffolk, creates a conceit by comparing the waters from her eyes, which indicate the undermining of her life, with rain that is generative in stimulating growth of crops: 'And with the southern clouds contend in tears, / Theirs for the earth's increase, mine for my sorrows?' (*2H6* 3.2.384–5).

In a pre-battle confrontation with Queen Margaret, George, Duke of Clarence, couches his argument, that the Yorkists put their claim in abeyance, in an extended simile, beginning, 'But when we saw our sunshine made thy spring, / And that thy summer bred us no increase, / We set the axe to thy usurping root' (*3H6* 2.2.163–5).

The early *SON*s are urgent in their appeal for the handsome young man to marry and produce children, commencing with the lines: 'From fairest creatures we desire increase, / That thereby beauty's rose might never die' (1.1–2).

In contrast to this appeal for generation, Lear's appeal to Nature is to obstruct Goneril's fertility: 'Into her womb convey sterility, / Dry up in her the organs of increase, / And from her derogate body never spring / A babe to honour her!' (*LR* 1.4.278–81).

The simple sense of increase as growing or extending can be illustrated by Desdemona's sublime anticipation of a continuing and growing love between herself and Othello: 'The heavens forbid / But that our loves and comforts should increase / Even as our days do grow!' (*OTH* 2.1.193–5).

(C) See Goldman, 'Acting and feeling' in *Acting and Action in Shakespearean Tragedy*; Kermode, *Shakespeare's Language*; and Schalkwyk, *Speech and Performance in Shakespeare's Sonnets and Plays*. On fertility in *TMP*, goddesses and symbolism, Orgel's fine Introduction to the World Classics edition is concise and insightful.

indent

(A) As a political term the verb, employed only once, means to enter an agreement or make a **bargain**; also to move in a zigzag – which perhaps surprisingly does not operate in the political sphere. As a noun the meaning is indentation – again unique. The adjective indented means sinuous.

(B) The wily Henry IV rejects the possibility of compromise with his antagonists and erstwhile allies, the Northumberland **faction**, so long as they persist in their demand that he ransom Mortimer (perceived to have surrendered in a cowardly way to Glendower, and, adding insult to injury, has married the Welsh rebel's daughter): 'Shall we buy treason? and indent with fears, / When they have lost and forfeited themselves?' (*1H4* 1.3.87–8). The King professes he has no desire to 'indent', or 'make a pact', or 'come to terms with' Mortimer because of his cowardice. The phrase 'indent with fears' means to make a pact with one whose cowardice brought about his capture. The choice of word contains the right balance of detachment and incisiveness in a speech which cunningly weaves together tones of indignation, irony and command, suffocating the implication of any desire to keep at a distance a figure who has a more legitimate right to the throne. The sense of indentation occurs in a politically charged situation though the word itself carries no political **freight**. When Hotspur disputes the boundaries proposed in the division of the kingdom he sees the prevailing course of the river Trent as disadvantageous: 'It shall not wind with such a deep indent, / To rob me of so rich a bottom here' (*1H4* 3.1.103–4).

(C) See Bulman, '*Henry IV, Parts 1 & 2* in Hattaway, ed., *Shakespeare's History Plays*, and McAlindon, *Shakespeare's Tudor History*.

indenture

(A) Operating in political and economic spheres this term refers to contracts or agreements.

(B) The term is used twice in the scene where the rebels meet to formulate their agreements prior to the Battle of Shrewsbury. Having described the proposed division of the kingdom between Hotspur, Glendower and himself, Mortimer says, 'And our indentures tripartite are drawn, / Which being sealed interchangeably / (A business that this night may execute)' (*1H4* 3.1.79–81). He then goes on to set out the arrangements for bringing the contingents together, but Hotspur holds up proceedings by cavilling at the appropriateness of the shares embodied in the articles or indentures. Eventually, however, Hotspur approves the agreement with the announcement, 'Are the indentures drawn? Shall we be gone?' (3.1.139).

In *JN*, Austria expresses the absolute nature of his commitment to young Arthur's cause by transmuting the legal term into a physical gesture: 'Upon thy cheek lay I this zealous kiss / As seal to this indenture of my love' (2.1.19–20). In the event the action proves to be more of a Judas kiss. In neither play do the indentures hold.

(C) See Salmon, 'Elizabethan colloquial English in the Falstaff plays' in Salmon and Burness, eds, *A Reader in the Language of Shakespearean Drama,* and Kinney, *Shakespeare's Webs.* Sokol and Sokol, *Shakespeare's Legal Language,* explore the legal dimensions of this word, pointing out that the parchment incorporating the agreement was torn in two with one half going to each participant. They point to the incongruity between the contractual precision of the rebels with respect to their agreement and the *illegality* of their enterprise

innovation, innovator

(A) Here is a word that takes the modern theatregoer by surprise, because, far from meaning some technical adaptation or transformation, it has the primary meaning of social or political upheaval. An innovator is a revolutionary or a political radical. In its only ambiguous application, *HAM,* there may be the suggestion of change in **fashion** rather than anything more subversive.

(B) Prior to the Battle of Shrewsbury, Henry dismisses Worcester's reasons for rebellion as opportunistic, designed, 'To face the garment of rebellion / With some fine color that may please the eye / Of fickle changelings and poor discontents, / Which gape and rub the elbow at the news / Of hurly-burly innovation' (*1H4* 5.1.74–8). The implication is that there will always be some popular support for an insurrection because there are those who possess a natural propensity for dissent.

Rosencrantz in explaining why the actors are on tour says, 'I think their inhibition comes by the means of the late innovation'. Later he adds: 'there is, sir, an aery of children, little eyases, that cry out on the top of question, and are most tyrannically clapp'd for't. These are now the fashion' (*HAM* 2.2.332–42). Uncertainty of interpretation reigns here, but it seems that the senior players have suffered some form of restraint and that boy companies have taken their place. 'Innovation' suggests some kind of upheaval or commotion, while the section cited involves the words 'tyrannically' and 'fashion', retaining a political colouration and the implication of new taste.

The sole use of 'innovator' is richly ironic because it is applied by the tribune, Sicinius, to Coriolanus. The tribunate is a new political office born out of political upheaval and granted by the patricians to the **plebeians** in a successful effort to quell the rebellion. Coriolanus has suggested a return to the *status quo ante* and so is denounced and threatened with arrest: 'Go call the people, in whose name myself / Attach thee as a traitorous innovator, / A foe to th' public weal' (*COR* 3.1.173–5). The innovator here, is, paradoxically a reactionary.

(C) On *HAM* and innovation see Riverside, fn 1204. Also of interest is Cavell, 'Who does the wolf love?' in Parker and Hartman, eds, *Shakespeare and the Question of Theory.* Hadfield, *Shakespeare and Renaissance Politics,* is of strong contextual significance.

intelligence

(A) A vigorous word that animates political discourse, it has the following applications: spying or secretly acquired information; the secret service or sources of information; communication which may or may not have political or military import; simple conversation.

(B) The Chorus in *H5* describes the English preparations and the French response to information acquired by efficient spying: 'The French, advis'd by good intelligence / Of this most dreadful preparation, / Shake in their fear' (Cho 2 12–14).

Being caught completely unawares by news of French preparation for invasion of England, King John expresses amazement that his secret service has let him down: 'O, where hath our intelligence been drunk?' (*JN* 4.2.116).

Where the term applies to information or news, it embraces military, political and sexual references. When Henry IV denounces Worcester for his failure to communicate the generous offer that had been made to Hotspur, he is not referring to anything clandestine. He rebukes him for the needless deaths arising from concealment of a genuine offer: 'A noble earl, and many a creature else / Had been alive this hour, / If like a Christian thou hadst truly borne / Betwixt our armies true intelligence' (*1H4* 5.5.7–10).

More pithy is Thersites' aside on Cressida's easy availability and Patroclus' seeming appetite: 'Patroclus will give me anything for the intelligence of this whore' (*TRO* 5.2.192–3).

Rosalind accused of treason by her uncle, protests that she has not communicated with anyone. The context is political but intelligence here refers not to illicit transactions but to conversation *per se*.

> I do beseech your Grace
> Let me the knowledge of my fault bear with me:
> If with myself I hold intelligence,
> Or have acquaintance with mine own desires;
> If that I do not dream, or be not frantic
> (As I do trust I am not), then, dear uncle,
> Never so much as in a thought unborn
> Did I offend your Highness.

The Duke's riposte is as incisive as it is misguided: 'Thus do all traitors: / If their purgation did consist in words, / They are as innocent as grace itself' (*AYL* 1.3.45–54). Though this usage resides outside the highly political applications, it is significant that it is quickly drawn into the sphere of politics.

(C) For the significance of rhetorical structures in *AYL* see Magnusson, 'Language and comedy' in Leggatt, ed., *Shakespearean Comedy*. Hadfield, *Shakespeare and Renaissance Politics*, and Eagleton, *William Shakespeare*, are also germane to this topic.

intelligencer, intelligencing

(A) The noun occurs only twice in Shakespeare's plays. The word's primary meaning is go-between, but attaching to this concept is the idea of underhand dealing on the part of the agent, so that rather than being passive the intermediary is actively iniquitous: insinuating, inciting and manipulating. In the drama of the period an intelligencer is generally a spy, informer or secret agent. Shakespeare's only deviation from this unsavoury conception is remarkable in that the role of intermediary is seen as wholesome (*2H4* 4.2.20). The adjective intelligencing, occurring only once, signifies a go-between.

(B) Intriguingly, Prince John of Lancaster, confronting the rebels at Gaultree Forest, castigates the Bishop of York for declining from his role as 'heaven's intelligencer':

> Who hath not heard it spoken
> How deep you were within the books of God?
> To us the speaker in his parliament,
> To us th'imagin'd voice of God himself,
> The very opener and intelligencer
> Between the grace, the sanctities of heaven,
> And our dull workings?
>
> *2H4* 4.2.16–22

This engagement abounds in ironies. John is swift to take the moral high ground and is thoroughly **Machiavellian** in engineering a pact which he promptly breaks – exculpating himself by means of a verbal quibble. He even orders the destruction of an army that has dispersed in the belief that the conflict has been peaceably resolved. Richard III is aptly denounced as 'hell's black intelligencer' (*R3* 4.4.71).

The madly jealous Leontes applies the expression 'intelligencing' to Paulina when she insists on bringing him his newly born daughter: 'A most intelligencing bawd!' (*WT* 2.3.69). Leontes believes that Paulina has been the go-between in the imagined adulterous relationship between Hermione and Polixenes.

(C) Relevant here are Howard and Dutton, eds, *A Companion to Shakespeare's Works – Volume II: The Histories*; McAlindon, *Shakespeare's Tudor History*; and Nuttall, *Shakespeare the Thinker*. Interesting are Felperin, 'Tongue-tied our Queen?' in Parker and Hartman, eds, *Shakespeare and the Question of Theory*; Sanders, *The Winter's Tale*; Hunt, ed., *The Winter's Tale*.

intelligent

(A) The word is used to mean either bearing **intelligence** that is politically significant information, or being frank, or straightforward.

(B) Cornwall assures his villainous associate Edmund that knowledge of all the political manoeuvres will be imparted to him by his agents: 'Our posts shall be swift and intelligent betwixt us' (*LR* 3.7.11). There is a superb compactness in the phrase 'swift and intelligent'. All the necessary state secrets will be delivered with despatch.

The nervous Polixenes means something different when he presses Camillo to explain why his friend Leontes suddenly shuns him: 'Be intelligent to me' (*WT* 1.2.378). In other words, be open and honest.

(C) Relevant here are Hunt, ed., *The Winter's Tale*; Heinmann, ' "Demystifying the mystery of state" ', in Alexander, ed., *Shakespeare and Politics*.

interess

(A) This unique usage means to lay claim to, but carries with it the additional implication of being conjoined or intertwined.

(B) Lear, in preparing to confirm his youngest daughter's rich inheritance of the best third of his kingdom, refers to the suitors who are pursuing Cordelia and her endowment: 'Now, our joy, / Although our last and least, to whose young love / The vines of France and milk of Burgundy / Strive to be interess'd' (*LR* 1.1.82–5). The conception of possession and inter-joining gives rise to and finds expression in 'interess'd'. The suitors and their territories are interwoven in such a way that the incipient union affords the prospect of a new and authentic entity.

(C) The chapters in Kermode, *Shakespeare's Language*, and Jones, *Shakespeare at Work*, are particularly germane to this topic. Foakes, Arden 3, 163, has the following footnote: 'lay claim. "Interest" is a variant spelling of this past participle, from the verb "interess", which gradually gave way to the modern form "interested" in the seventeenth century.'

interest

(A) The obvious economic significance of the term consists in the sum of **money** to be repaid on a loan over and above the sum borrowed. Secondly, there is the right of possession or title to property. Beyond this sphere there is the case of personal involvement or a special concern in a person or proceedings.

(B) The two plays most obviously concerned with 'interest' in the narrow financial sense are *MV* and *TIM*. The four occasions when the word is employed in *MV* occur during the money-saturated engagement between Shylock and Antonio over the question of the loan of 3,000 ducats. Shylock reflects on Antonio's past abuse – 'On me, my bargains, and my well-won thrift, / Which he calls interest' – before proceeding to highlight the incongruity of Antonio's quest to enter into an arrangement that he deplores. Employing a parable of Jacob and Laban, Shylock provokes Antonio to ask, 'And what of him? did he take interest?' This affords Shylock the opportunity of savouring the word, endowing it with a talismanic quality: 'No, not take interest, not as you would say / Directly int'rest' (1.3.50–77).

Timon's steward Flavius expresses his anguish that he is unable to restrain his master's reckless generosity, which has become so excessive that he has to borrow to finance it: 'He is so kind that he now / Pays interest for't; his land's put to their books' (*TIM* 1.2.199–200). When the senators reject Alcebiades' plea for clemency for one of his soldiers he gives vent to his disgust and opens a window on their activities: 'I have kept back their foes, / While they have told their money, and let out / Their coin upon large interest – I myself / Rich only in large hurts' (3.5.105–8). The picture of the rich Athenians counting their money and augmenting it by **usurious** rates of interest, while Alcibiades fought to defend the city, is a telling one.

Perhaps the supreme example of interest as property rights arises in the opening of *LR*. Relinquishing power, Lear strips himself of all rights of ownership: 'Since now we will divest us both of rule, / Interest of territory, cares of state' (1.1.49–50). King Charles of France accepts the conditions proposed by York, with the proviso, 'Only reserv'd, you claim no interest / In any of our towns of garrison' (*1H6* 5.4.167–8).

The idea of interest as personal involvement is well expressed by the Duke of Verona. Responding to the pleas of the Montague and Capulet families he alludes to the death of his kinsman Mercutio: 'I have an interest in your hearts' proceeding; / My blood for your rude brawls doth lie a-bleeding' (*ROM* 3.1.188–9).

Audrey's disclaimer to Touchstone's comment that 'a youth in the forest lays claim to you' is of special interest because it appears to conflate two meanings: 'he hath no interest in me in the world' (*AYL* 5.1.6–9). This implies that he has no valid claim; also that he is indifferent to her. Certainly to the modern ear the second meaning is the one that would register, whereas to Shakespeare's audience the first would be the active interpretation. William does in fact express an interest in Audrey only to be bamboozled by Touchstone. Audrey has obviously perceived the warm breath of William's desire, but evidently the matter has not proceeded to the point of any kind of arrangement or formal agreement. She considers herself a free agent. William has no title or claim to her.

(C) Of vital importance here are: Sullivan, *The Rhetoric of Credit*; Woodbridge, ed., *Money and the Age of Shakespeare*; Hawkes, *Idols of the Market Place*; Agnew, *Worlds Apart*; Long, *The Unnatural Scene*; Jones, *God and the Moneylenders*; Nelson, *The Idea of Usury*; Shell, *Money, Language and Thought*.

invest

(A) Surprisingly, the verb is not used in the modern financial sense, but, bearing political significance, the word means to install in office or to empower; clothe; permeate or impregnate; call upon or press.

(B) When Lear spurns Cordelia and divides his kingdom between Cornwall and Albany he says, 'I do invest you jointly with my power, / Pre-eminence, and all the large effects / That troop with majesty' (*LR* 1.1.130–2). 'Endow' is perhaps the best synonym here.

An intriguing exchange occurs when the ambitious and ruthless Antonio endeavours to overcome Sebastian's reluctance to murder his brother: 'If you but knew how you the purpose cherish / Whiles thus you mock it! how, in stripping it, / You more invest it!' (*TMP* 2.1.224–6). In other words, your protestations reveal your ambition rather than any disinclination: your very words clothe or adorn your desires while they assert naked innocence.

The Chorus in *H5* provides a highly evocative description of the English forces on the eve of the Battle of Agincourt: 'their gesture sad, / Investing lank-lean cheeks and war-worn coats, / Presented them unto the gazing moon / So many horrid ghosts' (Cho 4 25–8). As this is a unique usage, choice of the most apt synonym is open to question, but 'permeating' or 'impregnating' seem about right.

(C) See Kermode, *Shakespeare's Language*, and Jones, *Shakespeare at Work*.

investments

(A) The plural noun occurs only twice, both times signifying garments, which appears to be a Shakespearian coinage. It seems likely, however, that Polonius puns on the word so that its secondary meaning may well correspond to the modern usage, financial instruments.

(B) As the respective leaders parley at Gaultree Forest, Westmorland enumerates the attributes and functions of the Archbishop of York in such a way as to highlight the incongruity of this distinguished cleric appearing at the head of a rebel army: 'Whose beard the silver hand of peace hath touch'd, / Whose learning and good letters peace hath tutor'd, / Whose white investments figure innocence' (*2H4* 4.1.43–5). This is a politically adroit move, the image of the pristine garments symbolizing peace and godliness putting the Archbishop in a false position.

Polonius in a spectacular verbal *tour-de-force* inverts every one of Ophelia's representations of Hamlet's love, concluding,

> Do not believe his vows, for they are brokers,
> Not of that dye which their investments show,
> But mere implorators of unholy suits,
> Breathing like sanctified and pious bonds,
> The better to beguile.
>
> *HAM* 1.3.127–31

The presence of **brokers** and **bonds** in these lines, points in the direction of an innovative use of 'investments' as financial instruments. Thompson and Taylor, eds, *Hamlet*, Arden 3, 200, point out that 'Theobold's popular emendation of bonds to "**bawds**" destroys the *vows–suits–bonds* triplet, but "bawds" does go nicely with brokers'. Though broker is most active in the sense of bawd, it can signify *any* agent or go-between. Even acceptance of this emendation, therefore, does nothing to discredit the plausibility of investments operating in the financial as well as the sartorial field. Polonius reaches the peak of his intellectual ability in this speech, so the likelihood of a double-meaning attaching to investments is particularly strong.

(C) See the highly perceptive essay on the language of *HAM* by Ewbank, in Muir and Wells, eds, *Aspects of Hamlet*, esp. 99, for a discussion of the passage in question (reprinted in Alexander, ed., *Shakespeare and Language*). Also Kermode, *Shakespeare's Language*; Jones, *Shakespeare at Work*. Crucial to the etymology and context is Forman, 'Material dispossessions and counterfeit investments' in Woodbridge, ed., *Money and the Age of Shakespeare*. Of interest too is White's chapter on Ophelia in *Innocent Victims*.

jointress

(A) This term applies to a woman holding a property right from her deceased husband. The sole example possesses considerable political significance because it helps Claudius claim the Danish throne.

(B) Claudius' first appearance in the play requires a major public statement that involves a difficult balancing act. He has to justify his acquisition of the throne and the hasty marriage to his brother's widow. This masterpiece of political rhetoric contains the lines, 'Therefore our sometime sister, now our queen, / Th'imperial jointress to this warlike state' (*HAM* 1.2.8–9). She is 'jointress' by virtue of inheriting rights from her deceased husband and as consort to the reigning monarch, seamlessly linking the two regimes. In this way the dubious **practice** of brother rather than son succeeding to the throne appears natural. While there is no explicit statement in the play that the prevailing system is one of primogeniture, Hamlet makes it clear that he feels cheated out of his rightful inheritance. In addition to this seething resentment, apparent from the outset, Hamlet loathes Polonius as the political agent who has aided and abetted Claudius. Having escaped from Claudius' trap, Hamlet confides to Horatio the justification for **exacting** revenge for all the wrongs done to him: 'He that hath kill'd my king and whor'd my mother, / Popp'd in between th'election and my hopes, / Thrown out his angle for my proper life' (5.2.64–6). For all the subtlety and guile embodied in Claudius' key public speech – with its masterly deployment of assonance, alliteration, oxymoron and antithesis – it belongs to the category of utterance so despised by Cordelia, 'that glib and oily art' (*LR* 1.1.224).

(C) McAlindon, *Shakespeare's Tragic Cosmos*, and Watts, *Hamlet*, both engage with the concepts duality and unity. See entry on **jointure**. McDonald, *Shakespeare and the Arts of Language*, and Mack, *Renaissance Rhetoric*, are of particular interest here.

jointure

(A) This term indicates a marriage settlement designating the portion of a husband's estate to which his widow is entitled.

(B) When the French King Lewis consents to the proposal of marriage between his sister and the newly enthroned Yorkist, King Edward IV, he sets forth the necessary protocol: 'And now forthwith shall articles be drawn / Touching the jointure that your king must make, / With which her dowry shall be counterpois'd' (*3H6* 3.3.135–7). In this case the agreement is not ratified, because in the meantime Edward has become enamoured of the widow Grey and married her – with devastating political and military consequences.

In *WIV* Justice Shallow promises Anne Page on behalf of his dim-witted nephew Slender that, 'He will make you a hundred and fifty pounds jointure' (3.4.48–9). Like *WIV*, *SHR* is replete with financial transactions including the auction of Bianca Minola. Old Gremio, and Tranio disguised as Lucentio, engage in an active bidding war which provides an indication of the magnitude of possessions and sheer luxury involved. This scene possesses several interesting dimensions, but central to it is the transactional nature of social life with Bianca being sold, and the transformative nature of **money** whereby cash, ships and 'Turkey cushions' express the essence of 'commodification'. Baptista is explicit: ' 'Tis deeds must win the prize, and he of both / That can assure my daughter greatest dower / Shall have my Bianca's love' (2.1.342–4). In other words, possession of Bianca will be achieved by the individual with most possessions. But if she is sold, so too are the suitors: their identities become subsumed into their material possessions. Both bride and suitors are commodified. **Commodities**, in their turn, become articulate. Old Gremio, soon to be outbid by Tranio on behalf of Lucentio, lists his assets:

> First, as you know, my house within the city
> Is richly furnished with plate and gold,
> Basins and ewers to lave her dainty hands;
> My hangings all of Tyrian tapestry;
> In ivory coffers I have stuff'd my crowns;
> In cypress chests my arras counterpoints,
> Costly apparel, tents, and canopies,
> Fine linen, Turkey cushions boss'd with pearl,
> Valens of Venice gold in needle-work;
>
> 2.1.346–54

The game is far from over at this stage as capital assets such as land, farm, stock, ships and trading networks have yet to be brought forth: the guarantee of a continuing flow of consumer goods.

Petruchio is not burdened with such negotiations as he immediately cuts to the heart of the matter, stating his **wealth** and lineage, and requesting the sum of Kate's dowry (half Baptista's land on his demise 'And in possession twenty thousand crowns'). That stated he is generously unequivocal:

> And for that dowry, I'll assure her of
> Her widowhood, be it that she survive me,
> In all my lands and leases whatsoever.
> Let specialities be therefore drawn between us,
> That covenants may be kept on either hand.
>
> 2.1.121–7

However much or little affection is involved, marriage is part of a web of financial considerations taking account of risks in a carefully calculated **cost**–benefit analysis. From the Lord's description of his household (*Induction* 1.44.68) we enter a world of material possessions and a consciousness of its seductive pleasures.

(C) The Sokols' entry on jointure in *Shakespeare's Legal Language* is particularly informative about the legal aspects, historical and contextual. Jordan and Cunningham, eds, *The Law in Shakespeare*, is richly explorative; Jardine, *Worldly Goods*, Orlin, 'Shakespearean comedy and material life' in Dutton and Howard, eds, *Companion to Shakespeare's Works – Vol. III: The Comedies*, and Huebert, *The Performance of Pleasure in English Renaissance Drama*, provide valuable insights into the materiality and luxury of the Renaissance world. The interpenetration of the emotional and material worlds finds clear expression in several essays in Woodmansee and Osteen, eds, *The New Economic Criticism*. Important, too, are Korda, 'Household Kates: domestic commodities in *The Taming of the Shrew*', *Shakespeare Quarterly* 47 (1996): 110–31; Aspinall, ed., *The Taming of the Shrew*, Wynne-Davies, ed., *Much Ado About Nothing* and *The Taming of the Shrew*. It is worth noting Boas' insightful comment on Slender in *Shakespeare and his Predecessors*, 298: 'In Slender not only do we see intellect flickering with its last feeble glimmer, but the will attenuated almost to vanishing point. Palpitating on the brink of nonentity, he clings for support to the majestic personality of Shallow.' (Cited by Oliver, *The Merry Wives of Windsor*, Arden 2, Ixxiii.)

lean

(A) Primarily signifying land that is **barren** or unproductive, the adjective also means slight or insignificant. The verb has two facets, depend on or relate to, and incline towards or need the support of.

(B) Falstaff employs the word in its agricultural sense as a metaphor to explain why Hal is so different in temperament from his coldly calculating, humourless brother John: 'Hereof comes it that Prince Harry is valiant, for the cold blood he did naturally inherit of his father, he hath, like lean, sterile, and bare land, manur'd, husbanded, and till'd with excellent endeavour of drinking good and good store or fertile sherris, that he is become very hot and valiant' (*2H4* 4.3.117–22). Here the ironies are multiple. Falstaff extols what the King and court deplore as Hal's dissolute, unprincely behaviour. The reality is that tavern life is being employed fruitfully by Hal in ways that neither the court nor his drinking companions comprehend.

As Antony and Octavius prepare for an acrimonious encounter, the third member of the triumvirate, Lepidus, attempts to play the peacemaker, claiming that the source of their antipathy is slight compared with the significance of the political principle that unites them: 'Noble friends, / That which combin'd us was most great, and let not / A leaner action rend us' (*ANT* 2.2.17–19).

In a dialogue characterized by wordplay Falstaff puns on 'suits' in the sense of petitions and suits as garments: 'Yea for the obtaining of suits, whereof the hangman has no lean wardrobe' (*1H4* 1.2.72–3). Meagre is the meaning here as the victims' clothes were the perquisite of the hangman.

Giving instructions for Hamlet's immediate despatch to England, Claudius concludes, 'Away, for everything is seal'd and done / That else leans on th'affair' (*HAM* 4.3.56–7). 'Relates to' is the meaning here.

The Queen, in attempting to **suborn** Pisanio, cautions him that it is folly to depend upon or maintain fidelity to the exiled Posthumus: 'What shalt thou expect / To be depender on a thing that leans? / Who cannot be new built, nor has no friends / So much as but to prop him?' (*CYM* 1.5.57–60). This is an interesting configuration because it encapsulates the nature of court life and the whole process of patronage and interdependencies. The politic Queen spells out what would be obvious to anyone other than the scrupulously honest man.

(C) Denton, ed., *Orders and Hierarchies in Late Medieval and Renaissance Europe*, is the source of much interesting discussion on the intricacies of hierarchies and their transformations. Aughterson, ed., *The English Renaissance*, contains an informative section of contemporary writing on society and social life, urban and rural. Leibler, *Shakespeare's Festive Tragedy*, is central to this discussion. Insightful on language is Salmon, 'Elizabethan colloquial English in the Falstaff plays' in Salmon and Burness, eds, *A Reader in the Language of Shakespearean Drama*.

lendings
(A) Used only twice, the word means advance payments (for soldiers); applied metaphorically it indicates borrowings.

(B) Bolingbroke includes in his list of allegations against Mowbray, malfeasance:
'That Mowbray hath receiv'd eight thousand nobles / In name of lendings for your Highness' soldiers, / The which he hath detain'd for lewd employments' (*R2* 1.1.88–90). In other words the advance payments for military outlays have been misappropriated.

The mad Lear, confronted by the violent tempest, contemplates the nature of mankind and decides to discard his clothes which he perceives as illegitimate borrowings from nature – something Mad Tom in his loincloth is not guilty of, thereby providing a model to emulate: 'Thou ow'st the worm no silk, the beast no hide, the sheep no wool, the cat no perfume. Ha? here's three on's are sophisticated. Thou art the thing itself: unaccommodated man is no more but such a poor, bare, fork'd animal as thou art. Off, off, you lendings! Come, unbutton here' (*LR* 3.4.103–9).

(C) See Holderness, ed., *Shakespeare's History Plays*; Bolam, 'Richard II: Shakespeare and the language of the stage' in Hattaway, ed., *Shakespeare's History Plays*; Ryan ed., *King Lear*; Carroll, *Fat King, Lean Beggar*.

machiavel

(A) A generic term intimating extreme guile, ruthlessness and absence of morality, Shakespeare uses the word three times: once denoting the embodiment of guile and duplicity, once as a term of abuse, and on one occasion in a richly comic context. Characteristically, he employs the concept extensively. The term was coined in response to the presumed doctrines of Niccolo Machiavelli (1469–1527) whose *Il Principe* was completed in 1514, published in 1532 and translated into English as *The Prince* in 1640. Machiavelli's famous book was intended as a handbook for rulers and sought to make a distinction between effective action and moral behaviour. Having served in the new republic of Florence during the first decade of the sixteenth century, Machiavelli was consigned to the political wilderness with the change of regime in 1512. Forced retirement led him to devote the rest of his life to disquisitions on government and war: his analysis of republican government, *Discorsi sopra la prima deca di T. Livio*, was published in 1531 and translated into English in 1636 as *Discorses on Livy*; *Dell'arte della guerra* or *The Art of War* was published in 1521 and appeared in English in 1562. Witness to the lighter side of Machiavelli is his comic play of seduction *Mandragola*, which was completed around 1518 but not translated into English until 1940. Despite Machiavelli's careful distinction between moral acts and those designed to retain power, in the popular imagination he was the equivalent of the Devil himself. The conflation of Machiavelli and the Devil revitalized the term Old Nick (an epithet for the Devil predating Machiavelli). Shakespeare was probably acquainted with *Il Principe*, but the dramatic potentiality of the populist representation was greater than a sophisticated application of his ideas. This is probably why the dramatist entertains Machiavelli's concepts with great penetration without attaching the term to the actions of his *true* Machiavels: Octavius Caesar, Mark Antony, in *JC* and *ANT*; Bolingbroke/Henry IV, in *R2* and *1H4* and *2H4*; Prince Hal/Henry V; Prince John in *2H4*; and Edmund and the entire faction

165

consisting of Cornwall, Goneril, Regan and Oswald in *LR*. Cardinal Pandulph embodies the essence of the Machiavel in *JN* where the concept of Machievellianism enters the bloodstream of political life. Claudius (*HAM*) is another sturdy representative of the Machiavel. Shakespeare's populist Machiavels are Richard Gloucester who identifies himself as such in *3H6*, and Iago. The Host of the Garter uses the term playfully.

(B) Machiavel appeared as the prologue in Marlowe's *The Jew of Malta* enunciating his vision and his spirit as universal mover in the world:

> I count religion but a childish toy,
> And hold there is no sin but ignorance.
>
> . . .
>
> I come not, I,
> To read a lecture here in Britany,
> But to present the tragedy of a Jew,
> Who smiles to see how full his bags are crammed,
> Which money was not got without my means.
>
> Prologue, 14–32

Shakespeare employs the term sparingly but has characters who behave with all the amoral subtlety, guile and cynicism of the monster of popular imagination. Unlike Richard who celebrates his role as the very embodiment, the compound of Machiavellian iniquity, Iago plays the Machiavel with icy control. Significantly the word '**beguile**', used primarily by Shakespeare in the sense of to deceive, is used more frequently in *OTH* than in any other play. Iago is more coldly Machiavellian than Richard Ill, who does break down, suffers a crisis of identity and experiences remorse (*R3* 5.3.177–206): Iago evinces no such anguish or inwardness, giving vent to passion only through a jealousy, which, as he expresses it, 'Doth (like a poisonous mineral) gnaw my inwards' (*OTH* 2.1.297). Edmund is the complete Machiavel in that he cold-bloodedly plots the destruction of both his father and brother, and arranges the murder of Lear and Cordelia. He also uses his co-conspirators Goneril and Regan to maximize his own advantage. Unlike Iago, however, he does attempt to save Lear and Cordelia, though only when their deaths can be of no advantage to him. The perfect Machiavel? A strong contender for the position of supreme Machiavel in Shakespeare (though the term is never attached to him) is Octavius Caesar. Within the narrow confines of his 33 lines in *JC* he is evidently elbowing Antony aside, using his fallen enemy Brutus ('Within my tent his bones to-night shall lie, / Most like a soldier, ordered honourably' (5.5.78–9)), adopting the mantle of his great uncle Julius Caesar, and delivering the final lines of the play. In *ANT* his Machiavellianism is so breathtaking that critics still debate whether he is sincere in attempting a renewed alliance with Antony by promoting his marriage with Octavia. His icy calculation is responsible for the greatest piece of dramatic irony in Shakespeare. Entreating his fellow world-sharer to take a second cup of wine, Antony uses the phrase 'Be a child o'th'time' (2.7.100). Octavius is the supreme child of the time in that he sees life as a political chessboard and is always a move ahead of his advisors – and several moves ahead of his antagonists. This child of the time was to be the first Roman emperor and consequently master of the world at the time of the birth of Christ.

Significantly, the most authentic 'Machiavellian' characters are Henry IV and Prince Hal, both of whom, rather than indulging in vengeance, carefully balance severity and clemency with a view to long-term **advantage**. Hal displays his Machiavellian qualities early in *1H4* when he makes it clear to the audience that his 'loose behaviour' is merely a mask that will be removed when he becomes king – a strategy designed to create a heightened appreciation of his kingly qualities: 'So when this loose behaviour I throw off / And pay the debt I never promised, / By how much better than my word I am, / By so much shall I falsify men's hopes' (1.2.208–11).

He also requests the freedom of the Douglas after the Battle of Shrewsbury, presumably seeking an accommodation with the Scots by a display of magnanimity. His ice-cold brother, John of Lancaster, is utterly Machiavellian in persuading his opponents to surrender at Gaultree Forest under the pretence of affording them pardons before proceeding to execute them – justifying his action by means of a verbal quibble (*2H4* 4.2.54–123). The new King Henry V is often reviled for Machiavellianism when he publicly discards Falstaff with a harsh rebuke during his coronation (*2H4* 5.5.47–71), but arguably he is at his most Machiavellian in *H5* where he arranges matters so that the Archbishop of Canterbury has a strong vested interest in promoting the war with France. Canterbury removes all responsibility from Henry by responding to the King's caution, 'May I with right and conscience make this claim?' with the unequivocal statement, 'The sin upon my head, dread sovereign!' (1.2.96–7). Henry also sets up the traitors Cambridge, Scroop and Grey, luring them into censure of a drunken soldier before exposing their assassination plot, giving them no moral grounds to plead for clemency. Likewise Henry pursues his remorseless ambition to conquer France while constantly invoking God – not least by proclaiming God's hand as the decisive influence at the Battle of Agincourt: 'O God, thy arm was here' (4.8.107). That this is a family trait is demonstrated with striking force by Henry IV on his deathbed. He advises Hal to divert curiosity about the legitimacy of their title to the throne by engaging in foreign wars: 'Therefore, my Harry, / Be it thy course to busy giddy minds / With foreign quarrels, that action, hence borne out, / May waste the memory of the former days' (*2H4* 4.5.212–15).

In the popular sense, the quintessential Machiavellians are Richard III and Iago. Richard daringly declares this identity in *3H6* when enunciating his plans for the future. His speech, which is over 70 lines long, employs the word Machiavel in a way that gives the fullest colouration to the term:

> Why, I can smile, and murder whiles I smile,
>
>   . . .
> I'll play the orator as well as Nestor,
> Deceive more slily than Ulysses could,

> And like a Sinon, take another Troy.
> I can add colors to the chameleon,
> Change shapes with Proteus for advantages,
> And set the murderous Machiavel to school.
> 3.2.182–93

Here, the most notorious dissimulators, the very symbols of deception, are drawn together to culminate in the Machiavel. Curiously, the only other uses of the term Machiavel in the plays are trivial by comparison. As Joan Pucelle panics at the prospect of being burned alive by the English, she protests that she is pregnant, citing Alencon as the father, provoking the Duke of York to exclaim: 'Alanson, that notorious Machiavel? / It dies, and if it had a thousand lives' (*1H6* 5.4.74–5). What is a term of abuse here becomes the subject of a comic expression when the loquacious Host of the Garter, who delights in making language dance, celebrates his tricking of Evans the Welsh Parson and Caius the French Doctor, thereby preventing their duel, by exclaiming: 'Am I politic? Am I subtle? Am I a Machiavel?' (*WIV* 3.1.101).

Even Cassius displays a Machiavellian streak (Shakespeare's character, unlike his historical counterpart, manufactures the 'public' appeal to Brutus), but it is outweighed by a warm, emotional current which proves politically costly.

The Bastard Faulconbridge and King John can both lay claim to being Machiavels as can the majority of the characters in that play – though Cardinal Pandulph outdoes them all. For key aspects of their Machiavellianism see the entry on **commodity**. This list is not exhaustive and would inevitably include others such as Sicinius and Brutus the guileful tribunes in *COR*.

(C) Modern translations of Machiavelli are easily available. These include the Penguin edition of *The Prince* that contains a good Introduction with a commentary on detailed scholarly works. Likewise, some shrewd observations are made in Bondanella's Introduction to his translation in the Worlds Classics Series. Not to be missed is White's acclaimed recent study *Machievelli*. Coyle, ed., *Machievelli's The Prince*, is characterized by range and insight. An extended discussion of the evolution of the Machiavel in Shakespeare is provided by Danby, *Shakespeare and the Doctrine of Nature*. Ferroni's 'Transformation and adaptation in Machiavelli's *Mandragola*' in Ascoli and Kahn, eds, *Machiavelli and the Discourse of Literature* – a measured, sympathetic analysis – reveals the disparity between popular conceptions and the subtle, penetrating, engaging critique provided by Machiavelli. A rigorous appraisal of the significance of Machiavelli in the plays of Shakespeare and Marlowe can be found in Grady, *Shakespeare, Machiavelli and Montaigne*; Hadfield, *Shakespeare and Renaissance Politics*, esp. ch. 2; Agnew, *Worlds Apart*, esp. 126; Spivack, *Shakespeare and the Allegory of Evil*; Bawcutt, ed., *The Jew of Malta*, Introduction; Cheney, ed., *Christopher Marlowe*; Riggs, *The World of Christopher Marlowe*; Bushnell, *Tragedies of Tyrants*, esp. ch. 2; Spivak, *In Other Worlds*; Kamps, ed., *Materialist Shakespeare*; Foakes, *Shakespeare and Violence*; Barton, 'Livy, Machiavelli and Shakespeare in *Coriolanus*' in *Essays, Mainly Shakespearean*.

Admired for the clarity of his political thinking and lucidity of expression, Machiavelli's influence was wide ranging among political thinkers, literary figures and those in the forefront of public life. As Anne Barton comments:

> The notion that Machiavelli reached sixteenth century England only as a stock stage villain, a caricature agent of hell, has long since been exploded. Among Shakespeare's contemporaries, Sidney, Spenser, Gabriel Harvey, Nashe, Kyd, Marston, Bacon, Fulke Greville, Ralegh and Ben Jonson, to name only a few, were clearly familiar not only with the devilish practices and opinions popularly attributed to Machiavelli, but with what he had actually written. (148)

The following comments serve as a prologue to Grady's major study:

> No work has been more consequential for the classic post-Enlightenment practice of seeing in the Renaissance the beginnings of a modernity still in force than Niccolò Machiavelli's *The Prince*, and the literature on this topic is hundreds of years old, multidisciplinary, and extensive. In the present context, despite the great interest of Machiavelli's writings on numerous political and cultural topics, Machiavelli is most relevant as perhaps the most significant conduit for the dissemination in Tudor England of those two constitutive forms of modern rationality, instrumental and critical reason. (60)

> The last play of Shakespeare's *Henriad, Henry V,* is in many ways the most Machiavellian of them all, celebrating a Prince who succeeded in astonishing feats of conquest and national unification while coolly depicting how that Prince's heroic achievements were accomplished by political manipulation, image manufacture, violence, and the threat of violence. (204)

market

(A) This word can refer to the **market-place** or the network of transactions occurring there; **purchase**, spending, or outlay; profitable use; opportunity to make a **profit**.

(B) In the paradigm case of marketing, the brothel-keeper gives the servant Boult instructions: 'Search the market narrowly, Meteline is full of gallants. We have lost too much money this mart by being too wenchless' (*PER* 4.2.3–5). Pander's comment highlights the opportunity **cost** of having lots of potential customers but lacking the women to meet the demand. 'Market' applies not only to the physical space but also to transactional opportunities. Clearly, the **mart** is a time when **traders** and **customers** come together, affording the brothel-keeper the opportunity of purchasing working **capital**, i.e., women, and also attracting clients because the market acts as a magnet. Boult is in fact successful in purchasing Marina from the pirates, and so the first question Bawd asks him is, 'Now, sir, hast thou cried her through the market?' (4.2.93). Again there arises the double possibility of a market-place and the transactional flow of interactions.

When Antonio and Sebastian arrive in Illyria, the older man goes off to arrange accommodation. He gives his purse to his young friend, explaining, 'Haply your eye shall light upon some toy / You have desire to purchase; and your store / I think is not for idle markets, sir' (*TN* 3.3.44–6). The implication is that Sebastian lacks the wherewithal for frivolous purchases. Outlay seems the most appropriate synonym for market in this case.

'Profitable use' or 'outlay' is the meaning attaching to the word in *HAM*. Characteristic of the play is the figure hendiadys, in which a pregnant phrase is made up of seemingly parallel words. Hamlet asks the rhetorical question, 'What is a man, / If his chief good and market of his time / Be but to sleep and feed?' (4.4.33–5). Benefit and expenditure seems to capture the essence of the phrase 'good and market'. Typically, the figure hendiadys is untranslatable, but the element 'good' implying welfare by being harnessed to 'market' (relations governed by money) creates a tension, suggestive of the inadequacy of the material without the spiritual.

The Epilogue in *TNK* is fearful that the audience may 'hiss, and kill / Our market' (8–9). Opportunity to make a profit is the likely meaning here because a bad reception will preclude future performances and further takings.

(C) There is now a superabundance of material relating to the nature and role of the market in Shakespeare. The following are particularly important and contain extensive bibliographies: Agnew, *Worlds Apart*, esp. 18–56; Bruster, *Drama and the Market in the Age of Shakespeare*; Woodbridge, ed., *Money and the Age of Shakespeare*; Hawkes, *Idols of the Marketplace*, esp. 226–30; Turner, *Shakespeare's Twenty-First Century Economics*; Harris, *Sick Economies*; Woodmansee and Osteen, eds, *The New Economic Criticism*; Halpern, *The Poetics of Primitive Accumulation*; Muldrew, *The Economy of Obligation*; Hyde, *The Gift*; Howard and Shershow, eds, *Marxist Shakespeares*; Leinwand, *Theatre, Finance and Society in Early Modern England*.

market-maid, market-man

(A) These terms are derogatory, employed by someone of high standing and directed towards peasants or common people engaged in the **purchase** and sale of commonplace goods in the **market**.

(B) Suffolk strives to defend the astonishing announcement that Henry's wife-to-be comes without a dowry: 'So worthless peasants bargain for their wives, / As market men for oxen, sheep, or horse' (*1H6* 5.5.53–4).

The sole use of market-maid is both simple and fascinating. Octavia, having taken it upon herself to act as go-between in an attempt to resolve the differences between Mark Antony and Octavius, arrives in Rome with a modest entourage, even though her husband has invited her to 'command what cost / Your heart has mind to' (*ANT* 3.4.37–8). Octavius Caesar seizes on her natural dislike of display to denounce Antony for humiliating her and denying him the political **advantages** of an elaborate welcome:

> the dust
> Should have ascended to the roof of heaven,
> Rais'd by your populous troops. But you are come

A market-maid to Rome, and have prevented
The ostentation of our love, which, left unshown,
Is often left unlov'd.

3.6.48–53

This guileful piece of political rhetoric, in which public relations masquerades as personal affection, is balanced on this unique usage of 'market-maid'. Awareness of Caesar's guile is sometimes heightened in performance when Octavia arrives beautifully attired. The incongruity of attaching the term 'market-maid' to her comes close to provoking laughter.

(C) Deats, ed., *Antony and Cleopatra*, contains several essays that cast significant light on the political, theatrical and linguistic features of the conflicts in *ANT*. Marrapodi, ed., *Shakespeare, Italy and Intertextuality*, deals with important aspects of this topic as do the books on the Roman plays in the bibliography. See entry on **market**.

market-place

(A) Signifying the space where buying and selling takes place, the market-place is also the arena for public meetings and political events. Almost half the applications of this word occur in Shakespeare's most political play, *COR*. In all, the Roman plays account for two-thirds of the usages. Hence it is by no means a neutral term, but frequently accretes a socially opprobrious character.

(B) Brutus concurs with his fellow tribune that Coriolanus will not achieve political office:

I heard him swear,
Were he to stand for consul, never would he
Appear i'th'market-place, nor on him put
The napless vesture of humility,
Nor, showing (as the manner is) his wounds
To th'people, beg their stinking breaths.

COR 2.1.231–6

This time-honoured **practice** is repugnant to Coriolanus, especially the need to boast about heroic actions that he deems obligations, but to do such things in the market-place is utterly demeaning to a man who sees all economic activity as vulgar, the province of the **plebeians** or those undeserving of respect. Not only does Coriolanus participate in the ceremony, albeit gracelessly, but the market-place in Rome is the arena of his undoing when he is tried and exiled. Finally, having joined the Volscians, he is assassinated in the market-place. Thus the fundamental artery of economic life is an alien and fatal space for Shakespeare's mightiest warrior. Even Talbot expresses disgust at having been put on show as a prisoner in the market-place: 'In open market-place produc'd they me / To be a public spectacle to all' (*1H6* 1.4.40–1).

No less indignant is Octavius Caesar when describing Mark Antony's un-Roman antics in Egypt: 'Here's the manner of't: / I'th'market-place, on a tribunal silver'd, / Cleopatra and himself in chairs of gold / Were publicly enthron'd' (*ANT* 3.6.2–5).

The lesson to be derived from the majority of these references to the market-place is that though this great *public* space where *everyone* comes to **trade** and gossip is fundamental to the lifeblood of the society, its odour of **traffic** is offensive to the nostrils of the political and military elite. Nevertheless, the very centrality of the market-place as a physical space ensures that it doubles as commercial centre and political forum. The crown-offering scene in *JC* occurs there. As Casca explains, Julius Caesar 'fell down in the market-place, and foam'd at mouth, and was speechless' (1.2.252–3). Mark Antony, playing the humble petitioner to the assassins, requests that he may be allowed to reverence his friend and benefactor, Julius Caesar: 'Produce his body in the market-place, / And in the pulpit, as becomes a friend, / Speak in the order of his funeral' (3.1.228–30). The market-place is the perfect arena for the rhetorical skills of this accomplished orator. Caesar's will, his gown, his fame, his body all fill this transactional space in such a way that the very throb of everyday life coalesces with the high drama of political theatre. This audience becomes transformed into a force that re-**fashions** Rome.

The peculiar scope of the market-place receives striking expression by way of metaphor during a solemn funeral ceremony in *TNK*. The Third Queen says: 'This world's a city full of straying streets, / And death's the market-place, where each one meets' (1.5.15–16). It is hard to imagine a more emphatic acknowledgement of the centrality of the market-place: it registers the heartbeat of commercial, social, and even political life, contributing the perfect metaphor for the ultimate meeting place of high and low alike.

(C) Agnew's *World's Apart* contains an excellent analysis of the evolution and function of the market-place. See also Thomas 'Shakespeare's sources' in Zander, ed., *Julius Caesar*, esp. 103–7, for an exploration of the transformative features present in the forum scene. Keen insights are provided by Miola, 'Shakespeare's ancient Rome' in Hattaway, ed., *Shakespeare's History Plays*; Mulryne, 'Cleopatra's barge and Antony's body' in Marrapodi, ed., *Shakespeare, Italy and Intertextuality*. See entry on **market** for further references.

market-price

(A) Surprisingly, a unique usage indicating the **price** prevailing in response to conditions of supply and demand in the **market-place** as opposed to an object of special **value** not **traded** in a common way.

(B) In attempting to wriggle out of a humiliating situation, Bertram admits that he slept with Diana, claiming that his ring, a family heirloom, was the price he paid for her accommodation: 'She got the ring, / And I had that which any inferior might / At market-price have bought' (*AWW* 5.3.217–19). This ploy reduces Diana to the level of a prostitute. It is significant that the one use of the word occurs in the context of sex. As so often in the plays, a key area of **market** transactions is the brothel and its associated activities.

(C) Important here are Donawerth, *Shakespeare and the Sixteenth-Century Study of Language,* esp. ch. 7 and Zitner, *All's Well That Ends Well.* See entry on **market**.

mart

(A) This word applies to both the **market** as a physical place and to the transactions of buying, selling and dealing.

(B) The play in which the mart as **market-place** figures most prominently is *ERR,* where it occurs 10 times out of a total of 16 in the entire canon. Commerce is the lifeblood of Ephesus. Most expressive, however, is Shylock's comment on the crestfallen Antonio: 'a beggar, that was us'd to come so smug upon the mart' (*MV* 3.1.46–7).

The transactional use of the word is usually neutral, but it enters into the unsavoury arena of corruption in the quarrel scene of *JC* where Brutus lashes Cassius with the accusation, 'Let me tell you, Cassius, you yourself / Are much condemn'd to have an itching palm, / To sell and mart your offices for gold / To undeservers' (4.3.9–12).

Baptista having agreed with the seemingly mad Petruchio that he shall marry his equally wild daughter Kate, exclaims, 'now I play the merchant's part / And venture madly on a desperate mart' (*SHR* 2.1.326–7). He means 'transaction', 'arrangement' or '**bargain**'. Delivered lightly and with a sigh of relief, it nevertheless insinuates the market into a matrimonial arrangement. Later, of course, the dominant force of the commercial and pecuniary in relation to marriage becomes even more evident.

The significance of international **trade** is present in *HAM* when Marcellus seeks an explanation for the hectic military activity, including 'And why such daily cast of brazen cannon, / And foreign mart for implements of war' (1.1.73–4). Not only is domestic production proceeding apace but military hardware is being imported.

An interesting case occurs in *CYM.* When Iachimo offers himself as a replacement for Posthumus in Imogen's bed (having falsely denounced her husband for being unfaithful to her), she suddenly sees through him. Her disgust and indignation are not merely personal; she claims that Iachimo has defiled the court by employing the wiles and proposals characteristic of a brothel:

> The King my father shall be made acquainted
> Of thy assault. If he shall think it fit
> A saucy stranger in his court to mart
> As in a Romish stew, and to expound
> His beastly mind to us, he hath a court
> He little cares for and a daughter who
> He not respects at all. What ho, Pisanio!
>
> 1.6.149–55

To mart here is to 'bargain' or 'negotiate'. As so often, prostitution resides close to the centre of market transactions. The space Imogen creates between the court and a stew registers an important ideological point. For her the court represents a set of **values** totally at odds with the market, emphatically distanced from its more sordid **exchanges**.

(C) For the commercial dimensions of *ERR* and *SHR* see Wilson, 'Commerce, community, and nostalgia in *The Comedy of Errors*' in Woodbridge, ed., *Money and the Age of Shakespeare*; Parker, *Shakespeare from the Margins*, ch. 2; Miola, ed., *The Comedy of Errors*; Aspinall, ed., *The Taming of the Shrew*; Stevenson, *Praise and Paradox*. Cohen, *Shakespeare and Technology*, ch. 4, is highly informative on military technology. See entry on **market**.

mechanic, mechanical

(A) This is a word that has two distinctive aspects, one signifying a menial, manual worker or craftsman; the other stressing the commonplace or vulgar. Whether used in the sphere of economic life or of social relations, the term is active and strong, contempt being the animating feeling as comments are made by the socially elevated about the common people – though arguably pity is uppermost on at least one occasion. Admiration for their skills or craftsmanship is absent.

(B) A comprehensive overview of economic and social life is provided by the Archbishop of Canterbury. Having already delivered legal justification for Henry's invasion he advances the analogy of division of labour in his endeavour to provide a logistic validation of war with France. His representation of a functioning society includes the lines: 'The singing masons building roofs of gold, / The civil citizens kneading up the honey, / The poor mechanic porters crowding in / Their heavy burthens at his narrow gate' (*H5* 1.2.198–201). The contrast here is between skilled masons delighting in their tasks and the unskilled porters enduring back-breaking labour. In fairness, the Archbishop appears to feel pity rather than contempt for the 'mechanic porters'. A counterpoint to this incongruous application of a highly organized **commonwealth** working industriously as a means of justifying war is provided by Burgundy in his description of the economic and human destruction effected by Henry's invasion (5.2.32–67).

The most endearing mechanicals, consisting of several specialisms, occur in *MND*. Bottom the weaver and his associates are referred to by Puck as 'A crew of patches, rude mechanicals, / That work for bread upon Athenian stalls' (3.2.9–10). Even for a fairy this is singularly dismissive given that the skills in question embrace a carpenter, weaver, bellows-mender, tinker, joiner and a tailor.

Most characteristic of the overtly opprobrious references to common workmen is Cleopatra's anticipation of the humiliation she would suffer as a prisoner in Rome: 'Mechanic slaves / With greasy aprons, rules, and hammers shall / Uplift us to the view. In their thick breaths, / Rank of gross diet, shall we be enclouded, / And forc'd to drink their vapor' (*ANT* 5.2.209–13).

Accused of treason by one of his own servants, York denounces him as, 'Base dunghill villain and mechanical, / I'll have thy head for this thy traitor's speech' (*2H6* 1.3.193–4). The familiar disdain is present, though here York's predicament naturally predisposes him to be abusive.

The tribunes Marullus and Flavius are equally dismissive in their attitude towards Rome's mechanicals, though they, too, are angry because as antagonists of Caesar they are appalled that these common men have taken a holiday to celebrate Caesar's triumph over Pompey's sons: 'Hence! home, you idle creatures, get you home! / Is this a holiday? What, know you not, / Being mechanical, you ought not walk / Upon a labouring day without the sign / Of your profession?' (*JC* 1.1.1–5). 'Sign of your profession', of course, relates to aprons and tools or implements.

Pistol, who occupies the lower rungs of the social ladder, also expresses contempt for those who work with their hands. However, at the time he is adopting the persona of an elevated envoy, reporting to Falstaff on the misfortune of Doll and Nell. In anticipation of Falstaff's imminent elevation to chief advisor to the new-made King, Henry V, Pistol's sense of grandeur is all the more appropriate:

> My knight, I will inflame thy noble liver,
> And make thee rage.
> Thy Doll, and Helen of thy noble thoughts,
> Is in base durance and contagious prison,
> Hal'd thither
> By most mechanical and dirty hand.
>
> *2H4* 5.5.31–6

The humble instruments of the law are the 'mechanicals' in question. It is worth observing that Pistol wraps himself in the identities and language of the stage figures with whom he identifies, so that he leads a double life or even multiple lives. Theatre has infused Pistol's lowly, rather sordid existence, with magnificence. Cleopatra dreads the prospect of being portrayed and parodied by actors, but Pistol's existence is vitalized by emulation of theatrical creations – his own 'mechanical and dirty hand' barely visible.

A different aspect of affected social superiority occurs when Falstaff dismisses the wealthy Ford as a 'mechanical salt-butter rogue!' (*WIV* 2.2.278). Ford, despite his financial standing, is disparaged as menial or servile with the unrefined tastes of such a person – salt-butter being an inferior **commodity**.

The full sting of the term is rendered with admirable brevity by Coriolanus protesting that he would not stoop to negotiate a political agreement – '**capitulate**' – with the despised **plebeians**. Responding to his mother in her role as suitor for Rome, he says: 'Do not bid me / Dismiss my soldiers, or capitulate / Again with Rome's mechanics' (*COR* 5.3.81–3).

Finally in the Roman plays there is the interesting case of Antony's farewell to Cleopatra as he prepares to leave for a battle (from which neither expects him to return): 'This is a soldier's kiss; rebukable / And worthy shameful check it were, to stand / On more mechanic compliment. I'll leave thee / Now like a man of steel' (*ANT* 4.4.30–3). The antithesis is between the brevity and emotional compactness of a soldier's parting and the strained elaboration of the common citizen. Glow, aura and terse fertility of expression belong to the man of war;

uncomfortable, awkward, laboured speech characterize the common person – all but the most elevated civilians become merely 'mechanical' or base when set against soldiers. Antony and his men are effectively knights, figures from romantic literature, occupying a rarefied, sanctified space; all that is outside belongs to the mundane. Here is possibly a case where Shakespeare is giving the word an extra dimension: a linguistic mode is being characterized as inferior by means of its social residence, but additionally a distinction is being made between what is verbally adroit and what is maladroit. A verbal distinction is being born that will soon detach itself from the social origins that create it. In terms of social class this military/civilian distinction has already been made by Hotspur when he chastises Kate for employing the idiom of the citizen class (*1H4* 3.1.246–56).

(C) On *H5* see Brennan, *Henry V*, Parker, *Shakespeare from the Margins*, ch. 3, and Stevenson, *Praise and Paradox* – all are of interest here. Also relevant for the Roman plays are, for example, Drakakis, ed., *Antony and Cleopatra*; Cantor, *Shakespeare's Rome*; Thomas, *Shakespeare's Roman Worlds*, Zander, ed., *Julius Caesar*, Deats, ed., *Antony and Cleopatra*.

meed

(A) There are three meanings attaching to this word: reward or **recompense**; excellence or merit; gift or service.

(B) Responding to old Adam's offer of his life's savings, Orlando contrasts his attitude with that prevailing in the modern world: 'O good old man, how well in thee appears / The constant service of the antique world, / When service sweat for duty, not for meed!' (*AYL* 2.3.56–8). Here is a distinction Shakespeare frequently makes between a modern world obsessed with novelty and personal gain and a bygone age where the individual is deeply located in a community committed to human connectedness, duty and obligation.

When weighing the prospect of victory over Edward IV, Henry VI attaches great significance to his own merits as a just ruler: 'my meed hath got me fame' (*3H6* 4.8.38). Earlier in the play Edward has also cited his merits as making him worthy of the throne when he reflects on the strange appearance of three distinct suns that then coalesce:

> I think it cites us, brother, to the field,
> That we, the sons of brave Plantagenet,
> Each one already blazing by our meeds,
> Should not withstanding join our lights together,
> And over shine the earth as this the world.
>
> 2.1.34–8

Hall records that this phenomenon had a profound effect on Edward at the Battle of Mortimer's Cross, so that thereafter he took the sun as his emblem. The contrast between these parallel uses is striking. Henry VI reflects on his good governance that will rebound to his **advantage** in the form of popular support. Edward IV sees the heavens as emblematizing the merits of the Yorkists as rightful inheritors of the crown. 'Meed' signifies Henry's merits; lineage determines that of Edward and the Yorkists.

The Second Lord, expressing admiration for Timon's **bounty**, comments that any little gift or *service* bestowed on the wealthy Athenian is rewarded with a present of far greater **value:** 'No meed but he repays / Sevenfold above itself' (*TIM* 1.1.277–8).

(C) Bullough, *Narrative and Dramatic Sources of Shakespeare; Vol. III: Early English History Plays*, is a convenient source for Hall and other background material relating to the *H6–R3* cycle. Excellent and concise in relating source material to the plays are Saccio, *Shakespeare's English Kings*, and Norwich, *Shakespeare's Kings*. See also several relevant essays in Pendleton, ed., *Henry VI*; Goy-Blanquet, ed., *Shakespeare's Early History Plays*; Cavanagh, et al., *Shakespeare's Histories and Counter-Histories*; and Smallwood, ed., *Players of Shakespeare 6*.

meiny

(A) Employed only twice, the word is significant politically as it refers to the common multitude; economically, as it pertains to household servants or followers.

(B) Coriolanus' facility for vituperation is exhibited in response to the **plebeians'** withdrawal of support for his election as consul. Rejecting his friends' pleas for restraint he cries, 'For the mutable, rank-scented meiny, let them / Regard me as I do not flatter, and / Therein behold themselves' (*COR* 3.1.66–8). The multitude is guilty of that grievous fault, inconstancy. Moreover, they smell.

Kent, explaining to Lear how Regan and Cornwall set off for Gloucester's castle before he could deliver his message, gives a vivid picture of their hasty departure with their household servants: 'They summon'd up their meiny, straight took horse' (*LR* 2.4.35).

(C) McAlindon, *Shakespeare's Tragic Cosmos*, and *Shakespeare Minus 'Theory'*, contain vibrant essays on these topics; so too do Halio, ed., *Critical Essays on Shakespeare's 'King Lear'*, and Liebler, *Shakespeare's Festive Tragedy*.

mercenary

(A) Occurring only once in the sphere of finance, this word intimates an excessive appetite for financial gain. On three occasions it signifies military service undertaken for financial rather than patriotic reasons. Common soldier rather than foreigner is what is indicated here.

(B) Portia, disguised as Balthazar, declines the offer of financial **recompense** proposed by Bassanio and Antonio with the words, 'And therein do account myself well paid. / My mind was never yet more mercenary' (*MV* 4.1.417–18). She is, of course, well paid. Financial reward is not her aim; Bassanio is her target. She has had *personally* to free Antonio from Shylock in order to free Bassanio from Antonio – thereby transforming the emotional **bonds**.

At the end of the Battle of Agincourt the Herald Mountjoy approaches the English king for permission to remove the French nobility, who in death are being contaminated by their proximity to ordinary soldiers: 'For many of our princes (woe the while!) / Lie drown'd and soak'd in mercenary blood' (*H5* 4.7.75–6). This does not refer to foreigners, but to common Frenchmen. Such fastidiousness leaves a fetid taste in the mouth, particularly as the copious gore of the mercenaries is perceived as an unwonted offence rather than as dear lifeblood.

Intriguing in a different way is Aufidius' deep resentment at having been relegated from the leader of the Volsces to a place beneath the foreigner, Coriolanus. In enumerating the offences of his erstwhile colleague, and hence justifying his own jealous antipathy, he maintains that the Roman war-machine treated him as a mere 'mercenary' – a common soldier: 'till at the last / I seem'd his follower, not partner, and / He wag'd me with his countenance as if / I had been mercenary' (*COR* 5.6.37–40). The conception of an approving look as constituting a demeaning reward for **achievement** on the battlefield is well captured in the expression 'wag'd'. The entire 12-line speech is something to savour.

(C) Edelman, *Shakespeare's Military Language*, has interesting entries on mercenary and Mountjoy. He points out, for instance, 'the word soldier itself derives from the payment he receives, or in the case of Elizabeth's army, the payment he is meant to receive', 218. Woodbridge, ed., *Money and the Age of Shakespeare*, Mahon and Mahon, eds, *The Merchant of Venice*, Wheeler, ed., *Coriolanus*, and Scott, *Shakespeare and the Idea of the Book* all contain valuable commentary.

merchandise

(A) Most frequently this word applies to goods or **commodities** that are **traded**. A second meaning is the activity of trading itself rather than the items traded. This includes trading in **money** – moneylending. A particularly interesting metaphorical usage possesses the meaning to commercialize, to transform emotion into something marketable or advertised.

(B) Salerio, attributing Antonio's melancholy to anxiety about his valuable cargoes, comments: 'I know Antonio / Is sad to think upon his merchandise' (*MV* 1.1.39–40). Shylock, who despises trade in commodities because of the inherent risks, uses the term to cover moneylending. Because Antonio lends money without charging **interest** he reduces Shylock's **profits** (increasing the supply of loanable funds diminishes potential borrowing for loans at commercial rates, thereby, depressing the rate of interest). The moneylender, therefore, expresses delight at the prospect of Antonio's ruin: 'for were he out of Venice I can make what merchandise I will' (3.1.128–9). Merchandise here means 'financial transactions'.

When accounting for a love that is intense but articulated with delicacy or restraint, the speaker in *SON* 102 warns against expression that is ostentatious: 'That love is merchandis'd, whose rich esteeming / The owner's tongue doth publish every where' (3–4). Here is a case of affection being reduced to a saleable commodity. But the term also carries the suggestion of advertising: merchandised, therefore, means commercialized, the language of the **market-place** decidedly contaminating the authentic, intimate discourse of love.

Cleopatra uses the term metaphorically when she denounces the messenger who has brought the news of Antony's marriage to Octavia: 'Get thee hence; /

The merchandise which thou hast brought from Rome / Are all too dear for me. Lie they upon thy hand, / And be undone by 'em!' (*ANT* 2.5.103–6). What is particularly noteworthy about this example is the economic insight embedded in the Egyptian Queen's bitter resentment and dismay. The **trader** who invests in merchandise but then fails to find buyers at the appropriate **price** will be left with goods on his hands which may lead to his ruin.

Fascinating in a different way is Titania's description of her time shared with the mother of the Indian boy. Commerce enters the scene in a playful way, conveying a natural alliance between exotic ease and trade:

> And in the spiced Indian air, by night,
> Full often hath she gossip'd by my side,
> And sat with me on Neptune's yellow sands,
> Marking th'embarked traders on the flood;
> When we have laugh'd to see the sails conceive
> And grow big-bellied with the wanton wind;
> Which she, with pretty and with swimming gait,
> Following (her womb then rich with my young squire)
> Would imitate, and sail upon the land
> To fetch me trifles, and return again,
> As from a voyage, rich with merchandise.
>
> *MND* 2.1.124–34

The women initially laugh at the way in which the sails of a ship (trader) resemble a pregnant woman. Then that pregnant woman imitates a **merchant** ship, gathering up delights for the Queen of the Fairies as she sails on land. As Shakespeare's favourite image of complementarity is wind and sails, and as the description constitutes the unique case of a double image, the whole description becomes harmonious. Trade, exoticism and the music of human concord coalesce. This is an unexpected absorption of economic life into something mystical. Even in a play that more than any other celebrates melding, coalescing or merging.

(C) Calderwood, *A Midsummer Night's Dream*, along with Kehler, ed., *A Midsummer Night's Dream*, are particularly relevant here; so too is Drakakis, ed., *Antony and Cleopatra*. Aughterson, ed., *The English Renaissance*, contains an excellent section of contemporary documents on exploration and trade; Brenner, *Merchants and Revolution*, provides a wealth of fascinating information; Warley, *Sonnet Sequences and Social Distinction in Renaissance England*, is particularly rewarding with respect to the economic and social aspects of the *SONs*.

merchant, merchant-marring

(A) In addition to the obvious meaning of dealer or **trader**, the term is used for **merchant** ship. It is also used as a synonym for saucy fellow, young rascal. Although the most famous merchant is Antonio, the merchant of Venice, merchants pervade the plays. Merchant-marring is a hazard that threatens merchant ships.

(B) Gonzalo, attempting to console Alonso after the apparent shipwreck, comments on the commonplace nature of their circumstances, employing merchant as both ship and trader: 'Our hint of woe / Is common: every day some sailor's wife, / The masters of some merchant, and the merchant / Have just our theme of woe' (*TMP* 2.1.3–6).

Characters sometimes aim to make a distinction between merchants of great stature and more commonplace traders. In appealing to Shylock on Antonio's behalf, the Duke describes his losses as 'Enow to press a royal merchant down' (*MV* 4.1.29). Earlier in the play Gratiano asks, 'How doth that royal merchant, good Antonio?' (3.2.239). In *SHR*, Lucentio describes his father as 'A merchant of great traffic through the world' (1.1.12).

Juliet's nurse, having been flustered by Mercutio's waggish behaviour, asks: 'I pray you, sir, what saucy merchant was this, so full of ropery?' (*ROM* 2.4.145–6). 'Saucy' and 'ropery' (= roguery) make the sense clear. On only one other occasion is the word possibly used in this sense. The Countess of Auvergne, the would-be captor of the English hero Talbot, is perplexed by her guest's comments: 'This is a riddling merchant for the nonce' (*1H6* 2.3.57). She probably means 'dealer or trader in paradoxes', but that idea might well coalesce with an attempt to diminish him through a dismissive suggestion that he is not to be taken seriously.

Bassanio, having read Antonio's account of his losses, presses Salerio: 'And not one vessel scape the dreadful touch / Of merchant-marring rocks? (*MV* 3.2.270–1).

(C) See entries on **merchandise** and trader. Several essays in Salmon and Burness eds., *A Reader in the Language of Shakespearean Drama*, are relevant here. So too is Appadurai, *The Social Life of Things*. Further significant commentary is to be found in Castillo, *Performing America*; Loomba, *Shakespeare, Race and Colonialism*; Leinwand, *Theatre, Finance and Society in Early Modern England*; Stevenson, *Praise and Paradox*.

moiety

(A) This word can mean either share, portion, part or half. Used only once in its unabbreviated form (*SON* 46.12) its applications embrace economic, political and emotional spheres.

(B) The Duke, seeking to dissuade Shylock from **exacting** a pound of Antonio's flesh as penalty for failing to repay the loan of 3,000 ducats by the due date, suggests that the moneylender really intends to be magnanimous:

> And where thou now exacts the penalty,
> Which is a pound of this poor merchant's flesh,
> Thou wilt not only loose the forfeiture,
> But touch'd with humane gentleness and love,
> Forgive a moi'ty of the principal,
> Glancing an eye of pity on his losses,
>
> *MV* 4.1.22–7

Shylock is being requested not only to forgo the **interest** that is **owed** on the **debt** but also a part of the initial loan or 'principal'.

Just when the rebels appear to have reached an agreement on responsibilities and the distribution of territories in *1H4*, the fractious Hotspur suddenly objects that he has been short-changed: 'Methinks my moi'ty, north from Burton here, / In quantity equals not one of yours' (3.1.95–6). His initial solution, to redirect the river Trent, becomes a theoretical proposal to which he is indifferent once he has secured its acceptance. It is a bitter irony that this charismatic war-machine who squabbled over a piece of land needs only a small plot after falling victim to Hal in the Battle of Shrewsbury: 'Ill-weav'd ambition, how much art thou shrunk! / When that this body did contain a spirit, / A kingdom for it was too small a bound, / But now two paces of the vilest earth / Is room enough' (*1H4* 5.4.88–92).

Horatio provides a good example when he describes the famous challenge whereby Old Hamlet agreed to meet Fortinbras in single combat, each staking an equivalent portion of territory on the outcome of the contest. The defeated Fortinbras,

> Did forfeit (with his life) all those his lands
> Which he stood seiz'd of, to the conqueror;
> Against the which a moi'ty competent
> Was gaged by our king, which had return'd
> To the inheritance of Fortinbras,
> Had he been vanquisher;
>
> *HAM* 1.1.88–93

There is seldom any chance of ambiguity where 'half' is intended as opposed to 'portion' or 'share'. Henry V in conducting his courtship of the Princess Katherine of France anticipates their offspring: 'Shall not thou and I, between Saint Denis and Saint George, compound a boy, half French, half English, that shall go to Constantinople and take the Turk by the beard?' He rides over her hesitancy with the words, 'Do but now promise, Kate, you will endeavour for your French part of such a boy; and for my English moi'ty, take the word of a king and a bachelor' (*H5* 5.2.206–16).

At the time of his death Mark Antony controlled half the Roman world. His fellow world sharer, Octavius Caesar, on hearing of his adversary's death, declares: 'The breaking of so great a thing should make / A greater crack. / ... / The death of Antony / Is not a single doom, in the name lay / A moi'ty of the world' (*ANT* 5.1.14–19).

Queen Katherine insists on kneeling before Henry as she has a suit to plead. In response he graciously raises her up with the comment, 'Arise, and take your place by us. Half your suit / Never name to us; you have half our power. / The other moi'ty ere you ask is given' (*H8* 1.2.10–12). The meaning 'half' could hardly be clearer. Conceptually and rhetorically, this seemingly simple statement is perfectly structured to mirror the sentiment that Katherine has half the power of the kingdom by right; and the other half by virtue of her command over Henry's heart.

(C) The idea of parts, portions and disintegration is explored by Hunt, 'A thing of nothing' in Coyle, ed., *Hamlet.* See also Hillman, *Shakespeare's Entrails.* Hotspur's speech is analysed by Gillet, 'Me, U, and non-U' in Salmon and Burness, eds, *A Reader in the Language of Shakespearean Drama.* Relevant to the question of maps and divisions are Cohen, *Shakespeare and Technology;* Kinney, *Shakespeare's Webs;* Hopkins, *Shakespeare on the Edge.*

money

(A) Economics textbooks generally attribute four functions to money: a measure of **value**; a medium of **exchange**; a store of value; a standard of deferred payment. The meaning attaching to the word in the plays is coin of the realm or gold, and it is employed to distinguish liquidity, an immediate source of purchasing power, from other financial assets: **bills** of exchange, plate or other material assets including buildings and land. Shakespeare reveals how changes in the **conditions** of supply or demand can result in a change in the **price** of a product, but he does not engage with changes in the value of money, the phenomenon of inflation, something with which he would have been familiar. The word occurs most frequently in *ERR* followed by *WIV; TIM* and *MV* come next in terms of frequency, just ahead of *OTH*. 'Moneys', intimating quantity of cash, is a word favoured by Shylock, who employs it five times. It is also used in *WIV* and *TIM*. The most comprehensive account of **wealth** in all its forms occurs in *SHR*.

(B) Dismissing York's objections to his decision to confiscate Gaunt's property, thereby depriving Bolingbroke of his rightful inheritance, Richard II declares: 'Think what you will, we seize into our hands / His plate, his goods, his money, and his lands' (*R2* 2.1.209–10). Money as coin is clearly distinguished from other valuables and assets. This proves to be an expensive confiscation because it provides Bolingbroke with the pretext for returning from exile – a move that results in the loss of Richard's crown and his life.

The Pedant in *SHR* explains that it is imperative he enter Padua: 'For I have bills for money by exchange / From Florence, and must here deliver them' (4.2.89–90). The implication is that these bills of exchange have fallen due and are to be handed over in return for cash.

Money as the medium of exchange that exercises a command over real resources is made clear by the Messenger in *1H6*. When Exeter responds to the news of the loss of French territories, he ascribes the humiliation to treachery. The Messenger is terse: 'No treachery, but want of men and money' (1.1.69).

The King of Navarre, attempting to explain the reasons for the retention of part of Aquitaine, points out that it is held in lieu of an outstanding **debt** of a hundred thousand crowns. He adds that the value of the Aquitaine territory is less than the sum in question, so that he will happily relinquish it when the debt is paid: 'in surety of which / One part of Aquitaine is bound to us, / Although not valued to the money's worth' (*LLL* 2.1.134–6). Lying behind this comment is the matter of the **costs** and benefits associated with the land in question – though the function of the outstanding debt is to provide a pretext for the visitation of the French Princess and her party. Given the money-conscious age in which Shakespeare was writing, any kind of financial reference would arguably provoke consideration of the economic implications, thus providing a substantial subtext.

As Caliban, Stephano and Trinculo make their colourful entrance towards the close of *TMP* (two are attired in stolen clothes while Caliban is his 'normal' self), the malicious Sebastian laughs and asks, 'What things are these, my Lord Antonio? / Will money buy 'em?' (5.1.264–5). This crass, brazen, pecuniary mindset has been in evidence earlier when Stephano expressed delight in the magical music: 'This will prove a brave kingdom to me, where I shall have my music for nothing' (3.2.144–5). The money economy and the conception of all things in terms of marketability, the transformation of resources and people into **commodities**, is as striking as the propensity to create hierarchical political structures. Three of these exist on the island, with all of them racked by tensions and incipient **usurpation**.

An intriguing situation occurs in *ERR* when the goldsmith, appropriately named Angelo (in Shakespeare's England much was made of the gold coin referred to as an 'angel') hands over the chain to his client and requests payment:

> here's the note
> How much your chain weighs to the utmost charect,
> The fineness of the gold, and chargeful fashion,
> Which doth amount to three odd ducats more
> Than I stand debted to this gentleman.
> I pray you see him presently discharg'd,
> For he is bound to sea, and stays but for it.
>
> 4.1.27–33

Two things stand out: the careful documentation of the labour and materials involved in the creation of the chain, and the rapidity of the circulation of money. The goldsmith will not hold the money one second, as it is to be passed to the person to whom he **owes** an almost equivalent sum. Even a small delay in payment can prove hazardous as the man awaiting payment has to catch the tide. In the event Antipholus of Ephesus says:

> I am not furnish'd with the present money:
> Besides, I have some business in the town.
> Good signior, take the stranger to my house,
> And with you take the chain, and bid my wife
> Disburse the sum on the receipt thereof.
>
> 4.1.34–8

This moment is a prelude to comic confusion but it lays bare the transactional nature of this society. Antipholus does not carry that amount of cash on his person (in the play *Thomas More* the victim of theft is blamed as foolhardy for carrying around ten pounds). Moreover, he is too focused on his next transaction to return to his house immediately. He does, however, set out the necessary conditions for payment to be made by his wife. Here, a single reference to money reveals a network of **credit** based on trust, with narrow time-frames for closing transactions.

The numerous engagements with money in *MV* figure strongly under such entries as **value, worth** and **usury,** but it is worth noting here Launcelot's objection to Jessica becoming a Christian. If this precipitates a trend, he argues, the demand for pork will rise so rapidly that it will push up the price: 'This making of Christians will raise the price of hogs. If we grow all to be pork-eaters, we shall not shortly have a rasher on the coals for money' (3.5.23–6). The economic theory embodied in the joke is quite correct for the short run, though the long-term equilibrium price will depend on the elasticity of supply. What is so interesting here is the awareness of how social or cultural changes can influence relative prices in the **market-place**.

Even in the bucolic world of the Forest of Arden the need for money is in evidence. As the philosophical shepherd Corin puts it in response to Touchstone's prompting, 'I know that the more one sickens the worse at ease he is; and that he that wants money, means, and content is without three good friends' (*AYL* 3.2.23–6). The play is, of course, permeated by considerations of property and finance.

Given that it has a comment on 'bills for money by exchange' (4.2.89) and contains the most elaborate inventories of financial assets in the entire canon, a remarkable feature of *SHR* is that the word 'money' occurs on only two other occasions (1.1.130 and 1.2.82). However, in setting forth his inventory of wealth (designed to win Bianca who is auctioned off by her father), Gremio does refer to cash: 'In ivory coffers I have stuff'd my crowns' (2.1.350). Characteristic of a speech so heavily focused on the materiality of his affluence, the crowns are lodged in an expensive container – packed together tightly, asserting *their* physicality along with the other luxuries. Tranio, masquerading as his master Lucentio, provides an inventory which emphasizes not only fine houses (the contents taken for granted) but delineates the capital assets such as argosies which guarantee the continuing flow of income to support luxurious living. Even when he does mention cash it is directly in terms of yield from land: 'two thousand ducats by the year / Of fruitful land' (2.1.369–70). Much more delicate but equally physical is the Lord's description of his house and lifestyle in the Induction. Music, 'wanton pictures', 'a silver basin / Full of rose-water and bestrew'd with flowers', 'hounds and horse' are all part of this affluent social universe (*Ind* 1 35–61). Money is seldom mentioned. Where wealth is so abundant the physical manifestations become dominant.

The central feature of the relationship between Sir Toby Belch and Sir Andrew Aguecheek is financial exploitation. Sir Andrew is making a great investment in the pursuit of Olivia, a fantasy encouraged by Sir Toby. The cost of this enterprise is indicated when Sir Toby advises, 'Thou hadst need send for more money.' The anxious Andrew replies, 'If I cannot recover your niece, I am a foul way out.' The key word 'recover' intimates 'win'. Her wealth is to be the means of retrieving his outlays. Sir Toby reassures him, 'Send for more money, knight; if thou hast her not i'th'end, call me cut' (*TN* 2.3.182–7). By the end of the play Andrew is stripped of his money and his illusions.

The most concentrated repetition of the word also involves exploitation. In persuading Roderigo that he can still win Desdemona, Iago advises him to sell his land, turn everything into liquid assets and join the military force setting sail for Cyprus. In an exchange shaped by the refrain 'put money in thy purse' Iago uses the word 'money' ten times, before cynically congratulating himself, 'Thus do I ever make my fool my purse' (*OTH* 1.3.339–83). A short time into their Cyprian adventure the forlorn Roderigo complains, 'My money is almost spent' (2.3.364–5).

The problems of raising money to finance wars are highlighted in *R2* (2.2.104), *1H6* (1.1.69), and *2H6* (1.3.169). Interestingly, Brutus, complaining that Cassius has failed to provide a share of the funds he has exacted, claims that he personally is above such behaviour: 'For I can raise no money by vile means' (*JC* 4.3.71). The political difficulties associated with financial impositions requisite to fighting wars is also highlighted by Pompey when evaluating his prospects in anticipation of a clash with the Triumvirate: 'Caesar gets money where / He loses hearts' (*ANT* 2.1.13–14).

The role of trust, reputation and financial security in the complex network of financial obligations is given terse representation by a parasite who has **exploited** Timon's generosity, but is disinclined to aid his former benefactor when asked for assistance. Turning away Timon's servant he says, 'Thy lord's a bountiful gentleman, but . . . this is no time to lend money, especially upon bare friendship without security' (*TIM* 3.1.39–43). Timon has believed that there is only one realm: personal relationships; he is about to discover that the world is governed by financial expediency. The phrase 'bare friendship' is devastating in its clarity and brutality.

Cleopatra, presenting an inventory of her possessions to Octavius Caesar, distinguishes clearly between money and other valuables: 'This is the brief: of money, plate, and jewels / I am possess'd of; 'tis exactly valued, / Not petty things admitted' (*ANT* 5.2.138–40). This inventory, which Cleopatra's Treasurer claims covers only half her wealth, may be a ploy to persuade Caesar that she does not intend to commit suicide. The other great inventory in the plays is that of Cardinal Wolsey. When it falls into the King's hands it leaves him gasping in disbelief at the properties, income and expenditure contained therein. He refers to 'piles of wealth' but never employs the word money (*H8* 3.2.107).

The only character referred to as being 'money'd' is Doctor Caius in *WIV*. In selecting him as her ideal son-in-law, Mistress Page says, 'The doctor is well money'd, and his friends / Potent at court' (4.4.88–9). Accordingly, he is a sounder financial bet than the aristocratic but impecunious Fenton or the dim-witted Slender. Though Ford later declares, 'Money buys lands, and wives are sold by fate' (5.5.233), it is impossible to prevent the language of commerce ('sold') entering the marriage **market**.

(C) The available commentary on this topic is diverse and abundant. Some of the most significant discussions can be found in the following: Shell, *Money, Language and Thought*; Sullivan, *The Rhetoric of Credit*; Woodbridge, ed., *Money and the Age of Shakespeare*; Hawkes, *Idols of the Marketplace*; Simmel, *The Philosophy of Money*; Turner, *Shakespeare's Twenty-First Century Economics*; Woodmansee and Osteen, eds, *The New Economic Criticism*; Leinwand, *Theatre, Finance and Society*; Kamps, ed., *Materialist Shakespeare*; Heinzelman, *The Economics of the Imagination*. Crystal and Crystal, *A Shakespeare Glossary*, 286–7 provides concise and detailed tables of coins and values. See entries on **worth, value, wealth, market** and **price**.

monopoly

(A) Surprisingly, this is a unique usage signifying sole rights of sale or distribution granted by the monarch. At this time it was the source of much **money**-making and controversy. The fortunate recipient of an authorized monopoly was able to extract large **profits** at the **expense** of the consumer.

(B) Kent, commenting on the Fool's riddling critique of Lear's behaviour concedes, 'This is not altogether fool, my lord', eliciting the riposte, 'No, faith, lords and great men will not let me; if I had a monopoly out, they would have part an't' (*LR* 1.4.151–3). The Fool's sardonic response makes it clear that even the monarch's power to create monopolies could not confine folly. Given the significance of monopolies, both in terms of providing revenue for the monarch, and the commercial benefits for the recipient of the privilege to control the supply of a product in the **market,** not to mention the financial burdens imposed on the consumer, it is remarkable that this phenomenon – replete with economic and political implications – receives so little attention from Shakespeare. Clearly the whole point of a monopoly was that it enabled the supplier to charge a higher **price** than would have prevailed in competitive circumstances. So unpopular were monopolies that they were deemed responsible for exerting inflationary pressure, intensifying a problem of deep concern. Significantly the Queen's allocation of numerous grants of monopolies over two decades from the 1580s suffered a check and reverse in 1601.

(C) The whole question of monopolies set in the context of economic development is provided by Pallister, *The Age of Elizabeth*. See esp. 127, 168, 371, 375 for a list of products subject to the constraints of monopoly and listed in a parliamentary debate in 1601. For a useful provision of contemporary documents relating to trade and commerce see Aughterson, ed., *The English Renaissance*. Also of value here are Brenner, *Merchants and Revolution*; and Braudel, *Civilisation and Capitalism*.

mortgage

(A) The sole application of the word carries the modern suggestion of a contract whereby **debt** is incurred against collateral, which at this time took the form of a pledge of land.

(B) The speaker in *SON* 134 acknowledges that the woman he is addressing has already captured the affections of his friend. The whole sonnet turns on the concepts of debts, obligations and **usury**, but the opening lines convey the essence of the argument:

> So now I have confess'd that he is thine,
> And I myself am mortgag'd to thy will,
> Myself I'll forfeit, so that other mine
> Thou wilt restore to be my comfort still:
> But thou wilt not, nor he will not be free,
> For thou art covetous, and he is kind;
>
> 1–6

What is fascinating is the way in which Shakespeare draws on the language and concepts of economic life and utilizes them as instruments in his exploration of human relationships. In this sexual triangle the woman is in control. Much as the speaker is in thrall to her he makes a gesture which he recognizes as futile, to do anything to secure the release of his male friend – a relationship even more important to him. The speaker offers to sacrifice himself in order to gain the release of his friend from the embracement of the woman who is the object of desire by both men, but can't extricate himself from the power of the woman in question: the financial/legal obligation is the equivalent of surrender to the woman's sexual and emotional dominance, 'will' also meaning sexual organ.

(C) See Sokol and Sokol, 227–8, for the legal application and evolution of this financial instrument. They define the mortgage as follows:

> At common law a mortgage was a pledge of land as a security for borrowing. The debt was secured by the transfer of real property, either fee simple or lease (see conveyancing) from the borrower to the lender. If the borrower paid the debt on the agreed date, the redemption day, then by means of a covenant in the agreement he had the right to re-enter the land.

Vital here is Sullivan, *The Rhetoric of Credit*, 25–6. For a close analysis of the sonnets see Innes, '*Shakespeare and the English Renaissance Sonnet*'; Schiffer, ed., *Shakespeare's Sonnets*; Fineman, *Shakespeare's Perjured Eye*; Edmondson and Wells, *Shakespeare's Sonnets; Vendler, The Art of Shakespeare's Sonnets*; Warley, *Sonnet Sequences and Social Distinction in Renaissance England*, esp. ch. 6 which engages directly with Shakespeare's economic expertise. Leinwand, *Theatre, Finance and Society in Early Modern England*, devotes a chapter to mortgage payments.

mountebank

(A) The mountebank is a charlatan, fraud and generally a purveyor of quack medicines or remedies.

(B) This word would hardly merit a place in this volume were it not for Coriolanus' use of the term at a critical political juncture. Having delivered a magnificent speech revealing how any attempt to mollify the **plebeians** would corrupt his very spirit, and is, therefore, impossible, the warrior, incapable of defying his mother, makes a breathtaking promise: 'Chide me no more. I'll mountebank their loves, / Cog their hearts from them, and come home belov'd / Of all the trades in Rome' (*COR* 3.2.132–4). Only here is the word used as a verb, meaning something to the effect that he will put on such a dazzling display of hypocrisy or double-dealing that the plebeians will succumb to his pitch as eagerly as those gulled by mountebanks. Of course, far from achieving this outcome he drives the plebeians into a frenzy of hostility, albeit triggered by the manipulative tribunes, so that he is driven into exile. What makes Coriolanus' promise so politically and emotionally charged is its incongruity: he is incapable of duplicity. Here is the character who, when initially pleaded with to temporize, replies, 'For them? I cannot do it to the gods' (3.2.38).

(C) Poole, *Coriolanus* and Wheeler, ed., *Coriolanus*, contain relevant and insightful commentaries. Several of the volumes devoted to the Roman plays and listed in the bibliography are of importance here.

mystery

(A) The two economic meanings of the word are: first, **trade** or **occupation**; second, skill or mastery. Further applications are: a way of behaving; an essence, secret centre, source of perplexity, enigma.

(B) The most extensive discourse on the use of the word in the sense of occupation and also of skill, or artistry, occurs in *MM*, where Abhorson the hangman is reluctant to take on Pompey the bawd as a temporary assistant. He complains, 'he will discredit our mystery', implying that a bawd would contaminate the profession of hangman. Questioning the validity of attaching the word to the duties of a hangman Pompey retaliates by taking the word 'mystery' to signify 'skill' or 'artistry':

> Painting, sir, I have heard say, is a mystery;
> and your whores, sir, being members of my
> occupation, using painting, do prove my
> occupation a mystery; but what mystery
> there should be in hanging, if I should
> be hang'd, I cannot imagine.
>
> 4.2.28–40

In his artful deconstruction by this means of wordplay, Pompey is suggesting that painting is an art or a prized skill, in other words, a mystery, whereas the killing of a man, albeit as part of a judicial process, is an inferior skill, an occupation that doesn't even qualify as a trade. Given a general acknowledgement of the importance of the hangman's competence, the subtext here is the incongruity between an activity being designated with the suggestion of workmanship, even masterly skill, when its outcome is the death of a human being. As so often in Shakespeare, the surface stratum of a joke sits upon layers of complex suggestion.

There is no sliding between meanings when Parolles, outraged by friendly fire that has cost the loss of a drum, maintains that it ought to be retrieved as a matter of honour. Bertram responds 'if you think your mystery in stratagem can bring this instrument of honour again into his native quarter, be magnanimous in the enterprise and go on' (*AWW* 3.6.65–7). The reference here is to Parolles' supposed mastery of military arts.

The sense of 'mystery' as 'behaviour' occurs in an exchange on new-fangled **fashions** and mannerisms when the Lord Chamberlain comments, 'Is't possible the spells of France should juggle / Men into such strange mysteries?' (*H8* 1.3.1–2).

Having failed to induce Guildenstern to attempt to play a pipe, Hamlet turns on him with bitter mockery: 'Why, look you now, how unworthy a thing you make of me! You would play upon me, you would seem to know my stops, you would pluck out the heart of my mystery' (*HAM* 3.2.363–6). To probe his secret centre is the meaning here.

Seeking knowledge of her destiny at the shrine of Diana, Emilia responds to the symbolic happenings by asking for help in the interpretation of these enigmas: 'Unclasp thy mystery' (*TNK* 5.1.172).

(C) The mysteries attaching to trades and activities that were of singular significance in this period are well articulated in Cohen, *Shakespeare and Technology*; Kinney, *Shakespeare's Webs*; Mokyr, *The Lever of Riches*; Crosby, *The Measure of Reality*; Stevenson, *Praise and Paradox*; Kinney, ed., *A Companion to Renaissance Drama Part 1*.

nation

(A) With one exception, Shylock's reference in *MV* which signifies a racial group, this term relates to a clearly identifiable geographical entity.

(B) Shylock soliloquizes that Antonio 'hates our sacred nation' (*MV* 1.3.48). Defending his justification for claiming his **bond**, he says of his adversary that he has 'scorn'd my nation' (3.1.56). Responding to Jessica's extravagance, he protests, 'The curse never fell upon our nation till now' (3.1.85–6).

In all other cases, individual countries are alluded to: a colony such as Ireland; the city-state of Venice; England, France, Denmark, Rome and Troy. MacMorris responds vociferously to Fluellen's reference to his nation: 'What ish my nation? Who talks of my nation?' (*H5* 3.2.124). Responding to Coriolanus' change of allegiance, a Volscian comments, 'I would not be a Roman, of all nations' (*COR* 4.5.175). A French general refers to Talbot as 'Our nation's terror and their bloody scourge!' (*1H6* 4.2.16). The coherence and integrity of the state is suggested by Hector: 'There is a law in each well-order'd nation' (*TRO* 2.2.180).

(C) All of the following engage with this topic in ways that are informative and insightful: Shapiro, *1599*; Shapiro, *Shakespeare and the Jews*; Ackroyd, *Albion*; Greenblatt, *Learning to Curse*; Brotton, *The Renaissance Bazaar*; Lever, *The Tragedy of State*.

occupation

(A) There is the obvious meaning attaching to occupation of **trade**, handicraft or employment, often used in the pejorative sense of belonging to the lower orders, and the sense of a person's general way of carrying on, disposition, or manner of approaching matters.

(B) When Coriolanus has been condemned to exile, his mother Volumnia rages against the **plebeians** whose voices have determined his destiny: 'Now the red pestilence strike all trades in Rome, / And occupations perish!' (*COR* 3.4.13–14). This aristocratic contempt for common workmen is echoed by Menenius as he chides the tribunes on receiving news of the great warrior's return from exile at the head of an invading army: 'You have made good work, / You and your apronmen; you that stood so much / Upon the voice of occupation and / The breath of garlic-eaters! (4.6.95–8). Not all references to occupation are politically loaded in this way (see, for instance, the entry on **mystery**). *COR* is, after all, the prime example of a society riven by class antagonism.

Mark Antony makes fascinating use of the term as he arms for battle, expressing the wish that Cleopatra could observe him in action: 'O love, / That thou couldst see my wars to-day, and knew'st / The royal occupation, thou shouldst see / A workman in't' (*ANT* 4.4.15–18). Here is the other side of the coin: recognition of the **competence**, mastery of the task in hand and commitment attaching to **occupation** and workmanship. The phrase 'royal occupation', embracing as it does genuine skill and endeavour with a suggestion of the elevated nature of warfare, possesses a piquancy by virtue of carrying the term 'occupation' into this unusual realm.

Enraged by Oswald's cynicism and cowardice, the disguised Kent is chastized by Cornwall for his forthrightness. He responds by stating that it is his habitual manner to be direct: 'Sir, 'tis my occupation to be plain' (*LR* 2.2.92).

(C) Highly relevant are Carroll, *Fat King, Lean Beggar*, and 'Language, politics,

191

and poverty in Shakespearian drama' in Alexander, ed., *Shakespeare and Politics*. Aughterson, ed., *The English Renaissance*, contains important contemporary documents relating to 'Society and social life'. Palliser, *The Age of Elizabeth*, is also admirable in conveying the significance of various occupations and the social structure. A different angle of vision is provided by Stevenson, *Praise and Paradox*; Warley, *Sonnet Sequences and Social Distinction in Renaissance England*; and Woodbridge, *Vagrancy, Homelessness, and English Renaissance Literature*. See entry on **mystery**.

opinion(s)

(A) Playing a vital role in the political discourse of the plays, and employed about a hundred times, this word has several distinct – though frequently difficult to distinguish – meanings: popular judgement or public opinion; personal judgement, regard, belief or conviction; professional assessment; reputation, renown, stature, distinction, self-esteem or personal honour; arrogance, self-conceit or affectation; suspicion.

(B) Chastising Hal for his loose behaviour, Henry IV confides that it was by virtue of maintaining a carefully calculated demeanour that he enticed people to support him in supplanting Richard II: 'Had I so lavish of my presence been, / So common-hackney'd in the eyes of men, / So stale and cheap to vulgar company, / Opinion, that did help me to the crown, / Had still kept loyal to possession' (*1H4* 3.2.39–43). Here there is a sharp focus on the word. Placed for emphasis at the start of the line, and clearly meaning something more than the public at large, it relates especially to influential people. This example is particularly telling because it reveals 'opinion' as something politically strategic. The entire passage contrasts Richard's ill-considered flippancy and excessive public exposure with Bolingbroke, the image maker, attempting to convey the importance and method of the process to the heir apparent. Hal, of course, has already informed the audience (1.2.195–217) that his dissolute behaviour is a calculated ploy: when he ascends to the throne the transformation will amaze 'opinion'. The success of this strategy is clearly confirmed early in *H5* (1.1.22–69).

TRO is the play that features this word most prominently – ten times in all. Thesites is vociferous in denouncing the role of popular opinion in determining reputation and particularly its impact on Ajax: 'He's grown a very land-fish, languageless, a monster. A plague of opinion! a man may wear it on both sides, like a leather jerkin' (3.3.263–5). The big, brainless warrior, Thersites suggests, has suddenly become the darling of the Greeks. Yesterday's fool is today's hero without any discernible change, for the better, having been made. Reputation is besmirched. This interaction between public opinion and inflated self-esteem or arrogance precipitates Thersites' contemptuous attack on the incompetence of the Greek leadership when they fail in their sordid scheme designed to encourage Ajax and Achilles into emulative battle against the Trojans: 'and now is the cur Ajax prouder than the cur Achilles, and will not arm to-day; whereupon the Grecians began to proclaim barbarism, and policy grows to an ill opinion' (5.4.14–17). Thersites never had regard for the Greek leadership or their machinations so why is he agitated now that there is a general collapse of faith in their authority or political skills? If the Greeks are now embracing anarchy ('barbarism'), why does this provoke the play's misanthropic, voyeuristic cynic? Perhaps delight that the rottenness, all the while apparent to him, is now generally understood?

On his deathbed Henry IV strives to reassure Hal that the crown he will inherit, though a consequence of **usurpation** – a word he assiduously avoids while acknowledging the fact – will not be tarnished: 'To thee it shall descend with better quiet, / Better opinion, better confirmation, / For all the soil of the achievement goes / With me into the earth' (*2H4* 4.5.187–90). Public respect is the intended meaning, being neatly placed between the concepts of absence of civil broils, 'better quiet', and the validation of inheritance, 'better confirmation'.

King John expresses satisfaction after being crowned for a second time, but is quickly checked by Salisbury who claims that the **innovation** of a second coronation is more likely to call into question the monarch's legitimacy than to confirm it: 'Makes sound opinion sick, and truth suspected, / For putting on so new a fashion'd robe' (*JN* 4.2.26–7).

It is always informative when Shakespeare, repeating a word, changes its meaning. During the famous Temple Garden scene, Vernon offends Somerset and his supporters by picking a white rose to signify support for York: 'If I, my lord, for my opinion bleed, / Opinion shall be surgeon to my hurt, / And keep me on the side where still I am' (*1H6* 2.4.52–4). Vernon agues that if he has to bleed for the judgement he has made, the balm will be the validation of his personal evaluation by public approbation.

The sense of 'judgement' or 'assessment' is clearly present in Benedick's bantering reply to the love-struck Claudio on the merits of Hero: 'That I neither feel how she should be lov'd nor know how she should be worthy, is the opinion that fire cannot melt out of me; I will die in it at the stake' (*ADO* 1.1.229–33).

On receiving a negative reply to his question, 'Does your worship mean to geld and splay all the youth of the city?', Pompey, the bawd, attempts to enlighten Escalus on the folly of implementing the death penalty for the crime of fornication: 'Truly, sir, in my poor opinion, they will to't then' (*MM* 2.1.230–4). 'Personal view, assessment, judgement or modest prediction' equate to Pompey's expression.

Something much more formal and weighty than mere personal viewpoint is intimated by Bellario in his letter read by the Duke: ' "We turn'd o'er many books together. He is furnish'd with my opinion, which better'd with his own learning, the greatness whereof I cannot enough commend" ' (*MV* 4.1.156–9). This opinion is the embodiment of learning and experience; a professional judgement as opposed to a private estimate or evaluation.

Othello, drawn from his bed by the late-night disturbance, directs his outrage against Montano: 'What's the matter / That you unlace your reputation thus, / And spend your rich opinion for the name / Of a night-brawler?' (*OTH* 2.3.193–6). In this case renown or reputation is indicated by opinion, the phrase 'rich opinion' standing in stark contrast to 'night-brawler'.

After Roderigo has suddenly called Iago to **account** and threatened him, the devilish manipulator turns the outburst to his own **advantage**: 'Why, now I see there's mettle in thee, and even from this instant do build on thee a better opinion than ever before' (4.2.204–6). 'Make a higher estimation' is the meaning employed here.

Henry VIII, sending his Lord Chamberlain to Anne Bullen, transmits a message lavish in suggestion and substance: 'the King's Majesty / Commends his good opinion of you to you, and / Does purpose honor to you no less flowing / Than Marchioness of Pembroke' (*H8* 2.3.60–3). High regard is signified here, though a complication is imparted by the phrase 'of you to you': the estimation in which Anne is held is embodied in the title and the cash the King bestows on her. Here indeed, in the words of Pandarus, is 'a complimental assault' (*TRO* 3.1.39). Some editors, however – e.g. McMullen, Arden 3, 294 – perceive a printing error and so emend the phrase to read: 'his good opinion of you'.

In attempting to dissuade Sir Andrew Aguecheek from leaving, Sir Toby Belch incites him to a more vigorous pursuit of Olivia. Supported by Fabian, he warns Andrew that failure to prosecute his courtship with more passion has resulted in loss of the lady's esteem: 'you are now sail'd into the north of my lady's opinion, where you will hang like an icicle on a Dutchman's beard, unless you do redeem it by some laudable attempt either of valor or policy' (*TN* 3.2.26–9).

Venturing to coach the newly acquired Marina in the arts of prostitution, Boult tells her that she must appear coy and tremulous as such behaviour excites pity, so bringing her bigger financial rewards. He concludes with a homily: 'seldom but that pity begets you a good opinion, and that opinion a mere profit' (*PER* 4.2.120–1). The cynical **bawd** implies that objects of pity are generally objects of contempt and poverty. Only in the brothel is the rule reversed, because a satisfied client feels a degree of embarrassment when confronted by apparent distress and so pays more than the usual **fee**. The good opinion (estimation or regard) produces a 'mere' or clear **profit**.

When Prince Hal has rescued his father, Henry IV, from the hands of the fierce Douglas, he is rewarded with the assurance, 'Thou hast redeem'd thy lost opinion' (*1H4* 5.4.48). Reputation or honour is indicated here as the former frequenter of taverns becomes the hero of the Battle of Shrewsbury.

Having been let down by his father, who has failed to bring his forces to the Battle of Shrewsbury, Hotspur characteristically attempts to turn a liability into an asset by proclaiming that the rebels will **achieve** greater renown fighting without him: 'I rather of his absence make this use: / It lends a lustre and more great opinion, / A larger dare to our great enterprise, / Than if the Earl were here' (*1H4* 4.1.76–9). 'Higher stature' or 'enhanced distinction' is implied here.

The politic Earl of Worcester criticizes his nephew Hotspur for impatience and his dismissive attitude towards their ally Owen Glendower. Spelling out the requirements of a nobleman he cautions the young firebrand: 'You must needs learn, lord, to amend this fault; / Though sometimes it show greatness, courage, blood – / And that's the dearest grace it renders you – / Yet often times it doth present harsh rage, / Defect of manners, want of government, / Pride, haughtiness, opinion, and disdain' (3.1.178–83). The copius diction of the last line emphasizes the idea of an individual adopting a position of superiority that demeans others. 'Arrogance', 'self-complacency' or 'egotism' seems to be the meaning in this case.

There are very few occasions when the word is used to mean 'self-important', 'affected' or 'opinionated'. The most engaging case arises in *LLL* where several characters are addicted to displays of linguistic virtuosity. As the pedant Holofernes and his associates emerge from dinner, the curate, Sir Nathaniel, praises him on his acuity and discretion, attempting to emulate these qualities in his highly elaborate compliment: 'I praise God for you, sir. Your reasons at dinner have been sharp and sententious: pleasant without scurrility, witty without affection, audacious without impudency, learned without opinion, and strange without heresy' (5.1.2–6). The careful antitheses and balanced clauses exhibit the very parade of learning that Holofernes is being praised for avoiding. Opinion here means 'self-importance' or 'arrogance', which is a nice compliment confirmed by the subsequent suggestion, 'strange without heresy', that fresh theological ideas have been delivered without any affront to orthodoxy. Moth delivers his own crushing assessment of their discourse with the comment, 'They have been at a great feast of languages, and stol'n the scraps' (5.1.36–7). Put otherwise, they are all affectation, turning Nathaniel's skilfully crafted compliment on its head. Nathaniel's effusion is both precisely articulated and inflated; poised and balanced, yet showy. Here is an articulacy that is self-consciously striving, its deliberate artifice freezing what should be flowing. It leads us to the door of a paradox: the greatest art possesses the easy fluency of artlessness. When the King of Navarre mocks Armado as 'One who the music of his own vain tongue / Doth ravish like enchanting harmony' (1.1.166–7), he employs a verbal flashiness that exhibits the very fault it seeks to condemn. *LLL* is not a play where verbal infelicity and brilliance characterize low and high life respectively: both strands are mingled in both strata. Moreover, a single speech like Nathaniel's *simultaneously* calls forth admiration and criticism.

Desdemona provides a unique meaning when attempting to recover from Othello's denunciation of her as a strumpet. Bewildered, she asks Emilia, 'How have I behav'd, that he might stick / The small'st opinion on my least misuse?' (*OTH* 4.2.108–9). 'Doubt', or 'suspicion', appear to be the most accurate synonyms here. She simply can't think of any impropriety that might provoke such a brutal accusation of what to her is an unthinkable act: adultery.

The word is used once as a malapropism when Dogberry, giving instructions for the prisoners to be bound, says, 'Come let them be opinion'd' (*ADO* 4.2.67). Presumably he means 'pinioned'. Shakespeare, does, however, have a technique for suggesting a perceptive thought lying beneath the surface of the apparent verbal blunder that is highly suggestive or insightful. Has Dogberry alighted on the idea of 'opinion'd' as a mode of sifting the malefactors to discover their motivation – their opinions or beliefs?

(C) For pertinent comments on *LLL* and *TRO* see Schalkwyk, *Speech and*

Performance in Shakespeare's Sonnets and Plays, and Londres, ed., *Love's Labour's Lost.* Also of interest are Matthews, 'Language in *Love's Labour's Lost*', and Schlauch, 'The social background of Shakespeare's malapropisms', both in Salmon and Burness, eds, *A Reader in the Language of Shakespearean Drama*; McAlindon, *Shakespeare's Tudor History*; Harris, *Sick Economies*, esp. ch. 4; Donawerth, '*King John*: mutable speech' in *Shakespeare and the Sixteenth-Century Study of Language.* Bevington, ed., *Troilus and Cressida*, Arden 3 258 and 336 has interesting footnotes on Thersites' comments.

outsell
(A) This usage, unique to *CYM*, signifies to exceed in **worth** or **value**, surpass, transcend. The prefix 'out', used on several occasions, is a potent means of expressing 'to go beyond'.
(B) Surprisingly, the term is employed both by the silver-tongued Iachimo and by the blockhead Cloten. Having stolen Posthumus' love token from the arm of the sleeping Imogen, Iachimo proceeds to persuade his exiled adversary that the token was a gift subsequent to successful seduction. The description is delicately erotic, the commercial term insinuating just the right amount of contaminating colour: 'She stripp'd it from her arm. I see her yet: / Her pretty action did outsell her gift, / And yet enrich'd it too. She gave it me, and said / She priz'd it once' (2.4.101–4).
    The pictorial quality of this description is startling, the highly suggestive 'stripping' is heightened by the idea that the action of removing the armlet transcends the value of the object: 'stripp'd', 'outsell', 'gift', 'enrich'd' convey a heady feeling of a moment of intense sensuality, the 'sell' component exerting sufficient effect to transform the sanctuary of Imogen's bedchamber into a boudoir tainted by the **commerce** of the brothel.
    Cloten and subtlety never keep company, so his soliloquy provides none of Iachimo's guile. Even so, Imogen's grace and beauty are such as to impose themselves on this most arid of minds, pressing it into a seldom attained articulacy: 'I love her and hate her; for she's fair and royal, / And she hath all courtly parts more exquisite / Than lady, ladies, woman, from every one / The best she hath, and she, of all compounded, / Outsells them all' (3.5.70–4).
(C) Palfrey, *Late Shakespeare*, contains insightful commentary. Also richly suggestive are Thorne, *Vision and Rhetoric in Shakespeare*; Enterline, *The Rhetoric of the Body*.

outwork
(A) This unique usage, which acquires rich colouration from the language surrounding it, intimates workmanship or artistry of transcendent power.
(B) Enobarbus, in his celebrated description of Cleopatra's barge, produces a paradoxical concept: art producing beauty that goes beyond the **achievements** of nature – but which is then countered by a natural beauty transcending the most elaborate, and fanciful artistry: 'For her own person, / It beggar'd all description: she did lie / In her pavilion – cloth of gold, of tissue – / O'er picturing that Venus where we see / The fancy outwork nature' (*ANT* 2.2.197–201).

Those phrases 'O'er picturing' and 'outwork nature' effect a **counterpoise** that enables the mind's eye to dwell on the finest achievement of human creativity and artistic virtuosity, one that removes all flaws and so surpasses nature, only to be caught unawares by a reality that is even more wonderful – forcing the audience to visualize something almost beyond imagination. Cleopatra's surpassing beauty is rendered perfect by commandeering all the artistry available to her, which in turn is projected into our minds via Shakespeare's art – transforming and vivifying Plutarch's wonderful description. To analyse is to become dizzy with all the implications; to experience the moment on the stage or page is to enter a visionary zone that enables us to see beyond normal perception.

(C) Of interest here are Schalkwyk, *Speech and Performance in Shakespeare's Sonnets and Plays*, ch. 1; Goldman, *Acting and Action in Shakespearean Tragedy*, ch. 6; Mulryne, 'Cleopatra's barge and Antony's body' and Laroque, 'Rare Italian master(s)', both in Marrapodi, ed., *Shakespeare, Italy and Intertextuality*; and Thorne, *Vision and Rhetoric in Shakespeare*.

outworth

(A) The socio-economic significance of this unique usage is noteworthy. It means to exceed in **value**, to reach beyond the thing compared.

(B) Buckingham, giving vent to his loathing of Wolsey, uses a compacted expression to indicate that the low-bred Cardinal possesses a status (by virtue of his intellectual attainments) beyond that of the gentleman born: 'A beggar's book / Outworths a noble's blood' (*H8* 1.1.122–3). Whatever Wolsey's taints, and his Machiavellianism is beyond question, Buckingham has alighted on a dubious argument to denigrate the powerful churchman. The opposite view, or at least distaste for according primacy of **wealth** over intellect, finds expression in *TIM*, where the eponymous hero claims: 'The learned pate / Ducks to the golden fool' (4.3.17–18).

(C) For contemporary disquisitions on education, see Aughterson, ed., *The English Renaissance*. See also Denton, ed., *Orders and Hierarchies in Late Medieval and Renaissance Europe*. Fascinating and highly germane to this question is Warley, *Sonnet Sequences and Social Distinction in Renaissance England*.

overbuys

(A) Again unique and deeply engaged with relative **values**, this means to exceed in **worth**.

(B) Imogen, defending her choice of husband in the face of the King's disdain, exclaims: 'he is / A man worth any woman; overbuys me / Almost the sum he pays' (*CYM* 1.1.145–7). Noteworthy here is the double meaning of worth – worthy of and of equal value to – along with the transition to the specifics of the two people in question: Imogen pays or gives herself in this exchange of love and receives Posthumus in return, someone who is not just her equal but worth almost two of her. The language of the **market-place** enters into love via the transactional nature of the relationship, especially as one party is heir to the throne.

(C) Highly relevant here is McDonald, *Shakespeare's Late Style,* and Nuttall, *Shakespeare the Thinker.*

overhold

(A) Unique to *TRO*, this single usage means over-**value** or place too high an estimate upon.

(B) In a play abounding with references to measurement, calculation and values (financial and moral), Agamemnon, having exhausted his patience in attempts at luring Achilles back to the battlefield, finally concludes his unflattering assessment of the Greek hero by requiring Patroculus to, 'Go tell him this, and add, / That if he overhold his price so much, / We'll none of him' (2.3.132–4). In other words, he is not as valuable to the war effort as he thinks he is. The precise phrase transposes priceless heroism into **market-place** calculation. Even the mighty Achilles' worth must be measured by performance – and **priced** accordingly.

(C) For exploration of measurement and quantification in *TRO* see Thomas, *The Moral Universe of Shakespeare's Problem Plays*; Elton, *Shakespeare's Troilus and Cressida and the Inns of Court Revels,* esp. ch. 6.

overplus

(A) Surplus is the meaning of this word.

(B) *ANT* is the source of both applications of the word in the plays. The fading hero Antony resists the sound advice of his associates to fight on land, defending with dubious elaboration Cleopatra's decision to fight a sea battle. Responding to Enobarbus' objection 'Your ships are not well mann'd', he retorts, 'Our overplus of shipping we will burn, / And, with the rest full-mann'd, from th'head of Actium / Beat th'approaching Caesar' (3.7.34–52). The surplus ships are to be used as a fire hazard to Octavius Caesar's fleet.

If the first example exposes Antony's folly, the second reveals his generosity. On learning that his closest lieutenant has deserted him, Antony sends his treasure after him, the gesture enriching it in the process. The soldier informs the recipient, 'Enobarbus, Antony / Hath after thee sent all thy treasure, with / His bounty overplus' (4.6.19–21). The word **bounty** is associated with Antony throughout the play, but this act of magnanimity is such that even his attested capacity for generosity is surpassed. The overplus does not signify more material treasure, rather an overflowing of largesse or Antonian bounty.

Though different in tone, the same idea of superabundance occurs in the *SON*s. The speaker reassures the woman whose favours he seeks, that his commitment to her transcends even exceptional affiliation: 'Whoever hath her wish, thou hast thy *will*, / And *will* to boot, and *will* in overplus' (135.1–2). There is a pun on '**boot**' meaning 'in addition to' and 'bonus' – hence building up to the extravagance of overplus.

(C) See Schalkwyk, *Speech and Performance in Shakespeare's Sonnets and Plays*; Edmondson and Wells, *Shakespeare's Sonnets*; Deats, ed., *Antony and Cleopatra.*

owe, own

(A) Reaching beyond, but including current usage, this word is used to signify **debt** or obligation; it also means own or possess; repay in compensation; hold in **store**.

(B) The most common application of the word is clearly expressed by Bassanio. Requesting a further loan he acknowledges that he has already been the recipient of Antonio's largesse: 'To you, Antonio, / I owe the most in money and in love' (*MV* 1.1.130–1).

Antipholus of Ephesus is indignant when, on returning home, he finds the door locked against him. He calls to the servant inside: 'What art thou that keep'st me out from the house I owe?' (*ERR* 3.1.42). Owe, here, as on several other occasions, means own.

When the intransigent Coriolanus unleashes a torrent of vituperation against the **plebeians**, the **politic** Menenius attempts to calm him with the assurance that the present diplomatic defeat will in time be compensated for by a reversal of the situation: 'Put not your worthy rage into your tongue; / One time will owe another' (*COR* 3.1.240–1). This idea of owe as compensation is the least common application of the word, but finds expression in its colloquial counterpart today: 'I'll get my own back!'.

Attempting to justify the assassination of Coriolanus, Aufidius suggests to the political elite that he has protected them from a future evil: 'My lords, when you shall know (as in this rage, / Provok'd by him, you cannot) the great danger / Which this man's life did owe you, you'll rejoice / That he is thus cut off' (5.6.135–8). The meaning of this rare usage is far from obvious, but 'hold in store' seems to capture the sense here.

(C) Of particular interest here are Hyde, *The Gift*; Grady, *Shakespeare's Universal Wolf*; Kamps, ed., *Materialist Shakespeare*.

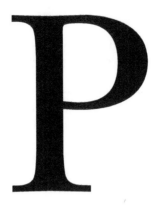

pack, pack'd, packing

(A) Used as a noun the word pack can refer to a gang or confederacy; it can also mean bundle. As a verb the word has four applications: to scheme or intrigue; enter into a covert arrangement; depart; load up (a wagon or horse) with goods. The adjective 'packed' intimates being in league with. Packing as a noun or adjective signifies underhand dealing or scheming; sudden departure; to transport.

(B) Gaining political ascendancy, Richard Gloucester arranges the executions of Queen Elizabeth's relatives and political allies. As he is led to his death Grey denounces his adversaries: 'God bless the Prince from all the pack of you! / A knot you are of damned blood-suckers' (*R3* 3.3.5–6). The amplification of 'pack' with 'knot' makes clear the political force of the word.

A deceptive example of the meaning to intrigue or scheme occurs when Hamlet tells his mother how clearly he understands the machinations of Claudius and his instruments, Rosencrantz and Guildenstern:

> an't shall go hard
> But I will delve one yard below their mines,
> And blow them at the moon. O 'tis most sweet
> When in one line two crafts directly meet.
> This man shall set me packing;
> I'll lug the guts into the neighbor room.
> *HAM* 3.4.207–12

These people will push him into guileful intrigue in order to outmanoeuvre them. As he has just killed Polonius, this act may hasten his departure (one meaning of packing). Moreover, he has to transport the body, which is another meaning of 'packing'. Here the word 'packing' calls for considerable unpacking.

No such complexity occurs when Cloten, finding Pisanio alone, snarls, 'What, are you packing, sirrah?' (*CYM* 3.5.80). He evidently means scheming.

Aaron the Moor, needing to effect a swift **exchange** of babies (white for black) to avoid the disgrace and political fall of Tamora, instructs her sons to undertake the negotiation: 'His child is like to her, fair as you are. / Go pack with him, and give the mother gold' (*TIT* 4.2.154–5). This transaction has to be covert, steeped in secrecy.

The disillusioned, desolate, Antony, believing Cleopatra has come to a political understanding with Octavius Caesar, prepares to commit suicide: 'she, Eros, has / Pack'd cards with Caesar's, and false-play'd my glory / Unto an enemy's triumph' (*ANT* 4.14.18–20). This expressive surrender resonates with deception: card-playing as a metaphor for political dealings and two master-players coming to an underhand agreement to sacrifice the third player, Antony. The full force of this comment emerges only when the sense of 'pack' as duplicitous dealing is understood.

Falstaff, offended by the reluctance of his erstwhile followers to act as go-betweens, dismisses them in language which is unambiguous, copious and emphatic: 'Rogues, hence, avaunt, vanish like hailstones; go! / Trudge! Plod away i'th'hoof! Seek shelter, pack!' (*WIV* 1.3.81–2).

(C) Young, *The Action to the Word*, esp. 39–43, makes some interesting comments on doubling and echoing in *Hamlet*; Barton's chapter on *ANT* in *Essays* is illuminating in terms of the above; likewise her essay 'Falstaff and the comic community'; White, *The Merry Wives of Windsor*, provides fascinating explorations of Falstaff in this middle-class milieu.

paction

(A) This is a word that signifies a **compact** or agreement.

(B) Queen Isabel, blessing the impending marriage of Henry and Katherine, expresses the hope, 'That never may ill office, or fell jealousy, / Which troubles oft the bed of blessed marriage, / Thrust in between the paction of these kingdoms, / To make divorce of their incorporate league' (*H5* 5.2.363–6). This elegant speech captures perfectly the aspiration for the success of the marriage in terms of personal attachment and the hope of political concord. 'Paction' positioned in the middle of the line, conveys the idea of the kingdoms being linked so tightly as to coalesce – something mirrored in the physical union of the marriage partners.

(C) Tennenhouse, *Power on Display*, explores diverse contextual aspects relating to marriage, power and staging. See also Cavanagh, '*Henry V* and the performance of the word' in *Language and Politics in the Sixteenth-Century History Play*.

palter, paltering

(A) Palter is a significant word in the political lexicon as it is the opposite of straightforward, upright dealing. There are shades of meaning in the six cases but equivocate, prevaricate, engage in underhand dealing, behave mischievously or unreliably, cover all of them. Paltering implies evasiveness.

(B) Emphasizing the Roman attributes of uprightness and fortitude, Brutus declares that his fellow conspirators have no need to take an oath. Their stated commitment to the cause is sufficient to ensure that they will not deviate from their task or behave in a way that will imperil the **venture**: 'what other bond / Than secret Romans, that have spoke the word / And will not palter? and what other oath / Than honesty to honesty engag'd / That this shall be, or we will fall for it?' (*JC* 2.1.124–8). The entire speech amounts to 26 lines, the fulcrum being the antithesis between the kind of men who could 'palter' and true Romans.

At the other extreme from the intellectual man of principle is the brainless Ajax, who having been manipulated into the position of the foremost Grecian warrior, denounces his superior rival, Achilles, for disdaining to talk with the Greek leadership. The incensed and puffed-up Ajax vociferates: 'A whoreson dog, that shall palter with us thus!' (*TRO* 2.3.233). Here the emphasis is less on unreliability than on mischievous evasiveness. Indeed, a virtually identical meaning occurs again in the same play when the recent arrival in the Greek camp, Cressida, declines to promise immediate physical surrender to the blunt courtship of Diomed. The impatient suitor begins to leave, dismissing her as a sexual tease: 'Fo, fo, adieu, you palter' (5.2.48).

In very different circumstances Macbeth makes a similar complaint against the weird sisters whose deception is far more sinister and calculated. Having already endured the experience of Birnan Wood coming to Dunsinane, he now discovers that Macduff is not 'of woman born' but was 'from his mother's womb / Untimely ripp'd' (*MAC* 5.8.13–16). Hence his frustrated outburst: 'And be these juggling fiends no more believ'd, / That palter with us in a double sense, / That keep the word of promise to our ear / And break it to our hope' (5.8.19–22). Equivocation is a major theme in the play. Here, 'palter' is sandwiched between 'juggling fiends' and 'double sense' gathering into itself the conception of a deception that is mocking: the hero has been seduced and toyed with by the weird sisters.

Coriolanus wins the voice of the common people to support his election to the position of consul, only to be stopped in the street by the tribunes indicating withdrawal of that support. Cominius protests: 'The people are abus'd, set on. This palt'ring / Becomes not Rome' (*COR* 3.1.58–9). The concepts 'palter' and 'Roman' are antithetical: a violation of the ethical principles proclaimed by the Romans. Hence Antony's distress after defeat at the Battle of Actium because he will have to resort to undignified, devious manoeuvring to survive politically against the all-conquering Octavius Caesar: 'Now I must / To the young man send humble treaties, dodge / And palter with the shifts of lowness, who / With half the bulk o'th' world play'd as I please'd, / Making and marring fortunes' (*ANT* 3.11.61–5). Here the unsavoury associations of the word are thrown into relief by the grandiose picture of Antony's former **condition** as master of half the world.

(C) Marrapodi, ed., *Shakespeare, Italy and Intertextuality*, contains a number of essays that are highly relevant here. See also Martindale and Martindale, *Shakespeare and the Uses of Antiquity*; Miola, *Shakespeare's Rome*; Thomas, *Shakespeare's Roman Worlds*; Sohmer, *Shakespeare's Mystery Play*.

pelf
(A) Employed twice in the sense of goods, possessions, property, on a single occasion the word intimates reward or riches.
(B) Apemantus, the cynic philosopher, in saying grace before his meal begins with the lines: 'Immortal gods, I crave no pelf, / I pray for no man but myself' (*TIM* 1.2.62–3). He clearly means 'possessions', just as Gower does when describing the wreck of Pericles' ship: 'All perishen of man, of pelf, / Ne aught escapend but himself' (*PER* Cho. 2 35–6).

The speaker in one of the poems in *The Passionate Pilgrim*, a miscellany containing contributions by Shakespeare, sorrows at being left alone for the night by the young woman. Contemplating the emptiness, he concludes the stanza: ' "Wander", a word for shadows like myself, / As take the pain but cannot pluck the pelf' (14.11–12). Reward of riches (beauty) would appear to be the required meaning here.
(C) An engaging exploration of the nature and articulacy of possessions is Jardine's *Worldly Goods*. Also relevant are Shell, *Money, Language and Thought*; Simmel, *The Philosophy of Money*; Heinzelman, *The Economics of the Imagination*; Bednarz, '*The Passionate Pilgrim*' in Cheney, ed., *Shakespeare's Poetry*.

perfidious
(A) An unusual word found only five times in the plays, with a single case of the adverb 'perfidiously', it signifies deep-seated treachery. In all cases the adjective is employed with such energy or disgust that none of the available synonyms quite do the work of this word, which has drifted to the periphery of the modern political lexicon. The various examples are not so much valuable for nuances of meaning, therefore, but rather to reveal the intensity of feeling attaching to the word: the ultimate expression of betrayal. To be perfidious is to be thoroughly treacherous.
(B) The two examples from *TMP* are instructive. Prospero narrates the **account** of his brother's **usurpation** of his dukedom. Even 12 years after the event, Prospero's disgust is evident at every turn but never more bitterly than in the parenthetical '– that a brother should / Be so perfidious!' (1.2.67–8).

The other example from the play is slightly odd as it appears in a comic context. The drunken butler Stephano has just come upon his associate Trinculo along with the islander, Caliban. Trinculo is offended by Caliban's enthusiastic worship of Stephano, albeit due to the influence of drink, especially as he himself has been frightened by the 'monster'. His recovery is effected by an outpouring of words – 'a very shallow monster! I afeard of him? A very weak monster! The man i'th'Moon? A most poor credulous monster!' – which culminate in his ultimate expression of disdain: 'a most perfidious and drunken monster! When's god's asleep, he'll rob his bottle' (2.2.145–51). Awareness of being placed at the bottom of this new political hierarchy in a community of three heightens Trinculo's antagonism towards Caliban. The worst charge he can level is treason based on the islander's greedy enthusiasm for the bottle – something for which he will betray his 'god' Stephano. Not even the comic context can diminish the force of this word, which serves to draw attention to this, seemingly absurd, grouping as a new political entity.

Venom and contempt are again present towards the close of *AWW* as Bertram undergoes a searching examination and public humiliation. When Parolles– a self-confessed liar, coward, traitor and underminer of his friend, Bertram – is summoned as a witness he is denounced with abhorrence by the young hero: 'He's quoted for a most perfidious slave, / With all the spots a'th'world tax'd and debosh'd, / Whose nature sickens but to speak a truth' (5.3.205–7). There could hardly be a more devastating vilification. This is a richly ironic situation with the audience attracted to the rogue, Parolles, while this self-admiring young man seems oblivious of his moral turpitude. The force of his vitriolic assault accentuates awareness of his moral blindness. Again, perhaps unexpectedly, this highly significant word is harnessed to a critical moment in which the moral and political are closely interlinked (Bertram has, of course, distinguished himself on the battlefield).

When the two close cousins fall into deadly hate through rivalry for the love of Emilia, Palamon, in shackles and having seen and heard his **rival** bathed in happiness, gives vent to a bitter and comprehensive denunciation of Arcite that includes the phrase, 'O thou most perfidious / That ever gently look'd!' (*TNK* 3.1.35–6).

The word sounds the hero's death knell in *COR* as his adversary, and erstwhile comrade-in-arms, Aufidius, denounces him for accepting the supplications of the Romans when they were at the mercy of the Volscians:

> You lords and heads a'th'state, perfidiously
> He has betray'd your business, and given up,
> For certain drops of salt, your city Rome,
> I say 'your city', to his wife and mother,
> Breaking his oath and resolution like
> A twist of rotten silk,
>
> 5.6.90–5

The verbal configuration in which this word is embodied conveys a clear sense of its vigour, the final simile in the quotation mirroring perfectly its overpowering force in this, Shakespeare's most visceral and kinetic tragedy.

(C) Interesting here is Parker, *Shakespeare from the Margins*, ch. 6. Palfry, *Late Shakespeare*, ch. 5, engages with language and power in *TMP*. Key texts are the essays on postcolonial Shakespeare in McDonald, ed., *Shakespeare: An Anthology of Criticism and Theory 1945–2000*; Castillo, *Performing America*; Gilles, *Shakespeare and the Geography of Difference*; Loomba, *Shakespeare, Race and Colonialism*.

pestiferous

(A) Appearing only twice and then in quite different contexts, this adjective plays a significant part in the political lexicon, not least because of the array of potential synonyms that can be invoked to capture its meaning. Essentially it means carrying moral contagion. The idea of vileness or poison that spreads through the system lies at the heart of the word. Pernicious is the obvious synonym, but pestiferous seems more specific to political life or to the military sphere where there is a fear of contamination or undermining of essential principles or **values**. Mischievous carries some of the force of the meaning, though that word may be too light.

(B) When employed by the Duke of Gloucester it is embedded in a vituperative speech directed at his deadly enemy, the cynical, Machiavellian Bishop of Winchester (later in the play made Cardinal):

> No, prelate, such is thy audacious wickedness,
> Thy lewd, pestiferous, and dissentious pranks,
> As very infants prattle of thy pride.
> Thou art a most pernicious usurer,
> Froward by nature, enemy to peace,
> Lascivious, wanton, more than well beseems
> A man of thy profession and degree;
>
> *1H6* 3.1.14–20

What is apparent from this quotation is that the words are carefully chosen. This is no piece of crude abuse. Each area of the Bishop's life is subjected to scrutiny and is exposed. Not only is he provocative, rancorous, and arrogant but his vices permeate every aspect of life, political, financial and sexual. His propensity for spreading a malign influence through these carefully delineated systems makes this word strategically important.

By comparison, the second application seems deceptively innocuous. It appears during the highly entertaining exposure of the braggart Parolles for betraying his comrades, so he believes, to the enemy. The blindfolded Parolles receives his sentence from a disguised associate: 'The general says, you that have so traitorously discover'd the secrets of your army, and made such pestiferous reports of men very nobly held, can serve the world for no honest use; therefore you must die' (*AWW* 4.3.304–7). Clearly these 'pestiferous reports' undermine the integrity of the soldiers. Once again the core idea is of an invasive, contaminating process. The seriousness of the meaning is easily missed here because an atmosphere of comedy pervades the scene.

(C) Goy-Blanquet, *Shakespeare's Early History Plays*, esp. ch. 4, provides interesting perspectives on the *H6* plays. Harris, *Sick Economies*, is conceptually significant, as is Hillman, *Shakespeare's Entrails*. Important too are Zitner, *All's Well That Ends Well*, and Engle, *Shakespearean Pragmatism*.

pittance

(A) This single usage means hospitality, **provision**, meal or fare rather than the current meaning of meagre financial reward.

(B) Tranio, in the guise of his master, Lucentio, whisks Baptista off to his lodgings with the caution that with such little time for preparation the hospitality will be insubstantial: 'The worst is this, that at so slender warning, / You are like to have a thin and slender pittance' (*SHR* 4.4.60–1). The doublet, 'thin and slender' is strongly suggestive that the fare will be plain and insufficient.

(C) Appelbaum, *Aguecheek's Beef*, provides a rich and varied feast on the subject of food in Shakespeare's world.

plebeians, plebeii, plebs

(A) The term in its various forms means common people or lower orders. Occasionally neutral, it is usually employed contemptuously. Predictably, all but one of the ten applications occurs in the Roman plays – six of them in *COR*. Even the exception, *H5*, draws a parallel between Henry V and Julius Caesar.

(B) The Chorus in *H5* depicts Henry's triumphant return to London after victory at Agincourt: 'The Mayor and all his brethren in best sort, / Like to the senators of th'antique Rome, / With the plebeians swarming at their heels, / Go forth and fetch their conqu'ring Caesar in' (5.25–8). In addition to drawing a parallel between the two great conquerors, the expression 'swarming' **plebeians** conveys the sense of multitudes: a torrent of people, insect-like, heedless of everything except catching a glimpse of the hero.

Twice each in *TIT* and *COR*, the term is used in a non-pejorative way. More usual are the following: Menenius' references to 'fusty plebeians' and 'beastly plebeians' (*COR* 1.9.7; 2.1.95); the enraged Mark Antony believing Cleopatra has betrayed him, warns she will be put on display in Rome by Octavius Caesar: 'Let him take thee / And hoist thee up to the shouting plebeians!' (*ANT* 4.12.33–4).

Contempt for the plebeians in the Roman plays finds expression in three ways. First, they are disdained for lacking a fundamental Roman **virtue**: constancy. Octavius Caesar comments, fairly dispassionately, 'This common body, / Like to a vagabond flag upon the stream, / Goes to and back, lackeying the varying tide, / To rot itself with motion' (1.4.44–7). Antony, Octavius Caesar's great adversary, makes a similar complaint: 'Our slippery people, / Whose love is never link'd to the deserver / Till his deserts are past, begin to throw / Pompey the Great and all his dignities / Upon his son' (*ANT* 1.2.185–9).

The second source of disparagement is that the common people are dirty. Casca, describing the crowd's response to the crown-offering, registers this perfectly: 'the rabblement hooted, and clapp'd their chopp'd hands, and threw up their sweaty night-caps, and utter'd such a deal of stinking breath because Caesar refus'd the crown, that it had, almost, choked Caesar, for he swounded, and fell down at it; and for mine own part, I durst not laugh, for fear of opening my lips and receiving the bad air' (*JC* 1.2.244–50). Here is a telling manifestation of the patrician's view of plebeians: they are coarse, have bad breath, and are best described as 'rabblement' or 'tag-rag people' (1.2.258).

Cleopatra, emphasizing their dirtiness, adds a third source of distaste – their engagement in menial **occupations**. Warning Charmian of their impending fate at the hands of the all-conquering Octavius Caesar, she paints a vivid picture of their destiny if taken alive: 'Mechanic slaves / With greasy aprons, rules, and hammers shall / Uplift us to the view. In their thick breaths, / Rank of gross diet, shall we be enclouded, / And forc'd to drink their vapor' (*ANT* 5.2.209–13).

There is a fourth characteristic implicit in these comments. The common people are unbridled as well as being uncouth – shouting is their natural mode of expression.

This commingling of disgust for people seen as devoid of merit, dignity, insight or cleanliness is exhibited by Menenius, the political wheeler-dealer. He is vociferous in denouncing the plebeians' recently acquired tribunes when the exiled Coriolanus returns at the head of a foreign army: 'You have made good work, / You and your apron-men; you that stood so much / Upon the voice of occupation and / The breath of garlic-eaters!' (*COR* 4.6.95–8). For Menenius plebeians are 'beasts' and 'clusters' (4.6.121–2). When addressing them directly, he hurls at them the kind of language favoured by Coriolanus himself: 'You are they / That made the air unwholesome, when you cast / Your strinking greasy caps in hooting at / Coriolanus's exile' (4.6.129–32).

COR is not only Shakespeare's most political play but it is also the one play in which class antagonism reaches the point where the only means of avoiding revolution is constitutional adjustment to accommodate the plebeians' demands. Hence they are bought off with the innovation of representatives called tribunes – only to be manipulated by them with a facility characteristic of the patricians. Until the moment when the intransigent exile seems about to annihilate Rome, the patricians conceal or at least moderate their contempt when confronted directly by the plebeians. The eponymous hero is withering in his loathing of the lower orders because he sees them as less than human. Moreover, blind to the inadequacy of their physical **condition** he despises their lack of military commitment. They are starving at the outset of the play, rioting in the quest for food – yet are expected to work and fight without having a voice in the **commonwealth**. Shakespeare balances the hero's purity, a total absence of hypocrisy or a capacity to play the politician, with plebeians who are vacillating and comic, but also generous in the circumstances.

(C) As Knowles, ed., *Henry VI Part 2*, Arden 3, points out in a discussion of the sumptuary laws and their relationship to Cade's rebellion, 'The dividing line between gentleman and plebeian was that between those whose annual income, after all taxes, was above or below five pounds' (93). He goes on to add, 'Unlike aristocratic dress, peasant wear changed relatively little during the Middle Ages. The one common innovation, particularly for smiths and tanners, was the leather apron. This remained an emblem of the lower orders.' For an excellent treatment of Shakespeare's engagement with this subject see Hadfield, *Shakespeare and Republicanism*, and Martindale and Taylor, eds, *Shakespeare and the Classics*. Of interest too are the numerous books on the Roman plays cited in the bibliography. Fascinating detail on this subject of class and status in Elizabethan England is to be found in Warley, *Sonnet Sequences and Social Distinction in Renaissance England*; Stevenson, *Praise and Paradox*.

policy

(A) 'Policy' can mean statecraft; amoral calculation; devious or **intelligent stratagem**. The term sometimes veers between wisdom and craft. Generally the words 'policy', '**politic**', '**politician**' and '**politicly**' are opprobrious. Although this group of closely affiliated words carry with them a suggestion of guileful, underhand or dishonourable dealing, this is true without exception only of the term politician. All the other terms can be used without suggestion of unscrupulous or ignoble behaviour. Occasionally the opposing meanings abut or coalesce. Sometimes the sense is rendered unambiguous by means of a qualifying epithet, e.g., 'scurvy', 'vile', 'base and rotten', 'devilish', 'grave'.

(B) The word is used on several occasions in the sense of prudence or sagacity with fine comic lightness. For instance, Berowne stands as advocate for Costard's proposal to put on the Pageant of the Nine Worthies for the Princess and her entourage. In brushing aside the King's fear of a fiasco, Berowne reminds him of their own embarrassment and proceeds to show the **advantage** of a worse display: 'We are shame-proof, my lord; and 'tis some policy / To have one worse show than the King's and his company' (*LLL* 5.2.512–13). Even here wisdom carries with it a smack of guile. In most cases the stress is on craft or guileful strategy. The least pejorative commingling of intelligent stratagem and mental adroitness is provided by Leonato in *ADO*. In threatening retribution for the disgrace inflicted on his daughter, Hero, he provides a list of resources available to him including 'Both strength of limb, and policy of mind' (4.1.198). Here policy means '**intelligence**' or 'mental adroitness' rather than implying subtle scheming.

By contrast, Touchstone, in his mock threat to his rival William, uses policy in the sense of stratagem stripped of scruple: 'I will deal in poison with thee, or in bastinado, or in steel; I will bandy with thee in faction; I will o'errun thee with policy; I will kill thee a hundred and fifty ways' (*AYL* 5.1.54–7).

When, after the tumultuous wooing, Petruchio employs the word in his mischievous speech to Kate's father, he assures his future father-in-law that Kate's abusive rejection is not really serious, nor is Kate genuinely wild and uncivil. Rather, her rough behaviour is employed as a screen to cover her affection: 'If she be curst, it is for policy, / For she's not froward, but modest as the dove' (*SHR* 2.1.292–3). Policy here means a 'social stratagem', a 'harmless deception'. A similar tone is struck by Helena in her jocular banter with Parolles when she asks, 'Is there no military policy how virgins might blow up men?' (*AWW* 1.1.121–2). But there is a playful suggestion of guile here. Any implication of mental dexterity or underhand dealing is abhorrent to Sir Andrew Aguecheek. Set on by Fabian to disgrace Cesario by means 'either of valour or policy' his riposte is immediate: 'And't be any way, it must be with valor, for policy I hate. I had as lief be a Brownist as a politician' (*TN* 3.2.29–32). Here the linking of policy and politician accentuates the element of deviousness and craft.

The slipperiness of the word as it teeters between wisdom and artful calculation is indicated when Northumberland responds to the Queen's appeal to allow the deposed King to accompany her into exile in France: 'That were some love, but little policy' (*R2* 5.1.84). The ugly nature of the word is given expression by several speakers. Hotspur in defending his brother-in-law Mortimer against Henry's accusation of betrayal responds passionately, 'Never did base and rotten policy / Color her working with such deadly wounds' (*1H4* 1.3.108–9). Here the adjectives violently expose the core of the noun. In *2H4* Mowbray claims that Prince John's offer to redress their grievances is the result of cynical calculation rather than an act of magnanimity: 'But he hath forc'd us to compel this offer, / And it proceeds from policy, not love' (4.1.145–6).

The delicacy of shading attaching to the word can be illustrated by examples suggesting that policy is a fundamental ingredient of political and military activities: a clear-eyed sifting of circumstances and the motivations of adversaries. The Archbishop of Canterbury, expressing his admiration for the suddenly revealed abilities of the newly crowned King, says: 'Turn him to any cause of policy, / The Gordian knot of it he will unloose, / Familiar as his garter' (*H5* 1.1.45–7).

A similar tone of approbation is conveyed by Canterbury in his famous beehive speech where he sweeps aside impediments to the invasion of France by proposing a division of English forces that will ensure safety at home and success abroad: 'If we, with thrice such powers left at home, / Cannot defend our own doors from the dog, / Let us be worried, and our nation lose / The name of hardiness and policy' (1.2.217–20). Here policy means 'skill and judgement as applied to military matters'. However, the English when speaking of the French never allow the word such immaculate usage. The Chorus insists that the French response to the imminent invasion is to prevent it by crafty manoeuvring: 'and with pale policy / Seek to divert the English purposes' (Cho 2 14–15). The epithet 'pale' indicates that French machinations are motivated by fear and cowardice. The Greeks likewise use policy as a term of approval when applied to themselves. In denouncing the mockery of Achilles and Patroclus, Ulysses is clearly thinking in terms of intelligent calculation, strategy and statecraft when he protests, 'They tax our policy, and call it cowardice, / Count wisdom as no member of the war, / Forstall prescience, and esteem no act / But that of hand' (*TRO* 1.3.197–200).

Diomed, greeting Aeneas during a truce, warns him, 'But when contention and occasion meet, / By Jove, I'll play the hunter for thy life, / With all my force, pursuit, and policy' (4.1.17–19). Here it would seem that policy implies tactical ingenuity.

When we come to Thersites, the situation is different. Launching an attack on the incompetence of the Greek leadership, he denounces the failure of strategy and statecraft rather than overtly questioning its morality:

> the policy of those crafty swearing rascals, that stale old mouse-eaten dry cheese, Nestor, and that same dog-fox, Ulysses, is not prov'd worth a blackberry. They set me up, in policy, that mongrel cur, Ajax, against that dog of as bad a kind, Achilles; and now is the cur Ajax prouder than the cur Achilles, and will not arm to-day; whereupon the Grecians begin to proclaim barbarism, and policy grows to an ill opinion. (5.4.9–17)

Thersites has the distinction of uttering the word policy three times in a single speech. The first and second applications mean 'scheming', the third, 'statecraft'. So for all the practised scheming of the Greek leadership (and in

Shakespeare's day Ulysses' name was synonymous with guile) their endeavours have proved to be totally ineffectual. Intriguingly, Thersites, who projects himself as witness to the ubiquity of vice and folly, does not directly censure policy, but rather seems to present it as a natural adjunct of devious characters – who aren't even bright enough to employ guile successfully. Because there is no morality in this social universe, as far as Thersites can see, the only test of policy or scheming is whether it produces the desired result.

Volumnia employs the word in an interesting way. Eager to persuade her son to soften his stance towards the **plebeians** in order to secure their goodwill, she attempts to brush aside his moral distaste for such actions by protesting, 'I have heard you say / Honor and policy, like unsever'd friends, / I'th' war do grow together' (*COR* 3.2.41–3). Policy evidently involves guile or even dissimulation. In response to his dismissive 'Tush, tush!' she argues,

> If it be honor in your wars to seem
> The same you are not, which, for your best ends,
> You adopt your policy, how is it less or worse
> That it shall hold companionship in peace
> With honor, as in war,
>
> 3.2.45–50

Here is a perfect example of the tension that resides in the word. Calculation and subtlety are necessary adjuncts in war and politics but at what point does an action cross the threshold to unworthiness or dishonour?

2H6 has several examples and they fall fairly neatly into two groups: policy as wisdom or policy as craft. When the Duke of Gloucester complains, 'And did my brother Bedford toil his wits, / To keep by policy what Henry got?' (1.1.83–4) the focus is on careful government and military **exploit**. Queen Margaret uses the term to mean 'wise' or 'judicious' when advising the King to keep his uncle Gloucester at arm's length (3.1.23). The Cardinal attaches the same sense to the word when advocating judicial murder: 'That he should die is worthy policy' (3.1.235). The meaning here is sound judgement or a wise course of action, but there is an unconscious slippage as employment of a euphemism hints at the ugly side of the word. Interestingly, Suffolk employs the same word when supporting the murder but rejecting the judicial part – 'But, in my mind, that were no policy' (3.1.238) – on the grounds that Gloucester will be reprieved by the King. There is a sliding towards the 'scheming' side of the meaning when Somerset defends his failure in France by claiming that the Duke of York would have encountered an even more ignominious defeat despite his much vaunted reputation as a strategist: 'If York, with all his far-fet policy, / Had been the Regent there instead of me, / He never would have stay'd in France so long' (3.1.293–5).

The phrase '**far-fet**' [fetched = far reaching] suggests cunning or subtlety but is poised delicately between unsavoury craft, and intelligent calculation, whereas the Lieutenant raging against Suffolk employs the harshest use of the term: 'By devilish policy art thou grown so great' (4.1.83). The darkest facet of the word is intensified here by the qualifying epithet attached to it. In *TIM* the self-interested, worldly side of the term is indicated by means of simple antithesis. The First Stranger recognizes the folly of attempting to aid Timon when all his former flatterers have deserted him: 'But I perceive / Men must learn now with pity to dispense, / For policy sits above conscience' (3.2.85–7).

A unique form is provided in *JN* where the Bastard encourages the English and French kings to establish a brief alliance to assault the fortified town of Angiers because the inhabitants have refused to submit to either side: 'Smacks it not something of the policy?' (2.1.396). The harshest significance attaching to the term is usually produced by means of a qualifying epithet. The use of the article here implies a mischievous pleasure in alighting on something deeply cynical: *the* policy seems to designate the ultimate instrument in political affairs; not just a clever ploy or stratagem but guile stripped of scruple. In other words, here is a celebration of a method or technique which has acquired notoriety.

(C) Cleansed of opprobrium this word eventually became a purely technical term for the articulation of a plan of action designed to achieve a clearly stated outcome. Although dictionaries provide several definitions that retain the element of guile and duplicity, economic and political publications, and even journalists, now employ the term in a purely neutral way, e.g. *The Penguin Dictionary of Economics, The Penguin Dictionary of Politics.* Fascinatingly, this carries the word's meaning back towards its earlier usage; for Elyot, in his celebrated book *The Governor* (1531), the word is synonymous with 'wisdom' (see Morris, *Political Thought in England,* 24). Spivack, *Shakespeare and the Allegory of Evil,* 374, comments on the way in which the word becomes associated with the Machiavel. Grady, *Shakespeare, Machiavelli and Montaigne,* is also insightful.

politic

(A) This word can describe behaviour that is anything from prudent to devious, though the emphasis is usually on craft and guile. Present usage of the term has almost freed the word of its unattractive associations so that its synonyms are words such as 'sagacious', 'prudent', 'judicious', 'expedient'. Dictionaries, however, keep open the unsavoury associations of the word, adding synonyms such as 'scheming' or 'crafty'. Perhaps the closest equivalent is 'expedient', which is finely balanced between 'astute' and 'unfettered by moral imperatives'. The term 'streetwise' is also apt here as it too intimates a necessary defensive awareness tilting towards a mental adroitness characterized by competitive self-interest. Significantly, in the USA, where the phrase originates, the term is 'street smart'. Additionally, the word signifies weighty, serious or impressive.

(B) Goneril's is the most striking application of the term in its neutral sense of 'prudence' when she excuses herself to her husband Albany for depriving Lear of half his entourage:

> This man hath had good counsel – a hundred knights!
> 'Tis politic and safe to let him keep
> At point a hundred knights; yes, that on every dream,

> Each buzz, each fancy, each complaint, dislike,
> He may enguard his dotage with their pow'rs,
> And hold our lives in mercy.
>
> *LR* 1.4.322–7

Here is one of the most ruthlessly **politic** characters in Shakespeare straining to soften the impact of the word. The more usual connotation is provided by the loquacious Host of the Garter in *WIV* when he prides himself on the success of his intrigue: 'Am I politic? Am I subtle? Am I a Machiavel? (3.1.101). His tone is jocular because his scheming is benign. The precise Jaques proclaims the singular, undefiled quality of his melancholy, insisting that all other types of melancholy are morally tainted: 'I have neither the scholar's melancholy, which is emulation; nor the musician's, which is fantastical; nor the courtier's, which is proud; nor the soldier's, which is ambitious; nor the lawyer's, which is politic' (*AYL* 4.1.10–14). Evidently the lawyer's melancholy is affected, a sobriety calculated to exert the desired impression on a client – seeming gravity designed to indicate the difficulty of the case – or on the judicial authority: a world-weariness that cries out for a sympathetic response. The word can also carry the connotation of being wise, serious, weighty, as in *AWW* where the First Lord cautions his associate about his conduct in the plot designed to deceive Parolles: 'As for you, interpreter, you must seem very politic' (4.1.20–1). On the other hand, he may be instructing his colleague to be cunning. The possible mixture of suggestions, the fluidity of the word, is brought out by Malvolio. Preparing for his new station he muses, 'I will be proud, I will read politic authors, I will baffle Sir Toby, I will wash off gross acquaintance, I will be point-devise the very man' (*TN* 2.5.161–3). Here the word politic above all implies 'weighty'. The Third Citizen in *R3*, reflecting on the more wholesome former days, protests, 'No, no, good friends, God wot, / For then this land was famously enrich'd / With politic grave counsel; then the King / Had virtuous uncles to protect his Grace' (2.3.18–21). These statesmen were perceptive and circumspect.

Close in meaning is Mortimer's use of the word in *1H6* when he advises his nephew the Duke of York to employ caution in his pursuit of the crown: 'With silence, nephew, be thou politic' (2.5.101). Here the word evidently implies wariness, caution, discretion, but not necessarily deceit or duplicity – though these meanings abut, and may be thought to coalesce.

Politic can also imply an assumed gravity, something imparted by Thersites' mocking description of the inflated Ajax, the newly nominated Greek champion, as he anticipates his forthcoming duel with Hector: 'Why, 'a stalks up and down like a peacock – a stride and a stand . . . bites his lip with a politic regard, as who should say there were wit in this head and 'twould out' (*TRO* 3.3.251–6).

The word can also mean 'discrete'. Desdemona reassures Cassio that her husband's present behaviour is a matter of necessary discretion rather than loss of affection for his friend: 'and be you well assur'd / He shall in strangeness stand no farther off / Than in a politic distance' (*OTH* 3.3.11–13).

Perhaps the most interesting application occurs in *HAM.* In baiting Claudius,

Hamlet says of the dead Polonius that 'a certain convocation of politic worms are e'en at him' (4.3.19–21). Here the word means 'shrewd', its precise weight being effected by use of 'convocation', which imparts the sense of a deliberative assembly. Part of the impact is attributable to the repetition of the 'c' sounds. So vivid is this phrase that these sly, eager, astute worms can be seen in the mind's eye dining enthusiastically on the carcass of the politic Polonius.

The sense of wisdom that occasionally attaches to the word is present in Parolles' denunciation of virginity. He protests to Helena: 'It is not politic in the commonwealth of nature to preserve virginity' (*AWW* 1.1.126–7). It is not 'politic' or 'sensible' because the continuation of the species depends on procreation. The choice of word is partially determined by the character, who uses a weighty expression whenever possible – affecting a raffish charm. Even when the word 'politic' seems stripped of association with guile or underhand dealing it generally retains the element of calculation and self-interest.

When Beatrice and Bendick finally confess their mutual love, the latter teasingly asks, 'for which of my bad parts didst thou first fall in love with me?', inviting the jocular rebuff: 'For them all together, which maintain'd so politic a state of evil that they will not admit any good part to intermingle with them' (*ADO* 5.2.62–4). Here the meaning is 'careful' or 'prudent', but there is an added edge to the word suggesting a ready self-awareness, a shrewdness which goes beyond mere prudence. Even in such light-hearted **exchanges**, then, the word carries a singular pressure.

The sense of 'dishonesty' or 'underhand dealing' is brought out in a comic moment when Touchstone ironically lists his accomplishments showing him to be a man of the world or a notable courtier: 'I have trod a measure, I have flatt'red a lady, I have been politic with my friend, smooth with mine enemy, I have undone three tailors, I have had four quarrels, and like to have fought one' (*AYL* 5.4.44–7). In other words, the worldly man employs guileful wariness with his friend and feigns affability with his enemy.

TIM affords two examples of the contemptible aspect of the word. Timon, having **bankrupted** himself through excessive generosity, discovers that all his ostensible friends turn their backs on him. His servant solicits financial assistance to no avail. Turned away with hypocritical excuses, he spits out his contempt, employing the word twice in one speech:

> Excellent! your lordship's a goodly villain. The devil knew not what he did when he made man politic; he crossed himself by't; and I cannot think but, in the end, the villainies of man will set him clear. How fairly this lord strives to appear foul! . . . like those that under hot and ardent zeal would set whole realms on fire; of such a nature is his politic love. (3.3.27–34)

The speech begins and ends with an oxymoron – 'politic' is the very antithesis of love; it is the attribute that makes man more wicked than the Devil himself. Here then, 'politic' receives its bleakest meaning: a total absence of human regard; a completeness of self-regard, self-interest, active duplicity and hypocrisy.

(C) Spivack, *Shakespeare and the Allegory of Evil*, esp. 374–8; Agnew, *Worlds Apart*, esp. 71; Jones, 'The Politics of Renaissance England' in Kinney, ed., *A Companion to Renaissance Drama*; Hadfield, *Shakespeare and Renaissance Politics*; Ingram, *Idioms of Self-Interest*, esp. ch. 3 on *TIM*, all provide significant commentary.

politician

(A) Here is someone who subscribes to a code of unprincipled self-interest and who engages in artful manipulation. For all the disparagement of today's politicians the term is clearly less opprobrious now than in Shakespeare's plays.

(B) It receives its fullest force when the mad Lear instructs the blind Duke of Gloucester, 'Get thee glass eyes, / And like a scurvy politician, seem / To see the things thou dost not' (*LR* 4.6.170–2).

Hotspur in denouncing Henry IV to his father, the Earl of Northumberland, and his uncle the Earl of Worcester, vociferates, 'Why, look you, I am whipped and scourg'd with rods, / Nettled and stung with pismires, when I hear / Of this vile politician Bullingbroke' (*1H4* 1.3.239–41).

The extent of the politician's deviousness is mocked by Hamlet when commenting on the gravedigger's rough treatment of a skull: 'This might be the pate of a politician, which this ass now o'erreaches, one that would circumvent God, might it not?' (*HAM* 5.1.78–80). In *TN*, being cautioned about provoking Malvolio, Sir Toby responds smugly, 'we are politicians' (2.3.75), implying that he and his entourage are cunning enough to outmanoeuvre the overbearing steward.

(C) See Alexander, ed., *Shakespeare and Politics*; Hadfield, *Shakespeare and Renaissance Politics*.

politicly

(A) Employed twice, 'politicly' means craftily, subtly or wisely. This word retains only a shadowy existence today, but when used its meaning is close to its original sense in Shakespeare.

(B) In *SHR*, as Petruchio prepares to retire on the first night in his matrimonial home he begins his famous speech, 'Thus have I politicly begun my reign' (4.1.188). Kate already subdued by her ordeal – cold, wet and hungry – is to be subjected to further deprivation in order to make her amenable. Here the word is finely apt, suggesting a carefully thought-out and well-executed strategy. The word 'politicly' contains the combined potency of shrewd calculation and awareness, setting the tone for the vigour, irony and harshness to which the rest of the speech gives expression. Reign conveys a clear sense of rule, authority and power, linking the domestic and political spheres. Having set out the rationale of his strategy, Petruchio challenges the audience in the concluding couplet of this colourful speech: 'He that knows better how to tame a shrew, / Now let him speak; 'tis charity to show' (4.1.210–11).

There is irony spilling over into contemptuous mockery in the Duke of York's reflection when contemplating a decision that has equipped him with a strong military force, nominally to be used against the Irish, but which can now be employed in his quest to secure the crown: 'Well, nobles, well; 'tis politicly done, / To send me packing with an host of men: / I fear me you but warm the starved snake, / Who, cherish'd in your breasts, will sting your hearts' (*2H6* 3.1.341–4).

One fascinating feature of the *H6–R3* cycle is the frequency with which characters stop, cogitate, analyse, evaluate and determine on a course of action. Here is Shakespeare from the earliest stage of his career exploring the political and psychological landscapes. Thoughts are sifted, words weighed, scenarios contemplated, and actions brutally executed.

(C) Some of the most recent contributions to this **politic** world are Goy-Blanquet, *Shakespeare's Early History Plays*; Cavanagh, et al., eds, *Shakespeare's Histories and Counter-Histories*; Hattaway, ed., *Shakespeare's Histories*; Pendleton, ed. *Henry VI*. Extracts from the political writings of the time are provided by Aughterson, ed., *The English Renaissance*. Other key aspects are explored in Foakes, *Shakespeare and Violence*; Leggatt, *Shakespeare's Tragedies*; Bushnell, *Tragedies of Tyrants*.

practice

(A) Functioning with singular force in the political sphere, the word's primary significance resides in actions that are devious, calculating, conspiratorial, subversive, underhand or exploitative. Equally, the term relates to 'doings' or to actions that are neutral or beneficent, such as mastery of technique, acquisition of theoretical or practical knowledge. Occupation is another meaning. Additionally, the verb can mean to work upon; engage; put to use; or rehearse. The noun is spelt with a 'c', the verb and adjective are sometimes spelt with an 's'.

(B) When Antony arrives in Rome to aid Octavius Caesar against Pompey, he finds himself embroiled in a confrontation:

> Ant: My being in Egypt, Caesar,
> What was't to you?
> Caes: No more than my residing here at Rome
> Might be to you in Egypt; yet if you there
> Did practice on my state, your being in Egypt
> Might be my question.
> Ant: How intend you, practic'd?
> Caes: You may be pleas'd to catch at mine intent
> By what did here befall me. Your wife and brother
> Made wars upon me, and their contestation
> Was theme for you – you were the word of war.
> *ANT* 2.2.35–44

This is particularly instructive because these are the preliminary manoeuvres in a game of cat and mouse. Octavius wants to push Antony onto the back foot while appearing discrete and restrained – no blusterer, he. Practice in the sense of to plot or scheme is blunt, affording little scope for ambiguity or nuance, yet Antony is reluctant to react too forcefully. Hence his demand for evidence of his supposed scheming rather than further exposition on the content of the term.

Octavius, the master political tactician, alights on precisely the right word to be both provocative and statesmanlike.

Having directed the assassination of the Duke of Gloucester, his political opponents present themselves before King Henry VI to justify the charges made against him. The King, ignorant of the deed, demands that Gloucester be treated fairly: 'Lords, take your places; and I pray you all / Proceed no straighter 'gainst our uncle Gloucester / Than from true evidence of good esteem / He be approv'd in practice culpable' (*2H6* 3.2.19–22). What is impressive here is the clarity of the King's insistence on what in today's political culture is referred to as 'transparency': the evidence must be verifiable and Gloucester's actions demonstrably treasonous. The key phrase 'in practice culpable' compresses the ideas of scheming or conspiracy being unequivocally directed at the state as opposed to the **factional** manoeuvring characteristic of ambitious individuals and groups surrounding the monarch. Without background knowledge of the word, an instinctive gloss would be 'action'. This would yield a comprehensible meaning but would fail to capture the stress on a devious scheme that has found expression in purposeful action.

The idea of practice as scheming occurs three times within the final act of *MM*. The newly returned Duke, feigning ignorance of Angelo's behaviour, affords him the opportunity of making a free and public confession of his actions. Addressing Isabella the Duke exclaims, 'By heaven, fond wretch, thou know'st not what thou speak'st, / Or else thou art suborn'd against his honor / In hateful practice' (5.1.105–7). 'Malicious scheming' is the meaning of 'hateful practice'. The Duke continues to reassure Angelo while allowing him the opportunity to clear his conscience: 'Shall we thus permit / A blasting and a scandalous breath to fall / On him so near us? This needs must be a practice' (5.1.121–3). The language employed by the Duke throws a huge weight on to 'practice'. The underhand conniving intimated by the word suggests activity that is politically subversive. In the wake of this emotional turmoil, with accusation and counter-accusation, Angelo displays a cool cynicism that is shocking:

> I did but smile till now.
> Now, good my lord, give me the scope of justice,
> My patience here is touch'd. I do perceive
> These poor informal women are no more
> But instruments of some more mightier member
> That sets them on. Let me have way, my lord,
> To find this practice out.
>
> 5.1.233–9

Here is the culmination of a process that makes the 'practice', or plot, something much more than a slanderous act of personal spite: it is an intrigue aimed at undermining the state. The *political* resonance of the word 'practice' is intensified to the point that Angelo is able to present himself not as an aggrieved party in a personal matter, but as an impartial public servant determined to protect the integrity of justice and the body **politic**. Political subversion not personal animus becomes the issue as Angelo picks up on the Duke's repeated use of 'practice' in a way that maximizes its potential.

This engagement reveals the richness and colouration provided by a word that can be free of political significance but is amenable to acquisition and exploitation by an adept **politician**. In addition, the repeated use of this word in Act 5 facilitates a close interweaving of the human, social and political strands of the play. Angelo has not merely sought sexual gratification by dishonest means: he has subverted the body politic.

It is significant that the word is used four times in the last two acts of *HAM*. First Claudius reassures Laertes that his scheme is so subtle that not even Gertrude will suspect foul play:

> I will work him
> To an exploit, now ripe in my device,
> Under the which he shall not choose but fall;
> And for his death no wind of blame shall breathe,
> But even his mother shall uncharge the practice,
> And call it accident.
>
> 4.7.63–8

Elaborating his **stratagem**, Claudius describes the nature of the treacherous device, including the calculated, underhand move – 'a pass of practice' – by which the Prince will be killed:

> He, being remiss,
> Most generous, and free from all contriving,
> Will not peruse the foils, so that with ease,
> Or with a little shuffling, you may choose
> A sword unbated, and in a pass of practice
> Requite him for your father.
>
> 4.7.134–9

Laertes is successful in killing Hamlet, but at the **cost** of a wounded conscience and his own life. Significantly, his confession acknowledges the true nature of the device: 'The treacherous instrument is in thy hand, / Unbated and envenom'd. The foul practice / Hath turn'd itself on me' (5.2.316–18).

After the shocking denunciation and rejection of Hero by Claudio, in *ADO*, family and friends contemplate the possibility of some calculated deception, leading Benedick to comment: 'Two of them have the very bent of honor, / And if their wisdoms be misled in this, / The practice of it lives in John the Bastard, / Whose spirits toil in frame of villainies' (4.1.186–9). The *plotting* of any scheme is ascribed to John, who revels in machinations.

The meaning 'treachery' occurs in *COR* when the eponymous hero attempts to console his mother as he is exiled from Rome: 'Your son / Will or exceed the common or be caught / With cautelous baits and practice' (4.1.31–3). The striking phrase 'cautelous baits and practice' means with crafty or underhand schemes and treachery. Here the supreme warrior is confident that he has no equal.

This moment is rich in dramatic irony because his loneliness, anguish and anger at Rome's ingratitude will drive him into the arms of his enemy, Aufidius, who will eventually bring about his death with 'cautelous baits and practice'. It is the emphasis on extreme guile devoid of honour which gives the word its potency – something reinforced by the interlocking phrase which is nowhere surpassed in crystallizing underhand, ignoble action.

In *JN*, Falconbridge the Bastard reflects on the ways of the world and the need to adapt: 'to deliver / Sweet, sweet, sweet poison for the age's tooth, / Which though I will not practice to deceive, / Yet to avoid deceit, I mean to learn' (1.1.212–15). It is essential to develop a defensive strategy to avoid being manipulated or outmanoeuvred. In this case, the use implies 'engage in', 'exercise' or 'work at'; but it could equally mean 'scheme'. What is interesting about this example is that Faulconbridge acknowledges that entry into the political sphere requires accommodation. Only a chameleon can hope to survive in this environment.

Having exposed Lord Scroop as one of the conspirators who sought to assassinate him, Henry V expresses his indignation against the man he had held in deepest trust: 'Thou that didst bear the key of all my counsels, / That knew'st the very bottom of my soul, / That (almost) mightst have coin'd me into gold, / Wouldst thou have practic'd on me, for thy use?' (*H5* 2.2.96–9). 'Worked upon' is the most suggestive meaning. This punning, compressed conceit involving 'use' as **interest** is remarkable because Henry reveals not only the magnitude of the betrayal but his own former subservience to the ends of Scroop.

Use of the term to signify 'worked upon' is admirably captured by the Lord Chief Justice when he chastises Falstaff for exploiting Mistress Quickly both financially and sexually: 'You have, as it appears to me, practic'd upon the easy-yielding spirit of this woman, and made her serve your uses both in purse and in person' (*2H4* 2.1.114–16). While the colouration of this moment is comic, the ugliness of exploitation emerges as strongly as in the previous example. A good deal of the aftertaste is occasioned by the potency of the word 'practic'd'.

There is no comic element to diminish the force of the term when Brabantio accuses Othello of winning Desdemona's affections by having worked upon her – not with the comic seductions of Falstaff but with exotic devices and potions: 'Judge me the world, if 'tis not gross in sense, / That thou hast practic'd on her with foul charms, / Abus'd her delicate youth with drugs or minerals / That weakens motion' (*OTH* 1.2.72–5). As 'practiced' is so often associated with guileful, devious actions, the idea of being manipulated surreptitiously acquires particular force. It also generates dramatic irony because the richly exotic Othello is singularly devoid of guile – and fatally fails to perceive it in others.

Having discovered Angelo's cynical abuse of authority by seeking a sexual favour from Isabella in return for her brother's life, the Duke delivers an exemplary soliloquy on justice. Employing rhyming couplets to reinforce the didactic force of the speech, he is scathing in his condemnation of Angelo: 'How may likeness made in crimes, / Making practice on the times, / To draw with idle spiders' strings / Most ponderous and substantial things!' (*MM* 3.2.273–6). The phrase 'making practice on the times' uniquely suggests action that transcends *personal* exploitation: the entire society, the epoch itself, is sullied and stained by corruption emanating from the very embodiment of justice.

The idea of direct and intimate engagement, as opposed to merely theoretical knowledge, occurs in the opening moments of the play. The Duke, before investing Angelo with his authority, enumerates Escalus' attributes: 'The nature of our people, / Our city's institutions, and the terms / For common justice, y'are as pregnant in / As art and practice hath enriched any / That we remember' (1.1.9–13). Escalus is clearly exemplary, his knowledge being sociological, constitutional, judicial and political. The key phrase is 'art and practice', which is probably the equivalent of our modern expression 'theory and practice' so that practice means practical experience. Escalus is no mere student of judicial and constitutional matters but has acquired a depth of understanding through long-standing application of the law.

In the famous quarrel scene between Cassius and Brutus the former demands primacy: 'Brutus, bait not me, / I'll not endure it. You forget yourself / To hedge me in. I am a soldier, I, / Older in practice, abler than yourself / To make conditions' (*JC* 4.3.28–32). More experienced is the implication of the key phrase, here, 'older in practice'.

Parolles' humiliation at having been exposed as a coward is compounded by the First Lord who mockingly describes him as 'the gallant militarist – that was his own phrase – that had the whole theoric of war in the knot of his scarf, and the practice in the chape of his dagger' (*AWW* 4.3.141–3). The mastery of theory and practice is intimated in this example, 'practice' being used to imply practical knowledge.

In *ANT*, the eponymous hero complains that though Octavius Caesar is now firmly in command, he was the fortunate beneficiary of Antony's generalship and fighting prowess at the crucial Battle of Philippi, failing to participate in any meaningful way: 'he at Philippi kept / His sword e'en like a dancer, / . . . / . . . He alone / Dealt on lieutenantry, and no practice had / In the brave squares of war; yet now – No matter' (3.11.35–40). No direct involvement in the 'doings' or 'actions' seems to be the meaning of 'practice' in this case.

Cerimon the physician, endowed with quasi-magical powers, reflects on the advantages of serious study:

> 'Tis known, I ever
> Have studied physic; through which secret art,
> By turning o'er authorities, I have,
> Together with my practice, made familiar
> To me and to my aid the blest infusions
> That dwells in vegetives, in metals, stones;
> *PER* 3.2.31–6

'Practice' here seems to be the opposite of 'theoretical studies', suggesting practical experiments or empirical work.

At the very moment he is soliciting their support to become Consul, Coriolanus, having been mildly rebuked for his antipathy to the **plebeians**, responds with biting irony: 'And since the wisdom of their choice is rather to have my hat than my heart, I will practice the insinuating nod and be off to them most counterfeitly' (*COR* 2.3.98–100). Characteristically, the Roman hero considers it a matter of rectitude to display open contempt towards those whom he disdains, expecting their support on the grounds of his exemplary military service. The politicians' 'nod' – insinuation and dissimulation – he scorns as beneath his code of honour. 'Practice' is a little slippery here, meaning emulate 'indulge in the action', 'carry out the performance' of humility, but it also carries the suggestion that he will make a point of undertaking this exercise regularly in an attempt to perfect the action. This conflation is typical of the man who strives to cram words with ideas and feelings that will give full vent to his intense emotions. Whereas here his expression is sardonic, even blatantly sarcastic, a little later the full force of his anger is embodied in a speech which emphasizes his inability to subdue his body into the corrupting action of political accommodation:

> Well, I must do't.
> Away, my disposition, and possess me
> Some harlot's spirit! My throat of war be turn'd,
> Which choir'd with my drum, into a pipe
> Small as an eunuch, or the virgin voice
> That babies lull asleep! The smiles of knaves
> Tent in my cheeks, and schoolboys' tears take up
> The glasses of my sight! A beggar's tongue
> Make motion through my lips, and my arm'd knees,
> Who bow'd but in my stirrup, bend like his
> That hath receiv'd an alms! I will not do't,
> Lest I surcease to honor mine own truth,
> And by my body's action teach my mind
> A most inherent baseness.
>
> 3.2.110–23

Panthio, advising Antonio on the education of his son, recommends that he be sent to court: 'There shall he practice tilts and tournaments' (*TGV* 1.3.30). The meaning of 'repeated exercise to gain proficiency' would seem the likely meaning to the modern ear, but in this case 'engage in' is probably the more accurate interpretation.

Hamlet, confident that he will win the duel with Laertes exclaims: 'since he went into France I have been in continual practice' (*HAM* 5.2.210–11). This is an example of the modern use of the term employed by anyone repeating an exercise with the aim of enhancing or perfecting their performance.

Viola/Cesario, arrested by Feste's wordplay, reflects on the demands imposed on a professional fool:

> He must observe their mood on whom he jests,
> The quality of persons, and the time;
> And like the haggard, check at every feather
> That comes before his eye. This is a practice
> As full of labor as a wise man's art;
>
> *TN* 3.1.62–6

As the terms 'practice' and 'art' are parallel, practice means activity, occupation or profession.

Boult, the pimp in *PER*, loses patience with the pure Marina. He tells Bawd, 'O, take her home, mistress, take her home. These blushes of hers must be quench'd with some present practice' (4.2.123–5). The action or activity implied by 'practice' in this case involves accommodating the customers' sexual requirements.

After the apparent death of Hero, her uncle Leonato threatens to fight with Claudio, 'Despite his nice fence and his active practice, / His May of youth and bloom of lustihood' (*ADO* 5.1.75–6). 'Nice fence' suggests new-fangled technique with 'active practice' constituting a parallel phrase (something mirrored in the next line), so that the meaning implied is of someone in top-class **condition** consequent on military training and a recent campaign. A superbly condensed phrase, 'active practice', indicates physical vitality dedicated to the mastery of swordsmanship. Practice means something more than repeated exercise of the activity; it intimates a honing of technique or vigorous mastery.

Cassandra, warning the Trojans of impending catastrophe, exclaims, 'practice your eyes with tears!' (*TRO* 2.2.108). 'Put to use or employ' might be the appropriate meaning here, but more likely is accustom or rehearse, because Cassandra is predicting that the weeping will soon be copious. When Falstaff cautions Prince Hal, 'Well, thou wilt be horribly chid to-morrow when thou comest to thy father. If thou love me, practice an answer' (*1H4* 2.4.373–5) he means either prepare or rehearse. He is, of course, alluding to the forthcoming interview between Hal and the King in which the Prince is to be chastised for his dissolute ways. Whereas Falstaff endeavours to tutor Hal in the art of evasion, the King provides his own master-class in the techniques of political manoeuvring.

(C) Elam, 'English bodies in Italian habits' in Marrapodi, ed., *Shakespeare, Italy and Intertextuality*, has an interesting comment on 'Osric his practice' including a reference 'to the most fashionable contemporary Anglo-Italian fencing manual of the day', *Vincentio Saviolo His Practise*, 32–3. Greenblatt, *Learning to Curse*, Bushnell, *Tragedies of Tyrants*, Bradshaw, *Shakespeare's Scepticism*, Alexander, ed., *Shakespeare and Politics*, Hadfield, *Shakespeare and Republicanism*, Vaughan, *Othello*, Alexander and Wells, eds, *Shakespeare and Sexuality*, and *Shakespeare and Race*, all provide important insights on this topic.

practicer
(A) Used only twice a 'practicer' is a practitioner, but in a rather special sense: no mere professional, but rather someone endowed with special powers arising from direct or indirect association with arcane knowledge, which may be benign or malign.
(B) Finally succumbing to the passionately persuasive pleas of Helena, the King agrees to submit to her treatment, holding her to the proposed penalty for failure: 'Sweet practicer, thy physic I will try, / That ministers thine own death if I die' (*AWW* 2.1.185–6). 'Practitioner' is the most obvious meaning attaching to 'practicer', but it is worth noting that the exchange brings to a conclusion a magical, incantatory moment partly given expression in rhyming couplets. Helena is not a doctor; merely a physician's daughter who possesses his most prized medication. Her virgin purity and grace are key elements attaching to the rendering of her father's gift. The word 'practitioner' is insufficiently expressive of the quasi-magical associations that animate the word '**practicer**'. The magical qualities inherent in the term can be positive or negative – white or black magic: a skill sanctified by a deep and profound knowledge of the workings of the natural world or a mystical engagement with dangerous and essentially evil forces. It is the latter that is intended by Brabantio when he denounces Othello for having lured Desdemona into his power:

> Damn'd as thou art, thou hast enchanted her,
> For I'll refer me to all things of sense,
> If she in chains of magic were not bound,
> . . .
> Judge me the world, if 'tis not gross in sense,
> That thou hast practice'd on her with foul charms,
> Abus'd her delicate youth with drugs or minerals
> That weakens motion . . .
> I therefore apprehend and do attach thee
> For an abuser of the world, a practicer
> Of arts inhibited and out of warrant.
>   *OTH* 1.2.63–79

The crucial feature of 'practicer' on the two occasions it is used in the singular, is as a possessor of arcane knowledge, whether inspired or acquired by virtuous or malign knowledge.
(C) Zitner, *All's Well That Ends Well*, Donawerth, *Shakespeare and the Sixteenth-Century Study of Language*, ch. 7, and Matar, *Turks, Moors and Englishmen*, all provide telling commentary relating to this topic.

practices
(A) The schemes, plots or endeavours intimated by this term can be benign or malign.
(B) The perfect contrast is between the reference made to the Duchess of

Gloucester, in *2H6*, who has been discovered participating in witchcraft, leading Suffolk to refer to her 'devilish practices' (3.1.46), and Guildenstern's expression of hope that his ministrations, and those of Rosencrantz, will be helpful to Hamlet: 'Heavens make our presence and our practices / Pleasant and helpful to him!' (*HAM* 2.2.38–9).

However, the suggestion of guileful activities occurs more frequently. Edmund expresses his complacent contempt towards his brother Edgar with the words: 'A credulous father and a brother noble, / Whose nature is so far from doing harms / That he suspects none; on whose foolish honesty / My practices ride easy' (*LR* 1.2.179–82). In contrast to the suave, smooth-tongued Edmund, the Duke of Gloucester is emphatic in delivering the oath to which the Governor of Paris must subscribe in swearing allegiance to Henry VI: 'Esteem none friends but such as are his friends, / And none your foes but such as shall pretend / Malicious practices against his state' (*1H6* 4.1.5–7).

Henry V denounces the conspirators for collaborating in the assassination plot manufactured by the French: 'sworn unto the practices of France / To kill us here in Hampton' (*H5* 2.2.90–1). He concludes his excoriation of the traitors by repeating the word: 'And God acquit them of their practices!' (2.2.144).

(C) Dutton and Howard, eds, *Shakespeare's Work: Vol. II – The Histories* contains insightful essays on the *H6* plays; Halio, ed., *Critical Essays on King Lear*, is highly relevant here.

practisants

(A) This is not only a unique usage in Shakespeare but also does not seem to be found anywhere else. It means associates but something more than that: conspirators, schemers, devious associates or even diabolical assistants.

(B) As Joan Pucelle, endeavouring to oust the English, gains entry into Rouen by disguising her followers as peasants, the Bastard comments: 'Here ent'red Pucelle and her practisants' (*1H6* 3.2.20). As Joan is already associated with magical **practices** – either divine or hellish – there might be a dimension present here that adds to the meaning of conspirators. On the other hand, disguising soldiers as peasants is a commonplace piece of guile. Joan refers to the exercise as '**policy**' (3.2.2) – devious behaviour but detached from supernatural activity. Unsurprisingly, the outmanoeuvred Talbot denounces her as 'Pucelle, that witch, that damned sorceress, / Hath wrought this hellish mischief unawares' (3.2.38–9).

Having tricked their way into the town, Joan signals to the French forces outside the wall by means of a flaming torch. Observing the signal, the Dauphin is almost visionary in celebrating destiny: 'Now shine it like a comet of revenge, / A prophet to the fall of all our foes!' (3.2.31–2). This play exhibits a commingling of the supernatural, charismatic and prosaic with the audience invited to sift these elements. For instance, Joan imposes the conception of herself as someone who has been chosen as the agent for the salvation of France, and is even shown surrounded by her spirit helpers (who appear to be servants of darkness rather than divinities). Even so, the French make salacious comments about their heroine; the English are relentless in denouncing her as a whore and witch.

(C) A fascinating discussion of the ambiguities surrounding Joan, drawing on the work of Marina Warner, and focusing especially on the range of suggestion embodied in the name Puzel, is to be found in Burns, ed., *Henry 6, Part 1*, Arden 3, 40–2. Commenting on 'practisants', he makes the interesting comment, 'The word's very obscurity lends it sinister connotations, perhaps of magic rites'.

price
(A) Conceptually critical, this commonplace word carries the following meanings: **worth** or **value; market** rate or **exchange** value; as a verb, to evaluate, value, or prize are the relevant meanings.
(B) Taking it quite simply to mean 'what is paid for a product in the market', Shakespeare explores with precision the various dimensions and perceptions of the term. A fundamental problem that exercised the ingenuity of economists for a considerable period of time is what determines the price of a product. The conclusion incorporated in a fully formulated theory was not given precise expression until long after Shakespeare's day. Leaving aside the subtleties, Shakespeare reveals a clear understanding that price is determined by the interaction of supply and demand. In the short run a change in taste in favour of say pork will lead to a rise in its price – which is precisely what Launcelot Gobbo tells Jessica when fearing a sudden upsurge in the number of Jews converting to Christianity: 'This making of Christians will raise the price of hogs. If we grow all to be pork-eaters, we shall not shortly have a rasher on the coals for money'. Jessica communicates the complaint to her husband, Lorenzo, elaborating the joke and amplifying the lesson in economics: 'he says you are no good member of the commonwealth, for in converting Jews to Christians, you raise the price of pork' (*MV* 3.5.23–36).

The most succinct expression of **market price** happens in *PER* when the intermediary Boult brings his new acquisition to the brothel, inviting Bawd's question: 'What's her price, Boult?' (4.2.50). This question, 'how much did she **cost**?' is precursive to an extensive seminar in business **practice**. Marina is a beautiful virgin, so this new **capital** asset has to be employed to maximize the return on the **investment**. As she will inevitably attract a high price for her first engagement, Marina is to be auctioned. The professional brothel-keeper is evidently capable of constructing a graph displaying the various prices she can charge for the use of a girl over her working life. In addition to the initial capital cost there will, of course, be running costs. When the weekly earnings fall below the level of running costs, the girl will be discarded. Because of limited accommodation, most brothels would discharge girls well before the critical point of minimum **profit** is reached unless unable to recruit new stock. For some reason this particular brothel has been unable to obtain new girls and has been operating on the working capital of a few diseased women. Market opportunities are being missed through lack of working capital. Responding to Pander's urgent appeal: 'Search the market narrowly, Meteline is full of gallants. We lost too much money this **mart** by being too wenchless', Bawd elaborates on their current predicament: 'We were never so much out of creatures. We have but poor three, and they can do no more than they can do; and they with continual action are even as good as rotten.' Agreement having been reached on their plight, Pander gives clear expression to the business plan: 'Therefore let's have fresh ones, what e'er we pay for them' (4.2.3–11).

It is more than a little surprising that the most extensive piece of economic analysis occurs in a brothel and in a Romance. The principles involved here are applicable to most business **ventures** and are easily transferable. Shakespeare sheds light on a significant portion of the 'black economy', illicit activities which reside outside official control, including the purview of taxation. Moreover, he raises key technical and moral issues. Those running the brothel do question the morality of their enterprise and consider closing down when returns are so low that they have reached a threshold where they barely compensate for the risks involved. The danger relates not only to the authorities but also to the gods. As Pander expresses it: 'O, our credit comes not in like the commodity, nor the commodity wages not with the danger' (4.2.30–1). (See entry on **commodity** for further elaboration on this.)

The Governor, Marina's future husband, is Pander's most respected customer, making the romantic engagement quite contrary to that prevailing in the other Romances where the young men are undefiled. The most overt expression of this innocence is found in *WT* where Florizel and Perdita share and celebrate a mutual purity (4.4.112–54). The reverberations of the brothel scenes in *PER* are, therefore, highly significant, ranging beyond the critical issues of the market and business enterprise.

The contrast between the differing prices paid for commodities of differing qualities is well brought out by Diana in *AWW*. In rebutting Bertram's accusation that his presumed sexual encounter with her was fleeting and commercial – 'She's impudent, my lord, / And was a common gamester to the camp' – her response is quick and incisive:

> He does me wrong, my lord; if it were so,
> He might have bought me at a common price.
> Do not believe him. O, behold this ring,
> Whose high respect and rich validity
> Did lack a parallel; yet for all that
> He gave it to a commoner a'th'camp,
> If I be one.
>
> 5.3.187–94

Common articles are bought at common prices – the gift of a family heirloom signifies the purchase of something special: Diana's virginity. Thanks to Helena's ingenuity and persistence in effecting the bed-trick, Bertram has not **purchased** Diana's virginity, but it is the price he has paid which catches him out in a shameful lie. What exposes his underdeveloped morality is trading an emblem of his family for sex: the lineage to which he attaches so much importance when disdaining 'A poor physician's daughter' (2.3.115).

Pistol's application is instructive. Announcing to Falstaff that his boon-companion is now King, he produces Pistolian lyricism appropriate to the value of his news: 'Sir John, I am thy Pistol and thy friend, / And helter-skelter have I rode to thee, / And tidings do I bring, and lucky joys, / And golden times, and happy news of price' (*2H4* 5.3.93–6). The 'golden times' promise earthly paradise abounding in the gold coins of the treasury. The news is of 'high value' indeed, his final word, aptly chosen, infects Falstaff with boundless expectations – only to culminate in cruel disappointment. Justice Shallow has already bought into the Falstaffian dream and sees himself about to be carried along by a bull market, only to lose his thousand pounds in the Falstaff bear market and be left bare, indeed.

In *H5* Pistol, hardly more terse in expression but certainly less exuberant in mood, makes an appeal to Fluellen on behalf of his associate Bardolph who is about to be executed for theft: 'Exeter hath given the doom of death / For pax of little price'. A disproportionate penalty, he feels, pleading, 'let not Bardolph's vital thread be cut / With edge of penny cord and vile reproach' (3.6.44–8). In this beguiling speech where comic deflation vies with aspirational pathos, the link between the 'pax of little price' and the 'penny cord' is conceptually effective and emotionally affecting. In both Hall and Holinshed the soldier in question steals a 'pix' not a 'pax'. As the latter is also Latin for 'peace' there appears to be a provocative contrast between the object stolen by Bardolph and Henry's somewhat more extensive depredations involved in stealing the peace – something elaborated in telling detail by Burgundy (5.2.24–67).

In *COR* the eponymous hero is justifiably perceived as an enemy of the people, one who opposes the distribution of corn at an artificially low price. Hence the enraged **plebeians** cry, 'Let us kill him, and we'll have corn at our own price' (1.1.10–11). They do nothing of the kind. Rather, they settle for the constitutional innovation of having their own representatives: tribunes. Later, a surly and reluctant hero seeking their support for election to the Consulship takes the economic term and transfers it to the political sphere: 'Well then, I pray, your price a'th'consulship?' The riposte, by the First Citizen, suggests a moral superiority proportional to social inferiority: 'The price is, to ask it kindly' (2.3.74–5). The cold economic calculus migrates to the manipulative political sphere only to emerge remade into dignified discourse. Coriolanus is still pre-occupied with the word when, having been outmanoeuvred by the guileful **politicians**, Brutus and Sicinius, he refuses to bend: 'I would not buy / Their mercy at the price of one fair word' (3.3.90–1). Coriolanus, a man of pure spirit uncontaminated by the machinations of politics, genuinely believes that common men are close to worthless, lacking the merit to be designated 'Romans'. His ruthless innocence is captured perfectly in his ignorance of hunger and the economics of everyday life. However, economic reality cannot be kept at bay: it even infiltrates his patrician discourse.

The idea of price moving from the **market-place** to ethics is nicely captured by Emilia when responding to Desdemona's expression of incredulity that any woman would commit adultery for 'all the world': 'The world's a huge thing; it is a great price / For a small vice' (*OTH* 4.3.64–70). Emilia makes some interesting distinctions in this dialogue while embracing sophistical argument to free herself from the taint of immorality:

> By my troth, I think I should, and undo't when I had done't. Marry, I would not do such a thing for a joint-ring, nor for measures of lawn, nor for gowns, petticoats, nor caps, nor any petty exhibition; but, for all the whole world – 'ud's pity, who would not make her husband a cuckold to make him a monarch? I should venture purgatory for't. (4.3.71–7)

She hypothesizes that every man and woman has his or her price; the premise is any injury done to the husband could be more than counterbalanced by the accession of the prize – a reward so great that it could even buy out the wrong. Even so, Emilia recognizes that the sin runs the risk of purgatory. This exchange, which is quiet and intimate, focuses on morality and rates of exchange: for Desdemona there can be no room for equivocation: adultery could not be contemplated or sanctioned in any circumstances. Seemingly, in the theology of the play she sacrifices her soul to protect Othello who says, 'She's like a liar gone to burning hell: / 'Twas I that kill'd her' (5.2.129–30). Yet in the action of the play Desdemona possesses a soul of transcendent beauty. The same theology will, of course, carry him to hell as a murderer and a suicide. What moral calculus can justify the damnation of the two most noble spirits in the play? The quiet discussion of infidelity, price and rates of **exchange** pushes the audience towards such questions. Actions, price, costs and benefits interpenetrate the spheres of morality and theology in a persistent and surprising way.

A perfect contrast to such a fascinating interweaving of the concept is to be found in *1H4*, where the First Carrier attributes the demise of his colleague Robin to the vagaries of the market-place: 'Poor fellow never joy'd since the price of oats rose, it was the death of him' (2.1.12–13).

'Price' meaning 'worth' is well illustrated by Troilus' protestation that Helen should not be surrendered in order to buy off the Greeks and end the Trojan War: 'Is she worth keeping? Why, she is a pearl, / Whose price hath launch'd above a thousand ships, / And turn'd crown'd kings to merchants' (*TRO* 2.2.81–3). This comment precipitates the most dense and systematic exploration of value, in both economic and philosophical terms, to be found anywhere in Shakespeare's works.

Troilus derives Helen's worth or value from *the cost incurred* in the pursuit and retention of her. Later the sagacious and clear-sighted Diomed draws the opposite conclusion, maintaining the enormous cost in lives of Greeks and Trojans expended in the quest to possess her makes her worthless – or more precisely turns a woman initially of dubious value into a negative sum. Pursuing his argument with intense emphasis on measurement and calculation he protests:

> For every false drop in her bawdy veins,
> A Grecian's life hath sunk; for every scruple

> Of her contaminated carrion weight,
> A Troyan hath been slain. Since she could speak,
> She hath not given so many good words breath
> As for her Greeks and Troyans suff'red death.
>
> 4.1.70–5

Before this devastating analysis, Hector has attempted to expose the flaw in Troilus' position, and does so with the same precise and ruthless arithmetic:

> Let Helen go.
> Since the first sword was drawn about this question,
> Every tithe soul, 'mongst many thousand dismes,
> Hath been as dear as Helen; I mean, of ours.
> If we have lost so many tenths of ours,
> To guard a thing not ours nor worth to us
> (Had it our name) the value of one ten,
> What merit's in that reason which denies
> The yielding of her up?
>
> 2.2.17–25

Hector, like Diomed, claims that far from validating the keeping of Helen, the enormous cost of doing so cries out for her surrender. But this provokes Troilus into shifting his ground: 'Fie, fie, my brother! / Weigh you the worth and honor of a king / So great as our dread father's in a scale / Of common ounces?' (2.2.25–8). Thus honour is something not amenable to the petty calculations of the market-place.

That the cost of human life cannot be so easily evaded is indicated in Hamlet's tangled analysis of Fortinbras' huge sacrifice of life 'for a fantasy and trick of fame' (*HAM* 4.4.61), even though he too concludes that honour is the ultimate test. When Hector cuts through the case for honour with another down-to-earth thrust – 'Brother, she is not worth what she doth cost / The keeping' – Troilus attempts to undermine any objective test of worth: 'What's aught but as 'tis valued?' (*TRO* 2.2.50–1). Even in this speech, which contains his crucial equation of cost equals worth, Troilus can hardly keep free of the shifting sands of costs and benefits, but he is finally rescued by his chief debating adversary, Hector, who perversely concurs that the war is a matter of principle, unconnected with Helen's worth: 'For 'tis a cause that hath no mean dependence / Upon our joint and several dignities' (2.2.192–3). Troilus embraces this verdict with enthusiasm: Helen is a mere symbol of Trojan honour, their quest for fame paramount. When celebrating this position, however, Troilus once more finds himself weighing honours against costs. But fame and honour are beyond price; they occupy a sphere above and beyond the commonplace of calculation: 'What's aught but as 'tis valued?'. This line of argument is also subjected to Hector's probing analysis: 'But value dwells not in particular will, / It holds his estimate and dignity / As well wherein 'tis precious of itself / As in the prizer' (2.2.51–6). One interpretation of this is that everything possessing a market value must have intrinsic worth, something *socially* generated. Troilus' attempt to escape objective valuation is thwarted, so he makes an appeal to the irrevocable nature of decisions.

The Trojans approved Paris' quest for retribution against the Greeks and applauded the prize, Helen. Therefore no re-evaluation is tenable without self-disparagement for the initial decision. Troilus' argument denies the pragmatic virtue of learning from experience. When acclaiming Paris' adventure and success, the Trojans had no conception of the consequences. The debate scene gives them the opportunity for reappraising the situation in the light of their losses to date and the prospective future losses. This moment possesses a powerful resonance because the audience knows that the price paid for persisting with the war was annihilation of Troy – an enormously powerful animating force in the Renaissance sensibility. For today's audience it offers a paradigm for the critical nature of political decision-making in a volatile and dangerous world.

Much simpler is Agamemnon's threatening message to Achilles:

> Much attribute he hath, and much the reason
> Why we ascribe it to him; yet all his virtues,
> Not virtuously on his own part beheld,
> Do in our eyes begin to lose their gloss,
>
>   . . .
>
>   Go tell him this, and add,
> That if he overhold his price so much,
> We'll none of him;
>
> 2.3.116–34

Thus the mighty Achilles can overestimate his value or worth to the Greek cause; the costs of attempting to mollify or cajole him exceed the benefits of having him fight.

Lear produces a nominally simple application when informing Cordelia's suitors that her value has fallen:

>   Right noble Burgundy,
> When she was dear to us, we did hold her so,
> But now her price is fallen. Sir, there she stands:
> If aught within that little seeming substance,
> Or all of it, with our displeasure piec'd,
> And nothing more, may fitly like your Grace,
> She's there, and she is yours.
>
> *LR* 1.1.195–201

Emotional devaluation has led to financial devaluation. Her value in the marriage market has collapsed to a negative sum: not only is she penniless but she is now 'dowered' with Lear's antagonism, or as he puts it, 'hate'.

Iago deftly links the meanings 'evaluated' and 'market price' in expressing his resentment at his failure to gain promotion: 'I know my price, I am worth no

229

worse a place' (*OTH* 1.1.11). Any *objective* evaluation of his attributes, he avers, would guarantee him the position as Othello's lieutenant.

The King, attempting to excuse Bertram for the ill-treatment of his, seemingly dead, wife, Helena, sees his behaviour as a universal weakness: 'Our rash faults / Make trivial price of serious things we have, / Not knowing them until we know their grave' (*AWW* 5.3.60–2). The true worth of those things we possess is not appreciated until they are gone.

(C) The exploration of 'value' in *TRO* and the intellectually exhilarating debate scene (2.2) has generated an abundance of fascinating critical work. It would be difficult to do better than to turn to Elton's stimulating study *Troilus and Cressida and the Inns of Court Revels*. Not only does he provide a rigorous critique of this topic, he also signposts the issues that lie behind the concept of value, esp. 128–30. Elton's study explores the philosophical and rhetorical context of the issues with remarkable thoroughness and erudition. What he aptly describes as 'a feast of unreason' achieves particularly sharp focus in ch. 6: *Value*. A propos the preceding discussion, it is worth citing a few of his telling comments:

> While the Trojans are fighting to retain a Helen Troilus claims is beyond price, he nevertheless implies (2.2.52) that valuations are ascribable by the valuing process. Yet he continues to proclaim Helen's value as absolute, as well as a requisite to honour and other absolutes (2.2.199–206). Hence, Troilus is in the paradoxical position of implying relative valuation (2.2.52) while urging that men commit themselves to die to preserve absolute honour and his own value views. (118)

> As Troilus brings to mind Lincoln's Inn's John Donne and his value relativism, his value question (2.2.52) recalls a relativistic Renaissance maxim: as cited critically in Agrippa of Nettesheim's sceptical *De incertitudine* (1530; ch. 91), among views accepted by lawyers: '*Tantum valet res quanti vendi possit*' (A thing is worth as much as it can be sold for). (120)
> As Cressid finds her own value reflected in what 'men prize' (1.2.290), Helen's 'value' is ironically implied in blood shed and lives sacrificed on her behalf (1.1.92–3). What men will give, her market price, Cressid renegotiates, by distributing or withholding her kisses among the exiled Greeks (4.5.), and by the competition and rivalry she excites. (121)

> Helen . . . is a figure around whom the play's value questions revolve. (121)

> Hector's opposition to Troilus' individualistic value-view recalls traditional scholastic attitudes. These stress value as dependent not on valuation by a single individual, but on communal estimation. (122)

Kermode, *Shakespeare's Language*, has a significant chapter on this topic, as illustrated by the following quotations:

> the language is almost everywhere concerned with questions relating to value – to puzzles arising from the difficulty that value is differently conceived by different people. A broad distinction exists between the view that value can be intrinsic, or that it depends on some transcendental criterion, and the sceptical view that it depends wholly upon attribution, that the value of anything is the value one places upon it. (129)

> *Troilus and Cressida* . . . dwells with exceptional concentration on these questions of

opinion, truth, and value . . . *Troilus* . . . is unique in the degree to which its language is saturated by 'opinion', and by the network of notions of which it is the centre. (130)

Words such as 'worthy', 'glory', 'fame', 'merit', 'esteem', 'estimate', 'estimation', 'value', 'cost', 'honour', are everywhere. And 'opinion' occurs ten times, far more than in any other Shakespeare play. It is a commonplace . . . that reputation, honour, fame, and all the rest depend on opinion . . . For a man to know he is famous he must look in the mirror of opinion; (134)

It is Troilus who asks the key question: 'What's aught but as 'tis valued?' (2.2.52). He has been saying that their honour is involved in keeping Helen and that their valuation of her when they approved the expedition of Paris was high; it would now be dishonourable to reduce it. (135)

The question of truth cannot be separated from that of worth or value. (138)

'Opinion', says Thersites, may be worn 'on both sides, like a leather jerkin' (3.3.264–5), and the tone of the whole play shares this ambivalence. (140)

The Matindales' admirable discussion in *Shakespeare and the Uses of Antiquity* provides a refreshing and necessary counterbalance to the critical overemphasis on the play's parody and burlesque, making an alert distinction between pastiche and parody. This self-reflexive, analytical play with its exposure of life, time, love, war and language displays a captivating awareness of beauty, courage, grandeur and delicacy. So while all values are interrogated and deconstructed, the play shimmers with fleeting moments of genuine feeling and humanity, usually when least expected, as when Agamemnon welcomes Hector to the Grecian camp (4.5.162–70). The Martindales' response to this moment is instructive:

It is not the least of this play's startling effects to see the stiff, perhaps absurd, certainly unglamorous and insensitive Agamemnon pour forth, if ever so briefly, such delicate, ravishing words . . . a play which seems so often to decry all value provides this and a few others which are not wholly nullified by their temporariness . . . nothing, no matter how strong and admired, has lasting power. But the tone, lyrical, wistful, elegiac, is wholly other, and Agamemnon, in particular, achieves, by acknowledging time's power, a temporary but important victory over it. (114–15)

See Craik, *Henry V*, Arden 2, 234–5, for footnote on the pix-pax question. For an appreciation of Pistol's verbal virtuosity see Hulme, 'The spoken language and the dramatic text' in Salmon and Burness, eds, *A Reader in the Language of Shakespearean Drama.* Samuels, et al., eds, *A Companion to the History of Economic Thought,* Gill, *Evolution of Modern Economics,* Forstater, *Little Book of Big Ideas: Economics,* and Robinson, *Economic Philosophy,* all provide clear explanations of the determination of price in the market-place and the evolution of economic thought on the subject. Of vital significance for this topic are: Agnew, *Worlds Apart*; Bruster, *Drama and the Market in the Age of Shakespeare*; Woodbridge, ed., *Money and the Age of Shakespeare*; Hawkes, *Idols of the Marketplace*; Turner, *Shakespeare's Twenty-First Century Economics*; Shell, *Money, Language and Thought*; Woodmansee and Osteen, eds, *The New Economic Criticism*; Meikle 'Quality and quantity in economics: the metaphysical construction of the economic realm', *New Literary History* 31 (2000): 247–68; Engle, *Shakespearean Pragmatism.*

proditor
(A) Used only once, this word means traitor or renegade.
(B) The baleful Winchester, having tried to prevent the Protector, the Duke of Gloucester, entering the Tower, rails at him as someone exceeding his authority and seeking to undermine the kingdom: 'thou most usurping proditor, / And not Protector, of the King or realm' (*1H6* 1.3.31–2). Rarely in these *H6* plays do opponents miss an opportunity to choose the most penetrating word and then reinforce it by some device, as here by alliteration and antithesis.
(C) McDonald, *Shakespeare and the Arts of Language*, and Hussey, *The Literary Language of Shakespeare*, are both exceptional in the clarity of their treatment of rhetoric and the fertility of their examples. Bevington, *Tudor Drama and Politics*, and Hadfield, *Shakespeare and Renaissance Politics*, are excellent on context. Burns, ed., *King Henry VI, Part 1*, Arden 3, has an exceptionally fine introduction.

profit, profitable, profited
(A) The word is used widely in the sense 'to derive benefit from', a meaning still current today. The other meaning is to achieve a pecuniary return in excess of outlays, either by a firm, organization or individual. Both applications are to be found in the plays, but the sense of a financial return appears only one-quarter as frequently as non-financial benefit. Occasionally either or both meanings could apply. Additionally, **advancement** and well-being are operative ideas. Profit appears on occasion to refer to *rate* of return rather than merely *total* return. The adjective suggests skilful.
(B) The Old Shepherd in *AYL* agrees to **purchase** the sheep farm on behalf of Celia, with the proviso, 'if you like upon report / The soil, the profit, and this kind of life' (2.4.97–8). The meaning here seems to be the *rate* of return on the **investment**. Eager to escape Macbeth's castle, the Doctor confides in an aside, 'Were I from Dunsinane away and clear, / Profit again should hardly draw me here' (*MAC* 5.3.61–2). His '**fee**' or 'financial **advantage**' is clearly the issue here. Henry VIII, recounting his relations with Cardinal Wolsey, is precise in delineating the latter's financial gains, including the suggestion of high *rates* of return – a specific economic concept: 'I have kept you next my heart, have not alone / Employ'd you where high profits might come home, / But par'd my present havings, to bestow / My bounties upon you' (*H8* 3.2.157–60).

The preponderance of applications, however, relate to non-pecuniary gains, with mental benefits heading the list. Orlando exclaims against his lack of education, protesting, 'My brother Jaques he keeps at school, and report speaks goldenly of his profit' (*AYL* 1.1.5–6). By contrast, Mistress Page complains, 'Sir Hugh, my husband says my son profits nothing in the world at his book' (*WIV* 4.1.14–15). Caliban is angrily dismissive in evaluating his relationship with Prospero: 'You taught me language, and my profit on't / Is, I know how to curse'

(*TMP* 1.2.363–4). Significantly, Prospero, though disdaining Caliban, finds him indispensable: 'We cannot miss him. He does make our fire, / Fetch in our wood, and serves in offices / That profit us' (1.2.311–13).

It is surprising that Caliban is vital as general factotum – 'We cannot miss him' – given Prospero's magical powers, but economic reality asserts itself here. This last comment possesses a sharp economic edge, but clearly profit here relates to general benefits rather than pecuniary gain, whereas Shylock makes a direct reference to pecuniary rate of return when complaining of Launcelot Gobbo: 'The patch is kind enough, but a huge feeder, / Snail-slow in profit' (*MV* 2.5.46–7). That the role of profit is fundamental to the very existence of Venice as a **mercantile** centre is clearly articulated by Antonio revealing why the authorities dare not create a precedent by cancelling a financial agreement: 'Since that the trade and profit of the city / Consisteth of all nations' (3.3.30–1).

Surprisingly, the clearest example of profit as a return on financial outlay occurs as a metaphor for physical love within marriage when the concept is employed by Othello in his tender address to Desdemona: 'Come, my dear love, / The purchase made, the fruits are to ensue; / That profit's yet to come 'tween me and you' (*OTH* 2.3.8–10). Equally, the metaphor might mean that the pleasures of consumption have yet to be derived from this expensive **purchase**. Here is another legitimate facet of an economic concept. Intriguingly, a concept is often to be seen at its sharpest or most complex when employed metaphorically so that what is elucidated by way of analogy becomes more expressive of itself.

The coalescing of a general benefit, with an economic return on outlay, in this case labour, is provided by Henry V in his idealized portrayal of the common man whose benefits far exceed those of a monarch: 'And follows so the ever-running year / With profitable labour to his grave' (*H5* 4.1.276–7). The speech pivots on the contrast between the careworn **condition** of a king whose rate of return on his responsibilities is mere 'ceremony' and the care free life of the working man who has the incalculable benefit of sleeping soundly: 'Who, with a body fill'd and vacant mind, / Gets him to rest, cramm'd with distressful bread, / Never sees horrid night, the child of hell; / . . . / Sleeps in Elysium' (4.1.269–74).

Henry IV expresses similar agitation when contrasting his inability to sleep with that of the ship-boy. His cry of anguish and frustration begins with the lines, 'How many thousand of my poorest subjects / Are at this hour asleep! O sleep! O gentle sleep! / Nature's soft nurse, how have I frighted thee . . .?' He then moves through evocative contrasts between the luxury of the King's palace and the violence of the seaman's existence:

> Wilt thou upon the high and giddy mast
> Seal up the ship-boy's eyes, and rock his brains
> In cradle of the rude imperious surge,
>
> . . .
>
> And in the calmest and most stillest night,
> With all appliances and means to boot,

> Deny it to a king? Then (happy) low, lie down!
> Uneasy lies the head that wears a crown.
> *2H4* 3.1.4–31

Henry IV is ill, confronting rebellions and deeply worried about the kind of king his son will be: 'therefore my grief / Stretches itself beyond the hour of death' (4.4.56–7). This preoccupation seems to be something of a family trait. Remarkably, Henry VI, in another consideration of these two worlds, exclaims:

> O God! Methinks it were a happy life
> To be no better than a homely swain,
> To sit upon a hill, as I do now,
>
> . . .
>
> So many years ere I shall shear the fleece:
> So minutes, hours, days, months, and years,
> Pass'd over to the end they were created,
> Would bring white hairs unto a quiet grave.
> *3H6* 2.5.21–40

Even this brief extract reveals a conception common to all three kings: what they lack is what the humble peasant enjoys, the ability to be solaced and caressed by the rhythms of life: the diurnal round. What they fail to acknowledge is the full extent of physical deprivation, but they make the revealing point that they are compelled to live outside the orbit of everyday life: they are obliged to project themselves elsewhere, envisaging anguish even beyond death – not spiritual but political.

The intensely explorative deployment of the word occurs in the narrative poem *LUC*, where it is embedded in a network of financial terms. The stanza provides a critique of self-defeating aspiration:

> Those that much *covet* are with *gain* so fond,
> That what they have not, that which they *possess*,
> They scatter and unloose it from their *bond*,
> And so by hoping more they have but less,
> Or *gaining* more, the *profit* of *excess*
>   Is but to *surfeit*, and such griefs sustain
>   That they prove *bankrout* in this poor *rich gain*.
> 134–40

It is significant that in setting out this human propensity for acquisition, which dulls awareness of the pleasures of being, of living in the moment with all its fullness, money is the poet's chosen symbolic instrument, the metaphoric field of articulation. '**Bond**', 'profit', 'excess' and '**bankrout**' are the key terms around which the stanza is structured. A paradoxical human characteristic captured in the idea of **lending** at **interest**, 'the profit of excess', parallels human failure of

234

seeking more when already replete, producing 'surfeit' – which not only 'cancels' the anticipated benefits of further gains but *diminishes* the pleasures attaching to enough. A social and moral sickness finds its most powerful expression in the language of the market-place. The paradoxical concept of the 'Profitless usurer' recurs in *SON* 4. 7.

(C) Siemon, *Shakespearean Iconoclasm,* has an interesting chapter 'Icon and iconoclasm in *Lucrece* and *Henry V*'. Cheney, ed., *Shakespeare's Poetry,* contains several fine essays. Enterline, *The Rhetoric of the Body from Ovid to Shakespeare,* ch. 5, explores interesting aspects of *LUC.* See, too, Hattaway, ed., *Shakespeare's History Plays,* and Ornstein, *A Kingdom for a Stage,* on the politics. Sullivan, *The Rhetoric of Credit,* and Bruster, *Drama and the Market in the Age of Shakespeare,* are two of the many fine books on financial profit. Also relevant here is Loomba, *Shakespeare, Race and Colonialism.* See entries on **use, price, value, worth** and **money** for commentary and further references.

provision

(A) In economic life provision means supplies of what is needful, e.g. to provision a ship or provide for a feast, and also financial resources. On one occasion it means foresight or prescience.

(B) Helicanus, arriving in port, requests that he be allowed to **purchase** fresh supplies: 'let us beseech you / That for our gold we may provision have' (*PER* 5.1.55–6). Similarly, when Capulet proposes that the wedding between Juliet and Paris take place on the morrow his wife protests: 'We shall be short in our provision' (*ROM* 4.2.38).

A financial dimension surfaces when the lords assemble for Timon's fake banquet. They provide excuses to one another for having rejected Timon's pleas for financial assistance: 'I am sorry, when he sent to borrow of me, that my provision was out' (*TIM* 3.6.15–16). His cash-flow problem is a result of the necessary financial resources being out on loan or otherwise tied up.

In reassuring Miranda that the shipwreck that has caused her such distress is not what it seems, Prospero says, 'I have with such provision in mine art / So safely ordered that there is no soul – / No, not so much perdition as an hair / Betid to any creature in the vessel' (*TMP* 1.2.28–31). Foresight or the facility to prepare in advance would seem to be the required meaning here.

(C) *TMP* and *TIM,* so close in chronology, are worlds apart in every other respect. See the relevant chapters in Alexander and Wells, eds, *Shakespeare and Race*; Bayley, *Shakespeare and Tragedy*; Bloom, *Shakespeare: The Invention of the Human*; and Nuttall, *Shakespeare the Thinker.* Appelbaum, *Auguecheek's Beef,* is excellent on all things culinary.

publican

(A) Nothing to do with tavern-keeping, the sole use of this word refers to a **tax-**collector.

(B) As Antonio approaches in his quest to secure a loan for Bassanio, Shylock, in an aside, comments on his old adversary, 'How like a fawning publican he looks!'

(*MV* 1.3.41). The phrase seems paradoxical in that tax-collectors would hardly be thought of as ingratiating, unless it was part of their technique to insinuate themselves in order to gain a clear picture of the tax-payer's resources. Perhaps, however, the implication is that there is something unbending or superior in Antonio's manner even when attempting to be civil. The phrase presents a fascinating crux.

(C) As the Riverside editors comment:

> Presumably Shylock regards Antonio as one who, like a publican (a tax collector for the Romans), deprives him of his rightful profits, but who now (like the publican in Luke 18:10–14 who prayed for mercy) assumes an ingratiating demeanour because he is asking a favour. (fn 292)

For a wide range of explorative probing of this provocative play see, for instance, Mahon and Mahon, eds, *The Merchant of Venice*; Woodbridge, ed., *Money and the Age of Shakespeare*; Shell's rightly acclaimed essay 'The Wether and the Ewe' in *Money, Language and Thought*.

purchase

(A) The modern meaning to obtain something in **exchange** for money is present but not dominant. Significant is the implication of ill-gotten gains: something acquired through theft or underhand dealings. A sense of acquisition, gaining possession through neither exchange nor theft, is also present: e.g., a woman or honour. Purchasing power is a fourth meaning. Fifth is a benefit or **advantage** gained. Sixth, there is a sense of return on **investment**, i.e. **profit**. Seventh is something earned or deserved – which, married to mockery, can be negative. One further meaning is to exert or endeavour. The adjective 'purchased' implies deliberately sought after.

(B) The simple sense of financial transaction occurs in *TIT*, but here with an ugly implication because Titus believes that in exchange for his hand he will purchase the freedom of his imprisoned sons. He tells the Emperor's messenger Aaron, 'As for my sons, say I account of them / As jewels purchas'd at an easy price, / And yet dear too, because I bought mine own' (3.1.197–9). Titus, unaware of the fraud inherent in the transaction, has no idea that an even more monstrous deal is in progress, as he will receive not his sons – only their heads.

A cant term for theft, 'purchase' was generally used euphemistically, even jauntily, but the Boy in *H5* reveals his contempt for this form of verbal dexterity, complaining that Nym and Bardolph, 'will steal any thing, and call it purchase' (3.2.42). Gadshill is relaxed in his promise to share the **booty** from the robbery: 'Thou shalt have a share in our purchase, as I am a true man' (*1H4* 2.1.91–2).

When Pericles seeks to explain his predicament to Helicanus he recounts the purpose of his recent journey: 'I went to Antioch, / Where, as thou know'st, against the face of death / I sought the purchase of a glorious beauty, / From whence an issue I might propagate' (*PER* 1.2.70–3). He sought to 'attain' rather than 'buy' her, winning her hand through solving a riddle, the penalty for failure being the forfeit of his life. So 'purchase' in this instance means 'attainment', 'prize' or 'acquisition'.

An instructive example occurs during Buckingham's scathing criticism of Lady Grey's conquest of King Edward: 'Even in the afternoon of her best days, / Made prize and purchase of his wanton eye' (*R3* 3.7.186–7). This evocative phrase presents her as a pirate capturing rich booty. The political implications of this event are profound, alienating Warwick and precipitating a return to civil war. Buckingham alights on a felicitous expression in his exercise of political theatre designed to secure the crown for Richard.

'Purchase' indicating the 'exchange **value** of money' is present in Falstaff's suggestion that Bardolph's nose shone like a bonfire during their escape from Gadshill: 'When thou ran'st up Gadshill in the night to catch my horse, if I did not think thou hadst been an *ignis fatuus* or a ball of wildfire, there's no purchase in money' (*1H4* 3.3.37–40). His oath is apt as Falstaff spends a great deal of time complaining about the lack of funds and the necessity of acquiring them by underhand means. He knows all too well that there is purchase in **money**.

As John of Gaunt bids farewell to his exiled son, Henry Bolingbroke, he tries to persuade him to treat the enforced departure as a deliberate action designed to reap a moral benefit: 'Go, say I sent thee forth to purchase honor' (*R2* 1.3.282).

The Chorus at the opening of *PER* explains that the function of the story is to impart an appreciation of human worth: 'The purchase is to make men glorious' (9). 'Purchase' here is 'profit' or 'benefit', albeit in a higher sense than the profit derived from **market** transactions.

'Purchase' as 'return on investment' can be illustrated in contrasting political and economic contexts. When in *JC* Metellus supports the proposal that Cicero be invited to join the conspiracy, he surmises that the political return on the investment will be substantial:

> O, let us have him, for his silver hairs
> Will purchase us a good opinion,
> And buy men's voices to commend our deeds.
> It shall be said his judgement rul'd our hands;
> Our youths and wildness shall no whit appear,
> But all be buried in his gravity.
>
> 2.1.144–9

Cicero's reputation will do the buying. This is instructive: Cicero is political **capital** the acquisition of which will provide a high return to the conspirators.

Feste, receiving money from Sebastian, expresses his delight by suggesting that a good tip buys the giver a favourable reputation – a good rate of return on his investment: 'By my troth, thou hast an open hand. These wise men that give fools money get themselves a good report – after fourteen years' purchase' (*TN* 4.1.21–3). The usual **price** for the purchase of a piece of land was the equivalent of 12 years' rental: 14 would be excessive payment. Sebastian has obviously given Feste a handout well above the average – a payment akin to paying over the odds for a piece of land. Alternatively Feste's oblique comment may imply that those who bestow charity had better not expect worthwhile thanks in the foreseeable future.

The meaning 'earned' or 'deserved' is clearly brought out in *COR*, where, in response to the letters praising the hero's achievements – 'there's wondrous things spoke of him' – Menenius claims that such praise has been thoroughly earned: 'Wondrous! ay, I warrant you, and not without his true purchasing' (2.1.137–40).

In the closing scene of *LLL*, the ladies congratulate themselves on their successful mockery of the men for, as they believe, courting them more in the spirit of masculine levity than true feeling. The Princess's graceful, 'We are wise girls to mock our lovers so' invites Rosaline's more astringent comment, 'They are worse fools to purchase mocking so' (5.2.58–9). Not only have they been mocked, Rosaline suggests, but they have paid for the indignity: they have earned or deserved their reward.

A possible meaning in *TIM* is 'to exert' or 'endeavour', but this example is ambiguous. When Timon's servant solicits financial assistance for his master, Lucius, a recipient of Timon's largesse, attempts to excuse himself with the words, 'How unluckily it happ'ned that I should purchase the day before for a little part, and undo a great deal of honour!' (3.2.46–8). This might be interpreted as saying that his financial *exertions* ('purchase') on the previous day, though bringing him *some* benefit, have left him with a liquidity crisis that precluded him attaining the greater honour of helping to rescue the noble Timon. Purchase could, however, be interpreted as expenditure or financial transaction. The meaning of the passage would be unchanged. The problem arises from Shakespeare's characteristic compression and his deep interest in the relationship or exchange rate between financial activities and moral values.

Two striking political moments reveal the elasticity of the term. On his deathbed, Henry IV attempts to motivate Hal to keep possession of the crown which he himself acquired by means of **usurpation**. He assiduously avoids that word in his very long speech, endeavouring to reassure the Prince that *inheritance* of the crown diminishes the hostility and rivalry arising from 'by-paths and indirect crook'd ways'. He says: 'for what in me was purchas'd / Falls upon thee in a more fairer sort; / So thou the garland wear'st successively' (*2H4* 4.5.184–201). He does not mean bought here, but gained by endeavour or exertion, which is both true and euphemistic.

Seeking to mollify Octavius Caesar, Lepidus claims that rather than being deliberate, Mark Antony's misdeeds arise from the grain of his nature, they are innate, a concomitant of his temperament: 'His faults, in him, seem as the spots of heaven, / More fiery by night's blackness; hereditary, / Rather than purchas'd; what he cannot change, / Than what he chooses' (*ANT* 1.4.12–15). 'Purchased' here means 'deliberately acquired' or 'sought after'.

(C) For an interesting engagement with the manipulative aspects of Henry IV see Grady, *Shakespeare, Machievelli and Montaigne*. Martindale and Taylor, eds, *Shakespeare and the Classics*, contains interesting commentary on *JC* and *TIM*.

Appadurai, ed., *The Social Life of Things*, and Jones, *God and the Moneylenders*, are both highly informative.

purchase out
(A) The verb purchase out means to buy off.
(B) The Prince expresses his anger and frustration at the continuing hostility between the Montagues and Capulets which has resulted in the death of his kinsman Mercutio. He exiles Romeo for killing Tybalt, adding, 'Nor tears or prayers shall purchase out abuses' (*ROM* 3.1.193). This unique use is unambiguous in meaning 'buy out' or 'buy off' penalties.
(C) Agnew, *Worlds Apart*, 142–3, charts the word's progress from 'pillage' to 'licit payment'.

putter-on
(A) The term relates to one who agitates, incites or instigates.
(B) Queen Katherine, setting out the case against new **taxes** that have caused severe economic disruption, singles out Cardinal Wolsey as the instigator of these impositions, which rebound against King Henry's reputation:

> wherein, although,
> My good Lord Cardinal, they vent reproaches
> Most bitterly on you as putter-on
> Of these exactions, yet the King our master –
> Whose honor heaven shield from soil! – even he escapes not
> Language unmannerly;
>
> *H8* 1.2.22–7

The only other application occurs in *WT* in a context that possesses political implications. Antigonus indignantly remonstrates with Leontes: 'You are abus'd, and by some putter-on / That will be damn'd for't' (2.1.141–2).
(C) The landscape of economic and political life is fundamental to *H8*. The role of decision-making in shaping or distorting religious, economic and political configurations is constantly brought into sharp focus. There have been two productions in recent years that have done much to heighten awareness of the play's intellectual and theatrical vigour: Greg Doran's 1996 production at the RSC's Swan Theatre and Gregory Thompson's A and BC Company at Holy Trinity Church, Stratford-upon-Avon, in 2006 (reviewed by Billington, *Guardian*, 26 August 2006).

See McMullan, ed., *King Henry VIII*, Arden 3, for an excellent essay. McDonald, *Shakespeare's Late Style*; Kermode, *Shakespeare's Language*; Barton, *Essays*, esp. ch. 8; Brigden, *New Worlds, Lost Worlds*, and Hamilton, *Shakespeare and the Politics of Protestant England*, are valuable for key concepts, language and context.

putter-out
(A) Used only once, the term refers to an investor, lender or insurance **broker**

who guaranteed a fivefold return on a deposit to a client on the successful completion of a foreign journey. Should the traveller fail to return, the deposit passed to the broker. The return seems high but the figure must represent a sound assessment of the probabilities of travellers returning and the rate of return on **investment** of those funds in the meantime.

(B) Easily missed, this term occurs obliquely when Gonzalo, reflecting on the strange creatures generated by Prospero's magic, refers to travellers who return with such fantastic accounts that nothing is deemed incredible: 'or that there were such men / Whose heads stood in their breasts? which now we find / Each putter-out of five for one will bring us / Good warrant of' (*TMP* 3.3.46–9). This sole reference provides a glimpse of the significance of brokers who borrowed and loaned funds, carefully balancing risks and probabilities. Implicit in this phenomenon is the importance to an economy of a free flow of finance between individuals and sectors so that funds are channelled to their most productive uses. Practical exigencies were clearly undermining attempts to maintain a legal maximum on **interest** rates.

(C) Sullivan, *The Rhetoric of Credit*, provides abundant detail on prevailing institutions and the ways in which they find expression in the plays. Turner, *Shakespeare's Twenty-First Century Economics*; Deng and Sebek, eds, *Global Traffic*; Brenner, *Merchants and Revolution*, also provide valuable information. See Vaughan and Vaughan, eds, *The Tempest*, Arden 3 237 for a concise and highly significant footnote.

quantity

(A) In addition to meaning an absolute amount, a ratio or proportion, quantity can also signify a small piece or fragment.

(B) The Painter, conversing with his associate, maintains that the apparently **bankrupt** Timon has been disbursing gold: 'He likewise enrich'd poor straggling soldiers with / Great quantity. 'Tis said he gave unto / His steward a mighty sum' (*TIM* 5.1.6–8). 'Quantity' here must mean 'amount'.

Both Hotspur and Orsino when using the term refer to land area. The wealthy Count wishes to assure Olivia that he 'Prizes not quantity of dirty lands' (*TN* 2.4.82), whereas the mercurial warrior protests that his share of the planned division of the kingdom is seriously curtailed: 'Methinks my moi'ty, north from Burton here, / In quantity equals not one of yours' (*1H4* 3.1.95–6).

Attempting to mollify Alcibiades, the Senator claims that they had sought to repeal his banishment *before* he acquired an army, their gesture of retraction, along with other unstated benefits, exceeding the initial offence: 'When thy first griefs were but a mere conceit, / Ere thou hadst power or we had cause to fear, / We sent to thee to give thy rages balm, / To wipe out our ingratitude with loves / Above their quantity' (*TIM* 5.4.14–18). The tone of this speech is totally at variance with the earlier contemptuous treatment of the military hero.

Guiderius is baffled by his instinctive affection for Fidele/Imogen, declaring: 'I love thee; I have spoke it; / How much the quantity, the weight as much, / As I do love my father' (*CYM* 4.2.16–18).

Helena, complaining of Demetrius' rejection of her in favour of Hermia, draws the conclusion that, 'Things base and vile, holding no quantity, / Love can transpose to form and dignity' (*MND* 1.1.232–3). She means lacking proportion or shapeliness.

Petruchio, during his feigned abuse of the tailor, employs the word in the sense of small piece: 'Away, thou rag, thou quantity, thou remnant' (*SHR* 4.3.111).

Reflecting on his great bulk and Shallow's meagre frame, Falstaff muses, 'If I were saw'd into quantities, I should make four dozen of such bearded hermits' staves as Master Shallow' (*2H4* 5.1.62–4).

(C) The advent and significance of quantification is set forth in Crosby, *The Measure of Reality*. Bates, 'Love and courtship' in Leggatt, ed., *Shakespearean Comedy*, is relevant. Klein, ed., *Timon of Athens*, and Nuttall, *Timon of Athens*, discuss key issues and significant elements of performance while McAlindon, *Shakespeare's Tudor History*, and Ruiter, *Shakespeare's Festive History*, capture another significant dimension. Relevant too is Taylor, *Shakespeare's Ovid*.

quietus

(A) The meaning here is simply the clearing or confirmation of accounts; signing them off as accurate.

(B) Hamlet, surveying life's torments in his most famous soliloquy, points to the means of securing relief by the closing of the book of life: 'When he himself might his quietus make / With a bare bodkin' (*HAM* 3.1.74–5). In this case the dagger replaces the auditor's pen.

SON 126 also sees the closure of life in terms of the audit of accounts. Here, Nature, though wishing to preserve the life of the 'lovely boy' as long as possible, will eventually have to relinquish him: 'Yet fear her, O thou minion of her pleasure, / She may detain, but still not keep, her treasure! / Her audit (though delay'd) answer'd must be, / And her quietus is to render thee' (9–12).

(C) See Long, *The Unnatural Scene*, Greenblatt, *Hamlet in Purgatory*, Warley, *Sonnet Sequences and Social Distinction in Renaissance England*, and Schiffer, ed., *Shakespeare's Sonnets*.

quittance

(A) The meanings attaching to the noun are: certification of a release from debt; requital or **recompense**; resistance. The verb intimates to requite.

(B) Slender, endeavouring to establish the social standing of Justice Shallow, describes him as one 'who writes himself *Armigero*, in any bill, warrant, quittance, or obligation, *Armigero*' (*WIV* 1.1.9–11). He repeats the word, signifying a gentleman with right to bear heraldic arms, but it is his powers of authorization of legal documents relating to financial matters that validates his strategic position in this bourgeois society.

Timon's largesse is such that when he receives gifts he disburses even more to the giver, thereby making it impossible for anyone to reciprocate his generosity – should they wish to do so: 'no gift to him / But breeds the giver a return exceeding / All use of quittance' (*TIM* 1.1.278–80).

Responding to Grey's affirmation of universal loyalty, Henry V is firm in his promise of requital: 'We therefore have great cause of thankfulness, / And shall forget the office of our hand / Sooner than quittance of desert and merit, / According to the weight and worthiness' (*H5* 2.2.32–5). As Henry has discovered the treachery of Grey and his associates he is being equivocal: for them the quittance or recompense will be execution. Talbot is direct in planning to repay or reciprocate French duplicity with English guile: 'Embrace we then this opportunity / As fitting best to quittance their deceit / Contriv'd by art and baleful sorcery' (*1H6* 2.1.13–15).

Morton, reporting the death of Hotspur, describes his resistance, offering blow for blow: 'Rend'ring faint quittance, wearied and outbreath'd / To Harry Monmouth, whose swift wrath beat down / The never-daunted Percy to the earth' (*2H4* 1.1.108–10).

(C) See Grady, *Shakespeare, Machiavelli and Montaigne*; Nuttall, *Timon of Athens*; and Muldrew, *The Economy of Obligation*.

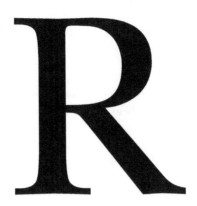

reckon

(A) This verb can mean either to calculate, measure, quantify or to add up. There is also the commonplace meaning, 'consider'.

(B) When Cleopatra asks Mark Antony, 'If it be love indeed, tell me how much' his response is unequivocal: 'There's beggary in the love that can be reckon'd' (*ANT* 1.1.13–15). Measurement or calculation is for the mundane world; love transcends such **values**.

The Steward of the **bankrupt** Timon, besieged by **creditors**, responds with the simple explanation, 'Believe't, my lord and I have made an end: / I have no more to reckon, he to spend' (*TIM* 3.4.55–6). The steward has no resources to count.

Cymbeline, repudiating the agreement to pay tribute to the Romans, exclaims,

> Caesar's ambition,
> Which swell'd so much that it did almost stretch
> The sides o'th'world, against all color here
> Did put the yoke upon's; which to shake off
> Becomes a warlike people, whom we reckon
> Ourselves to be.
> *CYM* 3.1.48–53

In the same play Arviragus declines Imogen's offer to pay for her food: 'All gold and silver rather turn to dirt, / As 'tis no better reckon'd, but of those / Who worship dirty gods' (3.6.53–5). Though the primary meaning appears to be considered, it carries the secondary meaning of counted or calculated.

(C) An interesting light is cast on this topic by Kinney, 'The Dramatic World of the Renaissance' in Kinney, ed., *Renaissance Drama*. Important here is Muir, '*Timon of Athens* and the cash-nexus' in Muir, *The Singularity of Shakespeare*.

reckoning

(A) Of the word's five applications, three are financial, two personal. First, there is the simple matter of counting or making a calculation; second, the settlement of a tavern **bill**; third, an evaluation of **debts** or the settlement of an **account**; fourth, there is the rendering of an account in the sense of setting forth one's actions for a moral **audit**; finally, the term can apply to personal qualities or attributes.

(B) In responding to Moth's invitation to engage in some simple arithmetic, the fantastic Spaniard, Armado, declines with an assertion of social superiority: 'I am ill at reck'ning, it fitteth the spirit of a tapster' (*LLL* 1.2.40–1). More pregnant because of its punning and allusive elements is Touchstone's complaint to Audrey that his intellectual brilliance is wasted on her. He likens the demoralizing effect to the receipt of a tavern bill: 'it strikes a man more dead than a great reckoning in a little room' (*AYL* 3.3.14–15). This startling allusion to Marlowe's murder in a tavern, supposedly in an argument over a 'reckoning', puns powerfully on the moral reckoning in the theological sense and on the colloquial sense of comeuppance. The 'little room' also alludes to Marlowe's *Jew of Malta* where Barabus the Jew refers to 'Infinite riches in a little room' (1.1.37). (Dusinberre, in her recent edition of the play, proffers: 'the "great reckoning" may be a scatological joke – Hanmer emended to "reeking" – with "little room" a euphemism for privy'; *As You Like It*, Arden 3, fn 266).

Hal is scornful of Frances, the drawer, for possessing no other quality but to carry drinks and to calculate tavern bills: 'His industry is up stairs and down stairs, his eloquence the parcel of a reckoning' (*1H4* 2.4.99–101).

As Flavius, Timon's steward, sets out the magnitude of his master's ruinous debts, he focuses on the contrasting time frames: 'The future comes apace; / What shall defend the interim? and at length / How goes our reck'ning?' (*TIM* 2.2.148–50). As soon as news of Timon's predicament becomes known, creditors will pour in on him, so what can they do in order to meet such an exigency? Finally, what assets do they have available to meet current **expenses**? 'How goes our reck'ning?' Here is a play that explores every aspect of finance, revealing elementary simplicity behind financial complexity.

The *locus classicus* for the meaning of rendering an account of one's actions is provided by the Ghost of Old Hamlet who complains,

> Thus was I, sleeping, by a brother's hand
> Of life, of crown, of queen, at once dispatch'd,
> Cut off even in the blossoms of my sin,
> Unhous'led, disappointed, unanel'd,
> No reck'ning made, but sent to my account
> With all my imperfections on my head.
> *HAM* 1.5.74–9

Had he time to repent and to receive absolution, his predicament when crossing the threshold into the other world would be much less grievous. In Shakespeare's plays there is a close link between the indisputable authority of the figures in an account book and the moral balance sheet.

Paris, deploring the feud between Capulet and Montague, refers to the high esteem in which they are both held: 'Of honourable reckoning are you both, / And pity 'tis you liv'd at odds so long' (*ROM* 1.2.4–5).

(C) For a thorough conceptual and contextual exploration of a spiritual reckoning see Greenblatt, *Hamlet in Purgatory*. De Grazia, *'Hamlet' without Hamlet*, is informative on this theme. A broad background account is provided by Bushby, *Paradise*, while the Hagens' *What Great Paintings Say*, vol. 1, 86–91, provides insights through the paintings of Hieronymous Bosch. Another dimension of reckoning is to be found in Bulman, *'Henry IV Parts 1 and 2'* in Hattaway, ed., *Shakespeare's History Plays*. For Marlowe see Riggs, *The World of Christopher Marlowe*, and Cheney, ed., *Christopher Marlowe*.

reckon with

(A) This term means to take fully into consideration what is owed.

(B) The final scene of *MAC*, replete with references to '**debt**', '**worth**', 'cheaply', 'measur'd', 'spend', '**expense**', closes with Malcolm's promise to take full **account** of all the services that have been rendered him (just as Duncan did in 1.4): 'We shall not spend a large expense of time / Before we reckon with your several loves,/ And make us even with you' (5.9.26–8).

(C) See Leggatt, *Shakespeare's Tragedies*; Foakes, *Shakespeare and Violence*; Long, *Macbeth*; Sinfield, ed., *Macbeth*; Moschovakis, ed., *Macbeth*.

recompense

(A) Here is a word that can mean either reward for services rendered, or compensation for personal sacrifice. If this seems like a fine distinction, there may be a third possibility where the stress is on making restitution.

(B) Fenton, thanking the Host of the Garter for his efforts in arranging the secret marriage with Anne Page, promises future benefits and *present reward for services rendered*: 'So shall I evermore be bound to thee; / Besides, I'll make a present recompense' (*WIV* 4.6.54–5).

As Coriolanus engages in an altercation with the tribunes for persuading the **plebeians** to withdraw their support for his elevation to consul, he justifies his opposition to the free distribution of corn: 'They know the corn / Was not our recompense, resting well assur'd / They ne'er did service for't' (*COR* 3.1.120–2). His point is that the corn was not a deserved payment in return for military services rendered, but rather a dubious act of political expediency in response to social unrest.

In pleading for aid from her spirits, Joan Pucelle promises to make restitution for this one last act of support by sacrificing her life: 'My body shall / Pay recompense, if you will grant my suit' (*1H6* 5.3.18–19). She has already offered to mutilate herself as a down payment ('earnest') for the full payment of her body. Reward may well be the meaning here or compensation for past services, but the urgency of her appeal pushes hard in the direction of restitution. The mystical energies expended by the spirits will be revivified by Joan's blood.

A fascinating case occurs when King Henry reinstates York to his property and titles, these having been withdrawn on the execution of his father for treason. Warwick, commending the gesture, declares, 'Let Richard be restored to his blood, / So shall his father's wrongs be recompens'd' (*1H6* 3.1.159–60). This must be taken to mean that Richard's father (Cambridge) paid for his wrongs with his life and so justice requires his true inheritor be restored to his birthright. 'Restitution' rather than 'payment for services rendered' is implied here. There may be a sly suggestion lurking in the ambiguous construction, namely that Cambridge was wrongly condemned, so making restitution obligatory.

(C) Burns, ed., *Henry VI, Part 1*, Arden 3, is highly informative on this play. Dutton and Howard, eds, *Shakespeare's Works – Vol. II: The Histories*, contains several highly relevant essays. Hamilton, *Shakespeare and the Politics of Protestant England*, is significant for context and language.

reformation

(A) This term signifies radical political change but also personal transformation, either superficial in terms of demeanour and **fashion** or more profoundly.

(B) Cade encourages his followers by enumerating the political changes he intends to bring about:

> Be brave then, for your captain is brave, and vows reformation . . . All the realm shall be in common . . . there shall be no money; all shall eat and drink on my score, and I will apparel them in one livery, that they may agree like brothers, and worship me their lord.
>
> *2H6* 4.2.64–75

The vision of egalitarianism and the annihilation of all the constraints of economics culminate in dictatorship.

At the other end of the political spectrum Lovell comments on the transformation in manners and fashions apparent in some courtiers subsequent to their return from France: 'The reformation of our travell'd gallants, / That fill the court with quarrel, talk, and tailors' (*H8* 1.3.19–20). The most politically significant transformation is that promised by Hal in his famous soliloquy:

> And like bright metal on a sullen ground,
> My reformation, glitt'ring o'er my fault,
> Shall show more goodly and attract more eyes
> Than that which hath no foil to set it off.
> I'll so offend, to make offence a skill,
> Redeeming time when men think least I will.
>
> *1H4* 1.2.212–17

(C) See Hattaway, ed., *Shakespeare's History Plays*, and Knowles, ed., *King Henry VI Part II*, Arden 3, Introduction, 89–106.

revenue

(A) The simple meaning of taxes or flow of income from productive assets, such as land, is usually present, but an alternative meaning of possession or control of assets that generate such an income flow also occurs. There are occasions when it is far from clear as to which meaning is applicable. Conceptually the distinction is an important one; in practice the ambiguity does not produce significant difficulties, not least because the **value** of assets and the income stream they generate are closely linked. There is also a legal-financial meaning: the right of inheritance or possession.

(B) When Richard II decides to embark on his Irish campaign, his mind immediately turns to the problem of finance: 'And for our coffers, with too great a court / And liberal largess, are grown somewhat light, / We are enforc'd to farm our royal realm, / The revenue whereof shall furnish us / For our affairs in hand' (*R2* 1.4.43–7). In order to secure ready money to pay for troops and supplies, Richard plans to sell entitlements to future income derived from crown lands, etc. This is analogous to the sale of **government bonds** to raise income to cover current expenditure. How satisfactory the arrangement is – Gaunt is horrified – depends on the details of the transaction. It does, however, provide one of the many examples of productive assets being sacrificed to military adventures.

Summarizing the complaints enumerated in Antony's letter, Octavius Caesar reveals a scramble for resources by allies about to become deadly enemies: 'Lastly, he frets / That Lepidus of the triumvirate / Should be depos'd; and being, that we detain / All his revenue' (*ANT* 3.6.27–30). The implication here is assets, including the scope for raising **taxes** in territories under his control, rather than the stream of income derivable from such assets – though with conflict on the horizon it is the need for cash to finance military preparations which is crucial.

Richard Gloucester, in a stage-managed scheme to secure the throne with popular support, feigns to decline the invitation to accept the crown, proffered by his henchman, Buckingham, on grounds of unworthiness: 'First, if all obstacles were cut away, / And that my path were even to the crown, / As the ripe revenue and due of birth' (*R3* 3.7.156–8). Possession or custody rather than income is the meaning here. The phrase 'ripe revenue' links the principle of authentic inheritance with the suggestion of a kingdom richly generative in its capacity to produce income and pleasure.

Richard II, having exiled Bolingbroke, moves swiftly when John of Gaunt dies. Foolishly, he decides to appropriate Gaunt's property to finance his impending Irish campaign: 'And, for these great affairs do ask some charge, / Towards our assistance we do seize to us / The plate, coin, revenues, and moveables / Whereof our uncle Gaunt did stand possess'd' (*R2* 2.1.159–62). This is a comprehensive survey of assets. Plate and movables may simply be purloined or sold; coin signifies ready cash; '**revenues**' suggest income in the form of rents etc., but must also mean possession of the assets which generate such an income flow. Hence both concepts seem present. As a consequence of Richard's action, a group sympathetic to Bolingbroke bewail the **usurpation** of his inheritance.

Willoughby says of the exiled Bolingbroke, and his newly inherited title of Duke of Lancaster: 'Barely in title, not in revenues' (2.1.226). Clearly he refers to his possessions in their *entirety*: manors, houses, **estates**, land, movables.

Plays as diverse as *LR, MND* and *AYL* all comment significantly on revenues, but one of the most interesting observations occurs in *2H6*. The Queen, repressing her jealousy and disgust at the ostentatious attire of the Duchess of Gloucester, comments, 'She bears a duke's revenues on her back' (1.3.80). No doubt the Duke's assets can easily support his wife's appetite for conspicuous consumption and her desire to emphasize her social standing.

(C) Grady, *Shakespeare, Machievelli and Montaigne*, and Scott, ' "Like to a Tenement": Landholding, Leasing and Inheritance in *Richard II*' in Jordan and Cunningham, eds, *The Law in Shakespeare*, are eloquent on the events in *R2*; other aspects are explored by Joughin, 'Richard II and the performance of grief' in Cavanagh, et al., eds, *Shakespeare's Histories and Counter-Histories*. Of real interest by way of parallels and contrasts is Corbin and Sharp, eds, *Thomas of Woodstock or King Richard the Second, Part One*.

rival

(A) Disconcertingly for the modern reader/**auditor**, rival can mean either associate or **competitor**. On one occasion Shakespeare uses the word in both senses in a vibrant piece of wordplay; on another the compression is such that both meanings are probably present. It can also mean equal.

(B) 'Partners' or 'associates' is the meaning when Bernardo tells Francisco, 'If you do meet Horatio and Marcellus, / The rivals of my watch, bid them make haste' (*HAM* 1.1.12–13).

When the Poet deconstructs his representation of Timon at the height of his fame, the very darling of Fortune, he concludes, 'Whose present grace to present slaves and servants / Translates his rivals' (*TIM* 1.1.71–2). 'Rivals' could mean either 'associates' or 'competitors'. They are rivals in the sense that all are aspiring to become the favourites of Fortune. As Timon is the source of much of their **wealth** they are nominally associates; as they seek to catch the eye of Fortune they look beyond him, being rivals for Fortune's favours. Both meanings seem present in this highly compacted expression.

A fascinating case arises when an angry and distressed Helena believes that the sudden competition for her favours (by the men who have been competing for Hermia's love) is a collusive ploy by Lysander and Demetrius calculated to make a fool of her: 'You both are rivals, and love Hermia, / And now both rivals, to mock Helena' (*MND* 3.2.155–6). The vitality of the wordplay hinges on '**rivals**' meaning *both* 'associates' *and* '**competitors**'. In the first line they are antagonists; in the second they are associates in their collusion, but also competitors in attempting to outdo each other in humiliating Helena. Two in oneness is the conceptual nucleus of the play and finds expression here in a way that is easily missed. When the Duke discovers the young people asleep on the ground there is no verbal ambiguity, merely his perplexity: 'I know you are two rival enemies / How comes this gentle concord in the world' (4.1.142–3).

A unique usage occurs in *MV* when Bassanio, seeking Antonio's financial assistance to compete for Portia, expresses confidence that he will win her: 'O my Antonio, had I but the means / To hold a rival place with one of them, / I have a mind presages me such thrift / That I should questionless be fortunate!' (1.1.173–6). In this situation of intense competition for Portia, Shakespeare employs this phrase 'rival place', an aspect of which must be 'equal place' yet enfolding within it the concept of rivalry.

Richard II, in pronouncing the sentence of banishment on Bolingbroke and Mowbray, delivers a masterly speech setting forth the dangers to the **commonwealth**. The key lines emphasize the destructive power of rivalry:

> And for our eyes do hate the dire aspect
> Of civil wounds plough'd up with neighbors' sword;
> And for we think the eagle-winged pride
> Of sky-aspiring and ambitious thoughts,
> With rival-hating envy, set on you
> To wake our peace, which in our country's cradle
> Draws the sweet infant breath of gentle sleep;
>
> . . .
>
> Therefore we banish you our territories.
>
> *R2* 1.3.127–39

What is so remarkable about this speech in its entirety is the vision it conjures up of noise, perturbation and violence of a kind which is enacted in the *H6* cycle consequent upon his deposition, in contrast to the 'sweet infant breath of gentle-sleep'. Passage from one state to another will arise from 'sky-aspiring and ambitious thoughts' and 'rival-hating envy'. This is political discourse at its most refined and sophisticated, seemingly devoid of malice or **Machiavel**lianism. An extra dimension is available because of Richard's prescience in his portrayal of deadly civil strife.

(C) Nuttall, *Timon of Athens*, and Hunt, 'Shakespeare and the Paragone: a reading of *Timon of Athens*' in Habicht, Palmer and Pringle, eds, *Images of Shakespeare*, explore rivalry in *TIM*. Also of relevance are Taylor, 'Ovid's myths and the unsmooth course of love in *A Midsummer Night's Dream*', and Roe, 'Character in Plutarch and Shakespeare', both in Martindale and Taylor, eds, *Shakespeare and the Classics*; Alexander, ed., *Shakespeare and Politics*; Grady, *Shakespeare, Machiavelli and Montaigne*.

rivality

(A) A unique usage, this word signifies shared power or equality of political authority.

(B) In a highly charged political situation, Eros reports that Octavius Caesar has removed Lepidus from power, depriving him of his status, and share of authority: 'Caesar, having made use of him in the wars 'gainst Pompey, presently denied him rivality, would not let him partake in the glory of the action' (*ANT* 3.5.7–9).

(C) See Roe, 'Character in Plutarch and Shakespeare' in Martindale and Taylor, eds, *Shakespeare and the Classics*; Foakes, *Shakespeare and Violence*.

rule

(A) Obviously relating to authority, order and fundamental principles or law, the word frequently occurs in contexts where compression strains meaning. It is possible to distinguish the following applications: **government** or legitimate authority including principles of good government; control, order, discipline; governing principle or controlling force or idea; method, manner; implement for measurement, or ruler. As a verb, to govern or control, direct or guide.

(B) Prospero's **usurping** brother Antonio attempts to entice Sebastian to murder his own brother, the King of Naples: 'There be they that can rule Naples / As well as he that sleeps' (*TMP* 2.1.262–3). 'Govern' or 'control' is the meaning here. Similarly, Coriolanus, when informed that the **plebeians** have revoked their election pledge, responds contemptuously to the tribunes: 'You being their mouths, why rule you not their teeth?' (*COR* 3.1.36).

During the quest for French support against the recently crowned Edward, Margaret warns Lewis that the incumbent is not the true king, nor is his government legitimate: 'For though usurpers sway the rule awhile, / Yet heav'ns are just, and time suppresseth wrongs' (*3H6* 3.3.76–7). Here rule, therefore, signifies state or government.

Blunt, responding to Hotspur in a parley before the Battle of Shrewsbury, proclaims he will remain opposed to the rebels: 'So long as out of limit and true rule / You stand against anointed majesty' (*1H4* 4.3.39–40). 'Legitimate government' must be the meaning of 'true rule'.

A testing case occurs in the closet scene during Hamlet's tirade against Claudius: 'A cutpurse of the empire and the rule, / That from a shelf the precious diadem stole' (*HAM* 3.4.99–100). The indictment relates to Claudius' usurpation, the phraseology reducing him to the level of a pickpocket, but rule is obviously a compressed form of expression which probably means principle of good government.

Caithness, reporting on Macbeth's preparations to repel the impending English attack, intimates a complete lack of unity and order, concluding: 'He cannot buckle his distemper'd cause / Within the belt of rule' (*MAC* 5.2.15–16).

Asked by Agamemnon why the Greeks have failed to capture Troy, Ulysses responds by citing the breach of a fundamental principle: the hierarchical concept of command and authority: 'The speciality of rule hath been neglected, / ... / Take but degree away, untune that string, / And hark what discord follows. Each thing meets / In mere oppugnancy' (*TRO* 1.3.78–111). 'Rule', then, means 'organizational principle'. All systems, entities, **values** and concepts are subject to assault or testing in this play – and they all splinter under the strain.

Troilus, having witnessed Cressida's betrayal, feels that this event has produced a breach in the order that governs life – and the very unity of the cosmos. 'Rule' here is a fundamental principle of order:

> This she? no, this is Diomed's Cressida.
> If beauty have a soul, this is not she;
> If souls guide vows, if vows be sanctimonies,
> If sanctimony be the gods' delight,
> If there be rule in unity itself,
> This was not she.
>
> 5.2.137–42

Portia, disguised as the lawyer, Balthazar, addresses the matter of Shylock's **bond**: 'Of a strange nature is the suit you follow, / Yet in such rule that the Venetian law / Cannot impugn you as you do proceed' (*MV* 4.1.177–9). The most difficult or teasing application, usually glossed as 'order', it seems to mean 'method or manner'.

Confronted by a group of plebeians who have taken a holiday, the tribune, Murellus, demands of a carpenter, 'Where is thy leather apron and thy rule?' (*JC* 1.1.7). This 'rule' is a measuring rod, but given the circumstances the suggestion of conduct is also present.

(C) Daniel, ed., *Julius Caesar*, Arden 3, fn 156, is suggestive with references to *JC*. Bains, 'The vicissitudes of language in *Julius Caesar*' in Zander, ed., *Julius Caesar*, is insightful and provocative; other essays in this volume also engage with the question of 'rule'. Of particular interest with reference to *TRO* is Freund, ' "Ariachne's broken woof" ' in Parker and Hartman, eds, *The Question of Theory*.

runagate

(A) The political meaning of the word is turncoat, but it also has the more general application of fugitive.

(B) Richard III denounces Richmond as 'White-liver'd runagate' (*R3* 4.4.464). As he is returning to England with an army to overthrow Richard, the denunciation probably carries the additional sting of 'turncoat' or 'rebel' to that of 'vagabond' or 'fugitive'.

By contrast, Cloten, in pursuit of Imogen and Pisanio, means runaways when he says, 'I cannot find those runagates' (*CYM* 4.2.62). Intriguing, especially as three of the five applications occur in *CYM*, is Iachimo's denunciation of Posthumus' unfaithfulness: 'I dedicate myself to your sweet pleasure, / More noble than that runagate to your bed' (1.6.136–7). As Imogen is, at this point, heir to the throne, such a betrayal would be both personal and political. Were the accusation true, Posthumus would, indeed, be a renegade.

(C) Key essays on rebellion and insurrection can be found in Alexander, ed., *Shakespeare and Politics*; Holstun, '*Damned Commotion*: Riot and Rebellion in Shakespeare's Histories' in Dutton and Howard, eds, *The Histories*. Palfrey, *Late Shakespeare*, and McDonald, *Shakespeare's Late Style*, have significant commentary on *CYM*.

satisfaction

(A) The financial meaning of satisfaction is the payment of a **debt**. In the political sphere the word signifies **recompense** or compensation. The general application is to assuage anxiety or remove doubt or meet a need. Finally, there is the specific meaning of gratifying sexual desire.

(B) A **merchant**, in urgent need of cash, accosts Angelo, the goldsmith, demanding instant repayment of a loan: 'Therefore make present satisfaction, / Or I'll attach you by this officer' (*ERR* 4.1.5–6). 'Present', of course, means 'immediate' payment.

King Edward, having triumphed over Margaret's forces at the Battle of Tewkesbury, makes a sardonic address to young Prince Edward requesting compensation for the trouble he has caused: 'Edward, what satisfaction canst thou make / For bearing arms, for stirring up my subjects' (*3H6* 5.5.14–15).

Although Angelo has been appointed deputy in the Duke's absence, the precise details of the distribution of responsibilities is yet to be determined. Eager to resolve doubts and uncertainties, he suggests to the elder statesman, Escalus, that they peruse their written instructions: 'Let us withdraw together, / And we may soon our satisfaction have / Touching that point' (*MM* 1.1.81–3).

The Duke, contriving the bed-trick in an attempt to save Claudio's life and secure Marianna the husband she craves, instructs Isabella to promise to meet Angelo's demands for sexual intercourse: 'if for this night he entreat you to his bed, give him promise of satisfaction' (3.1.262–3). Ford, disguised as Brooke, sets out his desperate desire to bed Mistress Ford. In response Falstaff asks, 'Have you receiv'd no promise of satisfaction at her hands?' (*WIV* 2.2.209–10).

(C) Miola, ed., *The Comedy of Errors*, provides extensive analysis of the contrasting dimensions of *ERR*, including its rich seam of commercial activity. Sanders, *The Winter's Tale*, reveals the sexual significance of 'satisfaction' – a word that carries

253

equally significant freight in *OTH*. Significant, too, are Charney, *Shakespeare on Love and Lust*, and Charnes, *Notorious Identity*.

scot, scot and lot

(A) A scot is a payment, financial contribution or small amount of **money**; scot and lot is a form of local **taxation**.

(B) Hotspur puns on a small sum of money and a Scotsman when he declares that he will not accommodate King Henry's demands that he hand over his Scottish prisoners: 'By God, he shall not have a Scot of them, / No, if a Scot would save his soul, he shall not!' (*1H4* 1.3.214–15).

Falstaff puns cleverly, after pretending to be killed when confronted by the fierce Scot, the Douglas. The extent of his wit is not fully appreciated without understanding the financial significance of a phrase which had come to mean 'completely', or more colloquially, 'done for me': ' 'Sblood, 'twas time to counterfeit, or that hot termagant Scot had paid me scot and lot too' (*1H4* 5.4.113–14).

(C) Blake's *Shakespeare's Non-Standard English* is revelatory in exploring the richness of such terms. See also Turner, *Shakespeare's Twenty-First Century Economics*, 123–4.

sect

(A) In modern parlance a term applied to a religious group (frequently with extreme views at variance with mainstream orthodoxies). In the plays the word possesses further meanings: any political group or association, a cabal, **faction** or party; category or assortment; horticultural cutting or offshoot.

(B) A servant expressing his admiration for the newly arrived Perdita sees her as capable of transforming worshippers into any religion she might choose to establish: 'This is a creature, / Would she begin a sect, might quench the zeal / Of all professors else, make proselytes / Of who she but bid follow' (*WT* 5.1.106–9).

A more contentious example occurs when Bishop Gardiner responds sharply to Cromwell's rebuke by referring to his protestant leanings: 'Do not I know you for a favorer / Of this new sect? You are not sound' (*H8* 5.2.115–16). Ironically, at the time the play was written Protestantism had become the orthodoxy.

A senator rejecting clemency for a murderer tells Alcibiades that violence displaced genuine valour, 'When sects and factions were newly born' (*TIM* 3.5.30). He sees the emergence of tight-knit groups with aggressive ideologies as responsible for authenticating violence. The relevance of this observation to the modern world is clear.

Lear also refers to cabals or factions when he consoles Cordelia with the satisfaction of being out of the fray in a world animated by political machinations: 'and we'll wear out, / In a wall'd prison, packs and sects of great ones, / That ebb and flow by th'moon' (*LR* 5.3.17–19).

Bewailing the harsh punishment imposed on Claudio for the crime of fornication and getting his fiancée with child, the Provost emphasizes the commonplace nature of the action: 'Alas, / He hath but as offended in a dream! / All sects, all ages smack of this vice, and he / To die for't!' (*MM* 2.2.3–6). 'Sects' seems particularly appropriate here as it signifies every conceivable kind of grouping: social, political and religious.

Iago, attempting to quell and redirect Roderigo's passion for Desdemona, assures him that the feeling he calls love is a mere offshoot of lust: 'But we have reason to cool our raging motions, our carnal stings, our unbitted lusts; whereof I take this that you call love to be a sect or scion' (*OTH* 1.3.329–32).

(C) Hassel, *Shakespeare's Religious Language*, has an entry on 'sect'. Important in this context are Hadfield, *Shakespeare and Renaissance Politics*; Hattaway, *Renaissance and Reformations*; Alexander and Wells, eds, *Shakespeare and Sexuality*; Hamilton, *Shakespeare and the Politics of Protestant England*.

state

(A) Crucially for this study, state designates **government** or ruling body; financial situation; well-being or prosperity; situation or plight; sovereignty. There are, however, many other meanings: status or rank; magnificence or stateliness; ceremony; ruler; throne; the canopy over the chair of state; bearing; elaborate expression.

(B) Norfolk cautions Buckingham, 'Like it your Grace, / The state takes notice of the private difference / Betwixt you and the Cardinal' (*H8* 1.1.100–2). Here is a clear reference to the government with the suggestion of its power to constrain or destroy individuals.

Bassanio, building up to an explanation of his **debt** to Antonio, confesses to Portia: 'when I told you / My state was nothing, I should then have told you / That I was worse than nothing' (*MV* 3.2.258–60). State here is financial situation.

Welfare or well-being is intimated by Henry VI when approving demands for Suffolk's banishment: 'For sure, my thoughts do hourly prophesy / Mischance unto my state by Suffolk's means' (*2H6* 3.2.283–4). Later the King refers to his precarious situation: 'Thus stands my state, 'twixt Cade and York distress'd' (4.9.31).

Henry V refers to kingship or majesty when responding to the gift of tennis balls. He advises the French ambassador: 'But tell the Dolphin I will keep my state, / Be like a king, and show my sail of greatness / When I do rouse me in my throne of France' (*H5* 1.2.273–5).

(C) Of interest here are Engle, *Shakespearean Pragmatism*; Lever, *The Tragedy of State*; Hadfield, *Shakespeare and Republicanism*; and McAlindon, *Shakespeare Minus 'Theory'*, ch. 3.

statist

(A) This term is applied to a statesman, **politician** or public officer.

(B) The first of the two applications of the word arises during Hamlet's account of how he substituted his own version of the death warrant for the one issued by Claudius: 'I once did hold it, as our statists do, / A baseness to write fair, and labor'd much / How to forget that learning, but sir, now / It did me yeoman's service' (*HAM* 5.2.33–6). This evidently refers to someone in authority, while conveying the impression more of a public officer than a politician. Significant is the indication of a perverse snobbery that disdains the virtue of good penmanship for the sake of displaying socio/political status.

A little different is Posthumus' comment to his host Philario regarding the Romans' demand for unpaid tribute: 'I do believe / (Statist though I am none, nor like to be) / That this will prove a war' (*CYM* 2.4.15–17). 'Councillor of state' appears to be indicated here.

(C) Useful here are de Grazia, *'Hamlet' without Hamlet*, and Pettegree, *Europe in the Sixteenth Century*.

sterling

(A) Occurring only three times, the noun signifies legal tender; the adjective genuine or authentic. The word is used in situations which are punningly generative.

(B) An emotionally turbulent Richard II is aggrieved at having formally to relinquish his crown to Bolingbroke. Veering away from the proposition that he no longer has an identity, he requests a means of validating his authority: 'And if my word be sterling yet in England, / Let it command a mirror hither straight' (*R2* 4.1.264–5). What makes the application so telling is that 'sterling' incorporates both the idea of a genuine identity and the conception of kingship as the ultimate authenticator of currency.

Intervening in the dispute between Falstaff and Mistress Quickly, the Lord Chief Justice advises the fat knight to be as good as his word by marrying the gullible hostess, and repaying the **money** he has borrowed: 'Pay her the debt you owe her, and unpay the villainy you have done with her. The one you may do with sterling money, and the other with current repentance' (*2H4* 2.1.118–21). The witty antithesis of pay and unpay, is followed by the punning complementarity of sterling and current, both possessing the meaning genuine.

More brutal than witty is Polonius' chastizement of Ophelia when he revels in turning the language of love into the language of commerce. One of his many moves occurs when Ophelia refers to Hamlet's 'tenders / Of his affection to me'. He comments derisively, 'think yourself a baby / That you have ta'en these tenders for true pay, / Which are not sterling' (*HAM* 1.3.99–107). Polonius scorns the Prince's offers or representations as deceptions, **counterfeit** money in the commerce of sex.

(C) See the entry on **investments** for further exploration of the Polonius–Ophelia exchange. Cavanagh's chapter 'The language of treason in *Richard II*' in *Language and Politics in the Sixteenth-Century History Play* merits attention along with Kinney, *Shakespeare's Webs* and Sullivan, *The Rhetoric of Credit*.

store

(A) This key economic term is characterized by a versatility that relates to resources such as stocks of food, income and **capital**; it migrates frequently into social, romantic and procreative contexts. Its distinctive meanings are **quantity**, supply, abundance, surplus, number, space; possessions, property, cash, capital; something carefully reserved, savings, accumulated **wealth**; company, party, assembly; lie in wait; procreate, supply with children.

(B) Antony, responding to Octavius' comment that Lepidus is 'a tried and valiant soldier', emphasizes the functionality of the relationship: 'So is my horse, Octavius, and for that / I do appoint him store of provender' (*JC* 4.1.29–30). Supply is the meaning here.

A paradoxical case arises in *SON* 64 when the speaker reflects on the changes wrought by time: 'When I have seen the hungry ocean gain / Advantage on the kingdom of the shore, / And the firm soil win of the wat'ry main, / Increasing store with loss, and loss with store' (5–8). Land that is flooded is lost to the sea, but the sea gains thereby; the reverse case arises when the sea recedes. The store, supply or abundance of land and sea exhibit a reciprocal relationship: either can be increased but only at the **expense** of the other.

Engaging Proteus in witty banter, Speed reveals consciousness of an optimum relationship between an area of land and the **quantity** of sheep it can support: 'Here's too small a pasture for such store of muttons' (*TGV* 1.1.100).

Octavius Caesar gives instructions for a special **provision** for the army as they ready themselves to overthrow Mark Antony: 'And feast the army; we have store to do't, / And they have earn'd the waste' (*ANT* 4.1.15–16). Clearly Octavius means that they possess sufficient supplies for this unusual expenditure or outlay. Unlike Antony, who is associated with **bounty**, his **rival** is niggardly, so that his choice of the word 'waste' is suggestive of a surplus that needs to be used up.

COR is peculiarly concerned with scarcity and plenty. Menenius defends the eponymous hero with the question, 'In what enormity is Martius poor in, that you two have not in abundance?' only to be countered by the tribune's insistence that Coriolanus abounds in faults: 'He's poor in no one fault, but stor'd with all' (2.1.16–18).

Shylock excuses his apparent failure to respond to Antonio's arrival by affecting a mental calculation of funds he has available for lending: 'I am debating of my present store' (*MV* 1.3.53).

Romeo, complaining of Rosaline's unwillingness to be wooed, fears that she will use up all her capital of beauty by failing to procreate: 'O, she is rich in beauty, only poor / That, when she dies, with beauty dies her store' (*ROM* 1.1.215–16).

In offering to provide the necessary resources for Orlando's escape from his murderous brother, Old Adam refers to his accumulated reserve or stored-up wealth: 'I have five hundred crowns, / The thrifty hire I sav'd under your father, / Which I did store to be my foster-nurse' (*AYL* 2.3.38–40).

Helena, explaining to the King the peculiar potency of the medicine she plans to apply to his seemingly incurable disease, comments, with respect to her father, the famous physician, 'He bade me store up, as a triple eye, / Safer than mine own two, more dear' (*AWW* 2.1.108–9). Keep in reserve, protected, is the sense conveyed here.

'Store' as 'increase' or 'procreation' finds expression in the injunction directed at the beautiful young man: 'As truth and beauty shall together thrive / If from thyself to store thou wouldst convert' (*SON* 14.11–12).

Assembly or party is the meaning employed by Capulet when he invites Paris to the family feast: 'Whereto I have invited many a guest, / Such as I love, and you, among the store / One more, most welcome, makes my number more' (*ROM* 1.2.22–4).

Queen Margaret, cursing her adversaries, leaves Richard Gloucester until last. She prays the evil that awaits him be kept back, until the moment of maximum pain: 'If heaven have any grievous plague in store / Exceeding those that I can wish upon thee, / O, let them keep it till thy sins be ripe, / And then hurl down their indignation' (*R3* 1.3.216–19).

When Julius Caesar tells Tribonius, 'I have an hour's talk in store for you' (*JC* 2.2.121), he means, in wait.

(C) Sorge, 'The failure of orthodoxy in *Coriolanus*' in Howard and O'Connor, eds, *Shakespeare Reproduced*, Kingsley-Smith, *Shakespeare's Drama of Exile*, Hillman, *Shakespeare's Entrails*, Schwyzer, *Archaeologies of English Renaissance Literature*, ch. 4, Edmondson and Wells, *Shakespeare's Sonnets*, and Schiffer, ed., *Shakespeare's Sonnets*, all contain significant commentaries.

stratagem
(A) In modern parlance strategy implies a well-thought-out scheme designed to achieve specific long-term objectives. Within this strategy there will be room for short-term adjustments aimed at thwarting temporary changes or unforeseen circumstances. Thus there is a crucial distinction between strategy and tactics. Originating in the military sphere, this terminology now encompasses government, business management and sporting activities. The meanings attaching to stratagems in the plays fall into three groups: military plans, tactics, schemes or well-governed actions; guileful **practices** or cunning schemes; violent or bloody actions. Whereas the first meaning is morally neutral the other two usually possess distasteful connotations.
(B) Surprisingly, *AWW* is the only play to employ the term three times and, even more remarkably, to utilize all three applications. When the Dumaine brothers endeavour to expose Parolles' swagger, his cover for cowardice, they propose that he be encouraged to attempt to recover the drum lost in the last action: 'O, for the love of laughter, let him fetch his drum; he says he has a stratagem for't' (3.6.34–5). The meaning is clear: he claims to have a carefully calculated plan of action. Bertram accepts the proposal, encouraging Parolles with the words, 'Why, if you have a stomach, to't, monsieur: if you think your mystery in stratagem can bring this instrument of honor again into his native quarter, be magnanimous in the enterprise and go on' (3.6.64–7). Here 'guileful practice', or 'subtle devices developed through arcane knowledge or mastery of military arts' ('**mystery**') is intimated. Having been puffed up, Parolles soliloquizes on the dangers inherent in the **venture** and the devices he might employ to make it appear that he made a valiant though failed attempt to retrieve the drum: 'I would the cutting of my garments would serve the turn, or the breaking of my Spanish sword . . . and to

say it was in stratagem' (4.1.46–50). In other words, he seeks to make it appear that he has been involved in a bloody conflict. In none of these examples is there any opprobrium attaching to the term.

Interestingly, Henry V, using the word in its second sense, protests that the Battle of Agincourt was won, against seemingly impossible odds, without resort to guile or trickery that might diminish the magnificence of the military achievement and the glory of God: 'When, without stratagem, / But in plain shock and even play of battle, / Was ever known so great and little loss, / On one part and on th' other? Take it, God, / For it is none but thine! (*H5* 4.8.108–12). Henry has used **intelligent** military strategy in the first sense of the word, but emphasizes that no crafty device was employed. This was nothing like the Trojan horse. In contrast to Henry, Charles, in *1H6*, delights in Joan's stratagem or crafty scheme of disguise that enables the French soldiers to gain access to the castle held by the English: 'Saint Denis bless this happy stratagem!' (3.2.18).

In *TIT* it is the villain, Aaron, who celebrates guile, linking 'stratagem' with '**policy**' and so doubling the taint of the word, when he plots the rape of Lavinia: ' 'Tis policy and stratagem must do / That you affect' (2.1.104–5). A little later he arranges yet another stage in his plan to destroy the Andronicii: 'Know that this gold must coin a stratagem, / Which cunningly effected will beget / A very excellent piece of villainy' (2.3.5–7). This archetypal villain celebrates his achievements, playfully punning as he anticipates further slaughter.

The untainted use of the term is given apt expression by the English hero Talbot in stating why he called his son to join him in France: 'O young John Talbot, I did send for thee / To tutor thee in stratagems of war, / That Talbot's name might be in thee reviv'd' (*1H6* 4.5.1–3). He means the techniques attaching to military campaigns, the arts of warfare, admirable rather than reprehensible.

An ambiguous use is to be found in *MV*, where in a moment of romantic serenity Lorenzo proclaims: 'The man that hath no music in himself, / Nor is not moved with concord of sweet sounds, / Is fit for treasons, stratagems, and spoils' (5.1.83–5). As the word resides between treacheries and pillage this could mean either subtle devices, devious, underhand practices, or bloody actions.

There is no such ambiguity in the tense opening scene of *2H4*, as Northumberland awaits the news from the Battle of Shrewsbury: 'Every minute now / Should be the father of some stratagem. / The times are wild, contention, like a horse / Full of high feeding, madly hath broke loose, / And bears down all before him' (1.1.7–11). Context indicates that 'bloody events' or 'accidents' is the required meaning here.

(C) Of particular interest here are '*All's Well That Ends Well*: words and things' in Donawerth, *Shakespeare and the Sixteenth-Century Study of Language*; Cavanagh, '*Henry V* and the reformation of the word' in *Language and Politics in the Sixteenth-Century History Play*; Foakes, *Shakespeare and Violence*; Gross, *Shakespeare's Noise*.

suborn, subornation, suborned

(A) Intimating bribery, corruption, or any action designed to induce or abet improper behaviour, this word is particularly active in the political sphere. A key strategy in manoeuvring to gain an **advantage** is persuading individuals to give evidence against, or contrive to damage an opponent. Even kings suborn individuals to act as assassins. The verb 'suborn' means to bribe or incite someone to commit perjury. The noun 'subornation' involves either instigating or collaborating in wrongdoing. The adjective 'suborned' describes someone bribed or corrupted.

(B) The most striking case of subornation in the drama of the period is that of Bosola in Webster's *The Duchess of Malfi*. His experience of being turned into his manipulators' 'creature' runs like poison through his system and gives him a sense of being violated. The phenomenon finds widespread expression in Shakespeare but it is never the central experience for any of his major characters.

The most emphatic admission of self-loathing arising from subornation is provided by Tyrrel, consequent upon the murder of the princes in the Tower:

> The tyrannous and bloody act is done,
> The most arch deed of piteous massacre
> That ever yet this land was guilty of.
> Dighton and Forrest, who I did suborn
> To do this piece of ruthless butchery,
> Albeit they were flesh'd villains, bloody dogs,
> Melted with tenderness and kind compassion,
> Wept like two children in their deaths' sad story.
>
> *R3* 4.3.1–8

Here is a case of double subornation because Richard has suborned Tyrrel who in turn suborned Dighton and Forrest.

The Shepherd who claims to be the father of Joan Pucelle is dismissed by her as an impostor. Turning on her captors, Warwick and York, she asserts: 'You have suborn'd this man / Of purpose to obscure my noble birth' (*1H6* 5.4.21–2).

Hotspur enraged by Henry IV's refusal to ransom his brother-in-law Mortimer, and indignant that his father and uncle, now being elbowed aside by the King, carry the stain of unseating Richard II to facilitate the **usurpation** by Bolingbroke, vociferates:

> But shall it be that you, that set the crown
> Upon the head of this forgetful man,
> And for his sake wear the detested blot
> Of murtherous subornation – shall it be
> That you a world of curses undergo,
> Being the agents or base second means,
> The cords, the ladder, or the hangman rather?
>
> *1H4* 1.3.160–6

The devastating phrase 'detested blot / Of murtherous subornation' compresses and crystalizes the sense of contamination attaching to a corrupted person. Here is a concept which exposes a poisoning of an individual that simultaneously contaminates the body **politic**. Once someone has been suborned, the Judas mark can never be erased.

Gloucester, hounded by his political adversaries, complains to the king of their underhand, corrupt **practices**: 'Foul subornation is predominant, / And equity exil'd your Highness' land' (*2H6* 3.1.145–6). The accusation is all the more powerful for the second component: corruption drives out probity.

One complaint of the Archbishop of York in his rambling, unpersuasive justification for armed rebellion is that he was prevented from speaking directly to the King: 'We are denied access unto his person / Even by those men that most have done us wrong'. In seeking to undermine the credibility of the Archbishop, Westmorland observes that the rebel has not been the victim of injury or false accusation: 'What peer hath been suborn'd to grate on you' (*2H4* 4.1.78–90). In other words, there has been no conspiracy against the Archbishop.

In his pursuit of Angelo, the Duke feigns an assault on Isabella, claiming she has been bribed to make false allegations: 'By heaven, fond wretch, thou know'st not what thou speak'st, / Or else thou art suborn'd against his honour / In hateful practice' (*MM* 5.1.105–7). Significant here is the proximity of the term 'practice', signifying a prearranged plot or device.

(C) Brennan, ed., *The Duchess of Malfi*, Lever, *The Tragedy of State*, Ornstein, *The Moral Vision of Jacobean Tragedy*, McAlindon, *English Renaissance Tragedy*, Wilson and Dutton, eds, *New Historicism and Renaissance Drama*, and Dollimore, *Radical Tragedy*, Simkin, ed., *Revenge Tragedy*, all cast light on this important subject.

subsidy

(A) In the modern world this is a negative tax, viz., a direct payment from the government to the citizen, or a concession reducing a tax obligation. Employed twice in the plays, it is a tax or levy. Moreover, such subsidies are special taxes imposed to meet particular needs rather than a regular, ongoing tax. A subsidy was also a parliamentary grant to the sovereign.

(B) Henry VI, citing the reasons why he should prevail over the Yorkist Edward, includes his financial restraint with respect to his subjects: 'I have not been desirous of their wealth, / Nor much oppress'd them with great subsidies' (*3H6* 4.8.44–5).

The other case occurs in *2H6* when one of Cade's men announces the capture of Lord Say, 'which sold the towns in France; he that made us pay one and twenty fifteens, and one shilling to the pound, the last subsidy' (4.7.21–3). The first part of this incongruous figure would constitute a tax of 140 per cent, the second 5 per cent. Characteristic of the violence and verbal inflation of the Cade scenes, this accusation bears little relationship to reality. (In the previous scene Cade commands that 'of the city's cost the pissing-conduit run nothing but claret wine this first year of our reign' (4.6.3–4).) Say rebuts the accusations with candour and dignity. His reward is to be decapitated.

(C) Sullivan, *The Rhetoric of Credit*, 65–8, affords fine detail and valuable context. Knowles, ed., *King Henry VI, Part II*, Arden 3, Introduction, provides perceptive commentary on Cade's rebellion and some interesting footnotes on this scene. A vital dimension is provided by Woodbridge, *Vagrancy, Homelessness, and English Renaissance Literature.*

sutler

(A) A sutler is one authorized to sell **provisions** to the army.

(B) Prior to setting sail for France, Pistol, the only character to hold this position, seals his compact with Nym by indicating gains in the offing: 'I'll live by Nym, and Nym shall live by me. / Is this not just? For I shall sutler be/ Unto the camp, and profits will accrue' (*H5* 2.1.110–12).

(C) Hussey, *The Literary Language of Shakespeare*, ch. 7, provides a fascinating exploration of the register and style of Pistol and his associates. Blake, *Shakespeare's Non-Standard English*, and Salmon and Burness, eds, *The Language of Shakespearean Drama*, are highly informative.

tag, tag-rag

(A) A contemptuous term for the common people, each of these words makes a single appearance – in the Roman plays.

(B) Casca, during his display of aristocratic contempt for the **plebeians**, describes their enthusiastic response to Caesar: 'If the tag-rag people did not clap him and hiss him, according as he pleas'd and displeas'd them, as they used to do the players in the theatre, I am no true man' (*JC* 1.2.258–61).

Cominius advises Coriolanus to make a tactical retreat when conflict with the plebeians spills over into violence: 'Will you hence / Before the tag return' (*COR* 3.1.246–7).

(C) Thomas, *Shakespeare's Roman Worlds*, Martindales', *Shakespeare and the Uses of Antiquity*, Miola, *Shakespeare's Rome*, and Sohmer, *Shakespeare's Mystery Play*, explore the language and context.

task

(A) The financial meaning is to impose a **tax**. Its other implications are: to challenge or test; set a task for; to censure or chastise.

Hotspur, justifying rebellion against Henry IV, includes among this monarch's wrongdoings the imposition of extensive taxation: 'he depos'd the King, / Soon after that, depriv'd him of his life, / And in the neck of that, task'd the whole state' (*1H4* 4.3.90–2).

The idea of being set a task draws on the sphere of economics when Volumnia compares her son in battle to an agricultural labourer on piece-work: 'His bloody brow / With his mail'd hand then wiping, forth he goes, / Like to a harvest-man that's task'd to mow / Or all or lose his hire' (*COR* 1.3.34–7).

Hotspur employs the word in the sense of 'test' or 'put me to my word' when affirming his admiration for the Douglas: 'Nay, task me to my word, approve me, lord' (*1H4* 4.1.9).

(C) See Engle, *Shakespearean Pragmatism*, esp. ch. 5, and McAlindon, *Shakespeare's Tudor History*.

tax, taxation(s)

(A) There are several references to tax in the sense of financial impositions, but more frequently the word is used to mean criticism, censure or slander. It can also mean command or burden.

(B) Being accused of malfeasance Gloucester protests, 'No; many a pound of mine own proper store, / Because I would not tax the needy commons, / Have I dispursed to the garrisons, / And never ask'd for restitution' (*2H6* 3.1.115–8). By contrast, as Ross makes clear, Richard II has no such defence: 'The commons hath he pill'd with grievous taxes' (*R2* 2.1.246).

Lear reassures the elements that he does not blame or censure them for afflicting him: 'I tax not you, you elements, with unkindness; / I never gave you kingdom, call'd you children; / You owe me no subscription' (*LR* 3.2.16–18).

(C) Of interest here are Elton, *King Lear and the Gods*; Leggatt, *King Lear*, and Hattaway, ed., *Shakespeare's History Plays*.

temporize(d)

(A) To temporize is to compromise, respond or adjust to circumstances, to sway with the breeze. Temporize is used only four times (which includes the form temporiz'd).

(B) During the easeful peace which has fallen upon Rome subsequent to the exile of Coriolanus, Sicinius the tribune greets Menenius, the banished hero's proxy father and greatest admirer, with a disparaging reference to the great warrior. In a singular act of betrayal Menenius responds, 'All's well; and might have been much better, if / He could have temporiz'd' (*COR* 4.6.16–17). Why the word is so shocking, and so perfect, is because the very thing that made Coriolanus the greatest warrior was precisely his inability to temporize. He is pure passion. The ways of the political world are not within his compass. Were he capable of bending with the breeze, responding to the eddies of the political current, he might well have made an effective **politician** but could not have become a force of nature, the supreme warrior. To use the word 'temporize' in conjunction with Coriolanus is oxymoronic. For the man who 'godded' Rome's saviour, trumpeting his incomparable deeds, to employ this word is not only a betrayal; it reveals incomprehension of the nature of his greatness. Thus this utterance is one of the most telling political comments in Shakespeare's most political play. By contrast Don Pedro's assertion that Benedick, despite his insistence to the contrary, will one day succumb to matrimony, is playful, if oblique: 'Well, you will temporize with the hours' (*ADO* 1.1.274–5). He will make the inevitable compromise; or in modern parlance, 'come round when the time is ripe'.

The applicability of the term to both politics and love makes the employment of the word by Cressida all the more fascinating in a play which so persistently interweaves these realms. Just as Menenius' comment reverberates to the utmost bounds of *COR*, so, too, does Cressida's in *TRO*. Her enforced separation from Troilus precipitates an anguish which cannot be assuaged or moderated: 'If I could temporize with my affections, / Or brew it to a weak and colder palate, / The like allayment could I give my grief: / My love admits no qualifying dross, / No more my grief, in such a precious loss' (*TRO* 4.4.6–10). Cressida expresses herself in terms of a love that is absolute and pure. To temporize is impossible. A few scenes later Troilus has to witness her easy surrender to Diomed. Like every quest for purity in this play, her love suffers 'maculation' or stain. Love like honour is destined to be contaminated.

The strongly political cast of this term is manifest in *JN* where the arch manipulator and emissary of the pope, Pandulph, expresses astonishment at the recalcitrance of the Dauphin: 'The Dolphin is too willful–opposite, / And will not temporize with my entreaties. / He flatly says he'll not lay down his arms' (5.2.124–6). The stinging compound 'wilfull–opposite' and emphatic 'flatly' neatly sandwich 'temporize', bringing out Pandulph's discomposure at being rebuffed, his proposed compromise rejected out of hand. No negotiations are possible. Clearly this rare word possesses real zest in the political lexicon of Shakespeare's plays.

(C) Miola, *Shakespeare's Rome*, contains an excellent chapter on *COR* and see 202 for a key summary. Cavanagh, *Language and Politics in the Sixteenth-Century History Play*, has an interesting chapter on *JN*. Charnes, *Notorious Identity*, Thomas, *The Moral Universe of Shakespeare's Problem Plays*, and Barker, ed., *Shakespeare's Problem Plays*, engage in a vigorous exploration of Cressida's plight and responses, locating her predicament in the thematic and dramatic pulse of the play.

temporizer

(A) On the basis of the exploration of the word temporize, temporizer ought to mean someone amenable to compromise. However, in the single use of this word the dramatist qualifies the noun with the adjective 'hovering', which suggests someone who is an equivocator or prevaricator.

(B) Leontes, overcome by jealousy, confides in his trusty counsellor Camillo. The latter rejects the imputation cast on Hermione's fidelity only to provoke a vitriolic onslaught: 'I say thou liest, Camillo, and I hate thee, / Pronounce thee a gross lout, a mindless slave, / Or else a hovering temporizer, that / Canst with thine eyes at once see good and evil, / Inclining to them both' (*WT* 1.2.300–4). Here is a compelling use of this unique phrase. Camillo is portrayed as one who accommodates all improprieties with compliant facility, being immune to distaste or disgust; indeed the phrase endows him with the easy moral tranquillity of the **bawd**. This scene relates to love and jealousy, but it is also a profoundly political matter. Leontes is about to commission Camillo to poison his lifelong friend, King Polixenes, the supposed adulterer. Thus this word, like its associate temporize, attaches itself to the sphere of politics.

(C) See Felperin, 'Tongue-tied our Queen', on *WT* in Parker and Hartman, eds, *Shakespeare and the Question of Theory*; Cavell, *Disowning Knowledge*; Sanders, *The Winter's Tale*; Hunt, ed., *The Winter's Tale*.

tenement

(A) The word signifies land held by a tenant, or a landholding.

(B) John of Gaunt's famous paean to England, which sanctifies the very soil of the land, contains a severe condemnation of Richard II for relegating his status from that of lordship to landlord: 'This land / ... / Is now leas'd out – I die pronouncing it – / Like to a tenement or pelting farm / ... / Landlord of England art thou now, not king' (*R2* 2.1.57–113). The various **taxes** and financial impositions have reduced the realm to the level of a petty farm with Richard as *rentier*, eagerly scrambling to maximize returns from leased land rather than nourishing a prosperous kingdom.

Gaunt's cited lines draw on the anonymous play *Thomas of Woodstock*. Here Richard contrasts his father's acquisition of territory in France with his own incessant pursuit of new sources of **revenue** to finance his profligacy: 'And we his son, to ease our wanton youth, / Become a landlord to this warlike realm, / Rent out our kingdom like a pelting farm' (4.1.146–8).

Suffolk informs Wolsey that, in addition to being relieved of his public offices, he is required 'To forfeit all your goods, lands, tenements' (*H8* 3.2.342).

(C) See Rossiter, *Angel with Horns*, 198–9. Dutton and Howard, eds, *Shakespeare's Works – Vol II: The Histories*, contains several essays relating to emergence of the history plays and the nature and significance of Shakespeare's contemporaries in this sphere. For concise exposition of the various forms of landholdings see the entry on land in Sokol and Sokol, eds, *Shakespeare's Legal Language*, and Scott, ' "Like to a tenement": Landholding, Leasing and Inheritance in *Richard II*' in Jordan and Cunningham, eds, *The Law in Shakespeare*. For a clear, convenient edition with a valuable Introduction see Corbin and Sedge, eds, *Thomas of Woodstock or Richard the Second, Part One*.

tenth

(A) Primarily a financial term with three contrasting aspects, it also has a significant political application: a tax or levy amounting to 10 per cent of the individual's income; the percentage taken (in some cases) by a creditor from a debtor unable to meet the full amount of his **debts**; an award of a tenth of **booty** taken in warfare; the killing of one prisoner in every ten as punishment, i.e. decimation.

(B) Henry VI, enamoured of Margaret by Suffolk's praise, awards him the responsibility of bringing her to England, and allows him to raise taxes to defray the costs of the enterprise: 'For your expenses and sufficient charge, / Among the people gather up a tenth' (*1H6* 5.5.92–3).

The remorseful Posthumus, praying to the gods, offers up his life as a sacrifice for Imogen. Contrasting this action with the strategy of **creditors** – who take only a percentage of their dues from **debtors** so that they are able to recuperate their fortunes – he pleads: 'I know you are more clement than vild men, / Who of their broken debtors take a third, / A sixt, a tenth, letting them thrive again / On their abatement' (*CYM* 5.4.18–21). Paradoxically, the generous creditors are vile from Posthumus' standpoint because he does not wish to survive.

Cominius, commending Coriolanus' heroics in the defeat of the Voscians, offers him a reward commensurate with his deeds (which he declines):

> Of all the horses –
> Whereof we have ta'en good and good store – of all
> The treasure in this field achiev'd and city,
> We render you the tenth, to be ta'en forth,
> Before the common distribution, at
> Your only choice.
>
> *COR* 1.9.31–6

The Second Senator in humbling himself before Alcibiades offers amends to the avenging general, even conveying a willingness to sacrifice a tenth of the citizenry: 'By decimation, and a tithed death, / If thy revenges hunger for that food / Which nature loathes, take thou the destin'd tenth, / And by the hazard of the spotted die / Let die the spotted' (*TIM* 5.4.31–5).

(C) Sullivan, *The Rhetoric of Credit*, and Turner, *Shakespeare's Twenty-First Century Economics*, are both informative. See also the entry on tithe in Hassel, *Shakespeare's Religious Language*.

thrift

(A) The diverse meanings of the word are: **profit** or financial gain; financial management; success; personal **advantage**; economical, provident, prudent – or parsimonious behaviour.

(B) When Shylock complains that Antonio denounces his 'well-won thrift, / Which he calls interest' (*MV* 1.3.50–1), he refers to what he sees as legitimate profit. Justifying the financial gain arising from his activities, he **ventures**, 'And thrift is blessing, if men steal it not' (1.3.90). When, however, Bassanio sets out his scheme to win Portia, he uses the word in the sense of 'success': 'I have a mind presages me such thrift / That I should questionless be fortunate!' (1.1.175–6).

Having gained access to Cardinal Wolsey's inventory of personal **wealth**, King Henry gasps in disbelief: 'What piles of wealth hath he accumulated / To his own portion! and what expense by th'hour / Seems to flow from him! How, i'th' name of thrift, / Does he rake this together?' (*H8* 3.2.107–10). Clearly, Wolsey's wealth does not arise from 'thrift' in the sense of being parsimonious or by the careful **husbandry** of resources, because his outlays are prodigious. The word could mean 'profit' but it seems to mean 'economic activity' or 'financial management'.

The Old Athenian who complains to Timon that his daughter is being wooed by a mere servant, defends his attitude by emphasizing the prudent behaviour that has enabled him to become wealthy: 'I am a man / That from my first have been inclin'd to thrift' (*TIM* 1.1.117–18).

Falstaff discharges his associates Pistol and Nym on the principle of economy: 'Falstaff will learn the humor of the age, / French thrift, you rogues' (*WIV* 1.3.83–4). The French fashion had led to the replacement of an entourage by a single page.

The most famous example of the word being used to signify 'economy' arises when Hamlet caustically explains to Horatio the reason for his mother's over-hasty marriage: 'Thrift, thrift, Horatio, the funeral bak'd meats / Did coldly furnish forth the marriage tables' (*HAM* 1.2.180–1).

The player-Queen, protesting against any inclination to take a second husband when widowed, says, 'The instances that second marriage move / Are base respects of thrift, but none of love' (3.2.182–3). '**Advantage**' is what is intimated here. The editors of Arden 3 (fns 179, 181 and fns 177, 310) see the two uses as identical, namely 'financial benefit'. However, while the first relates to financial advantage, the second signifies personal advantage that is not limited to, nor does it necessarily involve, financial gain. The other example that occurs in the play clearly refers to financial gain or profit. Hamlet, having praised Horatio, assures his friend that the evaluation is just. It is the poor who flatter the rich in the hope of financial gain: 'Why should the poor be flatter'd? / No, let the candied tongue lick absurd pomp, / And crook the pregnant hinges of the knee / Where thrift may follow fawning' (3.2.59–62).

(C) By far the most problematic application of the term occurs in *CYM* (5.1.15) though no economic or political significance attaches to it there. Nosworthy, ed., Arden 2, 146, provides a good summary of the discussion surrounding this example, which is generally interpreted as profit. For very interesting comments on the funeral baked meats in *HAM* see Appelbaum, *Auguecheek's Beef*, 15–27. Woodbridge, ed., *Money and the Age of Shakespeare*, contains important essays relating to *MV*.

thriftless

(A) The word can mean either unprofitable or unproductive.

(B) Ross, rejecting the suggestion that Duncan was murdered by his own sons, points to the unprofitable nature of such an action: 'Thriftless ambition, that will ravin up / Thine own live's means!' (*MAC* 2.4.28–9).

Viola expresses pity for Olivia who has been taken in by her male disguise: 'What thriftless sighs shall poor Olivia breathe!' (*TN* 2.2.39). Her longings will prove unproductive or unprofitable.

Old York, disinclined to accept the King's pardon for his son Aumerle as a reward for the Duke's own loyalty, claims, 'So shall my virtue be his vice's bawd, / An' he shall spend mine honour with his shame, / As thriftless sons their scraping fathers' gold' (*R2* 5.3.67–9). 'Unproductive' is the meaning here: wastrel sons squandering rather than augmenting their inheritance.

(C) Of interest for *TN* is Forman, 'Material dispossession and counterfeit investments' in Woodbridge, ed., *Money and the Age of Shakespeare*. Valuable too, are Sinfield, ed., *Macbeth*, and Long, *Macbeth*.

thrifty

(A) This word can mean provident, prudent or abstemious, but also, disparagingly, parsimonious or worthless.

(B) Old Adam assures Orlando that he has been provident and therefore has the financial means to enable them to flee: 'The thrifty hire I sav'd under your father' (*AYL* 2.3.39). This compacted phrase signifies carefully husbanded earnings.

The Duke conveys to Angelo the sense of a provident Nature, endowing individuals with talents in the knowledge that the outlay will be rendered back with **interest** ('**use**'): 'Nature never lends / The smallest scruple of her excellence, / But like a thrifty goddess, she determines / Herself the glory of a creditor, / Both thanks and use' (*MM* 1.1.36–40).

The rebel Cade contrasts the extravagant aristocrats, enemies of the people, with the abstemious common men who wear patched shoes or hobnailed boots: 'Spare none but such as go in clouted shoon, / For they are thrifty honest men' (*2H6* 4.2.185–6).

Thersites describes the contemptible Menelaus as a 'thrifty, shoeing-horn in a chain, hanging at his brother's leg' (*TRO* 5.1.55–6). 'Worthless' would appear to be the meaning here. Bevington (Arden 3, 309) interprets the phrase to signify 'a useful but stingy and pedestrian tool always at the beck and call of his brother, a hanger on not easily shaken off'. Riverside interprets the term to mean 'serviceable' (517). 'Thrifty' is pointing towards, or embracing, the idea of functionality with little intrinsic **worth**.

Shylock provides a tantalizing usage in a speech deriding the extravagance of the Christians and the poor returns deriving from employment of Launcelot Gobbo. Directing Jessica to lock up the house he concludes, 'Fast bind, fast find – / A proverb never stale in thrifty mind' (*MV* 2.5.54–5). Does this mean 'never fails to **profit** the prudent person'? The context suggests this: unlike the improvident for whom the crisp, compact wisdom of a proverb quickly loses its gloss or **value**, the abstemious person does not need to seek the new fangled. Shylock is a character profoundly concerned with rates of return, and he seems to apply this principle equally to the financial and linguistic fields. He delights in punning and compact phrasing, spending his wit shrewdly, so that his verbal **investment** secures an **advantage** over his adversaries.

(C) Szatek, '*The Merchant of Venice* and the politics of commerce' in Mahon and Mahon, eds, *The Merchant of Venice*, and Shell, *Money, Language and Thought*, are particularly insightful with respect to *MV*. Ward, *As You Like It*, is also relevant here.

tithe, tithed

(A) To tithe is to levy a tax or collect church **revenue**; a tithe is also a tenth or tenth part; finally, the sole use of tithed refers to the selection of one prisoner in every ten to be executed. See entry on **tenth**.

(B) King John, scornfully rejecting the authority of the Pope, informs his legate Pandulph, 'no Italian priest / Shall tithe or toll in our dominions' (*JN* 3.1.153–4). The Church's ability to **exact** revenue is now dependent on the monarch's approval.

During the famous debate scene in *TRO*, Hector states the case for returning Helen to the Greeks in return for peace. In a play deeply absorbed with quantification and measurement he pronounces:

> Let Helen go.
> Since the first sword was drawn about this question,
> Every tithe soul, 'mongst many thousand dismes,
> Hath been as dear as Helen; I mean, of ours.
> If we have lost so many tenths of ours,
> To guard a thing not ours nor worth to us
> (Had it our name) the value of one ten,
> What merit's in that reason which denies
> The yielding of her up?
>
> 2.2.17–25

In the antithesis of 'loss' and **'worth'** the 'tithe or tenth' is the fulcrum on which the argument is balanced; 'disme', meaning every tenth person is the tithe of war. And each one of those anonymous people, Hector claims, is as valuable as Helen. Already the **cost** of war has been so excessive that it is impossible to justify retention of Helen and continuation of the conflict.

(C) Bevington, in his admirable edition of *Troilus and Cressida*, Arden 3, 191, provides the following footnote on tithe: 'every human life exacted by the war as a tithe – and there have been many thousand such exactions'. '*Dismes* (Decimae) is made of the French *Decimes*, and signifieth *tithe*, or the tenth part of . . . our labour unto God.' (Minsheu, 148 cited in Var). Elton, *Troilus and Cressida and the Inns of Court Revels*, explores the intricacies; Kermode, *Shakespeare's Language*, has an interesting chapter; Peter Holland, *English Shakespeares*, 70–4, comments interestingly on performance. Cavanagh, *Language and Politics in the Sixteenth-Century History Play*, has a relevant chapter on *JN*.

tithing

(A) Parish is the meaning of tithing.

(B) Edgar, disguised as Mad Tom, describes the peregrinations of the social outcast, 'who is whipped from tithing to tithing' (*LR* 3.4.134). He is driven out from each parish not out of sheer malice, but to avoid the financial burden of relieving an outsider.

(C) For the relevant background see Agnew, *Worlds Apart*, 52. Of interest here is Carroll, *Fat King, Lean Beggar*, and Woodbridge, *Vagrancy, Homelessness, and English Renaissance Literature*.

toll

(A) The verb toll means to levy a **tax**; enter for sale in the toll book or tax-register of a **market**. See **tithe** for the sole example of 'toll' as a tax levied by the church.

(B) The single reference to the market tax-register arises when Lafew discovers something of Bertram's misdemeanours in Florence. He rejects him as a potential son-in-law with the comment, 'I will buy me a son-in-law in a fair, and toll for this. / I'll none of him' (*AWW* 5.3.147–8). He is prepared to pay the requisite 10 per cent tax for putting Bertram up for sale in the market. The nobleman,

Bertram, has declined markedly in public esteem, a process precipitated by exchanging his family ring for a sexual encounter.

(C) Mukherji's 'Consummation, custom and law in *All's Well*' in Alexander and Wells, eds, *Shakespeare and Sexuality*, provides a clear focus on the sexual-matrimonial dimension of the play. Donawerth, *Shakespeare and the Sixteenth-Century Study of Language*, has an excellent chapter on language in *AWW*. Zitner, *All's Well That Ends Well*, and Waller, ed., *All's Well that Ends Well*, provide insightful exploration.

tractable

(A) A key word that occurs six times, tractable means favourable, amenable, susceptible, willing, easily managed, persuadable or governable. For those with power, tractability is a critical quality in their associates or henchmen.

(B) The richly political context of the term is apparent when Buckingham directs Catesby to sound out Hastings about his willingness to support Richard's ascent to the throne: 'If thou dost find him tractable to us, / Encourage him, and tell him all our reasons; / If he be leaden, icy, cold, unwilling, / Be thou so too, and so break off the talk' (*R3* 3.1.174–7). Here the closest meaning of the word is 'favourable' or 'favourably disposed', but synonyms such as susceptible or amenable are also relevant. The superb line of copious diction generates an awareness of the ways in which a concept expands or fully manifests itself under the pressure of words closely related in meaning but with each one adding a peculiar flavour. In the event, Hastings proves recalcitrant rather than tractable – and is promptly executed.

A quite different but highly significant case arises in *H8* when Queen Katherine warns the King about the antagonism being provoked in his subjects by Cardinal Wolsey due to the imposition of a heavy tax or levy: 'Tongues spit their duties out, and cold hearts freeze / Allegiance in them; their curses now / Live where their prayers did; and it's come to pass / This tractable obedience is a slave / To each incensed will' (1.2.61–5). 'Willing' is probably the most accurate equivalent in this case. Here is a vivid picture of eager duty turned to grudging acquiescence. What should be treasured and nurtured by the King, 'tractable obedience', is now contaminated by ill will, so that it is a 'slave', something hardly endured. Obedience that goes against the grain can serve only to weaken the King's authority and his subjects' affection.

Two applications have a comic context, though in the case of *TRO* the situation is political inasmuch as Ulysses, Agamemnon and Nestor are manipulating Ajax into the role of Greek champion in order to lure Achilles back into action. In praising Ajax, and puffing him up, Agamemnon insists that he is Achilles' equal in all things but two, and in these Ajax is superior: 'No, noble Ajax, you are as strong, as valiant, as wise, no less noble, much more gentle, and altogether more tractable' (2.3.148–50). The key word is saved for the end and follows on the heels of gentle, so that the meaning is amenable or responsive. Ajax is being both flattered and mocked, so this sugar-coated word is perfect here. For the Greek leadership, tractability is a great quality in a hero. For them it means liable to manipulation. In the RSC's production in the Swan Theatre (directed by Michael Boyd, 1998) the actor playing Agamemnon (Sam Graham) squeezed Ajax's arm on the word 'tractable' causing him to swell with pride and satisfaction. The very sound of the word aids Ajax's delight at being so designated: it is muscular and flexible.

The word occurs in a purely comic context in *1H4*, where Falstaff survives the denunciation of Mistress Quickly for having falsely accused her of theft. Engaging in an outrageous gesture of magnanimity, he concludes, 'Thou shalt find me tractable to any honest reason; thou seest I am pacified still' (3.3.172–3). Here the meaning is 'susceptible' or 'amenable'. When it comes to repayment of **debts** Sir John is notoriously intractable so this false hope is dangled before the vulnerable hostess. This is not a copper-bottom promise to pay up (which would be implausible) but an intimation of a willingness to negotiate sensitively. Even in the one instance where the word does not belong to the political realm, then, it is intimately connected with finance.

Tamora, Queen of the Goths, having married the Emperor, engages in an act of outrageous duplicity, promising Titus and his family that she will play the peacemaker between them and Saturninus. She inserts one caveat: 'For you, Prince Bassianus, I have pass'd / My word and promise to the Emperor / That you will be more mild and tractable' (*TIT* 1.1.468–70). Doublets are of considerable significance in this play, and here 'mild and tractable' signifying 'gently mannered' and 'accommodating', is particularly appropriate in a speech that is the embodiment of that 'glib and oily art' so despised by Cordelia. Tamora is smoothing the feathers of the Andronicii preparatory to contriving their slaughter.

Boult, having become reconciled to the impossibility of forcing Marina into prostitution, accepts her proposal that she can make more **money** for them by employing her exceptional accomplishments – 'I can sing, weave, sew, and dance, / With other virtues' – in a rich household. He agrees to put the proposal to his employers: 'and I doubt not but I shall find them tractable enough' (*PER* 4.6.183–99). He is confident that they will take **advantage** of an opportunity for economic diversification. The prospect of gaining a rental income by leasing out their recent acquisition proves irresistible given her intractability in respect to the function for which she has been **purchased**.

(C) Particularly valuable here are Adamson, *Troilus and Cressida*; Leggatt, *Shakespeare's Tragedies*; Skeele, ed., *Pericles*; Ryan, ed., *Shakespeare: The Last Plays*.

trade

(A) The application of the term to everyday commercial activity is obvious. Likewise employed to designate occupations, there is little scope for ambiguity, though as the trade or **occupation** most frequently referred to in the plays is that of **bawd**, the odour of the brothel often clings to the word, thereby creating opportunities for sexual innuendos in seemingly innocent situations. The word is used significantly to designate the physical space in which commercial activity is undertaken. There is the distinctive application to non-commercial negotiations, affairs or business. There is also the suggestion of activity or **practice**, something akin to occupation, but not quite the same. Deal or 'engage in' is yet another application.

(B) The centrality of commercial activity to society, and the role of law in underpinning it, is given particular emphasis by Antonio when cautioning his associates against the expectation that the Duke will nullify Shylock's **bond**:

> The Duke cannot deny the course of law;
> For the commodity that strangers have
> With us in Venice, if it be denied,
> Will much impeach the justice of the state,
> Since that the trade and profit of the city
> Consisteth of all nations.
>
> *MV* 3.3.26–31

Here is a clear statement of trade as the lifeblood of the state, operating within an international network of commercial relations governed by a respected legal framework.

Edgar, providing a description of Dover Cliff, has the compassion to include a reference to a dangerous occupation: 'Halfway down / Hangs one that gathers samphire, dreadful trade!' (*LR* 4.6.14–15).

Most frequently the word is used to refer to the activities of the bawd: nine times in *MM*, with two further references to the trade of hangman. Among the other trades to get a mention in the plays are mason, surveyor, cobbler, women's tailor, tanner, glover, ostler and tapster – and even tapster is a disguise for bawd in *MM*. For instance, the bawd Pompey reassures the brothel-keeper Mistress Overdone that despite the biting constraints imposed by Angelo she need only change her location, not her business: 'Though you change your place, you need not change your trade' (1.2.107–8). Likewise, the jaunty go-between, Pandarus, whose very name becomes synonymous with bawd, 'pander', closes *TRO* with an address to his fellow practitioners, 'Brethren and sisters of the hold-door trade' (5.10.51). This mock lament for the low public esteem of the trade also contains two references to 'traders', the bawd being a **factor, merchant**, go-between, linking client and commodity so that the group can be cynically, though aptly, termed 'Good traders in the flesh' (5.10.45). This epilogue possesses a peculiar frisson, given the proximity of the theatres to brothels. If, as is widely believed, this play received its first, and possibly only, performance at The Inns of Court, the mockery of the audience would be received with hilarity – though the aftertaste might check the laughter as the legal profession consisted of go-betweens whose public standing was in some ways little better than that of bawds.

We may appear to be on relatively safe ground with Francis Feeble the 'woman's tailor', but the combination of his needle and being marked down ('pricked') for recruitment in the army provokes a pun on 'prick'. It seems that once the word 'trade' is mentioned – 'What trade art thou, Feeble?' asks Shallow

(*2H4* 3.2.149) – the odour of the brothel enters, or at the very least, sexual innuendo squeezes into the dialogue. When financial exigencies oblige Falstaff to dispense with his entourage he comments favourably on Bardolph's new situation as cellar-man and waiter: 'A tapster is a good trade. An old cloak makes a new jerkin; a wither'd serving man a fresh tapster' (*WIV* 1.3.16–18). Later in the scene Falstaff uses trade mischievously when contemplating the exploitation of Mistress Ford and Mistress Page (his asset being his physical attractions; theirs the fat purses of their husbands). Punning on escheators, 'officers appointed to oversee lands forfeited to the king, called *escheats*' and **exchequers** or treasuries, the escheator being 'an officer of the Exchequer' (*RIV* fn 329), Falstaff proclaims: 'I will be cheaters to them both, and they shall be exchequers to me. They shall be my East and West Indies, and 1 will trade to them both' (1.3.69–72).

Most unusual is Isabella's denunciation of her brother. Condemned to death for the crime of fornication, he has appealed to his sister to surrender her virginity to Angelo in **exchange** for a pardon: 'O fie, fie, fie! / Thy sin's not accidental, but a trade. / Mercy to thee would prove itself a bawd' (*MM* 3.1.147–9). The implication here is that Claudio's act was not a slip but part of a pattern of persistent licentious behaviour. Given the frequent association of 'trade' and 'bawd', there occurs a natural connection or a collocation with Shakespeare creating the startling notion of mercy playing bawd to vice.

'Trade' meaning 'affair' or 'business' arises in *TN* when Sir Toby in mock ceremony addresses Cesario/Viola: 'Will you encounter the house? My niece is desirous you should enter, if your trade be to her.' Viola seizes on the word 'trade' and elaborates on the mercantile suggestion. 'I am bound to your niece, sir; I mean she is the list of my voyage' (3.1.74–7). There is a tight and logical connection between trade and business, but given the now familiar association of 'trade' with 'bawd' it might seem that Sir Toby is making a sly play on bawd as Viola is acting as go-between for Orsino in his pursuit of Olivia.

The undertow attaching to this seemingly innocuous word is detectable in Hamlet's caustic comment to Rosencrantz and Guildenstern, now revealed as spies: 'Have you any further trade with us?' (*HAM* 3.2.334). The surface meaning is business or negotiation. The subterranean implication would not be apparent but for the way in which an association developed between bawd and trade. These go-betweens or agents of Claudius are exposed as bawds in the lurid world of political intrigue.

More wholesomely, trade as 'deal' is used by Cleopatra who calls, languidly, for 'music, moody food / Of us that trade in love' (*ANT* 2.5.1–2).

The concept of the space in which market activity takes place is apparent when Richard II, looking down from the castle walls and lamenting his imminent surrender to Bolingbroke, visualizes his grave in a **market-place**: 'Some way of common trade, where subjects' feet / May hourly trample on their sovereign's head' (*R2* 3.3.156–7).

One of the most complex examples is that which occurs in *H8* where Sir Thomas Cromwell's strategic position is referred to. After listing his various offices, Lovell adds, 'Further, sir, / Stands in the gap and trade of moe preferments, / With which the time will load him' (5.1.35–7). Editors variously gloss the phrase 'gap and trade' as 'open-road' (Riverside 1056), or 'opportunity and well-trodden path', *trade* meaning 'any road used by traders' (McMullan, *King Henry VIII*, Arden 3, fn 391). Clearly Cromwell is perceived as occupying a critical space into which or through which all preferment flows. A gap can be defined as 'an unfilled space or interval' (SOD), but also as a restricted or constricted space. Bearing these definitions in mind this superb hendiadys, 'gap and trade', suggests a confined space through which nothing can pass without the authority of Cromwell. In the use of hendiadys, meaning is generated by the cohabitation of its constituent parts. The image that emerges is of a *narrow* space dominated by one man. 'Open-road' doesn't quite fit the bill, here. The hendiadys produces an image more akin to a funnel.

MAC affords striking and contrasting applications. The eponymous hero describes the discovery of Duncan's body and the condition of the presumed murderers: 'Steep'd in the colors of their trade' (2.3.115). The suggestion is that these assassins were inured to their task, the blood with which they were smeared being natural to them. What is unexpected is the contrast between the commonplace nature of the idea and the startling impact of the line: the assonance creating a delicate euphony that repudiates the starkly violent image latent in the description. Artifice is the very essence of this speech, ostensibly giving expression to shock and grief. Here is studied elaboration that fails in its intention to deceive by calling attention to itself.

The meaning to have dealings or transactions with arises in a surprising context in this play when Hecate chastises her underlings for exceeding their authority: 'Saucy and overbold, how did you dare / To trade and traffic with Macbeth / In riddles and affairs of death' (*MAC* 3.5.3–5). Here there is an intriguing doublet, 'trade and **traffic**', two words which are close synonyms, followed by the hendiadys 'riddles and affairs' where the space or tension between the pairings is much greater. Hecate is evidently perturbed by an engagement that transcends the functions of mere messenger and **ventures** over an important threshold into active participation in the arcane. In a play which is profoundly engaged with thresholds, physical and psychological, this is an intriguing moment. It also suggests something less rarefied – a demarcation dispute relating to the division of labour, so that the weird sisters in addition to being sinister are slightly absurd.

A testing case is Edgar's reference to the anguish of having to play a role, maintaining the pretence of being Mad Tom, when confronted with his blind father: 'Bad is the trade that must play fool to sorrow, / Ang'ring itself and others' (*LR* 4.1.38–9). To translate 'trade' here is almost a violation of the poetry, but by attempting to do so the audience are lured into the strange **mysteries** of language. The word must mean something akin to 'activity' or 'practice'. Although there is no reference in Shakespeare to the role of the professional fool as a 'trade', the demanding nature of his labour is expounded by Viola in *TN*: 'He must observe their mood on whom he jests, / The quality of persons, and the time; / And like the haggard, check at every feather / That comes before his eye.

This is a practice / As full of labour as a wise man's art' (3.1.62–6). '**Practice**' is the word used here to describe the Fool's endeavours, art or trade.

Embedded in Edgar's term is the conception of something learned or achieved through burdensome endeavour. Linked with his later expression of anguish on behalf of the samphire collector making his way precariously along the cliff face, a 'dreadful trade', the role-playing Edgar (represented consecutively as Mad Tom, more refined common man, crude rustic and knight who challenges Edmund) appears to acquire a peculiar insight into the suffering attaching to various activities – the most painful of which is to 'play fool to sorrow'.

(C) For a fascinating analysis of Venice as a centre of trade routes see Brotton, *The Renaissance Bazaar*. On the English situation, Pallister, *The Age of Elizabeth*, provides a comprehensive survey and is complemented by Leinwand, *Theatre, Finance and Society in Early Modern England*. Another angle is provided by Matar, *Turks, Moors and Englishmen*. Brenner, *Merchants and Revolution*, contains a detailed picture of the commercial and political dimensions of London's overseas trade and is complemented by Carruthers, *City of Capital*, and Deng and Sebek, eds, *Global Traffic*. Wright, *Hearing the Measures*, analyses hendiadys with admirable clarity and has insightful commentary on *MM*. Also highly relevant here is Carroll, *Fat King, Lean Beggar*, and Gross, *Shakespeare's Noise*.

traded

(A) Used only twice the word means experienced, well practised or expert.

(B) Hubert, having been incited by King John to murder young Prince Arthur, gives way to pity. Unable to carry out the task he is later horrified to discover that Arthur has been killed. Overcome by tenderness and compassion, he is accused of crocodile tears by an incensed Salisbury: 'Trust not those cunning waters of his eyes, / For villainy is not without such rheum, / And he, long traded in it, makes it seem / Like rivers of remorse and innocency' (*JN* 4.3.107–10). The accomplished villain, maintains Salisbury, has mastered the art of dissimulation by experience and **practice**.

Troilus, setting out the case for the continuation of the Trojan War, uses an analogy to justify sticking firmly to a course of action once it has been agreed: 'I take to-day a wife, and my election / Is led on in the conduct of my will, / My will enkindled by mine eyes and ears, / Two traded pilots 'twixt the dangerous shores / Of will and judgement' (*TRO* 2.2.61–5). So, eyes and ears are experienced in navigating between those antithetical forces of will or passion and judgement or cold calculation.

(C) See Bradshaw, *Shakespeare's Scepticism*; Piesse, '*King John*' in Hattaway, ed., *Shakespeare's History Plays*.

trade-fall'n

(A) This term simply means unemployed: its single appearance occurs in *1H4*.

(B) Falstaff in soliloquy on the poor condition of his new recruits provides an inventory of their circumstances and **occupations**, finally arriving at, 'revolted tapsters, and ostlers trade-fall'n, the cankers of a calm world and a long peace' (4.2.29–30). A reasonable interpretation here is that these unemployed were formerly ostlers who are victims of a fall in the demand for their services. 'Cankers' means 'decayed', suggesting perhaps that war revitalizes the unemployed by creating new opportunities for them. This is, of course, pure sophistry because Falstaff later describes his recruits as 'food for powder' (4.3.65); indeed, they are almost all wiped out. The cynicism of associating 'a calm world' and a 'long peace' with cankers is breathtaking. The argument that war is superior to peace is not unique to Falstaff, as it is given sturdy expression by Aufidius' serving men in *COR*. Intriguingly, one of them denounces peace on the basis that it produces a maldistribution of economic opportunities: 'This peace is nothing but to rust iron, increase tailors, and breed ballad-makers' (4.5.219–20).

(C) See Knowles, '*1Henry IV*', and Crewe, '*Henry IV, Part 2*' both in Dutton and Howard, eds, *Shakespeare's Works – Vol. II: The Histories*; also McAlindon, *Shakespeare's Tudor History*.

traders

(A) The word has two meanings: merchants and trading ships. There is only one example of a legitimate commercial trader, and two of illegitimate traders. There are two references to ships.

(B) Poins, hoping to recruit Falstaff and Hal for highway robbery, advises them that there are 'pilgrims going to Canterbury with rich offerings, and traders riding to London with fat purses' (*1H4* 1.2.126–7).

Pandarus seemingly employs the term euphemistically twice, to describe **bawds** and brothel-keepers in his lubricious, deeply cynical epilogue. He commences with a plea for sympathy: 'O traders and bawds, how earnestly are you set a-work, and how ill requited!' He then follows his witty and sexually loaded ditty with an address to his fellow go-betweens: 'Good traders in the flesh' (*TRO* 5.10.37–45). Ironically, these practitioners in prostitution are not cleansed by the term traders, but the term itself becomes contaminated – something characteristic of the verbal virtuosity in this play.

Unproblematic is the meaning '**merchant** ships' in Titania's description of her friendship with the mother of the changeling boy: 'Full often hath she gossip'd by my side, / And sat with me on Neptune's yellow sands, / Marking th'embarked traders on the flood; / When we have laugh'd to see the sails conceive / And grow big-bellied with the wanton wind'. Not only does the ship imitate the pregnant woman as the wind fills its sails, but later the pregnant woman imitates the ship, 'and sail upon the land / To fetch me trifles, and return again, / As from a voyage, rich with merchandise' (*MND* 2.1.125–34). A fascinating aspect of this illustration is the double image, the ship and pregnant woman taking up a central position in this highly visual description. This is one of only two references to ships as traders. Antipholus of Syracuse, a merchant newly arrived in Ephesus, decides to do some sightseeing: 'I'll view the manners of the town, / Peruse the traders, gaze upon the buildings, / And then return and sleep within mine inn' (*ERR* 1.2.12–14). As peruse means inspect, examine or survey, it is a reasonable assumption that he is referring to ships rather than merchants, especially as the reference is made in conjunction with buildings.

(C) Miola, ed., *The Comedy of Errors*, Kehler, ed., *A Midsummer Night's Dream*, and Calderwood, *A Midsummer Night's Dream*, are highly relevant here.

trades

(A) This word, used only four times, has two meanings. Uniquely it is used in *MV* as a verb to describe the process of the ferry going to and fro. On the other three occasions it is used disparagingly, with reference to those belonging to a particular economic category, i.e. common workers. It appears to be sufficiently all embracing to include shopkeepers, carpenters and even unskilled workers associated with low-level economic activity without any suggestion of blue collar superiority over common labourers.

(B) 'Trades' in the sense of 'plies' or 'goes back and forth' arises in *MV* when Portia instructs Balthazar to bring the garments and documents she needs for the trial, 'Unto the traject, to the common ferry / Which trades to Venice' (3.4.53–4).

Unsurprisingly, two of the three applications of the term as an economic entity occur in *COR* because Coriolanus views the 'commonality' (to use the **plebeians**' self-description, 1.1.29) with contempt. Persuaded by his mother to attempt to redeem the political situation by placating the plebeians, he reveals his disdainful attitude while promising an effectual display of insincerity: 'Chide me no more. I'll mountebank their loves, / Cog their hearts from them, and come home belov'd / Of all the trades in Rome' (3.2.132–4). Having failed to win their hearts Coriolanus is exiled, provoking his mother, Volumnia, to employ the same term in her denunciation of the plebeians: 'Now the red pestilence strike all trades in Rome, / And occupations perish!' (4.1.13–14).

The only other occasion the term is used also involves vilification: Timon, turning his back on Athens, delivers the most comprehensive rejection of the whole of humanity to be found anywhere in Shakespeare. This magnificent speech, volcanic in its explosive energy, includes the lines,

> Piety, and fear,
> Religion to the gods, peace, justice, truth,
> Domestic awe, night-rest, and neighborhood,
> Instruction, manners, mysteries, and trades,
> Degrees, observances, customs, and laws,
> Decline to your confounding contraries;
> And yet confusion live!
>
> *TIM* 4.1.15–21

Mysteries is sometimes glossed as 'trade' but the suggestion that an activity which can be defined as a mystery is more sophisticated than a mere trade finds expression in the dispute between Abhorson the hangman and Pompey the **bawd** in *MM*. The latter rejects the assertion that the hangman's occupation is a **mystery** but elevates his own activity on the grounds that, 'Painting, sir, I have heard say, is a mystery; and your whores, sir, being members of my occupation, using painting, do prove my occupation a mystery' (4.2.36–8). The exchange reveals an interesting distinction: a mystery is superior to a mere trade.

(C) Wheeler, ed., *Coriolanus*, and Soellner, *Timon of Athens*, are both valuable here. Also relevant is Kamps, ed., *Materialist Shakespeare*.

tradesman's, tradesmen

(A) The possessive tradesman's occurs only once; the plural tradesmen twice. The only unequivocal use is in *COR* where it means workers. The other two cases arise in comic contexts. In *JC* the phrase 'tradesmen's matters' possesses a surface meaning of business dealings while carrying a covert reference to sexual impropriety. Most surprising is the application in *WT*, a late play, where the word seems to mean 'retailer'.

(B) The tribune Sicinius expresses his pleasure at the smooth running of civil society in Rome consequent upon the exile of Coriolanus: 'Our tradesmen singing in their shops, and going / About their functions friendly' (*COR* 4.6.8–9).

Autolycus, the 'snapper-up of unconsider'd trifles' (*WT* 4.3.26), adopts the posture of superior social status when seeking to awe the old shepherd and his son and so cautions them, 'Let me have no lying. It becomes none but tradesmen' (4.4.722–3). Here the term seems to mean 'retailers' or 'petty traders', lending a spice of comedy to the situation as the speaker is a seller of cheap trinkets in fairs. Strikingly, the phrase carries with it the smug condescension that later became a familiar feature of the English social landscape as the gentry and upper middle class adopted a similar attitude even to substantial men of **trade**. Autolycus is, therefore, a precursor of more high-minded and more absurd social pretenders. What is detectable in this late play is a shift in the application of the term from traders generally to retailers in particular.

Even more elusive is the cobbler's comment in *JC*. Being challenged by Flavius the tribune – 'Thou art a cobbler, art thou?' – the cobbler is intent on prolonging the baiting of his social superiors. His riposte includes the comment, 'I meddle with no tradesman's matters, nor women's matters' (1.1.20–3). No doubt part of the suggestiveness takes life from 'matters', as implied by Hamlet's 'country matters' (*HAM* 3.2.116). The conjunction of 'meddle' and 'matters' activates the sexual suggestion, but requires some input from 'tradesmen's', which is probably infected by its association with '**traders**', as in 'traders in the flesh' (*TRO* 5.10.45) or **bawd**. It would seem that the cobbler is stalking the tribunes, shooting off a whole quiverful of sexual innuendoes, to the amusement of his fellow workers, while taking refuge behind the double meaning. This kind of banter reveals the availability of commonplace words or expressions for appropriation by the joker, be they amateur or professional. The value of this kind of activity to the dramatist, apart from provoking laughter, is in stimulating audience alertness to the mobility of language.

(C) For an extensive exploration of the significance of the cobbler's comments see Dorsch, ed., *Julius Caesar*, Arden 2, fn 4–5; Toole, 'The cobbler, the disrobed image and the motif of movement in *Julius Caesar*' in *The Upstart Crow*, vol. IV

(Fall, 1982). See Williams, *Shakespeare's Sexual Language,* for the entries **trade** and **traders**.

traduc'd, traducement

(A) A fascinating word in the political lexicon, traduced appears five times in the plays with a further single form of 'traducement'. To be traduced is to endure denigration, to be the target of vituperative disdain, to be excoriated; it is an active condemnation rather than an adverse detached judgement or evaluation. Consequently, the recipient, either an individual or state, feels sullied, demeaned, stained, shamed, disgraced, defamed, dishonoured or degraded. While the concept is straightforward enough, exploration of the individual cases reveals subtleties that enhance appreciation of the term.

(B) A good idea of the company kept by the word, the conceptual verbal network in which it is enmeshed, is provided by Helena's appeal to the King to allow her to attempt a cure. In response to the King's question of what she might be prepared to stake on the efficacy of her medicine, she responds: 'Tax of impudence, / A strumpet's boldness, a divulged shame, / Traduc'd by odious ballads; my maiden's name / Sear'd otherwise' (*AWW* 2.1.170–3). What she is prepared to sacrifice is her dearest possession, her good name, and, critically, to have her name scandalized in public, her shame trumpeted by means of the most demeaning mockery, namely by ballad-mongers. The strategic location of the word leaves no doubt about its potency.

More central from a political standpoint is Cardinal Wolsey's response when challenged about the imposition of a heavy and unpopular tax about which the King is ignorant. His argument is that a person in high place is liable to vicious slanders:

> If I am
> Traduc'd by ignorant tongues, which neither know
> My faculties nor person, yet will be
> The chronicles of my doing, let me say
> 'Tis but the fate of place, and the rough brake
> That virtue must go through.
>
> *H8* 1.2.71–6

It is a neat defence, strongly portraying the ignorant as vociferous and the virtuous as vulnerable. The choice of word is precise because it embodies the idea of the vigorous nature of the calumny, voiced abroad with a lack of restraint characteristic of the uninformed.

Enobarbus, attempting to dissuade Cleopatra from her fateful decision to appear in person at the Battle of Actium, warns her of the damage this is likely to inflict on Antony's already declining reputation: 'He is already / Traduc'd for levity, and 'tis said in Rome / That Photinus an eunuch and your maids / Manage this war' (*ANT* 3.7.12–15). The essence of the attack on Antony is that he is no longer a Roman: he could hardly be castigated with a more serious weakness than levity, the very antithesis of Roman *gravitas*. It is significant that in the scene of drunkenness on Pompey's galley Caesar signals his distaste for the 'Egyptian Baccanals' with the comment, 'our graver business / Frowns at this levity' (2.7.120–1). To be 'traduc'd' for levity is to be scathed indeed.

By way of contrast there are two striking cases of injury to the whole society. Most famously Hamlet complains to Horatio about the consequences of the revels so enjoyed by Claudius: 'This heavy-headed revel east and west / Makes us traduc'd and tax'd of other nations. / They clip us drunkards, and with swinish phrase / Soil our addition' (*HAM* 1.4.17–20). Characteristically of *HAM*, 'traduc'd' appears as a component of hendiadys so that the Danes are subject to voluble scorn *and* sober criticism.

Othello, **fashioning** a **chronicle** to be delivered in Venice, describes the injury he has inflicted on the state: 'And say besides, that in Aleppo once, / Where a malignant and turban'd Turk / Beat a Venetian and traduc'd the state' (*OTH* 5.2.352–4).

The final word must be allocated to *COR*, which supplies the sole use of 'traducement'. Cominius is interrupted and rebuked by Coriolanus because he is proclaiming the astounding **achievements** of the hero in capturing Corioli. Cominius declares that to extol the achievements of the great warrior is a minimum requirement of Roman **virtue**: 'Rome must know / The value of her own. 'Twere a concealment / Worse than a theft, no less than a traducement, / To hide your doings' (1.9.20–3). Just as the vice of ingratitude is a heinous fault in the Roman world, to give a man less than due credit is actively to discriminate against him. That telling line, which makes theft a peccadillo by comparison to traducement, brings out the enormous significance of the term, particularly in the moral universe of such a self-conscious society.

(C) Pertinent here are Donawerth, *Shakespeare and the Sixteenth-Century Study of Language*, esp. chapters on *AWW, HAM*; McAlindon, *Shakespeare's Tragic Cosmos*; Wright, *Hearing the Measures*, ch. 1: 'Hendiadys and *Hamlet*'; Grady, *Shakespeare's Universal Wolf*.

traffic, traffickers

(A) The primary meaning of the term is **trade** or business, and it is employed either as a noun or verb. The modern suggestion of illicit activity is absent. It may also be used to suggest action, employment or engagement. Traffickers are ships.

(B) The word is usually applied in a direct and obvious way such as Lucentio's description of his father as 'A merchant of great traffic through the world' (*SHR* 1.1.12). Normally applied to legitimate trade, Autolycus, 'a snapper-up of unconsider'd trifles', purloins the word to describe his theft: 'My traffic is sheets; when the kite builds, look to lesser linen' (*WT* 4.3.23–6). This itinerant steals sheets left to dry on hedges but is prepared, at a pinch, to resort to lesser articles. Traffic here means business: Autolycus by a stealthy slight of hand seeks to pass off his theft as legitimate business. This is the closest case to traffic as illicit activity, but as the whole style is jaunty and cheeky there is no overt acceptance that traffic means illicit dealing. Normally applied to the trading of material objects there is a special application in *1H6* where Suffolk negotiates a marriage arrangement between Margaret of Anjou and Henry VI: 'Reignier of France, I give thee kingly thanks, / Because this is in traffic of a king' (5.3.163–4). Here the agreement is extolled as a transaction of great import either because a king is one of the components of the trade or because the **exchange** is in the service of a king – or both. The word occurs in *ROM* where the Chorus refers to 'the two hour's traffic' of our stage' (Prol. 12). Here the word seems to mean 'action', suggesting performance, with the stress on movement, or the business of the stage.

The application becomes metaphorical in *LUC* where the complex line, 'Despair to gain doth traffic oft for gaining' (131) conveys the suggestion of intellectual dealings or engagement. Apparent resignation is a condition that gives way to new thoughts or devices to **achieve** an end desperately desired – as when Tarquin contemplates various ways of overcoming the seemingly impossible impediments to the attainment of his lust. This idea of thoughts engaging in transactions acquires another twist in *TIM* when Timon graciously receives a painting with a commendation that emphasizes the commerce that takes place *within a character*, making him something other than merely outward appearance would suggest: 'The painting is almost the natural man; / For since dishonor traffics with man's nature, / He is but outside; these pencill'd figures are / Even such as they give out' (*TIM* 1.1.157–60). Ironically, the authenticity of the painting resides in its representation of externals only. It is notable here that dishonour does the trafficking, thereby diminishing honesty. We can perceive here the idea of trafficking as dubious, potentially staining.

The capacity for moral contamination arising out of traffic, its propensity for engendering sharp **practice** and extreme self-interest, is highlighted by Apemantus, the cynic philosopher, in the same play, when he chastises one of Timon's prosperous, guileful guests, 'Traffic's thy god, and thy god confound thee!' (1.1.239). For Apemantus, of course, the commerce of everyday life involves manoeuvring for **advantage**, so that perfectly licit activity produces moral debility.

The idea of commercial activity spilling over into other facets of human engagement finds powerful expression in *MAC*. Hecate denounces her minions for exceeding their authority: 'how did you dare / To trade and traffic with Macbeth / In riddles and affairs of death' (3.5.3–5). The hendiadysdic 'trade and traffic' suggests that traffic is a more complex activity than mere trade: more subtle, artful and disreputable. Evidently the dramatist, as so often, stretches out a term, using it in a way that ranges from moral neutrality, a purely technical designation, to an activity which is morally contaminated. This leads us in the direction of the modern use of the word 'traffickers' as those who engage in illegal and/or immoral transactions.

Shakespeare's only use of 'traffickers' is free of such a taint, as Antonio's ships are described as being superior to other trading vessels:

> There where your argosies with portly sail
> Like signiors and rich burghers on the flood,
> Or as it were the pageants of the sea,

Do overpeer the petty traffickers
That cur'sy to them, do them reverence,
As they fly by them with their woven wings.
MV 1.1.9–14

In 1601 John Wheeler conveyed a heartfelt sense of the grip traffic had taken on the world: 'all the world choppeth and changeth, runeth and reveth after Martes, Markettes, and Merchandising, so that all things come into Commerce, and pass into Trafficque (in a maner) in all times'.

(C) Significant in diverse ways are Wheeler, *A Treatise of Commerce*, quoted by Netzloff, 'The lead casket' in Woodbridge, ed., *Money and the Age of Shakespeare*; Kahn, 'Publishing shame: *The Rape of Lucrece*' in Dutton and Howard, eds, *Shakespeare's Works, Vol. IV*; Muldrew, *The Economy of Obligation*; Brenner, *Merchants and Revolution*; Carruthers, *City of Capital*; Deng and Sebek, eds, *Global Traffic*.

treasury

(A) Surprisingly, this term is not used to describe the repository of state funds, but rather to indicate **wealth**. Of the six applications two refer to private riches, one to public finance and three relate to wealth that is non-financial.

(B) Somerset, in his contribution to the assault on Gloucester's probity, claims: 'Thy sumptuous buildings and thy wive's attire / Have cost a mass of public treasury' (*2H6* 1.3.130–1). This is the only case where the word is used to indicate public treasure or finance. At the other end of the spectrum is the reference to Autolycus' stock of knick-knacks. The disguised Polixenes chastises his son for failing to **purchase** presents for Perdita, claiming, 'I would have ransack'd / The pedlar's silken treasury' (*WT* 4.4.349–50). Bolingbroke, having returned from exile to reclaim his confiscated property and title, tells his supporters: 'All my treasury / Is yet but unfelt thanks, which more enrich'd / Shall be your love and labor's recompense' (*R2* 2.3.60–2).

The treasury of words is light and insubstantial compared with the material rewards that are to ensue. For Henry VI the only riches to be really esteemed is 'The treasury of everlasting joy' (*2H6* 2.1.18).

Aaron encourages Chiron and Demetrius to rape the woman they desire and to 'revel in Lavinia's treasury' (*TIT* 2.1.131). Edgar, having ostensibly led Gloucester to the edge of Dover cliff reflects: 'And yet I know not how conceit may rob / The treasury of life, when life itself / Yields to the theft' (*LR* 4.6.42–4). The references to 'treasury' in the plays engage with large and small sums of **money** and also with more precious properties of physical purity and integrity, earthly existence and the prize of heaven.

(C) See Enterline, *The Rhetoric of the Body*; Hattaway, ed., *Shakespeare's History Plays*; Jordan and Cunningham, *The Law in Shakespeare*.

truster

(A) The word means **creditor** in *TIM*, but probably signifies believer in *HAM* – the only other use.

(B) Timon, turning his back on Athens and cursing all its inhabitants, incites **debtors** to kill their creditors: 'Bankrupts, hold fast; / Rather than render back, out with your knives, / And cut your trusters' throats!' (*TIM* 4.1.8–10). Hamlet, rejecting Horatio's claim that his visit to Elsinor has been prompted by a 'truant disposition', protests, 'Nor shall you do my ear that violence / To make it truster of your own report / Against yourself' (*HAM* 1.2.171–3). 'Believer' must be the meaning here.

(C) See Long, *The Unnatural Scene*, and de Grazia, *'Hamlet' without Hamlet*, for *HAM*, and G. Wilson Knight, 'The pilgrimage of hate' in *The Wheel of Fire*, for *TIM*.

tyrant

(A) This term, along with its numerous adjuncts, tyrannically, tyrannize, tyrannous, tyranny, is used in a powerfully pejorative rather than technically narrow sense. It signifies behaviour characterized by individual licence unconstrained by moral or institutional impediments. Here is authority exercised in an oppressive, overbearing, intemperate **fashion**. Macbeth is most frequently referred to as a tyrant, and he does, indeed, seem free from any constitutional restraint. He is followed by Richard III, and, perhaps surprisingly, Leontes. In the Roman plays, where the term acquires a lively political sting, it is Julius Caesar and Coriolanus who attract the politically potent accusation. Unsurprisingly, the concept is particularly energized in *MM*. In *3H6* the word appears as a synonym for usurper, and in other cases, too, it often carries this suggestion. Frequently, especially when giving rise to a vituperative outburst in response to an act of injustice or cruelty, it means 'barbarous', 'villainous', 'remorselessly violent'. Coriolanus uses the term simply to signify harshness or cruelty. Not just rulers or humans wielding power are embraced by this term. Lovers are also seen as tyrannous. But Time, fever, war, seas, wind, might and custom are all denounced as tyrannical, thereby emphasizing the significance of extremity, or a quality that is remorseless and overwhelming.

(B) Malcolm refers to Macbeth as 'This tyrant, whose sole name blisters our tongues' (*MAC* 4.3.12). Richmond, whose claim to the English throne is weak, emphasizes that his cause is validated by Richard's tyrannical behaviour. Denouncing him as 'A bloody tyrant and a homicide', he declares, 'If you do sweat to put a tyrant down, / You sleep in peace, the tyrant being slain' (*R3* 5.3.246–56). Leontes, eager to acquit himself of abuse of power or injustice in the cruel treatment of his queen, Hermione, begins her trial with the words, 'Let us be clear'd / Of being tyrannous, since we so openly / Proceed in justice' (*WT* 3.2.4–6).

Queen Margaret, having been thrust from power by Edward, attempts to thwart a French Alliance by protesting that Henry VI is the legitimate monarch, and moreover, that he in turn has a living heir: 'For how can tyrants safely govern home, / Unless abroad they purchase great alliance? / To prove him tyrant this reason may suffice, / That Henry liveth still; but were he dead, / Yet here Prince Edward stands, King Henry's son' (*3H6* 3.3.69–73). Here 'tyrant' means 'usurper'. Warwick, who suddenly switches sides, also uses the word in this sense, promising to 'force the tyrant from his seat by war' (3.3.206).

Julius Caesar is assassinated on the grounds that he is, or is about to become, a tyrant. Caesar has assumed a dominant position in Rome, although the democratic structure remains operative. Cassius, drawing Casca into the conspiracy, asks the rhetorical question, 'And why should Caesar be a tyrant then?' (*JC* 1.3.103). The answer is because the servile Romans have allowed him such latitude. Cinna, observing the fall of Caesar, cries 'Liberty! Freedom! Tyranny is dead!' (3.1.78). The First Plebeian, having been persuaded by Brutus' oration exclaims, 'This Caesar was a tyrant' (3.2.69). Indeed, the play pivots on this very word, though it operates in close alliance with 'ambition'.

The strategic significance of the word in Rome is manifested in the scheming of the tribunes to bring down Coriolanus: 'In this point charge him home, that he affects / Tyrannical power' (*COR* 3.3.1–2), an accusation critical in their successful public assault on him. Coriolanus does not aspire to political office but rather surrenders to his mother's ambitions. Rich in name and fame, and possessed of an aristocratic contempt for the **plebeians**, he employs the word in a personal sense when returning from exile at the head of an invading army. Incapable of resisting the emotional pressure of his family, he turns to his wife with the words, 'Best of my flesh, / Forgive my tyranny; but do not say / For that, "Forgive our Romans" ' (5.3.42–4). 'Cruelty' is what the word signifies here.

Caliban, who is acutely aware of his status as a slave, has no hesitation in referring to Prospero as a 'tyrant'. Committing himself to his new master Stephano, he repeats the mistake he made when revealing to Prospero the island's secret **bounty**: 'I'll show thee the best springs; I'll pluck thee berries; / I'll fish for thee, and get thee wood enough. / A plague upon the tyrant that I serve! / I'll bear him no more sticks, but follow thee / Thou wondrous man' (*TMP* 2.2.160–4).

The intensity of the islander's hostility finds clear expression in a speech where he embraces further servitude but one in which the nature of the **bond** is not alienating. Caliban appears to have alighted on the term 'tyrant' and employed it with considered precision. For him it is not authority per se that antagonizes him, but an exercise of control that humiliates and degrades him. Indeed, Caliban refers to Stephano as 'my noble lord' and, repeating his hatred of Prospero, he uses the word with the added sense of **usurp**: 'I am subject to a tyrant, / A sorcerer, that by his cunning hath / Cheated me of the island' (3.2.38–44).

Intriguingly, there is a further application in the play. The magical hounds set upon Stephano and his associates by Prospero and Ariel are called, 'Mountain', 'Silver', 'Fury' and 'Tyrant' (4.1.255–7). Here, remorseless and unbridled ferocity seem to be signalled. Indeed, it resides at the dynamic centre of the term.

Rumour, disclosing a facility for infinite mischief and misrepresentation, refers to the greatest tyrant of all: 'Whiles the big year, swoll'n with some other grief, / Is thought with child by the stern tyrant war' (*2H4*, Induction 13–14).

SON 115 refers to 'Time's tyranny' (9), while Lord Bardolph cautions against grandiose plans insufficiently matched by resources so that the half-built house is left 'for churlish winter's tyranny' (*2H4* 1.3.62). As he attempts to steer Lear into a hovel, Kent insists, 'The tyranny of the open night's too rough / For nature to endure' (*LR* 3.4.2–3). Just as war, Time or the elements with their irresistible force can crush men, so too can they be discomposed by the tyranny of the loved one who, like Olivia, declines to reciprocate the fervour of Orsino's feelings: 'Live you the marble-breasted tyrant still' (*TN* 5.1.124).

Both in the Renaissance and in classical times, discussions of the origins of the term 'tyrant' and the office are characterized by uncertainty. Intimating bravery and fortitude, it would appear that the name was originally honorific, attaching to a person endowed with the requisite attributes for protecting the community from invasion and maintaining justice and prosperity within the realm. When such rulers or kings abused their prerogatives, the name of 'tyrant' became opprobrious, being reserved for those rulers who were unfit to occupy a position of absolute power. Given the particular historical conjunction of the expulsion of the Tarquins from Rome, the word 'king' acquired the stain attaching to tyrant – something made much of in *JC*. Likewise tyrant became a key word in the lexicon of political invective.

Tyrants made their entry on the stage as early as fifth-century Athens where their threat to democracy was rendered vivid, though many Greek tragedians accepted the hospitality of tyrants. The same is true of Roman tragedians, with Seneca acting as speech writer for Nero. Violence, cruelty, effeminization and histrionics were perceived as shared characteristics by tragic actors and tyrants.

A vital contribution is made by Aristotle, who contrasts monarchy with tyranny: the former acquires power by succession or election. Even so, the monarch can become a tyrant by resorting to repression and wielding power over unwilling subjects. A monarch is accountable to the people; the tyrant may retain power by force or guile. Competent governance and the *appearance* of decency is all that is required to make tyranny acceptable.

The Romans had their own tradition, with *tyrannus* attaining the status of political abuse. It was Seneca who provided the tyrant with an expressive language consonant with his malign propensities. For Seneca, clemency is what distinguishes the king from the tyrant. Seneca's primary concern is the offence tyrants caused to morality and to the gods. His Elizabethan and Jacobean counterparts focused on their impact on the commonweal. Seneca's tyrant penetrates the Renaissance sensibility as a fantasist exhibiting limitless desire: someone unrestrained in the exercise of power.

Inevitably, a key question during the Renaissance was distinguishing between the prince and tyrant. One approach was to identify legitimacy as the crucial **factor**: a usurper was a tyrant. Another was to suggest that it was purely a matter of nomenclature: king was uncontaminated by the accretions time had laid on the word tyrant.

Erasmus' distinction was between one who served his people (meriting the name of 'prince') and one who pursued his own gratification. A powerful strand running from Plato through to Humanist writings was the identification of the tyrant with the beast. Given the strength of this connection in Renaissance writing, **Machiavelli**'s allowance of all behaviour conducing to the retention of power was treated as an affront to the conception of a true monarch. Machiavelli's instruction that the prince simulate virtue, so that were he wolf in appetite he should emulate the fox in guile, produced deep antagonism on a wide front from those who saw the art of dissimulation as intrinsically vile. Special attention was given to the Roman emperors notorious for tyrannical behaviour and sexual excess while still delighting in theatre. Effeminacy, deemed a fundamental feature of the tyrant and of the theatre, was, in turn, linked with bestiality.

(C) Bushnell, *Tragedies of Tyrants*, is meticulous in her exploration of the writing on 'tyrant', its etymology and status, from classical times through to the Renaissance. Her study supplies and analyses a rich store of commentary including consideration of the relationship between the Roman dictator – technically a temporary and emergency magistracy attained by Julius Caesar in 48 BC, but four years later illegally accorded to him for life – and tyrant. Significant here is Miola, '*Julius Caesar* and the tyrannicide debate', *Renaissance Quarterly* 38 (1985): 271–89; also Armstrong, 'The influence of Seneca and Machiavelli on the Elizabethan tyrant', *Review of English Studies* 24 (1948): 19–35. For further exploration of the topic see Frye, *The Renaissance Hamlet: Issues and Responses in 1600*. Bevington, *Tudor Drama and Politics*, esp. ch. 12; Hadfield, *Shakespeare and Republicanism* and *Renaissance Politics*; Martindale and Taylor, eds, *Shakespeare and the Classics*; Kraye, ed., *Renaissance Humanism*; Morris, *Political Thought in England*; Loomba, *Shakespeare, Race and Colonialism*; Coyle, ed., *Niccolò Machiavelli's* The Prince.

U

uncrossed

(A) This term refers to debts not cleared on the **account** book; not cancelled.

(B) Belarius, in the sole use of this application, contrasts the honesty and innocence of life in the wilderness with the indulgence and corruption of the court, concluding with reference to the well-dressed man who fails to pay his creditors: 'Prouder than rustling in unpaid-for silk: / Such gain the cap of him that makes him fine, / Yet keeps his book uncross'd. No life to ours' (*CYM* 3.3.24–6).

There is an interesting contrast between the pastoral world and its sophisticated opposite to that found in its sister Romance, *WT*. The pastoral world of Wales lacks the vital social engagement and material well-being found in the sheep-shearing feast in *WT*. There the spirit of the **market**, with its meretriciousness and slight of hand, enters in the form of Autolycus. A huckster and petty thief, he nevertheless brings with him a colourful energy and vitality that is stimulating to the rustics and audience alike. In *CYM* the court is portrayed as duplicitous, the elaborate unpaid-for clothes tawdry. The tailors, so often ruined by courtiers, feel obliged to do obeisance to their social superiors in the hope of encouraging **custom**. The sequestered life lacks colour and excitement; it is precarious and demanding; but it possesses the quintessence of pastoral and the world removed: innocence or purity.

(C) For contrasting views of Autolycus see Correll, 'Scene stealers: Autolycus, *The Winter's Tale* and economic criticism' in Woodbridge, ed., *Money and the Age of Shakespeare*, and Turner, *Shakespeare's Twenty-First Century Economics*, 88–90. The potential contemporary resonances of *CYM* are discussed by Marcus, 'Cymbeline and the unease of topicality' in Ryan, ed., *Shakespeare: The Last Plays*.

uncurrent

(A) Occurring only three times, the meanings attaching to the word are: not legal tender, devoid of **exchange value**, worthless, unacceptable; also improper, exceptional, unlawful or out of the ordinary.

(B) Sebastian, profuse in thanks to his protector, Antonio, concludes with an acknowledgement of the unsubstantial nature of verbal gratitude: 'and ever oft good turns / Are shuffled off with such uncurrent pay' (*TN* 3.3.15–16).

Hamlet, engaging in banter with the players, comments on the transformation of the boy actor playing the woman's part: 'Pray God your voice, like a piece of uncurrent gold, be not crack'd within the ring' (*HAM* 2.2.427–8). 'A coin with a crack extending far enough from the edge to cross the circle surrounding the stamp of the sovereign's head was unacceptable for exchange (uncurrent)' (Riverside, fn 1205).

At her trial Hermione attempts to fathom the cause of Leontes' jealousy, asking in what way her behaviour transgressed the **bounds** of hospitality towards Polixenes: 'since he came, / With what encounter so uncurrent I / Have strain'd t' appear thus' (*WT* 3.2.48–50). 'Unlawful' or 'improper' is the sense here.

(C) Relevant here is Barton, 'Leontes and the spider: language and speaker in Shakespeare's last plays' in Barton, *Essays*. On coinage see Sullivan, *The Rhetoric of Credit*, esp. 78–9. Turner, *Shakespeare's Twenty-First Century Economics*, is highly informative on technicalities. Shell, *Money, Language and Thought*, and Woodmansee and Osteen, eds, *The New Economic Criticism*, explore the boundaries of these concepts with insight and panache.

usance, use, usurer, usury

(A) These words all relate to the **practice** of lending money at interest, though 'use' has several meanings not directly relevant to the present study, except in the sense 'to hold in trust' which occurs in *MV* 4.1.380 and arguably in *ANT* 1.3.44. Throughout Shakespeare's lifetime usury was synonymous with charging **interest** on a loan – frequently with the presumption of exploitation. The usurer is simply a moneylender. However, from medieval times through to the beginning of the seventeenth century usury was legally defined as entering into a contract that involved the return of payment in excess of the principal, where the lender was not subject to risk. The special case for the lender being reimbursed for risk or serious inconvenience could not be determined when the loan was agreed so that theoretically *no advance arrangement* for a return over and above the principal was tolerable. By the early Jacobean period, and certainly by the passage of the 1624 legislation, a semantic shift had occurred so that usury was perceived as the exaction of 'excessive' interest. The twin sources of doctrine were biblical and Aristotelian as transmitted via Aquinas. The key biblical texts to which disputants inevitably referred were Exodus 22:25; Deuteronomy 23:20–1; Ezekiel 18:7–8, 18:13; Leviticus 25:35–6; Psalms 15:5. The conclusion generally derived from these texts was that interest should not be charged to your brother or the needy. Strangers or outsiders afforded dispensation for interest but, as Christians believed they were brothers that possible exception was ruled out. The matter of whether the Old Testament should constitute a **rule** or merely a guide to conduct still left the matter of the New Testament to contend with in the form of Luke 6:35, which prescribed the giving of loans without any intention of gain.

Aristotle saw the taking of interest as the most extreme form of employing **money** to gain **advantage** at someone else's **expense**. As money is only a medium of **exchange**, a facilitator of transactions, it does not possess 'use **value**', though as Meikle points out, Aristotle did not use the term 'barren metal' so frequently ascribed to him. By definition, therefore, someone should not be expected to pay back more than he received. Aristotle's society was worlds apart from sixteenth-century England. Social reality was one in which **trade**, commerce, enterprise, **commodities** and **profits** reigned supreme. In such a world the objections to usury or the taking of interest appeared spurious. The **market** was now at the centre of human engagement rather than an adjunct of the *polis*. As early as the thirteenth century practical considerations had imposed themselves on Aquinas, who agreed in Question 78 of the *Summa Theologica* that a lender who shared the borrower's risk was entitled to part of the profits that accrued from the **venture**. Here the lender became investor so was not guilty of the sin of usury. This critical principle was seized on by those wrestling with the realities of economic life and the restraints imposed by the Bible. The underpinning of this concession by Aquinas arose from analysis of two sets of circumstances. First, the loan had to be freely given, but if the borrower was deficient in repaying the loan, thereby imposing an additional burden on the lender, compensation was allowable. The technical title was *damnun emergens.* The second case amounted to what is now known as 'opportunity **cost**'. If the lender sacrificed a profit he could have attained during the period of the loan he was entitled to receive compensation, designated *lucrum cessans.* After careful consideration Aquinas opposed this latter principle on the grounds that the missed profits could not have been known at the time the loan was made. Despite this dubious objection the principle gained acceptance subject to certain specified criteria (see Jones, 107). Aquinas, a theologian of enormous stature, played a role in opening the door to the taking of interest by authenticating *damnum emergens* or compensation.

As possibilities for the productive use of ready money grew, awareness of the principle of 'opportunity cost' with regard to loans became increasingly appreciated. The taking of interest came to be not only aceptable but respectable. The odour surrounding usury eventually changed when usury began to appear more like compensation than exploitation. Moreover, the scholastics accepted the legitimacy of insurance, and receiving a return for risk.

As the cracks in the restrictive edifice opened up, the beginning of the sixteenth century witnessed an acknowledgement that a fundamental objection to usury during the Middle Ages was the assumption of evil intent on the part of the lender: the arrangement was designed to be exploitative. As economic circumstances provided increasing opportunities for *mutual* gains this position seemed at least questionable. Conservatives, however, rejected anything broader than acceptance of *damnum emergens* and *lucrum cessans.* Even so, the territory of debate had expanded and the issue of the *intention* of the lender assumed greater significance. Where no injury was intended, no usury occurred.

Debates about the status of lending money at interest during this period provide fascinating insights into the interweaving of theology, economics and semantics. Here was an activity that was ubiquitous, embracing all social classes, becoming ever more important as a **factor** in economic activity and social relations, but one that was viewed at the beginning of the period as contrary to God's law. In order to accommodate this **practice**, theologians interrogated the key texts, provided contrasting exegeses and asked whether Old Testament principles should be accepted as absolute rules or merely as guidelines to good conduct. Theologians who allowed economic arguments to infiltrate their discourse found themselves carried ever further into the landscape of economics. God was eventually ushered from the scene for the newly emerging science of economics to shape the debate. Close scrutiny of this process provides a vivid representation of economic realities refashioning ideological perspectives. As in the natural sciences, empiricism was the guiding principle. Theoretical constructions or 'economic models' were derived from observations drawn from the economic realities of everyday life.

Despite the presumed Aristotelian and biblical injunctions against taking interest on loans, the middle of the sixteenth century witnessed a major reappraisal of the theological and economic arguments relating to usury. The one common point of agreement was that usury was not wrong or sinful in all circumstances. It was unequivocally wrong when the strong sought to **exploit** the weak and poor, but could be justified where the returns derived from charging interest were directed towards the socially vulnerable, such as charities for orphans. The critical test was motivation. Where the aim of the loan was benevolent, guided by the spirit of fellowship and good conscience, it could not be designated as sinful. Given this position the question arose as to the legitimacy of legal sanctions: should the adjudication of intention be left to God without the intervention of the ecclesiastic or secular authorities? Clearly, for many, man's law should match or reflect God's law. Only if the textual foundations of biblical interpretation could be shown as questionable could there be a case for legitimizing usury.

During the Middle Ages usury was deemed a spiritual offence subject to the jurisdiction of Church Courts, a power confirmed by Edward III in 1341. This situation changed in 1487 with the enactment of the first general statute against usury. Usury was defined as the receipt of anything in excess of the sum loaned. Deemed ineffective it was replaced in 1545 by an Act of Henry VIII which allowed the taking of interest up to 10 per cent. The penalty for violation was triple forfeiture of the principal. The statute omitted any reference to God and His law. Likewise there was no mention of Church Courts. It was repealed and replaced by the Statute of Edward VI in 1552. The taking of interest was prohibited. The law was framed with reference to God and the scriptures. Inevitably the rich and sophisticated found ways around the law but the poor and needy were injured rather than aided by the legislation. Dissatisfaction with the situation culminated in vigorous debate which drew heavily on earlier Continental explorations of the subject. The most strenuous opposition to allowing the receipt of any sum in excess of the loan was provided by Thomas Wilson, distinguished for his *Discourse on Usury.* The debate produced a thoroughgoing analysis of biblical authority and economic circumstances. The resulting legislation of 1571 was termed the Act Against Usury. It did not signal a return to the Henrican legislation, though it did allow for the taking of a maximum rate of interest of 10 per cent subject to clearly stated **conditions**. God had returned centre stage and jurisdiction was given to ecclesiastical courts. Only courts of orphans were allowed to charge interest on loans. However, a special Commission sent to Devon and Cornwall in 1571 discovered rates ranging from a low of 25 per cent to a high of 180 per cent. At the less exploitative end of the market, lenders felt confident of steering clear of trouble so long as rates did not exceed 10 per cent. A significant feature of the case for **exacting** substantial interest was the phenomenon of inflation. A loan that did not carry an interest rate equal to the rate of inflation would result in the lender receiving less **purchasing** power than he had parted with. Clearly this could not be considered equitable and would certainly discourage lending. The Act, designed to restrain lending at interest, achieved nothing of the sort as the requirements of the expanding economy ensured a growing **money** market. Dissimulation, camouflage and a display of financial virtuosity ensured that a smokescreen was thrown over usurious activities. One device was to include the interest in the principal when the bond was transacted. Sometimes the interest was paid up front and repayments covered the principal. So fertile were the schemes devised to evade the law that one observer commented wryly that usurers practised a **mystery** rather than a craft. The Act stimulated subterfuge rather than restraint.

The twist of silk which constituted the case against usury was braided from Aristotle commingled with Christian interpretation by Aquinas and the contemporary interpretations of the scriptures. However, just as the waves of economic forces beat ever harder against the rocks of ideology, so too were the rocks becoming more friable under the influence of Puritan thinking. By the 1590s the combination of economic turbulence and theological revisionism generated a new perspective with respect to financial dealings. Gibbon was one among many reluctantly accepting that those who loaned to the wealthy, thereby facilitating large profits, were entitled to a respectable return. Moreover, the matter was one of conscience rather than one of external regulation. Increasingly, even stark opponents of toleration recognized that supplies of loanable funds were essential to meet the needs of productive enterprises. The blanket opposition to 'usury' began to appear antagonistic to the release of human energy and imagination. These theologians were not detached from social and economic realities and felt the ground shifting beneath their feet. The financial requirements of economic activity in all sectors, many of which were experiencing severe strains, made the conservatives engage with new realities.

Whereas in earlier debates theology was paramount, the high ground of debate was now occupied by economists such as Gerard de Malyne, Assay Master of the English Mint; Edward Misselden, a merchant of distinction; and Thomas Mun, a prominent member of the East India Company. By the last decade of the sixteenth century theology was surrendering to economics. The transition from Elizabeth to James witnessed a series of intense debates about how to reconcile the needs of the economy with restraint on usury. The economic arguments became increasingly sophisticated, revealing a veritable eclipse of theology as the governing principle of human endeavour.

Francis Bacon was particularly insightful and politically astute, focusing on the ways in which moneylending could be made to yield a return to the Crown. His conception was of a highly developed and licensed money market servicing the needs of agriculture, industry and commerce – while contributing to the public purse. The debate encompassed comparisons of interest rates, the condition of coinage and the relationships between sectors of the economy. Culpepper showed a clear awareness of the significance of supply and demand in determining interest rates. Low interest rates, he rightly averred, were essential to maximize economic activity.

An important semantic shift occurred during this period. Initially the legal definition of usury was to contract for a loan with repayment of a sum greater than the principal without any risk to the lender. Usury did not take place where the sum in excess of the principal reflected justifiable compensation for risk experienced by the lender. By the passage of the 1624 Act the very word 'usury' had come to mean the taking of *excessive* interest – the meaning obtaining to this day. So long as the exaction of interest was allowable up to a legal maximum in certain circumstances, lenders were able to devise a multiplicity of techniques to make the transaction accord with the law, while enabling them in practice to charge whatever the particular circumstances of the borrower allowed. Those in authority continually denounced interest being **exacted** at the expense of the poor and needy, but it was the most desperate and least sophisticated who were most severely exploited. Moreover, the activities of **brokers** and scriveners, who also took a slice of the returns arising from these contracts, increased the financial burden further. Ironically, the best hope for facilitating the demand for liquidity, for trading ventures or tiding people over short-term crises, was the development of a sophisticated, transparent money market with licensed lenders, who, as Francis Bacon astutely observed, could then be taxed.

The Act of 1624 was the product of a series of debates that were vigorous and perceptive. It signalled that the world had changed. It was no longer possible to determine economic matters by reference to theology. Lending at interest was a matter for the state rather than the Church. Such measures as were necessary were to be determined by the dynamics of economic realities. 'Usury' no longer meant lending at interest, but the taking of *excessive* interest, engaging in manifestly exploitative activities. Moneylending had a new name and smelled all the sweeter for it. One significant feature of the Act was the squeezing of middlemen: brokers' rates were reduced and penalties for violation increased. It should be mentioned that a persistent note struck throughout these discussions was the disgust felt at the exploitation of the poor. However, many like Thomas Lodge were more concerned for the wealthy who might fall into the hands of cynical moneylenders, thereby losing much of their property or entire estates. Intriguingly, this duality of commercial **credit** and consumer credit pertains today: credit-card holders accumulate **debts** way beyond their means and the very poor are preyed upon by back-street lenders exacting prodigious rates of interest. In traditional rural communities in third world countries, moneylenders frequently establish such a firm hold on peasants that they become virtual slaves. The role of interest in modern economic life is so fundamental as to be considered entirely natural and is fully legitimized by economic theory, but 'usury' retains the odour of exploitation.

(B) Shakespeare takes up the issue directly in *MV* (c.1597) where the highly successful merchant Antonio expresses contempt for the moneylender, Shylock, while having to resort to his services because of a cash-flow problem. Significantly, Shylock considers *trading* foolish because it is so risky. 'Usance' is used only three times, each time by Shylock and without ambiguity. First, he complains about the financial consequences of Antonio's eccentricity: 'in low simplicity / He lends out money gratis, and brings down / The rate of usance here with us in Venice' (1.3.43–5).

Antonio's provision of *free* loans reduces demand for *interest-bearing* loans thereby lowering the going rate of interest and Shylock's profits. Secondly, in response to Antonio's request for a loan, Shylock reminds him, 'many a time and oft / In the Rialto you have rated me / About my moneys and my usances' (1.3.106–8).

In commencing his game of cat and mouse with Antonio, Shylock slips in a little pun: rated meaning denounced or excoriated, but marrying with it the suggestion of rate or level of interest, i.e. interest rate. Finally, he makes his offer of an interest-free loan, ostensibly as a means of diminishing personal antagonism: 'I would be friends with you, and have your love, / Forget the shames that you have stain'd me with, / Supply your present wants, and take no doit / Of usance for my moneys, and you'll not hear me' (1.3.138–41).

TIM contains a perplexing passage in which there is a subtle play on 'use' as usury. Timon's flatterers congratulate themselves on the rates of return secured by their gifts: 'no gift to him / But breeds the giver a return exceeding / All use of quittance' (1.1.278–80). '**Quittance**' is repayment, so the paradoxical situation is one in which gifts function as loans because they are given in an assurance that they will earn a 'return' far above the market rate of interest. The reality is even more startling because Timon is financing his gift-giving by borrowing from those he endows with his largesse.

It is worth noting the frequent occurrence of 'breed' in connection with usury in Shakespeare. Antonio's mordant thrust, 'Was this inserted to make interest good? / Or is your gold and silver ewes and rams?', is parried by Shylock by means of the familiar collocation: 'I cannot tell, I make it breed as fast' (*MV* 1.3.94–6). At one level this is a joke, but Shylock is also providing a riposte to the Aristotelian view that interest is illegitimate because it cannot breed. Whatever theory proclaims, in practice money *does* breed.

In the opening scene of *MM* the Duke praises Nature in terms of an astute creditor rewarded both by thanks and by the receipt of interest, or 'use': 'nor Nature never lends / The smallest scruple of her excellence, / But like a thrifty goddess, she determines / Herself the glory of a creditor, / Both thanks and use' (1.1.36–40). This moral is addressed to Angelo who is being presented with the opportunity of deputizing for the Duke. The 'use' in question involves a compacted comparison: Nature lends talents so that they may be exercised or used; the beneficiaries of such generosity display their gratitude ('thanks'); Nature's endowment produces benefits of such magnitude that they are equivalent to interest on loans. Usury is here perceived as both natural and beneficial.

When Romeo threatens suicide as a consequence of his banishment, the Friar chastises him for the wild excesses of his emotional outburst, drawing a parallel with the usurer: 'Fie, fie, thou shamest thy shape, thy love, thy wit, / Which like a usurer, abound'st in all, / And usest none in that true use indeed / Which should bedeck thy shape, thy love, thy wit' (*ROM* 3.3.122–5). 'Usurer', 'usest', 'use' are packed together in a way that reveals the folly of usury: an activity that augments wealth for a person who lacks the discrimination to disburse it in a way that is wholesomely advantageous or that produces benefits surpassing the mere accumulation of coin. It is important to draw attention to Shakespeare's punning on 'use', as its application is so subtle that it may easily be missed. For instance, Romeo makes a clever pun when praising Juliet's beauty. Failure to recognize the double meaning of 'use' diminishes both the sense and impact of the comment: 'Beauty too rich for use, for earth too dear!' (1.5.47). Her beauty is so incomparable that it could not be enhanced or augmented, therefore it could not be put out to interest, i.e. it is impossible to add anything to what is infinite. The second clause maintains the aesthetic/financial dichotomy: she is simply too wonderful (dear) for this world and is beyond **price**, i.e. the world's capacity to yield a sum equal to her beauty. The lynch pin of the 'argument' is, of course, 'use'.

On several occasions Shakespeare makes a punning use of 'use'. Valentine, praising Proteous to the Duke, claims that he has 'Made use and fair advantage of his days' (*TGV* 2.4.68). Unlike most young men, he implies, he has put his time to such good use that it has yielded him high interest. 'Advantage', another word for interest in the financial sense, activates the pun. Later, he reflects on how easy it is to become accustomed to the seclusion of living in the woods: 'How use doth breed a habit in a man!' (5.4.1.). The pun is triggered by the familiar collocation of 'use' and 'breed'. Much more overtly Beatrice confides to Don Pedro her former fleeting romantic engagement with Benedick in which she seemed to win his heart: 'Indeed, my lord, he lent it me awhile, and I gave him use for it, a double heart for a single one' (*ADO* 2.1.278–80). Wrapped up in the pert comment is the bitter suggestion that she paid interest for the loan of Benedick's heart. Both meanings of use indict Benedick for abusing Beatrice's trust. This is one of those situations where the financial metaphor does not shed its unappealing qualities when it is transferred to the romantic sphere but still retains its exploitative character. Regrettably, the recent enthusiasm for tampering with the text resulted in 'use' being replaced by the word 'interest' in the admirable National Theatre production of 2007–8. (During the same season the RSC replaced 'deracinate' (*H5* 5.2.47) with 'uproot'.)

The connection between usury and breeding arises in Orsino's witty response to Feste's plea for a second coin in *TN*. When Feste says, 'Would not a pair of these have bred, sir?' the riposte involves a pun on breeding and lending money at interest: 'Yes, being kept together, and put to use' (3.1.49–50).

The concept of a parallel between love's increase, the attainment of emotional augmentation, and the taking of interest, became a literary commonplace and runs through Shakespeare's sonnets. Another aspect of this connection is physical increase in the form of childbearing. A strong and highly developed theme in the sonnets is the appeal to the young man to procreate so that his beauty does not become lost forever. As the opening lines of the first *SON* express it, 'From fairest creatures we desire increase, / That thereby beauty's rose might never die'.

The folly of achieving a childless old age is denounced in the second sonnet, again drawing on the financial parallel, with a specific reference to usury in 'use': 'How much more praise deserv'd thy beauty's use, / If thou couldst answer, "This fair child of mine / Shall sum my count, and make my old excuse" ' (*SON* 2 9–11).

The analogy is driven home with great force in *SON* 4 where the whole of nature is seen as a system of borrowing, lending and bequeathing:

> Unthrifty loveliness, why dost thou spend
> Upon thyself thy beauty's legacy?
> Nature's bequest gives nothing, but doth lend,
> And being frank she lends to those are free:
> Then, beauteous niggard, why dost thou abuse
> The bounteous largesse given thee to give?
> Profitless usurer, why dost thou use
> So great a sum of sums, yet canst not live?
>
> 1–8

In the second quatrain of *SON* 6 the reference to usury is explicit, paying attention to the restrictions on lending and the high rates of return yielded by the transaction: 'That use is not forbidden usury, / Which happies those that pay the willing loan; / That's for thyself to breed another thee, / Or ten times happier be it ten for one'. Thus in the *SON*s Shakespeare is invoking a paradox: if usury is morally tainted because metal cannot breed, there is a special kind of usury that is essential for the perpetuation of the individual – namely, breeding. Venus piles argument on argument in an endeavour to persuade Adonis to engage with her in amorous rapture. Denouncing ' "fruitless chastity" ' she makes a telling contrast: ' "Foul cank'ring rust the hidden treasure frets, / But gold that's put to use more gold begets" ' (*VEN* 751–68). This is perhaps the best example of Shakespeare taking a term that is generally perceived as opprobrious in its literal application and giving it a new and vitalizing energy through metaphorical transformation in the sphere of sexual love. Indeed, this is only one aspect, albeit a striking one, of Shakespeare's transformation of the entire lexicon of commerce to the sphere of romantic love, something elaborated with verve in the exchange between Portia and Bassanio in their declaration of love (*MV* 3.2.139–74).

Surprisingly, the word 'usury' is used only four times in Shakespeare's plays with two further cases of 'usuries'. In *MM* the word is used flippantly by Pompey the bawd, who protests against the suppression of fornication and prostitution (which might result in 'increase') while the respectable members of the community are allowed to thrive by the taking of interest: ' 'Twas never merry world since of two usuries the merriest was put down, and the worser allow'd by order of law' (3.2.5–7). Written and staged in 1604, this play gives a powerful sense of usury being institutionalized to the extent that it is primarily the province of the wealthy. Paradoxically, it provides a rare instance of the technique of evading the legal maximum rate of interest by the device of a covering transaction by means of which the lender sells goods to the borrower above their market value so that the combined transaction of lending and selling produces a real rate of interest much higher than the legal maximum. In delineating the inmates of the prison and their crimes, Pompey refers to young Master Rash who has engaged in this type of transaction: 'he's in for a commodity of brown paper and old ginger, ninescore and seventeen pounds, of which he made five marks ready money' (4.3.4–7). Hence evasion of the implicit maximum rate of interest is *not* tolerated in Vienna unless the law is invoked only against those at the lower end of the moneylending profession. This oblique reference suggests that a great deal is rotten in the state of Vienna and that Angelo's clean-up **policy** is somewhat selective, catching only the small fry.

Strikingly, the first Citizen in *COR* denounces the patricians for their support of usurers: 'Suffer us to famish, and their store-houses cramm'd with grain; make edicts for usury, to support usurers; repeal daily any wholesome act establish'd against the rich, and provide more piercing statutes daily to chain up and restrain the poor' (1.1.80–5). Performed around 1608 and set between 494 and 491 BC, the play's contemporary resonance has long been recognized. Here it is the poor who are the victims of usury, not, as is frequently suggested with reference to Shakespeare's England, wealthy noblemen living beyond their means. Again in *TIM* there is a clear implication of collusion between the rulers of the state and unscrupulous but respectable moneylenders, designed to facilitate the exploitation of the less fortunate. It is the general Alcibiades who indignantly exposes this social evil: 'banish usury, / That makes the Senate ugly!' (3.5.98–9). *CYM*, the latest of these plays (about 1609), continues this theme, albeit more lightly. Belarius, in response to Arviragus' expressed longing for escape from their rural retreat into the wider world, cautions, 'Did you but know the city's usuries, / And felt them knowingly' (3.3.45–6).

Usury in all these cases is portrayed as an exploitative mechanism practised by the rich and sophisticated against the needy. It is all the more remarkable, therefore, that this perspective is absent in *MV*, where the borrower is a rich merchant contemptuous of usury but operating in a society where the very shortage of moneylenders drives up the rate of interest. Shakespeare sees the rate of interest in that society as a consequence of supply and demand. As Shylock puts it succinctly in listing his reasons for hating Antonio: 'I hate him for he is a Christian; / But more, for that in low simplicity / He lends out money gratis, and brings down / The rate of usance here with us in Venice' (1.3.42–5). He repeats the point later in an aside: 'for were he out of Venice I can make what merchandise I will' (3.1.127–8). (Shylock is responsible for the two applications of 'usance' and the sole example of 'usances'.) What is surprising about this play, compared to the other cases of moneylending in the rest of Shakespeare's plays, is that the practice is seen as a necessary requirement of a commercial world in which cash-flow problems are inevitable, and the rate of interest is seen as the consequence of the supply and demand for loanable funds. To fix a legally binding maximum rate in such circumstances is simply to impair the smooth operation of trade and commerce, and to encourage wasteful methods of circumventing the law. Moreover, by showing how all prices are the outcome of the interaction of supply and demand (which he does in the joke between Launcelot and Jessica about the price of pork: 'This making of Christians will raise the price of hogs' (3.5.23–4)), Shakespeare puts usury or moneylending on the same footing as other business transactions – something not understood by Antonio. There is rich irony and considerable ambiguity when Antonio, playing his part in the 'mercy' rendered Shylock, seeks his allotment of 50 per cent of the Jew's wealth, not to keep but rather to retain it 'in use'. As he is apparently devoid of resources, Antonio wishes to take his entitlement and employ it as working capital in re-establishing his business. The 'use' in question – to hold in trust – will not be moneylending, which he despises, but trading. (See the Sokols' entry on 'use' for details of this legal term.) Having re-established himself, Shylock's money will be passed on to Lorenzo and Jessica provided that Shylock leaves his remaining assets to them in his will. The usurer is used but not used up. Ecclesiasticus 34:22, 'He that taketh away his neighbour's living, slayeth him', provides the foundation for Shylock's complaint that: 'You take my house when you do take the prop / That doth sustain my house; you take my life / When you do take the means whereby I live' (4.1.375–7).

The Christians do leave Shylock with sufficient resources to continue in business, but whether he will be able to continue as a moneylender given his new status as a Christian is another matter. Here is a solution that is inherently contradictory.

TIM has several references to usury but one of the most telling is Alcibiades' response to the Senators who condemn him to exile:

> I have kept back their foes,
> While they have told their money, and let out
> Their coin upon large interest – I myself
> Rich only in large hurts. All those, for this?
> Is this the balsom that the usuring Senate
> Pours into captains' wounds? Banishment!
> 3.5.105–10

Evidently moneylending is firmly institutionalized in Athens and is in the hands of the political elite. Here the sense of exploitation rather than the provision of needful financial liquidity is apparent. Additionally, there is a suggestion that this activity is unobtrusive to the point of being surreptitious. The money market and the calculated friendships that characterize Athens are linked when Timon, so perplexed by finding one honest man, has to press him: 'But tell me true / (For I must ever doubt, though ne'er so sure), / Is not thy kindness subtle, covetous, / If not a usuring kindness, and, as rich men deal gifts, / Expecting in return twenty for one?' (4.3.506–10). Unlike Shylock, who stands forthright in his trade, Athenians are ruthlessly usurous both in their commerce and in friendship. Indeed, here is an example of the market mindset becoming so dominant that no space is left for friendship. This is a truly acquisitive world.

Intriguingly, the outburst against usury in *COR* (1.1.80–2), is precipitated by hunger and provocation. Like Alcibiades' accusation, criticism is called forth only by extreme circumstances. In both plays there is a feeling that an institutionalized injustice is momentarily exposed. *LR* contains a similar allusion to those in political authority engaging in financial practices that are unconscionable. Lear, who has endured the miseries of the world, acknowledges bitterly, 'The usurer hangs the cozener / Through tatter'd clothes small vices do appear; / Robes and furr'd gowns hide all' (4.6.163–5).

The impression gained from these four cases (*MM, COR, TIM, LR*) is that here is an activity indulged in by a powerful elite to the detriment of the weak. Usury in these societies is an adjunct of political power. There is no implication that these cliques are meeting the urgent needs of trade and commerce by providing much needed liquidity; rather, they are preying on those desperate enough to have to resort to them. The fact that these activities are so opaque makes them all the more sinister and suspicious.

(C) The literature on usury is superabundant, with *MV* figuring prominently in analyses of Shakespeare's work. For a masterly discussion of this topic see Jones, *God and the Moneylenders*, and Meikle, *Aristotle's Economic Thought*. Critical, too, are Noonan, *The Scholastic Analysis of Usury*; Carruthers, *City of Capital*; Nelson, *The Idea of Usury*; Stevenson, *Praise and Paradox*; Brenner, *Merchants and Revolution*; Braudel, *Civilisation and Capitalism*; Wilson, *A Discourse on Usury*, ed. Tawney; Hyde, *The Gift*; Shell, *Money, Language and Thought* (which contains the remarkable essay 'The wether and the ewe'); Woodmansee and Osteen, eds, *The New Economic Criticism*; Muldrew, *The Economy of Obligation*; Simmel, *The Philosophy of Money*; Woodbridge, ed., *Money and the Age of Shakespeare*; Sullivan, *The Rhetoric of Credit*; Hawkes, *Idols of the Marketplace*; Bruster, *Drama and the Market in the Age of Shakespeare*; Jordan and Cunningham, eds, *The Law in Shakespeare*; Lyon, *The Merchant of Venice*, esp. 26–8; Szatek, '*The Merchant of Venice* and the Politics of Commerce' in Mahon and Mahon, eds, *The Merchant of Venice: Critical Essays*; Vendler, *The Art of Shakespeare's Sonnets*; Herman, 'What's the Use? Or, The Problematic of Economy in Shakespeare's Procreation Sonnets' in Schiffer, ed., *Shakespeare's Sonnets*; Warley, *Sonnet Sequences and Social Distinction in Renaissance England*; Kolin, ed., *Venus and Adonis*; Aughterson, ed., *The English Renaissance,* esp. part 8 for contemporary discussions of trade and usury. A fascinating exploration on this topic – including Shakespeare's perspectives on fertility, reproduction, natural expansion and rates of return – is to be found in Turner, *Shakespeare's Twenty-First Century Economics*, esp. 59–70. Sokol and Sokol's entry on usury in *Shakespeare's Legal Language*, 388, emphasizes that as early as 1545 a statute 'although nominally punitive, effectively allowed the taking of interest, as long as it was set at less than 10%'. See this entry for succinct examination of the evolution of the legal situation with respect to usury. They also analyse several cases where Shakespeare draws on the concept of usury or the taking of interest in both the literal and metaphorical senses, concluding, 'There are clearly varied attitudes to monetary interest-taking shown in Shakespeare's plays' (392). Their analysis of 'use' in the sense of 'to hold in trust' is particularly valuable.

usurp

(A) This word in its various forms – usurpation, usurped, usurper, usurping – means to effect an illegitimate claim to a title, property or identity. Most obviously concerned with the misappropriation of the crown it is used with great frequency in *JN* and in the Wars of the Roses cycle, *1H6–R3*. In the *R2–H5* tetralogy usurpation is of strategic significance. Curiously, the sense of taking on someone's identity by means of disguise is a frequent application, as is the more abstract conception of death prematurely ousting life.

(B) The indignant English hero Talbot, having been betrayed in battle, strips the famous Garter from Sir John Falstaff or Fastolfe, declaring that he 'Doth but usurp the sacred name of knight' (*1H6* 4.1.40). Unlike his more illustrious dramatic namesake, this Sir John is unable to wriggle out of the consequences of his ignominious act of cowardice and so suffers public humiliation.

As the two contending forces confront each other in the parliament house, complete with emblematic roses, young Richard incites his father, the Duke of York, to take immediate possession of the throne occupied by Henry VI (grandson of the usurper Bolingbroke/Henry IV): 'Father, tear the crown from the usurper's head' (*3H6* 1.1.114). Ironically, Richard himself becomes a usurper in the next play of the cycle by arranging the murders of his nephews in the Tower, drawing forth Richmond's denunciation of, 'The wretched, bloody, and usurping boar' (*R3* 5.2.7).

Richard II chastizes Northumberland for failing to kneel before him, going on to argue that no king can be dethroned: 'For well we know no hand of blood and bone / Can gripe the sacred handle of our sceptre, / Unless he do profane, steal, or usurp' (*R2* 3.3.79–81). The quest for wrongful acquisition of the crown is registered as sacrilege, common theft and an infamous political act.

A fine example, and one with at least a strong undertow of political significance, occurs in *LR*, when the frustrated Goneril, already enthralled by Edmund, expresses contempt for her too kindly husband: 'O, the difference of man and man! / To thee a woman's services are due, / A fool usurps my bed' (4.2.26–8).

'Usurps' means to take unrightful or unlawful possession. In Goneril's eyes legitimacy is determined by merit rather than by contract: Edmund, Duke of

Gloucester, possesses the charisma and ruthlessness that exercise magnetic attraction; Albany's compassion is equated with weakness; his reticence with lack of resolve.

Engaging is the usage in *SHR*, where the Lord gives instructions for the playful illusion designed to test Christopher Sly's sense of his own identity. The servant boy is to disguise himself as Sly's wife, the lady of the house. The Lord expresses his confidence that he will play the role to perfection: 'I know the boy will well usurp the grace, / Voice, gait, and action of a gentlewoman' (Induction 1.131–2).

This idea of usurpation as taking on someone else's identity occurs again in *TN*. When Viola disguised as the page Cesario, asks for confirmation of Olivia's identity – 'Are you the lady of the house?' – she is reassured by means of a tart response: 'If I do not usurp myself, I am' (1.5.184–6). This idea of a false imposition, of taking on another's identity, might seem a purely playful application of the term, but it would have had a strong resonance for Elizabethan and Jacobean audiences given the hostility to the very idea of acting by the puritan religion. The political significance of the concept here relates to its offstage implications. Viola picks up the word in her denunciation of Olivia: 'Most certain, if you are she, you do usurp yourself; for what is yours to bestow is not yours to reserve' (*TN* 1.5.187–9). The inference is that anyone in possession of such beauty has no right to conceal it from the world: this gift from God is to be rendered forth for the world's enjoyment and no doubt, following the line of argument pursued in the *SON*s, should be perpetuated through procreation. Thus even in this witty, playful context the notion of misappropriation inherent in the word is being strongly exercised.

The idea of territory being wrongfully appropriated occurs in *AYL*. In response to Duke Senior's expressed pity – 'Come, shall we go and kill us venison? / And yet it irks me the poor dappled fools, / Being native burghers of this desert city, / Should in their own confines with forked heads / Have their round haunches gor'd' – the First Lord comments, 'Indeed, my lord, / The melancholy Jaques grieves at that, / And in that kind swears you do more usurp / Than doth your brother that hath banish'd you' (2.1.21–8). The anthropomorphism might well give rise to a smile, but the immediate juxtaposition with the ducal usurpation diminishes the obvious sentimentality while casting a critical glance at the human assumption of authority over all things and places – a tension given more vigorous expression by Caliban in *TMP* (1.2.331–44).

Whenever the word occurs it produces a spillage that, while not confounding the comic moment, transforms it.

Of particular interest is the comment made by the remarkable Cerimon who brings his powerful gifts of healing to bear on the 'coffin'd', apparently dead, Thaisa: 'Death may usurp on nature many hours, / And yet the fire of life kindle again / The o'erpress'd spirits' (*PER* 3.2.82–4). The most natural substitution for usurp in this context is trespass, but the conception intrinsic to the word remains present: to effect an illegitimate claim on life. Death has not only attempted to cross the threshold of life but has been premature in attempting to encompass it.

301

The illegitimacy is such that with careful management the incipient possession can be cancelled. This is a fine example of an unlikely word being chosen because of the suggestion it carries as it is stretched in an improbable situation. The lovely Thaisa, who was presumed to have died in childbirth, was placed in a casket and thrown overboard with great haste in response to the sailors' superstition. It is as if death cannot wait patiently but trespasses on life, seeking to dethrone life before nature is ready to relinquish possession. Cerimon cannot bring someone back from the dead, but has the art to recognize the persistent sparks of life and to rekindle the fire – driving back the usurper, death.

The play within a play in *HAM* offers another example of this mysterious application. Lucianus describes the process of poisoning the king: 'Thou mixture rank, of midnight weeds collected, / With Hecat's ban thrice blasted, thrice infected, / Thy natural magic and dire property / On wholesome life usurps immediately' (3.2.257–60). Again there is a theft of life; nature does not make a willing surrender. Not only is this incident a replication of the murder of King Hamlet; it is also a representation of the usurpation that animates the play. Both life and kingdom are usurped. The word resonates between the deeply personal and the intensely political.

HAM provides another example of violation, when the Ghost of Old Hamlet crosses the threshold from the realm of the dead to the world of the living. Horatio accosts the apparition with the words, 'What art thou that usurp'st this time of night, / Together with that fair and warlike form / In which the majesty of buried Denmark / Did sometimes march?' (1.1.46–9). Night-time is, of course, the very time when spirits can walk abroad, but the rational or sceptical Horatio does not believe that the dead can do so. A breach of this principle is, indeed, usurpation, a breach in nature. Moreover, the identity of the dead king is being usurped. Hence this striking example links one form of usurpation with a second.

A surprising case occurs in *MM*. The flippant, waggish rogue Lucio denounces the Duke for leaving Vienna and delegating authority to his severe deputy, Angelo: 'It was a mad fantastical trick of him to steal from the state, and usurp the beggary he was never born to' (3.2.92–4). Here is an inversion of the usual process of usurpation: people normally usurp a crown or position; to usurp beggary is oxymoronic. Yet Lucio has method in his madness – punning on steal: by stealing away the Duke is also stealing from the Viennese the authority they have come to depend on. For the Duke to affect beggary is to turn the world upside-down; to commit a bizarre usurpation.

VEN offers a purely metaphorical usage when the lovely goddess is suddenly terrified on receiving information that Adonis intends to hunt the wild boar: ' "The boar!" quoth she, whereat a sudden pale, / Like lawn being spread upon the blushing rose, / Usurps her cheek' (589–91). This elegant simile achieves the energy of compression by means of the last phrase: the essence of her cheek is suffused colour – just like that of the rose, but the unnatural whiteness suddenly extinguishes all traces of delicate pink. Lawn itself, a fine white linen, is diaphanous, so Venus' face remains exquisite. The blanching, however, is violent and comprehensive; every suggestion of colour has been banished. Such a violent overthrow can only be conceived as usurpation.

Given the historical significance of issues of usurpation the frequent appearance of the concept in the plays is unsurprising. It is all the more remarkable, therefore, that the physical action of transferring the crown from one head to another, as is so graphically represented in *R2*, was not allowed on the stage in Shakespeare's own day – nor could it be printed in the Q texts. The play gathered around it further political significance when it was performed at the request of the plotters of the intended *coup d'etat* on the day before their uprising, the so-called Essex rebellion of 1599.

(C) For an account of the Essex affair and discussion relating to the above comment on *HAM* see Shapiro, *1599*, esp. chs 13–15. Bushnell, *Tragedies of Tyrants*, explores the concept with vigour including the vexed question of the circumstances in which usurpation might be considered legitimate. The following are also all of interest on this topic: Bevington, *Tudor Drama and Politics*; Dollimore, *Radical Tragedy*; Grady, *Shakespeare, Machiavelli and Montaigne*; Hadfield, *Shakespeare and Renaissance Politics* and *Shakespeare and Republicanism*; McAlindon, *Shakespeare's Tudor History*; Cavanagh, *Language and Politics in the Sixteenth-Century History Play*; Schwyzer, *Archaeologies of English Renaissance Literature*; Boehrer, *Shakespeare Among the Animals*; Skeele, ed., *Pericles*.

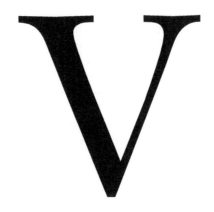

V

value

(A) Generally, value and its adjuncts relate to **market price** or moral **worth**. The noun signifies worth, valuation or estimation. The verb can have the meaning 'to **consider**' or 'to take into **account**'; also 'to estimate'; consider to be equal in value. 'Discriminating' is intimated by the adjective 'valued'. The overriding human necessity of making evaluations generates powerful tensions as incomparable and immeasurable values are set against each other. The market exerts pressure to make value equal price or to sum individual prices. Shakespeare's numerous subtle and provocative applications of the word anticipates the requirement for '**cost**-benefit analysis' (a theoretical tool of economics that gained significant application only in the second half of the twentieth century); 'cultural value', 'shadow value', 'honorific value' (Troilus' view of Helen), 'spiritual value' and 'human value'. This little word contains within it the capacity to impregnate political, economic and social decision-making in diverse and contradictory ways. Troilus' 'What's aught but as 'tis valued?' (*TRO* 2.2.52) is protean, insinuating its way into unlikely places.

(B) 'Value' as 'moral weight', 'purity' or 'worthiness' finds emphatic expression in diverse situations, such as Fenton's declaration to Anne that, though initial pursuit of her was for her dowry, he has discovered her moral worth: 'I found thee of more value / Than stamps in gold' (*WIV* 3.4.15–16).

Cominius claims that despite Coriolanus' unwillingness to have his praises sung in public, his *worth* to Rome must be acknowledged: 'Rome must know / The value of her own' (*COR* 1.9.20–1).

The financial use of the term is equally clear. Antonio attempts to reassure Bassanio that Shylock's proposed 'merry sport' in which he is to risk a pound of flesh, is not foolhardy: 'Within these two months, that's a month before / This bond expires, I do expect return / Of thrice three times the value of this bond' (*MV* 1.3.157–9). Unsurprisingly, 'value' as a financial measure is used more frequently in this play than in any other. At the end of the Trial scene Shylock is baited by Gratiano: 'thy wealth being forfeit to the state, / Thou hast not left the value of a cord' (4.1.365–6). When the disguised Portia seeks Bassanio's ring in recompense for her services, he makes a distinction between its financial and sentimental value: 'There's more depends on this than on the value' (4.1.434).

It would be surprising, however, if Shakespeare did not probe the complexities of the word. In *TRO*, for instance, the dramatist is relentless in his pursuit of the concept. Hector, in his debate with Troilus on the merits of continuing the war, points out that no matter how highly he or Paris rate Helen there is a distinction between a private evaluation (what we might term sentimental value) and social estimate of worth – and it is the latter that is germane to public debate or to the determination of price in the **market-place**. When Troilus protests, 'What's aught but as 'tis valued?', Hector's response is immediate: 'But value dwells not in particular will, / It holds his estimate and dignity / As well wherein 'tis precious of itself / As in the prizer' (2.2.52–6). Here is an insistence on intrinsic value or worth, something that can only be tested or ratified by a general acceptance of that estimate rather than by an individual evaluation. This contrast between personal evaluation and social worth or market price is also explored in *TIM* where a flattering jeweller's knotty syntax leaves the reader or auditor perplexed when Timon is assured that the jewel is not beyond his means: 'My lord, 'tis rated / As those which sell would give; but you well know, / Things of like value differing in their owners / Are prized by their masters. Believ't, dear lord, / You mend the jewel by the wearing it' (1.1.168–72).

Oliver, ed., *Timon of Athens*, Arden 2, makes the following interpretation: 'its price is determined by what those who sell it would themselves be prepared to pay for it'. This is, no doubt, one aspect of the meaning, but the Jeweller seems also to be saying that Timon's valuation is above the market price because he possesses an aesthetic sensibility beyond that prevailing in the market-place. Moreover, the value of the jewel is enhanced by being worn by a man as impressive (gracious, lordly) as Timon. Here there seems to be a dazzling exploration of 'shadow value': an overestimate brought about by a man who enhances the monetary value by virtue of the complementary value he brings to the item. Another way of interpreting the comment is to see this as a simpler piece of flattery: the Jeweller is intimating that Timon himself has value – moral and/or financial – which is transferred to the jewel merely because he wears it. Thus although the dramatist generally employs the term value in one of two unambiguous ways, moral or financial worth, he is eager in some cases to alert the audience to complex aspects of monetary value. Likewise, there is at least one case where there may be a coalescing of moral and monetary worth. In a dialogue between the Painter and the Poet, the latter explains his allegory by describing a man of **wealth** and nobility surrounded by men of at least equal stature, who nevertheless do obeisance to him while he is still prosperous: 'All those which were his fellows but of late – / Some *better than his value* – on the moment / Follow his strides, his lobbies fill with tendance, / Rain sacrificial whisperings in his ear' (1.1.78–81). 'Better than his value' could mean both financial superiority and/or of better social standing. The moral of the story is that they all discard their prosperous patron when he loses his wealth. If 'value' here relates only to their wealth the story is bleak in its implication, but if it includes moral worth it is even bleaker because nobody of substance (social or financial) is ever to be trusted. Here Shakespeare is employing the term ambiguously to provoke such questioning. To Timon's cost the rest of the action confirms that all the men of financial value are devoid of moral worth. Thus 'courtesy' is mere outward show, an instrument of cynical self-seeking.

Henry IV provides an unusual application when giving instructions for the ensuing Battle of Shrewsbury: 'And, Harry, you shall march / Through Gloucestershire; by which account, / Our business valued, some twelve days hence / Our general forces at Bridgenorth shall meet' (*1H4* 3.2.175–8). 'Considered' is the meaning of 'valued' here. Richard Gloucester, estimating Queen Margaret's army, says, 'The Queen is valued thirty thousand strong' (*3H6* 5.3.14).

MAC has an interesting case of the adjective 'valued', which means the esteemed or those of genuine quality. In response to the First Murderer's assertion of manhood, Macbeth responds testily:

> Ay, in the catalogue ye go for men,
> As hounds and greyhounds, mongrels, spaniels, curs,
> Shoughs, water-rugs, and demi-wolves are clipt
> All by the name of dogs; the valued file
> Distinguishes the swift, the slow, the subtle,
> The house-keeper, the hunter, every one,
> According to the gift which bounteous nature
> Hath in him clos'd; whereby he does receive
> Particular addition, from the bill
> That writes them all alike; and so of men.
>
> 3.1.91–100

Remarkable in many ways, this speech is a variant on Lady Macbeth's accusatory question when her husband wavers in his determination to kill Duncan: 'When you durst do it, then you were a man' (1.7.49). In both cases to belong to the 'valued file' is to possess the willingness and capacity to undertake brutal murder.

The range or fixity of value is given expression by the Duke in his opening speech of *ERR*. Indicating that Egeon is the victim of an embargo on Syracusians he points out that putting the highest possible valuation on the prisoner's assets they fail to come anywhere near the appropriate fine: 'Thy substance, valued at the highest rate, / Cannot amount unto a hundred marks' (1.1.23–4). Significant here is the immutable nature of market judgements: there is *some* leeway in determining a price or valuing assets, but it is very circumscribed. As so often in the plays human values attempt to evade the shackles of law and the market, and the tension is particularly strong in a play where Egeon enters fettered and where physical and human bonds are in a state of contestation.

A striking case occurs in *CYM* when Iachimo, demonstrating to Posthumus that he has gained access to Imogen's bedchamber, provides a description that celebrates the rich materials and exquisite workmanship:

> it was hang'd
> With tapestry of silk and silver; the story
> Proud Cleopatra, when she met her Roman,
> And Cydnus swell'd above the banks, or for
> The press of boats or pride. A piece of work
> So bravely done, so rich, that it did strive
> In workmanship and value, which I wonder'd
> Could be so rarely and exactly wrought,
> Since the true life on't was –
>
> 2.4.68–76

The idea is that the viewer is so profoundly affected by this perfectly realized representation – a mobility captured in the masterly conceit of the river threatening the banks, possibly because it was swollen with pride – that he is arrested by the dazzlingly precious and malleable materials and the human skill and ingenuity that **fashioned** them. Such is this fixation that he is stimulated to assess the relative worth of skill and materials. Intrinsic to the impact on the audience or reader is the power of the narrative with its burgeoning intertextuality – a new layer of which is provided by Iachimo's description: its tone and cadence. The passage calls forth a consideration of all the aspects of value – including the aural experience in the theatre.

Isabella provides an interesting example when appealing to Angelo on behalf of her brother. Offering a 'bribe' of prayers, she contrasts their efficacy with the dubious worth of costly jewels whose market price is the product of mere 'fancy': 'Not with fond sicles of the tested gold, / Or stones, whose rate are either rich or poor / As fancy values them; but with true prayers' (*MM* 2.2.149–51). There is a contrast between the material and the spiritual, but the dismissive reference to precious stones that derive value primarily from competitive demand by the whim of the wealthy, constitutes a questioning of market values in the sense of potential disparities between value as pride and worth as utility. This comment is particularly interesting in a play replete with the imagery of coining, authentic and **counterfeit**, where even human flesh is a highly marketable commodity. Values, secular and theological, financial and human, are constantly juxtaposed and then tested.

Bassanio having refused to part with Portia's ring is prevailed upon by Antonio to gratify the clever lawyer who has saved his life: 'My Lord Bassanio, let him have the ring. / Let his deservings and my love withal / Be valued 'gainst your wive's commandment' (*MV* 4.1.449–51). Antonio is requesting that Bassanio set Balthazar's service and Antonio's love above Portia's injunction. There are two values which have to be weighed against each other. The meaning is clear, though the compactness of 'valued 'gainst' concentrates the conceptual principle of values being of different kinds but being commensurable.

Cleopatra, handing the inventory of her valuables to the triumphant Caesar, declares, 'This is the brief: of money, plate, and jewels / I am possess'd of; 'tis exactly valued, / Not petty things admitted'. Here is the total valuation of her liquid assets, or so it appears, until her Treasurer (in what is probably a ploy to reassure Caesar that she has no intention of committing suicide) responds that what she has kept back is 'Enough to purchase what you have made known' (148). Here we have two mighty rulers engaged in drawing up accounts with the precision of **merchants** or **debt**-collectors – albeit Caesar, playing his own game, protests, 'Caesar's no merchant, to make prize with you / Of things that merchants sold' (*ANT* 5.2.138–84). The interesting expression 'make prize' means to '**bargain**' or 'wrangle'.

Values meaning 'equals' arises in *H8*. As the courtiers weigh up the enormous expenditure required of individuals for the treaty celebrated at the Field of the Cloth of Gold, Norfolk sums up their sentiments: 'Grievingly I think / The peace between the French and us not values / The cost that did conclude it' (1.1.87–9). This scene is noteworthy not least because it sets out in great detail the lavish theatricality of the competitive entertainments, the magnitude of financial burdens imposed on participants (some of whom will never recover their financial strength), and the commercial implications of the success or failure of the agreement: 'For France hath flaw'd the league, and hath attach'd / Our merchants' goods at Bordeaux' (1.1.95–6). For these critics, subjecting the diplomatic engagement to cost-benefit analysis demonstrates the folly of the affair.

LLL provides a highly specific case. The King of Navarre explains to the Princess of France the reason for his retention of part of Aquitaine. It is being held in lieu of a debt owed by the French King, but he is eager to release the territory as it is **worth** less than the outstanding debt: 'Yet there remains unpaid / A hundred thousand more, in surety of the which / One part of Aquitaine is bound to us, / Although not valued to the money's worth' (2.1.133–6). In this slightly odd construction 'not valued' means 'not equivalent to'.

A peculiar phrase occurs in *TNK* when the anguished Emilia contemplates the incomparable worth of the combatant-cousins, rivals for her love:

> Were they metamorphos'd
> Both into one – O why? there were no woman
> Worth so compos'd a man! Their single share,
> Their nobleness peculiar to them, gives
> The prejudice of disparity, value's shortness,
> To any lady breathing.
>
> 5.3.84–9

No woman living is equal in value to either man: any woman would fall short when set against one of these men – or would suffer 'value's shortness'. This seemingly awkward, infelicitous phrase, arises, perhaps, from the staccato jolting process of thought precipitated by divided loyalties and consciousness that one of these men is about to die.

This probing of value and evaluation recurs a few lines later when the triumphant Arcite claims his prize but at the price of having killed his cousin: 'Emily, / To buy you I have lost what's dearest to me / Save what is bought, and yet I purchase cheaply, / As I do rate your value' (5.3.111–14). The distasteful nature of the sentiment whereby love of a woman based purely on physical attraction is set against the love and life of the dearest friend is accentuated by the intrusion of the vocabulary of the market-place. Friendship and love have been debased to expose a depleted sensibility.

Given Shakespeare's subtle and wide-ranging application of 'value', it is necessary to make a brief comment on the evolution of the concept in the sphere of economics.

Aristotle introduced a problem that presented subsequent economists with a seemingly intractable obstacle, namely, what is the relationship between **use** value and **exchange** value? For Aristotle an artefact is fashioned to fulfil a purpose. The function it fulfils or the use to which it is put is its 'use value'. Its natural properties constitute its use value. However, Aristotle believed that there was a metaphysical distinction between use value, both in the item's creation and acquisition, and 'exchange value', which is what it could be **traded** for in the market-place. Moreover, the determination of exchange value was in itself problematic as somehow or other the market established relationships, prices, between the multifarious products traded. Heterogeneity gives way to commensurability. The key element here is **money**. Finally, if this question could be answered, what was the nature of the relationship between use value and exchange value?

The Aristotelian ideal is based on an ethical principle, an aspect of which is the concept of 'having enough'. Accumulation and limitless consumption reside outside the Aristotelian orbit. Aristotle was not opposed to development in terms of human invention and ingenuity being employed to generate more use value for the community, but the accumulation of wealth in the form of exchange value, the accumulation of money or exchangeable assets, he saw as spurious wealth. Marx adopted the duality of 'use value' and 'exchange value', a distinction expunged by modern economic theory. It was Marx who adopted the formulaic distinction between pre-capitalist forms C-M-C and the capitalist form M-C-M'. In other words, the pre-capitalist individual brings a commodity to the market and acquires money (M) in order to obtain another commodity (C). The capitalist situation is one where money (M) is brought to the market-place to **purchase** commodities (C) for resale in order to make a profit: (M) becomes (M'). Capitalism is the end-game that Aristotle feared. Paradoxically, Marx praised capitalism for its achievements in the realm of **capital** accumulation because it had wrought the means of lifting the entire population to a level of material comfort: profits transmuted into capital equipment and driven by technological **advance** laid the foundations of a prosperous industrial population – a world beyond the vision of Aristotle. Marx, however, shared Aristotle's goal of the welfare of the community as a whole rather than a system or model designed to increase the wealth of the few at the **expense** of the many. Marx's model makes it explicit that capitalism functions by means of systematic exploitation of the many, not out of malice, but as an inevitable consequence of the system of ownership and control. Marx inherited or chose to adopt the Aristotelian dichotomy of use value and exchange value, while mainstream economics expunged use value or collapsed the two values into exchange value, which can be seen as escaping from a false dilemma or finding a convenient way of eliding an inconvenient problem which was at bottom metaphysical and of no practical import. Whereas Aristotle was exploring a community – whose welfare was paramount – that *contained* a market, by the sixteenth century it was apparent that the market was a great abstract mechanism that dominated social relations and was not merely an aspect of the *polis*. In other words, Aristotle had no conception of the nature of a modern economy. His consideration of economic relations interested him in the ways in which he conceived of the 'good life'. The trajectory of modern economic analysis by contrast, was in the direction of jettisoning value judgements or ethical principles and focusing on the interconnections between economic variables. 'Positive' economics sought to be *value free.* Understanding the operations of this vast impersonal mechanism, the core of which consisted of market relations, was the task economists set themselves. A theory of value eventually came to mean a theory of prices. Aristotle could provide no meaningful guidance to the sixteenth-century world because his judgements were determined by ethical principles antithetical to an economic theatre which he could not have imagined. The embryonic features of market opportunism were totally alien to his conception of the ideal *polis* in which pursuit of 'enough' was governed by ethical principles of 'fairness, mutuality, and common purpose' (Meikle, 153). Adam Smith validated the market and circumvented some of these considerations by proposing that though the *motives* of the participants in the market-place were self-interest and, *wherever possible* collusive and exploitative, the *outcome* for the consumer was benign. Subject to certain caveats, the pursuit of private interest produced public good. Of course, this is not equivalent to Aristotle's notion of public good because Smith is dealing with effective demand or demand backed by money operating within an economic and social structure quite alien to Aristotle's world. As Meikle points out, in 'utilitarian or neo-classsical economics, use value and exchange value are conceptually connected in the notion of utility' (86). This conceptual conflation is neat, concise and effective in removing ethical considerations arising from the Aristotelian duality.

At the heart of modern economic thinking is the concept of the atomized individual entering the market-place and seeking to optimize his position through the marketing of his attributes or assets and the acquisition of money and commodities in quantity and variety that maximizes his perceived benefits. The social economy is an adjunct to the market-place of firms, corporations and individuals. From Aristotle, through such diverse thinkers as Marx, Veblen and J. K. Galbraith, the social economy is central. Galbraith's representation of the issue as public squalor versus private affluence highlights a fundamental feature of the dichotomy. Aristotle's idea of 'having enough' rather than the desire for 'too much' clearly relates to a worldview far removed from the epoch of consumerism.

(C) Value is a word deeply implicated in the spheres of philosophy, metaphysics, economics, sociology and social policy. A thorough exposition of Aristotle's theory of value and the relationship of his commentaries on economics to Marx and modern theory is provided by Meikle, *Aristotle's Economic Thought*. Vital to this question are Egan, *Shakespeare and Marx*; Shell, *Money, Language and Thought*; Halpern, *The Poetics of Primitive Accumulation*; Woodmansee and Osteen, eds, *The New Economic Criticism*; Appadurai, ed., *The Social Life of Things*; Veblen, *The Theory of the Leisure Class*; Galbraith, *The Affluent Society*; Smith, *The Wealth of Nations*; Gill, *Evolution of Modern Economics*; Samuels, Biddle and Davis, eds, *A Companion to the History of Economic Thought*; Simmel, *The Philosophy of Money*; Heinzelman, *The Economics of the Imagination*. Other relevant critical commentaries are: Thorne, *Vision and Rhetoric in Shakespeare*, esp. ch. 5, on *TRO*; Hawkes, *Idols of the Marketplace*, 22–32, 40–2, 118–24, 200–8 has particularly pungent commentary on 'value'; Spencer, 'Taking Excess, Exceeding Account: Aristotle Meets *The Merchant of Venice*' in Woodbridge, ed., *Money and the Age of Shakespeare*; Elton, *Shakespeare's Troilus and Cressida and the Inns of Court Revels*, ch. 6; and Kermode, *Shakespeare's Language*. All are rigorous and explorative. Williams, ' "Time for such a word": verbal echoing in *Macbeth*' in Alexander, ed., *Shakespeare and Language* merits scrutiny. Also see entries on **worth** and **price**.

vendible

(A) Marketable is the clear meaning of the first of the two usages; on the second occasion the word possibly straddles marketable and marriageable.

(B) Parolles, attempting a display of witty insouciance, exclaims against virginity: ' 'Tis a commodity will lose the gloss with lying: the longer kept, the less worth. Off with't while 'tis vendible' (*AWW* 1.1.153–5). Virginity is perceived as a marketable commodity. The implication is that the best opportunity of selling a perishable commodity at a high **price** is while it is fresh. This playful argument is flawed because the loss of virginity before marriage can destroy marriage prospects.

More unsavoury is Gratiano's quip, 'silence is only commendable / In a neat's tongue dried and a maid not vendible' (*MV* 1.1.111–12). Here again is the idea of a woman as a marketable commodity. If she lacks the minimum of attractiveness she cannot find a buyer or husband. Such a woman is not entitled to a voice.

(C) Schalkwyk, *Speech and Performance in Shakespeare's Sonnets and Plays*, ch. 5, Zitner, *All's Well That Ends Well*, Donawerth, *Shakespeare and the Sixteenth-Century Study of Language*, ch. 7, and Alexander and Wells, eds, *Shakespeare and Sexuality*, are all of interest here.

venter (at a), venture, venturous

(A) Venter is an alternative spelling of venture. Impregnating the very fabric of commerce and politics, the distinctive meanings of venture are: cargo;

commercial activity, enterprise or undertaking; daring, courageous or hazardous endeavour; prostitute. The verb signifies to run the risk or dare to act. The adjective venturous intimates adventurous, daring, or even presumptuous behaviour. The phrase 'at a venter' means guessingly or recklessly.

(B) Antonio reassures his friends that his melancholy does not arise from anxiety that his cargoes might be lost at sea: 'My ventures are not in one bottom trusted, / Nor to one place; nor is my whole estate / Upon the fortune of this present year: / Therefore my merchandise makes me not sad' (*MV* 1.1.42–5).

Doll, protesting against Mistress Quickly's assertion that being the 'weaker vessel' she should accept subordination, comments wittily on Falstaff's cargo: 'Can a weak and empty vessel bear such a huge full hogshead? There's a whole merchant's venture of Bordeaux stuff in him, you have not seen a hulk better stuff'd in the hold' (*2H4* 2.4.62–5).

A curious case of ventures as commercial activities arises when Shylock chooses to emphasize the precariousness of Antonio's financial position. Enumerating these activities he concludes 'and other ventures he hath squand'red abroad' (*MV* 1.3.21). Here is the moneylender expressing disdain for something as risky as mercantile activity. Ironically, Antonio's careful spreading of risks evades the narrow view of certitude attaching to the moneylender. When Shylock cites Jacob's method of prospering by opting for the 'parti-color'd lambs', Antonio makes a distinction between divine intervention and calculation in determining the outcome of an enterprise or undertaking: 'This was a venture, sir, that Jacob serv'd for, / A thing not in his power to bring to pass, / But sway'd and fashion'd by the hand of heaven' (1.3.88–93).

A coalescing of the commercial and political occurs in *JC*. Brutus, in pressing the case to fight at Philippi, rather than holding their ground as Cassius proposes, engages in a commercial metaphor:

> There is a tide in the affairs of men,
> Which taken at the flood, leads on to fortune;
> Omitted, all the voyage of their life
> Is bound in shallows and in miseries.
> On such a full sea are we now afloat,
> And we must take the current when it serves,
> Or lose our ventures.
>
> 4.3.218–24

Every one of Brutus' decisions is wrong. He seems particularly inept in his employment of imagery (as, for example, his insistence that the assassination of Caesar be conducted with decorum: 'Let's carve him as a dish fit for the gods, / Not hew him as a carcass fit for hounds' (2.1.173–4)). What is unusual here is his choice of commercial imagery, 'ventures' signifying merchandise risked in **trade**. The political 'ventures' involve the conspiracy, assassination and subsequent creation of an army to face Antony and Octavius. This high-minded character strays inadvertently into a sphere that dilutes or even contaminates the purity of his political endeavours.

Iachimo in his attempted seduction of Imogen claims that her husband, Posthumus, diverts himself with prostitutes: 'with diseas'd ventures / That play with all infirmities for gold' (*CYM* 1.6.123–4).

The idea of a risky enterprise is best expressed by Lord Bardolph as he rebukes Northumberland for indulging his grief at the loss of his son, Hotspur:

> We all that are engaged to this loss
> Knew that we ventured on such dangerous seas
> That if we wrought out life 'twas ten to one,
> And yet we ventur'd for the gain propos'd,
> Chok'd the respect of likely peril fear'd,
> And since we are o'erset, venture again.
>
> *2H4* 1.1.180–5

The daring and precarious nature of the action is emphasized by this word being used three times in a short speech.

The word occurs twice within a few lines in *TNK*. Arcite decides to disguise himself in order to enter the tournament, despite the risk involved: 'I'll venture, / And in some poor disguise be there' (2.3.78–9). Take a risk is the meaning here. When, however, the Jailer's daughter contemplates freeing Palemon from prison, she reflects, 'Say I ventur'd / To set him free? What says the law then?' (2.4.30–1), 'ventur'd' could mean 'attempted' or 'dared', with the latter seeming more likely.

Heroic daring is intimated by Rosse when proclaiming to Macbeth the King's response to 'Thy personal venture in the rebels' fight' (*MAC* 1.3.91). In a deeply moving and insightful soliloquy Cardinal Wolsey reflects on his sudden fall from greatness. In a key simile he sees his life as a daring or risky enterprise:

> I have ventur'd,
> Like little wanton boys that swim on bladders,
> This many summers in a sea of glory,
> But far beyond my depth. My high-blown pride
> At length broke under me, and now has left me,
> Weary and old with service, to the mercy
> Of a rude stream that must forever hide me.
>
> *H8* 3.2.358–64

Here is Wolsey's recognition that success in an ambitious political quest produces complacency so that the perilous nature of manoeuvres becomes apparent only in the face of catastrophe. It is worth setting this example alongside an earlier usage in the play. Queen Katherine, in attempting to expose Wolsey's surreptitious and burdensome taxes, presses her case to the King with the words: 'I am much too venturous / In tempting of your patience; but am bold'ned / Under your promis'd pardon' (1.2.54–6). 'Venturous' seems to possess not only the sense of 'daring' but also of 'being presumptuous', something detectable in Wolsey's rueful response to his fall.

Cynically, Suffolk advises the murderers of Gloucester 'I will reward you for this venturous deed' (*2H6* 3.2.9).

As Northumberland and Lord Bardolph attempt to reconcile the contradictory information about the outcome of the Battle of Shrewsbury, the latter states that the horseman who **conveyed** bad news spoke thoughtlessly, guessingly or recklessly: a 'hilding fellow' who 'spoke at a venter' [venture] (*2H4* 1.1.57–9).

(C) See Rudnytsky, 'Henry VIII and the deconstruction of history' in Alexander, ed., *Shakespeare and Politics*; Salmon, 'Elizabethan colloquial English in the Falstaff plays' in Salmon and Burness, eds, *A Reader in the Language of Shakespearean Drama*. Vital here for a sense of commercial ventures are Brenner, *Merchants and Revolution*; and Braudel, *Civilisation and Capitalism*.

victual, victualler

(A) The noun (usually plural) means provisions; the verb, to supply with food; a vict'ler is an inn-keeper.

(B) Preparing to besiege Calais, Edward III commands 'That neither victuals nor supply of men / May come to succour this accursed town' (*E3* 4.2.4–5).

Joan Pucelle (or Puzel) undertakes the opposite action as she breaks off her fight with Talbot, 'I must go victual Orleans forthwith' (*1H6* 1.5.14).

Responding to Falstaff's threat of damnation 'for suffering flesh to be eaten in thy house, contrary to the law', the Hostess of the tavern responds, 'All vict'lers do so. What's a joint of mutton or two in a whole Lent?' (*2H4* 2.4.344–7).

(C) For a superb compendium of the social, religious, political and family structures and patterns of behaviour consult Aughterson, ed., *The English Renaissance*. A fascinating culinary exploration is provided by Appelbaum, *Aguecheek's Beef*. Also of interest here is Ruiter, *Shakespeare's Festive History*.

virtue, virtuous, virtuously

(A) The range of meanings and nuances attaching to the noun, adjective and adverb is striking, several of them possessing political or economic significance. The noun encompasses: attribute, quality; power, authority, jurisdiction; efficacy, property, capability; integrity or personal **worth**; true **value** or excellence; principle; courage; essence; goodness, benevolence; chastity or sexual purity; selfhood; forgiveness, mercy. The adjective includes powerful or efficacious; displaying admirable qualities, praiseworthy; fecund or beneficial; growing out of virtuous actions, well justified. The adverb means steadfastly.

(B) Cominius, praising Coriolanus' deeds, specifies the most highly valued attribute of a Roman: 'It is held / That valor is the chiefest virtue' (*COR* 2.2.83–4). Coriolanus employs the same usage with reference to the **plebeians**, but for him their essential virtue or quality is a vice: 'Your virtue is / To make him worthy whose offence subdues him, / And curse that justice did it' (1.1.174–6). For the eponymous hero the characteristic attribute of the common people is to misplace their admiration, directing it towards a wrongdoer and denouncing the justice that brings him to book.

In denying him access to Coriolanus, the guard devalues the quality of Menenius' name: 'The virtue of your name / Is not here passable' (*COR* 5.2.12–13). His name possesses no power or authority; it is not legal tender, but a mere **counterfeit** coin.

Responding to Angelo's corrupt proposition, Isabella highlights the nature of his power or authority: 'I know your virtue hath a license in't' (*MM* 2.4.145).

As the contending parties encounter each other at Gaultree forest, Hastings asks whether Prince John has the jurisdiction or delegated authority for a peace agreement: 'In very ample virtue of his father' (*2H4* 4.1.161).

As King John experiences the agonies of his death throes, his son, Prince Henry, wishes his tears possessed the power or efficacy to ameliorate the suffering: 'O that there were some virtue in my tears, / That might relieve you!' (*JN* 5.7.44–5).

Likewise, the Friar talks of the divers powers and efficacious properties of plants: 'Many for many virtues excellent' (*ROM* 2.3.13).

Artemidorus, having discovered the conspiracy against Julius Caesar, is grieved that integrity or personal worth inevitably falls victim to envious **rivalry**: 'My heart laments that virtue cannot live / Out of the teeth of emulation' (*JC* 2.3.13–14).

In the play most deeply engaged with the issue of personal **worth, value** or moral centre, Ulysses warns Achilles, 'Let not virtue seek / Remuneration for the thing it was'. Even the purity of selfhood is subject to 'envious and calumniating Time' (*TRO* 3.3.169–74).

Agamemnon, rationalizing the Greeks' failure to defeat the Trojans after seven years of siege, claims that it is a test arranged by the gods to discover or bring out the true worth or intrinsic excellence in men of genuine worth: 'Distinction, with a broad and powerful fan, / Puffing at all, winnows the light away, / And what hath mass or matter, by itself / Lies rich in virtue and unmingled' (1.3.27–30).

Paris seems to mean 'principle', when responding to Diomed's disparagement of Helen: 'But we in silence hold this virtue well, / We'll not commend what we intend to sell' (4.1.78–9).

Falstaff, exclaiming against the desertion of Hal and Poins at Gad's Hill, bewails the absence of courage: 'Is there no virtue extant?' (*1H4* 2.4.118–19).

Responding to Ariel's feeling of compassion for his enemies, Prospero acknowledges the value of forgiveness: 'The rarer action is / In virtue than in vengeance' (*TMP* 5.1.27–8).

When Alcibiades pleads for the life of his condemned colleague he maintains that 'pity is the virtue of the law' (*TIM* 3.5.8), meaning 'essence'.

Servilius, appealing for funds on behalf of his master, Timon, assures Lucius that his request is justifiable or honourable: 'If his occasion were not virtuous, / I should not urge it half so faithfully' (3.2.40–1).

Lafew reassures Bertram that he will be received by the King with kindness or benevolence on his arrival at court: 'He that so generally is at all times good must of necessity hold his virtue to you, whose worthiness would stir it up where it wanted rather than lack it where there is such abundance' (*AWW* 1.1.7–10).

In his denunciation of practitioners of vices in the storm scene, Lear includes, 'thou simular [dissembler] of virtue / That art incestuous!' (*LR* 3.2.54–5). 'Integrity' or 'honesty' is the possible meaning here but the more specific suggestion of 'chastity' or 'sexual purity' is more likely.

Duke Frederick justifies the banishment of his niece Rosalind on the grounds that his daughter will be the beneficiary of this action: 'And thou wilt show more bright and seem more virtuous / When she is gone' (*AYL* 1.3.81–2). More 'praiseworthy' or 'admirable' appears to be the required meaning here.

Angelo, having been overcome by sexual desire consequent upon his first encounter with the novice, Isabella, expresses his bewilderment – which is such that he wonders who is to blame: 'Not she; nor doth she tempt; but it is I / That, lying by the violet in the sun, / Do as the carrion does, not as the flow'r, / Corrupt with virtuous season' (*MM* 2.2.164–7). The last phrase suggests the season conducive to growth and generation. Paradoxically, the season conducive to beneficial growth is also favourable to corruption or putrefaction.

The adverb is hypocritically employed by the First Lord when expressing his gratitude for Timon's largesse: 'We are so virtuously bound' (*TIM* 1.2.226). He means steadfastly or strongly attached to his benefactor.

(C) For virtue in the classical world see Brower, *Hero and Saint*; Martindale and Taylor, eds, *Shakespeare and the Classics*; Miola, *Shakespeare and Classical Tragedy*; Bulman, *The Heroic Idiom of Shakespearean Tragedy*. See also Bull, ed., *Machievelli, The Prince*, Introduction, esp. 24–5; Danson, ed., *On King Lear*, and Elton, *'King Lear' and the Gods*. Kermode, ed., *The Tempest*, Arden 2, Introduction, esp. lii–liv is of particular interest here.

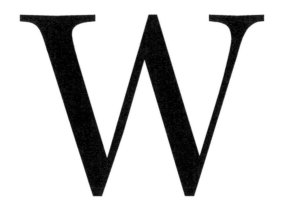

wage

(A) The noun, singular or plural, indicates payment made, usually at regular intervals, in return for work undertaken. In addition to the obvious meaning to pay or **recompense**, the verb also has the following applications: to risk or **venture** upon; hazard or stake; to equal or measure up to; to struggle against.

(B) Aufidius, having harboured the exiled Roman and made him coequal, complains that Coriolanus 'wag'd me with his countenance as if / I had been mercenary' (*COR* 5.6.39–40). This is a peculiar example of paid or rewarded: the currency is a mere look of approval in a master–servant relationship. Indignation at Coriolanus' ingratitude – whether the charge be true or false – is expressed with a sourness that is compelling.

A very different note is struck by Celia, the new landowner, who jauntily promises the shepherd 'And we will mend thy wages' (*AYL* 2.4.94).

The First Senator expresses disbelief that the Turks would risk or venture to capture Rhodes rather than Cypress, 'Neglecting an attempt of ease and gain / To wake and wage a danger profitless' (*OTH* 1.3.29–30).

Posthumus, having been lured into a gamble on Imogen's virtue, declines to stake or hazard his ring, but proposes, 'I will wage against your gold, gold to it' (*CYM* 1.4.132).

Pander, making the case for retirement from brothel-keeping, admits that there is still **profit** in it, but complains that the returns are not proportionate to the risks: 'the commodity wages not with the danger' (*PER* 4.2.31).

Maecenas, responding to the death of Antony declares, 'His taints and honors / Wag'd equal with him'. This was a man whose virtues and vices battled against or vied with one another for supremacy. This supremely balanced and economical judgement contrasts with Agrippa's rather more expansive eulogy, 'A rarer spirit never / Did steer humanity; but you gods will give us / Some faults to make us men' (*ANT* 5.1.30–3). This in turn provides the platform for

Caesar's elaborate encomium – though abandoned in midstream by more urgent business.

Lear rejects the suggestion that he returns to the protection of Goneril, choosing instead to contend with or do battle against the elements: 'I abjure all roofs, and choose / To wage against the enmity o'th'air' (*LR* 2.4.208–9).

(C) Dollimore, *Radical Tragedy*, is germane to the issues in *COR*, *ANT* and *LR*. Relevant, too, are the contributions of Serpieri, 'The breakdown of medieval hierarchy in *King Lear*', Evans, 'Albion's confusion', and Eagleton, 'Value: *King Lear, Timon of Athens* and *Antony and Cleopatra*', all in Drakakis, ed., *Shakespearean Tragedy*.

weal, wealsman

(A) The primary meaning of weal is state or **commonwealth**; wealsman, therefore, is a servant of the commonwealth or someone who is devoted to the well-being of the state. The secondary meaning of weal is well-being, welfare.

(B) Henry VI, attempting to reconcile Gloucester and Winchester, emphasizes their responsibility as 'The special watchmen of our English weal' (*1H6* 3.1.66). Responding to Coriolanus' advocacy of return to the *status quo ante* and the removal of the tribuneship, Sicinius denounces him as 'a traitorous innovator, / A foe to th'public weal' (*COR* 3.1.174–5). This particular public servant and his fellow tribune Brutus have already been disparaged by Menenius, who refers to them as 'two such wealsmen as you are' (2.1.54). It is unsurprising that the only application of the term 'wealsmen' occurs in *COR*, because the play is deeply engaged with the nature of the state and its constitution. The sense of 'public welfare' also emerges in this play. Having delivered his famous fable of the belly, thereby quelling the riotous **plebeians**, Menenius tries to drive home his argument by attributing the provision of public welfare exclusively to the patricians: 'digest things rightly / Touching the weal a'th'common, you shall find / No public benefit which you receive / But it proceeds or comes from them to you, / And no way from yourselves' (1.1.150–4). This wily **politician** prevails, though during a later outburst the revolutionary utterance reveals the continuing tensions: 'The people are the city' (3.1.199).

Despite being mortally wounded, Bedford expresses to Talbot his wish to keep the field, and 'be partner of your weal or woe' (*1H6* 3.2.92). Intriguingly, this construction, with its sense of the gulf between well-being and suffering, occurs with particular force in the world of love. Juliet, agitated by the Nurse's exclamations, demands concise and immediate news of Romeo: 'Brief sounds determine my weal or woe' (*ROM* 3.2.51). Similarly, Venus wavers between fear that Adonis has been killed by the boar and hope that he has survived the encounter:

> O hard-believing love, how strange it seems!
> Not to believe, and yet too credulous:
> Thy weal and woe are both of them extremes;
> Despair and hope makes thee ridiculous:

The one doth flatter thee in thoughts unlikely,
In likely thoughts the other kills thee quickly.
VEN 985–90

These last two examples drawn from the sphere of love intensify awareness of the magnitude of the conceptual duality inherent in Bedford's expression: the sense of a boundary where one side is immense relief and joy; the other where all engulfing grief resides.

(C) See Hadfield, *Shakespeare and Republicanism*; Cantor, *Shakespeare's Rome*; Hattaway, ed., *Shakespeare's History Plays*; Smallwood, ed., *Players of Shakespeare 6: Essays in the Performance of Shakespeare's History Plays*; Cheney, ed., *Shakespeare's Poetry*; Alexander and Wells, eds, *Shakespeare and Sexuality*; Andrews, ed., *Romeo and Juliet: Critical Essays*.

wealth

(A) Used frequently to indicate well-being or personal welfare, the most general application of the word is to material resources or financial assets, either in terms of an entire portfolio or as cash. 'Blood' or social status is another form of wealth.

(B) Considering the impending military encounter between Norway and Poland over a worthless piece of land, Hamlet comments, 'This is th' imposthume of much wealth and peace' (*HAM* 4.4.27). He means, here, a feeling of comfort and well-being rather than personal riches. Likewise, Antonio, offering himself as guarantor for Bassanio keeping safe Portia's ring, exclaims: 'I once did lend my body for his wealth' (*MV* 5.1.249). It is Bassanio's welfare he is alluding to rather than **money**.

Rationalizing the failure of Northumberland to arrive with his force at the Battle of Shrewsbury, Hotspur exclaims: 'Were it good / To set the exact wealth of all our states / All at one cast?' (*1H4* 4.1.45–7). Here 'wealth' signifies 'total resources'. Likewise when Henry VIII has inspected Wolsey's inventory he refers to all his assets: 'What piles of wealth hath he accumulated / To his own portion!' (*H8* 3.2.107–8). As Celia prepares to escape from the court she draws a distinction between valuables and wealth as cash: 'Let's away, / And get our jewels and our wealth together' (*AYL* 1.3.133–4).

Bassanio provides an interesting expression when he reminds Portia that he had confessed his impoverishment: 'I freely told you all the wealth I had / Ran in my veins: I was a gentleman' (*MV* 3.2.254–5). High social standing is a genuine form of wealth – and a marketable asset. A distinction between material wealth and social standing also occurs in *AWW*. The King is indignant at Bertram's rejection of Helena – 'A poor physician's daughter my wife! Disdain / Rather corrupt me ever!' – completing his remarkable speech on social equality with the words: 'Virtue and she / Is her own dower; honor and wealth from me' (2.3.115–44). Not only can the King make her wealthy but he can bestow honour on her: becoming noble without being of noble birth.

There are dramatic cases of people stripped of their wealth. Timon becomes **bankrupt**; Shylock retains some of his assets only by the benevolence of the Duke;

Cordelia is stripped of her third of the kingdom and the goodwill of her father. Withdrawing her dowry, his love and protection, Lear announces to Burgundy: 'I tell you all her wealth' (*LR* 1.1.208).

(C) For an exploration of the various manifestations of wealth and attitudes towards possessions see Jardine, *Worldly Goods*, and Halpern, *The Poetics of Primitive Accumulation*. Conditions experienced by the lower echelons of society are summarized by Pallister, *The Age of Elizabeth*, ch. 4; Carroll, *Fat King, Lean Beggar*, Warley, *Sonnet Sequences and Social Distinction in Renaissance England*; Woodbridge, *Vagrancy, Homelessness, and English Renaissance Literature*.

working-day, workyday

(A) These terms simply mean workaday, mundane, the opposite of holiday. Implicit in working-day is the idea of efficient, down-to-earth, unelaborated endeavour. Workyday suggests commonplace, run of the mill, undistinguished.

(B) When Rosaline sighs to Celia, 'O, how full of briars is this working-day world!' (*AYL* 1.3.12) she is stressing the risk of complications that arise even in the daily round – because she has fallen in love. Celia plays off her term with its antithesis: 'They are but burs, cousin, thrown upon thee in holiday foolery' (1.3.13–14).

Beatrice rejects Don Pedro's (possibly teasing) proposal of marriage, with the playful riposte: 'No, my lord, unless I might have another for working-days. Your Grace is too costly to wear every day' (*ADO* 2.1.327–9).

Henry V employs the term to stress the practical, efficient, undecorated nature of his army: 'For that I have laid by my majesty, / And plodded like a man for working-days' (*H5* 1.2.276–7). This is a sentiment he reiterates later when rejecting the French offer of ransom and reparations: 'We are but warriors for the working-day; / Our gayness and our gilt are all besmirch'd / With rainy marching in the painful field' (4.3.109–11). Here Henry makes a virtue of necessity, contrasting his unglamorous but tried and trusty soldiers with adversaries more colourful than potent.

In her banter with Iras, Charmian instructs the Soothsayer, 'tell her but a worky-day fortune' (*ANT* 1.2.54).

(C) Various aspects of this topic are explored in Wynne-Davies, ed., *Much Ado About Nothing* and *The Taming of the Shrew*; Barber, *Shakespeare's Festive Comedy*; Kamps, ed., *Materialist Shakespeare*; Brennan, *Henry V*; McAlindon, *Shakespeare Minus 'Theory'*; Dollimore and Sinfield, eds, *Political Shakespeare*; Kinney, ed., *A Companion to Renaissance Drama*. The conflicts between the mundane and the realms of imagination, fortune, destiny, prediction, sexuality and fertility articulated in the dialogue between Charmian and the Soothsayer are explored in Deats, ed., *Antony and Cleopatra*; McAlindon, *Shakespeare's Tragic Cosmos*; Adelman, *The Common Liar*; Kahn, *Roman Shakespeare*.

working-house

(A) The sole use is metaphorical, relating to the mind, which is perceived as analogous to a workshop.

(B) The Chorus in *H5* encourages the audience to relocate from France to England, picturing the nature of the triumphant monarch: 'But now behold, / In the quick forge and working-house of thought, / How London doth pour out her citizens!' (Cho 5 22–4).

(C) For a discussion of *Henry V* in the context of Shakespeare's England see Shapiro, *1599*, ch. 5 (n.b. 110 for comments on language). See also Hapgood, 'Shakespeare's thematic modes of speech: *Richard II* to *Henry V*' in Alexander, ed., *Shakespeare and Language*; Mason, '*Henry V*: "the quick forge and working house of thought" ' in Hattaway, ed., *Shakespeare's History Plays*.

workman, workmanly, workmanship
(A) The singular form 'workman' signifies craftsman rather than labourer, embracing a range of occupations from cobbler to painter or artist. Despite the generally dismissive attitude towards common workmen, the concept of workmanship embodies the idea of skilful application, something finding clear expression in the term 'workmanly', but also attaching to 'workman' when referring to human endeavour such as soldiership. Paradoxically, there is a genuine respect and admiration for any task well executed, fine workmanship, especially in an elevated activity, even though workmen are not highly regarded. 'Workmanship' signifies artistry applying to both the master-craftsman and nature.
(B) When the workmen are interrogated by the tribunes about the nature of their '**trade**', the truculent cobbler is far more voluble than his neighbour the carpenter, explaining, 'Truly, sir, in respect of a fine workman, I am but, as you would say, a cobbler' (*JC* 1.1.10–11). This trade, of course, allows a pun on cobbler as 'botcher', thereby enabling this 'mender of bad soles' to lead his social superior a verbal dance.

The sense of skill involved in the term is apparent in Antony's boast to Cleopatra about his impending performance in soldiership: 'O love, / That thou couldst see my wars to-day, and knew'st / The royal occupation, thou shouldst see / A workman in't' (*ANT* 4.4.15–18).

Having overheard the painter reveal the depth of his cynicism Timon expresses his disdain in an aside: 'Excellent workman! thou canst not paint a man / So bad as is thyself' (*TIM* 5.1.31–2).

Seeking to turn the world upside-down, two of Cade's rebels use the term to encompass working men, whatever their skill:

Bevis:	O miserable age! virtue is not regarded in handicrafts-men.
Holland:	The nobility think scorn to go in leather aprons.
Bevis:	Nay more, the King's Council are no good workmen.
Holland:	True; and yet it is said, labor in thy vocation; which is as much to say as, let the magistrates be laboring men; and therefore should we be magistrates.
Bevis:	Thou hast hit it; for there's no better sign of a brave mind than a hard hand.

2H6 4.2.10–20

This critique engages with the idea of all activity being judged for competence, workmanship, and the dignity or indignity attaching to the 'leather apron', emblem of the skilled workman, down to the intrinsic merit of the 'hard hand', of the labourer. Here is a discourse designed to shake out the complacency attaching to the traditional hierarchy.

Timon produces an unusual example when exposing the villainy of the bandits. He commences his exposition on the ubiquity of theft: 'Like workmen, I'll example you with thievery' (*TIM* 4.3.435). He will instruct them as all **practitioners** are taught in the principles of their craft.

The sole application of workmanly is in *SHR*. A servant describes a picture of Daphne and Apollo that is so skilfully wrought 'that one shall swear she bleeds, / And at that sight shall sad Apollo weep, / So workmanly the blood and tears are drawn' (Induction 2.58–60).

Iachimo takes peculiar delight describing Imogen's bedchamber, concluding with admiration of the precious materials incorporated in a work of art: 'A piece of work / So bravely done, so rich, that it did strive / In workmanship and value, which I wonder'd / Could be so rarely and exactly wrought, / Since the true life on't was –' (*CYM* 2.4.72–6). Here is workmanship of the highest order. See entry on **value**.

Two applications occur in *VEN*, where there is an expression of awe for Nature's power, ' "the curious workmanship of Nature" ' (734), and a celebration of the artist's emulative skill: 'Look when a painter would surpass the life / In limning out a well-proportioned steed, / His art with nature's workmanship at strife, / As if the dead the living should exceed' (289–92). Hence workmanship deals with the highest powers of the skilled craftsman and of nature. There is nothing commonplace attaching to this term, which is deeply situated in the realm of aesthetics.

(C) See entry on **occupation**. Braudel, *Civilisation and Capitalism*, Pallister, *The Age of Elizabeth*, Mokyer, *The Lever of Riches*, Aughterson, ed., *The English Renaissance*, and Engle, *Shakespearean Pragmatism*, are all informative on this topic. Of particular interest in the exploration of the relationship between narrative, the verbal and pictorial, are Enterline, *The Rhetoric of the Body*; Laroque, 'Rare Italian master(s)' in Marapodi, ed., *Shakespeare, Italy and Intertextuality*; Thorne, *Vision and Rhetoric in Shakespeare*; Hammill, *Sexuality and Form*.

worth

(A) A deceptive word that requires detailed exploration to tease out the socio-political hinterland implicit in each application. Not only does it possess highly specific meanings that are economic, political, social or personal, but it has the more general colloquial application of 'What is that worth?' This usage can carry the suggestion of **market value** – 'What could I get in exchange for this?' – or 'To what use could I put this?' However loosely formed, the inquiry essentially relates to the relative or **exchange** value of the object. Secondly, there is the meaning of worth as moral value, merit or human excellence. Thirdly, the term is applied to personal **wealth** – a concept familiar today and easily defined as the sum total of a person's assets minus liabilities. The fourth application pertains to social status or standing. A fifth meaning relates to the assertion of rights or authority – to demand one's fill or full ration. There is the rare but potentially confusing sixth meaning of the verb, 'happen to' or 'fall on'. Finally, the adjective means deserving or meriting.

(B) When using 'worth' in the sense of 'relative value' there are many examples. These range from comparing the value of a person, or thing, in terms of another, to the market value of virginity, to the price of ewes and the value of rich cargoes. 'Worth' meaning '**price**' or 'financial equivalence' is clearly illustrated by Silence's comment, that, 'a score of good ewes may be worth ten pounds' (*2H4* 3.2.50–1). Parolles cynically points out that virginity is highly prized in a young woman but that its value diminishes with increasing age: ' 'Tis a commodity will lose the gloss with lying: the longer kept, the less worth' (*AWW* 1.1.153–4). Most commodities lose value as they become stale by being kept in store ('lying') too long; with the loss of youth the esteem with which virginity is held indubitably diminishes; gradually at first, then steeply. Social and monetary evaluations converge in a culture where young women are perceived as marketable objects. Even in a very sophisticated society such as that portrayed in the novels of Jane Austen there is a marriage market where women are carefully evaluated in accordance with their wealth (dowry), social standing and beauty, the weighting attaching to each of these variables being dependent on the requirements and circumstances of the suitor. Parolles' witty, cynical comment contains within it an essay on the socio-economics of sex (and age). Moreover, he provides a richly suggestive subtext by intimating that sexual engagement is the means of rational increase: 'Within the year it will make itself two, which is goodly increase, and the principal itself not much the worse' (1.1.147–9) – an argument for procreation analogous to the function of moneylending and the achievement of '**interest**'.

Salerio tells Antonio that he too would be in low spirits if his wealth were subject to the hazards of the sea. A richly furnished ship of enormous value might be transformed within minutes by 'dangerous rocks' into something worthless: 'Which touching but my gentle vessel's side / Would scatter all her spices on the stream, / Enrobe the roaring waters with my silks, / And in a word, but even now worth this, / And now worth nothing?' (*MV* 1.1.32–6). Here is a vivid representation as valuable commodities momentarily display themselves before disappearing under the sea. At the same moment a seemingly prosperous **merchant** is reduced to a man of little worth. A shrewd merchant like Antonio diversifies so that the statistical probability of all his **ventures** failing at once is remote. Implicit is the concept of spreading risks. Rates of return on each cargo would be sufficiently high to compensate for occasional disasters. Something else emerges from this example: the wealthy Antonio is so biased towards **profit** maximization that he is prepared to operate with a low cash reserve. In modern parlance he experiences a cash-flow problem precipitated by a high ratio of **investment** to total assets. His behaviour is perfectly rational in economic terms, but also points up the need for moneylenders like Shylock who must step into the breach. The availability of moneylending enables **traders** to maximize their economic activity. In this economic model financiers like Shylock play a key role in liberating merchant ventures and maximizing trade and profits. Indeed, an expansion of moneylenders would stimulate economic activity by pushing down interest rates through competition.

When, in *1H4*, the Hostess denounces Falstaff for claiming that the Prince owed him a thousand pounds, the old rogue quickly responds: 'A thousand pound, Hal? a million, thy love is worth a million; thou owest me thy love' (3.3.136–7). Falstaff's wit transforms a slander into a declaration of esteem, extolling the true worth of the Prince's love – something that is of infinite value.

Menenius, chastizing the manipulative tribunes, effectively places them on a weighing scale to compare their relative value or worth in terms of the Roman hero: 'When you speak best unto the purpose, it is not worth the wagging of your beards, and your beards deserve not so honorable a grave as to stuff a botcher's cushion, or to be entomb'd in an ass's pack-saddle. Yet you must be saying Martius is proud; who, in a cheap estimation, is worth all your predecessors since Deucalion, though peradventure some of the best of 'em were hereditary hangmen' (*COR* 2.1.86–93). Menenius demonstrates his mental acuity and polemical skill, because this comparison, for all its rancorous tone, is about relative *social worth* or value to Rome.

Human excellence or intrinsic value finds widespread expression in the plays and sonnets. The Friar, when proposing to pretend that Hero is dead, makes a profound statement about human nature which could be taken as an epigraph for Shakespeare's Romances: 'That what we have we prize not to the worth / Whiles we enjoy it, but being lack'd and lost, / Why then we rack the value; then we find / The virtue that possession would not show us / Whiles it was ours' (*ADO* 4.1.218–22). What is possessed is taken for granted – rather than being esteemed for its true worth.

Conceptions of personal integrity and public standing find expression in the Duke's feigned defence of Angelo as a man and public servant. Seeming to dismiss Isabella's complaints against the guilty deputy, the Duke exclaims: 'think'st thou thy oaths, / Though they would swear down each particular saint, / Were testimonies against his worth and credit / That's seal'd in approbation?' (*MM* 5.1.242–5). 'Worth' here is 'personal integrity'; '**credit**' is the 'respect with which he is held consequent on the performance of his duties'.

Cordelia and Sebastian in *LR* and *TN*, respectively, provide good examples of worth as personal wealth. The distressed Cordelia contemplating Lear's madness expresses a willingness to part with all her material wealth to anyone who can restore her father's sanity: 'What can man's wisdom / In the restoring his bereaved sense? / He that helps him take all my outward worth' (4.4.8–10).

Sebastian expressing gratitude to the man who has been lavish with his aid and friendship regrets that he lacks the financial wherewithal to **recompense** his friend:

> My kind Antonio,
> I can no other answer make but thanks,
> And thanks; and ever oft good turns
> Are shuffled off with such uncurrent pay;
> But were my worth as is my conscience firm,
> You should find better dealing.
>
> 3.3.13–18

When, towards the close of *1H6*, Lucy is confronted with the bodies of the English hero Talbot and his son, he says to the French, 'Give me their bodies, that I may bear them hence / And give them burial as beseems their worth' (4.7.85–6). Evidently, Lucy is conscious of the dead hero's *social standing* whose long list of titles he has just enumerated. It is inevitable, however, that the audience, having witnessed Talbot's courage and leadership and young John's bravery in his first battle, will feel another pull attaching to the term. Here are warriors of true mettle or worth: effectively irreplaceable.

Leontes, welcoming the young Prince Florizel and the apparently low-born Perdita, regrets that she, 'is not so rich in worth as beauty' (*WT* 5.1.214). Here 'worth' means 'breeding', 'social status'.

A marriage of personal qualities and social status occurs in *TGV*. Valentine, responding to the Duke's inquiry about Don Antonio, gives his warranty for the man's personal qualities and social standing: 'I know the gentleman / To be of worth and worthy estimation, / And not without desert so well reputed' (2.4.55–7). Though rather inflated this is Valentine's conception of courtly discourse.

A peculiar case is Mark Antony's opening address to the crowd following Brutus' oration. He begins by stressing his absence of position – 'worth' – or persuasive gifts before then producing one of the most telling displays of the power of rhetoric in Shakespeare. The man who at this point claims that he has no standing, goes on to become one of the 'triple pillars of the world'. Even before attaining that height his manipulative self-deprecation is breathtaking in its audacity, but completely successful in gaining the enthusiastic support of his audience:

> I come not, friends, to steal away your hearts.
> I am no orator, as Brutus is;
> But (as you know me all) a plain blunt man
> That love my friend, and that they know full well
> That gave me public leave to speak of him.
> For I have neither wit, nor words, nor worth,
> Action, nor utterance, nor the power of speech
> To stir men's blood; I only speak right on.
>
> *JC* 3.2.216–23

His lack of 'worth' or social standing might seem wholly implausible. The suggestion is that Antony is only a soldier, powerless and therefore no threat; a suppliant seeking the goodwill of the common people towards their former leader and benefactor, Julius Caesar.

'Worth' as an adjective to mean 'meriting' or 'worthy of' in *H8* is problematic. The difficulty arises more from the verbal structure of the speech than from any peculiar application of the word. The King, having inadvertently discovered Cardinal Wolsey's inventory of possessions, casts doubt on the balance between the cleric's spiritual and material concerns, implying that the former seem 'not worth' or not to merit his serious consideration:

> If we did think
> His contemplation were above the earth,
> And fix'd on spiritual object, he should still
> Dwell in his musings, but I am afraid
> His thinkings are below the moon, not worth
> His serious considering.
>
> 3.2.130–5

It is the spiritual matters that the King feels Wolsey considers 'not worth' or not deserving of his deep musings – the opposite of what should be the case.

The sense of worth as a full or over-full share is brought out sharply when the calculating tribunes seek to provoke Coriolanus into an outburst that will be politically disastrous to him. Brutus' scheme is based on Coriolanus' history of laying down the law or having his own way:

> Put him to choler straight, he hath been us'd
> Ever to conquer, and to have his worth
> Of contradiction. Being once chaf'd, he cannot
> Be rein'd again to temperance; then he speaks
> What's in his heart, and that is there which looks
> With us to break his neck.
>
> *COR* 3.3.25–30

'Worth' is evidently 'full quantity', demanding the last iota of attention or sway in any dispute.

A problematic application occurs in *TNK*. Emilia is deeply distressed that her beauty has provoked a deadly rivalry between Palamon and Arcite that has culminated in Theseus' decision to execute them. She begs for compassion towards the young men on the grounds that her name will be irrevocably tarnished if they die for loving her. Indeed, everyone will 'cry woe worth me' or call down curses on her:

> O Duke Theseus,
> The goodly mothers that have groan'd for these,
> And all the longing maids that ever lov'd,
> If your vow stand, shall curse me and my beauty,

And in their funeral songs for these two cousins
Despise my cruelty, and cry woe worth me,
Till I am nothing but the scorn of women.

3.6.244–50

The foregoing distinctions are mainly straightforward. However, Shakespeare was singularly engaged with probing the difficult aspects of worth. Here there is room for only the briefest commentary, but a few pointers will aid the reader in approaching specialist discussions. This is especially so in the exploration of worth and value in *TRO*, a play haunted by these concepts. This play, more than any other, provokes the question of what we mean by intrinsic worth. In Achilles case it is his killing capacity that is esteemed; his personal attributes are meagre, but irrelevant. During the course of the Greek leadership's analysis of their continued failure to defeat Troy, Nestor sets out the argument that adversity is the test of true merit or intrinsic value. Arguing by analogy he declares that both flimsy and stout ships look equally impressive on a calm sea; it takes a tempest to distinguish one from the other:

> Where's then the saucy boat
> Whose weak untimber'd sides but even now
> Corrivall'd greatness? Either to harbour fled,
> Or made a toast for Neptune. Even so
> Doth valor's show and valor's worth divide
> In storms of fortune;

1.3.42–7

Aeneas, having praised the Trojans, draws back a little on the principle that: 'The worthiness of praise distains his worth, / If that the prais'd himself bring the praise forth' (1.3.241–2). No matter how accurately represented, the intrinsic merit attaching to an individual or group loses something of its gloss when self-praise is involved. Ulysses, manoeuvring to draw Achilles into action, points to a paradox: a person of genuine merit may be overlooked while someone almost worthless is rated highly: 'Nature, what things there are / Most abject in regard, and dear in use! / What things again most dear in the esteem, / And poor in worth!' (3.3.127–30).

In a rigged ballot, Ajax has drawn the right to represent the Greeks against Hector. He will be the object of great esteem though his intrinsic worth as a warrior is inferior to that of Achilles. The supreme warrior Achilles is being disregarded. The syntax and terminology exert intense pressure on the concepts of intrinsic worth and popular **opinion**.

Ulysses, attempting to explain Achilles' withdrawal from fighting, focuses on reputation and self-esteem: 'The great Achilles, whom opinion crowns / The sinew and the forehand of our host, / Having his ear full of his airy fame, / Grows dainty of his worth, and in his tent / Lies mocking our designs' (1.3.142–6). Achilles has become so conceited that he no longer deigns to collaborate in the

327

common objective. He is above them: conception of his intrinsic worth detaches him from his associates.

A frequent tension in the play is between the desire to bestow infinite value on something and the propensity for measuring the value so that a price is placed on it.

Intrinsic worth once transformed to relative worth becomes exchange value. Thersites, in calculating Ajax's worth, remarks, 'I will buy nine sparrows for a penny, and his *pia mater* is not worth the ninth part of a sparrow' (2.1.70–2). Troilus, however, is outraged by Hector's application of quantification to an issue he believes to reside in a different realm from that of everyday consideration. Hector places Helen within the calculus of cost-benefit analysis:

> Let Helen go.
> Since the first sword was drawn about this question,
> Every tithe soul, 'mongst many thousand dismes,
> Hath been as dear as Helen; I mean, of ours.
> If we have lost so many tenths of ours,
> To guard a thing not ours nor worth to us
> (Had it our name) the value of one ten,
> What merit's in that reason which denies
> The yielding of her up?
>
> 2.2.17–25

What appears to be an unassailable proposition when subjected to the scrutiny of measuring benefits (Helen's worth or value) against costs (lives lost) is countered by the proposition of absolute worth, value which cannot be determined by reference to anything else. As Troilus puts it: 'Fie, fie, my brother! / Weigh you the worth and honor of a king / So great as our dread father's in a scale / Of common ounces? Will you with counters sum / The past-proportionate of his infinite' (2.2.25–9). For Troilus, to surrender Helen is to sacrifice the honour of King Priam and Troy.

Metaphorically, Troy's honour and Helen coalesce. Hector, however, insists on separating them and so reduces the glamorous icon to something more prosaic: 'Brother, she is not worth what she doth cost / The keeping'. Troilus then strikes at the conceptual nucleus of Hector's argument: 'What's aught but as 'tis valued?' There is no such thing as objective worth – something that can be valued in the market-place in relation to other objects. An entity is worth the value we arbitrarily choose to ascribe to it. Not so, says Hector:

> But value dwells not in particular will,
> It holds his estimate and dignity
> As well wherein 'tis precious of itself
> As in the prizer. 'Tis mad idolatory
> To make the service greater than the god,
> And the will dotes that is attributive

To what infectiously itself affects,
Without some image of th'affected merit.
2.2.51–60

One person may decide that an eggshell is a pearl beyond price, but the irrational commitment of one opinion will not bend reality: there is such a thing as objective value. Having won the argument, Hector decides to retain Helen and continue the war – not because her worth is beyond rational calculation, but because she is a symbol of Trojan honour and a pretext for gaining fame on the battlefield. Her intrinsic worth might be zero, but the heroic deeds to which her capture has given rise belong outside the realm of commonplace calculations. Her 'worth' is bestowed on her by the heroic actions to which her presence in Troy gives rise. Helen is a mere emblem: personally or intrinsically she may be worth little. Viewed prosaically in terms of cost-benefit analysis – lives lost and future dangers incurred by keeping her – her value or worth is negative. Perceived as the embodiment of Trojan fame and heroism she is a pearl beyond price: of supreme worth.

(C) The analyses of value in *TRO* are so rich that it is difficult to limit recommended texts. However, most relevant in terms of this entry are: Elton, *Shakespeare's* Troilus and Cressida *and the Inns of Courts Revels*, ch. 6; Kermode, *Shakespeare's Language*; Grady, *Shakespeare's Universal Wolf*; Thomas, *The Moral Universe of Shakespeare's Problem Plays*. Serpieri, 'Reading the signs' in Drakakis, ed., *Alternative Shakespeares*, provides a penetrating analysis of Antony's forum speech, while other essays in the volume cast significant light on this topic. Of vital significance too are Shell, *Money, Language and Thought*; Woodbridge, ed., *Money and the Age of Shakespeare*. Simmel, *The Philosophy of Money*; Leinwand, *Theatre, Finance and Society in Early Modern England*; Woodmansee and Osteen, eds, *The New Economic Criticism*; Howard and Shershow, eds, *Marxist Shakespeares*; Heinzelman, *The Economics of the Imagination*; Hyde, *The Gift*; Appadurai, ed., *The Social Life of Things*; Engle, *Shakespearean Pragmatism*; Waller, ed., *Shakespeare's Comedies*; Grantly, *London in Early Modern English Drama*. See entry on **value**.

Bibliography

Editions of Shakespeare's Works
The Riverside Shakespeare, ed., G. Blakemore Evans, 2nd edn, Boston: Houghton Mifflin, 1997.

Bate, Jonathan, ed., *Titus Andronicus*, London and New York; Routledge, Arden Shakespeare, Third Series, 1995.

Bevington, David, ed., *Troilus and Cressida*, London and New York: Arden Shakespeare, Third Series, 1998.

Brockbank, Philip, ed., *Coriolanus*, London, Methuen, Arden Shakespeare, Second Series, 1976.

Burns, Edward, ed., *King Henry VI, Part 1*, London and New York: Arden Shakespeare, Third Series, 2000.

Carroll, William C., ed., *The Two Gentlemen of Verona*, London and New York: Arden Shakespeare, Third Series, 2004.

Cox, John D. and Rasmussen, Eric, eds, *King Henry VI, Part 3*, London and New York: Arden Shakespeare, Third Series, 2001.

Craik, T. W., ed., *King Henry V*, London and New York: Routledge, Arden Shakespeare, Third Series, 1995.

Daniell, David, ed., *Julius Caesar*, London and New York: Arden Shakespeare, Third Series, 1998.

Dorsch, T. S., ed., *Julius Caesar*, London and New York: Methuen, Arden Shakespeare, Second Series, 1955.

Dusinberre, Juliet, ed., *As You Like It*, London and New York: Arden Shakespeare, Third Series, 2006.

Foakes, R. A., ed., *King Lear*, London and New York: Arden Shakespeare, Third Series, 1997.

Forker, Charles R., ed., *King Richard II*, London and New York: Arden Shakespeare, Third Series, 2002.

Gossett, Suzanne, ed., *Pericles*, London and New York: Arden Shakespeare, Third Series, 2004.

Honigmann, E. A. J., ed., *Othello*, London and New York: Arden Shakespeare, Third Series, 1997.

Humphreys, A. R., ed., *King Henry IV, Part 2*, London, Methuen, Arden Shakespeare, Second Series, 1966.

Jenkins, Harold, ed., *Hamlet*, London and New York: Methuen, Arden Shakespeare, Second Series, 1982.

Kastan, David Scott, ed., *King Henry IV, Part 1*, London and New York: Arden Shakespeare, Third Series, 2002.

Kermode, Frank, ed., *The Tempest*, London and New York: Arden Shakespeare, Second Series, 1964.

Klein, Karl, ed., *Timon of Athens*, Cambridge and New York: Cambridge University Press, New Cambridge Shakespeare, 2001.

Knowles, Ronald, ed., *King Henry VI, Part 2*, London and New York: Arden Shakespeare, Third Series, 2000.

Lever, J. W., ed., *Measure for Measure*, London and Cambridge, MA: Methuen, Arden Shakespeare, Second Series, 1965.

Lothian, J. M. and Craik, T. W., eds. *Twelfth Night*, Methuen, Arden Shakespeare, Second Series, 1975.

McEachern, Claire, ed., *Much Ado About Nothing*, London and New York: Arden Shakespeare, Third Series, 2006.

McMullan, Gordon, ed., *King Henry VIII*, London and New York: Arden Shakespeare, Third Series, 2000.

Melchiori, Giorgio, ed., *The Merry Wives of Windsor*, London and New York: Arden Shakespeare, Third Series, 2000.

—— , *King Edward III*, Cambridge and New York, Cambridge University Press, The New Cambridge Shakespeare, 1998.

Morris, Brian, ed., *The Taming of the Shrew*, London and New York: Routledge, Arden Shakespeare, Second Series, 1994.

Nosworthy, J. M., ed., *Cymbeline*, London and New York: Methuen, Arden Shakespeare, Second Series, 1955.

Orgel, Stephen, ed., *The Tempest*, Oxford and New York: Oxford University Press, The World's Classics, 1994.

Oliver, H. J., ed., *Timon of Athens*, London: Methuen, Arden Shakespeare, Second Series, 1969.

—— , *The Merry Wives of Windsor*, London: Methuen, Arden Shakespeare, Second Series, 1971.

Pafford, J. H. P., ed., *The Winter's Tale*, London and New York: Arden Shakespeare, Second Series, 1966.

Potter, Lois, ed., *The Two Noble Kinsmen*, London and New York: Arden Shakespeare, Third Series, 1997.

Sams, Eric, ed., *Shakespeare's Edward III: An Early Play Restored to the Canon*, New Haven and London: Yale University Press, 1996.

Thompson, Ann and Taylor, Neil, eds, *Hamlet*, London and New York: Arden Shakespeare, Third Series, 2006.

Vaughan, Virginia Mason and Vaughan, Alden T., eds, *The Tempest*, London and New York: Arden Shakespeare, Third Series, 1999.

Warren, Roger, ed., *Edward III*, London: Nick Hern Books in association with the Royal Shakespeare Company, 2002.

Wilders, John, ed., *Antony and Cleopatra*, London and New York: Routledge, Arden Shakespeare, Third Series, 1995.

Woudhuysen, H. R., ed., *Love's Labour's Lost*, London and New York: Arden Shakespeare, Third Series, 1998.

Non-Shakespeare Texts

Bawcutt, N. W., ed., *The Jew of Malta: Christopher Marlowe*, Manchester and New York: Manchester University Press, 1978.

Bevington, David, ed., *The Spanish Tragedy: Thomas Kyd*, Manchester and New York: Manchester University Press, 1996.

Bolton, W. F., ed., *Sejanus, his Fall*, London: Ernest Benn, 1966.

Brennan, Elizabeth M., ed., *The Duchess of Malfi: John Webster*, London and Tonbridge; Ernest Benn, 1964.

Brockbank, Philip, ed., *Volpone: Ben Jonson*, London: Ernest Benn, 1968.

Brown, Douglas ed., *The Alchemist: Ben Jonson*, London: Ernest Benn, 1966.

Corbin, Peter and Sedge, Douglas, eds, *Thomas of Woodstock or King Richard the Second, Part One*, Manchester and New York: Manchester University Press, 2002.

Edwards, Philip, ed., *The Spanish Tragedy: Thomas Kyd*, London: Methuen, 1959.

Van Fossen, Richard, ed., *The Jew of Malta: Christopher Marlowe*, London: Edward Arnold, 1965.

Critical Studies

Abbott, E. A., *A Shakespearian Grammar*, New York: Dover Publication Inc., 1966.

Ackroyd, Peter, *Albion: The Origins of the English Imagination*, London: Chatto & Windus, 2002.

——, *Shakespeare: The Biography*, London: Chatto & Windus, 2005.

Adamson, Jane, *Troilus and Cressida*, Harvester New Critical Introductions to Shakespeare, Brighton: The Harvester Press, 1987.

Adelman, Janet, *The Common Liar: An Essay on 'Antony and Cleopatra'*, New Haven and London: Yale University Press, 1973.

Agnew, Jean-Christophe, *Worlds Apart: The Market and the Theater in Anglo-American Thought, 1550–1750*, Cambridge and New York: Cambridge University Press, 1986.

Alexander, Catherine M. S. and Wells, Stanley, eds, *Shakespeare and Race*, Cambridge: Cambridge University Press, 2000.

——, eds, *Shakespeare and Sexuality*, Cambridge: Cambridge University Press, 2001.

Alexander, Catherine M.S., ed., *Shakespeare and Politics*, Cambridge: Cambridge University Press, 2004.

——, ed. *Shakespeare and Language*, Cambridge: Cambridge University Press, 2004.

Allen, Graham, *Intertextuality: The New Critical Idiom*, London and New York: Routledge, 2000.

Alvis, John and West, Thomas G., eds, *Shakespeare as Political Thinker*, Durham: Carolina Academic Press, 1981.

Andrews, John F., ed., *Romeo and Juliet: Critical Essays*, New York and London: Routledge, 1993.

Andrews, Kenneth R., *Trade, Plunder and Settlement: Maritime Enterprise and the*

Genesis of the British Empire, 1480–1630, Cambridge: Cambridge University Press, 1984.

Appadurai, Arjun, ed., *The Social Life of Things: Commodities in Cultural Perspective*, Cambridge and New York: Cambridge University Press, 1986.

Appelbaum, Robert, *Aguecheek's Beef, Belch's Hiccup, and Other Gastronomic Interjections: Literature, Culture, and Food among the Early Moderns*, Chicago and London: University of Chicago Press, 2006.

Appleby, Joyce Oldham, *Economic Thought and Ideology in Seventeenth-Century England*, Princeton, NJ: Princeton University Press, 1978.

Aristotle, *Nichomachean Ethics*, trans. Martin Oswald, Indianapolis: Bobbs-Merrill, 1962.

Armstrong, W. A., 'The influence of Seneca and Machiavelli on the Elizabethan tyrant', *Review of English Studies* 24 (1948): 19–35.

Ascoli, Albert Russell and Kahn, Victoria, eds, *Machiavelli and the Discourse of Literature*, Ithaca and London: Cornell University Press, 1993.

Aspinall, Dana E., ed., *The Taming of the Shrew, Critical Essays*, New York and London: Routledge, 2001.

Aughterson, Kate, ed., *The English Renaissance: An Anthology of Sources and Documents*, London and New York: Routledge, 1998, 2002.

Bacon, Francis, *The Advancement of Learning*, ed., G. W. Kitchin (1861); J. M. Dent & Sons Ltd.

Bamborough, J. B., *The Little World of Man*, London, New York and Toronto: Longman, Green and Co., 1952.

Barber, C. L., *Shakespeare's Festive Comedy: A Study of Dramatic Form and its Relation to Social Custom*, Princeton: Princeton University Press, 1959.

Barbour, Violet, 'Marine risks and insurance in the seventeenth century', *Journal of Economic and Business History* 1 (1928–9): 561–96.

Barfoot, C. C., '*Troilus and Cressida:* "Praise us as we are tasted" ', *Shakespeare Quarterly* 39 (1988): 45–57.

Barker, Simon, ed., *Shakespeare's Problem Plays, All's Well That Ends Well, Measure for Measure, Troilus and Cressida: Contemporary Critical Essays*, Basingstoke and New York: Palgrave Macmillan, 2005.

Barnhart, Robert K., ed., *Chambers Dictionary of Etymology*, Edinburgh and New York: Chambers Harrap Publishers, 2000–2006.

Barton, Anne, *Essays, Mainly Shakespearean*, Cambridge and New York: Cambridge University Press, 1994.

Bate, Jonathan, 'The performance of revenge: *Titus Andronicus* and *The Spanish Tragedy*', *The Show Within: Dramatic and Other Insets, English Renaissance Drama 1550–1642*, ed., Francois Laroque, Montpellier: Université Paul Valery, 1992, II, 274.

——, *Shakespeare and Ovid*, Oxford and New York: Clarendon Paperbacks Press, 1993, reprinted 2001.

——, *The Genius of Shakespeare*, London and Basingstoke: Picador, 1997.

Baugh, Albert C. and Cable, Thomas, eds, *A History of the English Language*, Abingdon: Routledge, 1951–2006.

Bayley, John, *Shakespeare and Tragedy*, London, Boston and Henley: Routledge & Kegan Paul, 1981.

Beier, A. L., *Masterless Men: The Vagrancy Problem in England, 1560–1640*, New York: Methuen, 1985.

—— and Findlay, Roger, eds, *London 1500–1700: The Making of the Metropolis*, London: Longman, 1986.

——, Cannadine, David and Rosenheim, James M., eds, *The First Modern Society: Essays in English History in Honour of Lawrence Stone*, Cambridge: Cambridge University Press, 1989.

Bentley, Greg W., *Shakespeare and the New Disease: The Dramatic Function of Syphilis in Troilus and Cressida, Measure for Measure and Timon of Athens*, New York: Peter Lang, 1989.

Bevington, David M., *From Mankind to Marlowe: Growth of Structure in the Popular Drama of Tudor England*, Cambridge, MA: Harvard University Press, 1962.

——, *Tudor Drama and Politics: A Critical Approach to Topical Meaning*, Cambridge, MA: Harvard University Press, 1968.

Billington, Michael, Review of *Henry VIII*, *Guardian*, 26 August 2006. 'Exciting trilogy with limitations: *Richard II/Henry IV Parts One and Two*', *Guardian*, 18 August 2007.

Black, John, *A Dictionary of Economics*, Oxford, New York: Oxford University Press, 1997.

Blake, Norman, *Shakespeare's Non-Standard English; A Dictionary of his Informal Language*, London and New York: Continuum, 2006.

Blaxton, John, *The English Usurer, or Usury Condemned*, London, 1634.

Bloom, Harold, *Shakespeare: The Invention of the Human*, London: Fourth Estate, 1999.

Boehrer, Bruce, *Shakespeare among the Animals: Nature and Society in the Drama of Early Modern England*, New York and Basingstoke: Palgrave, 2002.

Booth, Stephen, ed., *Shakespeare's Sonnets*, New Haven and London: Yale University Press, 1977.

Bosing, Walter, *The Complete Paintings of Bosch*, Cologne and London: Taschen, 2000.

Boughner, Daniel C., 'Sejanus and Machiavelli', *Studies in English Literature*, 1 (2) (1961): 84.

Bradbrook, M. C., *Shakespeare the Craftsman: The Clark Lectures, 1968*, London: Chatto & Windus, 1969.

Bradshaw, Graham, *Shakespeare's Scepticism*, Brighton: The Harvester Press, 1987.

Braudel, Fernand, *Civilization and Capitalism, 15th–18th Century, Volume 1, The Structures of Everyday Life*, rev., trans. by Sian Reynolds, London: Collins, 1981.

Braunmuller, A. R. and Hattaway, Michael, eds, *English Renaissance Drama*, Cambridge and New York: Cambridge University Press, 1990.

Brennan, Anthony, *Henry V*, Harvester New Critical Introductions to Shakespeare, Hemel Hempstead: Harvester Wheatsheaf, 1992.

Brenner, Robert, *Merchants and Revolution: Commercial Change, Political Conflict,* and London's Overseas Traders, 1550–1653, Princeton: Princeton University Press, 1993; London and New York: Verso, 2003.

Brewer, John and Porter, Roy, eds, *Consumption and the World of Goods*, London: Routledge, 1994.

Brigden, Susan, *New Worlds, Lost Worlds: The Rule of the Tudors 1485–1603*, London: Penguin Books, 2000.

Bristol, Michael D., *Carnival and Theater: Plebeian Culture and the Structure of Authority in Renaissance England*, New York and London: Routledge, 1985, paperback 1989.

Brockbank, Philip, ed., *Players of Shakespeare 1: Essays in Shakespearean Performance by Twelve Players with the Royal Shakespeare Company*, Cambridge and New York: Cambridge University Press, 1985.

Brotton, Jerry, *The Renaissance Bazaar: From the Silk Road to Michelangelo*, Oxford and New York: Oxford University Press, 2002.

Brower, Reuben A., *Hero and Saint: Shakespeare and the Graeco-Roman Heroic Tradition*, Oxford: Oxford University Press, 1971.

Bruster, Douglas, *Drama and the Market in the Age of Shakespeare*, Cambridge and New York: Cambridge University Press, 1992; paperback 2004.

——, *'To Be Or Not To Be'*, London: Continuum, 2007.

Bullough, Geoffrey, *Narrative and Dramatic Sources of Shakespeare*, 8 vols, New York: Columbia University Press, 1957–75.

Bulman, James C., *The Heroic Idiom of Shakespearean Tragedy*, University of Delaware Press; London and Toronto: Associated Universities Press, 1985.

Burckhardt, Jacob, *The Civilization of the Renaissance in Italy*, London: Penguin Books, 1990.

Burton, Robert, *The Anatomy of Melancholy*, New York: New York Review of Books, 2001.

Bushnell, Rebecca, W., *Tragedies of Tyrants: Political Thought and Theater in the English Renaissance*, Ithaca and London: Cornell University Press, 1990.

Calderwood, James L., *A Midsummer Night's Dream*, Harvester New Critical Introductions to Shakespeare, Hemel Hempstead: Harvester Wheatsheaf, 1992.

Cantor, Paul A., *Shakespeare's Rome: Republic and Empire*, Ithaca and London: Cornell University Press, 1976.

Carroll, William C., *Fat King, Lean Beggar: Representations of Poverty in the Age of Shakespeare*, Ithaca: Cornell University Press, 1996.

Carruthers, Bruce G., *City of Capital: Politics and Markets in the English Financial Revolution*, Princeton: Princeton University Press, 1996, 1999.

Castiglione, Baldassare, *The Book of the Courtier*, trans. Sir Thomas Hoby, London and New York: J. M. Dent, 1974.

Castillo, Susan, *Colonial Encounters in New World Writing 1500–1786: Performing America*, London and New York: Routledge, 2006.

Cavanagh, Dermot, *Language and Politics in the Sixteenth-Century History Play*, Basingstoke and New York: Palgrave Macmillan, 2003.

——, Hampton-Reeves, Stuart and Longstaffe, Stephen, eds, *Shakespeare's Histories and Counter-Histories*, Manchester and New York: Manchester University Press, 2006.

Cavell, Stanley, *Disowning Knowledge in Six Plays of Shakespeare*, Cambridge and New York: Cambridge University Press, 1987.

Cawdrey, Robert, *The First English Dictionary 1604: Robert Cawdrey's A Table Alphabeticall*, Oxford: Bodleian Library, 2007.

Charnes, Linda, *Notorious Identity: Materializing the Subject in Shakespeare*, Cambridge, MA and London: Harvard University Press, 1993, 1995.

Chartres, J. A., *Internal Trade in England, 1500–1700*, London: Macmillan Press, 1977.

Charney, Maurice, *Shakespeare on Love and Lust*, New York: Columbia University Press, 2000.

Cheney, Patrick, ed., *The Cambridge Companion to Christopher Marlowe*, Cambridge and New York: Cambridge University Press, 2004.

——, ed., *The Cambridge Companion to Shakespeare's Poetry*, Cambridge: Cambridge University Press, 2007.

Chorost, Michael, 'Biological finance in Shakespeare's *Timon of Athens*', *English Literary Renaissance* 21 (Autumn, 1991): 349–70.

Clark, Sandra, *Renaissance Drama*, Cambridge and Malden, MA: Polity, 2007.

Clemen, Wolfgang, *The Development of Shakespeare's Imagery*, 2nd edn, London: Methuen, 1977.

Cohen, Adam Max, *Shakespeare and Technology: Dramatising Early Modern Technological Revolutions*, New York and Basingstoke: Palgrave, 2006.

Coleman, D. C., *The Economy of England 1450–1750*, Oxford: Oxford University Press, 1977.

Cook, Ann Jennalie, *The Privileged Playgoers of Shakespeare's London 1576–1642*, New Jersey and Guildford: Princeton University Press, 1981.

Cook, Elizabeth, *Seeing Through Words: The Scope of Late Renaissance Poetry*, New Haven and London: Yale University Press, 1986.

Corfield, Penelope, ed., *Language, History and Class*, Oxford: Basil Blackwell, 1991.

Courtney, Richard, *Shakespeare's World of War: The Early Histories*, Toronto and Oxford: Simon and Pierre, 1994.

Cox, Murray and Theilgaard, Alice, *Mutative Metaphors in Psychotherapy: The Aeolian Mode*, London and New York: Tavistock Publications, 1987.

Coyle, Dale, *Pronouncing Shakespeare's Words: A Guide from A to Zounds*, New York and London, Routledge, 2002.

Coyle, Martin, ed., *Hamlet: Contemporary Critical Essays*, Basingstoke and London: Macmillan, 1992.

——, ed., *Niccolo Machiavelli's The Prince: New Interdisciplinary Essays*, Manchester and New York: Manchester University Press, 1995.

Craig, Hardin, *The Enchanted Glass: The Renaissance Mind in English Literature*, Oxford: Basil Blackwell, 1952.

Crewe, Jonathan, 'Reforming Prince Hal: the sovereign inheritor in *2Henry IV*', *Renaissance Drama*, n.s. 21 (1990): 225–42.

Crosby, Alfred W., *The Measure of Reality: Quantification and Western Society, 1250–1600*, Cambridge and New York: Cambridge University Press, 1997.

Crystal, David and Crystal, Ben, *Shakespeare's Words: A Glossary and Language Companion*, London, New York: Penguin Books, 2002.

Crystal, David, *'Think on my words': Exploring Shakespeare's Language*, Cambridge and New York: Cambridge University Press, 2008.

Danby, John F., *Shakespeare's Doctrine of Nature: A Study of King Lear*, London: Faber & Faber, 1948.

Danson, Lawrence, *The Harmonies of The Merchant of Venice*, New Haven: Yale University Press, 1978.

——, ed., *On King Lear*, New Jersey and Guilford: Princeton University Press, 1981.

——, *Shakespeare's Dramatic Genres*, Oxford and New York: Oxford University Press, 2000.

Dawson, Anthony B. and Yachnin, Paul, *The Culture of Playgoing in Shakespeare's England: A Collaborative Debate*, Cambridge and New York: Cambridge University Press, 2001, reprinted 2002, paperback 2005.

Deats, Sara Munson, ed., *Antony and Cleopatra: New Critical Essays*, New York and London: Routledge, 2005.

de Grazia, Margreta, *'Hamlet' without Hamlet*, Cambridge and New York: Cambridge University Press, 2007.

——, Quilligan, Maureen and Stallybrass, Peter, eds, *Subject and Object in Renaissance Culture*, Cambridge: Cambridge University Press, 1996.

Deng, Stephen and Sebek, Barbara, eds, *Global Traffic: Discourse and Practices of Trade in English Literature and Culture from 1550 to 1700*, Basingstoke and New York: Palgrave Macmillan, 2008.

Denton, Jeffrey, ed., *Orders and Hierarchies in Late Medieval and Renaissance Europe*, Basingstoke and London: Macmillan Press, Ltd, 1999.

Dessen, Alan C., *Recovering Shakespeare's Theatrical Language*, Cambridge and New York: Cambridge University Press, 1995.

Divine, Thomas F., *Interest: An Historical and Analytical Study in Economics and Modern Ethics*, Milwaukee: Marquette University Press, 1959.

Dollimore, Jonathan, *Radical Tragedy: Religion, Ideology and Power in the Drama of Shakespeare and his Contemporaries*, Brighton: The Harvester Press, 1984.

—— and Sinfield, Alan, eds, *Political Shakespeare: New Essays in Cultural Materialism*, Manchester: Manchester University Press, 1985.

Donawerth, Jane, *Shakespeare and the Sixteenth-Century Study of Language*, Urbana and Chicago: University of Illinois Press, 1984.

Dorfman, Joseph, *Thorstein Veblen and his America*, New York: Augustus M. Kelley, 1966.

Dowden, Edward, *Shakspere: A Critical Study of his Mind and Art*, London: Routledge & Kegan Paul, reprinted 1967. First published 1875.

Drakakis, John, ed., *Alternative Shakespeares*, London and New York: Methuen, 1985.

——, ed., *Shakespearean Tragedy*, London and New York: Longman, 1992.

——, ed., *Antony and Cleopatra: Contemporary Critical Essays*, Basingstoke and London: Macmillan, 1994.

Draper, R. P., ed., *Tragedy: Developments in Criticism*, Basingstoke and London: Macmillan, 1980.

Duncan-Jones, Katherine, *Ungentle Shakespeare: Scenes from his Life*, London: The Arden Shakespeare, 2001.

Durston, Christopher and Eales, Jacqueline, eds, *The Culture of English Puritanism 1560–1700*, New York: St Martin's Press, 1996.

Dutton, Richard, ed., *A Midsummer Night's Dream: Contemporary Critical Essays*, Basingstoke and New York: Palgrave, 1996.

—— and Howard, Jean E., eds, *A Companion to Shakespeare's Works – Volume I: The Tragedies*, Malden and Oxford: Blackwell, 2003.

——, eds, *A Companion to Shakespeare's Works – Volume II: The Histories*, Malden and Oxford: Blackwell, 2003.

——, eds, *A Companion to Shakespeare's Works – Volume III: The Comedies*, Malden and Oxford: Blackwell, 2003.

——, eds, *A Companion to Shakespeare's Works – Volume IV: The Poems, Problem Comedies, Late Plays*, Malden and Oxford: Blackwell, 2003.

Eagleton, Terry, *Marxism and Literary Criticism*, London: Methuen, 1976.

——, *William Shakespeare*, Cambridge, MA: Basil Blackwell, 1986.

Eatwell, John, Milgate, Murray and Newman, Peter, *The New Palgrave: Marxian Economics*, New York: W. W. Norton, 1990.

Edelman, Charles, *Shakespeare's Military Language*, London and New Brunswick, NJ: The Athlone Press, 2000; paperback Continuum, 2004.

Edmondson, Paul and Wells, Stanley, *Shakespeare's Sonnets*, Oxford: Oxford University Press, 2004.

Egan, Gabriel, *Shakespeare and Marx*, Oxford: Oxford University Press, 2004.

Elton, William R., *King Lear and the Gods*, California: The Henry E. Huntington Library and Art Gallery, 1966, 1968.

——, *Shakespeare's Troilus and Cressida and the Inns of Court Revels*, Aldershot, Brookfield, USA: Ashgate, 2000.

Engle, Lars, *Shakespearean Pragmatism: Market of his Time*, Chicago and London: University of Chicago Press, 1993.

Enterline, Lynn, *The Rhetoric of the Body from Ovid to Shakespeare*, Cambridge and New York: Cambridge University Press, 2000.

Erickson, Amy, ed., *Working Life of Women in the Seventeenth Century*, by Alice Clark, New York and London: Routledge, 1992.

——, *Women and Property in Early Modern England*, New York: Routledge, 1993.

Erasmus, *Praise and Folly and Letter to Martin Dorp 1515*, trans. Betty Radice, Harmondsworth and New York: Penguin Books, 1971.

Erne, Lukas, *Beyond The Spanish Tragedy: A Study of the Works of Thomas Kyd*, Manchester and New York: Manchester University Press, 2001.

Feingold, Mordechai, *The Mathematician's Apprenticeship: Science, Universities and Society in England, 1560–1640*, Cambridge: Cambridge University Press, 1984.

Felperin, Howard, *Shakespearean Representation: Mimesis and Modernity in*

Elizabethan Tragedy, New Jersey and Guildford: Princeton University Press, 1977.

Fineman, Joel, *Shakespeare's Perjured Eye: The Invention of Poetic Subjectivity in the Sonnets*, Berkeley, LA and London: University of California Press, 1986, paperback 1988.

Finkelstein, Andrea, *Harmony and Balance: An Intellectual History of Seventeenth-Century English Economic Thought*, Ann Arbor: University of Michigan Press, 2000.

Fischer, David Hackett, *The Great Wave: Price Revolutions and the Rhythm of History*, New York: Oxford University Press, 1996.

Fischer, Sandra K., *Econolingua: A Glossary of Coins and Economic Language in Renaissance Drama*, Newark: University of Delaware Press, 1985.

——, ' "He means to pay": value and metaphor in the Lancastrian tetralogy', *Shakespeare Quarterly* 40: 149–64.

Fisher, F. J., 'The development of London as a centre of conspicuous consumption in the sixteenth and seventeenth centuries', *Transactions of the Royal Historical Society*, 4th series, 30 (1948): 37–50.

——, *London and the English Economy, 1500–1700*, ed., P. J. Cornfield and N. B. Harte, London: Hambledon Press, 1990.

Florio, John, *Second Frutes* (1591); Gainesville: Scholars' Facsimilies, 1953.

——, *A Worlde of Wordes*, first published by Edw. Blount, 1598; Hildesheim, Zurich and New York: Georg Olms Verlag, 2004.

Foakes, R. A., *Shakespeare and Violence*, Cambridge and New York: Cambridge University Press, 2003.

Forkerth, Wes, *The Sound of Shakespeare*, London and New York: Routledge, 2002.

Forman, Valerie, 'Marked angels: counterfeits, commodities, and *The Roaring Girl*', *Renaissance Quarterly* 54 (2001): 1531–60.

Forstater, Mathew, *Little Book of Big Ideas: Economics*, London: A&C Black Publishers Ltd, 2007.

Frazer, Elizabeth, *Shakespeare and the Political Way*, London and New York: Continuum, 2007.

Freedman, Penelope, *Power and Passion in Shakespeare's Pronouns*, Aldershot and Burlington: Ashgate, 2007.

Frye, Roland, *The Renaissance 'Hamlet': Issues and Responses in 1660*, Princeton: Princeton University Press, 1984.

Galbraith, J. K., *The Affluent Society*, Harmondsworth: Pelican Books, 1962.

Garber, Marjorie, ' "Infinite riches in a little room", closure and enclosure in Marlowe' in Kernan, Alvin, ed., *Two Renaissance Mythmakers: Christopher Marlowe and Ben Jonson*, Baltimore: Johns Hopkins University Press, 1977.

Gardner, Helen, *Religion and Literature*, London: Faber & Faber, 1971.

Gifford, Terry, *Pastoral: The New Critical Idiom*, London and New York: Routledge, 1999.

Gill, Richard T., *Evolution of Modern Economics*, Englewood Cliffs, NJ: Prentice-Hall Inc., 1967.

Gillespie, Stuart, *Shakespeare's Books: A Dictionary of Shakespeare Sources*, London and New Brunswick, NJ: The Athlone Press, 2001.

Gillies, John, *Shakespeare and the Geography of Difference*, Cambridge and New York: Cambridge University Press, 1994.

Golding, Arthur (1567), *Ovid's Metamorphoses*, ed., John Frederick Nims, Philadelphia: Paul Dry Books, 2000.

Goldman, Michael, *Acting and Action in Shakespearean Tragedy*, Princeton, NJ and Guildford: Princeton University Press, 1985.

Goux, Jean-Joseph, *Symbolic Economies: After Marx and Freud*, trans. Jennifer Curtiss Gage, Ithaca, New York: Cornell University Press, 1990.

——, *The Coiners of Language*, Norman: University of Oklahoma Press, 1994.

Goy-Blanquet, Dominque, *Shakespeare's Early History Plays: From Chronicle to Stage*, Oxford and New York: Oxford University Press, 2003.

Grady, Hugh, *Shakespeare's Universal Wolf: Studies in Early Modern Reification*, Oxford: Clarendon Press, 1996, reprinted Oxford University Press, 2006.

——, *Shakespeare, Machiavelli & Montaigne: Power and Subjectivity from Richard II to Hamlet*, Oxford and New York: Oxford University Press, 2002.

Grantley, Darryll, *London in Early Modern English Drama*, Basingstoke and New York: Palgrave Macmillan, 2008.

Grassby, Richard, *The Idea of Capitalism before the Industrial Revolution*, Oxford: Oxford University Press, 1999.

Greenblatt, Stephen, ed., *Representing the English Renaissance*, Berkeley: University of California Press, 1988.

——, *Learning to Curse: Essays in Early Modern Culture*, New York and London: Routledge, 1990; Routledge Classics, 2007.

——, *Hamlet in Purgatory*, Princeton and Oxford: Princeton University Press, 2001.

——, *Renaissance Self-Fashioning: From More to Shakespeare*, Chicago and London: University of Chicago Press, 1980; with a new Preface, 2005.

——, *Will in the World: How Shakespeare Became Shakespeare*, USA: W. W. Norton & Company, 2004; London: Jonathan Cape, 2004.

Greene, Gayle, 'Language and value in Shakespeare's *Troilus and Cressida*', *Studies in English Literature* 21 (1981): 271–85.

Gross, Kenneth, *Shakespeare's Noise*, Chicago and London: University of Chicago Press, 2001.

Gurr, Andrew, *Playgoing in Shakespeare's London*, Cambridge: Cambridge University Press, 1987.

Habicht, Werner, Palmer, David John and Pringle Roger, eds, *Images of Shakespeare: Proceedings of the Third International Congress of the Shakespeare Association, 1986*, London and Newark: University of Delaware Press and United Associated Presses, 1988.

Hacking, Ian, *The Emergence of Probability*, Cambridge: Cambridge University Press, 1975.

Hadfield, Andrew, *The English Renaissance 1500–1620*, Malden, USA: Blackwell Publishers, 2001.

——, *Shakespeare and Renaissance Politics*, London and New York: Arden Shakespeare, Thomson Learning, 2004.

——, *Shakespeare and Republicanism*, Cambridge and New York: Cambridge University Press, 2005.

—— and Hammond, Paul, eds, *Shakespeare and Renaissance Europe*, London and New York: Arden Shakespeare, 2004, Thomson Learning, 2005.

Hagen, Rose-Marie and Rainer, *Bruegel: The Complete Paintings*, Germany: Midpoint Press, 2001.

——, *What Great Paintings Say*, vol. 1. Cologne and London: Taschen, 2003.

——, *What Great Paintings Say*, vol. 2. Cologne and London: Taschen, 2003.

Halio, Jay L., ed., *Critical Essays on Shakespeare's 'King Lear'*, New York: G. K. Hall & Co., 1996.

Hall, Kim F., *Things of Darkness: Economies of Race and Gender in Early Modern England*, Ithaca: Cornell University Press, 1995.

Halpern, Richard, *The Poetics of Primitive Accumulation: English Renaissance Culture and the Genealogy of Capital*, Ithaca: Cornell University Press, 1991.

——, *Shakespeare among the Moderns*, Ithaca: Cornell University Press, 1997.

Hamilton, Donna B., *Shakespeare and the Politics of Protestant England*, Lexington, Kentucky: The University Press of Kentucky, 1992.

Hammill, Graham L., *Sexuality and Form: Caravaggio, Marlowe, and Bacon*, Chicago and London: University of Chicago Press, 2000.

Hardy, Barbara, *Shakespeare's Storytellers*, London and Chester Springs: Peter Owen, 1997.

Harris, Jonathan Gil, *Sick Economies: Drama, Mercantilism and Disease in Shakespeare's England*, Philadelphia: University of Pennsylvania Press, 2004.

Hartwig, Joan, *Shakespeare's Tragicomic Vision*, Baton Rouge: Louisiana State University Press, 1972.

Hassel, R. Chris, Jr, *Shakespeare's Religious Language: A Dictionary*, London and New York: Thoemmes Continuum, 2005; paperback, Continuum, 2007.

Hattaway, Michael, ed., *The Cambridge Companion to Shakespeare's History Plays*, Cambridge and New York: Cambridge University Press, 2002.

——, *Renaissance and Reformations: An Introduction to Early Modern English Literature*, Malden, USA, Oxford: Blackwell Publishing, 2005.

Hawkes, David, *Ideology*, London and New York: Routledge, 1996.

——, *Idols of the Marketplace: Idolatry and Commodity Fetishism in English Literature, 1580–1680*, New York and Basingstoke: Palgrave, 2001.

Hayward, Maria, *Dress at the Court of King Henry VIII*, Leeds, London and Cambridge, MA; Maney, 2007.

Heilbroner, Robert L., *The Worldly Philosophers*, 6th edn, New York: Simon & Schuster, 1986.

Heinzelman Kurt, *The Economics of the Imagination*, Amherst: University of Massachusetts Press, 1980.

Hicks, Carola, *The King's Glass: A Story of Tudor Power and Secret Art*, London: Chatto & Windus, 2007.

Hillman, David, *Shakespeare's Entrails: Belief, Scepticism and the Interior of the Body*, Basingstoke, New York: Palgrave Macmillan, 2007.

Holderness, Graham, ed., *Shakespeare's History Plays: Richard II to Henry V: Contemporary Critical Essays*, Basingstoke and London: Macmillan, 1992.

Holland, Peter, *English Shakespeares: Shakespeare on the English Stage in the 1990s*, Cambridge and New York: Cambridge University Press, 1997.

——, ed., *Shakespeare, Memory and Performance*, Cambridge: Cambridge University Press, 2006.

Honan, Park, *Shakespeare: A Life*, Oxford and New York: Oxford University Press, 1998.

——, *Christopher Marlowe: Poet and Spy*, Oxford and New York: Oxford University Press, 2005.

Honigmann, E. A. J., *Shakespeare's Impact on his Contemporaries*, London and Basingstoke: The Macmillan Press Ltd, 1982.

——, ed., *Shakespeare and his Contemporaries: Essays in Comparison*, Manchester and New Hampshire: Manchester University Press, 1986.

Hooker, Richard, *Of the Laws of Ecclesiastical Polity*, ed., Arthur Stephen McGrade, Book 1, Cambridge: Cambridge University Press, 1989.

Hopkins, Lisa, *Shakespeare on the Edge: Border-crossing in the Tragedies and the Henriad*, Aldershot and Burlington, VT: Ashgate, 2005.

—— and Steggle, Matthew, *Renaissance Literature and Culture*, London and New York: Continuum, 2006.

Houston, John Porter, *Shakespearean Sentences: A Study in Style and Syntax*, Baton Rouge and London: Louisiana State University Press, 1988.

Howard, Jean E. and O'Connor, Marion F., eds, *Shakespeare Reproduced: The Text in History and Ideology*, New York and London: Methuen, 1987.

—— and Rackin, Phyllis, *Engendering a Nation: A Feminist Account of Shakespeare's English Histories*, London: Routledge, 1997.

—— and Shershow, Scott Cutler, eds, *Marxist Shakespeares*, London and New York: Routledge, 2001.

Huebert, Ronald, *The Performance of Pleasure in English Renaissance Drama*, Basingstoke and New York: Palgrave Macmillan, 2003.

Hulme, Hilda M., *Explorations in Shakespeare's Language: Some Problems of Word Meaning in the Dramatic Text*, New York: Longman, 1962, 1977.

Hunt, Maurice, ed., *The Winter's Tale: New Critical Essays*, New York and London: Routledge, 1995.

Hutchinson, Terence, *Before Adam Smith: The Emergence of Political Economy 1622–1776*, Oxford: Blackwell, 1988.

Hussey, S. S., *The Literary Language of Shakespeare*, London and New York: Longman, 1982.

Hyde, Lewis, *The Gift: How the Creative Spirit Transforms the World*, Edinburgh, New York, first published in US and Canada: 1979; Canongate, 2006.

Ingram, Jill Phillips, *Idioms of Self-Interest: Credit, Identity, and Property in English Renaissance Literature*, New York and London: Routledge, 2006.

Innes, Paul, *Shakespeare and the English Renaissance Sonnet: Verses of Feigning Love*,

Basingstoke and London: Macmillan Press Ltd, St Martin's Press, Inc., 1997.

——, *Class and Society in Shakespeare*, London and New York: Continuum, 2008.

Jackson, Russell and Smallwood, Robert, eds, *Players of Shakespeare 2: Further Essays in Shakespearean Performance by Players with the Royal Shakespeare Company*, Cambridge and New York: Cambridge University Press, 1988.

James, Heather, *Shakespeare's Troy: Drama, Politics, and the Translation of Empire*, Cambridge: Cambridge University Press, 1997.

James, Mervyn, ed., *Society, Politics, and Culture: Studies in Early Modern England*, Cambridge: Cambridge University Press, 1986.

Jardine, Lisa, *Worldly Goods: A New History of the Renaissance*, London and Basingstoke: Macmillan, 1996.

Johns, Adrian, *The Nature of the Book: Print and Knowledge in the Making*, Chicago: Chicago University Press, 1998.

Jones, Ann Rosalind and Stallybrass, Peter, *Renaissance Clothing: The Materials of Memory*, Cambridge: Cambridge University Press, 2001.

Jones, Emrys, 'London in the early seventeenth century: an ecological approach', *The London Journal* 6 (1980): 123–33.

Jones, John, *Shakespeare at Work*, Oxford: Clarendon Press, 1995, paperback, 1999.

Jones, Norman, *God and the Moneylenders: Usury and Law in Early Modern England*, Oxford: Blackwell, 1989.

——, *The Birth of the Elizabethan Age: England in the 1560s*, Oxford: Blackwell, 1993.

Jordan, Constance and Cunningham, Karen, eds, *The Law in Shakespeare*, Basingstoke and New York: Palgrave Macmillan, 2007.

Joughin, John J., ed., *Shakespeare and National Culture*, Manchester: Manchester University Press, 1997.

Kahn, Coppelia, ' "Magic of bounty": *Timon of Athens*, Jacobean patronage, and maternal power', *Shakespeare Quarterly* 38 (1987): 34–57.

——, *Roman Shakespeare: Warriors, Wounds and Women*, London and New York: Routledge, 1997.

Kamps, Ivo, ed., *Materialist Shakespeare: A History*, London and New York: Verso, 1995.

Kehler, Dorothea, ed., *A Midsummer Night's Dream: Critical Essays*, New York and London: Routledge, 1998, paperback 2001.

Kelly, Henry Ansgar, *Divine Providence in the England of Shakespeare's Histories*, Cambridge, MA: Harvard University Press, 1970.

Kermode, Frank, 'Opinion, truth and value', *Essays in Criticism* 5 (1955): 181–7.

——, *Shakespeare's Language*, London and New York: Allen Lane/Penguin Press, 2000.

Kerridge, Eric, *Trade and Banking in Early Modern England*, Manchester: Manchester University Press, 1988.

Kettle, Arnold, ed., *Shakespeare in a Changing World*, London: Lawrence & Wishart, 1964.

Keynes, J. M., *A Treatise on Money*, 2 vols, New York: Macmillan, 1930.

——, *The General Theory of Employment, Interest and Money*, London: Macmillan, 1936.

Kingsley-Smith, Jane, *Shakespeare's Drama of Exile*, Basingstoke and New York: Palgrave Macmillan, 2003.

Kinney, Arthur F., *A Companion to Renaissance Drama*, Malden, USA., Oxford: Blackwell, 2002, paperback 2004, reprinted 2005.

——, ed., *Hamlet: New Critical Essays*, New York and London: Routledge, 2002.

——, *Shakespeare's Webs: Networks of Meaning in Renaissance Drama*, New York and London: Routledge, 2004.

Klamer, Arjo, McCloskey, Donald N. and Solow, Robert M., eds, *The Consequences of Economic Rhetoric*, Cambridge: Cambridge University Press, 1988.

Knight, G. Wilson, *The Wheel of Fire: Interpretations of Shakespearian Tragedy with Three New Essays*, London: Methuen & Co. Ltd, 1930.

——, *The Crown of Life: Essays in Interpretation of Shakespeare's Final Plays*, first published by Oxford University Press, 1947; London: Methuen, 1948.

——, *The Imperial Theme*, first published by Oxford University Press, 1931; London: Methuen, 1951.

——, *Shakespearian Dimensions*, Brighton: Harvester Press, 1984.

Knights, L. C., *Some Shakespearean Themes*, London: Chatto & Windus, 1966. First edn 1959.

——, *Drama and Society in the Age of Jonson*, London: Chatto & Windus, 1937.

Kolin, Philip C., ed., *Titus Andronicus: Critical Essays*, New York and London, Routledge, 1995.

——, ed., *Venus and Adonis: Critical Essays*, New York and London: Garland Publishing, Inc., 1997.

——, ed., *Othello: New Critical Essays*, New York and London: Routledge, 2002.

Korda, Natasha, 'Household Kates: domesticating commodities in *The Taming of the Shrew*', *Shakespeare Quarterly* 47 (1996): 110–31.

Kott, Jan, *Shakespeare our Contemporary*, trans. Boleslaw Taborski, Bristol: Methuen, 1965.

Kraye, Jill, ed., *The Cambridge Companion to Renaissance Humanism*, Cambridge and New York: Cambridge University Press, 1996, reprinted 1998.

Lachmann, Richard, *From Manor to Market: Structural Change in England, 1536–1640*, Madison: University of Wisconsin Press, 1987.

——, *Capitalists in Spite of Themselves: Elite Conflict and Economic Transitions in Early Modern Europe*, Oxford: Oxford University Press, 2000.

Lander, Jesse M., ' "Crack'd crowns" and counterfeit sovereigns: the crisis of value in *1 Henry IV*', *Shakespeare Studies* 30 (2002): 137–61.

Lavoie, Don, ed., *Economics and Hermeneutics*, London and New York: Routledge, 1990.

Leggatt, Alexander, *Citizen Comedy in the Age of Shakespeare*, Toronto: University of Toronto Press, 1973.

——, *Shakespeare's Comedy of Love*, London: Methuen & Co., 1974.

——, *Shakespeare's Political Drama: The History Plays and the Roman Plays*, London and New York: Routledge, 1988.

——, *King Lear*, Harvester New Critical Introductions to Shakespeare, Hemel Hempstead: Harvester Wheatsheaf, 1988.

——, ed., *The Cambridge Companion to Shakespearean Comedy*, Cambridge and New York: Cambridge University Press, 2002.

——, *Shakespeare's Tragedies: Violation and Identity*, Cambridge and New York: Cambridge University Press, 2005.

Leijonhufvud, Axel, *On Keynesian Economics and the Economics of Keynes*, Oxford: Oxford University Press, 1979.

Leinwand, Theodore B., *Theatre, Finance and Society in Early Modern England*, Cambridge: Cambridge University Press, 1999.

Lever, J. W., *The Tragedy of State*, London: Methuen, 1971.

Liebler, Naomi Conn, *Shakespeare's Festive Tragedy: The Ritual Foundations of Genre*, London and New York: Routledge, 1995.

Lloyd Pritchard, M. F., ed., *Original Papers Regarding Trade in England and Abroad drawn up by John Keymer for Information of King James I about 1620*, New York: Augustus M. Kelly Publishers, 1967.

Londré, Felicia Hardison, ed., *Love's Labour's Lost: Critical Essays*, New York and London: Routledge, 2001.

Long, Michael, *The Unnatural Scene: A Study in Shakespearean Tragedy*, London: Methuen & Co. Ltd, 1976.

——, *Macbeth*, Harvester New Critical Introductions to Shakespeare, Hemel Hempstead: Harvester Wheatsheaf, 1989.

Loomba, Ania, *Shakespeare, Race, and Colonialism*, Oxford: Oxford University Press, 2002.

Lyne, Raphael, *Shakespeare's Late Work*, Oxford and New York: Oxford University Press, 2007.

Lyon, John, *The Merchant of Venice*, Harvester New Critical Introductions to Shakespeare, Hemel Hempstead: Harvester Wheatsheaf, 1988.

MacDonald, Joyce Green, ed., *Race, Ethnicity, and Power in the Renaissance*, London: Associated University Presses, 1997.

Machiavelli, Niccolo, *The Prince*, trans. George Bull, Harmondsworth and Baltimore: Penguin Books, 1961.

——, *The Prince*, trans. Peter Bondanella and Mark Musa, Oxford and New York: Oxford University Press, 1984.

Mack, Peter, ed., *Renaissance Rhetoric*, Basingstoke and London: St Martin's Press, 1994.

Magnusson, Lars, *Mercantilism: The Shaping of an Economic Language*, London: Routledge, 1994.

Magnusson, Lynne, *Shakespeare and Social Dialogue: Dramatic Language and Elizabethan Letters*, Cambridge: Cambridge University Press, 1999.

Mahon, John W. and Mahon, Ellen Macleod, eds, *The Merchant of Venice: New Critical Essays*, New York and London: Routledge, 2002.

Mahood, M. M., *Shakespeare's Wordplay*, London and New York: Methuen, 1957.

Mallin, Eric S., *Inscribing the Time: Shakespeare and the End of Elizabethan England*, Berkeley: University of California Press, 1995.

Manning, Roger B., *Village Revolts: Social Protest and Popular Disturbances in England, 1509–1640*, Oxford: Clarendon Press, 1988.

Marrapodi, Michele, ed., *Shakespeare, Italy, and Intertextuality*, Manchester and New York: Manchester University Press, 2004.

Marshall, Peter, ' "The map of God's world": geographies of the afterlife in Tudor and early Stuart England' in Gordon, Bruce and Marshall, Peter, eds, *The Place of the Dead: Death and Remembrance in Late Medieval and Early Modern Europe*, Cambridge: Cambridge University Press, 2000: 110–30.

Martindale, Charles and Michelle, *Shakespeare and the Uses of Antiquity*, London and New York: Routledge, 1990.

—— and Taylor, A. B., eds, *Shakespeare and the Classics*, Cambridge and New York: Cambridge University Press, 2004.

Marx, Karl, *Capital: A Critique of Political Economy*, 3 vols, trans. Samuel Moore and Edward Aveling, New York: The Modern Library, 1906.

Marx, Steven, *Shakespeare and the Bible*, Oxford and New York: Oxford University Press, 2000.

Matar, Nabil, *Turks, Moors, & Englishmen in the Age of Discovery*, New York and Chichester: Columbia University Press, 1999.

Mattelart, Armand and Siegelaub, Seth, eds, *Communication and Class Struggle, Volume 2: Liberation, Socialism*, New York: International General, 1983.

Maus, Katherine Eisamen, *Inwardness and Theater in the English Renaissance*, Chicago: University of Chicago Press, 1995.

McAlindon, Tom, *English Renaissance Tragedy*, Vancouver: The University of British Columbia Press, 1986.

——, *Shakespeare's Tragic Cosmos*, Cambridge and New York: Cambridge University Press, 1991.

——, *Shakespeare's Tudor History: A Study of* Henry IV, Parts 1 and 2, Aldershot and Burlington: Ashgate, 2001.

——, *Shakespeare Minus 'Theory'*, Aldershot and Burlington: Ashgate, 2004.

McCloskey, Donald N., *The Rhetoric of Economics*, Madison: University of Wisconsin Press, 1985.

McDonald, Russ, *Shakespeare and the Arts of Language*, Oxford and New York: Oxford University Press, 2001.

——, ed., *Shakespeare: An Anthology of Criticism and Theory 1945–2000*, Malden, USA, Oxford: Blackwell, 2004.

——, *Shakespeare's Late Style*, Cambridge and New York: Cambridge University Press, 2006.

McEachern, Claire, ed., *A Companion to Shakespearean Tragedy*, Cambridge and New York: Cambridge University Press, 2002.

Mc Mullan, John L., *The Canting Crew: London's Criminal Underworld, 1550–1700*, New Brunswick, NJ: Rutgers University Press, 1984.

Meikle, Scott, *Aristotle's Economic Thought*, Oxford: Oxford University Press, 1995.

——, 'Quality and quantity in economics: the metaphysical construction of the economic realm' *New Literary History* 31 (2000): 247–68.

Metz, G. Harold, *Shakespeare's Earliest Tragedy: Studies in Titus Andronicus*, London: Associated University Presses, 1996.

Minchinton, W. E, ed., *The Growth of English Overseas Trade in the Seventeenth and Eighteenth Centuries*, London: Methuen, 1969.

Miola, Robert S., *Shakespeare's Rome*, Cambridge, London and New York: Cambridge University Press, 1983.

——, '*Julius Caesar* and the tyrannicide debate' *Renaissance Quarterly* 38 (1985): 271–89.

——, *Shakespeare and Classical Tragedy: The Influence of Seneca*, Oxford: Clarendon Press, 1992.

——, *Shakespeare's Reading*, Oxford: Oxford University Press, 2000.

——, ed., *The Comedy of Errors: Critical Essays*, New York and London: Routledge, 2001.

Misselden, Edward, *The Circle of Commerce: Or, the Balance of Trade, in Defence of Free Trade: Opposed to Malynes Little Fish and His Great Whale, and Poized Against Them in the Scales*, London: 1623.

Mokyr, Joel, *The Lever of Riches: Technological Creativity and Economic Progress*, New York and Oxford: Oxford University Press, 1990.

de Montaigne, Michel, *The Complete Essays of Montaigne*, trans. Donald M. Frame, Stanford: Stanford University Press, 1958.

Morris, Christopher, *Political Thought in England: Tyndale to Hooker*, London and New York: Oxford University Press, 1953.

Moschovakis, Nick, ed., *Macbeth: New Critical Essays*, London and New York: Routledge, 2008.

Muir, Kenneth, '*Timon of Athens* and the cash-nexus' in *The Singularity of Shakespeare and Other Essays*, Liverpool: Liverpool University Press, 1977.

—— and Edwards, Philip, eds, *Aspects of Othello*, Cambridge and New York: Cambridge University Press, 1977.

——, eds, *Aspects of Macbeth*, Cambridge and New York: Cambridge University Press, 1977.

—— and Wells Stanley, eds, *Aspects of Hamlet*, Cambridge and New York: Cambridge University Press, 1979.

——, eds, *Aspects of Shakespeare's 'Problem Plays': All's Well that Ends Well, Measure for Measure, Troilus and Cressida*, Cambridge and New York: Cambridge University Press, 1982.

——, eds, *Aspects of King Lear*, Cambridge and New York: Cambridge University Press, 1982.

Muldrew, Craig, *The Economy of Obligation: The Culture of Credit and Social Relations in Early Modern England*, Basingstoke and New York: Palgrave, 1998.

Mun, Thomas, *A Discourse of Trade, From England Vnto the East-Indies: Answering to Diuerse Obiections Which Are Usually Made Against the Same*, London: 1621; New York: Facsimile Text Society, 1930.

Murphy, Patrick, ed., *The Tempest: Critical Essays*, New York and London: Routledge, 2001.

Neill, Anna, *British Discovery Literature and the Rise of Global Commerce*, New York: Palgrave, 2002.

Neill, Michael, *Issues of Death: Mortality and Identity in English Renaissance Tragedy*, Oxford: Clarendon Press, 1997.

Nelson, Benjamin, *The Idea of Usury: From Tribal Brotherhood to Universal Otherhood*, 1949; 2nd edn, enlarged, Chicago and London: University of Chicago Press, 1969.

Nelson, Julie A., 'Value-free or valueless? Notes on the pursuit of detachment in economics' *History of Political Economy* 121 (Winter, 1993): 121–45.

Nelson, Robert H., *Reaching for Heaven on Earth: The Theological Meaning of Economics*, Savage, MD: Rowan and Littlefield, 1991.

Nicholl, Charles, *The Reckoning: The Murder of Christopher Marlowe*, London and Basingstoke: Picador, 1993.

Nightingale, Pamela, *Trade, Money and Power in Medieval England*, Abingdon: Ashgate, 2007.

Noonan, John T., *The Scholastic Analysis of Usury*, Cambridge, MA: Harvard University Press, 1957.

Norwich, John Julius, *Shakespeare's Kings*, Penguin Books, London: Viking, Penguin, 1999.

Nowottny, Winifred M. T., ' "Opinion" and "Value" in *Troilus and Cressida*', *Essays in Criticism* 4 (1954): 282–96.

Nuttall, A. D., *A New Mimesis: Shakespeare and the Representation of Reality*, London and New York: Methuen, 1983.

——, *Timon of Athens*, Harvester New Critical Introductions to Shakespeare, Hemel Hempstead: Harvester Wheatsheaf, 1989.

——, *Why Does Tragedy Give Pleasure?*, Oxford: Clarendon Press, 1996, reprinted 2003.

——, *Shakespeare the Thinker*, New Haven and London: Yale University Press, 2007.

O'Connor, John and Goodland, Katherine, eds, *A Directory of Shakespeare in Performance, 1970–2005*, Vol 1, Basingstoke and New York: Palgrave Macmillan, 2007.

Orlin, Lena Cowen, *Othello: Contemporary Critical Essays*, Basingstoke and New York: Palgrave, 2004.

Ornstein, Robert, *A Kingdom for a Stage: The Achievement of Shakespeare's History Plays*, Cambridge, MA: Harvard University Press, 1972.

Orwell, George, *Collected Essays*, London: Secker & Warburg, 1970.

Palfrey, Simon, *Late Shakespeare: A New World of Words*, Oxford and New York: Clarendon Press, 1997, paperback 1999.

Pallister, D. M., *The Age of Elizabeth: England under the Later Tudors. 1547–1603*, London and New York: Longman, 1983, 1992.

Palmer, D. J., *Comedy: Developments in Criticism*, Basingstoke and London: Macmillan, 1984.

Parker, Patricia and Hartman, Geoffrey, eds, *Shakespeare and the Question of Theory*, New York and London: Methuen, 1985.

——, *Shakespeare from the Margins: Language, Culture, Context*, Chicago and London: University of Chicago Press, 1996.

Parry, Jonathan and Bloch, Maurice, eds, *Money and the Morality of Exchange*, Cambridge: Cambridge University Press, 1989.

Partridge, Eric, *Shakespeare's Bawdy*, London and New York: Routledge Classics, 2001: first published Routledge & Kegan Paul, 1947.

Paster, Gail Kern, *The Idea of the City in the Age of Shakespeare*, Athens, GA: University of Georgia Press, 1985.

Peltonen, Markku, *Classical Humanism and Republicanism in English Political Thought 1570–1640*, Cambridge: Cambridge University Press, 1995.

——, ed., *The Cambridge Companion to Bacon*, Cambridge: Cambridge University Press, 1996.

Pendleton, Thomas A., ed., *Henry VI: Critical Essays*, New York and London: Routledge, 2001.

Pendry, E. D., ed., *Thomas Dekker*, Stratford-upon-Avon Library, Volume 4, Cambridge, MA: Harvard University Press, 1968.

Perry, Curtis, ed., *Material Culture and Cultural Materialism in the Middle Ages and the Renaissance*, Turnhout, Belgium: Brepols, 2001.

Pettegree, Andrew, *Europe in the Sixteenth Century*, Malden and Oxford: Blackwell Publishing, 2002.

Pocock, J. G. A., *The Machiavellian Moment: Florentine Political Thought and the Atlantic Republican Tradition*, Princeton: Princeton University Press, 1975.

——, *Politics, Language and Time: Essays on Political Thought and History*, Chicago: University of Chicago Press, 1989.

Poole, Adrian, *Coriolanus*, Harvester New Critical Introductions to Shakespeare, Hemel Hempstead: Harvester Wheatsheaf, 1988.

Poovey, Mary, *A History of the Modern Fact: Problems of Knowledge in the Sciences of Wealth and Society*, Chicago: University of Chicago Press, 1998.

Pressman, Steven, *Fifty Major Economists*, London and New York: Routledge, 1999.

Pullen, Brian, 'Charity and usury: Christian and Jewish lending in renaissance and early modern Italy', *Proceedings of the British Academy* 125 (2003): 19–40.

Rackin, Phyllis, *Stages of History: Shakespeare's English Chronicles*, Ithaca: Cornell University Press, 1990.

Ramsay, G. D., *The City of London in International Politics at the Accession of Elizabeth Tudor*, Manchester: Manchester University Press, 1975.

Ramsey, Peter H., ed., *The Price Revolution in Sixteenth-Century England*, London: Methuen, 1971.

Rhodes, Neil, ed., *English Renaissance Prose: History, Language and Politics*, Tempe: 1997.

——, *Shakespeare and the Origins of English*, Oxford and New York: Oxford University Press, 2004.

Ribner, Irving, *Patterns in Shakespearian Tragedy*, London: Methuen & Co. Ltd, 1960, paperback 1969, reprinted 1971.

Richmond, Hugh Macrae, *Shakespeare's Theatre: A Dictionary of His Stage Context*, London and New York: Continuum, 2002, reprinted 2004.

Riggs, David, *The World of Christopher Marlowe*, London: Faber & Faber, 2004.

Righter, Anne, *Shakespeare and the Idea of the Play*, Harmondsworth and Baltimore: Chatto & Windus, 1962, Penguin Books, 1967.

Robertson, David, *The Penguin Dictionary of Politics*, London and New York: Penguin Books, 1993.

Robinson, Joan, *Economic Philosophy*, London: C. A.Watts & Co. Ltd, 1962.

Rollins, Peter C. and Smith, Alan, eds, *Shakespeare's Theories of Blood, Character and Class: A Festschrift in Honor of David Shelley Berkeley*, New York: Peter Lang, 2001.

Rossiter, A. P. *Angel with Horns*, ed., Graham Storey, London: Longman, 1961.

Ruiter, David, *Shakespeare's Festive History: Feasting, Festivity, Fasting and Lent in the Second Henriad*, Aldershot and Burlington, VT: Ashgate, 2003.

Rushby, Kevin, *Paradise: A History of the Idea that Rules the World*, London: Constable, 2006.

Ryan, Kiernan, ed., *King Lear: Contemporary Critical Essays*, Basingstoke and London: Macmillan, 1993.

——, ed., *Shakespeare: The Last Plays*, London and New York: Longman, 1999.

Sabine, George H., *A History of Political Theory*, 3rd edn, London: George G. Harrap & Co. Ltd, 1963.

Saccio, Peter, *Shakespeare's English Kings: History, Chronicle, and Drama*, 2nd edn, Oxford: Oxford University Press, 1977, 2000.

Salinger, Leo, *Dramatic Form in Shakespeare and the Jacobeans*, Cambridge: Cambridge University Press, 1986.

Salmon, V. and Burness, E., *A Reader in the Language of Shakespearean Drama*, Amsterdam/Philadelphia: John Benjamins Publishing Company, 1987.

Sams, Eric, *The Real Shakespeare: Retrieving the Early Years, 1564–1594*, New Haven and London: Yale University Press, 1995, paperback 1997.

Samuels, Warren J., Biddle, Jeff E. and Davis, John B., eds, *A Companion to The History of Economic Thought*, Malden and Oxford: Blackwell Publishing, 2003, paperback, 2007.

Sanders, Wilbur, *The Winter's Tale*, Harvester New Critical Introductions to Shakespeare, Brighton: The Harvester Press, 1987.

Schalkwyk, David, *Speech and Performance in Shakespeare's Sonnets and Plays*, New York and Cambridge: Cambridge University Press, 2002.

Schama, Simon, *The Embarrassment of Riches: An Interpretation of Dutch Culture in the Golden Age*, London: Fontana Press, 1991.

Schiffer, James, ed., *Shakespeare's Sonnets: Critical Essays*, New York and London: Garland Publishing, 2000.

——, ed., *Twelfth Night: New Critical Essays*, New York and London, Routledge, 2008.

Schlueter, June, ed., *Two Gentlemen of Verona: Critical Essays*, New York and London: Garland Publishing, 1996.

Schumpeter, Joseph A., *Ten Great Economists: From Marx to Keynes*, first published 1952; London: George Allen & Unwin, 1966.

——, *History of Economic Analysis*, first published 1954; London: George Allen & Unwin, 1967.

Schwyzer, Philip, *Archaeologies of English Renaissance Literature*, Oxford and New York: Oxford University Press, 2007.

Scott, Charlotte, *Shakespeare and the Idea of the Book*, Oxford and New York: Oxford University Press, 2007.

Shapiro, James, *Shakespeare and the Jews*, New York and Chichester: Columbia University Press, 1996.

——, *1599: A Year in the Life of William Shakespeare*, London: Faber & Faber, 2005.

Shell, Marc, *The Economy of Literature*, Baltimore: Johns Hopkins University Press, 1978.

——, *Money, Language, and Thought: Literary and Philosophical Economies from the Medieval to the Modern Era*, Berkeley: University of California Press, 1982, Softshell Books edition, 1993.

Shrank, Cathy, *Writing the Nation in Reformation England, 1530–1580*, Oxford and New York: Oxford University Press, 2004.

Shuger, Debora Kuller, *Political Theologies in Shakespeare's England: The Sacred and the State in Measure for Measure*, Basingstoke and New York: Palgrave, 2001.

Siemon, James R., *Shakespearean Iconoclasm*, Berkeley, LA and London: University of California Press, 1985.

Simkin, Stevie, ed., *Revenge Tragedy: Contemporary Critical Essays*, Basingstoke: Palgrave, 2001.

Simmel, Georg, *The Philosophy of Money*, ed., trans. Tom Bottomore and David Frisby, London: first published Routledge, 1978; 3rd edn, 2004.

Simmons, J. L., *Shakespeare's Pagan World: The Roman Tragedies*, Charlottesville, VA: University of Virginia Press, 1973.

Sinfield, Alan, ed., *Macbeth: Contemporary Critical Essays*, Basingstoke and London: Macmillan, 1992.

Skeele, David, ed., *Pericles: Critical Essays*, New York and London: Garland Publishing, 2000.

Smallwood, Robert, ed., *Players of Shakespeare 6: Essays in the Performance of Shakespeare's History Plays*, Cambridge and New York: Cambridge University Press, 2004.

Smith Adam, *An Inquiry into the Nature and Causes of the Wealth of Nations* (1776), New York: Modern Library, 1937.

Smith, David L., Strier, Richard and Bevington, David, eds, *The Theatrical City: Culture, Theatre and Politics in London, 1576–1649*, Cambridge: Cambridge University Press, 1995.

Smith, Peter J., *Social Shakespeare*, Basingstoke: Macmillan, 1995.

Soellner, Rolf, *Timon of Athens: Shakespeare's Pessimistic Tragedy*, Columbus: Ohio State University Press, 1979.

Sohmer, Steve, *Shakespeare's Mystery Play: The Opening of the Globe Theatre 1599*, Manchester and New York: Manchester University Press, 1999.

Sokol, B. J. and Sokol, Mary, *Shakespeare's Legal Language: A Dictionary*, London and New York: Continuum, 2000, reprinted 2004.

Solomon, Julie Robin, *Objectivity in the Making: Francis Bacon and the Politics of Inquiry*, Baltimore: Johns Hopkins University Press, 1998.

Spencer, T. J. B., *The Roman Plays*, London and Tonbridge: Longman, 1963, revised 1976.

Spiegel, H. W., ed., *The Development of Economic Thought: Great Economists in Perspective*, abr. edn, New York: John Wiley & Sons, 1964.

Spivack, Bernard, *Shakespeare and the Allegory of Evil: The History of a Metaphor in Relation to his Major Villains*, New York and London: Columbia University Press, Oxford University Press, 1958.

Spivak, Gayatri Chakravorty, *In Other Worlds: Essays in Cultural Politics*, New York and London: Methuen, 1987; Routledge Classics, 2006.

Spurgeon, Caroline, *Shakespeare's Imagery and What It Tells Us*, Cambridge: Cambridge University Press, 1971, 1st edn 1935.

Stafford, T. J., 'Mercantile imagery in *Troilus and Cressida*' in Stafford, T. J., ed., *Shakespeare in the Southwest: Some New Directions*, El Paso: Texas Western Press, 1969.

Stanivukovic, Goran V., ed., *Remapping the Mediterranean World in Early Modern English Writings*, New York and Basingstoke: Palgrave Macmillan, 2007.

Stevenson, Laura, *Praise and Paradox: Merchants and Craftsmen in Elizabethan Popular Literature*, Cambridge: Cambridge University Press, 1984, paperback 2002.

Stone, Lawrence, 'Inigo Jones and the new exchange', *Archaeological Journal* 114 (1957): 106–7.

——, *The Crisis of the Aristocracy 1558–1641*, first published 1965; Oxford: Oxford University Press, 1967, abridged.

Strathern, Paul, *The Medici: Godfathers of the Renaissance*, London: Pimlico, 2005.

Sullivan, Ceri, *The Rhetoric of Credit: Merchants in Early Modern Writing*, New York and London: Rosemont Publishing, 2002.

Sullivan, Garrett A., Jr, *The Drama of Landscape: Land, Property and Social Relations on the Early Modern Stage*, Stanford; Stanford University Press, 1998.

Supple, Brian E., *Commercial Crisis and Change in England 1600–1642: A Study in the Instability of a Mercantile Economy*, Cambridge: Cambridge University Press, 1959.

Tawney, R. H., *Religion and the Rise of Capitalism*, 1926; reprinted Gloucester, MA: Peter Smith, 1962.

Taylor, A. B., ed., *Shakespeare's Ovid: The Metamorphoses in the Plays and Poems*, Cambridge and New York: Cambridge University Press, 2000.

Taylor, Dennis and Beauregard, David, eds, *Shakespeare and the Culture of Christianity in Early Modern England*, New York: Fordham University Press, 2003.

Taylor, Michael, *Shakespeare Criticism in the Twentieth Century*, Oxford: Oxford University Press, 2001.

Tennenhouse, Leonard, *Power on Display: The Politics of Shakespeare's Genres*, New York and London: Methuen, 1986.

Thirsk, Joan, *Economic Policy and Projects: The Development of a Consumer Society in Early Modern England*, Oxford: Clarendon Press, 1978.

Thomas, Vivian, *The Moral Universe of Shakespeare's Problem Plays*, London and Sydney: Croom Helm, 1987, Routledge paperback 1991.

——, *Shakespeare's Roman Worlds*, London and New York: Routledge, 1989.

——, *Julius Caesar*, Harvester New Critical Introductions to Shakespeare, New York: Twayne Publishers, 1992; Hemel Hempstead: Harvester Wheatsheaf, 1992.

——, ' "Thus from the heart's abundance speaks the tongue": review of the Royal Shakespeare Company's *Edward III*', *Shakespeare at the Centre*, Vol. 2 (August, 2002), 4–6.

Thomas, William, *The Historye of Italye*, London: 1561.

Thorne, Alison, *Vision and Rhetoric in Shakespeare: Looking through Language*, New York and Basingstoke: Macmillan Press Ltd, St Martin's Press, LLC, 2000.

Toole, William B., 'The cobbler, the disrobed image and the motif of movement in *Julius Caesar*', *The Upstart Crow*, vol. IV (Fall 1982).

Turner, Henry S., *Shakespeare's Double Helix*, London and New York: Continuum, 2008.

Turner, Frederick, *Shakespeare and the Nature of Time: Moral and Philosophical Themes in Some Plays and Poems of William Shakespeare*, Oxford: Clarendon Press, 1971.

——, *Shakespeare's Twenty-First Century Economics: The Morality of Love and Money*, New York and Oxford: Oxford University Press, 1999.

Ullmann, Walter, *Medieval Foundations of Renaissance Humanism*, London: Paul Elek, 1977.

Vaughan, Virginia Mason, *Othello: A Contextual History*, Cambridge and New York: Cambridge University Press, 1994.

Veblen, Thorstein, *The Place of Science in Modern Civilisation*, New York: Russell & Russell, 1961.

——, *The Vested Interests*, New York: reprints of Economic Classics, Augustus M. Kelley, 1964.

——, *The Theory of Business Enterprise*, New York: reprints of Economic Classics, Augustus M. Kelley, 1965.

——, *The Theory of the Leisure Class*, New York: reprints of Economic Classics, Augustus M. Kelley, 1965.

Velz, John W. 'The ancient world in Shakespeare: authenticity or anachronism? A retrospect' *Shakespeare Survey* 31 (1978): 1–12.

Vendler, Helen, *The Art of Shakespeare's Sonnets*, Cambridge, MA: Harvard University Press, 1997.

Vickers, Brian, *The Artistry of Shakespeare's Prose*, rev. edn, London: Methuen, 1968.

Vitkus, Daniel J., *Turning Turk: English Theater and the Multicultural Mediterranean, 1570–1630*, Basingstoke: Palgrave Macmillan, 2003.

Walker, Greg, *The Politics of Performance in Early Renaissance Drama*, Cambridge: Cambridge University Press, 1998.

Waller, Gary, ed., *Shakespeare's Comedies*, London and New York: Longman, 1991.

——, ed., *All's Well That Ends Well: New Critical Essays*, New York and London: Routledge, 2006.

Walter, John and Wrightson, Keith, 'Dearth and the social order in early modern England', *Past and Present* 71 (1976): 22–42.

Ward, John Powell, *As You Like It*, Harvester New Critical Introductions to Shakespeare, Hemel Hempstead: Harvester Wheatsheaf, 1992.

Warley, Christopher, *Sonnet Sequences and Social Distinction in Renaissance England*, Cambridge: Cambridge University Press, 2005.

Warneke, Sara, 'A taste for newfangledness: the destructive potential of novelty in early modern England', *Sixteenth Century Journal* 26 (1995): 881–96.

Watts, Cedric, *Hamlet*, Harvester New Critical Introductions to Shakespeare, Hemel Hempstead: Harvester Wheatsheaf, 1988.

——, *Literature and Money: Financial Myth and Literary Truth*, New York and London: Harvester Wheatsheaf, 1990.

——, *Romeo and Juliet*, Harvester New Introductions to Shakespeare, Hemel Hempstead: Harvester Wheatsheaf, 1991.

Weber, Max, *The Protestant Ethic and the Spirit of Capitalism*, trans. Talcott Parsons, London: Routledge, 1992.

Weis, Rene, *Shakespeare Revealed: A Biography*, Great Britain: John Murray (Publishers), 2007.

Wells, Robin Headlam, *Shakespeare and Politics: A Contextual Introduction*, London and New York: Continuum, 2008, 2nd edn.

Wells, Stanley, *Shakespeare and Co.*, London and New York: Penguin Group, 2006.

Wheeler, David, ed., *Coriolanus: Critical Essays*, New York and London: Routledge, 1995.

Wheeler, John, *A Treatise of Commerce, Wherin Are Shewed the Commodities Arising by a Well Ordered, and Ruled Trade, Such As That of the Societie of Merchantes Adventureres Is Proved to Bee*, London, 1601; Facsimile: New York: Columbia University Press, 1931.

White, Michael, *Machiavelli: A Man Misunderstood*, London: Little, Brown, 2004.

White, R. S., *Innocent Victims: Poetic Injustice in Shakespearean Tragedy*, London: Athlone Press, revised 1986.

——, *The Merry Wives of Windsor*, Harvester New Introductions to Shakespeare, Hemel Hempstead: Harvester Wheatsheaf, 1991.

Williams, Gordon, *Shakespeare's Sexual Language: A Glossary*, London and New York: Athlone Press, 1997, reprinted Continuum, 2006.

Wilson, Christopher R. and Calore, Michela, *Music in Shakespeare: A Dictionary*, London and New York: Thoemmes Continuum, 2005; paperback, 2008.

Wilson, John Dover, *Life in Shakespeare's England*, London: Cambridge University Press, 1911, Pelican Books 1944, reprinted 1949.

Wilson Richard and Dutton, Richard, eds, *New Historicism and Renaissance Drama*, London and New York: Longman, 1992.

——, *Will Power: Essays on Shakespearean Authority*, Hemel Hempstead: Harvester Wheatsheaf, 1993.

Wilson, Thomas, *A Discourse Upon Usury*, 1572; ed., R. H. Tawney, London: G. Bell and Sons, 1925.

Witmore, Michael, *Shakespearean Metaphysics*, London and New York: Continuum, 2008.

Wood, Ellen Meiksins, *The Origin of Capitalism: A Longer View*, London: Verso, 2002.

Wood, Michael, *In Search of Shakespeare*, London: BBC Worldwide Ltd, 2003.

Woodbridge, Linda, *Women and the English Renaissance: Literature and the Nature of Womankind 1540–1620*, Urbana: University of Illinois Press, 1984.

——, *Vagrancy, Homelessness, and English Renaissance Literature*, Urbana: University of Illinois Press, 2001.

——, ed., *Money and the Age of Shakespeare: Essays in New Economic Criticism*, New York and Basingstoke: Palgrave, Macmillan, 2003.

Woodmansee, Martha and Osteen, Mark, eds, *The New Economic Criticism: Studies at the Intersection of Literature and Economics*, London and New York: Routledge, 1999.

Woodward, Donald, 'Wage rates and living standards in pre-industrial England', *Past and Present* 91 (1981): 28–46.

Wright, George T., *Shakespeare's Metrical Art*, Berkeley, Los Angeles and Oxford: University of California Press, 1988, paperback 1991.

——, *Hearing the Measures: Shakespearean and Other Inflections*, Madison and London: University of Wisconsin Press, 2001.

Wrightson, Keith, *English Society 1580–1680*, London: Hutchinson, 1982.

——, *Earthly Necessities: Economic Lives in Early Modern Britain*, New Haven, CT: Yale University Press, 2000.

Wynne-Davies, Marion, ed., *Much Ado About Nothing and The Taming of the Shrew: Contemporary Critical Essays*, Basingstoke and New York: Palgrave, 2001.

Young, David, *The Action to the Word: Structure and Style in Shakespearean Tragedy*, New Haven and London: Yale University Press, 1990.

Zander, Horst, ed., *Julius Caesar: New Critical Essays*, New York and London: Routledge, 2005.

Zelizer, Viviana A., *The Social Meaning of Money*, New York: Basic Books, 1994.

Zitner, Sheldon P., *All's Well That Ends Well*, Harvester New Critical Introductions to Shakespeare, Hemel Hempstead: Harvester Wheatsheaf, 1989.

Žižek, Slavoj, *The Sublime Object of Ideology*, London: Verso, 1989.

List of Headwords

Abound
Accompt, account
Achieve, achievement
Advance, advanced, advancement
Advantage, advantageable, advantaging
After-debts
Agent
Assay
Audit, auditor

Band
Bankrout, bankrupt
Bargain(s)
Barren, barren-spirited
Bate, bated, bate-breeding, bateless
Bawd
Beguile, beguiling
Bill
Bond, bondage
Boot(s), to boot, to give the boots, make
  boot, overboots
Bootless
Booty, booties
Bound, bounded, bounding
Bountiful, bountifully, bounty
Bourn
Break, broken
Broker

Capital
Capitulate
Cashier(ed)
Caterpillar
Chapman
Cheap, cheapen
Chronicle, chronicled, chronicler
Clipper
Coffer, coffers up
Commerce
Commission, commissioner
Commodity

Commonality
Commonweal, commonwealth
Compact
Competence
Competency
Competent, computent
Competitor(s)
Complice(s)
Complot
Compose
Composition
Compt
Compter, counter
Comptless
Condition
Consort, consorted
Contumelious(ly), contumely
Convent, conventicle
Convey, conveyance, conveyers
Corrival, co-rival
Cost, costly
Counter-caster
Counterfeit
Counterpoise
Cozen, cozener
Credit, creditor
Current
Custom, custom-shrunk
Customer

Dearth
Debt, debitor, debtor
Detention

Earnest, earnest-penny
Engage
Engross
Estate
Exact, exacted, exacting, exaction, exactly
Excess
Exchange

Exchequer

Exhibiter

Exhibition

Expense

Exploit, exploits

Faction, factionary. factious

Factor

Far-fet

Fashion, fashionable, fashion-mongers, fashion-monging

Fedary, federary, feodary

Fee

Fee-grief, fee-simple, in fee

Fifteen, fifteenth

Fraught, fraughtage, fraughting

Garner

Government

Hade land, head land

Having

Hire

Husbandry

Impeach, impeachment

Imprese

Impress

Increase

Indent

Indenture

Innovation, innovator

Intelligence

Intelligencer, intelligencing

Intelligent

Interess

Interest

Invest

Investments

Jointress

Jointure

Lean

Lendings

Machiavel

Market

Market-maid, market-man

Market-place

Market-price

Mart

Mechanic, mechanical

Meed

Meiny

Mercenary

Merchandise

Merchant, merchant-marring

Moiety

Money

Monopoly

Mortgage

Mountebank

Mystery

Nation

Occupation

Opinion(s)

Outsell

Outwork

Outworth

Overbuys

Overhold

Overplus

Owe, own

Pack, pack'd, packing

Paction

Palter, paltering

Pelf

Perfidious

Pestiferous

Pittance

Plebeians, plebeii, plebs

Policy

Politic

Politician

Politicly

Practice

Practicer

Practices

Practisants

Price

Proditor

Profit, profitable, profited

Provision

Publican

Purchase

Purchase out

Putter-on

Putter-out

Quantity

Quietus

Quittance

Reckon

Shakespeare's Works Index

All's Well That Ends Well
achieve, advantage, after-debts, bountiful, break, commodity, compt, counterpoise, cozen, customer, exact, exploit, market-price, mystery, perfidious, pestiferous, policy, politic, practice, practicer, price, store, stratagem, toll, traduc'd, vendible, virtue, wealth, worth

Antony and Cleopatra
band, beguile, boot, bounty, bourn, chronicle, competitor(s), compose, convey, dearth, exactly, faction, factor, impress, lean, machiavel, market-maid, marketplace, mechanic, merchandise, moiety, money, occupation, outwork, overplus, pack'd, palter, plebeians, practice, purchase, reckon, revenue, rivality, store, trade, traduc'd, value, wage, worky-day, workman

As You Like It
assay, bond, bound, bountiful, counter, cost, estate, faction, fashion, husbandry, intelligence, interest, meed, money, policy, politic, profit, reckoning, revenue, store, thrifty, usurp, virtuous, wage, wealth, working-day

The Comedy of Errors
band, bargain, bond, convey, credit, exploit, factor, fashion, fee, mart, money, owe, satisfaction, traders, value

Coriolanus
account, achieve, advanced, band, bate, bond, bound, bountiful, capital, capitulate, cheap, chronicle, commission, commonality, competency, condition, condition, convent, convey, counterpoise, dearth, estate, factionary, fashion, garner, hire, husbandry, innovator, machiavel, market-place, mechanic, meiny, mercenary, mountebank, nation, occupation, owe, paltering, perfidious, plebeians, policy, practice, price, purchase, recompense, rule, store, tag, task, temporize, tenth, trade-fall'n, trades, tradesmen, traducement, tyrant, usurers, usury, value, virtue, wage, weal, wealsmen, worth

Cymbeline
advantage, agent, band, bond, broken, counterfeit, credit, custom, debitor, exactly, exhibition, factor, fashion, feodary, fraught, lean, mart, outsell, overbuys,

packing, quantity, reckon, runagate, statist, tenth, thrift, uncrossed, usury, value, venture, wage, workmanship

Edward III
conventicler, cost, custom, victual

Hamlet
account, achievement, advantage, assay, audit, band, barren, bawd, bound, bourn, broker, capital, chronicle, compact, competent, counter, contumely, convey, current, dearth, engage, exact, exactly, exchange, fashion, fee, innovation, investments, jointress, lean, machiavel, market, mart, moiety, mystery, packing, politic, politician, practice, practices, price, quietus, reckoning, rival, rule, statist, sterling, thrift, trade, tradesmen, traduc'd, truster, uncurrent, usurp, wealth

The First Part of Henry IV
advantage, assay, auditor, beguile, boots, booty, bound, bountiful, capitulate, caterpillar, coffer, commodity, commonality, condition, corrival, cost, counterfeit, counterpoise, credit, current, debt, engage, engross, exact, exchequer, exploit, factor, government, hade land, impress, indent, indenture, innovation, intelligence, lean, machiavel, mechanic, moiety, opinion, policy, politician, practice, price, purchase, quantity, reckoning, reformation, rule, scot, subornation, task, trade-fall'n, traders, value, virtue, wealth, worth

The Second Part of Henry IV
achievement, advancement, bate, boot, to boot, commission, competence, complice, cost, debt, engage, engross, exploit, fashion, hade land, husbandry, intelligencer, investments, lean, machiavel, mechanical, opinion, policy, practice, price, profit, purchase, quantity, quittance, sterling, stratagem, suborned, trade, tyrant, venter, venture, victualler, virtue, worth

Henry V
achieve, advantage, advantageable, bargain, bate, bawd, bill, make boot, capital, clipper, commissioner, condition, convey, counterfeit, debt, earnest, estate, exhibiter, exploits, fashion, husbandry, impeachment, intelligence, invest, machiavel, mechanic, mercenary, moiety, nation, opinion, paction, plebeians, policy, practice, practices, price, profitable, purchase, quittance, state, stratagem, sutler, usurp, working-day, working-house

The First Part of Henry VI
achieve, advantage, band, bargain, bounded, caterpillar, commission, expense, exploit, fation, factious, fashion, interest, machiavel, market-man, market-place, merchant, money, nation, pestiferous, politic, practices, practisants, proditor, quittance, recompense, stratagem, suborn, tenth, traffic, usurp, victual, weal, worth

The Second Part of Henry VI

acompt, achieve, assay, bargain, make boot, broker, caterpillar, commonweal, complice, complot, contumelious, conventicles, convey, counterpoise, credit, exacted, factious, far-fet, fee-simple, fifteen, fifteenth, husbandry, increase, mechanical, money, policy, politicly, practice, practices, reformation, revenue, state, subornation, subsidy, tax, thrifty, treasury, venturous, workman

The Third Part of Henry VI

achieve, assay, band, bootless, booty, condition, cost, counterfeit, faction, factious, impeach, increase, jointure, machiavel, meed, profit, rule, satisfaction, subsidy, tyrant, usurp, value

Henry the Eighth

abound, agent, chronicle, chronicler, commission, commonality, convent, costly, counterfeit, current, exaction, expense, fashion, having, moiety, money, , mystery, opinion, outworth, profit, putter-on, reformation, sect, state, tenement, thrift, tractable, trade, traduc'd, value, venture, wealth, worth

Julius Caesar

advantage, barren-spirited, bill, bond, bootless, coffer, commonwealth, compact, counter, condition, consorted, costly, credit, debt, engage, exploit, faction, factious, fashion, machiavel, market-place, mart, mechanical, money, palter, plebeians, practice, purchase, rule, store, tag-rag, tradesmen, tyrant, venture, virtue, workman, worth

King John

advantage, agent, bawd, bound, broker, commodity, composition, counterfeit, excess, impeach, indenture, intelligence, machiavel, opinion, policy, practice, temporize, tithe, traded, usurp, virtue

King Lear

advantage, assay, bond, boot, to boot, bound, bourn, compact, consort, convey, counterfeit, cozener, exact, excess, exhibition, fashion, increase, intelligent, interess, interest, invest, jointress, lendings, machiavel, meiny, monopoly, occupation, politic, politician, practices, price, revenue, sect, tax, tithing, trade, treasury, tyrant, usurer, usury, usurp, virtue, wage, wealth, worth

Love's Labour's Lost

advance, bargain, chapmen, commonwealth, competitors, consort, fashion, money, opinion, policy, reckoning, value

A Lover's Complaint

assay, having

Macbeth
abound, agent, audit, beguile, bond, to boot, bountiful, compose, compt, consort, convey, debt, earnest, estate, exploits, fee, fee-grief, husbandry, impress, palter, profit, reckon with, rule, thriftless, trade, traffic, tyrant, value, venture

Measure for Measure
account, advantage, agent, assay, bawd, bond, commodity, commonwealth, composition, convey, cost, credit, custom-shrunk, debt, exacting, fedary, government, husbandry, mystery, opinion, practice, satisfaction, sect, suborn, thrifty, trade, trades, tyrant, usury, usurp, value, virtue, virtuous, worth

The Merchant of Venice
account, advantage, bankrout, bargain, barren, bate, bated, bond, bootless, break, commodity, competency, condition, counterfeit, creditor, custom, engage, earnest, estate, exact, excess, exchange, fraught, hire, husbandry, impeach, interest, mart, mercenary, merchandise, merchant, merchant-marring, moiety, money, nation, opinion, owe, price, profit, publican, rival, rule, state, store, stratagem, thrift, thrifty, trade, trades, traffickers, usance, value, vendible, venture, wealth, worth

The Merry Wives of Windsor
advantage, assay, bate-breeding, bill, cashier, cashiered, coffer, convey, cozen, exchequer, expense, having, jointure, machiavel, mechanical, money, pack, politic, profit, quittance, recompense, satisfaction, thrift, trade, value

A Midsummer Night's Dream
advantage, barren, beguiling, bond, chronicled, debt, exploit, mechanical, merchandise, quantity, revenue, rival, traders

Much Ado About Nothing
cheapen, commodity, custom, exchange, exhibition, fashion, fashion-monging, opinion, policy, politic, practice, temporize, use, working-day, worth

Othello
accompt, achieve, advantage, assay, beguile, beguiling, cashiered, chronicle, coffer, composition, compt, counter-caster, current, customer, exchange, exhibition, fraught, garner, increase, machiavel, money, opinion, politic, practice, practicer, price, profit, satisfaction, sect, traduc'd, wage

The Passionate Pilgrim
Pelf

Pericles
bargain, bawd, bourn, caterpillar, cheapen, commodity, cost, custom, earnest,

estate, husbandry, market, opinion, pelf, practice, price, provision, purchase, tractable, usurp, wage

The Rape of Lucrece
bateless, coffer, excess, exploits, profit, traffic

Richard II
barren, beguile, boot, bounty, broken, caterpillar, chronicled, coffer, commonality, complot, condition, consorted, convey, conveyers, cozen, custom, engage, exactly, exchequer, fashion, government, impeach, imprese, lendings, machiavel, money, policy, purchase, revenue, rival, sterling, tax, tenement, thriftless, trade, treasury, usurp

Richard III
account, advance, advancement, advantaging, barren, boot, competitor, complot, consort, convey, cozen, current, debt, earnest, engross, estate, exploit, factious, factor, fee, intelligencer, machiavel, pack, politic, politicly, purchase, revenue, runagate, store, subornation, tractable, tyrant, usurp

Romeo and Juliet
abound, account, advance, bankrout, bargain, bounty, break, consort, counterfeit, engross, excess, fashion-mongers, hire, interest, merchant, provision, purchase out, reckoning, store, traffic, usurer, virtue, weal

Sonnets
bankrout, barren, cheap, dearth, exchequer, expense, husbandry, increase, increase, merchandise, moiety, mortgage, overplus, profit, quietus, store, tyrant, use, usurer, usury, usurp

The Taming of the Shrew
credit, custom, exchange, fashion, jointure, mart, merchant, money, pittance, policy, politicly, quantity, traffic, usurp, workmanly

The Tempest
advantage, barren, bate, bound, bountiful, bourn, chronicle, commonwealth, debt, exact, exactly, fraughting, garner, increase, invest, merchant, money, perfidious, profit, provision, putter-out, rule, tyrant, usurp, virtue

Timon of Athens
accompt, advance, auditor, bankrupt, bawd, bill, bond, bounded, bountiful, bounty, broken, cashier, commodity, condition, contumelious, counterfeit, counterpoise, credit, creditor, debt, detention, engage, estate, exact, faction, fashionable, fee, husbandry, interest, meed, money, outworth, pelf, policy, politic, provision, purchase, quantity, quittance, reckon, reckoning, rival, sect, tenth, thrift, trades, traffic, truster, use, usury, value, virtue, virtuously, wealth, workman

Titus Andronicus
beguile, booty, commonweal, compact, competitor, complot, exploits, pack, plebeians, purchase, stratagem, tractable, treasury

Troilus and Cressida
achievement, agent, bargain, bond, boot, bounty, bourn, broker, chapmen, chronicle, commerce, condition, corrival, cost, custom, debt, earnest, engage, exact, exchange, exploit, faction, factious, fashion, fraughtage, husbandry, intelligence, nation, opinion, overhold, palter, policy, politic, practice, price, rule, temporize, thrifty, tithe, tractable, trade, traded, traders, tradesmen, value, virtue, worth

Twelfth Night
achieve, advanced, barren, coffer, compact, competent, competitors, credit, estate, having, market, money, opinion, policy, politic, politician, practice, purchase, quantity, thriftless, trade, tyrant, uncurrent, use, usurp, worth

The Two Gentlemen of Verona
achieve, advantage, bargain, chronicled, competitor, convey, dearth, exchequer, exhibition, faction, impress, practice, store, use, worth

The Two Nobel Kinsmen
account, advanced, advantage, bargain, fee, market, market-place, mystery, perfidious, value, venture, worth

Venus and Adonis
bargains, bate-breeding, bound, caterpillar, comptless, dearth, use, usurp, weal, workmanship

The Winter's Tale
accompt, account, agent, barren, boot, booties, bourn, commodity, compter, cozener, custom, customer, exchange, fashion, federary, intelligencing, intelligent, price, putter-on, satisfaction, sect, temporizer, tradesmen, traffic, treasury, tyrant, uncrossed, uncurrent, worth

General Index